Baseball's All-Time Best Sluggers

MICHAEL J. SCHELL

Baseball's All-Time Best Sluggers

Adjusted Batting Performance from
Strikeouts to Home Runs

PRINCETON UNIVERSITY PRESS   PRINCETON AND OXFORD

Library of Congress Cataloging-in-Publication Data

Schell, Michael J., 1957–
    Baseball's all-time best sluggers : adjusted batting performance from strikeouts
to home runs / Michael J. Schell
        p.   cm.
    Includes bibliographical references and index.
    ISBN 0-691-11557-5 (alk. paper)
        1. Batting (Baseball)—United States—Statistics.   2. Baseball players—Rating
of—United States.   3. Baseball players—United States—Statistics.   I. Title.
GV869.S345   2005
796.357′26′021—dc22   2004059994

This book has been composed in Electra by Princeton Editorial Associates, Inc.,
Scottsdale, Arizona

Printed on acid-free paper. ∞
pup.princeton.edu
Printed in the United States of America
10 9 8 7 6 5 4 3 2 1

To Noreen and our daughter Charis Irene

CONTENTS

CONTENTS

PREFACE

In the early 1970s, my brothers Kevin, Patrick, and I designed our own baseball game to play with the best players in baseball history. Each of us scoured our baseball encyclopedias in order to plan our draft picks. Yet a major obstacle complicated our quest. Because of striking differences between eras in the game, the raw numbers in the encyclopedias did not truly reflect the performance ability of the players if placed on the same field.

We decided to adjust player averages by comparing them to the overall league average for each season. That adjustment resulted in baseball's early stars claiming the best averages for most offensive events. To overcome that problem, we then assumed that the "average player" improved over the course of baseball history. For our league, the batting average of the average player improved until 1920; for home runs, improvement continued until around 1940. Stolen bases and triples, however, went the opposite way, with the average player being better in the early days.

Even after the improved adjustment, we found that players like Babe Ruth and Lou Gehrig still had too many home runs to be believable, while Rube Waddell and Dazzy Vance struck out too many batters. Each of these players needed a further "personal adjustment."

With all that settled, we drafted our players and played a baseball season. Prior to the draft, however, we needed to "work up" the players of interest to us, computing their adjusted averages in order to assess their relative strengths.

In the years since my boyhood, I became a statistician. Although the rudimentary adjustments that we used many years ago were remarkably good, my training now allows me to ground an adjustment procedure in a more objective and defensible way.

Baseball's All-Time Best Sluggers "works up" all 1140 players in major league history with 4000 or more at-bats plus walks plus hit-by-pitches. Four adjustments are used: for the league average, for the spread in averages, for the ballpark effect, and for aging. The league average and aging adjustments are easy to understand and apply;

the other two adjustments require more development. A power transformation model is used to handle the spread in averages, eliminating the need for "personal adjustments." Park effects likewise demand a statistically sophisticated approach. My goal in this book is to both make the adjustments and explain them in reasonable detail.

This book completes the work that I began with *Baseball's All-Time Best Hitters*. In that book, the rationale for the four adjustments was established and applied to batting average and walks. In this book, that work is extended to eight other offensive events as well: doubles, triples, home runs, runs, RBIs, strikeouts, stolen bases, and hit-by-pitches.

Baseball's All-Time Best Sluggers focuses on the batting abilities of baseball players, and hence does not establish an overall ranking of players, since running and fielding skills have not been accounted for. Other authors, most notably John Thorn and Pete Palmer, and Bill James, have established all-around player rankings. As part of their work, they rank the batting component of play. The rankings in this book do not differ greatly from theirs, which should re-assure readers familiar with their fine work. This book, however, is the first to adjust each offensive event separately, also allowing for park effect. As a result, the averages provided here can be used to play simulation baseball games.

The more detailed statistical methods have been placed in the appendices. In that way, casual readers do not need to get caught up in them. Teachers may find this book useful in presenting statistical ideas to students in an interesting context. A glossary summarizes the main statistical concepts as well as many baseball terms introduced in the book.

I thank Jim Albert, Dan Levitt, Cy Morong, Tom Ruane, Joseph Schell, John Steele, David Stephan, and Mike Symons, who read sections of the book and provided me with many useful suggestions. The principal data source for this book is the Lahman Baseball Database, version 5.1 (available at www.baseball1.com). Pete Palmer and David Vincent provided me with valuable home and road ballpark data, some of which were obtained from Retrosheet, a project led by David Smith with the ambitious goal of computerizing the play-by-play data for every 20th-century major league game.

Three people played especially valuable roles in helping me with this book. My colleague Dominic Moore lent his critical eye to the statistical methods that I developed to identify eras in the game and when ballpark changes occurred. He also assisted with all the figures and with the presentation of some of the tables. My editor, Vickie Kearn, was a constant source of encouragement and gave me valuable suggestions on the organization and overall flow of the book. Most significantly, I thank my wife, Noreen, who edited nearly every page of the manuscript, and was frequently the first person I turned to for feedback as I sifted through various options. She also relieved me of some duties in parenting our daughter Charis Irene, now a year and a half old, so that I could complete this work.

ABBREVIATIONS

AB	at-bat	**K**	strikeout
AL	American League	**LF**	left field or left fielder
API	adjusted park index	**LHB**	left-handed batter
Avg	average	**LOR**	log odds ratio
1B	single or first baseman	**NFP**	net-facing pitcher
2B	double or second baseman	**NL**	National League
3B	triple or third baseman	**OBP**	on-base percentage
BA	batting average	**OOB**	outs on base
BATBH	*Baseball's All-Time Best Hitters*	**OPS**	on-base-plus-slugging
BB	bases on balls	**OR**	odds ratio
C	catcher	**PA**	park-adjusted
CBR	Career Batter Rating	**Pct**	percentage
CF	center field or center fielder	**PN**	park-neutral
CHI	clutch hitting index	**R**	runs
CS	caught stealing	**RBIs**	runs batted in
DH	designated hitter	**REC**	rare events correction
DPT	doubles-plus-triples	**RF**	right field or right fielder
EBH	extra-base hits	**RHB**	right-handed batter
ESBR	Event-Specific Batting Runs	**SB**	stolen base
E.R.A.	earned run average	**SD**	standard deviation
G	games	**SLG**	slugging average
H	hits	**SLS**	significance-level-to-stay
HBP	hit-by-pitch	**SO**	strikeout
HR	home run	**SS**	shortstop
IP	inside-the-park	**Yr**	year

Baseball's All-Time Best Sluggers

CHAPTER 1

Fair Ball!

Why Adjustments
Are Needed

King Arthur's quest for it in the Middle Ages became a large part of his legend. Monty Python and Indiana Jones launched their searches in popular 1974 and 1989 movies. The mythic quest for the Holy Grail, the name given in Western tradition to the chalice used by Jesus Christ at his Passover meal the night before his death, is now often a metaphor for a quintessential search.

In the illustrious history of baseball, the "holy grail" is a ranking of each player's overall value on the baseball diamond. Because player skills are multifaceted, it is not clear that such a ranking is possible. In comparing two players, you see that one hits home runs much better, whereas the other gets on base more often, is faster on the base paths, and is a better fielder. So which player should rank higher?

In *Baseball's All-Time Best Hitters*, I identified which players were best at getting a hit in a given at-bat, calling them the *best hitters*. Many reviewers either disapproved of or failed to note my definition of "best hitter." Although frequently used in baseball writings, the terms "good hitter" or *best hitter* are rarely defined.

In a July 1997 *Sports Illustrated* article, Tom Verducci called Tony Gwynn "the best hitter since Ted Williams" while considering only batting average. With the likes of Willie Mays, Hank Aaron, and Mickey Mantle as candidates to rival Gwynn, it is clear that Verducci used *best hitter* in the same, limited way.

Best Batters and the Offensive Events Used to Determine Them

A broader category is *best batters*. These are the players with the best all-around ability to produce runs based on events emerging from their plate appearances. Those in the "holy grail" category would be the *best players*, the players who are best in all-around play.

The goal of *Baseball's All-Time Best Sluggers* is to identify the *best batters* in baseball history. Consequently, neither pitching nor fielding is considered in this book.

When a player steps up to the plate, one of more than a dozen events can happen. Here are the major ones. The player can get a single, double, triple, or home run, based on the number of bases earned on a hit. Home runs can be either inside or outside the park. Players also make outs. Outs, like hits, can be divided into several categories, including strikeouts, groundouts, and flyouts. Another major event is a base on balls, sometimes subcategorized into intentional or nonintentional. Additional events include sacrifice flies, sacrifice hits, hit-by-pitch, and reached-base-on-an-error.

The currency of baseball is runs. Since scoring more runs than one's opponent wins ballgames, a batter's primary role is to produce runs. A value could be placed on each offensive event, based on how it contributes to or hampers run scoring. A batter's overall value would then be calculated by multiplying the values of these events by the rate at which he gets them.

This concept, known as linear weights, dates back to the early 1960s and the pioneering work of George Lindsey. In the 1980s, John Thorn and Pete Palmer expanded on this idea with their "Batting Runs" formula, which plays a central role in their "Total Player Rating" in *Total Baseball*. Batting Runs has adjustments for both era-of-play and ballpark effects.

The study in this book extends the work of Thorn and Palmer. The basic formula, called Event-Specific Batting Runs, is developed. For the adjustment process, we will look at 10 *basic offensive events*: batting average, *doubles-plus-triples* (the sum of doubles and triples), triples, home runs, runs, RBIs, walks, strikeouts, stolen bases, and hit-by-pitches. Four adjustments are applied to these events: the effects of aging, ballpark effects, and two factors based on the era of play, as described later in this chapter.

Seven offensive events are used to rank the batters—the four kinds of hits, walks, and total outs. Four of these—triples, home runs, walks, and hit-by-pitches—are basic offensive events. The other three are derived from basic offensive events.

Singles are obtained from subtracting Extra-Base Hits (doubles-plus-triples plus home runs) from hits, where hits equals the batting average multiplied by at-bats. Doubles are obtained by subtracting triples from doubles-plus-triples. Total outs are obtained by subtracting hits from at-bats.

The reasons why doubles-plus-triples (DPTs), rather than doubles, are considered a basic offensive event are discussed in Chapters 4 and 8. In brief, a double is a hit intermediate between a single and a triple, but more like a triple in nature. The answer to the question of which batted balls become doubles versus triples is blurry, and depends significantly on the speed of the batter. Thus it is better to apply the four adjustments to doubles-plus-triples and to triples and obtain adjusted doubles by subtracting the latter from the former.

Why not use the other four basic offensive events in the Event-Specific Batting Runs formula? Individual run and RBI totals depend on the ability of one's teammates and the batter's position in the lineup, not just on the relative abilities of pitcher and batter. Batters fortunate to have teammates on base more often can garner RBIs more easily; a single hit with a man on third nets an RBI, but a bases-empty single doesn't.

Hence runs and RBIs are not used in the best-batter ranking system. They are used, however, to build a case for the existence of clutch hitters, with Yogi Berra, Pie Traynor, and Joe DiMaggio all ranking among the top 10.

Strikeouts, like other outs, hurt run scoring. They haven't been shown, however, to have a significantly different negative value from non-strikeout outs. Consequently they are not needed in the valuation.

Stolen bases are not used for two reasons. First, although they are an offensive event, they are not a batting event. Second, to evaluate stolen bases fairly, one also needs caught stealing data. Caught stealing data, however, have been consistently available only since 1951. Thus it becomes difficult to compare players from before and after that time.

Rankings are also provided for five additional *derived offensive events*: OBP, slugging average, OPS, Event-Specific Batting Runs (ESBRs), and Career Batter Rating (CBR). The first three events are popular ways to evaluate players, while the final two are the main formulas developed in this book—to identify the best batters and get a preliminary ranking of baseball's best players. Finally, position-adjusted results are also given for ESBRs and CBR.

Philosophy of Player Comparison Over Time

It is a tall order to develop a method that can compare athletic performance fairly over time. For most running and swimming events, race times have progressively declined over time. Does this mean that recent world record holders are better than their forebears? Not necessarily. To ensure fairness, the philosophy of this study involves a complete time-transport of players. In other words, the athlete from bygone times needs to have all the modern advantages today's stars enjoy—such as current equipment, today's sports medicine, training advances, new techniques, and nutritional advances. How can this be done?

The basic strategy is first to rank players within their own eras and then to integrate these era-restricted rankings into an overall ranking. We could develop a statistical method to test whether the collective abilities of players in the league are stable, improve, or decline over time. Such a method would be quite complex, however, and is therefore not attempted. Instead the rankings in this book are based on the assumption that the players from each era are equally talented, as described in Chapter 2.

The Evolving Game of Baseball

To the casual fan, baseball is a game that seemingly has changed little over time. Baseball announcers and reporters encourage this view, often unwittingly, when the accomplishments of current players are compared to those achieved in bygone eras without any caveats. Record-breaking performances—heralded events in the lore of baseball—invite such misperceptions. For example, Mark McGwire's 70 home runs and Sammy

Sosa's 66 home runs in 1998 vaulted them to the top of the single-season home run list—past Roger Maris's 61 in 1961 and Babe Ruth's 60 in 1927. Then in 2001 Barry Bonds established a new mark, with 73 home runs. Constancy is only a thin veneer, however, and among the most enduring features of more than a century of major league baseball play is that the game is constantly changing. In Chapter 3, we look at how offensive events have varied across baseball history.

Adjusting Player Averages

In this book, four principal adjustments are applied to a batter's raw statistical data in order to rank his overall batting ability. These adjustments are for hitting feasts and famines, ballpark differences, the talent pool, and late career declines, which are conceptually the same as those used in *Baseball's All-Time Best Hitters.* Since the rationale for each adjustment is explained in that book, only a brief description suffices here.

Hitting Feasts and Famines: Across time, different aspects of the game are in the ascendancy. For example, batting averages were quite high in the 1920s and 1930s. In today's game, power events such as doubles and home runs are at or near all-time highs. These shifts are adjusted out under the assumption that they have occurred as a result of changes other than shifts in player ability, such as rules, training, equipment, or ballparks. This adjustment makes the performance of the average *regular player* (defined in Chapter 2) equivalent across time.

Ballpark Effects: It is much easier to collect hits, hit home runs, and score runs in some ballparks than in others. Since players play half their games at home, their true value is more fairly appraised by adjusting out the effects of their home parks. In this book, the adjustments are made using ballpark effects that will be obtained for every basic offensive event except stolen bases and HBPs.

Talent Pool: A key consideration in comparing players from different eras is whether play has remained the same or has improved or declined over time. In *Full House,* Stephen J. Gould considered the standard deviation of the offensive event being studied to be a measure of the talent pool from which players in that season were selected: a large standard deviation means greater variability in performance among the players, implying that they were drawn from a smaller talent pool.

Although I believe that the standard deviation for a given event only imperfectly measures the talent pool for it, it is still an appropriate adjustment under a "percentile equivalence" assumption explained in Chapter 2.

Late Career Declines: Age and experience certainly play roles in the seasonal performances of ballplayers. Although experience is beneficial, the abilities of most players decline at the end of their careers. I believe that a better comparison can be made between players by discounting late career plate appearances of players with long careers. An aging profile for each offensive event is shown, and a cutoff based on number of at-bats or at-bats plus walks plus hit-by-pitches is used to define a player's "productive career" average.

The 100 Best Batters

Let's take a sneak preview of the best batters through the 2003 season (Table 1.1). It will surprise few baseball fans that Babe Ruth and Ted Williams claim the top two spots. Next comes Rogers Hornsby, who was the standout player in the National League in the 1920s, counterbalancing Ruth's American League dominance. In fourth place is the greatest star from our time, Barry Bonds, who fashioned three seasons—2001, 2002, and 2003— to cap an already fabulous career. Lou Gehrig, Ruth's longtime teammate, claims fifth place. Mickey Mantle places sixth, giving the Yankees three of the top six batters. Stan Musial, Ted Williams' National League counterpart, ranks seventh. Ty Cobb, who received more votes than Babe Ruth in the inaugural Hall of Fame class, ranks as the eighth best batter of all-time. Jimmie Foxx and Willie Mays round out the top 10.

As the four adjustments are further developed and applied throughout this book, we will see how this ranking was obtained.

Organization of the Book

In this book, a number of statistical and baseball terms are used. They are italicized at their point of first definition in the text. In other chapters, they are italicized when first used. All such terms are defined in the glossary, in addition to the chapter or appendix in which they are presented in detail.

The book is divided into two major sections: "The Methods" and "The Findings."

The Methods

A summary of the method for adjusting player averages is given in Chapter 2, with the detailed statistical aspects provided in Appendices A–G. The four adjustments are discussed in detail in Chapters 3–6. Because the adjustments are based on statistical principles, these chapters necessarily contain some references and descriptions of statistical methods, although the more technical details are provided in the appendices.

Chapters 3–6 provide additional insights into how the method detailed in Chapter 2 works. However, the essential ingredients for actually making the adjustments are given in Chapter 2 using data given in Appendices H–J. Readers anxious to see the findings may choose to skip those chapters.

The Findings

The basic offensive events are discussed in Chapters 7–12. Throughout the book, the basic offensive events are presented in the following order: batting average, doubles-plus-triples, triples, home runs, runs, RBIs, walks, strikeouts, and stolen bases. In each chapter, some additional results that go beyond the adjusted averages approach defined in "The Methods" are given. At the end of each chapter, the top 10 single-season and *productive career* performances based on the adjustment methods are highlighted. Lists of the top 100 single-season and productive career averages are given in Appendices L and M.

Table 1.1 The 100 Best Batters

1	Babe Ruth	34	Dick Allen	68	Cap Anson
2	Ted Williams	35	Eddie Murray	69	Reggie Smith
3	Rogers Hornsby	36	**Gary Sheffield**	70	Billy Hamilton
4	**Barry Bonds**	37	Rickey Henderson	71	Boog Powell
5	Lou Gehrig	38	Harry Heilmann	72	Sherry Magee
6	Mickey Mantle	39	Carl Yastrzemski	73	**John Olerud**
7	Stan Musial	40	Jesse Burkett	74	Joe Medwick
8	Ty Cobb	41	Wade Boggs	75	Keith Hernandez
9	Jimmie Foxx	42	Paul Waner	76	Norm Cash
10	Willie Mays	43	Duke Snider	77	Arky Vaughan
11	Mel Ott	44	**Fred McGriff**	78	Ralph Kiner
12	Honus Wagner	45	Al Kaline	79	Bob Johnson
13	Frank Robinson	46	Jack Clark	80	**Larry Walker**
14	Tris Speaker	47	Harry Stovey	81	Orlando Cepeda
15	Hank Aaron	48	**Ken Griffey Jr**	82	**Jason Giambi**
16	**Frank Thomas**	49	Rod Carew	83	Charlie Gehringer
17	Mike Schmidt	50	Tony Gwynn	84	Hack Wilson
18	Joe DiMaggio	51	**Manny Ramirez**	85	Joe Kelley
19	**Jeff Bagwell**	52	Joe Morgan	86	Jack Fournier
20	Roger Connor	53	Eddie Collins	87	Fred Clarke
21	Dan Brouthers	54	Joe Jackson	88	**Albert Belle**
22	Mark McGwire	55	Will Clark	89	Babe Herman
23	Reggie Jackson	56	Hank Greenberg	90	Elmer Flick
24	Willie McCovey	57	Dave Winfield	91	Pete Browning
25	Eddie Mathews	58	Zach Wheat	92	**Chipper Jones**
26	Nap Lajoie	59	**Jim Thome**	93	Tim Raines
27	**Edgar Martinez**	60	Al Simmons	94	Dolph Camilli
28	Harmon Killebrew	61	**Rafael Palmeiro**	95	Cy Williams
29	Ed Delahanty	62	Goose Goslin	96	Roberto Clemente
30	George Brett	63	**Mike Piazza**	97	Chuck Klein
31	Willie Stargell	64	Mike Tiernan	98	**Alex Rodriguez**
32	Johnny Mize	65	Billy Williams	99	Bill Terry
33	Sam Crawford	66	Ken Singleton	100	Paul Molitor
		67	Frank Howard		

Note: Active players are shown in bold.

Chapters 13–17 close in on the major goal of this book—determining the 100 best batters. Chapter 13 begins with two traditional, derived offensive event measures—OBP and slugging average—and their sum, OPS. Chapter 14 introduces two new methods, *Event-Specific Batting Runs* and *Career Batter Rating*, which yield the 100 best batters. Chapter 15 lists the 25 best batters at each position. Later, a list of the 100 best batters after adjustment for fielding position is provided. This list accounts for the fact that offensive performance tends to be lower for positions that have greater defensive demands.

Because of the involved nature of the adjustments, the findings are given through the 2003 season. However, Chapter 16 provides a brief update of the top performances and players from the 2004 season. Chapter 17 compares the Career Batter Rating to the work of Pete Palmer and Bill James, and maps a course for further improving the ranking of batting ability across baseball history.

Appendix N contains a complete list of all 1140 players who qualified for inclusion in this book, along with their adjusted averages and Career Batter Ratings.

PART ONE

The Methods

CHAPTER 2

Manager's Game Plan

Method for Identifying
the Best Batters

Who's the best doubles hitter in major league history?

Honus Wagner, but only because he didn't leg out enough of his inside-the-park smashes into triples. You should ask: Who's the best at hitting doubles-plus-triples?

OK, who's the best at hitting doubles-plus-triples?

Stan Musial edged out Honus Wagner for the top spot after playing era, park effects, and player aging were accounted for.

Back up. How can one account for era of play, park effects, and player aging in order to claim that Wagner and Musial are nearly equivalent in ability? After all, their careers are more than 40 years apart and they played in largely different ballparks.

The first two of these questions, "Who's the best . . . ?" and many others like them, are the questions on which we would most like to spend time—and we will in later chapters. The final question, "How can one account for era of play and park effect . . . ?", however, needs to be resolved first and is the main subject of this chapter.

This chapter describes the statistical method used to compare players over time. All statistical methods rely on assumptions, and users of statistically analyzed data should be aware of them. If the assumptions aren't valid, the conclusions based on them may be invalid as well. One can truly say that in statistical analyses "The devil is in the details."

Summary of the Game Plan

The overall game plan has seven steps, based on one primary assumption.

Primary Assumption: *After adjusting for ballpark effects, a pth percentile player in one year is equal in ability to a pth percentile player in another year for each basic offensive event.*

Identifying the Eligible Players

Step 1. Establish guidelines for deciding which players are eligible for the single-season and career lists.

Adjustment 1: For Hitting Feasts and Famines

Step 2. Calculate the *mean-adjusted averages* using standardizing averages.

Adjustment 2: For Ballpark Effects

Step 3. Obtain good estimates of the park effects for all basic offensive events and calculate the *park-adjusted averages* for players.

Adjustment 3: For the Talent Pool

Step 4. For each season, assess the performance spread for each basic offensive event.
Step 5. Obtain means and standard deviations from transformed distributions, and stabilize them using 5-year *moving averages*.

Calculating the Fully Adjusted Average

Step 6. Calculate the *fully adjusted average*.

Adjustment 4: For Late Career Declines

Step 7. For career performances, add the single-season totals together for the defined number of ABs or NFPs established as the productive career length for each offensive event.

That's it in a nutshell. The plan will now be explained in greater detail.

The Primary Assumption Explained

Primary Assumption: *After adjusting for effects, a pth percentile player in one year is equal in ability to a pth percentile player in another year for each basic offensive event.*

A *pth percentile player* is a player who is better than p out of 100 players in accomplishing the offensive event being considered, where p is any number between 0 and 100. Taking $p = 95$, this assumption means that the 95th percentile player in any one year, say 1910, is equal in ability to a 95th percentile player from any other year, say 2003.

This percentile equilibration for a given offensive event shouldn't be made simply by ranking the players, though. If that were done, every champion would rank no. 1 for the season and (given the same number of eligible players) receive the same percentile score. It wouldn't be possible then to distinguish historic performances from more "ordinary" championship seasons. Let's see how percentile rankings should be obtained.

Percentile Ranking and the Normal Distribution

Some powerful statistical theorems crown the *normal distribution* as the reigning queen of distributions. A *distribution* is a complete listing of the possible values of the variable, with their relative frequency of occurrence—batting average, for example. The percentile ranking method has been applied most routinely when the data have a normal distribution. Normal distributions are completely characterized by two numbers, the *mean* (or average) and the *standard deviation.* In other words, if two data sets have a normal distribution and have the same mean and standard deviation, then the distributions are identical. For normally distributed data, a percentile ranking for a given data point is obtained by subtracting from the mean and dividing by the standard deviation, a procedure known as *standardization,* yielding a result known as the *z-score.* As we will see later in the chapter, though, none of the basic offensive events have normal distributions. Consequently, to illustrate the idea, we'll look at a classic situation for which data are generally believed to be normally distributed.

Suppose we want to rank the heights of boys from two different fifth-grade classes for which we believe the heights are normally distributed, with the same mean and standard deviation. The tallest boy in one class is probably not exactly the same height as the tallest boy in the other. By measuring the two heights, we could identify which child is taller.

Alternatively, we could measure the height of the tallest child in each of the two classes and obtain their standardized heights, by subtracting the mean and dividing by the standard deviation of the entire population of fifth-grade boys. This "adjusted height" *z*-score, though, is much more general because it can be used to compare the height of the fifth-grade boys to the expected fifth-grade height of third-grade boys, as long as an assumption that boys maintain their percentile ranking from third to fifth grade holds.

Is this primary assumption true for baseball? Although it is doubtful that a 20th percentile player in, say, 1910 would even be a major leaguer today, our primary focus is on the best batters. Since more than 1000 players qualify for consideration, the top 100 players for a given offensive event are all at or above the 90th percentile. For these elite players, such an assumption may be reasonable. If the primary assumption is rejected, statistical methods that are more involved than those used here would be needed to establish a method to compare players across eras in a fair way.

Rankings Based on Other Assumptions

Let's examine the underlying assumptions on which other ranking methods are based. In most baseball encyclopedias, averages or event totals from one year are directly compared with totals from other years. Such rankings are based on an assumption that averages from different years are directly comparable.

An adjusted batting average, called *relative batting average,* is based on a different assumption. Relative batting average equals 100 times the player's batting average divided by the league batting average of players whose primary position was not pitcher. Relative batting average can be converted to look more like a batting average by multiplying it by some standardizing batting average, as shown in the final column of Table 2.1.

While Cobb tops the list under both assumptions, the rankings of other players shift around. Three players—Delahanty, Hamilton, and Ruth—drop out and are replaced by Gwynn, Lajoie, and Carew. Relative batting average represents a significant change from the raw batting average since the most recent player in the raw batting average list is Ted Williams, whereas Tony Gwynn (raw rank 16) and Rod Carew (raw rank 32) are more recent players who rank among the top 10 for relative batting average.

The basic assumption behind the relative batting average is that the league batting average rises or falls as a result of inherent changes in the game, not because players have become better or worse. According to this assumption, players should be ranked by their average *relative* to that of the average player, not by the raw averages themselves.

Relative batting average does not yield percentile equivalence over baseball history, though. While it does adjust for the mean league batting average, it fails to adjust for the spread of the batting averages in a given season. Consequently it is possible that nearly all of the top performances would come from seasons with very large spreads. For example, suppose that in one season, half of the players bat .300, while the other half bat .200. In a second season, all players bat .250. In both seasons, the league batting average is .250. Thus the players with .300 averages all have much higher RBAs (1.20 = .300/.250) than all players from the second season, who have RBAs of 1.00.

Since neither the raw batting average nor the relative batting average contains adjustments for the parks in which player played, the rankings in Table 2.1 assume that park effects are negligible.

Table 2.1   Top 10 Career Raw and Relative Batting Averages

Raw Batting Average			Relative Batting Average			
Rank	Player	Avg.	Rank	Player	RBA	Adj. Avg.
1	Ty Cobb	.366	1	Ty Cobb	134.8	.354
2	Rogers Hornsby	.358	2	Joe Jackson	133.1	.349
3	Joe Jackson	.356	3	Pete Browning	130.8	.343
4	Dan Brouthers	.349	4	Dan Brouthers	128.3	.337
5	Pete Browning	.349	5	Ted Williams	128.1	.336
6	Ed Delahanty	.346	6	Tony Gwynn	127.7	.335
7	Tris Speaker	.345	7	Nap Lajoie	127.4	.334
8	Billy Hamilton	.344	8	Rod Carew	127.0	.333
9	Ted Williams	.344	9	Rogers Hornsby	126.2	.331
10	Babe Ruth	.344	10	Tris Speaker	125.4	.329

Note: RBA = relative batting average, Adj. Avg. = .2625 × RBA/100, where .2625 is the standardizing average used, which is the non-pitchers' batting average for NL players from 1969 to 1992.

Source for RBA: Total Baseball, Seventh Edition, p. 2294.

THE METHODS

Each of the seven steps of the game plan will now be explained.

Step 1. Establish guidelines for which players are eligible for the single-season and career lists.

Regular Players

A league average is a composite of averages of individual players who have different abilities. The foremost difference is that between pitchers and non-pitchers. The percentage of plate appearances amassed by pitchers has declined throughout history—and has dropped to very low levels in the American League since the designated hitter was introduced in 1973. Thus the league average increasingly has reflected the batting experience of non-pitchers. In addition, everyday players generally bat better than those riding the bench or late season call-ups. Consequently we will divide the players into three groups: *regulars*, non-regulars, and pitchers.

A plate appearance is the fundamental turnstile of a player's batting experience. Plate appearances, which can also be called times facing pitcher, include at-bats, bases on balls, hit-by-pitches, sacrifice hits, sacrifice flies, and catcher's interference. Unfortunately we lack a complete accounting of plate appearances throughout baseball history. We do have at-bats, bases on balls, and hit-by-pitches though, which comprise the vast majority of times facing pitcher. Hence at-bats plus walks plus hit-by-pitches are called *net-facing pitchers* (NFPs), a term that was coined by David Stephan.

How should *regular players* be defined? One could require that regulars have a minimum number of NFPs per game. However, the average number of NFPs per game per player has declined over time.

In this book, regular players are defined using the following approach. For each season, the minimum number of NFPs was found such that players with this number of NFPs or more accounted for 75% of the non-pitcher NFPs. For example, in 2000, there were 99,376 NFPs in the National League. Of these, 5438 were by pitchers and 93,938 were by non-pitchers. Of all the non-pitcher NFPs, 75.2% were by players with at least 272 NFPs.

Using the *multiple changepoint regression* model (see Appendix C), NFP eras were identified, and a minimum number of NFPs per game established for each era, as shown in Table 2.2. For example, to be a regular in the National League between 1904 and 1938, a player needed 2.2 NFPs per game. Since there were 154 games in a season, this translates to 339 NFPs for the year. During these years, there was an average of 7.4 regulars and 12.3 non-regulars per team.

A *regular player-season* is a given season for which a given player was a regular. For example, Mickey Cochrane was a regular every year from 1925 to 1935, so he had 11 regular player-seasons in his career.

The minimum number of NFPs per game of regular players generally drops over time, while the numbers of regulars and non-regulars per team rise. The strongest exception to these trends occurred in the American League from 1908 to 1916, when the numbers of both regulars and non-regulars jumped dramatically. Perhaps the supe-

Table 2.2 Minimum Number of NFPs to Be Considered a Regular Player
          in a Given Season

Years	League	Minimum NFPs per Game	Minimum NFPs	Number of Regulars per Team	Number of Others per Team
1876–84	NL	3.4	*	6.2	7.6
1885–95		2.6	*	6.5	9.3
1896–1903		2.2	*	7.2	10.0
1904–38		2.2	339	7.4	12.3
1939–61		2.0	308	7.9	13.9
1962–83		2.0	324	8.0	13.7
1984–2003		1.7	275	8.9	13.6
1901–03	AL	2.4	*	6.9	9.1
1904–07		2.4	370	6.9	10.0
1908–16		1.9	293	7.8	14.5
1917–24		2.4	370	7.2	11.7
1925–30		2.1	323	7.6	12.5
1931–41		2.4	370	7.3	11.2
1942–60		2.0	308	7.9	13.7
1961–2003		2.0	324	8.5	13.6
1882–91	AA	2.4	*	6.9	10.2
1884	UA	1.4	150	8.0	20.9
1890	PL	3.1	409	6.9	5.8
1914–15	FL	2.2	339	7.4	11.3

Note: Number of Others Per Team = Average number of nonregulars per team with 1 or more NFPs.

*NFPs are not given for years in which the number of games varied regularly. NFPs differ from the listed values for 1918, 1919, 1972, 1981, 1994, and 1995.

rior performance of the stars of this period—Ty Cobb, Tris Speaker, Nap Lajoie, and Joe Jackson—led to dissatisfaction with the lackluster play of some league-mates and resulted in a search for other superior players. The large *performance spread* during these years may explain why these four hitters from this narrow slice of baseball history rank among the 11 best in *Baseball's All-Time Best Hitters*.

Qualifying Players and Career Position

A minimum amount of play will now be chosen for a player to qualify for the career average lists presented later in the book. Common standards are 4000 at-bats or 1000 games. Since walks are positive contributions to a player's offensive output, it doesn't make sense to exclude Ferris Fain, who had 3930 at-bats but amassed 904 walks, while including, say, Mark Koenig, who had 4271 at-bats but only 222 walks. So we'll adopt 4000 at-bats plus walks plus hit-by-pitches as the minimum standard.

The players who meet this standard are *qualifying players*. Through the 2003 season, there are 1140 qualifying players, including more than 100 active players.

Since we will look at the top all-around batters by position as well as overall, we need to define a player's career position. A player's *career position* is the position at which he played the most games through his 9000th NFP. Outfielders are handled in a special way. First, they must have played more games in the outfield than any other position. Then the particular outfield location (left, center, right) at which they played most is defined as their career position.

Step 2. Calculate the mean-adjusted averages using standardizing averages.

We will look at nine basic offensive events. For four of them—hits, doubles-plus-triples, triples, and home runs—the raw event average is obtained by dividing by the player's at-bats. For the other five events—runs, RBIs, bases on balls, strikeouts, and stolen bases—the raw event average is obtained by dividing the offensive event counts by NFPs. NFPs are used for the latter five since they provide a better basis on which to evaluate the event rate (e.g., a player can score a run or steal a base as often after drawing a walk as after hitting a single).

Formula 2.1   **Mean-adjusted average**

Mean-adjusted average = (Raw average + REC) × season factor, where the season factor = *standardizing average*/season average and REC is the *rare events correction*.

Notes:
1. The standardizing average is the regular players' average for the offensive event in National League seasons from 1977 to 1992. These averages are: BA, .270; DPT, .0547; 3B, .0077; HR, .025; R, .119; RBI, .111; BB .091; SO, .132; SB, .027, HBP, .0047.
2. The season average is the regular players' average for the offensive event in the season of interest.
3. The rare events correction term is used for triples, home runs, and stolen bases. It is defined as 0.5/AB if the player has 0 of the given events for the season, and 0.5/{Avg. no. of ABs for regular players in season}, for players with at least 1 event. For SBs, NFPs are used rather than ABs. The rationale for this correction term is given in Appendix E.
4. When mentioning adjusted averages later in the text, the particular offensive event will often be inserted before the word "average," for example, mean-adjusted batting average.

The mean-adjusted batting average is simply the relative batting average (in which the league average is limited to regular players) multiplied by the standardizing average. A recent book, *Leveling the Field* by G. Scott Thomas, essentially applies this adjustment across baseball history to other offensive events besides batting average. While it is a good starting place, mean-adjusted averages are insufficient to provide a fair comparison of baseball players.

Step 3. Obtain good estimates of the park effects for all offensive events and calculate park-adjusted averages for all players.

The park effects for various offensive events can be quite substantial, thereby impacting the performances of players from different teams. Although the need for a park adjustment is widely appreciated—especially since Coors Field in Colorado is recognized as a hitter's heaven—it has rarely been applied, except in the case of run scoring, which Thorn, Palmer, and Gershman do in *Total Baseball*.

Appendix E shows how to obtain park effects and Appendix J gives adjusted park indices for all offensive events.

Step 4. For each season, assess the performance spread for each basic offensive event.

Our knowledge about which players are the best in a given season comes through comparison with their peers. Comparisons between players from different seasons are much more difficult, though. A superior player who plays in a weak league will stand out much more than he would if the competition were stiffer.

For batting average, Stephen J. Gould established the basic rationale for using the standard deviation as a measure of the talent pool. In *Full House*, he wrote:

> Two arguments, and supporting data, convince me that shrinkage of variation (with consequent disappearance of 0.400 hitting) must be measuring a general improvement of play. . . .

Formula 2.2   **Park-adjusted average**

Park-adjusted average = mean-adjusted average ÷ park factor

Formula 2.1 is used to obtain the mean-adjusted average. The park factor formula is

$$\text{Park factor} = 1 + M \times (\text{API}/100 - 1),$$

where $M = .429$, when $n = 8$; $M = .444$, when $n = 10$; $M = .455$, when $n = 12$; $M = .462$, when $n = 14$; and $M = .467$, when $n = 16$, n is the number of teams in the league, and the adjusted park index (API) is obtained from Appendix J. (See Definitions 6.1 for more explanation of the park factor.)

---

1. Complex systems improve when the best performers play by the same rules over extended periods of time.
   . . .

2. As play improves and bell curves march toward the right wall, variation must shrink at the right tail.

In this book, we apply this idea to all basic offensive events. We will call the season standard deviation of the park-adjusted average the *performance spread*, and will use it as a measure of the talent pool. A further discussion of this adjustment is given in Chapter 5.

Positive Skewness and Its Change over Time

When data are highly skewed, the standard deviation is highly affected by the extreme performances and is therefore not an ideal measure of performance spread. All of the nine basic offensive events have positive *skewness*, which indicates that the most extreme averages are more likely to be above the mean, rather than below. For example, the top hitters for average in a given season are likely to be farther away from the overall batting average than the worst hitters. For baseball data, the standard deviation becomes a more useful number if the skewness is close to zero, a key property of normally distributed data. Before the standard deviations are calculated, therefore, the park-adjusted averages need to be "transformed" to be more normal-like.

Two examples show how the most extreme averages from one era have been much farther from the league average than in another because of transitions in skewness over time.

In 1920 Babe Ruth smashed 54 home runs, personally out-homering each team other than the Yankees. Ruth's tally was 14.6% of the 8-team American League home run total. In 2001, 2952 home runs were hit in the 16-team National League, which is 1476 per 8 teams. For Barry Bonds to have attained the same fraction of league home runs as Ruth in 2001, he would have needed to hit 216 home runs!

Stolen bases have gone the opposite way over time. In 1982, American League players stole 1394 bases in a 14-team league, the equivalent of 797 SBs per 8 teams. Rickey Henderson stole 130 bases, 16.3% of the 8-team total. Seventy years earlier, in 1912, American League players swiped 1809 bases, led by Clyde Milan's 88. Milan would have had to steal 295 bases to have had the same percentage of the total.

Unfortunately, standard deviation adjustments alone are not sufficient to bring Ruth and Henderson down from the stratosphere, because the skewnesses from the years being compared are so different—for home runs, 4.29 in 1920, compared to 1.81 in 2001, while for stolen bases, 1.31 in 1912, compared to 3.71 in 1982.

Transformation Time

Appendix E describes the method used to transform the park-adjusted event averages into more normal-like distributions. The results of that work are shown in Table 2.3. The *transformations* are characterized by a number between 0 and 1, called the *trans-*

Table 2.3   Transformation Powers over Baseball History

Event	Initial Year								
	1876	1901	1920	1931	1947	1963	1969	1977	1993
BA	0.50								
R	0.50	0.75							
DPT	0.50		0.75						
SO	0.33				0.50				
RBI	0.50					0.75			
BB	0.50								
3B	0.50						0.33		
HR	0.33	0.20	0.25	0.33	0.50				
SB (NL)	0.33		0.25	0.20		0.15		0.33	
SB (AL)	0.33		0.25	0.20					0.25

Notes: For blank cells in the table, the previous number in the row gives the transformation power. Stolen base transformations differ by league from 1963 to 2003.

formation power. If a lower transformation power is needed to render the distribution bell shaped, it strongly suggests that the original data had more positive skewness.

Some interesting insights about baseball performance can be gleaned from Table 2.3. For example, a single power suffices for batting average and bases on balls over baseball history, indicating that the forces leading to the distributional shape of these events have changed little over time. The power for three other events—runs, doubles-plus-triples, and RBIs—improved from 0.50 to 0.75, the highest power in the table. This signifies that forces in the game have required more clustering of these offensive events over its history—all regulars have been expected to excel at run scoring since 1901, doubles-plus-triples since 1920, and RBI production since 1963.

Events whose powers are 0.33 or lower could be called "specialty" events. By that definition, base stealing is the specialty event par excellence. In nearly every era, base-stealing has been at the bottom of the transformation power "food chain." Home runs and strikeouts were specialty events prior to 1947. Since 1969, triples have been specialty events, with such notable players as Mark McGwire and Mike Piazza not even hitting one for years!

Home runs and stolen bases are the only offensive events requiring more than one transformation power shift. Home runs increased in positive skewness at the turn of the 20th century but declined through the first half of the 20th century, before stabilizing after World War II. Stolen bases became more highly skewed with the onset of the lively ball era in 1920, increased in positive skewness after World War II, but reversed that trend toward the end of the 20th century, around 1977 in the National League and 1993 in the American League.

Step 5. Obtain means and standard deviations from transformed distributions, and stabilize them using 5-year moving averages.

Having transformed the offensive events to achieve approximate normality, the means and standard deviations for each season are computed. With these numbers, we are almost ready to compute z-scores for player performances. However, these means and standard deviations show considerable variation from year to year. While some of the variation over time reflects true changes in the game, some is random variation. If we could selectively smooth out the random component of variation, while leaving the true variation component, a better estimate of the standard deviation—that is, the performance spread—could be made. The smoothing out is done using a 5-year moving average. The statistical details for this approach are given in Appendix B.

Step 6. Calculate the fully adjusted average.

The fully adjusted average is obtained in two steps: (1) computing the player's z-score and (2) re-scaling it based on standardizing seasons. First, we obtain the player's z-score:

Formula 2.3   **Player's z-score**

Player's z-score

= (player's park-adjusted average − regular players' park-adjusted mean)/regular players' park-adjusted SD, where all right-hand terms are transformed as described in step 4.

Why should we do this? Normal distributions are specified by their means and standard deviations. The z-score is a very special normal distribution, one with a mean of 0 and a standard deviation of 1, which allows us to put all normal distributions on the same scale!

The z-scores can be translated into percentile rankings, as described earlier in the chapter. Using the player's z-scores, all seasons can now be combined together, since the data are scaled the same. Then, given the primary assumption set forth at the outset of this chapter, a 95th percentile player from 1904 is comparable to a 95th percentile player from 2003.

Rescaling the z-Score Based on Standardizing Seasons

Statistically, the z-score is nice. It is more difficult, however, to interpret than a number that is more familiar to baseball fans. Thus the z-scores will be rescaled. This is done using the formula:

Formula 2.4   **Fully adjusted average**

Fully adjusted average = {standardizing regulars' PA mean + player's z-score $\times$ standardizing regulars' PA SD$\}^{1/\text{TP}}$ – REC,

where PA = "park-adjusted," TP is the transformation power that was in effect for the standardizing seasons, and REC is the "rare events correction" term given in Table 2.4.

The standardizing regulars' park-adjusted means and SDs are given in Table 2.4.

Technical Note: The part of the fully adjusted average formula outside the braces is called a *back transformation*. It reverses the transformation step. The benefits of the transformation, however, have been achieved, since all three terms inside the braces were computed on the transformed scale.

Table 2.4   **Regular Players' Park-Adjusted Means and Standard Deviations for Standardizing Years**

Offensive Event	Transformation			Percentiles		
	Mean	**SD**	**Power**	**1%**	**50%**	**99%**
BA	.5191	.0263	.50	.210	.269	.337
DPT	.1123	.0198	.75	13	27	43
3B*	.1968	.0459	.333	0	3.3	14
HR*	.1508	.0577	.50	0	11	40
R	.2012	.0326	.75	34	65	99
RBI	.1901	.0455	.75	20	60	109
BB	.2954	.0569	.50	15	48	101
SO	.3567	.0631	.50	24	70	140
SB*	.2718	.0963	.333	0	11	67
HBP*	.1683	.0430	.333	0	2.1	10

Notes: Data are from the 1648 regular player-seasons in the NL from 1977 to 1992. The percentiles are computed using the back transformation and normal distribution theory; counts are per 500 ABs for DPT, 3B, and HR, and per 550 NFPs for R, RBI, BB, SO, SB, and HBP.

*These means and SDs for these events have the REC added in.

Since the standardizing regulars' park-adjusted SD and the transformation power are both positive, mathematically the fully adjusted average yields the same player ranking as the z-score itself. Hence the rankings for the ten *basic offensive events* adjusted for in this book do not depend on whether we standardize the z-scores to the deadball era, the power era (defined in Chapter 3), or any other era.

The standardizing season or era we choose, though, *does* matter when we look at *derived offensive events,* such as slugging average. In the deadball era, home runs were relatively rare. As a result, the slugging average was dependent more on the number of hits (measured by batting average) than on the quality of hits (such as home runs), compared to today.

The most comprehensive ranking in this book, Event-Specific Batting Runs, is a *derived offensive event.* As such, the chosen standardizing seasons will have some effect on the relative ranking of players. In this book, standardizing averages are obtained from the 1977–92 National League seasons. These seasons were chosen as the standardizing seasons since they are relatively recent, and thus will be familiar to many readers, and they represent arguably the most stable period in baseball history for all of the basic offensive events. These seasons are described in greater detail in Chapter 3.

Step 7. For career performances, cumulate the single-season totals for the defined number of ABs or NFPs established as the productive career length for each offensive event.

All the steps so far have applied to single seasons. To obtain career performance results, one needs to combine data from different seasons. For adjusted career event counts, such as adjusted career home runs, one simply sums the fully adjusted totals from one year to the next. The fully adjusted total for a season is obtained by multiplying the fully adjusted average by the number of at-bats or NFPs.

A player's performance changes over his career, mainly because of two forces: development of baseball skills and physical ability. These forces generally oppose each other—skills improve with age and experience, while physical ability tends to decline. Performance on the field is a result of the magnitude and proportion of each of these opposing forces.

Since there is a selection process regarding which players continue to play, it is most useful to track the effect of age in the same players over time. The results provided here are based on *longtime players,* those with 8000 at-bats or 9000 NFPs, depending on the event being considered. Table 2.5 gives the *milestone* at-bats (or NFPs) at which the event averages peak (peak AB or NFP), and are maintained at near the *peak average,* called the *productive career length.* These terms and results are all explained in detail in Chapter 4.

Table 2.5   Productive Career Lengths for Offensive Events

Event	Peak AB	Productive Career Length (ABs)
Batting average	5000	8000
Doubles-plus-triples	4000	6000
Triples	2000	4000
Home runs	6000	7000
Slugging average	5000	8000

Event	Peak NFP	Productive Career Length (NFPs)
Runs	6000	8000
RBIs	8000	9000
Walks	9000	9000
Strikeouts	9000	9000
Stolen bases	4000	5000
On-Base Percentage	8000	9000
OPS	7000	9000
Event-Specific Batting Runs	7000	9000

Note: Peak AB (NFP) is the milestone at-bat (NFP) at which the offensive event average peaks.

The seven-step game plan outlined at the beginning of the chapter has now been described. The method is applied to Rogers Hornsby's 1924 season for batting average in the Stats Time box on the next page.

Is the Power Transformation Approach Really Needed?

The transformation in step 4 is admittedly complex. Is it really needed? In short, yes, as will now be shown.

For well-behaved distributions, there are an infinite number of *moments*. The first is the mean, the second is the standard deviation, the third is the skewness, and the fourth is the kurtosis. Each moment in the sequence is less important in characterizing the distribution than the previous one. The mean-adjusted average adjusts only for the first moment. In *Baseball's All-Time Best Hitters*, the case was made that the square root of the second moment, the standard deviation, was also needed. Power transformations adjust for the third and fourth moments as well.

Table 2.6 shows the productive career home run rate per 500 at-bats under three approaches: no power transformation (None), a square root ($\sqrt{}$) power transformation across all history, or a variable power transformation (Var) by era, as given in step 4. All career rates among the top 20 for any method are presented. The results can vary considerably for players who played before 1947. For example, Babe Ruth had

Let's work through the 7 steps identified in Chapter 2 for Rogers Hornsby's 1924 season. In 1924, Hornsby rapped out 227 hits in only 536 ABs, for a batting average of .4235.

Step 1. Hornsby's 1924 season easily passes the threshold of 339 NFP for him to be considered a regular.

Step 2. The season factor is .9094 = (.270/.2969), since the standardizing batting average is .270 and the mean batting average of regulars in 1924 was .2969 (from Table H.2 in Appendix H). Thus Hornsby's mean-adjusted batting average is .3851 = .4235 × .9094. If we multiply the season factor, .9094, by Hornsby's raw hit total of 227, we get his mean-adjusted hits, 206.4.

Step 3. The adjusted park index for batting average for St. Louis for 1924 is 102 (from Appendix J), yielding a park factor of 1.0086. So Hornsby's 1924 park-adjusted batting average is .3818 = .3851 ÷ 1.0086.

Steps 4, 5. The *transformation power* for all years is 0.50 for batting average (from Table 2.3). The standardizing park-adjusted mean and SD for the 1924 National League season were .5180 and .0271, respectively (from Tables I.2 and I.5 in Appendix I).

Step 6. The player's z-score (see Formula 2.3) removes the context of the 1924 season and produces a term that can be compared across eras:
Player's z-score = $(.3818^{.50} - .5180)/.0271 = (.6179 - .5180)/.0271 = 3.686$.

The fully adjusted batting average puts the z-score into the context of the 1977–92 National League season averages (see Formula 2.4 and Table 2.4):
Fully adjusted batting average = $(.5191 + 3.686 \times .0263)^{1/.50} = .3795$, since the mean and SD for batting average from Table 2.4 are .5191 and .0263.

Step 7. This step applies to career performance and does not apply to the fully adjusted single-season batting average.

---

between 50 and 66 adjusted HRs/500 ABs, depending on the method used. Over a career, this translates to between 803 and 1037 adjusted home runs, a range of more than 230 home runs!

Table 2.6 shows that although the rank of the top 10 players does not change that much for the three different methods, there is considerable movement among the next 10 batters. Mantle ranks 11th with the variable method but is 23rd when no transformation is used. Ralph Kiner rises eight spots when using the variable power transformation method, while Charlie Hickman, Rogers Hornsby, Harry Stovey, and Cy Williams all drop at least nine spots.

Clearly the adjustments matter. Since the variable power transformation method equalizes the distributions more than the other two, I claim that it is best one to use.

Table 2.6   Productive Career Adjusted Home Runs per 500 At-Bats for Three
Possible Transformations

Player	Adj. HRs/500 ABs			Rank		
	None	$\sqrt{}$	Var	None	$\sqrt{}$	Var
1 Babe Ruth	59	66	50	1	1	1
2 Mark McGwire	41	41	41	2	2	2
3 Ted Williams	39	40	39	3	3	3
4 Barry Bonds	35	36	36	7	7	4
5 Mike Schmidt	35	35	35	5	9	5
6 Lou Gehrig	35	37	34	6	4	6
7 Harmon Killebrew	33	34	34	13	12	7
8 Jimmie Foxx	35	36	33	8	5	8
9 Dave Kingman	33	33	33	12	13	9
10 Bill Nicholson	34	34	32	11	10	10
11 Mickey Mantle	31	32	32	23	17	11
12 Ralph Kiner	31	32	32	20	18	12
13 Willie Stargell	32	32	32	16	21	13
14 Darryl Strawberry	31	32	32	18	22	14
15 Hack Wilson	35	35	32	9	8	15
16 Reggie Jackson	31	31	31	19	23	16
17 Rogers Hornsby	35	36	31	4	6	17
18 Joe DiMaggio	32	32	31	17	16	18
19 Willie McCovey	31	31	31	24	24	19
20 Wally Berger	32	33	31	15	14	20
23 Harry Stovey	33	33	30	14	15	23
25 Mel Ott	31	32	29	22	20	25
27 Charlie Hickman	34	34	29	10	11	27
32 Cy Williams	31	32	28	21	19	32

Note: None = no power transformation used; $\sqrt{}$ = square root transformation for all players; Var = variable transformation powers, given in Table 2.3.

Even greater changes can be seen among the top single-seasons shown in Table 2.7. Using the variable transformation power method, Barry Bonds' 2001 season was the best for adjusted home runs rate in baseball history. That season drops to third with no power transformation.

Babe Ruth's 1919 season yields 103 and 86 adjusted HRs/500 ABs using the two cruder methods, compared to 62 HRs/500 ABs for the variable power transformation method. McGwire's 1998 and Bonds' 2002 seasons rank much higher with the variable transformation power method, while Tim Jordan's 1906 season drops from 4th to 12th.

Table 2.7 Single-Season Adjusted Home Runs per 500 At-Bats for Three Possible Transformations

Player-Season	Adj. HRs/500 ABs			Rank		
	None	$\sqrt{\ }$	Var	None	$\sqrt{\ }$	Var
Barry Bonds, 2001	69	74	74	3	5	1
Babe Ruth, 1920	64	79	64	6	3	2
Babe Ruth, 1919	86	103	62	1	1	3
Barry Bonds, 2002	58	62	62	13	14	4
Mark McGwire, 1998	57	59	59	15	17	5
Babe Ruth, 1927	71	80	58	2	2	6
Babe Ruth, 1921	60	71	56	10	6	7
Buck Freeman, 1899	62	65	54	5	6	8
Babe Ruth, 1926	64	72	54	5	6	9
Ed Delahanty, 1893	61	64	54	9	11	10
Tim Jordan, 1906	68	75	52	4	4	12
Babe Ruth, 1928	58	65	50	14	10	15
Rogers Hornsby, 1922	62	66	50	7	8	16

Note: $\sqrt{\ }$ = square root transformation for all players; None = no power transformation used; Var = variable transformation powers, given in Table 2.3.

CHAPTER 3

New Ball!

Historical Changes
in Offensive Events

Baseball is a continually evolving game. Rates of home runs, strikeouts, and other offensive events change as a result of innovations in baseball equipment and in the style of play, including new pitches, new batting methods, and new offensive and defensive strategies. Change in the talent pool, which occurs most dramatically at times of expansion or contraction in the number of major league teams, also plays a role. Finally, the baseball field itself affects the rates of offensive events. Field effects are quite dramatic, because ballparks can and do differ so much. Fence distances, field surface (Astroturf versus natural grass), and visibility of the ball by the hitter (the part of the park in direct center field from which the pitch needs to be seen is known as the "batter's eye") are among the key park differences. A detailed account of changes across baseball history is given in "The Changing Game," a chapter by Bill Felber and Gary Gillette in the seventh edition of *Total Baseball*.

One of the four adjustments in our game plan, presented in the last chapter (Step 2), is an adjustment for the averages of regular players for the various offensive events. In this chapter, using graphics, we look at how league averages for the 9 basic offensive events (and several derived ones) have changed over the 20th century. Our principal interest is to identify major eras in the history of baseball. The graphs play no direct role in the adjustment. Only the identification of the eras for the transformation fitting (Step 4) and the selection of the 1977–92 National League seasons as the *standardizing years* (Steps 2 and 6) are used.

In *The Evolution of Baseball*, Russell Wright also used graphs to examine the "history of the major leagues." Wright combined data over 5-, 10-, and roughly 20-year intervals. A simple *linear regression* model provides a single measure of the rate of change in series of values, known as a *slope*. In this chapter, a more statistically advanced method, *piecewise linear regression* (see Appendix A for a detailed description), is used, since a series of upturns and downturns in event averages have occurred over time. This method helps to identify when shifts in the slope have occurred. From the regression, we can identify major shifts in average from one year to the next as well as long periods of stability. Years in which major shifts occur for several offensive events help us to identify eras in the game's history.

In this chapter, six eras are identified. Then, piecewise linear regression plots are shown for all basic offensive events, as well as percentage Extra-Base Hits (EBHs), On-Base Percentage (OBP), slugging average, and On-Base-Plus-Slugging (OPS).

Eras in Baseball History

Baseball history can be divided into different eras of play, and many baseball writers have done so. Post-19th century baseball has been divided into six eras. The transition from one era to the next is marked by some historical event leading to changes in the averages on the field, sometimes gradually, sometimes dramatically.

Tables 3.1 and 3.2 help to identify differences between the eras. In Table 3.1, the differences are shown numerically. For example, run scoring has differed by a run per game, from 3.86 in the big strike zone era (big K zone, for short) to 4.86 in the ongoing power era.

Table 3.2 identifies the periods of the six eras and provides a relative comparison of the various event averages across them, by indicating whether they are in the lowest, middle, or highest third of the range.

Deadball Era (1901–19)

During this era, baseballs were not constantly replaced during a game, and so became soiled, scuffed, or mushy. The condition of these baseballs favored the pitchers and made it particularly difficult to smash home runs. This era, therefore, was the lowest in run scoring, EBHs, bases on balls, and OPS. It had high records for speed, though, being the best era for both stolen bases and triples.

Table 3.1   Offensive Event Averages by Era, 1901–2003

Era	R/G	BA	2B	3B	HR	BB	SO	SB	OBP	SLG	OPS
Deadball	3.93	.254	18.1	7.0	2.3	42	56	18.0	.316	.332	.649
Lively ball	4.70	.276	23.8	6.0	6.8	47	46	6.7	.340	.389	.729
Post–WWII	4.46	.259	20.6	4.2	12.0	52	65	4.6	.333	.390	.723
Big K zone	3.86	.245	18.7	3.5	11.6	44	88	6.3	.310	.366	.676
DH	4.20	.257	21.4	3.3	11.3	48	79	10.3	.326	.381	.706
Power	4.85	.267	25.8	2.9	15.4	51	93	9.7	.340	.423	.762

Notes: Values for 2B, 3B, and HR are per 500 ABs; values for BB, SO, and SB are per 550 NFPs.

Years for the eras are given in Table 3.2.

Table 3.2   Relative Level of Various Offensive Events by Era

Era	Years	R/G	BA	2B	3B	HR	BB	SO	SB	OPS
Deadball	1901–19	L	L	**L**	**H**	**L**	L	L	**H**	**L**
Lively ball	1920–46	**H**	**H**	**H**	H	M	M	**L**	L	H
Post–WWII	1947–62	M	M	M	L	H	**H**	M	L	H
Big K zone	1963–68	**L**	**L**	L	L	H	**L**	H	L	**L**
DH	1969–92	M	M	M	L	H	M	H	**M**	M
Power	1993–	**H**	**H**	**H**	**L**	**H**	**H**	**H**	M	**H**

Note: L, M, or H = average in lowest, middle, or highest third of range, with the highest and lowest averages for each event (column) highlighted in bold.

Lively Ball Era (1920–46)

Starting in 1920, baseballs were replaced more frequently during the game. Babe Ruth immediately took advantage of the change, using a full swing with an uppercut to loft balls over the outfield fences. Within this era, there are two main shifts in the event averages. The first occurred after the 1930 season, when the National League made a change in the type of baseball used, leading to dramatic declines in offense. Second, during World War II, many of the game's best players served in the military. Consequently, the averages were substantially lower during 1942–45. The main characteristics of the lively ball era are shown in Table 3.3, where they are partitioned into three sub-eras.

Table 3.3   Offensive Event Averages by Sub-Era, 1920–46

Era	R/G	BA	2B	3B	HR	BB	SO	SB	OBP	SLG	OPS
1920–30	4.88	.286	24.4	7.1	6.1	44	42	8.4	.347	.400	.747
1931–41	4.81	.275	24.6	5.6	7.8	47	49	5.5	.340	.393	.732
1942–46	4.07	.256	20.9	4.5	6.2	49	51	5.6	.326	.353	.679

Note: Values for 2B, 3B, HR are per 500 ABs; BB, SO, SB are per 550 NFPs.

Post-World War II Era (1947–62)

In 1947, Jackie Robinson became the first black to play major league baseball in the 20th century. In the coming years, major black stars such as Willie Mays ('51), Ernie Banks ('53), Hank Aaron ('54), and Frank Robinson ('56) exploded onto the scene, principally in the National League. The year 1946 does not mark the start of the post–WWII era because, in many ways, it was a transitional year, as team lineups were jockeyed and the baseball skills of returning players were reassessed. OBP, SLG, and OPS averages are very similar to those in the lively ball era, while home runs were substantially higher. Even so, run scoring is lower, primarily because of the decline in batting average.

Big Strike Zone Era (1963-68)

In 1963, the strike zone was expanded. Predictably, batting averages and walks declined, while strikeouts rose (especially in the American League). Even though the home run rate was the same as in the post–WWII era, run scoring dropped by half a run per game. All the events except home runs and strikeouts were low during this era. This is the shortest of any of the six eras. It was deliberately brought to an end by baseball management decisions because the fewer runs and hits that characterized the era contributed to a decline in fan interest.

Designated Hitter Era (1969-92)

In 1969, the strike zone was reduced and the pitching mound was lowered from 15 inches to 10 inches above the home plate level. This led to an immediate jump in run scoring. The rise, however, was relatively short lived, and run scoring again began declining in 1971. Run scoring in the National League leveled out on its own, while run scoring from the American League received a big jolt in 1973 from the introduction of the designated hitter (DH).

Perhaps the defining characteristic of the DH era is its moderateness. It is the only era without any extreme averages, and 6 of the 9 events presented in Table 3.2 are in the middle third of the range. This era is used in this book to standardize the adjusted player averages. As a consequence, closer inspection of the era is helpful. Let's take a closer look at the era by dividing it into three sub-eras (Table 3.4) and evaluating the effect on both leagues separately.

While the National League averages are remarkably stable over the sub-eras, the American League shows progressive gains in offense. The average number of runs per game in the American League jumped by a quarter of a run with the introduction of the DH in 1973. For the years 1973–76, the American League and National League averages are remarkably similar. However, between 1977 and 1992, as the DH became a more established position in the American League, the average runs per game exceeded those in the National League by a third of a run.

Table 3.4 Offensive Event Averages by Sub-Era, 1969–92

Era	R/G	BA	2B	3B	HR	BB	SO	SB	OBP	SLG	OPS
					American League						
1969–72	3.90	.245	18.6	2.8	11.7	50	82	7.0	.319	.364	.683
1973–76	4.17	.258	19.8	3.2	10.5	49	72	10.1	.327	.373	.700
1977–92	4.45	.263	22.7	3.2	12.7	48	76	9.7	.331	.397	.728
					National League						
1969–72	4.10	.252	19.3	3.7	11.3	49	85	7.1	.322	.373	.695
1973–76	4.10	.255	20.2	3.4	9.8	50	75	9.0	.326	.368	.694
1977–92	4.10	.255	21.9	3.5	10.6	47	82	12.9	.322	.376	.698

Note: Values for 2B, 3B, and HR are per 500 ABs; values for BB, SO, and SB are per 550 NFPs.

The stolen base is the offensive event with the largest percentage change in the NL over the sub-eras. In particular, the jump of nearly 6 stolen bases per 550 NFPs with the 1977–92 sub-era (an 82% rise) over the average from 1969–72 is striking. The rise in the American League was a more modest 39%, some of which is attributable to the DH rule.

Because of the differences between leagues attributable to the DH, and the dramatic rise in stolen bases across sub-eras, the years 1977–92 for the National League are used to standardize the adjusted averages in this book.

Power Era (1993–2003+)

Today's game is a high-octane one. Most of the main areas of hitting are on the rise: runs, batting average, doubles, home runs, strikeouts, and walks. These are leading to record-breaking performances, especially in home runs.

Colorado and Florida entered the National League in 1993. Colorado's thin air leads to a ton of offense, which caused many National League event averages to shoot up. American League averages, though, have also climbed significantly.

In the remainder of this chapter, piecewise linear regression plots are shown for the 9 basic offensive events and for 4 derived offensive events, EBHs, OBP, slugging average, and OPS. The piecewise linear sections indicate where statistically detectable changes in the rate of annual change in an event occur. Sometimes more global trends can be seen as well. For example, in Table 3.9 and Figure 3.5, 4 rate changes can be seen for National League triples/500 at-bats from 1921 to 2003. More globally, we can see that triples have generally declined over the 83-year period.

The remainder of this chapter consists of piecewise linear regression fits (Figures 3.1–3.24). The piecewise linear regression model is described in Appendix A. Tables that identify the changeyears and rates of change can be found at http://pup .princeton.edu/schell/chap3tables.pdf.

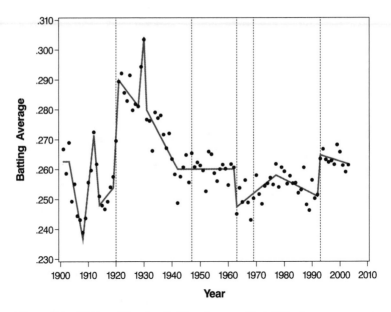

Figure 3.1   National League Batting Average Time Chart

Figure 3.2   American League Batting Average Time Chart

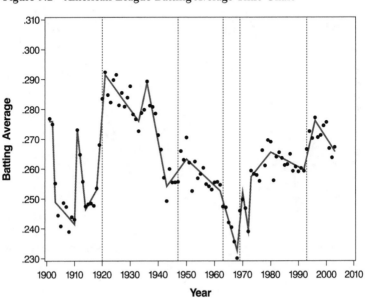

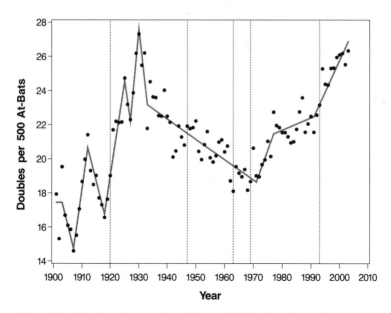

Figure 3.3   National League Doubles per 500 At-Bats Time Chart

Figure 3.4   American League Doubles per 500 At-Bats Time Chart

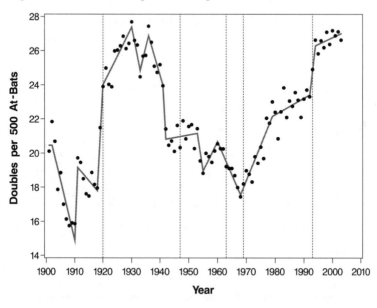

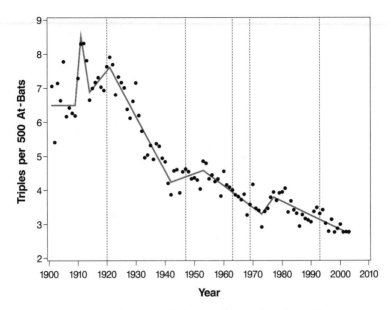

Figure 3.5   National League Triples per 500 At-Bats Time Chart

Figure 3.6   American League Triples per 500 At-Bats Time Chart

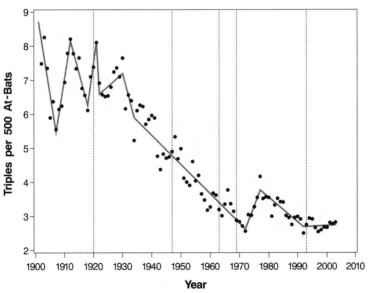

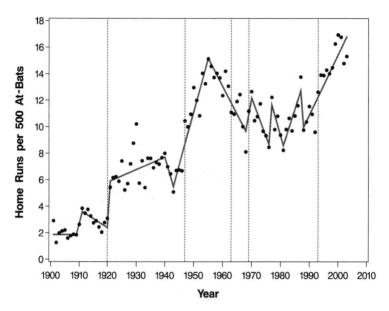

Figure 3.7   National League Home Runs per 500 At-Bats Time Chart

Figure 3.8   American League Home Runs per 500 At-Bats Time Chart

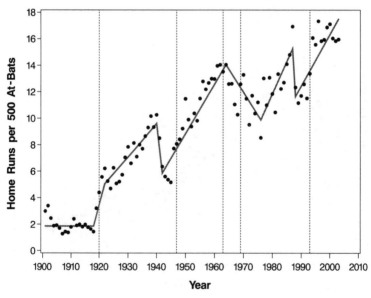

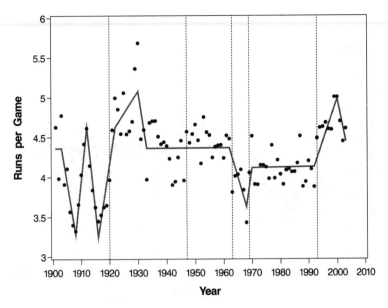

Figure 3.9   National League Runs per Game Time Chart

Figure 3.10   American League Runs per Game Time Chart

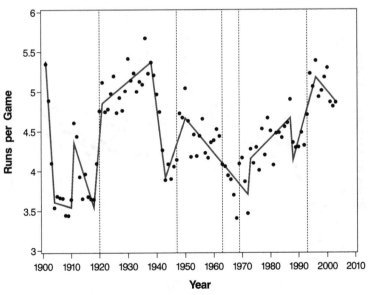

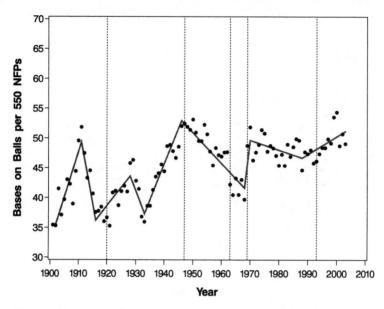

Figure 3.11   National League Bases on Balls per 550 NFPs Time Chart

Figure 3.12   American League Bases on Balls per 550 NFPs Time Chart

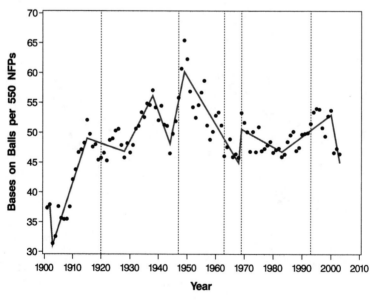

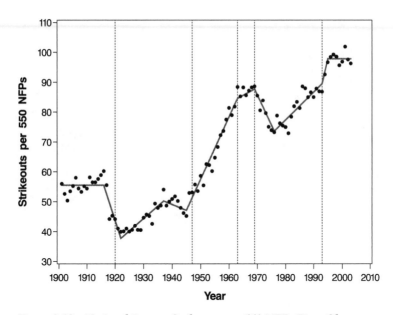

Figure 3.13   National League Strikeouts per 550 NFPs Time Chart

Figure 3.14   American League Strikeouts per 550 NFPs Time Chart

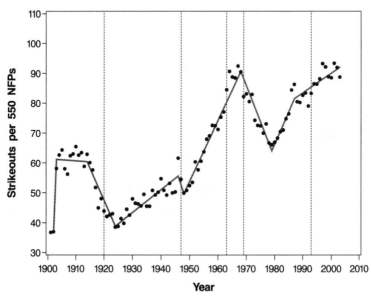

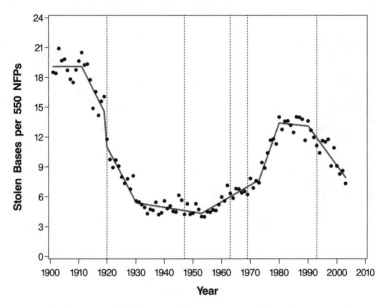

Figure 3.15   National League Stolen Bases per 550 NFPs Time Chart

Figure 3.16   American League Stolen Bases per 550 NFPs Time Chart

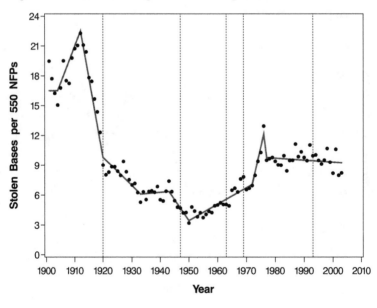

THE METHODS

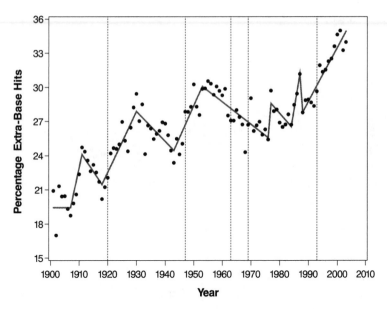

Figure 3.17   National League Percentage Extra-Base Hits Time Chart

Figure 3.18   American League Percentage Extra-Base Hits Time Chart

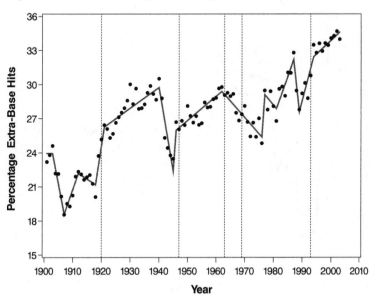

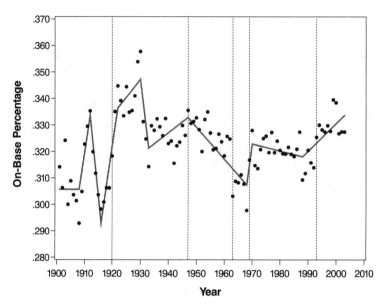

Figure 3.19   National League On-Base Percentage Time Chart

Figure 3.20   American League On-Base Percentage Time Chart

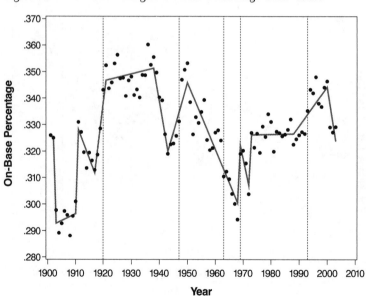

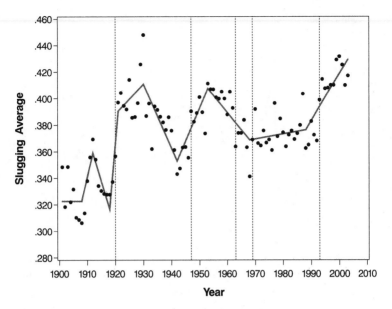

Figure 3.21   National League Slugging Average Time Chart

Figure 3.22   American League Slugging Average Time Chart

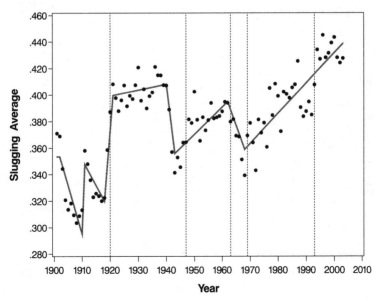

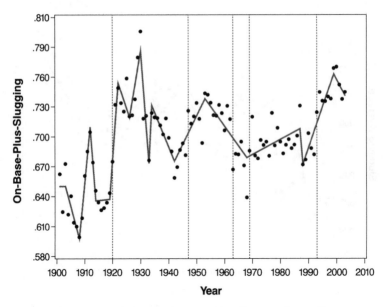

Figure 3.23   National League On-Base-Plus-Slugging Time Chart

Figure 3.24   American League On-Base-Plus-Slugging Time Chart

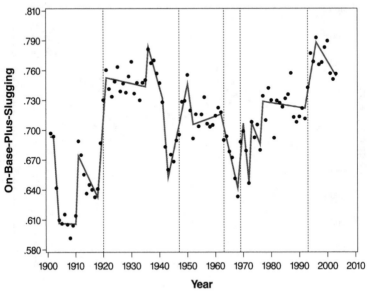

CHAPTER 4

Calling It a Career

Examining Player Aging

Each season, general managers face difficult choices in building a team they hope will need to be sized for championship rings in October. Often the choice centers on the issue of player age. Should an aging star remain as a regular, or be replaced with an eager rookie or an established mid-career regular acquired from another team?

Although players' individual aging trajectories are critical to such decisions, overall aging tendencies play an important role in the decisions as well. In this chapter, we explore these tendencies, primarily through plots and tables.

Player aging is examined in two ways for each event: the "age profile plot" and the "milestone average table." The first approach relates performance to player age; the second approach relates performance to batting experience. The age profile plot is shown for illustration only. The aging adjustment (Step 7 of the game plan presented in Chapter 2) is based on the milestone average table.

Age profile plot

The age profile plot shows the fully adjusted average for a given offensive event for regular players by age. A player's age is defined as his age on June 30th.

Two cohorts of *player-seasons* are shown: *early player-seasons*, between 1876 and 1946, and *modern player-seasons*, on or after 1947. Only regular player-seasons are used in the averages. A *piecewise linear regression* model (see Appendix A) was fit to each cohort (a dashed line fitting the asterisks for early player-seasons and a solid line fitting the circles for modern player-seasons).

The solid horizontal line shows the standardizing average. Data are shown only for players between ages 20 and 38, since there are relatively few regular player-seasons for younger or older players (less than 100 for a given age). Of the 18,681 regular player-seasons between 1876 and 2002, only 43 (0.2%) were from players younger than 20 and only 170 (0.9%) for players 39 and older.

The age profile plot does not provide the best insight as to how aging affects individual players. Players are part of the profile at a given age only if they are regulars. Since players who perform better tend to remain regulars and have longer careers, what might appear as improving or declining play with age in the profile is partly a selection process regarding which players continue to play. The milestone average table avoids this potential bias by tracking an elite group of batters, called *longtime players*, through milestone at-bats, in which each batter contributes the same 1000 at-bats (or NFPs) of batting experience over the entire table. Even so, the age profile plots do show useful information, since they accurately depict the average offensive performance of the players who happen to be regulars between age 20 and age 38.

The table below shows the average age at milestones for longtime players. Note that 8000 ABs and 9000 NFPs are reached by age 37, on average.

Average Age of Longtime Players at Various Milestones

	1000	2000	3000	4000	5000	6000	7000	8000	9000
ABs	23.2	25.1	27.0	28.8	30.7	32.5	34.5	36.6	—
NFPs	23.0	24.8	26.4	28.1	29.8	31.4	33.1	34.8	36.8

Age Profile for Batting Average

Figure 4.1 shows that the fully adjusted batting average rose modestly with player age for both early and modern player-seasons. The gain, although visible, is quite small—only 0.06% per year for the early player-seasons and 0.09% for the modern player-seasons.

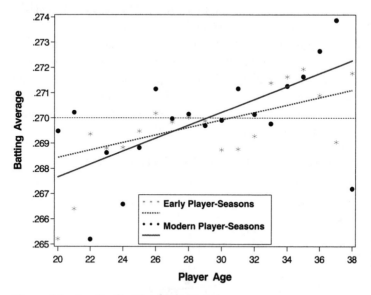

Figure 4.1   Age Profile Plot for Batting Average

From Figure 4.1, one can see that averages were fairly stable starting at age 33 among early players, but continued to climb through age 37 for modern players. This older age peak reflects in part the selection process regarding which players have longer careers, mentioned previously. Table 4.1, which tracks a single group of players, shows that the peak occurs between at-bats 2001 and 3000.

Table 4.1   Milestone Average Table for Batting Average

	Milestone At-Bats							
	1000	2000	3000	4000	5000	6000	7000	8000
Slice Avg	.2767	.2890	.2931	.2930	.2930	.2885	.2862	.2803
Cum Avg	.2767	.2828	.2862	.2879	.2890	.2889	.2885	.2875
% of peak	95.7	97.9	99.1	99.6	100	100	99.8	99.5

The peak cumulative batting average is reached at the 5000th at-bat milestone. However, the decline is sufficiently slow that the productive career length is 8000 at-bats.

Age Profile for Doubles-Plus-Triples

The previous age profile showed that the batting average of regular players tended to increase with age. One expects the rate of doubles-plus-triples (DPTs) to likewise increase, since they represent about 20% of all hits. To eliminate the effect attributable to overall batting ability, we will look at the age profile for the "doubles-plus-triples fraction," in which the DPT fraction is the fraction of non–home run hits that are Extra-Base Hits (that is, doubles-plus-triples divided by the sum of singles, doubles, and triples). For regulars, the average DPT fraction is 22.3%.

Figure 4.2 shows how the DPT fraction varies with age. The trend line for early player-seasons declines steadily at 0.36% per year. For modern player-seasons, the decline was minimal through age 31, but dropped more quickly at that point.

As Table 4.2 shows, the peak slice for DPTs was the third (2001–3000 AB). The peak average occurred 1000 at-bats later, at 4000, with the productive career length running through the 6000th at-bat.

Figure 4.2　Age Profile Plot for Doubles-Plus-Triples Fraction

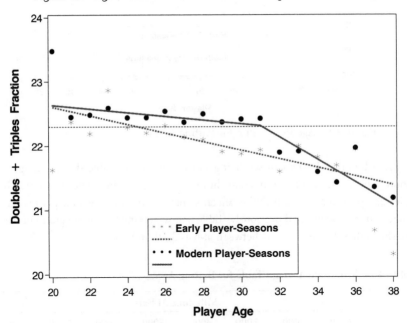

Table 4.2　Milestone Average Table for Doubles-Plus-Triples per 500 At-Bats

	Milestone At-Bats							
	1000	2000	3000	4000	5000	6000	7000	8000
Slice Avg	29.1	30.9	31.6	31.3	30.4	29.4	29.3	27.5
Cum Avg	29.1	30.0	30.5	30.7	30.7	30.4	30.3	29.9
% of peak	94.7	97.6	99.4	100	99.8	99.1	98.6	97.4

Age Profile for Triples Fraction

Figure 4.3 shows the decline with age in triple fraction, defined as the fraction of non–home run hits that are triples (that is, triples divided by the sum of singles, doubles, and triples). Overall, 3.1% of the non–home run hits by regulars are triples. However, the decline with age is quite steep—1.5% per year for early player-seasons and a more striking 2.9% for modern player-seasons. Visually, the data suggest that the "triples fraction" peaks for modern player-seasons at 4% for 22-year-old hitters, although the fitting model did not pick up the initial rise.

The peak slice and peak average both occur at the 2000th at-bat (Table 4.3). Since the smallest allowable productive career length is 4000 at-bats and the percentage of peak is closer to 99% at 4000 at-bats than at higher milestones, 4000 at-bats is the productive career length.

Figure 4.3 Age Profile Plot for Triples Fraction

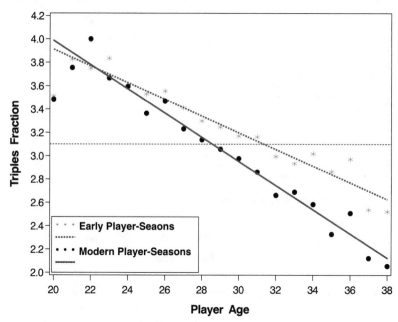

Table 4.3 Milestone Average Table for Triples per 500 At-Bats

	Milestone At-Bats							
	1000	2000	3000	4000	5000	6000	7000	8000
Slice Avg	5.5	5.7	5.3	5.0	4.6	4.3	3.8	3.4
Cum Avg	5.5	5.6	5.5	5.4	5.2	5.1	4.9	4.7
% of peak	98.3	100	98.2	95.7	93.0	90.3	87.2	83.8

Age Profile for Home Runs

The age profile for home runs is quite interesting (Figure 4.4). Modern players improve as they age, gaining 1.2% per year. By contrast, home run percentage fell 1.3% per year of age for early player-seasons. Many 19th century and deadball era home runs were inside-the-park home runs. As we just saw, triples declined strongly with player age, so inside-the-park home runs likely do as well.

Table 4.4 gives cumulative averages for home runs for four eras. The peak average for the earliest hitters was 2000 at-bats, compared to 4000 at-bats for lively ball era (1920–46) batters, and 6000–8000 at-bats for modern players. Overall, 7000 at-bats is the productive career length.

Figure 4.4   Age Profile Plot for Home Runs per 500 At-Bats

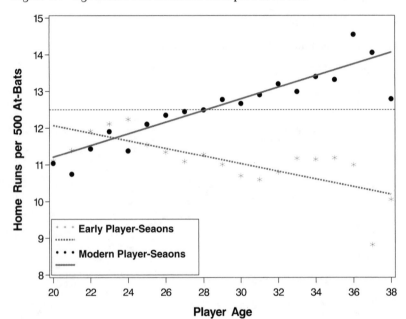

Table 4.4   Cumulative Average Table for Home Runs per 500 At-Bats

	Milestone At-Bats							
	1000	2000	3000	4000	5000	6000	7000	8000
1876–1919	14.5	*15.9*	15.7	15.5	14.9	14.6	14.2	13.9
1920–46	17.2	19.2	20.0	*20.4*	20.4	20.0	19.3	18.7
1947–76	13.2	14.2	15.1	15.9	16.3	*16.5*	*16.5*	16.3
1977–2003	12.2	12.8	13.7	14.4	14.7	15.0	*15.1*	*15.1*
Total	13.6	14.7	15.3	15.9	16.0	*16.1*	15.9	15.7

Note: Sample sizes for groups: 1876–1919 (N = 22), 1920–46 (N = 16), 1947–76 (N = 31), 1977–2003 (N = 44).

Age Profile for Runs

Run scoring and batting average are the two most stable offensive events across player ages, as Figure 4.5 shows. While batting average shows a modest gain with age, run scoring shows a modest decline, 0.07% per year for modern player-seasons, and –0.16% for early player-seasons. The slight decline seen is most likely attributable to the decline in speed as players age, which is somewhat offset by the gains in getting on base with a hit or a walk. Closer inspection of Figure 4.5 reveals that fairly substantial drops in run scoring occur at age 37 (early player-seasons) or 38 (modern player-seasons).

As shown in Table 4.5, the peak slice averages for run scoring are at 3001–5000 NFPs. That ability is maintained rather well among older players, leading to a peak average at 6000, and a productive career length of 8000 NFPs.

Figure 4.5 Age Profile Plot for Runs per 550 NFPs

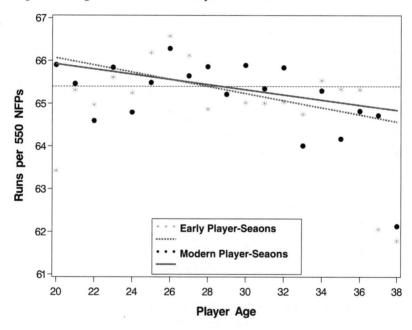

Table 4.5 Milestone Average Table for Runs per 550 NFPs

	Milestone NFPs								
	1000	2000	3000	4000	5000	6000	7000	8000	9000
Slice Avg	69.8	75.5	77.5	78.2	78.2	77.2	75.0	72.4	69.5
Cum Avg	69.8	72.6	74.3	75.2	75.8	76.1	75.9	75.5	74.8
% of peak	91.8	95.5	97.6	98.9	99.7	100	99.8	99.2	98.4

Age Profile for RBIs

The age profile for RBIs is the most intricate of any offensive event (see Figure 4.6). For modern players, we see a close-fitting model with three periods of increase separated by two short periods of stability. The final period of increase, from age 33 to 36, has the greatest per-year rise and is following by a decline in years 37 and 38. The early player-seasons show a very stable pattern through age 33 followed by a 2-year rise and then a decline beginning at age 35.

RBIs production peaks in the seventh slice, 6001–7000 NFPs, as shown in Table 4.6. The peak average occurs at the 8000th NFP, while the productive career length is a full 9000 NFPs.

Figure 4.6   Age Profile Plot for RBIs per 550 NFPs

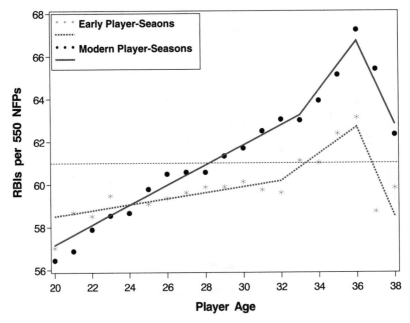

Table 4.6   Milestone Average Table for RBIs per 550 NFPs

	Milestone NFPs								
	1000	2000	3000	4000	5000	6000	7000	8000	9000
Slice Avg	60.8	66.0	68.1	69.6	69.3	70.7	70.4	68.9	67.3
Cum Avg	60.8	63.4	64.9	66.1	66.7	67.4	67.8	68.0	67.9
% of peak	89.5	93.3	95.6	97.3	98.2	99.2	99.8	100	99.9

Age Profile for Bases on Balls

Modern players improve 1.5% per year on their walk average (Figure 4.7). Early players likewise show improvement, although it is less striking. Averages improve 2.0% per year from age 20 to age 25 and 0.8% thereafter. Of the 9 basic offensive events, the walk average is the one in which players gain the most based on experience.

Experience is crucial to the plate discipline needed to collect walks. The baseball adage "Nobody walks off the island!" reflects the anxiousness of young Caribbean island players to swing the bat. To remain in the major leagues, however, the skill of drawing valuable walks needs to be acquired.

Table 4.7 shows that the bases on balls peak slice is not reached until 6001–7000 NFPs. Through each milestone, the cumulative average climbs, resulting in a productive career length of 9000 NFPs.

Figure 4.7 Age Profile Plot for Bases on Balls per 550 NFPs

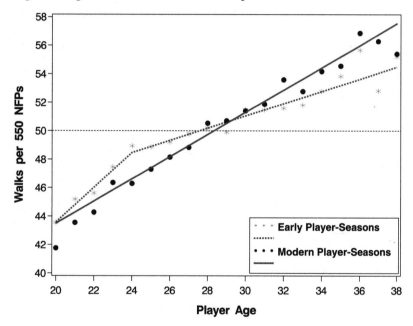

Table 4.7   Milestone Average Table for Bases on Balls per 550 NFPs

	Milestone NFPs								
	1000	2000	3000	4000	5000	6000	7000	8000	9000
Slice Avg	46.4	53.1	55.5	56.4	58.6	60.0	61.8	60.8	59.4
Cum Avg	46.4	49.7	51.6	52.8	54.0	55.0	56.0	56.6	56.9
% of peak	81.5	87.4	90.8	92.9	94.9	96.7	98.4	99.4	100

Age Profile for Strikeouts

Players improve their strikeout averages as they age, as can be seen in Figure 4.8. Strikeout averages drop 1.2% per year of age for modern hitters and an even more striking 2.2% for hitters prior to 1947.

The combination of these two age-related trends, "More walks, fewer strikeouts" renders the battle between pitcher and seasoned hitter into a real test of wills. Although the rookie may have more bat speed than the grizzled veteran, the latter can work the pitcher more and wear him down.

Owing to the lack of strikeout data from the 19th and early 20th centuries, only 89 players rate as longtime players for strikeouts. The learning curve continues throughout a player's career, with the peak slice, peak average, and productive career length all aligning at the 9000th NFP (Table 4.8).

Figure 4.8 Age Profile Plot for Strikeouts per 550 NFPs

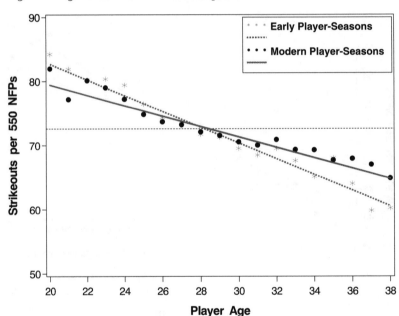

Table 4.8   Milestone Average Table for Strikeouts per 550 NFPs

	Milestone NFPs								
	1000	2000	3000	4000	5000	6000	7000	8000	9000
Slice Avg	78.0	69.1	67.2	62.9	61.6	63.0	61.6	*61.0*	*61.0*
Cum Avg	78.0	73.6	71.5	69.3	67.8	67.0	66.2	65.6	*65.1*
% of peak	119.9	113.1	109.8	106.5	104.1	102.9	101.7	100.7	*100*

Age Profile for Stolen Bases

The age profile plot for stolen bases (Figure 4.9) shows that performance declines steadily as players age. For players since 1947, the decline is dramatic since the stolen base average of 38-year-old players is only about half of what it is for 21-year-old players. The age profile for early player-seasons is somewhat different. The modeled average rises to a peak at age 24 followed by a less steep decline. The rise suggests a learning curve was associated with stolen bases in the early years of the game.

As Table 4.9 shows, the peak slice for stolen bases occurs at 3001–4000 NFPs, the peak average occurs at the 4000th NFP, and the productive career length runs through the 5000th NFP. Base stealing represents a tradeoff between speed, which declines rather quickly with age, and the skill of reading the pitcher. Consequently, the aging effect for base stealing is somewhat less pronounced than it was for triples, an offensive event that relies more purely on speed.

Figure 4.9 Age Profile Plot for Stolen Bases per 550 NFPs

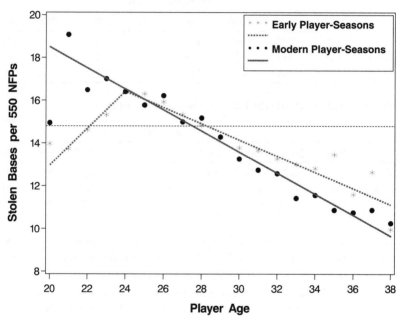

Table 4.9   Milestone Average Table for Stolen Bases per 550 NFPs

	Milestone NFPs								
	1000	2000	3000	4000	5000	6000	7000	8000	9000
Slice Avg	18.1	21.3	**22.3**	21.2	20.2	19.2	17.9	14.6	12.4
Cum Avg	18.1	19.7	20.6	**20.7**	20.6	20.4	20.0	19.4	18.6
% of peak	87.1	95.0	99.2	100	99.5	98.4	96.7	93.4	89.6

Milestone Average Tables for Derived Offensive Events

Since batters will be ranked for several offensive events derived from the basic offensive events, we need to obtain productive career lengths for them as well. As Tables 4.10–4.12 show, the productive career lengths for OBP and OPS are both 9000 NFPs, and 8000 ABs for slugging average.

Table 4.10   Milestone Average Table for On-Base Percentage

	Milestone NFPs								
	1000	2000	3000	4000	5000	6000	7000	8000	9000
Slice Avg	.340	.361	.368	.369	.372	.372	.371	.368	.362
Cum Avg	.340	.350	.356	.359	.362	.364	.365	.365	.365
% of peak	93.1	96.0	97.5	98.4	99.1	99.6	99.9	100	99.9

Table 4.11   Milestone Average Table for Slugging Average

	Milestone At-Bats							
	1000	2000	3000	4000	5000	6000	7000	8000
Slice Avg	.428	.457	.467	.470	.463	.454	.444	.427
Cum Avg	.428	.442	.450	.455	.457	.456	.454	.451
% of peak	93.6	96.8	98.6	99.7	100	99.9	99.5	98.7

Table 4.12   Milestone Average Table for On-Base-Plus-Slugging

	Milestone NFPs								
	1000	2000	3000	4000	5000	6000	7000	8000	9000
Slice Avg	.765	.817	.834	.841	.840	.834	.826	.811	.792
Cum Avg	.765	.791	.805	.814	.819	.822	.822	.821	.818
% of peak	93.0	96.2	97.9	99.0	99.6	99.9	100	99.8	99.4

Event-Specific Batting Runs (ESBRs) is the key derived offensive event developed in this book (Chapter 14), and Table 4.13 provides the milestone table for it. Since the number of ESBRs of an average player is set to zero and negative values are possible, the 99% of peak rule for defining the productive career length should not be applied to it. Since ESBRs are very highly correlated with OPS, 9000 NFPs is used as the productive career length for ESBRs.

Table 4.13   Milestone Average Table for Event-Specific Batting Runs per 550 NFPs

	Milestone NFPs								
	1000	2000	3000	4000	5000	6000	7000	8000	9000
Slice Avg	13.7	23.4	26.4	27.3	27.8	27.0	25.9	23.5	20.3
Cum Avg	13.7	18.6	21.2	22.7	23.7	24.3	24.5	24.4	23.9
% of peak	56.1	75.8	86.5	92.7	96.8	99.1	100	99.5	97.7

Summary of Results

In this chapter, we have looked at the age trends for the 9 basic offensive events. In some cases, a simple linear trend was seen. In others, one or more shifts in trend slope were found. Table 4.14 summarizes the overall trend based on a simple linear regression fit.

Table 4.14   Linear Trends of Offensive Events with Player Age

Event	Early Player-Seasons % Change per 10 yrs	Modern Player-Seasons % Change per 10 yrs
Bases on balls	11*	18
Home runs	−9	15
Strikeouts	−15	−10
RBIs	3*	9*
Batting average	1	1
Runs	−1*	−1
DPT fraction	−3	−3*
Triple fraction	−18	−26
Stolen Bases	−16*	−27

Notes: Results based on regular player-seasons.

The % change values were determined using age 20 as the baseline value.

Events listed by decreasing improvement with age for modern seasons.

* Indicates that a nonlinear trend was detected as shown in the age profile plots.

For modern player-seasons, the events can be classified into three types, based on their percentage change per year. For four events—bases on balls, strikeouts, home runs, and RBIs—the averages improve at least 9% per 10 years of age, say between a 25-year-old and 35-year-old player. The first two events reflect plate discipline; the latter two events reflect power. Three events—batting average, runs, and doubles-plus-triples—are relatively stable. The final two events—triples and stolen bases—decline sharply with player age. In these speed events, the decline is 5% for every 2 years.

CHAPTER 5

Talent Search

Measuring the Spread
in Player Performance

As noted in Chapter 2, Stephen J. Gould introduced the notion of using the season standard deviation as a measure of the talent pool from which ball players were selected. In both *Baseball's All-Time Best Hitters* and this book, I have interpreted the standard deviation (SD) similarly. Its use in the adjustment procedure proposed in Chapter 2, though, is problematic, as the following argument scheme indicates.

1. The variability in batting averages was greater in the 19th and early 20th centuries than it is today (see Figure 5.1).
2. This implies that the talent pool was weaker in those early days of professional baseball.
3. The SD adjustment pulls down the high batting averages of early players, which is appropriate given the assumption in (2).
4. The fully adjusted average pulls up the batting averages of below-average hitters, to satisfy the "hitting feasts and famines" adjustment requiring the overall average of players be the same across baseball history.
5. However, that contradicts the claim in (2) that the early players were worse.

I see three ways out of this quagmire. First, one may regard the variability as some accident of baseball needing adjustment, not a measure of talent. Second, one can consider that the adjustment method works only for some fraction of the best players, say, the top 30%. Third, one can abandon the use of the SD as a talent pool adjustment altogether and search for another talent pool adjustment method.

The method developed for this book relies on the second explanation, but it comes at a cost. Ultimately, it is an incomplete explanation, leaving us on unstable ground. Someday we will need to move to the third explanation requiring a different talent pool adjustment, likely involving more difficult statistical methods than those used in this book.

Even if the SD is ultimately discarded as a measure of the talent pool for a given event, it still has a natural role to play. The single-season standard deviations still measure the variability in performance for the event, which is why they are called *performance spreads*.

Guide to the performance spread plots and tables

The performance spread plots (Figures 5.1–5.9) show the 5-year moving averages of the SDs of regular player averages obtained yearly from 1885–2003 for the 9 power-transformed 9 basic offensive events. The National League data are shown using a solid line, while the American League data are shown with a dashed line. Vertical dashed lines divide the data into five eras: 1885–1900, 1901–19, 1920–46, 1947–76, and 1977–2003. The horizontal line shows the park-adjusted SD for regular players from the standardizing years (1977–92 National League). This is given in Table 2.4 for each of the basic offensive events.

In adjusting player averages, different power transformations are used for different eras for 7 of the 9 basic offensive events, as described in Appendix E. Unfortunately, SDs obtained using different power transformations cannot be compared easily numerically. The plots in this chapter are constructed simply to help the reader visualize how the performance spread changes over time. For that purpose, use of a single power transformation for each basic offensive event over time is suitable. The power transformations used for the plots are the ones needed for the standardizing years, as given in Table 2.4.

The performance spread tables accompany the plots. For each era, they identify the years when the SD was the lowest and highest, and give the average SD over the entire era.

Performance Spread Plot for Batting Average

American League

American League and National League performance spreads were fairly similar through 1907, before diverging. The American League performance spread rise coincides with the emergence of batting stars Cobb, Speaker, and Jackson. The sharp contrast in ability between them and their league mates led to an elevated SD of around .036 in the second half of the deadball era, which did not drop to the National League level until 1930. In 1962, the performance spread reached an all-time low, before rising for a decade. The SD has remained fairly flat since the introduction of the DH in 1973.

National League

The National League performance spread reached an all-time high in 1886, then dipped sharply through 1892, before spiking up in 1901. The SDs dropped sharply to .026 in 1913 and have vacillated between .025 and .030 ever since. The greater performance spreads of the late 1960s and early 1970s may be due to the 1962 and 1969 expansions.

Figure 5.1   Performance Spread Plot for Batting Average

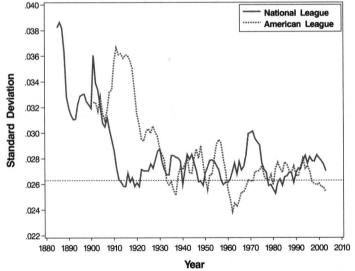

Years	American League			National League		
	Low Yr	High Yr	Avg SD	Low Yr	High Yr	Avg SD
1885–1900	—	—	—	1892	1886	.034
1901–19	1906	1911	.034	1915	1901	.029
1920–46	1937	1920	.028	1921	1930	.027
1947–76	1962	1956	.027	1949	1969	.027
1977–2003	2003	1993	.027	1981	1999	.027
Overall	1962	1911	.028	1981	1886	.028

Performance Spread Plot for Doubles-Plus-Triples

American League

The performance spread reached its highest levels in the 1910s. A sharp decline occurred in 1920, ending the deadball era and coinciding with the shift in the transformation power for DPTs from 0.50 to 0.75 (see Table 2.3). The performance spread dropped to an all-time low in 1937, before climbing during the World War II years. The SD hovered between .020 and .022 from the 1950s to 1970s, before beginning a decline around 1980 that still continues. The 2003 performance spread is approaching the all-time low from 1937.

National League

The National League performance spread peaked in 1901, the year the American League became a major league and weakened the National League talent pool. From 1908 to 1912, however, the standard deviation declined rapidly from .027 to .022. Since then, the SD has never risen above .023. The SD has been declining since the early 1990s, and is now at an all-time low.

Figure 5.2   Performance Spread Plot for Doubles-Plus-Triples

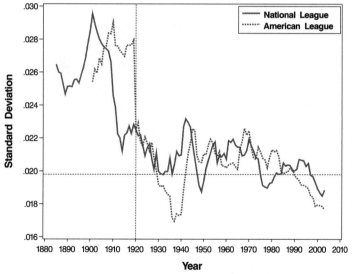

Years	American League			National League		
	Low Yr	High Yr	Avg SD	Low Yr	High Yr	Avg SD
1885–1900	—	—	—	1889	1900	.026
1901–19	1901	1910	.027	1914	1901	.025
1920–46	1937	1921	.020	1932	1942	.021
1947–76	1965	1968	.021	1949	1970	.021
1977–2003	2003	1980	.020	2002	1992	.020
Overall	1937	1910	.022	2002	1901	.022

Performance Spread Plot for Triples

American League

The American League performance spread shows a now familiar increase from 1901 to the 1910s with a drop at the end of the deadball era. Between 1940 and 1944, the SD rose sharply. Since then, the performance spreads have continued to climb to the all-time high in 2001. Since 1969, a more powerful cube-root transformation has been needed to normalize the triple average distribution, compared to the square-root transformation required for earlier years.

National League

The performance spread spiked in 1901, similar to the spike seen in the DPT plot. The spike for triples, though, is more pronounced. From there, the SD declined markedly, reaching an all-time low in 1921. Then, the performance spread rose steadily to .044 in 1943, before dropping to .036 in 1947. Since 1947, the performance spread has risen rather consistently, reaching an all-time high in 2001.

Figure 5.3   Performance Spread Plot for Triples

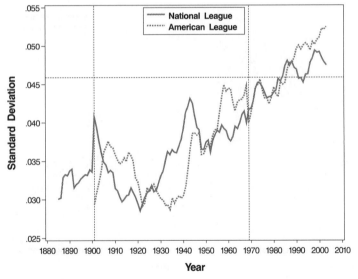

Years	American League			National League		
	Low Yr	High Yr	Avg SD	Low Yr	High Yr	Avg SD
1885–1900	—	—	—	1885	1891	.033
1901–19	1901	1907	.035	1913	1901	.033
1920–46	1934	1945	.032	1921	1943	.035
1947–76	1948	1974	.042	1952	1974	.040
1977–2003	1978	2003	.048	1977	1998	.047
Overall	1934	2003	.039	1921	1998	.038

Performance Spread Plot for Home Runs

American League

Between 1913 and 1919, the American League performance spread skyrocketed. Babe Ruth was a key contributor to this increase. The spread declined steeply with the advent of the lively ball era, resulting in spreads comparable to the National League. Post–WWII, the performance spread showed continued declines until 1964, before rising again. Since 1991, the spread has declined to an all-time low in 2003. Since the early 1960s, the American League has generally shown less performance spread than the National League.

National League

The performance spread jumped dramatically around 1901 to an all-time peak in 1904, before declining to 19th century levels in 1915. Between 1915 and 1946, it vacillated between the 1904 and 1915 spreads. After World War II, the spread declined to a new low in 1952, before climbing back to a postwar high in 1980. Since then, the performance spread has continued to drop and is now at an all-time low.

Figure 5.4   Performance Spread Plot for Home Runs

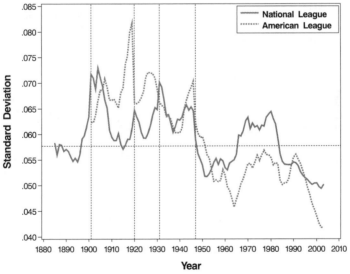

Years	American League			National League		
	Low Yr	High Yr	Avg SD	Low Yr	High Yr	Avg SD
1885–1900	—	—	—	1895	1900	.057
1901–19	1902	1919	.069	1915	1904	.064
1920–46	1940	1926	.066	1925	1931	.064
1947–76	1964	1947	.053	1952	1970	.057
1977–2003	2003	1977	.051	2002	1980	.055
Overall	2003	1919	.059	2002	1904	.059

Performance Spread Plot for Runs

American League
The performance spread in 1901, .030, was the lowest SD until 1960. Starting in 1907, the SDs rose rapidly to all-time highs in 1914–15, while those in the National League dropped to lower levels. The American League and National League performance spreads converged in 1923, when the two leagues tracked each other for 20 years. In 1957, the American League performance spread dropped below that of the National League. Since then, the American League has consistently had lower spreads, averaging 12% lower.

National League
The performance spread dropped rapidly from 1885 to 1891 and was relatively stable for 10 years before skyrocketing in 1901. The SD remained high through 1908, before dropping to a new low in 1913. The SD has vacillated above and below .033 since that time. The SD has been in fairly stable decline since 1990.

Figure 5.5   Performance Spread Plot for Runs

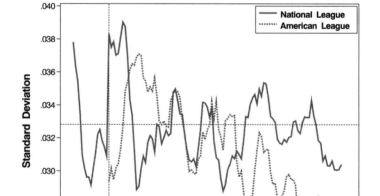

Years	American League			National League		
	Low Yr	High Yr	Avg SD	Low Yr	High Yr	Avg SD
1885–1900	—	—	—	1893	1885	.032
1901–19	1901	1914	.034	1913	1907	.034
1920–46	1939	1921	.033	1939	1930	.033
1947–76	1962	1948	.031	1951	1970	.032
1977–2003	2002	1980	.027	2001	1990	.032
Overall	2002	1914	.031	1951	1907	.033

Performance Spread Plot for RBIs

American League

Performance spreads rose to all-time highs in the 1910s before plummeting at the deadball era's end. American League and National League SDs were close between 1920 and 1954. Since then, the American League SD has been 10% lower on average. Recent league up/down swings have coincided: 1970 ↑, 1975 ↓, 1979 ↑, 1988 ↓, 1996 ↑, 2003 ↓. The DH partly explains the American League's smaller spreads in runs and RBIs. However, the separations began in the 1950s, perhaps because of league style differences, with the National League being the "speed league" and the American League being the "3-run homer" league.

National League

The National League performance spread for RBIs slipped from 1885 to an all-time low in 1893, the year the pitching box was moved to its current distance of 60 feet, 6 inches. From there, the SD skyrocketed to a high in 1907, before declining again. Since then, the performance spreads have wandered around .046, the standardizing level.

Figure 5.6   Performance Spread Plot for RBIs

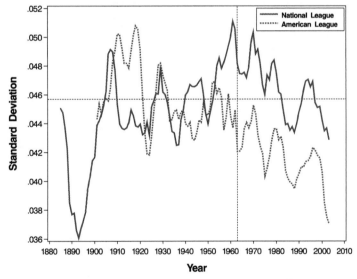

Years	American League			National League		
	Low Yr	High Yr	Avg SD	Low Yr	High Yr	Avg SD
1885–1900	—	—	—	1893	1885	.040
1901–19	1901	1918	.048	1913	1907	.045
1920–46	1924	1920	.045	1936	1929	.045
1947–76	1975	1953	.044	1950	1961	.048
1977–2003	2003	1979	.041	2003	1979	.045
Overall	2003	1918	.044	1893	1961	.045

Performance Spread Plot for Bases on Balls

American League

The American League performance spreads closely tracked those of the National League through 1918. Since that time the two leagues have taken turns at having the lowest SDs. In 2003, the American League had the highest performance spread in 70 years. The all-time lowest performance spread was achieved in 1950, 1 year after the all-time highest walk average in 1949.

National League

The performance spread peaked at .078 in 1886 and fell rapidly to .055 in 1892. After the pitching box was moved back in 1893, the SD rose, reaching a more modest peak of .066 in 1901. Within a decade, the SD dropped past .057—the standardizing SD from 1977 to 1992, around which it has meandered ever since.

Figure 5.7   Performance Spread Plot for Bases on Balls

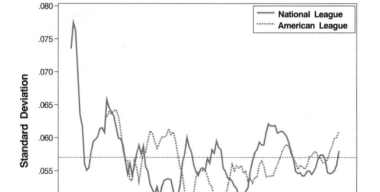

Years	American League			National League		
	Low Yr	High Yr	Avg SD	Low Yr	High Yr	Avg SD
1885–1900	—	—	—	1892	1886	.063
1901–19	1915	1905	.059	1912	1901	.059
1920–46	1936	1928	.057	1931	1936	.054
1947–76	1950	1969	.054	1960	1972	.057
1977–2003	1985	2003	.057	1987	1978	.057
Overall	1950	1905	.056	1931	1886	.057

Performance Spread Plot for Strikeouts

American League

The performance spreads for strikeouts are a roller coaster ride for both the American League and National League. The increase from 1913 to the end of the deadball period followed by a decline in the 1920s parallels the National League figures. A long decline in spread occurred between 1950 and 1974. From a recent high in 1990, performance spreads dropped to an all-time low in 2002. The lower spreads in recent eras may be due to the fact that today strikeouts are less a mark of shame than they were in previous eras.

National League

Performance spreads were high throughout the 19th century. Strikeout totals were not routinely kept from 1897 to 1909. When records resumed, the spread remained low through 1915, before skyrocketing to .083 in 1921. Between 1939 and 1963, performance spreads generally declined, before climbing to a 5-year plateau in the 1970s. The spread has declined since then, nearing the all-time low.

Figure 5.8   Performance Spread Plot for Strikeouts

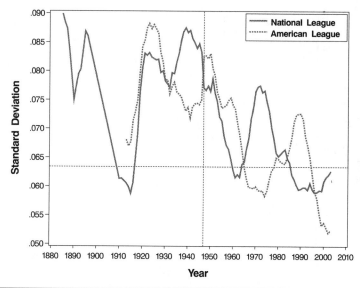

Years	American League			National League		
	Low Yr	High Yr	Avg SD	Low Yr	High Yr	Avg SD
1885–1900	—	—	—	1890	1885	.083
1901–19	1914	1919	.072	1915	1919	.063
1920–46	1941	1923	.079	1932	1939	.083
1947–76	1974	1950	.069	1961	1951	.071
1977–2003	2002	1989	.063	1996	1977	.062
Overall	2002	1923	.071	1915	1885	.072

Performance Spread Plot for Stolen Bases

American League

Overall, performance spreads in both the American League and National League have tended to increase. A striking increase in spreads occurred at the onset of the lively ball era in 1920. From there, the SDs in both leagues continued to rise until about 1977. Since then, the American League SD has remained stable, while the National League SD has declined slightly. The plot demonstrates the strong relationship between higher performance spreads and lower transformation powers needed for normality as given in Table 2.3. For example, the SD jump in 1920 is accompanied by a downshift in the transformation power from .33 to .20.

National League

Stolen bases have had the greatest spreads of performance spreads of the basic offensive events. There is a 2.3-fold spread of SDs, from a low of .046 in the National League in 1903 to a high of .108 in the American League in 1983. Home runs have the next greatest spread, at 1.9-fold.

Figure 5.9   Performance Spread Plot for Stolen Bases

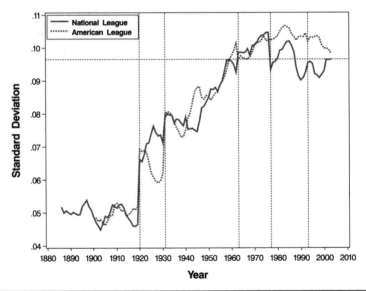

Years	American League			National League		
	Low Yr	High Yr	Avg SD	Low Yr	High Yr	Avg SD
1885–1900	—	—	—	1900	1897	.051
1901–19	1905	1910	.050	1903	1912	.049
1920–46	1928	1946	.073	1921	1932	.075
1947–76	1951	1974	.094	1947	1976	.095
1977–2003	2003	1983	.103	1990	1985	.095
Overall	1905	1983	.083	1903	1976	.077

CHAPTER 6

Home Park Advantage

A Closer Look at Park Effects

Colorado Rockies hitters are the current Rodney Dangerfields of baseball—they "get no respect." Their numbers are frequently discredited by baseball fans because their home park, Coors Field, is well known to be a great park for a hitter. Through the 2003 season, the Rockies have won all but one National League team batting average title since moving into Coors Field in 1995. Meanwhile, Rockies pitchers have had the highest National League team E.R.A. in all but two Coors Field years.

Similarly, sabermetricians discredit the hitting marks of such players as Chuck Klein, who racked up great numbers in Philadelphia's Baker Bowl, and home run champions such as Mel Ott, Ralph Kiner and Gavy Cravath, who had advantageous parks for home runs. Less obvious are the players who *didn't* post gaudy totals, since they were hampered with poor hitters' parks. How many home runs might Joe DiMaggio have hit, if he hadn't called Yankee Stadium home, or Roberto Clemente, if he hadn't played so much in Forbes Field?

In Appendix D, a methodology is presented that provides good estimates of ballpark effects throughout major league history. In this chapter, we look at three things:

1. The greatest park effect transitions for home runs and runs
2. Home run park effects for six teams with interesting stories
3. The most extreme parks in major league history for all basic offensive events.

Greatest Year-to-Year Park Effect Transitions

Sometimes dramatic changes occur in a given park from one year to the next, or when a club moves into a new park. In this section, we look at the most dramatic park effect transitions in history.

Baseball at the Polo Grounds. (National Baseball Hall of Fame Library, Coopers-town, NY.)

Home Runs

Table 6.1 shows the most dramatic park effects transitions for home runs. Seven of the fourteen transitions shown involve changes from one ballpark to another, including three occasions when the franchise moved to a new city. The other seven involved changes within the lifespan of a given ballpark. Here are the top transitions:

1. **Crosley Field, 1938.**   The greatest transition occurred at Crosley Field in 1938. In 1938, the outfield fences were reduced by 20 feet, leading to a dramatic rise in home runs. From 1912 to 1937, only 24% of the home runs hit in Reds' games were hit at Crosley Field. From 1938 to 1969, 52% of the home runs were hit at Crosley Field.

2. **Griffith Stadium to Metropolitan Stadium, 1961.**   Griffith Stadium, in Washington, was a terrible park for home runs for most of its history. Metropolitan Stadium, which was an above-average park for home runs, stands in sharp contrast. Overall, 34% of home runs in games involving the Senators were hit in Griffith Stadium compared to 52% at Metropolitan (1961–81) for Twins' games.

3. **South End Grounds to Braves Field, 1915.**   Braves Field was a large park that was not conducive to home runs. Overall 67% percent of the home runs in Braves' games were hit at South End Grounds from 1894–1914. By contrast, only 40% of the home runs in Braves' games between 1915 and 1952 were hit at Braves Field.

Table 6.1 Greatest Park Effect Transitions for Home Runs

Team	Park 1	Park 2	Changeyear(s)	LR χ²	Dir
1 Cin–N	Crosley	—	1938	486	↑
2 Min–A	Griffith	Metropolitan	1961	386	↑
3 Bos–N	South End Gds	Braves Field	1915	329	↓
4 Was–A	Griffith	—	1956	264	↑
5 Phi–N	Baker Bowl	Shibe Park	1938	234	↓
6 Bal–A	Sportsman's	Memorial Stadium	1954	182	↓
7 Pit–N	Forbes Field	—	1947, '54	173	↑↓
8 Atl–N	County Stadium	Atlanta/Fulton Co.	1966	167	↑
9 Bos–A	Fenway Park	—	1934	164	↑
10 Phi–N	Baker Bowl	—	1911	143	↑
11 Bos–A	Huntington Ave.	Fenway Park	1912	139	↓
12 Pit–N	Forbes	Three Rivers	1970	125	↑
13 Bos–N	Braves Field	—	1942, '46, '59	105	↑↓↑
14 KC–A	Municipal	—	1965	103	↓

Notes: LR χ² is the *likelihood ratio* χ² value for the change using *backward elimination* until only forced *changeyears* and those with LR χ² ≥ 100 remain.

See Appendix C for details of the statistical analysis.

Dir = direction of the change: ↑ for up, ↓ for down, ↑↓ for up, then down.

4. Griffith Stadium, 1956. Griffith Stadium was home to the Washington Senators from 1911 through 1960. From 1911 to 1955, only 28% of home runs were hit there. After the stadium was redesigned in 1956, 53% of the home runs were hit at Griffith Stadium.

Griffith Stadium is ranked above (no. 2) for its striking contrast to Metropolitan Stadium. Actually, there was very little change in park effect from the 1956–60 Griffith Stadium years to those at Metropolitan Stadium. The striking transition above applies if one contrasts the entire experience in Griffith Stadium with that of Metropolitan Stadium.

5. Baker Bowl to Shibe Park, 1938. The Baker Bowl was a great home run park. When the Phillies left there in 1938, the home run rate declined dramatically. While the Phillies were in the Baker Bowl (1895–1937), 62% of their and their opponents' home runs were hit at the Baker Bowl. While they were in Shibe Park (1938–70), only 47% of their and their opponents' homes runs were hit at home.

Runs

Table 6.2 shows the most dramatic park effect changes for runs. This list is quite close to the home run list, with 7 of the top 10 transitions in common.

Table 6.2 Greatest Park Effect Transitions for Runs

Team	Park 1	Park 2	Changeyear(s)	LR χ^2	Dir
1 Bal–A	Sportsman's	Memorial Stadium	1954	259	↓
2 Atl–N	County	Atlanta/Fulton Co.	1966	210	↑
3 Bos–N	South End Gds	Braves Field	1915	207	↓
4 Phi–N	Baker Bowl	—	1911	204	↑
5 Phi–N	Baker Bowl	Shibe Park	1938	159	↓
6 Chi–N	Wrigley Field	—	1961, 2000	129	↑↓
7 Bos–A	Fenway Park	—	1934	127	↑
8 Cin–N	Crosley Field	—	1953	115	↑
9 Oak–A	Municipal	Oakland/Ala. Co.	1968	112	↓
10 Min–A	Griffith	Metropolitan	1961	87	↑
11 LA–N	LA Coliseum	Dodger Stadium	1962	79	↓
12 Hou–N	Astrodome	Minute Maid Park	2000	66	↑
13 Cin–N	Palace of Fans	—	1907	57	↓
14 Cle–A	Cleveland	—	1954	56	↑

Notes: LR χ^2 is the *likelihood ratio* χ^2 value for the change using *backward elimination* until only forced *changeyears* and those with LR $\chi^2 \geq 50$ remain.

See Appendix C for details of the statistical analysis.

Dir = direction of the change: ↑ for up, ↓ for down, ↑↓ for up, then down.

Notable Ballpark Effects for Home Runs

In this section, we examine home run park effects for 6 franchises. A guide to the tables and figures used is given below, exemplified by the Giants franchise.

Guide to the park percentage tables

From 1911 to 1930, right-handed Giants hit 62% of their home runs at the Polo Grounds compared to 56% for left-handed Giants (see Table 6.3). Right- and left-handed opponents hit 60% and 53% there.

Over baseball history, 50.3% of right-handed batter (RHB) and 50.7% of left-handed bater (LHB) home runs are hit at home. Consequently, differences of 5–9 percentage points between a team and its opponents are underlined; those = 10 are in boldface since they represent larger imbalances worthy of further investigation.

An *odds ratio* (defined in Appendix D) of 1.3R indicates that the odds that a RHB hits a home run at the Polo Grounds is 1.3 times greater than the odds for a LHB. If "L" follows the number, the odds ratio favors the left-hander.

THE METHODS

Guide to the figures

The top figure (see Figure 6.1) shows the year-by-year percentage of home runs (one dot per year) of the stated team and their opponents that were hit at the team's home park (normalized for the number of games played). The park effect estimates are shown by the nonstraight line, which is flat where the estimates remain constant and jump or drop where a new park effect begins. Vertical lines show when the team moved into a new park.

The bottom figure (see Figure 6.2) shows the odds ratio (OR) of hitting a home run for a right-handed hitter compared to a left-hander. The base-2 logarithm (LOR) is shown rather than the OR itself since the OR is not graphically symmetric. If LOR = 0, the park does not favor either right- or left-handed players. A positive LOR favors right-handed hitters, while a negative OR favors left-handers. An LOR of 1 means that the right-handed hitter is favored with an odds ratio of 2; an LOR of –1 means that a LHB is favored with an OR of 2. LOR values –1, 0, and 1 are indicated with horizontal lines.

Polo Grounds, 1911-57

The Polo Grounds, during the years 1936–44, has the highest home park home run percentage of a post-deadball era park with a 5-year minimum period—71%. During these 9 years, the Polo Grounds were the stomping grounds of left-handed power hitter Mel Ott, who tied for or won the home run race 4 times. He hit 161 of his 247 homers in these years at the Polo Grounds—a 65% home percentage. Ott's career home percentage, 63%, is the highest percentage of any player with at least 400 home runs.

Table 6.3 shows the park home run percentages for the Polo Grounds. During the years 1936–44, Giant left-handers hit 69% of their home runs at the Polo Grounds. Ott's left-handed teammates, however, hit 72% of their home runs at the Polo Grounds, compared to Ott's 65%. Giant left-handed opponents hit 67% at the Polo Grounds. Notably, right-handers enjoyed an even greater advantage there, hitting a combined 74% of their home runs at the Polo Grounds.

During the years 1945–57, the park percentage dropped considerably for right-handed hitters, to a combined 59%, while the left-handed percentages remained roughly the same. Consequently, the park shifted from favoring right-handed hitters to favoring left-handers.

Table 6.3   Percentage of Home Runs Hit at the Polo Grounds by Team and Handedness

| | Giants | | Opponents | | |
Years	RHB	LHB	RHB	LHB	OR
1911–25	57	59	58	54	1.0
1926–35	71	58	67	55	1.7R
1936–44	77	69	72	67	1.3R
1945–57	59	68	58	61	1.3L

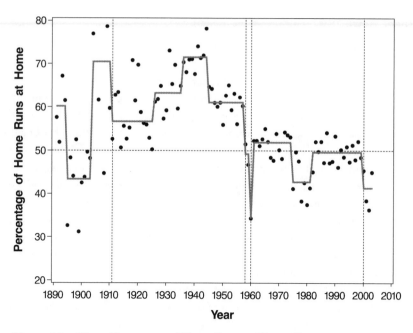

Figure 6.1   Giants Percentage of Home Runs at Home Plot

Figure 6.2   Giants Right-Handed Batter to Left-Handed Batter Home Run Log
Odds Ratio Plot

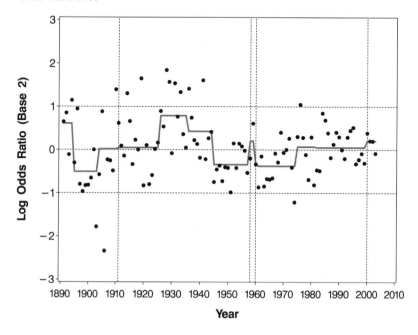

Baker Bowl, 1897-1937

The Baker Bowl was one of the best places to hit home runs between 1911 and the last full year it was used, 1937. The major jump that occurred starting in 1911 can be seen in Figure 6.3. Table 6.4 shows the park percentages by team and handedness. One can see that the park percentages jumped for both right- and left-handed batters, with the odds ratio shifting in favor of right-handers. Rich Westcott in *Philadelphia's Old Ballparks* (pp. 49–50) described a "significant change [to Baker Bowl] in 1910 when new bleachers were installed in the outfield. . . . The left field line was reduced from 415 feet to 335, and the right field line became one foot longer at 273 feet." It is not clear whether the park changes occurred before or after the 1910 season. In any event, the effect shows up most notably starting in 1911.

In 1926, home plate was moved closer to the stands, effectively lengthening the distance to left field to 341 feet and right field to 280 feet. Table 6.4 shows corresponding drops in the park percentages and a reversal of the odds ratio back in favor of left-handed power hitters.

Note that the park percentages were always higher for Phillies players, ranging from 3% to 9% higher. This suggests that the Phillies were able to take particular advantage of the quirky park, perhaps by altering their hitting style to fit it.

Three notable Phillies home run hitters were Gavy Cravath, Cy Williams, and Chuck Klein. Cravath played for the Phillies between 1912 and 1920, winning 6 home run titles. The right-handed Cravath hit 92 of his 117 Phillie home runs—79%—at the Baker Bowl, including all 19 of his league leading home runs in 1914.

From 1918 to 1929, left-handed power hitter Cy Williams hit 139 of his 217 Phillie home runs (64%) at Baker Bowl. Left-handed-hitting Chuck Klein's record was strikingly similar. Between 1928 and 1937, Klein hit 153 of his 226 home runs (68%) at the Baker Bowl, including more than 2 seasons as a Chicago Cub! Westcott notes that, the visiting left-handed Giant Mel Ott hit 40 home runs at the Baker Bowl.

Table 6.4   Percentage of Home Runs Hit at the Baker Bowl by Team and Handedness

	Phillies		Opponents		
Years	RHB	LHB	RHB	LHB	OR
1897–1910	37	45	29	39	1.4L
1911–25	75	70	71	61	1.4R
1926–37	59	64	56	61	1.2L

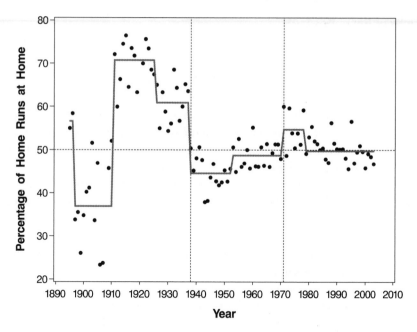

Figure 6.3   Phillies Percentage of Home Runs at Home Plot

Figure 6.4   Phillies Right-Handed Batter to Left-Handed Batter Home Run
Log Odds Ratio Plot

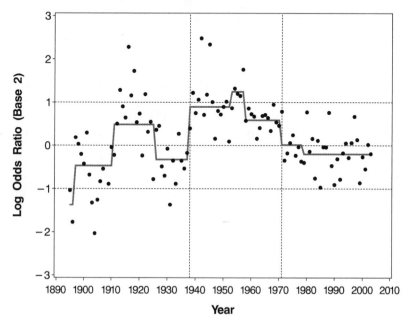

Fenway Park, 1934-49

Fenway Park, current home of the Boston Red Sox, was opened in 1912. Initially, it was a very bad park for hitting home runs, as shown in Figure 6.5. The most significant change to the ballpark occurred in 1934, with the installation of a 37-foot wall in left field, known affectionately as the "Green Monster" for its color and size.

Although the percentage of home runs hit at home did not jump until 1937, the park immediately became very asymmetrically favorable to a right-handed power hitter, as shown in Figure 6.6. Table 6.5 shows the percentages of home runs hit at Fenway Park by batting handedness during several brief eras of play.

From 1934 to 1938, right-handers hit 54% of their home runs at Fenway while left-handers hit only 15–18% of their home runs there. In 1939, left-handed power hitter Ted Williams joined the Red Sox and belted 14 of his 31 homers at Fenway. In 1940, the right field fence distance was shortened (from 332 feet to 304 feet at the foul pole). From 1939 to 1942, the percentage of right-hander's home runs was roughly the same, while that of left-handers jumped to a combined 46% at Fenway.

Many of baseball's best power hitters served in the military during the 1943–45 seasons. During these 3 seasons, the home run rate of the right-handers rose to a combined 63%, while that of left-handers fell to 26%. Consequently, the odds ratio skyrocketed to 4.8.

After players in military service returned in 1946, the percentage of home runs hit by right-handers declined to 59%, while that of left-handers jumped to 44%, lowering the odds ratio to 1.8. The table shows that these changes occurred for both the Red Sox and their opponents.

While Ted Williams accounted for most of the Red Sox left-handed home runs in the 1939–42 (127 of 154 home runs) and 1946–49 eras (138 of 185 home runs), the left-handed Red Sox home park percentages are nearly the same without Williams (44% and 51%, respectively). Thus, Williams is not skewing the findings.

Table 6.5   Percentage of Home Runs Hit at Fenway Park by Team and Handedness

Years	Red Sox		Opponents		OR
	RHB	LHB	RHB	LHB	
1934–38	54	15	54	18	5.5R
1939–42	54	45	57	46	1.4R
1943–45	64	32	62	23	4.8R
1946–49	60	49	57	38	1.8R

THE METHODS

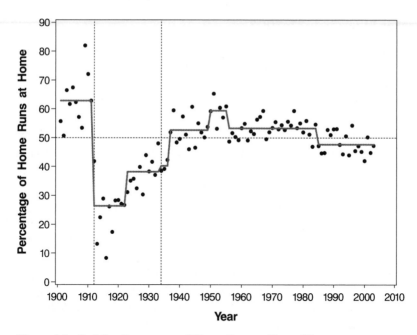

Figure 6.5   Red Sox Percentage of Home Runs at Home Plot

Figure 6.6   Red Sox Right-Handed Batter to Left-Handed Batter Home Run
Log Odds Ratio Plot for Yankee Stadium

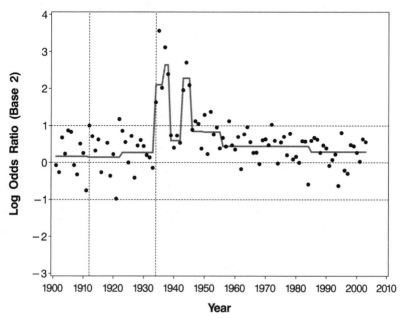

Yankee Stadium, 1923-2003

A *changeyear* was detected for Yankee Stadium in 1933 when the odds of hitting a home run shifted dramatically in favor of left-handed hitters, even though the overall home run rate did not change, as Figures 6.7 and 6.8 illustrate. What caused this shift? Let's look for clues in the park percentage table for the major eras in Yankee Stadium.

In 1933, the odds ratio favoring left-handers jumped from 1.2 to 2.4. The odds ratio remained at or above 2 until 1985, when the fences were moved up in left center field to put the monuments out of play.

From 1923 to 1932, left-handed Yankees hit 52% of their home runs at home, while their visitors hit 69% of their home runs against them there—a striking contrast. During those years, Babe Ruth and Lou Gehrig accounted for 78% of Yankee LHB home runs (722 of 923) and hit slightly more home runs on the road, while the other left-handers hit two thirds of their home runs at Yankee Stadium (see Table 6.7). As preeminent sluggers, Ruth and Gehrig were less park determined. In their later years, they and other left-handers converged to about 62% Yankee Stadium home runs. Meanwhile, right-handers dropped substantially to about 40% (see Table 6.6), leading to the striking odds ratio favoring LHBs.

Table 6.6   Percentage of Home Runs Hit at Yankee Stadium by Team and Handedness

| | Yankees | | Opponents | | |
Years	RHB	LHB	RHB	LHB	OR
1923–32	50	52	57	69	1.2L
1933–38	42	63	39	61	2.4L
1939–49	44	64	46	66	2.2L
1950–73	37	56	36	56	2.2L
1976–84	35	56	41	55	2.0L
1985–2003	47	52	49	54	1.2L

Table 6.7   Left-Handed Home Run Hitting in Yankees Games

| | Ruth | | Gehrig | | Yankees | | Other Opponents | | Overall Total |
Years	HR	Pct in NY	HR	Pct in NY	HR	Pct in NY	HR	Pct in NY	Pct in NY
1923–32	455	49%	267	46%	201	67%	381	69%	57%
1933–38	56	62%	226	57%	281	68%	200	61%	62%

Note: Pct in NY is the percent of the home runs hit at the Yankees' home park.

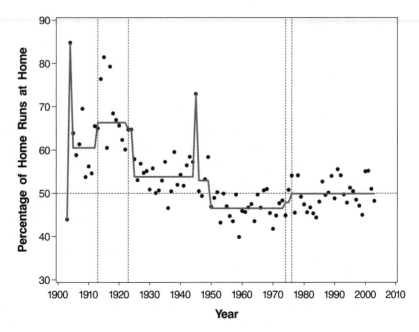

Figure 6.7   Yankees Percentage of Home Runs at Home Plot

Figure 6.8   Yankees' Right-Handed Batter to Left-Handed Batter Home Run
Log Odds Ratio Plot

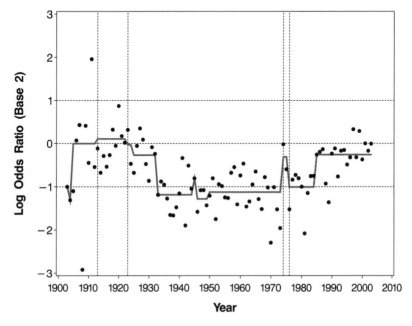

Forbes Field, 1909-70

The Pittsburgh Pirates called Forbes Field home from 1909 to June, 1970. In 1947, the Pirates decided to relocate one of the pitchers' bullpen areas from the left field foul line into left field. Consequently, they placed a fence in front of the bullpen area, which was 30 feet closer to home plate than the left field wall—335 feet away. Balls hit over the makeshift wire fence were home runs. Figure 6.9 shows the dramatic rise in the percentage of home runs hit at Forbes Field in 1947. This ballpark change "just happened" to coincide with the acquisition of right-handed power hitter Hank Greenberg. Figure 6.10 and Table 6.8 show that the jump in home runs at Forbes was enjoyed exclusively by right-handed hitters.

In 1947, the 36-year-old Greenberg, playing his final season, hit 18 of his 25 home runs at Forbes Field. Twenty-four-year old right-handed-hitting Pirate Ralph Kiner smacked 28 of his league-leading 51 home runs at the modified park. This was the second of 7 consecutive seasons in which Kiner won or tied for the most home runs in the National League.

Although initially called "Greenberg Gardens," the area behind the left-field fence was renamed "Kiner's Korner." In 1953, Kiner was traded to the Chicago Cubs. The following season, the owners decided to return the bullpen to the sidelines and remove the fence.

At Forbes, Kiner hit 167 of 278 home runs (60%) in front of the home crowd, while teammate Wally Westlake hit 63% percent of his homers at home. From 1947 to 1953, the other right-handed Pirate hitters hit 66% of their 294 home runs at home. Meanwhile, right-handed opponents of the Pirates hit 60% of their 712 home runs against the Pirates at Forbes. Among left-handed Pirates and opponents, only 38% of 496 home runs from Pirate games were hit at Forbes.

Table 6.8   Percentage of Home Runs Hit at Forbes Field by Team and Handedness

| Years | Pirates | | Opponents | | |
	RHB	LHB	RHB	LHB	OR
1909–31	40	41	34	29	1.1R
1932–46	29	46	36	39	1.5L
1947–53	63	37	60	39	2.5R
1954–58	30	39	32	34	1.2L
1959–70	37	43	39	43	1.2L

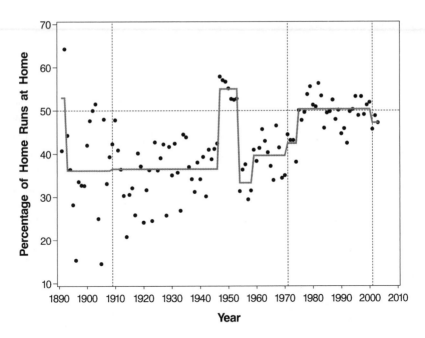

Figure 6.9   Pirates Percentage of Home Runs at Home Plot

Figure 6.10   Pirates Right-Handed Batter to Left-Handed Batter Home Run
Log Odds Ratio Plot

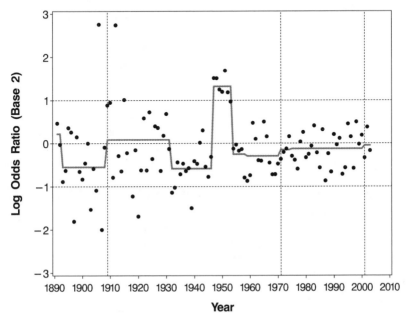

LA Coliseum, 1958-61

When the Dodgers moved to Los Angeles in 1958, the LA Coliseum became their temporary home. LA Coliseum, the best park for home runs in Dodger history (see Figure 6.11), was wildly asymmetric, favoring left field clouts, as Table 6.9 shows. Over the 4-year period, 83% were hit to left field, 15% to right field and only 2% to center field. Home plate was 250 feet from the left field foul pole and 320 feet to left center before stretching back to 425 feet away at center. The fences closed to 390 feet in right center before angling in to 301 feet at the right field foul pole. In 1959, the right center field distance was cut to 333 feet, leading to the increase in home runs in right field.

Park percentages in LA Coliseum (Table 6.10) were stable for right-handers in 1958 and 1959–61. By contrast, those of left-handers jumped in 1959, dramatically reducing the odds ratio (Figure 6.12). Left-hander Dodger Duke Snider, who had hit at least 40 home runs in each of his 5 previous seasons, hit only 15 in 1958—6 at LA Coliseum, 9 away. From 1959 to 1961, however, 60% of Snider's 53 home runs were hit at home.

Home runs are typically hit to the "pull" field of the batter. At the Coliseum, however, since only 127 homers were hit to center field or right field, left-handers hit at least 38% (77/204) of their home runs to left field. Indeed, left-hander Wally Moon joined the Dodgers in 1959 and ushered in the "Moon Shot"—an opposite field home run to take advantage of the short LF fence. From 1959 to 1961, Moon hit 76% of his 49 home runs at home.

Table 6.9 Direction of Home Runs in LA Coliseum

Year	HRs	LF	CF	RF	RHB	LHB
1958	193	182	3	8	177	16
1959	172	132	1	39	114	58
1960	186	155	3	28	127	59
1961	192	147	7	38	121	71
Total	743	616	14	113	539	204

Sources: RHB, LHB home runs were obtained from David Vincent. LF, CF, RF home runs are from *Green Cathedrals* by Philip Lowry.

Table 6.10 Percentage of Home Runs Hit at the LA Coliseum by Team
and Handedness

	Dodgers		Opponents		
Years	RHB	LHB	RHB	LHB	OR
1958	61	27	66	21	5.4R
1959–61	60	58	65	54	1.3R

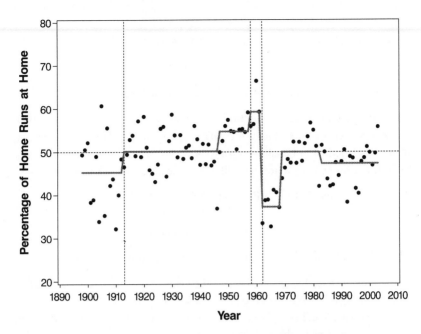

Figure 6.11   Dodgers Percentage of Home Runs at Home Plot

Figure 6.12   Dodgers Right-Handed Batter to Left-Handed Batter Home Run Log Odds Ratio Plot

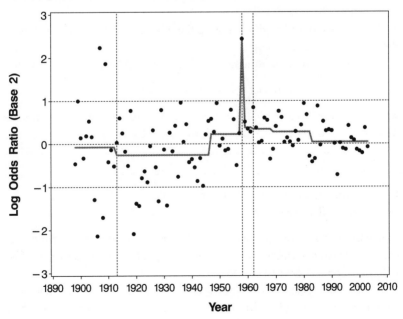

Definitions 6.1 **Park index, adjusted park index, park factor**

The simplest way one can define a park factor is:

Park index = 100 × home average/road average, based on both teams

This is the definition used in the *Bill James Presents. . .* annual guides. If the park index is greater than 100, the home park is above average. Hence, the average of the road parks must mathematically be below average, since they do not include the home park. Thus, we will define the adjusted park index as:

Adjusted park index (API)   = Park index/$[(R + n - 1)/n]$
                              = $100 \times R/[(R + n - 1)/n]$,
                              = 100 × home average/ league average

where R = Park index/100, and n is the number of teams in the league.

Total Baseball calls the term $(R + n - 1)/n$, the "other parks corrector." The adjusted park index compares the home park to an "average park."

If one wishes to adjust a player's raw average to account for the ballpark effect, one should divide it by the park factor, defined as:

$$Park\ factor = [(R + 1)/2]/[(R + n - 1)/n],$$

using the same definitions for R and n as above. Here is the rationale for the park factor. Scale the average for all road teams to be 1. The corresponding home average is R, as seen by the park index. Then, since a player plays half of his ballgames in his own park, his average is a half–half mixture of home and road averages, which equals $[(R + 1)/2]$.

This average must be adjusted using the other parks corrector, which gives the park factor formula above.

One can easily adjust from adjusted park index to park factor using the formula:

$$Park\ factor = 1 + M \times (API/100 - 1),$$

where $M = .429$, when $n = 8$; $M = .444$, when $n = 10$; $M = .455$, when $n = 12$; $M = .462$, when $n = 14$; and $M = .467$, when $n = 16$.

**Guide to the tables for the best and worst parks
for the basic offensive events**

The remainder of this chapter is comprised of tables that show the best and worst parks for the basic offensive events. In order to make the list, the same park effect must have applied for at least 5 years.

Some parks appear in the tables several times, since park effect changes were identified over time, as has already been illustrated in this chapter. Parks which appear in the list for at least 20 seasons for a given team are shown in bold for easy identification.

For each park in the list, the home average and the API are shown. The home averages have all been adjusted to a standardizing league average, as given at the top of each table.

The API values are shown in whole numbers. More accurate values can be obtained by dividing the home averages by the league average. For example, the API for Coors Field (1995–2002) for batting average is given as 121. A more accurate figure of 121.3 is obtained by dividing .3093 by .255 and multiplying the result by 100.

The home run tables (Tables 6.18 and 6.19) are dominated by parks from earlier eras, when home runs were rarer and ballparks varied more across the league. Consequently, additional tables (Tables 6.21 and 6.22) indicate the best and worst parks from 1961 to the present.

No park effects were identified for walks or strikeouts prior to 1969, the first year for which home and away park data are available. As explained in Appendix D, park effect estimation before that time is unreliable for walks, so an API of 100 is given to all parks. API estimates are provided for strikeouts, with the best and worst parks shown in Tables 6.25 and 6.26. Because of the improved data from 1969 to the present, APIs for the best and worst parks are shown in Table 6.27 for walks and Table 6.28 for strikeouts. For these tables, only the top and bottom 10 parks are shown.

Park effects can change over the lifespan of a given park. For each offensive event, APIs are estimated as being constant between changeyears. A detailed discussion of this approach is given in Appendix D and a complete listing of APIs is provided in Appendix J.

Table 6.11   Best Parks for Batting Average

Team	Years	Park	No. of Years	BA	API
1 Col–N	1995–2003	Coors Field	9	.3060	120
2 Phi–N	1922–37	Baker Bowl	16	.2787	109
3 Bos–A	1969–84	**Fenway Park**	16	.2761	108
4 Cin–N	1965–69	Crosley Field	5	.2737	107
5 Pit–N	1959–70	**Forbes Field**	12	.2721	107
6 Chi–N	1969–85	Wrigley Field	17	.2711	106
7 Buf–N	1879–83	Riverside Park	5	.2709	106
8 Bal–N	1892–99	Union Park	8	.2709	106
9 Bos–A	1985–2003	**Fenway Park**	19	.2707	106
10 Cin–N	1953–59	Crosley Field	7	.2701	106
11 Bos–A	1937–68	**Fenway Park**	32	.2699	106
12 Cle–A	1910–29	**League Park II**	20	.2682	105
13 KC–A	1959–65	Municipal Stadium	7	.2680	105
14 Atl–N	1966–91	**Atlanta/Fulton Co. Stadium**	26	.2678	105
15 Det–A	1912–31	**Navin Field**	20	.2675	105
16 Pit–N	1932–46	**Forbes Field**	15	.2669	105
17 Ari–N	1998–2003	Bank One Ballpark	6	.2666	105
18 Tex–A	1994–2003	Ballpark at Arlington	10	.2662	104
19 Phi–a	1883–90	Jefferson Street Grounds	8	.2661	104
20 NY–N	1904–10	Polo Grounds IV	7	.2658	104

Note: Average park = .255.

Table 6.12   Worst Parks for Batting Average

Team	Years	Park	No. of Years	BA	API
1 Cle–N	1879–84	Kennard Street Park	6	.2332	91
2 Chi–A	1901–09	South Side Park III	9	.2359	93
3 LA–N	1994–2003	Dodger Stadium	10	.2364	93
4 Chi–N	1899–1907	West Side Park II	9	.2376	93
5 Cin–N	1938–45	Crosley Field	8	.2377	93
6 NY–N	1964–70	Shea Stadium	7	.2379	93
7 SD–N	1998–2003	Qualcomm Stadium	6	.2381	93
8 Bal–A	1974–79	Memorial Stadium	6	.2383	94
9 Bal–A	1954–63	Memorial Stadium	10	.2388	93
10 Bos–N	1929–40	Braves Field	12	.2390	94
11 Chi–A	1964–68	Comiskey Park I	5	.2400	94
12 Oak–A	1968–95	**Oakland Coliseum**	28	.2405	94
13 NY–A	1969–73	Yankee Stadium	5	.2407	94
14 LA–N	1962–68	Dodger Stadium	7	.2412	95
15 Chi–A	1910–18	Comiskey Park I	9	.2415	95
16 Bro–N	1902–12	Washington Park	11	.2416	95
17 Mil–A	1980–84	County Stadium	5	.2416	95
18 Bal–a	1883–89	Union Park	7	.2418	95
19 Phi–N	1999–2003	Veterans Stadium	5	.2419	95
20 Bos–A	1912–33	**Fenway Park**	22	.2427	95

Note: Average park = .255.

Table 6.13   Best Parks for Doubles-Plus-Triples

Team	Years	Park	No. of Years	DPTs/500	API
1 Bos–A	1969–84	**Fenway Park**	16	32.3	129
2 Phi–A	1883–90	Jefferson Street Grounds	8	31.8	127
3 Cin–N	1965–69	Crosley Field	5	31.7	127
4 Chi–N	1878–82	Lake Front Park I	5	31.7	127
5 Phi–A	1901–908	Columbia Park	8	31.1	124
6 KC–A	1973–94	**Kaufmann Stadium**	22	30.9	124
7 Cle–A	1901–09	League Park I	9	30.8	123
8 Bos–A	1956–68	**Fenway Park**	13	30.5	122
9 Cle–A	1910–31	**League Park II**	22	30.4	122
10 StL–N	1920–57	**Sportsman's Park III**	38	30.0	120
11 Phi–N	1897–1925	**Baker Bowl**	29	29.9	119
12 Col–N	1995–2003	Coors Field	9	29.8	119
13 Tor–A	1977–88	Exhibition Stadium	12	29.5	118
14 Bos–A	1985–2003	**Fenway Park**	19	29.5	118
15 Phi–N	1887–94	Philadelphia Baseball Grounds	8	29.4	118
16 Cin–N	1902–06	Palace of the Fans	5	29.2	117
17 Hou–N	1966–71	Astrodome	6	28.8	115
18 Bkn–N	1936–46	Ebbets Field	11	28.8	115
19 Cin–N	1970–83	Riverfront Stadium	14	28.8	115
20 Min–A	1982–2003	**Metrodome**	22	28.7	115

Note: Average park = 25.0 DPTs/500 ABs.

Table 6.14   Worst Parks for Doubles-Plus-Triples

Team	Years	Park	No. of Years	DPTs/500	API
1 Bos–N	1936–40	Braves Field	5	18.6	74
2 NY–N	1926–57	**Polo Grounds V**	32	18.9	76
3 LA–N	1969–2003	**Dodger Stadium**	35	19.2	77
4 Chi–A	1901–09	South Side Park	9	19.7	79
5 NY–A	1961–68	**Yankee Stadium**	8	19.8	79
6 SF–N	1961–68	Candlestick Park	8	20.1	80
7 Bal–A	1996–2003	Camden Yards	8	20.2	81
8 Oak–A	1968–95	**Oakland Coliseum**	28	20.3	81
9 Cin–A	1884–89	League Park I	6	20.3	81
10 Chi–A	1910–18	Comiskey Park I	9	20.4	82
11 SD–N	1998–2003	Qualcomm Stadium	6	20.5	82
12 Cal–A	1970–79	Edison International Stadium	10	20.6	82
13 StL–A	1902–08	Sportsman's Park II	7	20.7	83
14 NY–A	1923–45	**Yankee Stadium**	23	20.9	83
15 NY–N	1883–88	Polo Grounds I	6	20.9	84
16 LA–N	1962–68	**Dodger Stadium**	7	21.0	84
17 Cin–N	1907–11	Palace of the Fans	5	21.4	86
18 Pro–N	1878–85	Messer Street Grounds	8	21.5	86
19 Cle–A	1947–69	**Cleveland Stadium**	23	21.6	87
20 Bos–N	1894–1909	South End Grounds III	16	21.7	87

Note: Average park = 25.0 DPTs/500 ABs.

Table 6.15 Best Parks for Doubles

Team	Years	Park	No. of Years	2Bs/500	API
1 Chi–N	1878–82	Lake Front Park I	5	29.5	137
2 Phi–A	1901–08	Columbia Park	8	29.0	135
3 Phi–A	1883–90	Jefferson Street Grounds	8	28.7	133
4 Bos–A	1969–84	**Fenway Park**	16	28.6	133
5 Cin–N	1965–69	Crosley Field	5	28.1	131
6 Phi–N	1897–1925	**Baker Bowl**	29	27.8	129
7 Cle–A	1910–31	**League Park II**	22	27.6	129
8 Bos–A	1956–68	**Fenway Park**	13	27.5	128
9 Cle–A	1901–09	League Park I	9	27.2	126
10 Phi–N	1887–94	Philadelphia Baseball Grounds	8	26.6	124
11 StL–N	1920–57	**Sportsman's Park III**	38	26.1	121
12 Bos–A	1985–2003	**Fenway Park**	19	25.8	120
13 Phi–N	1926–37	**Baker Bowl**	12	25.7	120
14 Bos–A	1939–1955	**Fenway Park**	17	25.7	119
15 KC–A	1973–94	**Kauffman Stadium**	22	25.5	119
16 Hou–N	1966–71	Astrodome	6	25.2	117
17 Cin–N	1894–1901	League Park II	8	25.0	116
18 Bal–A	1964–68	Memorial Stadium	5	25.0	116
19 Tor–A	1977–88	Exhibition Stadium	12	24.8	116
20 Col–N	1995–2003	Coors Field	9	24.7	115

Note: Average park = 21.5 2Bs/500 ABs.

Table 6.16 Worst Parks for Doubles

Team	Years	Park	No. of Years	2Bs/500	API
1 Cin–A	1884–89	League Park I	6	15.7	73
2 Bos–N	1936–40	Braves Field	5	15.9	74
3 NY–N	1926–57	**Polo Grounds V**	32	16.0	75
4 Chi–A	1910–18	Comiskey Park I	9	16.2	75
5 Cin–N	1907–11	Palace of the Fans	5	16.3	76
6 NY–A	1923–45	**Yankee Stadium**	23	16.9	79
7 NY–A	1961–68	**Yankee Stadium**	8	17.2	80
8 LA–N	1969–2003	**Dodger Stadium**	35	17.3	80
9 Was–A	1911–29	Griffith Stadium	19	17.4	81
10 NY–N	1884–88	Polo Grounds I	5	17.4	81
11 SD–N	1998–2003	Qualcomm Stadium	6	17.4	81
12 Chi–A	1901–09	South Side Park III	9	17.5	82
13 Bal–A	1996–2003	Camden Yards	8	17.7	82
14 StL–A	1902–08	Sportsman's Park II	7	17.8	83
15 Oak–A	1968–95	**Oakland Coliseum**	28	17.8	83
16 Pit–N	1891–1900	Exposition Park III	10	18.0	84
17 Cal–A	1970–79	Edison International Stadium	10	18.0	84
18 LA–N	1962–68	**Dodger Stadium**	7	18.0	84
19 SF–N	1960–68	Candlestick Park	9	18.1	84
20 Cle–A	1947–53	Cleveland Stadium	7	18.2	85

Note: Average park = 21.5 2Bs/500 ABs.

Table 6.17 Best Parks for Triples

Team	Years	Park	No. of Years	3Bs/500	API
1 Ari–N	1998–2003	Bank One Ballpark	6	5.6	161
2 Col–N	1995–2003	Coors Field	9	5.5	156
3 Pit–N	1921–46	**Forbes Field**	26	5.5	156
4 KC–A	1973–2000	**Kauffman Stadium**	28	5.4	155
5 Pit–N	1954–70	**Forbes Field**	17	5.1	146
6 Hou–N	1977–84	Astrodome	8	5.0	142
7 Cin–N	1902–11	Palace of the Fans	10	4.9	139
8 Min–A	1969–81	Metropolitan Stadium	13	4.8	138
9 Was–A	1951–60	**Griffith Stadium**	10	4.8	138
10 Pit–N	1891–1908	Exposition Park III	18	4.8	137
11 Chi–A	1974–90	Comiskey Park I	17	4.8	136
12 Was–A	1930–41	**Griffith Stadium**	12	4.7	136
13 StL–N	1966–91	**Busch Stadium**	26	4.7	136
14 Tor–A	1977–88	Exhibition Stadium	12	4.7	135
15 Tex–A	1994–2003	Ballpark at Arlington	10	4.7	134
16 NY–A	1969–73	Yankee Stadium	5	4.7	134
17 Min–A	1982–2003	**Metrodome**	22	4.6	130
18 Cin–N	1912–37	**Crosley Field**	26	4.6	130
19 Fla–N	1993–2003	Pro Player Stadium	11	4.5	129
20 Pit–N	1909–20	**Forbes Field**	12	4.5	129

Note: Average park = 3.5 3Bs/500 ABs.

Table 6.18 Worst Parks for Triples

Team	Years	Park	No. of Years	3Bs/500	API
1 LA–N	1969–2003	**Dodger Stadium**	35	1.9	54
2 Cle–A	1954–69	**Cleveland Stadium**	16	2.0	57
3 Cle–A	1970–75	**Cleveland Stadium**	6	2.0	58
4 Bal–A	1974–91	Memorial Stadium	18	2.1	59
5 Chi–A	1902–09	South Side Park III	8	2.1	60
6 StL–a	1882–91	Sportsman's Park I	10	2.1	61
7 Phi–N	1911–37	**Baker Bowl**	27	2.2	61
8 Atl–N	1966–82	Atlanta/Fulton Co. Stadium	17	2.3	65
9 Bos–N	1894–1914	**South End Grounds III**	21	2.3	67
10 Cal–A	1970–2003	**Edison International Stadium**	34	2.4	69
11 NY–N	1926–44	Polo Grounds V	19	2.4	69
12 Bal–A	1992–2003	Camden Yards	12	2.4	70
13 SF–N	1961–68	Candlestick Park	8	2.4	70
14 NY–A	1913–22	Polo Grounds V	10	2.4	70
15 Oak–A	1968–1995	**Oakland Coliseum**	28	2.4	70
16 Bos–N	1936–52	Braves Field	17	2.5	70
17 Cin–N	1938–64	**Crosley Field**	27	2.5	70
18 Chi–N	1916–37	**Wrigley Field**	22	2.6	74
19 NY–A	1961–68	Yankee Stadium	8	2.6	75
20 Tex–A	1972–84	Arlington Stadium	13	2.6	75

Note: Average park = 3.5 3Bs/500 ABs.

Table 6.19   Best Parks for Home Runs

Team	Years	Park	No. of Years	HRs/500	API
1 Bos–N	1894–1902	South End Grounds III	9	24.8	236
2 Phi–A	1915–22	Shibe Park	8	23.7	225
3 NY–N	1936–44	**Polo Grounds V**	9	22.2	211
4 Phi–N	1911–25	**Baker Bowl**	15	21.5	205
5 NY–N	1904–10	Polo Grounds IV	7	21.1	201
6 StL–A	1920–28	Sportsman's Park III	9	19.8	188
7 StL–N	1895–99	Robison Field	5	18.9	180
8 NY–A	1913–22	Polo Grounds V	10	18.4	175
9 Atl–N	1977–82	Atlanta/Fulton Co. Stadium	6	17.9	171
10 Cin–a	1884–89	League Park I	6	17.1	163
11 NY–N	1926–35	**Polo Grounds V**	10	16.6	158
12 Col–N	1995–2003	Coors Field	9	16.3	155
13 Bos–A	1901–11	Huntington Ave. Grounds	11	16.3	155
14 Cle–A	1970–75	Cleveland Stadium	6	16.1	153
15 NY–N	1945–1957	**Polo Grounds V**	13	15.4	146
16 Phi–N	1926–37	**Baker Bowl**	12	15.2	145
17 NY–A	1905–12	Hilltop Park	8	15.0	143
18 Det–A	1938–46	Tiger Stadium	9	14.8	141
19 Bos–N	1903–09	South End Grounds III	7	14.6	139
20 Bos–A	1950–55	Fenway Park	6	14.5	138

Note: Average park = 10.5 HRs/500 ABs.

Table 6.20   Worst Parks for Home Runs

Team	Years	Park	No. of Years	HRs/500	API
1 Cin–N	1895–99	League Park II	5	2.4	23
2 Chi–A	1902–09	South Side Park III	8	2.8	27
3 Cin–N	1920–33	**Crosley Field**	14	2.8	27
4 Was–A	1914–29	**Griffith Stadium**	16	3.9	37
5 Was–A	1942–55	**Griffith Stadium**	14	4.1	39
6 Bos–A	1912–22	Fenway Park	11	4.1	30
7 Cle–N	1891–99	League Park I	9	4.2	40
8 Cin–N	1907–11	Palace of the Fans	5	4.4	42
9 Bos–N	1915–27	Braves Field	13	4.4	42
10 Buf–N	1879–83	Riverside Grounds	5	4.5	43
11 Cle–N	1879–84	National League Park I	6	4.6	44
12 Was–A	1930–41	**Griffith Stadium**	12	4.9	46
13 Cin–N	1912–19	**Crosley Field**	8	5.0	48
14 Bal–N	1892–99	Oriole Park III	8	5.1	48
15 Hou–N	1977–84	Astrodome	8	5.3	50
16 Was–A	1904–10	American League Park II	7	5.4	52
17 Bos–N	1936–41	Braves Field	6	5.6	53
18 Pit–N	1954–58	Forbes Field	5	5.6	53
19 NY–N	1884–88	Polo Grounds I	5	6.2	59
20 Pit–N	1893–1908	Exposition Park III	16	6.2	59

Note: Average park = 10.5 HRs/500 ABs.

Table 6.21   Best Parks for Home Runs, 1961–2003

Team	Years	Park	No. of Years	HRs/500	API
1 Atl–N	1977–82	**Atlanta/Fulton Co. Stadium**	6	17.9	171
2 Col–N	1995–2003	Coors Field	9	16.3	155
3 Cle–A	1970–75	Cleveland Stadium	6	16.1	153
4 Sea–A	1977–89	Kingdome	13	14.3	136
5 Atl–N	1966–76	**Atlanta/Fulton Co. Stadium**	11	14.0	134
6 Chi–N	1961–83	**Wrigley Field**	23	14.0	133
7 Cin–N	1965–69	Crosley Field	5	13.4	127
8 Det–A	1947–81	**Tiger Stadium**	35	13.1	124
9 Cin–N	1984–92	Riverfront Stadium	9	12.8	122
10 Phi–N	1971–78	Veterans Stadium	8	12.4	119
11 Mon–N	1969–76	Parc Jarry	8	12.4	118
12 SD–N	1982–97	Qualcomm Stadium	16	12.4	118
13 Chi–N	1986–99	**Wrigley Field**	14	12.3	117
14 Bos–A	1965–84	**Fenway Park**	20	12.2	117
15 Det–A	1982–99	**Tiger Stadium**	18	12.2	117
16 Atl–N	1983–96	**Atlanta/Fulton Co. Stadium**	14	12.1	115
17 Min–A	1961–68	Metropolitan Stadium	8	12.0	115
18 Cal–A	1980–97	Edison International Field	18	12.0	115
19 Chi–A	1969–73	Comiskey Park I	5	11.9	114
20 Tex–A	1995–2003	Ballpark at Arlington	9	11.7	111

Note: Average park = 10.5 HRs/500 ABs.

Table 6.22   Worst Parks for Home Runs, 1961–2003

Team	Years	Park	No. of Years	HRs/500	API
1 Hou–N	1977–84	**Astrodome**	8	5.3	50
2 LA–N	1962–68	Dodger Stadium	7	6.5	62
3 Hou–N	1966–71	**Astrodome**	6	6.7	64
4 Hou–N	1985–91	**Astrodome**	7	7.0	66
5 Chi–A	1964–68	Comiskey Park I	5	7.1	68
6 Pit–N	1959–69	Forbes Field	12	7.2	68
7 KC–A	1973–94	**Kauffman Stadium**	22	7.9	75
8 SD–N	1969–81	Qualcomm Stadium	13	8.0	76
9 Bal–A	1958–63	Memorial Stadium	6	8.1	77
10 Chi–A	1986–90	Comiskey Park I	5	8.2	78
11 Cal–A	1970–79	Edison International Field	10	8.3	79
12 Mil–A	1980–84	County Stadium	5	8.4	80
13 Hou–N	1992–99	**Astrodome**	8	8.4	80
14 StL–N	1966–91	**Busch Stadium**	26	8.4	80
15 Hou–N	1972–76	**Astrodome**	5	8.6	82
16 Chi–A	1974–82	Comiskey Park I	9	8.6	82
17 SD–N	1998–2003	Qualcomm Stadium	6	8.9	85
18 Bal–A	1969–79	Memorial Stadium	11	9.1	87
19 Fla–A	1993–2003	Pro Player Stadium	11	9.1	87
20 Tex–A	1972–84	Arlington Stadium	13	9.1	87

Note: Average park = 10.5 HRs/500 ABs.

Table 6.23 Best Parks for Runs

Team	Years	Park	No. of Years	Runs/500	API
1 Col–N	1995–2003	Coors Field	9	93.7	141
2 Phi–N	1926–37	**Baker Bowl**	12	79.9	120
3 Bos–A	1950–55	**Fenway Park**	6	78.2	117
4 Cin–N	1902–06	Palace of the Fans	5	77.6	117
5 Chi–N	1969–83	**Wrigley Field**	15	76.8	115
6 Bos–A	1965–84	**Fenway Park**	20	75.8	114
7 StL–N	1958–65	Sportsman's Park III	8	75.8	114
8 Atl–N	1977–91	Altanta/Fulton Co. Stadium	15	75.4	113
9 NY–A	1904–12	Hilltop Park	9	75.2	113
10 Cin–N	1965–69	Crosley Field	5	75.2	113
11 Bos–N	1894–1902	South End Grounds III	9	73.6	111
12 Det–A	1938–46	Tiger Stadium	9	73.2	110
13 Phi–N	1911–21	**Baker Bowl**	11	73.1	110
14 StL–A	1920–53	**Sportsman's Park III**	34	72.9	110
15 Tex–A	1995–2003	Ballpark at Arlington	9	72.9	110
16 Cin–N	1895–99	League Park II	5	72.9	110
17 Bos–A	1956–64	**Fenway Park**	9	72.6	109
18 Cin–N	1953–59	Crosley Field	7	72.6	109
19 Pit–N	1947–53	Forbes Field	7	72.2	109
20 Chi–N	1961–68	**Wrigley Field**	8	72.2	109

Note: Average park = 66.6 Runs/550 NFPs.

Table 6.24 Worst Parks for Runs

Team	Years	Park	No. of Years	Runs/500	API
1 Mil–N	1953–58	County Stadium	6	56.0	84
2 LA–N	1962–68	Dodger Stadium	7	56.0	84
3 SD–N	1998–2003	Qualcomm Stadium	6	57.0	86
4 LA–N	1994–2003	Dodger Stadium	10	57.1	86
5 Hou–N	1977–84	**Astrodome**	8	57.7	87
6 Chi–A	1964–68	Comiskey Park I	5	58.7	88
7 Mil–A	1980–84	County Stadium	5	58.8	88
8 Bos–N	1929–41	**Braves Field**	13	58.9	88
9 Cle–A	1947–53	Cleveland Stadium	7	59.2	89
10 Bal–A	1954–63	Memorial Stadium	10	59.4	89
11 Cal–A	1970–79	Edison International Stadium	10	59.6	89
12 Oak–A	1968–95	**Oakland Coliseum**	28	59.7	90
13 SD–N	1969–81	Qualcomm Stadium	13	59.8	90
14 NY–A	1950–60	Yankee Stadium	11	60.1	90
15 Chi–A	1901–09	South Side Park III	9	60.3	91
16 Bos–N	1946–52	**Braves Field**	7	60.3	91
17 Cle–A	1937–46	League Park II	10	60.6	91
18 Bos–N	1915–27	**Braves Field**	13	60.7	91
19 NY–A	1925–32	Yankee Stadium	8	60.9	91
20 Hou–N	1985–99	Astrodome	15	61.0	92

Note: Average park = 66.6 Runs/550 NFPs.

Table 6.25   Parks for Highest Strikeouts

Team	Years	Park	No. of Years	SOs/550	API
1 Phi–A	1901–08	Columbia Park	8	107.4	121
2 NY–N	1891–1910	**Polo Grounds IV**	20	103.8	117
3 NY–A	1923–36	Yankee Stadium	14	102.5	116
4 Bro–N	1922–35	**Ebbets Field**	14	101.6	115
5 Was–A	1911–20	Griffith Stadium	10	101.5	115
6 Phi–N	1999–2003	Veterans Stadium	5	100.6	114
7 Bal–A	1883–89	Union Park	7	100.0	113
8 StL–N	1929–37	Sportsman's Park III	9	99.6	112
9 Hou–N	1992–99	Astrodome	8	99.6	112
10 Bos–N	1876–87	South End Grounds I	12	99.3	112
11 Chi–N	1885–91	West Side Park I	7	98.4	111
12 Cle–A	1937–46	League Park II	10	98.1	111
13 Bro–N	1947–57	**Ebbets Field**	11	97.8	110
14 Det–A	1938–46	Tiger Stadium	9	97.5	110
15 StL–A	1942–53	Sportsman's Park III	12	96.8	109
16 Chi–N	1916–60	**Wrigley Field**	45	96.8	109
17 Phi–A	1915–34	**Shibe Park**	20	96.1	109
18 NY–A	1913–22	Polo Grounds V	10	96.1	109
19 SF–N	1975–81	Candlestick Park	7	95.9	108
20 Lou–N	1893–99	Eclipse Park II	7	95.8	108

Note: Average park = 88.6 SOs/550 NFPs.

Table 6.26   Parks for Lowest Strikeouts

Team	Years	Park	No. of Years	SOs/550	API
1 Cin–N	1894–99	League Park II	6	72.6	82
2 Pit–N	1921–31	**Forbes Field**	11	73.4	83
3 Was–A	1930–41	Griffith Stadium	12	74.6	84
4 Cle–A	1918–31	League Park II	14	75.8	86
5 Det–A	1912–22	Navin Field	11	76.4	86
6 Col–N	1995–2003	Coors Field	9	76.5	86
7 Bro–a	1884–88	Washington Park	5	76.6	86
8 StL–a	1882–88	Sportsman's Park II	7	77.1	87
9 Cin–N	1912–33	**Crosley Field**	22	77.2	87
10 KC–A	1973–2003	**Kauffman Stadium**	31	77.3	87
11 Pit–N	1932–46	**Forbes Field**	15	78.2	88
12 Cin–N	1902–11	Palace of the Fans	10	78.3	88
13 StL–N	1895–1908	Robison Field	14	78.5	89
14 Cin–a	1884–89	League Park I	6	79.5	90
15 Phi–A	1943–54	Shibe Park	12	80.2	91
16 Det–A	1901–11	Bennett Park	11	80.4	91
17 Cin–N	1953–59	**Crosley Field**	7	80.7	91
18 Chi–A	1919–68	**Comiskey Park I**	50	80.8	91
19 Chi–A	1902–09	South Side Park III	8	81.6	92
20 NY–A	1903–12	Hilltop Park	10	81.9	93

Note: Average park = 88.6 SOs/550 NFPs.

Table 6.27   Best and Worst Parks for Base on Balls, 1969–2003

Team	Years	Park	No. of Years	BBs/550	API
1 Chi–A	1983–90	Comiskey Park I	8	51.4	108
2 Cin–N	1984–2002	Cinergy Field	19	51.0	107
3 Mon–N	1977–99	**Olympic Stadium**	23	50.6	106
4 Sea–A	1977–99	**Kingdome**	23	50.0	104
5 Cle–A	1970–75	Cleveland Stadium	6	50.0	104
6 Bos–A	1969–84	Fenway Park	16	50.0	104
7 Fla–N	1993–2003	Pro Player Stadium	11	49.8	104
8 Phi–N	1971–2003	**Veterans Stadium**	33	49.7	104
9 StL–N	1998–2003	Busch Stadium	6	49.6	104
10 SF–N	1969–1977	Candlestick Park	9	49.6	104
1 Mil–A	1980–84	County Stadium	5	44.9	94
2 SD–N	1969–81	Qualcomm Stadium	13	45.1	94
3 KC–A	1973–2000	**Kauffman Stadium**	28	45.2	95
4 LA–N	1969–2003	**Dodger Stadium**	35	45.4	95
5 Bal–A	1969–79	Memorial Stadium	11	46.2	96
6 Hou–N	1985–99	Astrodome	15	46.3	97
7 Cal–A	1970–2003	**Edison International Stadium**	34	46.5	97
8 NY–A	1976–2003	**Yankee Stadium**	28	46.6	97
9 StL–N	1966–97	**Busch Stadium**	32	46.6	97
10 Tex–A	1972–93	Arlington Stadium	22	46.6	97

Note: Average park = 47.9 BBs/550 NFPs.

Table 6.28   Best and Worst Parks for Strikeouts, 1969–2003

Team	Years	Park	No. of Years	SOs/550	API
1 Phi–N	1999–2003	Veterans Stadium	5	100.6	114
2 Hou–N	1992–99	Astrodome	8	99.6	112
3 SF–N	1975–81	Candlestick Park	7	95.9	108
4 SD–N	1982–2003	**Qualcomm Stadium**	22	94.5	107
5 Fla–N	1993–2003	Player Pro Stadium	11	93.4	105
6 Det–A	1969–76	Tiger Stadium	8	93.0	105
7 Tex–A	1972–93	**Arlington Stadium**	22	92.8	105
8 Sea–A	1977–99	**Kingdome**	23	92.8	105
9 Bal–A	1974–91	Memorial Stadium	18	92.7	105
10 Hou–N	1966–71	Astrodome	6	92.7	105
1 Col–N	1995–2003	Coors Field	9	76.5	86
2 KC–A	1973–2003	**Kauffman Stadium**	31	77.3	87
3 StL–N	1966–91	**Busch Stadium**	26	82.1	93
4 Atl–N	1966–96	**Atlanta/Fulton Co. Stadium**	31	82.3	93
5 Ari–N	1998–2003	Bank One Ballpark	6	83.8	95
6 Tex–A	1994–2003	Ballpark at Arlington	10	84.2	95
7 Chi–A	1969–83	**Comiskey Park I**	15	84.3	95
8 Cle–A	1976–93	Cleveland Stadium	18	84.3	95
9 Chi–A	1991–2003	Comiskey Park II	13	85.2	96
10 Chi–A	1986–90	**Comiskey Park I**	5	85.6	97

Note: Average park = 88.6 SOs/550 NFPs.

Table 6.29   Best Parks for On-Base-Plus-Slugging

Team	Years	Park	No. of Years	OPs	API
1 Col–N	1995–2003	Coors Field	9	.840	121
2 NY–N	1904–1910	Polo Grounds IV	7	.780	112
3 Phi–N	1911–21	**Baker Bowl**	11	.777	112
4 Phi–A	1915–22	Shibe Park	8	.771	111
5 Phi–N	1926–37	**Baker Bowl**	12	.771	111
6 Bos–A	1969–84	**Fenway Park**	16	.763	110
7 StL–A	1920–28	Sportsman's Park III	9	.762	110
8 Cin–N	1965–69	Crosley Field	5	.762	110
9 Bos–N	1894–1902	South End Grounds III	9	.761	110
10 Atl–N	1977–82	Atlanta/Fulton Co. Stadium	6	.756	109
11 Bos–A	1950–55	**Fenway Park**	6	.755	109
12 Chi–N	1969–83	Wrigley Field	15	.749	108
13 StL–N	1895–99	Robison Field	5	.747	107
14 NY–N	1936–44	Polo Grounds V	9	.745	107
15 Cin–N	1953–59	Crosley Field	7	.742	107
16 NY–A	1905–12	Hilltop Park	8	.739	106
17 Bos–A	1956–64	**Fenway Park**	9	.738	106
18 Bos–A	1939–49	**Fenway Park**	11	.737	106
19 Cin–a	1884–89	League Park I	6	.734	106
20 StL–N	1924–28	Sportsman's Park III	5	.733	105

Note: Average park = .695.

Table 6.30   Worst Parks for On-Base-Plus-Slugging

Team	Years	Park	No. of Years	OPs	API
1 Chi–A	1902–09	South Side Park III	8	.599	86
2 Cle–N	1879–84	National League Park I	6	.618	89
3 Bos–N	1936–40	**Braves Field**	5	.620	89
4 Was–A	1914–20	Griffith Stadium	7	.627	90
5 Was–A	1921–29	Griffith Stadium	9	.628	90
6 Cin–N	1920–33	**Crosley Field**	14	.632	91
7 Chi–N	1899–1907	West Side Grounds	9	.634	91
8 LA–N	1994–2003	Dodger Stadium	10	.635	91
9 LA–N	1962–68	Dodger Stadium	7	.635	91
10 Bos–A	1912–22	Fenway Park	11	.636	91
11 Chi–A	1910–18	Comiskey Park I	9	.636	92
12 Chi–A	1964–68	Comiskey Park I	5	.640	92
13 SD–N	1998–2003	Qualcomm Stadium	6	.642	92
14 Bos–N	1929–35	**Braves Field**	7	.643	92
15 Bos–N	1915–27	**Braves Field**	13	.643	93
16 Cin–N	1938–45	**Crosley Field**	8	.644	93
17 Bal–A	1958–63	Memorial Stadium	6	.644	93
18 Bal–A	1974–79	Memorial Stadium	6	.646	93
19 Cal–A	1970–79	Edison Internationl Stadium	10	.647	93
20 Mil–A	1980–84	County Stadium	5	.648	93

Note: Average park = .695.

PART TWO

The Findings

On previous page: Babe Ruth. (National Baseball Hall of Fame Library, Coopers-town, NY.)

CHAPTER 7

Swing, Batter!

Adjusting Batting
Average

A crowd roars with delight when the home team's leadoff hitter laces a single to right. They are less enthusiastic if the player draws a walk. Still, from a run scoring point of view, the two outcomes are equivalent—runner on first, nobody out. In baseball, as with any sport, winning is important. Sports are also a form of entertainment, though. When the batter hits the ball, the fans enjoy hearing the crack of the bat; tracking the flight, speed, and arc of the ball; and seeing the athleticism of the fielder trying to shag it. By comparison, a walk is often viewed as an anticlimactic failure on the part of the pitcher to throw enough pitches into the strike zone.

Many baseball fans would prefer to replace batting average with *on-base percentage*. On-base percentage combines hits, walks, and hit-by-pitches together into a single statistic. All hits have a basic similarity—the batter makes contact with the ball and places it where the fielders can't catch it. How many bases a hit nets is a matter of degree, not essential character. Hits and walks are of different character.

Many fans also deride the batting average statistic for giving the same weight to the lowly single as to the mighty home run. On-base percentage, however, would only heighten such a criticism since a walk is even less valuable than a single. Slugging average, an early attempt to weight the value of hits, overemphasizes the effect of a home run compared to a single. Adding on-base percentage and slugging average together, it turns out, happens to produce just about the right weighting of walks and the different hits—but it is an even more complex offensive event. For these reasons, batting average will and should always remain a fundamental statistic in baseball.

Later in this book, a composite rating of a player is developed, appropriately weighting the relative importance of different kinds of hits and walks. Calculating the adjusted batting average is important, because an adjusted average for singles can then be obtained by subtracting out the adjusted averages for doubles, triples, and home runs.

In *Baseball's All-Time Best Hitters*, I developed a method for obtaining the adjusted batting average and identified Tony Gwynn as the *best hitter* in baseball history. "Best hitter" was defined as the hitter with the highest probability to get a hit in a given at bat. The more self-evidently restrictive term *best hitter for average* could be used instead.

Comparison of Current Method to That in
Baseball's All-Time Best Hitters

In *Baseball's All-Time Best Hitters* (abbreviated *BATBH*), a methodology adjusting the raw batting averages for the league batting average, the talent pool, the ballpark effects, and late-career declines was established for comparing players across baseball history. While the same four adjustments form the basis for this book as well, differences in how they are applied yields a modestly different list of best hitters for average. Here are the differences, with a brief rationale for the change:

Regular Players. The era of play adjustment in *BATBH* was based on the league average, with an adjustment to account for the designated hitter (DH) in the American League since 1973. This book limits the average to *regular players*, therefore eliminating some cross-era concerns, such as the declining proportion of NFPs attained by pitchers, which make it harder to exceed the league average today than in previous eras.

Qualifying Players. For the career lists, *BATBH* required a player to have a minimum of 4000 ABs. In this book, the minimum is 4000 NFPs, which allows more players to "qualify." Since walks and HBPs are also plate appearances, NFPs are a fairer turnstile of batting experience.

Park Effect Estimates. The park effect estimates have been improved substantially. In *BATBH*, Level 1 data were used for the years 1876–1981, and Level 3 data for 1982–1998 (see Appendix E for a description of the data levels). In this book, Level 2 data are used for 1876–1968, and Level 4 data for 1969–2003. Higher level data provides better park estimates. Moreover, the changeyears are more closely aligned with ballpark dimension and fence changes than before.

Transformation. In *BATBH*, no transformation was applied to the raw batting average before applying the adjustments. In this book, a square root transformation is used when calculating the performance spread.

Although the improvement for batting average for this adjustment is modest, it plays a critical role in producing cross-era fairness for many other offensive events.

Year-by-Year Standard Deviations Based on Regular Players. The adjustment for talent pool used the year-by-year standard deviation for the park-adjusted batting average. In *BATBH*, all player-seasons with 200 or more at-bats were included, whereas only regular player-seasons are included here. Table 3.4 shows minimum NFP requirements for various eras of play. The current requirements are 292 NFP for the National League and 324 NFP for the American League. The new approach includes a near-constant 75% of all non-pitcher NFPs per season in the SD calculation, leading to better fairness for seasons of different average number of games.

Standardizing Seasons. In *BATBH*, the average National League batting average from 1969 to 1992 was used, with an adjustment for the American League from 1973 on to account for the impact of the DH. In this book, the average National League batting average of regular players from 1977 to 1992 is used. Since no pitcher during these years was a *regular*, no adjustment for the DH is needed. The years were chosen to be a period when the offensive event averages were relatively constant. The smaller period especially improved the constancy of the stolen base averages.

Table 7.1 shows the impact that changes between the approach presented here and in *BATBH* had on the ranking of the best 12 hitters in baseball history. Overall, the

Table 7.1 Best Career Performances for Adjusted Batting Average Compared to Those in *Baseball's All-Time Best Hitters*

Rank	Player	Adj. BA	*BATBH* Adj. BA	Change	*BATBH* Rank
1	Tony Gwynn	.338	.342	−4	1
2	Ty Cobb	.336	.340	−4	2
3	Rod Carew	.332	.332	0	3
4	Stan Musial	.327	.325	+2	8
5	Rogers Hornsby	.327	.330	−3	5
6	Nap Lajoie	.324	.322	+2	10
7	Joe Jackson	.324	.331	−7	4
8	Honus Wagner	.324	.326	−2	7
9	Ted Williams	.322	.327	−5	6
10	Wade Boggs	.322	.324	−2	9
11	Pete Browning	.321	.317	+4	12
12	Tris Speaker	.319	.322	−3	11

Note: The change, in batting points, is (Adj. BA − BATBH Adj. BA) × 1000.

Guide to the top 100 seasons tables

The actual number of player-seasons that rank among the top 100 are identified for each of six eras, under the column entitled "Seasons." The "expected" number of top 100 seasons for the era is calculated as the percentage of player-seasons of regular players that falls within that era. The deviation between the actual and expected numbers is considered to be "significant" if the value $q = $ (actual number − expected number)^2/expected number is 3.84 or larger. Hall of Fame players with multiple top 100 seasons are listed in italics.

adjusted averages in this book are 2 batting points lower than in *BATBH*. Gwynn, Cobb, and Carew remain 1, 2, and 3. Jackson loses 7 points and drops from fourth to seventh, allowing Musial and Hornsby to move up. Musial and Lajoie gain 2 batting points each, and slip past Ted Williams. Pete Browning posted the largest gain, 4 points, but is able to move up only one spot into eleventh place.

Best Single-Season Hitters for Average

Here is a summary of the top 100 seasons for batting average. The complete list of seasons is given in Appendix L.1.

Table 7.2   Top 100 Seasons—Adjusted Batting Average
63 Different Players with Average Age = 28.3

Era	Seasons	Expected	Era	Seasons	Expected
1876–1900	10	9.9	1947–68	10	16.5
1901–19	21↑	13.4	1969–92	24	26.8
1920–46	22	19.4	1993–2003	13	14.0

No. of Seasons	Players with Multiple Top 100 Seasons
7	*Ty Cobb*, Tony Gwynn
6	*Rogers Hornsby*
4	Wade Boggs, *Rod Carew, Nap Lajoie*
3	*Stan Musial, Honus Wagner*
2	Pete Browning, *Joe DiMaggio*, Edgar Martinez, John Olerud, *George Sisler, Tris Speaker, Ted Williams*

Notes: Hall of Fame players are listed in italics.

The symbol ↑ means that the number of seasons is significantly higher than expected.

See the guide to the top 100 seasons tables on page 103.

10. Stan Musial, 1948   .364 Adjusted Batting Average

1948 was Stan Musial's greatest season. Missing the triple crown by a single home run, Musial led the National League in hits, doubles, triples, runs, RBIs, batting average, and slugging average. As such, it is a near duplicate of the performance of Tip O'Neill in 1887, which is described below.

9. Barry Bonds, 2002   .365 Adjusted Batting Average

In 2002, Barry Bonds smashed the major league single-season bases on balls mark with 198 walks, breaking his own record of 177 walks set in 2001. Bonds' high walk totals stem from his refusal to swing at bad pitches. In further developing this discrimination between good and bad pitches, Bonds hit for one the highest averages in the history of the game.

8. Ted Williams, 1957   .366 Adjusted Batting Average

Ted Williams put in an amazing performance at age 38, winning the batting crown with one of the 10 best seasons of all time. Williams has only 2 seasons among the top 100, but both of them are also among the top 10.

7. Tip O'Neill, 1887   .366 Adjusted Batting Average

In 1887, walks counted the same as hits when computing the batting average. For historical fairness, however, only his hits are counted here. Tip O'Neill's .435 raw batting average towered over that of his peers. In 1887, O'Neill led the American Association in hits, doubles, triples, home runs, runs, RBIs, batting average, and slugging average.

6. Ted Williams, 1941   .370 Adjusted Batting Average

Ted Williams is the only player with two seasons in the top 10. This year is the benchmark to which all great recent batting performances are compared, since it was the last season that a player who qualified for the batting title hit at least .400. After adjustments, however, 3 more recent performances have bettered this mark.

5. Nap Lajoie, 1901   .372 Adjusted Batting Average

In 1901, Lajoie hit for an unadjusted .426 average, the highest average since the 19th century. Lajoie was so far ahead of his peers that the second best average was Mike Donlin's .340.

4. George Brett, 1980   .375 Adjusted Batting Average

George Brett won both the batting title and the slugging title, while battling an injury.

3. Tony Gwynn, 1994   .376 Adjusted Batting Average

In the strike-shortened season, Gwynn hit for the highest unadjusted average since 1941, a .394 mark. Rated as the best single-season adjusted average in *Baseball's All-Time Best Hitters*, the changes in the adjustment procedures drop it into third place.

2. Rod Carew, 1977   .377 Adjusted Batting Average

Carew's season was frequently compared to Williams' 1941 campaign as Carew sought to hit .400. Even though his unadjusted mark of .388 fell short, after the adjustments, Carew's season topped that of Williams.

1. Rogers Hornsby, 1924   **.379 Adjusted Batting Average**

Rogers Hornsby is perhaps best remembered for a 5-year stretch (1921–5) when he averaged more than .400. His best season for average among them was his 1924 season, which ranks as the all-time best.

Best Productive Career Hitters for Average (8000 At-Bats)

Complete lists of the top 100 players for career hits and adjusted batting average are given in Appendix M.1. The top 12 are listed below. Players separated by at most 0.1 hit per 500 ABs are given tied ranks (see the guide at the top of page 104).

12. Tris Speaker, 1907–28   **.319 Adjusted Batting Average**

The top 12 hitters for average are given here since the gap between Speaker and the no. 13 hitter, Mike Piazza, is as great as his gap to the sixth best hitters: Lajoie, Jackson, and Wagner.

11. Pete Browning, 1882–94   **.321 Adjusted Batting Average**

The adjusted career BAs of the top hitters are remarkably close. Per 8000 at-bats, only 7 hits separate Browning, Boggs, and Williams. Browning is the only 19th century representative in the top 12.

10. Wade Boggs, 1982–99   **.322 Adjusted Batting Average**

Wade Boggs had a remarkable first half of his career. Through 4000 at-bats, Boggs held a .340 adjusted average (3 points higher than Gwynn's), having won 5 batting titles in 6 years. For the second 4000 ABs, Boggs batted a respectable, but much lower .303, placing him 10th.

9. Ted Williams, 1939–60   **.322 Adjusted Batting Average**

Compared to Ruth, Ted Williams has a higher adjusted BA and a lower HR rate. Although we can adjust for park effects, baseball success is still earned on the field. Fenway Park rewarded left-handed hitters with hits, but was stingier with home runs. Yankee Stadium was the opposite. Perhaps these park effects led the two men to craft their games a bit differently.

6T. Honus Wagner, 1897–1917   **.324 Adjusted Batting Average**

Two hits per 8000 ABs is the total gap separating deadball hitters Jackson, Wagner, and Lajoie. Wagner and Lajoie played concurrently. They overlapped for 4 seasons in the National League, before Lajoie jumped to the American League in 1901. Afterward, Wagner and Lajoie never again faced each other in a major league game.

6T. Joe Jackson, 1908–20   **.324 Adjusted Batting Average**

Shoeless Joe is the only top 12 hitter without a batting title. With the increased offense of the lively ball era that began in 1920, fans have wondered what numbers Jackson, banned after the 1920 season, could have posted. It's no wonder that Jackson is the biggest star to emerge from the "Field of Dreams" cornfield.

6T. Nap Lajoie, 1896–1916   .324 Adjusted Batting Average

Jackson, Wagner, and Lajoie forged different paths to the same career average. Both Lajoie and Wagner had slow starts. Through 2000 ABs, they stood: Jackson, .333; Wagner, .306; Lajoie, .303. Lajoie had 3 "monster years"—1901, '04, and '10—the first two catapulting him to the top. Through 4000 ABs, they stood: Lajoie, .325; Jackson, .323; Wagner, .311. In his second 4000 ABs, Wagner hit .336 to catch up.

4T. Stan Musial, 1941–63   .327 Adjusted Batting Average

Through 8000 at-bats, the adjusted number of hits for Stan Musial and Rogers Hornsby differ by only 0.3. Musial and Hornsby also won the same number of batting crowns, 7, and placed one season in the adjusted top 10.

4T. Rogers Hornsby, 1915–37   .327 Adjusted Batting Average

In the 20th century, there were 4 great batters in the National League—Wagner in the 1900s, Hornsby in the 1920s, Musial in the 1940–50s, and Gwynn in the 1980–90s. Between them, these four hitters combined for 30 batting titles between 1900 and 1997.

3. Rod Carew, 1967–85   .332 Adjusted Batting Average

There is a bit more separation among the top 3 hitters. Through 8000 at-bats, Carew picked up 38 more adjusted hits than Hornsby.

2. Ty Cobb, 1905–28   .336 Adjusted Batting Average

Ty Cobb and Tony Gwynn both placed 7 seasons among the 100 best in history. Cobb's adjusted batting average is 28 hits higher than Carew's.

1. Tony Gwynn, 1982–2001   .338 Adjusted Batting Average

In *Baseball's All-Time Best Hitters*, Gwynn edged out Cobb by 9 hits for the highest career batting average. With the slight modifications in the adjustment procedure, Gwynn's edge is now a more sizable 22 hits.

CHAPTER 8

Hit . . . and Run

Adjusting Double
and Triple Totals

The casual baseball fan may believe that the kind of hit a player gets is straightforward, given where the ball lands. Balls hit in front of the outfielders are singles. Balls hit between outfielders or in the corners of the park are either doubles or triples depending on how far from the fielders they land and how they bounce. Balls hit over the fence are home runs.

In 2002, 38-year-old Mark Grace remarked that he has a great knack "for turning triples into doubles." Indeed, as players age and their speed declines, would-be triples do become doubles. This is illustrated by the age-profile plot for triples fraction (defined as triples divided by hits minus home runs), presented in Chapter 4 and duplicated here as Figure 8.1. The figure shows that, for modern player-seasons, the triples fraction peaks at 4% at age 22 and declines steadily to 2% at age 38.

Do older players also turn "doubles" into singles? The evidence says "Yes." Figure 8.2 shows that, for modern player-seasons, the doubles-plus-triples fraction was fairly constant through age 31 before declining.

Extra-Base Hits of the Pittsburgh Pirates, 1900-1908

Let's take a closer look at the sharpness of separation between singles, doubles, and triples by looking in detail at a particular team, the 1900–1908 Pittsburgh Pirates. Table 8.1 shows the Pirate base hit totals, with players having at least 3000 at-bats listed individually. Playing in Exposition Park, the Pirates boasted a major league best .625 winning percentage from 1900 to 1908.

This team was selected for three reasons. First, Pirate Honus Wagner ranks among the best *inside-the-park* (IP) extra base hitters in baseball history. Second, the team composition was quite stable. Third, by comparing teammates, we avoid park effects complications.

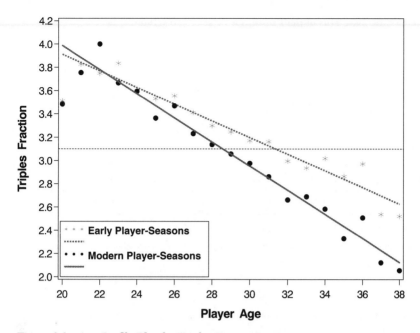

Figure 8.1   Age Profile Plot for Triples Fraction

Figure 8.2   Age Profile Plot for Doubles-Plus-Triples Fraction

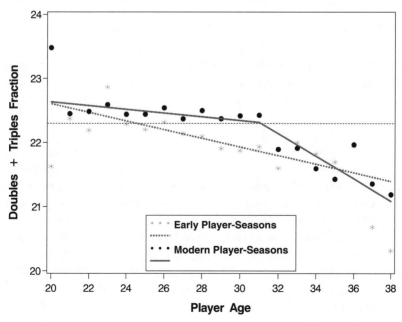

Table 8.1   Base Hits of the Pittsburgh Pirates, 1900–1908

						HR	
Player	Age	AB	H	2B	3B	IP	Out
Honus Wagner	30	4759	1679	333	138	19	27
Fred Clarke	31	4084	1238	173	123	14	9
Tommy Leach	26	4239	1172	121	115	26	4
Claude Ritchey	29	3488	955	150	46	3	2
Ginger Beaumont	26	3588	1138	112	49	19	9
Other Pirates	28	24,955	5921	688	362	26	43
Total	28	45,113	12,113	1577	833	107	93

Source for IP HRs: SABR Presents the Home Run Encyclopedia.

Notes: Age = age in 1904. IP HR = inside-the-park home run, Out HR = out-of-the-park home run.

Let's contrast the performance of Honus Wagner to that of his four principal teammates. Thirty-one percent of Wagner's hits went for extra bases, compared to only 22% for his teammates. However, only 32% of his inside-the-park Extra-Base Hits (EBHs) were more than doubles, compared to 42% for his teammates. Had Wagner's percentage been as high, he would have hit 47 more triples + IP home runs over the 9 seasons.

What are we to make of these facts? Three alternative possibilities seem plausible:

1.   Wagner was better at the "stretch double"—where a well-hit "single" is stretched into a double by aggressive base running.
2.   Wagner legged out a lower percentage of equally well hit balls into triples and IP home runs than did his principal teammates.
3.   A smaller percentage of Wagner's hits were deep ones, the kind likely to lead to triples and IP home runs.

The third explanation can be discounted, however, since 59% of Wagner's home runs were out-of-the-park, compared to 28% for his teammates. Wagner's profile of higher EBHs and out-of-the-park home runs coupled with a lower 3B plus IP home run percentage provides evidence that he relied more upon power than speed in garnering EBHs. Thus, the second explanation has the greatest plausibility.

Inside-the-park home runs are quite rare in the modern game; in 2002, there were only 12. Moreover, they are not yet completely tallied across baseball history. Consequently, *doubles-plus-triples*, which comprise most of the IP EBHs, will be adopted as a basic offensive event. To avoid rewarding players who hold up at second base on would-be triples, a list of the top players for doubles-plus-triples is given instead of a list of top doubles hitters.

Park Adjustment for Doubles and Triples

Given the weak separation between doubles and triples, how should the park adjustments be made? Two methods merit comparison:

1. The DPT method: First, obtain park effect estimates for doubles-plus-triples and for triples. Next, adjust a player's DPT total for park effects; then obtain his adjusted triple average using the park effect for triples. Finally, adjusted doubles are obtained by subtraction.
2. The separate-events method: Obtain separate park effect estimates for doubles and triples. Then, estimate the adjusted doubles and triples separately, using the park effect estimates.

Appendix F demonstrates that the DPT method is best.

Best Single-Season Doubles-Plus-Triples Performances

The doubles-plus-triples rate is arguably the most competitive offensive event in baseball. As evidence, in Table 8.2 notice the small number of players with multiple seasons among the best 100. The list of top seasons is given in Appendix L.2. The top 10 are given below. Players separated by at most 0.1 DPTs/500 ABs are given tied ranks (see the guide at the top of page 104).

Table 8.2   Top 100 Seasons—Adjusted Doubles-Plus-Triples per 500 At-Bats
79 Different Players with Average Age = 27.8

Era	Seasons	Expected	Era	Seasons	Expected
1876–1900	7	9.9	1947–68	17	16.5
1901–19	10	13.4	1969–92	22	26.8
1920–46	27	19.4	1993–2003	17	14.0

No. of Seasons	Players with Multiple Top 100 Seasons
5	*Stan Musial, Honus Wagner*
3	Edgar Martinez, *Tris Speaker, Robin Yount*
2	*Ty Cobb, Lou Gehrig, Hank Greenberg,* Hal McRae, Kevin Millar, *Paul Waner, Robin Yount*

Notes: Hall of Fame players are listed in italics.

See the guide to the top 100 seasons tables on page 103.

10T. Tip O'Neil, 1887   48.3 Adjusted DPTs/500 ABs
In his career year, 1887, Tip O'Neil led the American Association in batting average, doubles, triples, home runs, runs scored, and RBIs (RBIs).

10T. Fred Lynn, 1975   **48.3 Adjusted DPTs/500 ABs**

In his rookie season, Lynn won his only doubles crown. He was never able to match this season, but very few other players have been able to achieve this either.

9. Jay Johnstone, 1976   **48.4 Adjusted DPTs/500 ABs**

In the 11th season of a 20-year career, but the last one meeting the eligibility criterion for best single-season performance (that is, 450 or more NFPs), Johnstone had a superb year for EBHs.

7T. Honus Wagner, 1900   **48.6 Adjusted DPTs/500 ABs**

Wagner is the only player to have 2 seasons among the top 10. In 1900, Wagner led the league in both doubles with 45 and triples with 22, for a raw total of 67 DPTs. The second best total in 1900 was only 48, by Elmer Flick.

7T. Joe Medwick, 1936   **48.7 Adjusted DPTs/500 ABs**

1936 was the first of 3 years in which Medwick led the National League in doubles and RBIs. This was his best for inside-the-park EBHs.

4T. Craig Biggio, 1994   **48.9 Adjusted DPTs/500 ABs**

A catcher in his first 4 seasons, Biggio made the switch to second baseman in 1992. Two years later, he put together a terrific year for DPTs which was short circuited with the players' strike.

4T. Stan Musial, 1946   **49.0 Adjusted DPTs/500 ABs**

One of 2 players to appear in the top 100 in 5 different seasons, Musial's hustle out of the box netted him 8 doubles titles and 5 triples crowns between 1943 and 1954. In 1946, he achieved his best combined total.

4T. Honus Wagner, 1904   **49.0 Adjusted DPTs/500 ABs**

In 1904, Wagner led the National League in doubles with 44 and was second in triples with 14. Again, his total of 58 DPTs greatly outpaced those of his closest competitor, Harry Lumley, who hit only 41 DPTs.

3. Paul Molitor, 1987   **49.1 Adjusted DPTs/500 ABs**

In the middle of a 21-year career, Molitor led the league in doubles even though he only had 465 at-bats. This season rejuvenated a career that had begun to stall.

2. Lou Brock, 1968   **49.3 Adjusted DPTs/500 ABs**

In mid-career in 1968, Lou Brock led the league in both doubles and triples. In 1968, Brock had 15 fewer home runs than he did in 1967, but apparently cashed them in for his 16 additional DPTs, leading to the second best DPT season ever.

1. Carl Yastrzemski, 1965   **49.6 Adjusted DPTs per 500 ABs**

In the low offensive 1960s, Carl Yastrzemski fashioned a season that rates as the best season for DPTs in baseball history.

Best Single-Season Triples Performances

Table 8.3 summarizes the top 100 seasons for triples. Significantly more top 100 seasons occurred in the 19th century than expected. The complete list of top seasons is given in Appendix L.3. A countdown of the top 10 seasons is given below. Players separated by at most 0.1 3Bs/500 ABs are given tied ranks.

Table 8.3   Top 100 Seasons—Adjusted Triples per 500 At-Bats
85 Different Players with Average Age = 27.1

Era	Seasons	Expected	Era	Seasons	Expected
1876–1900	19↑	9.9	1947–68	20	16.5
1901–19	13	13.4	1969–92	17↓	26.8
1920–46	19	19.4	1993–2003	12	14.0

No. of Seasons	Players with Multiple Top 100 Seasons
3	Lance Johnson, Harry Stovey
2	Brett Butler, *Earle Combs*, *Sam Crawford*, Cristian Guzman, Jeff Heath, Minnie Minoso, *Stan Musial*, Dave Orr, Mickey Rivers

Notes: Hall of Fame players are listed in italics. The symbols ↑ (↓) mean the number of seasons is significantly higher (or lower) than expected.

See the guide to the top 100 seasons tables on page 103.

10. Earle Combs, 1933   18.2 Adjusted Triples/500 ABs

Earle Combs won 3 triples titles. His triple rate was greatest, however, in 1933, his last season as a regular, when he hit 16 triples in just 417 at-bats.

8T. Dave Orr, 1886   18.6 Adjusted Triples/500 ABs

In major league baseball's 11th year, 1886, Dave Orr set a new mark for triples in a season with 31. In more than a century of play since then, that mark has been exceeded only once, by Chief Wilson in 1912 (see later).

8T. Lance Johnson, 1996   18.6 Adjusted Triples/500 ABS

In 1996, Johnson's raw triple total, 21, was 11 more than the runners-up. Only 9 times in history has the edge been 8 or more, with 6 ranking among the top 10. The others are: Dave Orr, 1886 AA; Chief Wilson, 1912 NL; Tom Long, 1915 NL; Kiki Cuyler, 1925 NL; Stan Musial, 1946 NL; Dale Mitchell, 1949 AL; Willie Mays, 1957 NL; and Cristian Guzman, 2000 AL.

7. Ival Goodman, 1939   19.4 Adjusted Triples/500 ABs

Cincinnati's Ival Goodman won triples titles in 1935–6—his first 2 seasons. The Crosley Field fences were shortened in 1938, however, reducing the number of triples hit there. Thus, it is Goodman's 16 triples in 470 at-bats in 1939 that stands out as among the best triples performances in major league history, after the park effect adjustment.

5T. Walt Wilmot, 1889   20.1 Adjusted Triples/500 ABs

In his second season in 1889, with the Washington Statesmen, Walt Wilmot won the triples title, hitting 19 in just 432 at-bats.

5T. Harry Davis, 1897   20.1 Adjusted Triples/500 ABs

In 1897, Harry Davis hit 28 triples but only 10 doubles. The triples-to-doubles ratio, 2.8, is the highest in any season at least 10 triples. It is fitting that such a year would rank among the best ever.

4. Willie Mays, 1957   20.2 Adjusted Triples/500 ABs

In 1957, 26-year-old Willie Mays won the triples title for the third time in 4 years. The 20 triples he hit were a personal best by 7 triples and represented the largest National League total until Lance Johnson hit 21 in 1996.

3. Tom Long, 1915   21.5 Adjusted Triples/500 ABs

Tom Long had a short career, with only 3 seasons as a regular player. In his first full season at age 25, though, he fashioned one of the best seasons ever for triples.

2. Chief Wilson, 1912   21.7 Adjusted Triples/500 ABs

Pittsburgh's Forbes Field was a great park for triples. In 1912, 28-year-old Pirate out-fielder Chief Wilson posted the highest mark ever for triples—36—greatly outstrip-ping his total of 19 doubles. Not surprisingly, 24 of them were hit in Forbes Field. The second highest raw total was 31, shared by Dave Orr in 1886 and Heinie Reitz in 1894. On a percentage basis, this is the largest gap between the highest two raw totals of any of the main offensive events.

1. Dale Mitchell, 1949   22.9 Adjusted Triples/500 ABs

Dale Mitchell's season is certainly a standout one. His raw total of 23 triples has not been equaled in more than 50 years in either league. It was also a year like no other for Mitchell himself. Except for the 1949 season, Mitchell hit 4 times as many doubles as triples (153 to 38). In 1949, though, he hit only 16 doubles to accompany his 23 triples.

Best Productive Career Doubles-Plus-Triples Performances (6000 At-Bats)

Lists of the top 100 players for career doubles-plus-triples and DPTs/500 ABs are given Appendix M.2. The top 11 are listed below. Players separated by at most than 0.1 DPTs/500 ABs are given tied ranks.

10T. Hal McRae, 1968–87   37.2 Adjusted DPTs/500 ABs

After 4 seasons of part-time play with Cincinnati, McRae embarked on a 15-year career with Kansas City, primarily as a designated hitter. As a DH, the first to reach 1000 games, McRae could focus on hitting. Through a solid career, McRae earned his spot tied for the 10th best productive career for DPTs.

10T. Babe Herman, 1926–45   37.3 Adjusted DPTs/500 ABs

Between 1929 and 1932, Babe Herman struck at least 55 DPTs per year. These prime seasons propelled him into a 10th place tie with Hal McRae.

7T. Joe Medwick, 1932–48   37.6 Adjusted DPTs/500 ABs

For 7 consecutive seasons, from 1933 to 1939, Medwick had at least 50 DPTs each year. During those years, he averaged 49 doubles and 11 triples, while winning 3 doubles titles and 1 triples title. This consistent, solid production netted Medwick a seventh place tie on the list.

7T. Ty Cobb, 1905–28   37.7 Adjusted DPTs/500 ABs

For a deadball era player, home runs were relatively rare and hence not a major emphasis of the game, as they are today. Thus, the events that separated superstars from average players were batting average and IP EBHs. Ty Cobb is the first of 5 deadball stars in this countdown. During his career, Cobb won 3 doubles and 4 triples titles.

7T. George Brett, 1973–93   37.7 Adjusted DPTs/500 ABs

George Brett is the second Kansas City Royal to make the top 10. In Brett's time, Kauffman Stadium favored doubles and triples, while disadvantaging home run hitting. Royals' hitters may have stylized their game to gain a park advantage. Brett won 2 doubles and 3 triples titles.

6. Joe Jackson, 1908–20   38.0 Adjusted DPTs/500 ABs

Shoeless Joe was a great deadball era slugger, but somewhat obscured by the exploits of Cobb and Ruth. Cobb claimed 4 slugging titles and Ruth garnered 3 more in Jackson's 10 seasons as a regular, while Jackson netted a lone slugging crown in 1914, 1 doubles, and 3 triples titles. Over a career, however, Jackson slipped past both on this prestigious list.

5. Nap Lajoie, 1896–1916   38.2 Adjusted DPTs/500 ABs

Napoleon Lajoie is the third of the 5 deadball-era hitters among the top 8 in DPTs. Although he didn't win any triple titles, Lajoie led the league in doubles 5 times. He also led the league in slugging 4 times. In 3 of those 4 seasons, he led the league in DPTs.

4. Tris Speaker, 1907–28   39.1 Adjusted DPTs/500 ABs

Tris Speaker holds the record for the most doubles with 792, with many coming in his 11 years (1916–26) with the Cleveland Indians. During those years, he capitalized on League Park's short right field fence (290 feet), with its unusual caroms, hitting 306 doubles at home compared to 179 on the road. Even so, his career DPT ranking is fourth best.

3. Dan Brouthers, 1879–1896, 1904   39.3 Adjusted DPTs/500 ABs

Dan Brouthers was the best extra-base hitter from the 19th century. He won 3 doubles title in his 3 years with Detroit.

2. Honus Wagner, 1897–1917   41.2 Adjusted DPTs/500 ABs

Honus Wagner was the premier slugger of the first decade of the 20th century. Between 1900 and 1909, Wagner won 6 slugging titles, led the league in doubles 7 times, and added 3 triples crowns, beautifully complementing his 7 batting titles. His EBHs stand out more strongly from his peers than perhaps those of any other player. Ballpark and distributional transformation adjustments are critical to equitably comparing Wagner's performance to other great IP extra-basemen.

1. Stan Musial, 1941–63   41.3 Adjusted DPTs/500 ABs

Stan Musial was cut from the same cloth as Honus Wagner. Between 1943 and 1952, Musial won 6 slugging titles, 7 doubles crowns, and 5 triples titles to accompany his 6 batting crowns. The only 20th century players with at least 2 slugging average titles who never led the league in home runs are: Musial, Wagner—6 titles; George Brett—3 titles; and Manny Ramirez—2 titles. Musial's secret weapon—doubles and triples.

Best Productive Career Triples Performances (4000 At-Bats)

Complete lists of the top 100 players for career triples and adjusted 3Bs/500 ABs are given Appendix M.3. The top 12 are listed below. Players separated by at most 0.1 3Bs/500 ABs are given tied ranks.

9T. Earle Combs, 1924–35   9.4 Adjusted Triples/500 ABs

(Adj SBs/550 = 13.7, Rank = 501) Earle Combs won 3 triples crowns between 1927 and 1930 and had the 10th best individual season in 1933.

9T. Elmer Flick, 1898–1910   9.4 Adjusted Triples/500 ABs

(Adj SBs/550 = 25.6, Rank = 193) While triples is a speed event in the modern game, power played a greater role earlier in history. Of the 5 players in this list whose careers began after 1946, none ranks below 69th for career SB rate. Of the 7 earlier players, Flick , at 193rd, ranks best.

9T. Luis Polonia, 1987–   9.4 Adjusted Triples/500 ABs

(Adj SBs/550 = 42.2, Rank = 51) Luis Polonia is a player with no "black ink"—that is, he never led the league in any event. One reason: Polonia topped 500 only NFPs in 3 seasons. If I had lowered the minimum single-season NFP total to 300 from 450, Polonia's '87, '90, and '99 seasons would all place among the top 100.

9T. Jeff Heath, 1936–49   9.5 Adjusted Triples/500 ABs

(Adj SBs/550 = 12.7, Rank = 538) Jeff Heath won 2 triples titles in his first 4 seasons as a regular ('38, '41). Both rank among the top 100 seasons in history, propelling Heath into the career top 10.

8. Bill Bruton, 1953–64   10.1 Adjusted Triples/500 ABs

(Adj SBs/550 = 45.6, Rank = 41) Speedy Bill Bruton led the National League in SBs his first 3 seasons. In later years, he won 2 triples titles.

7. Willie Mays, 1951–73   10.2 Adjusted Triples/500 ABs

(Adj SBs/550 = 48.7, Rank = 34) Willie Mays is known for his enthusiasm for the game and for having all "five skills" wanted in a player, including the rather rare combination of hitting for power and speed. Mays, who won 3 triples titles in 4 seasons from 1954 to 1957, channeled these talents and his enthusiasm into seventh place.

5T. Brett Butler, 1981–97   10.4 Adjusted Triples/500 ABs

(Adj SBs/550 = 38.3, Rank = 69) Brett Butler and Lance Johnson were the only players to place 3 seasons in the top 100. Butler won 4 triples titles, 2 early in his career—1983 and 1986—and 2 later, in 1994–95.

5T. Sam Crawford, 1899–1917   10.4 Adjusted Triples/500 ABs

(Adj SBs/550 = 11.1, Rank = 609) Sam Crawford holds the record for the most career triples, had 10 or more triples for 17 straight seasons, and led the league 6 times. Hence, it is *apropos* that he ranks among the best.

4. Joe Jackson, 1908–20   10.6 Adjusted Triples/500 ABs

(Adj SBs/550 = 12.3, Rank = 554) Jackson picked up the eponym "Shoeless Joe" in a minor league game in which he tripled while in stocking feet since the shoes he was wearing caused blisters. In his major league career, he showed that that name fit him well. While not a prolific base stealer, Jackson, who won 3 triples titles, ranks fourth best over a career.

2T. Buck Ewing, 1880–1897   11.0 Adjusted Triples/500 ABs

(Adj SBs/550 = 21.0, Rank = 286) It is rather surprising that a catcher places among the top three in this list—but Buck Ewing does. The best explanations are that he played catcher only about half the time and that his lofty triple average is probably attributable more to powerful hits than to exceptional speed.

2T. Stan Musial, 1941–63   11.1 Adjusted Triples/500 ABs

(Adj SBs/550 = 12.5, Rank = 545) Stan Musial was made in the mold of the deadball era triples stars. He was an average stolen base threat, with 78 career steals. However, he jolted out of the batter's box after hitting the ball. That hustle netted Musial 5 triples titles and second place on the career triples rate list, nicely enhancing his first-place finish in DPTs.

1. Lance Johnson, 1987–   13.2 Adjusted Triples/500 ABs

(Adj SBs/550 = 40.4, Rank = 57) *Baseball: The Biographical Encyclopedia* says:

> Lance Johnson was a master of hitting triples. He tied for the league lead with 13 in 1991, and led the American League four straight seasons. . . . His 21 triples [in 1996] were the most in the National League since Adam Comorsky's 23 in 1930. . . . [Johnson] had the most triples of any major leaguer during the 1990s.

Using the methods in this book, one sees that Johnson was *the* master of hitting triples.

CHAPTER 9

This One's Outta Here!
Adjusting Home Run Totals

Home runs are the glamour events in baseball. They are also relatively rare, though; even today, home runs are struck in only 3% of all plate appearances. Nonetheless, they fix the imagination of both fan and writer like no other baseball event. Fans are constantly reminded of Bill Mazeroski's 1960 and Joe Carter's 1993 World Series–ending blasts. In 1997 and 2001, Edgar Renteria and Luis Gonzalez made Game 7 World Series champions of their teams—by hitting walk-off singles. It is doubtful that those singles, notable as they are, will stand the test of time so well.

Of the top 30 "memorable moments" sponsored by Major League Baseball in 2002 and voted on by fans, 11 involve home run hitting. Among the "memorable moments," 8 involved a single play and included 5 walk-off home runs in critical games—the 2 home runs listed earlier, Bobby Thomson's in 1951, Carlton Fisk's in 1975, and Kirk Gibson's in 1988. From these rankings, the primacy of the home run over other baseball events is clear.

Recent Books Featuring Home Run Hitters

In his 1989 book, *The Power Hitters,* Donald Honig featured "the 18 men who dominate the all-time power-hitting charts": Babe Ruth, Lou Gehrig, Jimmie Foxx, Mel Ott, Hank Greenberg, Ted Williams, Ralph Kiner, Mickey Mantle, Willie Mays, Eddie Mathews, Ernie Banks, Hank Aaron, Harmon Killebrew, Frank Robinson, Willie McCovey, Willie Stargell, Reggie Jackson, and Mike Schmidt. All but one rank among the top 50 in adjusted home run rate presented in this chapter (Ernie Banks, who fails to make the top 100), with 6 among the top 10.

In *The King of Swat,* William McNeil sought to obtain a single list containing the best home run hitters from the major, minor, Negro, and Japanese leagues, after leveling the playing field. By his own admission, McNeil's effort is an early attempt.

Hopefully, in future years, more in-depth studies will be conducted concerning the same topic. A detailed statistical analysis will either verify or contradict the findings of this rudimentary work.

McNeil's major league top 10 major leaguers are:

Rank	Player	Estimated HRS/500 ABs	Rank	Player	Estimated HRs/500 ABs
1	Babe Ruth	50	6T	Jimmie Foxx	36
2	Gavy Cravath	43	6T	Mickey Mantle	36
3T	Harmon Killebrew	39	6T	Dave Kingman	36
3T	Ralph Kiner	39	6T	Mike Schmidt	36
5	Ted Williams	37	10	Sam Thompson	35

Seven of these players rank among the top 10 listed at the end of this chapter. Adjusting for ballpark effects (which McNeil did not do), plus a more detailed statistical approach to home run hitting in different eras undoubtedly accounts for many of the differences in the lists.

Inside-the-Park Home Runs

In the earliest days of baseball, players really had to move on the base paths to garner a home run—hence the term home "run." Today, for the most part it's a home trot—a celebratory time to acknowledge the joy or shock on the faces of the fans, exchange high-fives with teammates, and see the fireworks display.

These days, the hustle home runs—known as *inside-the-park* (IP) home runs—occur only about 5–15 times each season. It was much different, however, in the 19th and early 20th centuries. In 1901, 37% (168 of 455) of home runs were IP home runs. Thus, to better understand home run hitting at the turn of the 20th century, we need some understanding of IP homers.

Table 9.1 shows the 12 times that the number of IP home runs hit by a team shifted by 10 or more from one year to the next for National League teams from 1890 to 1910. New ballparks can explain 2 of the changes—Pittsburgh in 1891 and Cincinnati in 1902. The other 10 cases are all worthy of further investigation.

The jumps in Cincinnati in 1900 and 1901 are most interesting. The Reds played in League Park II from 1894 through 1901, before moving into the Palace of the Fans in 1902. David Vincent provided me with a list of IP home runs hit in League Park II over its history. There were 14 IP homers in its first 5 years, from 1894 through 1898—about 3 per year.

In 1899, Pittsburgh's Sam Leever hit the lone IP home run at League Park on April 17. The next IP home run at League Park was struck more than 1 year later, on June 30, 1900. Then the floodgates opened—8 were hit in July, 3 in August, and 3 more in October.

Table 9.1 Teams with Shifts of 10+ Inside-the-Park Home Runs, 1890–1910 National League

	Previous Year				Previous Year		
Team	Year	IP HR	IP HR	Team	Year	IP HR	IP HR
Cin	1900	19	3	Pit	1895	8	25
Cin	1901	29	19	Pit	1904	8	20
Cin	1902	14	29	StL	1894	13	3
Phi	1894	3	14	StL	1899	11	0
Pit	1891	16	3	StL	1902	7	20
Pit	1892	33	16	Was	1893	6	21

Source: David Vincent, co-editor of SABR *Presents the Home Run Encyclopedia.*

In 1901, 7 were hit at League Park by the end of June. Between July 4, 1901 and the season's close on October 6, 1901, a whopping 39 IP home runs were hit in League Park, including 4 on August 5 and 5 and 4 in doubleheader games in September and October! *Cincinnati Enquirer* sports writers considered only 1 or 2 of the IP home runs to be the result of fielding miscues coupled with generous calls by the official scorer.

Sam Crawford of Cincinnati won the 1901 National League home run crown with 16. Of these, 12 were IP home runs, of which 7 were hit at League Park, including 3 over a 4-game stretch in August.

The likely explanation for this sudden burst in IP home runs is provided by Michael Gershman in *Diamonds* (p. 71): "On the night of May 28, 1900, a fire burned most of the grandstand and was hurriedly replaced with temporary seating so that the Reds could finish their schedule." This fire undoubtedly changed the dimensions of the field and resulted in the sudden jump in IP home runs. Indeed, some accounts talk of balls being hit into the lumber pile in the outfield!

Unfortunately, a complete accounting of IP home runs has not yet been done. In this book, therefore, IP and over-the-fence home runs are not adjusted for separately.

Park Effects by Batting Handedness

Through the efforts of many SABR members, we have very good data on park effects for home runs, including separate data for left- and right-handed hitters. Thus, park effects for home runs are estimated by batting handedness.

How would we establish a park effect for switch-hitters, such as Mickey Mantle? In recent years, right-handers have accounted for 70% of all innings pitched. Thus, we will use the formula

$$0.70 \times \text{HR park factor for LHB} + 0.30 \times \text{HR park factor for RHB}.$$

Park-Neutral Home Runs

Of the 4 adjustments needed to level the playing field, only the park effects adjustment is needed to compare players fairly within a given season. *Park-neutral home runs* provide that adjustment.

Park-neutral home runs is a home run total that has been adjusted only for the ballpark effect. Two formulas to estimate park-neutral home runs are described here, with the second being more accurate.

Park-Neutral Home Runs Based on a Player's Seasonal HR Total

In 1940, Joe DiMaggio socked 31 home runs to tie for fourth place in the American League. With a HR park factor of .906, DiMaggio struck 34.2 approximate park-neutral. Table 9.2 shows the number of approximate park-neutral home runs of the American League players who hit at least 30 in 1940.

Table 9.2 Approximate Park-Neutral Home Runs for 1940 American League Players with 30+ Home Runs

Player	Hand	Team	Raw HRs	API	Park factor	Approx PN HRs
Hank Greenberg	R	Det	41	144	1.189	34.5
Jimmie Foxx	R	Bos	36	133	1.142	31.5
Rudy York	R	Det	33	144	1.189	27.8
Joe DiMaggio	R	NY	31	78	.906	34.2
Bob Johnson	R	Phi	31	133	1.142	27.2
Joe Gordon	R	NY	30	78	.906	33.1

Notes: API values are given in Appendix J. Park factors are obtained using the park factor formula at the bottom of Definitions 6.1.

Park-Neutral Home Runs Based on Player Home/Road Splits

SABR Presents the Home Run Encyclopedia gives the home and road home run breakdowns for all major league home runs through 1995. This allows for an improved way to calculate park-neutral home runs.

Formula 9.1 **Approximate park-neutral home runs**

We can adjust out their effects using the simple formula:

Approximate park-neutral HRs = HRs ÷ HR park factor.

Formula 9.2   Park-neutral home runs

First, compute a park's home run ratio by dividing the number of home runs hit at the home park by both teams by the number of home runs hit at the road parks for players with the same handedness as the batter whose home runs are being adjusted. Then the road home run park factor is computed as:

$$\text{Road HR park factor} = \{\text{HR ratio} + (k - 1)\}/k,$$

where k is the number of teams in the league. Then

$$\text{Park-neutral road HRs} = \text{road HRs} \times \text{road HR park factor},$$

and

$$\text{Park-neutral home HRs} = \text{home HRs/HR ratio} \times \text{road HR park factor}$$

Finally,

$$\text{Park-neutral HRs} = \text{PN home HRs} + \text{PN road HRs}.$$

In 1940, Joe DiMaggio hit 16 home runs at home and 15 on the road (Table 9.3). Yankee Stadium's HR ratio for left-handed hitters for 1940 is .759. Thus, the road HR park factor is .970 and DiMaggio hit 20.4 park-neutral home home runs and 14.6 park-neutral road home runs, giving him 35.0 total park-neutral home runs.

The results obtained using the 2 park-neutral home run formulas are generally within 2 home runs of each other. For the 1940 home run leaders, the difference ranged from −0.8 to +0.9. Interestingly, using the preferred home/road split method, DiMaggio slips past Hank Greenberg to claim the park-neutral home run championship.

For the book, formula 9.2 is used for every batter who hit at least 300 home runs, won a home run title since 1893, or appears in the best 100 lists for single-season or career in this book. For all other players, formula 9.1 is used.

Table 9.3   Park-Neutral Home Runs for 1940 American League Players with 30+ Home Runs

	HRs		HR ratio	PN HRs		PN HRs
Player	Home	Road		Home	Road	
Hank Greenberg	27	14	1.559	18.5	15.0	33.5
Jimmie Foxx	19	17	1.397	14.3	17.8	32.1
Rudy York	19	14	1.559	13.0	15.0	28.0
Joe DiMaggio	16	15	.759	20.5	14.5	35.0
Bob Johnson	15	16	1.397	11.3	16.8	28.1
Joe Gordon	15	15	.759	19.2	14.5	33.7

Players Most Affected by Park Adjustments

Table 9.4 shows the players who lose the most home runs and the greatest percentage of home runs with park adjustment over their careers.

Table 9.4   Players with the Largest Drops in Home Runs and Percentage Home Runs after Adjusting for Park Effect

Rank	Player	HR Drop	Rank	Player	% HR Drop
1	Mel Ott	−96	1	Hugh Duffy	−39%
2	Ken Williams	−64	2	Gavy Cravath	−39%
3	Johnny Mize	−59	3	Ken Williams	−33%
4	Jimmie Foxx	−56	4	Tilly Walker	−30%
5	Babe Ruth	−56	5	George Sisler	−24%
6	Cy Williams	−53	6	Sam Thompson	−21%
7	Norm Cash	−51	7	Cy Williams	−21%
8	Ron Santo	−51	8	Bob Horner	−20%
9	Lou Gehrig	−49	9	Tommy Henrich	−19%
10	Dante Bichette	−46	10	Bill Dickey	−19%

Notes: HR Drop = PN$^+$ HR − Raw HRs. % HR Drop = HR Drop ÷ Raw HRs (Minimum: 100 Raw HRs).

Table 9.5 shows the players with the greatest gains. Nearly all of Bonds' gains occurred since the Giants moved into Pacific Bell Park in 2000.

Table 9.5   Players with the Largest Gains in Home Runs and Percentage Home Runs after Adjusting for Park Effect

Rank	Player	HR Gain	Rank	Player	% HR Gain
1	George Brett	+57	1	Paul Waner	+25%
2	Roberto Clemente	+54	2	Ed Delahanty	+23%
3	Bill Nicholson	+53	3	Bill Nicholson	+23%
4	Barry Bonds	+52	4	Roberto Clemente	+23%
5	Joe DiMaggio	+48	5	Vince DiMaggio	+22%
6	Ted Williams	+46	6	Thurmon Munson	+22%
7	Eddie Mathews	+45	7	Jose Cruz	+21%
8	Jimmy Wynn	+43	8	Ken Keltner	+19%
9	Joe Adcock	+35	9	George Brett	+18%
10	Willie Stargell	+35	10	Glenn Davis	+17%

Notes: HR Gain = PN$^+$ HR − Raw HRs. % HR Gain = HR Drop ÷ Raw HRs (Minimum: 100 Raw HRs).

Classifying Home Run Hitters

We will classify home run hitters using two criteria: (1) whether their home park is favorable to home runs or not and (2) whether they hit more park-neutral home runs at home or not.

For the first criterion, a player whose raw home run total is at least 10% higher than his park-neutral home runs has played in a "Good Park." A player whose total is at least 10% lower has played in a "Bad Park." The remaining players have played in an "Average Park." Categories for the second criterion are defined in formula 9.3.

Classifying Hitters with 300 or More Home Runs

Table 9.6 shows the cross-classification table based on these criteria, listing players with 300 or more career home runs. Players in the top row launch more home runs at home than expected. Those in the top-left cell are "sluggers," since they overcame the adversity of their parks to a greater degree than did their fellow players. Ted Williams is the lone slugger in a bad park—Fenway Park, for a left-handed hitter.

The top-right cell has "opportunists"—Ron Santo, Chuck Klein, and Hank Greenberg—who played in good parks but picked up even more home runs at home than an average player. Players in the top-center cell, such as Frank Robinson and Duke Snider, are "homebodies."

More than 80% (77 of the 98 players) fall into the second row. These players, including Hank Aaron, Willie Mays, Mark McGwire, and Harmon Killebrew, show no strong favoritism in hitting at home or on the road.

The bottom row lists players who hit especially well on the road. No bad park "opportunist" has hit 300 home runs. Left-handed Yankee teammates Ruth and Gehrig, and Willie Horton are the "sluggers" from good parks. Mike Schmidt and Juan Gonzalez are the "roadbodies."

Classifying Selected Other Hitters

Through the deadball era, no player hit more than 150 home runs. Era adjustments boost their adjusted home run totals considerably. Thus, it is useful to look at how some of the most prolific home run hitters from these early eras are classified. Table 9.7 lists some of these and other selected players.

Formula 9.3   **Home/road HR z-score**

Home/Road HR z-score = (PN HRs at home − PN HRs on road) ÷ (PN HRs at home + PN HRs on road)$^{0.5}$.

"Home HR Hitter" =	z-score ≥ 1.28
"Location-Balanced HR Hitter" =	$-1.28 < z\text{-score} < 1.28$
"Road HR Hitter" =	$z\text{-score} \leq -1.28$

Table 9.6   Classification of Players with 300 or More Home Runs

Home/Road HR z-score	Park Type		
	Bad Park	**Average Park**	**Good Park**
Home HR Hitter	Sluggers	Homebodies	Opportunists
	Mo Vaughn	10 Players	Ron Santo
	Barry Bonds	Frank Robinson	Chuck Klein
	Ted Williams	Frank Thomas	Hank Greenberg
		Duke Snider	
Location-Balanced HR Hitter	11 Players	43 Players	23 Players
	Eddie Mathews	Mark McGwire	Ernie Banks
	Dave Winfield	Hank Aaron	Mel Ott
	Willie Stargell	Willie Mays	Sammy Sosa
	Joe DiMaggio	Harmon Killebrew	Jimmie Foxx
Road HR Hitter	Opportunists	Roadbodies	Sluggers
		Mike Schmidt	Willie Horton
		Juan Gonzalez	Lou Gehrig
			Babe Ruth

Notes: Players are listed in order of decreasing *z*-score; players in groups not completely listed are those who have the most lifetime home runs in the group.

Table 9.7   Classification for Selected Players with Fewer than 300 Home Runs

Home/Road HR z-score	Park Type		
	Bad Park	**Average Park**	**Good Park**
Home HR Hitter	Sluggers	Homebodies	Opportunists
	Ed Delahanty	Hank Sauer	Frank Baker
	Jimmy Wynn	Hack Wilson	Wally Moon
	Bill Nicholson	Jason Giambi	Bobby Doerr
	Roberto Clemente	Harry Davis	Bill Dickey
Location-Balanced HR Hitter	Tris Speaker	Roger Connor	Gavy Cravath
	Joe Gordon	Harry Stovey	Ken Williams
	Honus Wagner	Dan Brouthers	Cy Williams
	Joe Morgan	Jason Giambi	Tilly Walker
Road HR Hitter	Opportunists	Roadbodies	Sluggers
	Goose Goslin	Tino Martinez	George Sisler
	Bob Watson	Pedro Guerrero	Bob Meusel
	Ty Cobb	Tony Oliva	Charlie Keller
	Eddie Yost	Jack Fournier	Roger Maris

Note: Players are listed in order of decreasing *z*-score.

"Opportunistic" players in bad parks are particularly interesting, since they must have stylized their play differently for different parks. Eddie Yost is the most extreme example. A singles hitter, Yost hit only 7 of his 73 home runs from 1948 to 1955 at Washington's cavernous Griffith Stadium (before it was redesigned in 1956). The home and road walk totals for Yost—"The Walking Man"—are nearly equal, though (451 and 467, provided to me by Pete Palmer).

Ty Cobb was also an opportunist. While calling Detroit's Navin Field home, Cobb struck 16 home runs there and 59 on the road.

Wally Moon is a chronicled "opportunist in a good park." While playing for the Dodgers, Moon hit 37 home runs at the LA Coliseum and only 12 on the road from 1959 to 1961. Most, if not all, of his Coliseum home runs were to the opposite field (left field for him) to take advantage of the close fence there.

Home Run Rate Rankings

The raw home run rate, obtained as the number of home runs per at-bat, is one of the most prominent of baseball rankings. It is also sometimes called the home run percentage or home run average. Frequently, the rate is turned upside down and expressed as the number of at-bats per home run. Through the early 1990s, Babe Ruth held the highest mark, hitting 1 home run per 11.8 at-bats. Through 1992, Mark Mc-Gwire had hit 1 home run per 14.0 at-bats (238 home runs in 3342 at-bats)—and held second place, just ahead of Ralph Kiner. Then, during the power era, which began in 1993, Big Mac hit 1 home run per 8.2 at-bats (345 home runs in 2845 at-bats). This allowed him to surge ahead of Ruth to a lifetime rate of 1 home run per 10.6 at-bats.

Table 9.8 **Ranks of the 20 Players with the Highest Raw Lifetime Home Run Rates by Era of Mid-Career Year**

Lively Ball Era (1920–46)
2. Babe Ruth; 17. Jimmie Foxx
World War II and Big Strike Zone Eras (1947–68)
6. Ralph Kiner; 7. Harmon Killebrew; 11. Ted Williams; 16. Mickey Mantle
Designated Hitter Era (1969–92)
1. Mark McGwire; 15. Dave Kingman; 18. Mike Schmidt
Power Era (1993–2003+)
3. Barry Bonds; 4. Jim Thome; 5. Sammy Sosa; 8. Manny Ramirez; 9. Alex Rodriguez; 10. Ken Griffey, Jr.; 12. Mike Piazza; 13. Carlos Delgado; 14. Juan Gonzalez; 19. Jose Canseco; 20. Albert Belle

Note: Raw HR rate = HRs/ABs.

Three other active qualifying players—Barry Bonds, Jim Thome, and Sammy Sosa—are also posting better rates than Kiner—who now holds sixth place. Table 9.8 shows the ranked order of the 20 players with the highest raw home run rates, organized by the era of their mid-career year.

It is easy to see that the list is heavy with power era players—with 11 of the 20 players. This striking presence of recent players, though, depends partly on the fact that home run rates are at all-time highs in both the American and National Leagues. After adjusting using the methods of this book, 9 of these 20 players will make the top 10 list. Who will they be? It's time to find out.

Best Single-Season Home Run Performances

Table 9.9 summarizes the best 100 seasons for home runs in baseball history. An exceptionally high number of top seasons were produced from 1947 to 1968, perhaps the heyday for home runs. A complete list of top seasons is given in Appendix L.4, with the top 10 given below.

Table 9.9   Top 100 Seasons—Adjusted Home Runs per 500 At-Bats
58 Different Players with Average Age = 29.1

Era	Seasons	Expected	Era	Seasons	Expected
1876–1900	8	9.9	1947–68	28↑	16.5
1901–19	8	13.4	1969–92	18	26.8
1920–46	23	19.4	1993–2003	15	14.0

No. of Seasons	Players with Multiple Top 100 Seasons
13	*Babe Ruth*
7	Barry Bonds
6	*Ted Williams*
4	Mark McGwire
3	*Willie Stargell*
2	*Jimmie Foxx*, *Lou Gehrig*, *Rogers Hornsby*, Frank Howard, *Reggie Jackson*, Tim Jordan, *Ralph Kiner*, Dave Kingman, *Mickey Mantle*, *Eddie Mathews*, *Willie Mays*, Bill Nicholson, *Mike Schmidt*, Harry Stovey, Jim Thome

Notes: Hall of Fame players are listed in italics. The symbol ↑ means the number of seasons is significantly higher than expected.

See the guide to the top 100 seasons tables on page 103.

10. Babe Ruth, 1926   53.7 Adjusted HRs/500 ABs

This is one of Ruth's 5 seasons among the top 10. In 1926, Ruth hit 46 four-baggers, easily outdistancing runner-up Al Simmons, who had 19.

9. Buck Freeman, 1899   54.0 Adjusted HRs/500 ABs

Freeman's 25 home runs in 1899 were the second highest single-season HR total until Ruth's 29 in 1919. Those 25 home runs were more than double the runner-up's total of 12. There were 4 other times in history when this has occurred, all produced by Babe Ruth—in 1919, '20, '21, and '26. All 5 seasons are among the top 10.

8. Babe Ruth, 1921   56.0 Adjusted HRs/500 ABs

For the third year in a row, Ruth set a new record for the most home runs in a season. Again his competition was sparse, with runners-up Bob Meusel and Ken Williams belting out only 24 each.

7. Babe Ruth, 1927   57.7 Adjusted HRs/500 ABs

Ruth's 60 home runs in 1927 set the mark of excellence in home run hitting. On an adjusted basis, it has now been topped 3 times in recent years, once by McGwire and twice by Barry Bonds.

6. Barry Bonds, 2003   60.3 Adjusted HRs/500 ABs

Bonds hit 45 home runs in only 390 at-bats. He has been such a dangerous hitter since 2001 that he has been collecting walks at record rates, thereby reducing the number of at-bats he attains.

5. Barry Bonds, 2002   61.4 Adjusted HRs/500 ABs

This stellar season may be underappreciated by casual fans. This is the only top 10 season in which the player did not win the home run title—with Bonds' 46 home runs finishing second to Sammy Sosa's 49. However, Bonds only had 403 at-bats. Moreover, his home park was the hardest in which to hit home runs across the National League. After adjusting for that, this season ranks fifth, justifying why Bonds received 198 walks, including 68 intentional ones.

4. Mark McGwire, 1998   61.6 Adjusted HRs/500 ABs

Mark McGwire caught the attention of the entire country as he broke Roger Maris's 37-year-old record with 70 home runs. That season holds up after adjustment as the fourth best in history.

3. Babe Ruth, 1919   61.8 Adjusted HRs/500 ABs

In his final season with Boston, Ruth set a new home run record, hitting 29 home runs, while playing at the toughest home run park in the American League—Fenway Park. Not surprisingly, 20 of Ruth's home runs were hit on the road.

2. Babe Ruth, 1920   63.7 Adjusted HRs/500 ABs

In 1920, Ruth smashed his own home run record of 29, belting out 54. This major surge was principally the result of two factors. First, more frequent replacements of baseballs led to a 54% jump in home runs. Second, Ruth moved from the worst to the best home run park in the American League. After adjustments, the 2 seasons differ by only 2 adjusted home runs.

1. Barry Bonds, 2001   **73.5 Adjusted HRs/500 ABs**

In 2001, Barry Bonds broke McGwire's home run record by three, hitting 73 home runs in 33 fewer at-bats. Moreover, Pacific Bell Park was the hardest park in 2001 in which to homer, particularly for left-handers. As a result, this season ranks as the best in baseball history.

Best Productive Career Home Run Performances (7000 ABs)

Complete lists of the top 100 players for career home runs and adjusted HRs/500 ABs are given in Appendix M.4. The top 11 are given below. Players separated by at most 0.1 HRs/500 ABs are given tied ranks (see the guide at the top of page 104).

10T. Bill Nicholson, 1936–53   **32.0 Adjusted HRs/500 ABs**

Bill Nicholson is certainly a surprise member of this elite list. Nicholson's best 2 seasons occurred in the war years 1943 and 1944, when home run totals were rather low. Nicholson's principal home park, Wrigley Field, was also a bad park to hit in for left-handers. Both of these factors obscured Nicholson's accomplishments.

10T. Reggie Jackson, 1967–87   **32.0 Adjusted HRs/500 ABs**

Reggie Jackson won 4 home runs crowns over his career. In 1969, Jackson had 45 home runs by September, but hit only 2 afterward to finish third that year, with 47.

9. Dave Kingman, 1971–86   **33.1 Adjusted HRs/500 ABs**

Kingman is the odd-man out in this list. Eight of the remaining 10 players place among the top 100 players for career OBP, with 4 in the top 25. Jackson and Nicholson, rank 165th and 340th, respectively. By contrast, Kingman ranks 1031st out of 1140 qualifying players. His poor OBP undermines Kingman's candidacy for the Hall of Fame. Fans should, however, keep in mind his strength—home run hitting, in which he ranks ahead of such luminaries as Aaron, Mantle, and Mays.

8. Jimmie Foxx, 1925–45   **33.3 Adjusted HRs/500 ABs**

Jimmie Foxx, known as "The Beast," was the main interloper to Ruth and Gehrig's home run party. From 1927 to 1931, Ruth and Gehrig claimed the top 2 spots for most home runs, with Foxx finishing fourth 3 times. Foxx climbed to the top in 1932–33. Between 1929 and 1937, both Foxx and Gehrig placed among the top 4 home run hitters every year.

7. Harmon Killebrew, 1954–75   **33.5 Adjusted HRs/500 ABs**

Harmon Killebrew was the premier American League home run hitter during the 1960s, when he averaged 39.3 home runs a season and won 5 of his 6 titles.

6. Lou Gehrig, 1923–39   **33.7 Adjusted HRs/500 ABs**

Gehrig is one of the big winners after the adjustments for home runs are made. His raw home rate puts him in 27th place. Although Gehrig played in Yankee Stadium, which was favorable to left-handers, the rate of home run hitting in his day was much lower than it is now.

5. Mike Schmidt, 1972–89   34.7 Adjusted HRs/500 ABs

Mike Schmidt was a dominant home run force in the 1970s and 1980s. Between 1974 and 1986, Schmidt won 8 home run titles. Only one other man has at least 8 home run titles—Babe Ruth.

4. Barry Bonds, 1986–   35.7 Adjusted HRs/500 ABs

Not too bad for a player who began as a leadoff hitter. For the first 2000 at-bats of his career, during which he primarily batted leadoff, Bonds hit an average of 19.6 HRs/500 ABs. Since then, his rate has been 40.4 HRs/500 ABs. For 2001–3, Bonds' rate was 65.6 HRs/500 ABs, beating the previous high rate of 60.2 HRs/500 ABs for Ruth in 1919–21.

3. Ted Williams, 1939–60   38.7 Adjusted HRs/500 ABs

It has long been known that Ted Williams' raw home run totals were hurt by playing half his games in Fenway Park, which was an adverse park for left-handed hitters. The adjusted averages better reveal Williams' ability. He places third behind the 2 men whose names are synonymous with home runs.

2. Mark McGwire, 1986–2001   41.5 Adjusted HRs/500 ABs

Mark McGwire had the highest raw home run rate in baseball history—1 per 10.6 at-bats. Plagued with foot and knee problems throughout his career, McGwire took home run hitting to new heights by averaging more than 61 home runs over 4 years, from 1996 to 1999, while setting a new home record with 70 home runs in 1998.

1. Babe Ruth, 1914–35   49.8 Adjusted HRs/500 ABs

It is certainly no surprise that Ruth tops this list, but his margin is rather staggering. Ruth's adjusted home run rate is 20% higher than McGwire's. Ruth's domination in this list occurred in spite of the strong transformation adjustments applied to his playing years. Ruth dominated his era like no other player—winning 12 home run titles in 14 years from 1918 to 1931.

CHAPTER 10

Changing the Score
Adjusting Run and RBI Totals

Runs and RBIs, a pair of traditional baseball statistics, have been maligned in recent years. The principal criticism against them is that they are "context-dependent," whereas true ability should be measured using "context-independent" information.

For example, the runs Pete Rose scored as a Cincinnati Red depended not just on his ability to get on base but also on the ability of the lineup behind him—Joe Morgan, Johnny Bench, and Tony Perez—to drive him in. Thus, the claim is that runs scored and RBIs are virtually worthless numbers, better ignored. Instead, the argument continues, a player's ability to "produce runs" should be computed from "context-independent" data, such as his own singles, doubles, triples, home runs, walks, and outs. Such a claim, however, assumes that *clutch performance* does not exist.

Jim Albert and Jay Bennett devote a chapter in *Curve Ball* to the various models used to assess clutch performance, but fail to demonstrate its existence in major league baseball. They are not alone. To date, no widely accepted study has shown that it exists. On the other hand, no one has proven that clutch performance, however defined, doesn't exist. While the lists at the chapter's end are obtained from the methods presented in Chapter 2, we begin by looking at how the adjusted run and RBI totals can suggest the existence of clutch performance.

Total Baseball's Clutch Hitting Index

Total Baseball uses a measure called "Clutch Hitting Index" (CHI) for assessing which players obtain more RBIs than the authors expect, given a formula predicting RBI totals. The formula is based on the number of singles, doubles, triples, and home runs a player hits, adjusted for his average position in the lineup.

There are two main problems with CHI. First, the formula used to identify the player's average lineup position is flawed. Second, CHI does not work well for major home run hitters. Both failures will now be described in greater detail, since they provide insight into the construction of an improved measure of clutch performance.

Problems with the Lineup Position Formula

The number of RBIs a player chalks up depends partly on his position in the lineup. CHI adjusts for a player's estimated average lineup position by contrasting the player's plate appearances per game with the team average. Fifth-place hitters should have an average number of plate appearances, while others should have approximately one ninth greater or fewer plate appearances, depending on how many slots they are above or below the fifth-place slot. Unfortunately, both pinch hitting appearances and substitutions involving the player reduce his plate appearances per game, yielding a lineup position number that is too low.

CHI Doesn't Work Well for Home Run Hitters

The second major problem with the Clutch Hitting Index is that it is biased against big home run hitters. Of the 100 hitters with the highest CHI, only 2 of the top 100 home run hitters appear—Boog Powell (337 home runs) and Rusty Staub (292 home runs)—with neither among the top 50. Among the top 25 CHI performers, only Tommy Davis (153 home runs) has more than 100 home runs. It seems quite odd that almost none of the game's best home run hitters would be "clutch hitters."

The "power outage" at the top of the CHI list may have to do with a statistical concept known as "expectation." The CHI formula compares a player's RBIs with his expected total given the number of singles, doubles, triples, and home runs he hit.

When a player hits a home run, we have a good idea of what to expect—the player gets one sure RBI and an additional RBI for each player on base. The impact of a single is much less certain. It depends not only on the number of base runners, but also on what bases they occupy, how fast they are, and the quality of the hit—for example, a solid single to center versus an infield hit.

Predicting Runs-Plus-RBIs

Suppose 9 clones placed in a lineup averaged 100 RBIs for the season. According to the CHI formula, the leadoff clone would have an expected total of only 88 RBIs. The expectations for the remaining lineup positions in order are: 90, 98, 108 (cleanup), 108, 104, 104, 104, and 102.

Batters who frequently hit early in an inning, or with few men on base, score more runs than they drive in, while the opposite conditions favor RBIs over runs scored. As a result, batters in the first and second positions are key run scorers, while batters in the cleanup and fifth positions are key RBI men. By adding runs and RBIs together, however, we significantly reduce the effect that lineup position has on runs and RBIs individually. We call this sum *runs-plus-RBIs* (RPRBIs).

The number of runs, RBIs, and RPRBIs that a player obtains in a given season can be predicted quite well using linear regression models (details are given in Appendix

G). Three formulas were developed for each statistic, for the eras 1893–1919, 1920–1946, and 1947–2003. The factors included in the formulas are: singles, doubles, triples, home runs, walks-plus-HBPs, stolen bases, and three other factors that need additional explanation: *catcher-on-firsts, team OBP edge,* and *league error difference.*

Catcher-on-firsts is the number singles, walks, and HBPs that catchers obtain in a season. This factor was included in the model because catchers were found to have fewer RPRBIs than non-catchers. The deficit was 7.8 RPRBIs/550 NFPs for catchers before 1947 and 4.3 RPRBIs/550 NFPs for catchers since 1947. No striking differences were found between the other player positions.

Team OBP edge gives the difference in the player's team OBP and .319 (the average team OBP for the standardizing seasons—1977–92 National League) multiplied by the number of NFPs for the player. This term adjusts the expectation for producing runs based on the team's on-base percentage. With this adjustment, full-time players on top OBP teams are expected to produce roughly 8 more RPRBIs than players on average teams.

League errors difference is the difference in the number of league errors per NFP and the average rate of league errors from 1893 to 1919 multiplied by the number of NFPs for the player. This factor, used only for the 1893–1919 era, estimates that 1.5 additional RPRBIs are gained for each additional error.

The r^2 values for all models are at least 97%, meaning that the models account for at least 97% of the variability of the data. From them, we can obtain Run%, RBI%, and RPRBI% values for each player by computing the ratio of their actual to their expected totals.

Over their careers, most players have RPRBI% values close to 100, with one third of the players falling between 99 and 101, and more than three quarters falling between 96 and 104. However, some players deviate substantially from their expected totals. Pie Traynor (RPRBI% = 115) had 314 more RPRBIs than expected. Even if two thirds of Traynor's additional RPRBIs could be attributed to random variation, that would still leave 100 RPRBIs to be accounted for. On the negative side, Jack Tobin, Wally Moses, and Jesse Burkett all fell more than 200 RPRBIs short of their expectations.

Adjusting the RPRBI% to Get the Additional Scoring Rating

The RPRBI% formula, like the CHI, is less likely to rank big home run hitters at the extremes. This fact is demonstrated in Table 10.1, where the mean RPRBI% values are consistent as the number of career home runs increases, but the RPRBI% SD declines. We can adjust out most of the impact of career home runs using the *Additional Scoring Rating (ASR)*, a modified version of RPRBI% defined in Appendix G. Thus, ASR remedies two key problems that beset CHI—lineup position and bias against major home run hitters.

Table 10.1 Variability in Career RPRBI% by Player Home Runs

| Career HRs | Number of Players | RPRBI% | | ASR SD |
		Mean	SD	
0–49	305	99.9	4.41	0.96
50–99	240	99.8	4.08	1.02
100–149	156	100.5	3.39	0.96
150–199	107	101.3	3.15	0.98
200–299	152	100.5	2.76	0.98
300+	98	100.4	2.42	1.10

Extreme Career Additional Scoring Ratings

Table 10.2 shows the 5 players with the highest Run% and RBI% values. We can see how the RPRBI% adjusts for lineup position problems that affect both Run% and RBI%. For example, Red Rolfe scored 24% more runs than expected but had 24% fewer RBIs. As a result, his RPRBI% is exactly average. Similar results are seen for Beckert, Smith, and Adams. However, Mickey Cochrane's positive run edge is much greater in size than his negative RBI edge. This suggests that his Run% was most responsible for his overall RPRBI edge of +7. Since we have an adjustment for catchers, who tend to be slow-footed, we could claim a la Yogi Bear that "Cochrane is faster than the average catcher!"

Table 10.2 Players with the Highest Run and RBI% Values

Player	Run %	RBI %	RPRBI %	Run edge	RBI edge	RPRBI edge
	Players with Highest Run% Values					
1 Mickey Cochrane	126	90	107	+26	−10	+7
2 Glenn Beckert	126	79	104	+26	−21	+4
3 Red Rolfe	124	74	100	+24	−26	0
4 Jack Smith	121	79	103	+21	−21	+3
5 Bobby Adams	118	79	101	+18	−21	+1
	Players with Highest RBI% Values					
1 Earl Sheely	82	130	104	−18	+30	+4
2 Pie Traynor	103	129	115	+3	+29	+15
3 Tommy Davis	92	126	108	−8	+26	+8
4 Sam Mertes	91	125	106	−9	+25	+6
5 Tommy Thevenow	84	125	103	−16	+25	+3

Note: Run edge = Run% − 100; RBI edge = RBI% − 100; RPRBI edge = RPRBI% − 100.

Three of the five players with the highest RBI% values have even higher RPRBI% values than Cochrane—Pie Traynor, Tommy Davis, and Kid Elberfeld. In fact, all 3 rank among the top 20 for RPRBI%.

Define the *RBI gap* as the absolute value of the RBI edge (which is RBI% − 100)—so RBI% values of 90 and 110 both have RBI gaps of 10. Then, a player whose RBI gap exceeds his *run gap* by 10 or more has an *excessive RBI gap*, where similar definitions are used for *run gap* and *excessive run gap*. (The choice of a difference of 10 for an excessive gap is subjective; given random variation, smaller differences are less compelling.) For players with excessive RBI gaps (14% of qualifying players), I consider the RBI component most responsible for the overall RPRBI edge. Those whose RBI% values exceed 100 are good "clutch hitters"; those whose RBI% are less than 100 are poor in "clutch" situations. By contrast, only 22 (2%) players have excessive run gaps.

The players with the 50 highest ASRs are shown in Table 10.3. Yogi Berra leads the way, by both scoring more runs than expected of a catcher with his offensive numbers and driving in more runs. Hall of Famers Pie Traynor, Joe DiMaggio, and Enos Slaughter also rank among the top 10.

Pie Traynor has an excessive RBI gap of 26, strongly suggesting that his superior ASR came primarily from driving in additional runs. Yogi Berra and Joe DiMaggio have roughly equal Run% and RBI% values. Thus, it is unclear which component is most responsible for their superior RPRBI% values.

Manny Mota, a premier pinch hitter for the Pittsburgh Pirates and Los Angeles Dodgers in the 1960s and 1970s, ranks 42nd. Thirteen percent of Mota's 3779 lifetime at-bats were pinch hit appearances. It seems likely that use of Mota in selective pinch hitting spots at least partially accounts for his elevated ASR.

The players with the 50 lowest ASRs are shown in Table 10.4. Outfielders Jack Tobin and Wally Moses, who have the lowest ratings, both scored runs at the expected rate but drove in at most three fourths of their expected RBIs. Catchers Spud Davis, Del Rice, and Mike Scioscia all placed in the bottom 10. In each case, they were particularly hurt by their poor Run% scores. This suggests that especially slow-footed catchers still have roles on major league teams because of their offsetting defensive strengths.

Mark McGwire is perhaps a surprise member of the bottom 10. Other prominent home run hitters also rank among the bottom 50—Jim Thome, Rafael Palmeiro, Frank Howard, Babe Ruth, Barry Bonds, Stan Musial, and Joe Adcock. All but Howard and Adcock were hurt primarily by lower-than-expected RBI production. These low ASRs may be partially explained by the use of intentional and "semi-intentional" bases on balls by opposing pitching staffs to work around these batters in key run-producing situations. It is important to remember that although the ASRs of these home run hitters are quite low, their RPRBI% values are not as low as those of other bottom 50 players.

Players can have elevated RPRBI% values by being superior at scoring runs, driving them in, or both. Without knowing the player's typical lineup position, we can't

Table 10.3 Players with the Highest Additional Scoring Ratings

Rank/Name	Position	HRs	Run%	RBI%	RPRBI%	ASR
1 Yogi Berra	C	358	111	109	110	4.28
2 Pie Traynor	3B	58	103	**129**	115	3.54
3 Jeff King	3B	154	104	**120**	112	3.54
4 Vern Stephens	SS	247	103	**113**	108	2.91
5 Ted Simmons	C	248	100	**114**	108	2.75
6 Joe DiMaggio	OF	361	107	106	106	2.72
7 Minnie Minoso	OF	186	104	**114**	108	2.63
8 Frank McCormick	1B	128	97	**121**	109	2.63
9 Tommy Davis	OF	153	92	**125**	108	2.50
10 Enos Slaughter	OF	169	99	**118**	108	2.49
11 Luke Sewell	C	20	110	113	111	2.42
12 Frank Chance	1B	20	104	**123**	111	2.36
13 Joe Carter	OF	396	99	**110**	105	2.35
14 Terry Pendleton	3B	140	99	**118**	108	2.32
15 Earl Torgeson	1B	149	103	**113**	108	2.31
16 Julio Cruz	2B	23	105	**123**	111	2.29
17 Brian Jordan	OF	173	103	112	107	2.26
18 Darren Daulton	C	137	102	**113**	108	2.25
19 Hugh Duffy	OF	66	102	**117**	109	2.23
20 Dots Miller	1B	32	104	**117**	110	2.22
21 Bob Elliott	3B	170	97	**118**	107	2.21
22 Eric Davis	OF	282	101	**111**	106	2.19
23 Keith Hernandez	1B	162	102	**113**	107	2.15
24 Darrell Porter	C	188	105	108	107	2.15
25 Greg Vaughn	OF	355	107	103	105	2.12
26 Jimmie Wilson	C	32	111	108	109	2.10
27 Sherry Magee	OF	83	99	**119**	108	2.09
28 Al Simmons	OF	307	100	**110**	105	2.07
29 Dave Winfield	OF	465	100	108	104	2.06
30 Thurman Munson	C	113	111	104	107	2.05
31 Del Ennis	OF	288	96	**114**	105	2.04
32 Cleon Jones	OF	93	106	110	108	2.04
33 Vic Wertz	OF	266	92	**118**	105	2.02
34 Darren Lewis	OF	27	109	110	109	2.01
35 Larry Doby	OF	253	105	106	106	2.00
36 Otis Nixon	OF	11	110	110	110	2.00
37 Mickey Cochrane	C	119	**126**	90	107	1.97
38 Roy Sievers	1B	318	100	109	105	1.95
39 Scott Fletcher	SS	34	108	109	108	1.90
40 Roger Maris	OF	275	110	100	105	1.89
41 Joe Medwick	OF	205	104	107	106	1.89
42 Jimmy Williams	2B	49	102	**114**	108	1.88
43 Fred Schulte	OF	47	108	109	108	1.88
44 Sal Bando	3B	242	100	**111**	105	1.88
45 Manny Mota	OF	31	102	**116**	108	1.83
46 Mel Hall	OF	134	106	106	106	1.83
47 Charlie Gehringer	2B	184	110	101	106	1.82
48 Johnny Bench	C	389	103	105	104	1.81
49 Kevin Young	1B	144	101	**111**	106	1.81
50 Julio Franco	SS	155	102	111	106	1.79

Note: Excessive RBI and run gaps (see text for definition) are in bold.

Table 10.4 Players with the Lowest Additional Scoring Ratings

Rank/Name	Position	HRs	Run%	RBI%	RPRBI%	ASR
1 Jack Tobin	OF	64	101	**72**	88	−2.99
2 Wally Moses	OF	89	102	**75**	90	−2.75
3 Spud Davis	C	77	**77**	101	90	−2.50
4 Vinny Castilla	3B	268	93	94	93	−2.45
5 Ralph Garr	OF	75	104	**73**	90	−2.44
6 Del Rice	C	79	**83**	97	91	−2.42
7 Billy Cox	3B	66	99	**81**	90	−2.41
8 Eddie Bressoud	SS	94	99	**83**	91	−2.40
9 Don Slaught	C	77	88	93	91	−2.33
10 Dick Bartell	SS	79	103	**77**	91	−2.32
11 Mike Scioscia	C	68	**86**	96	91	−2.27
12 Ron Oester	2B	42	95	**85**	90	−2.23
13 Mark McGwire	1B	583	98	95	96	−2.22
14 Lee Magee	OF	12	101	**75**	89	−2.17
15 Leo Cardenas	SS	118	88	97	92	−2.16
16 Warren Cromartie	OF	61	94	89	92	−2.03
17 Jesse Burkett	OF	65	105	**75**	92	−2.01
18 Brady Anderson	OF	210	97	90	94	−2.00
19 Barry Bonds	OF	658	100	94	97	−1.99
20 Earl Battey	C	104	92	94	93	−1.92
21 Topsy Hartsel	OF	31	104	**70**	91	−1.91
22 Rafael Palmeiro	1B	528	98	95	97	−1.91
23 Jim Thome	1B	381	100	92	96	−1.91
24 George Gibson	C	15	90	92	91	−1.90
25 Mike Pagliarulo	3B	134	93	94	93	−1.89
26 Javy Lopez	C	214	94	95	94	−1.87
27 Frank Howard	OF	382	92	99	96	−1.87
28 Steve O'Neill	C	13	**85**	96	91	−1.85
29 Charlie Jamieson	OF	18	104	**74**	91	−1.84
30 Ken Reitz	3B	68	**75**	109	93	−1.82
31 Mike Easler	OF	118	90	97	94	−1.82
32 Davey Johnson	2B	136	90	98	94	−1.76
33 Mike Donlin	OF	51	98	87	93	−1.74
34 Bill Virdon	OF	91	104	**81**	93	−1.73
35 Dickie Thon	SS	71	**88**	100	93	−1.70
36 Burt Shotton	OF	9	103	**72**	91	−1.69
37 Vladimir Guerrero	OF	234	95	95	95	−1.68
38 Babe Ruth	OF	714	102	94	98	−1.68
39 Harry Hooper	OF	75	103	**80**	93	−1.66
40 Lloyd Waner	OF	27	114	**67**	92	−1.65
41 Milt May	C	77	**83**	103	94	−1.65
42 Chet Lemon	OF	215	98	92	95	−1.64
43 Jimmy Austin	3B	13	95	87	92	−1.62
44 Monte Cross	SS	31	**84**	105	93	−1.61
45 Frank Snyder	C	47	**81**	103	93	−1.61
46 Bernie Friberg	3B	38	90	97	93	−1.59
47 Stan Musial	OF	475	98	96	97	−1.58
48 Aurelio Rodriguez	3B	124	93	96	94	−1.58
49 Randy Velarde	2B	100	104	**83**	94	−1.57
50 Dale Mitchell	OF	41	97	88	93	−1.57

Note: Excessive RBI and run gaps (see text for definition) are in bold.

tell for sure which aspect of play was most responsible for the superior RPRBI% result. Use of the excessive RBI and run gaps, however, provides reasonable clues. Among the players with the 50 highest ASR values, 28 had excessive RBI gaps, but only two had excessive run edges. Among the players with the 50 lowest ASR values, 17 had excessive RBI gaps, while 10 had excessive run gaps. Thus, it appears to be much easier to stand out because of exceptionally high or low RBI% values than Run% values.

Does Clutch Performance Exist?

What Is Clutch Performance?

The biggest problem with determining whether "clutch performance" exists is that the baseball research community has not yet clearly defined what it is. "Clutch performance" measures can be categorized into three major types. The measures either: (1) use all batting data without regard for inning or closeness of game, (2) divide batting data into clutch and nonclutch situations and compare them, or (3) weight the batting data by game impact.

Both CHI and ASR are examples of the first type. The contrasting of "Close and Late" data (used in STATS *Player Profiles* annuals) against the remaining data is an example of the second type, and the player-game-percentage method presented in *Curve Ball* is an example of the third.

Although the second and third type methods can define "clutch" situations in a better way than the first type, such data are not easily available across baseball history. While the first type can use seasonal data, the second type needs data at the game level, and the third type requires play-by-play data. Thus, if one is willing to accept the first type as a legitimate measure of "clutch performance," it currently has the greatest likelihood of being able to demonstrate the existence of clutch performance.

By successfully answering two questions, I claim that clutch performance exists in baseball. The questions are: Does ASR measure clutch performance? Is the variation in ASR completely random?

Does ASR Measure Clutch Performance?

The argument that ASR measures clutch performance is that if one drives in significantly more runs than expected, then the hits must have come at especially opportune times—that is, in clutch situations. The most serious weakness of ASR as a clutch performance measure is that the player may be exceptional in the runs component, rather than in the RBI component, and the runs component is more likely to reflect an overall ability rather than a clutch ability. This no doubt applies with regard to some players. The runs component was principally included as part of ASR, however, to adjust for a player's lineup position, allowing truly exceptional RBI differences to manifest themselves more clearly. Indeed, many more players have excessive RBI edges than run edges, suggesting that the RBI component of RPRBI% is generally more important.

I believe that ASR measures a mixture of overall ability differences, mainly through the runs component and clutch ability differences, measured primarily through the RBI component. Ultimately, we will want to examine the detailed batting records of individual players, using a method such as player-game-performance to corroborate the evidence that is statistically suggested using ASR.

Is the Variation in ASR Completely Random?

If no true differences in additional scoring existed, random variation would allow some players to top the ASR list, while others would be relegated to the bottom. Were Yogi Berra and Pie Traynor the lottery winners in the random game of ASR scores, while Jack Tobin and Wally Moses were the hapless losers—or were there intrinsic differences in their RPRBI producing performances?

We could get the answer by knowing how much spread to expect from randomness alone and then determine whether the variation seen exceeds that amount. Unfortunately, it is not clear how much spread to expect in a season. Assuming random variation, however, the SD for the career RPRBI % can be determined mathematically from the single-season SD.

The single-season SD for RPRBI % is 8.64 for players who had at least 450 NFPs, as shown in Table 10.5. Assuming random variation of the single-season data, the career RPRBI% SD should be 2.62 = 8.64/(10.9, where 10.9 is the average number of "full seasons of play," = 6275/577, from Table 10.5). The actual average career RPRBI% SD, however, is 42% higher than the expected value. Thus, the ASR values are not completely random.

Perhaps the easiest way for the RBI% to vary from player to player in clutch situations is for the walk rate to vary depending on the number of players on base. Sometimes pitchers intentionally walk batters to set up a double play or to avoid a particularly dangerous batter. Other times, pitchers work around batters, giving them little to hit. Whether a batter should take the walk or swing at a "bad ball" depends on whether the players behind the batter can be expected to bring the run home.

Additional factors may need to be included in the RPRBI models to "explain" more of the nonrandom variation. Undoubtedly lineup position differences still exist. Eighth-place batters probably gain fewer RPRBIs per event than other batters. Even so, that would mean that their hits were less valuable to the team than batters earlier in the lineup. Thus, it is useful for ASR to reveal such differences.

Table 10.5   Standard Deviation of RPRBI%

	N	SD	Average No. of NFPs	Range of NFPs
Single-season	11,633	8.64	577	450–768
Career	1058	3.73	6275	4000–15,726

Notes: The single-season data include all player-seasons from 1893 to 2003 with at least 450 NFPs. The career data include all players with at least 4000 NFPs.

Extreme Single-Season Additional Scoring Ratings

I have argued that ASR provides modest evidence in favor of the existence of clutch performance. Additional insights into the existence of clutch performance can be gleaned from further study of the single-season performances that yielded RPRBI totals the most deviant from the expected totals, shown in Table 10.6.

Interestingly, in 13 of the best 25 single-season for RPRBI%, the player's team won at least a divisional title. By contrast, only 2 players with the largest single-season deficits in RPRBI% were on championship teams—Max Carey (1925) and Earle Combs (1927). Three examples from Table 10.6 are highlighted below.

Tommy Davis had an amazing campaign in 1962, driving in 153 runs, while scoring 120. Compare Davis's numbers with those of Frank Robinson. Given their batting records and the fact that Robinson beat his own expected total by 21 RPRBI, it is hard to figure out how Davis managed to top him.

	AB	1B	DPT	HR	BB + HBP	RPRBI Expected	RPRBI Actual
Tommy Davis	665	167	36	27	32	221	273
Frank Robinson	609	116	53	39	87	249	270
Difference	+56	+51	−17	−12	−55	−28	+3

Barry Bonds's 2001 season was certainly one of the best seasons in baseball history. He fell short of his expected RPRBI total by 51, however. In 2001, Bonds broke the single-season records for both home runs and walks, including 35 intentional walks. Pitchers worked around Bonds in key situations; it will certainly be interesting to know what impact this had on Bonds' run and RBI totals and on his San Francisco Giants overall.

Ted Williams' 1957 season also shows up as having the 12th greatest deficit in RPRBIs from the expected total. Williams walked frequently throughout his entire career. In 1957, though, pitchers may have more deliberately worked around him, limiting the scoring damage that he might have caused.

Table 10.6 Seasons with the Largest Gaps Between Actual and Expected RPRBIs

			Actual – Expected		
Rank/Player	Year	Pos	Runs	RBIs	RPRBIs
1 Tommy Davis	1962	LF	10	42	52
2 Hughie Jennings	1895	SS	31	17	49
3 Al Simmons	1930	LF	30	16	46
4 Maurice Van Robays	1940	LF	7	38	45
5 Hugh Duffy	1893	CF	24	20	45
6 Tom Herr	1985	2B	2	43	44
7 Zeke Bonura	1936	1B	5	38	43
8 Sherry Magee	1910	LF	1	42	43
9 Billy Nash	1893	3B	5	37	43
10 Farmer Vaughn	1893	C	1	42	42
11 Mickey Cochrane	1929	C	34	8	42
12 Pie Traynor	1928	3B	–1	42	42
13 Luke Appling	1936	SS	0	41	42
14 Kirby Puckett	1994	RF	9	33	42
15 Sal Bando	1974	3B	13	30	42
16 Dixie Walker	1945	RF	3	38	41
17 Julio Franco	1985	SS	16	25	41
18 Tom Herr	1987	2B	4	37	40
19 Frank LaPorte	1914	2B	9	31	40
20 Manny Ramirez	1999	RF	12	28	40
21 Frankie Frisch	1931	2B	14	26	40
22 Gary Carter	1986	C	15	25	40
23 Vern Stephens	1950	SS	15	25	39
24 Enos Slaughter	1946	RF	3	36	39
25 Sam Crawford	1910	RF	1	38	39
1 Brook Jacoby	1987	3B	–16	–33	–50
2 Barry Bonds	2001	LF	–14	–35	–50
3 Jesse Burkett	1900	LF	–30	–20	–49
4 Ducky Holmes	1899	LF	–28	–20	–48
5 Richie Ashburn	1958	CF	–14	–31	–45
6 Chick Stahl	1899	RF	0	–45	–44
7 Ken Williams	1923	LF	–12	–30	–41
8 Max Carey	1925	CF	–8	–33	–40
9 Wally Moses	1937	RF	1	–39	–38
10 Johnny Mostil	1926	CF	0	–39	–38
11 Ted Williams	1957	LF	–8	–30	–38
12 Cy Seymour	1903	CF	–15	–24	–38
13 Johnny Mize	1939	1B	–16	–22	–38
14 Alfonso Soriano	2003	2B	–5	–32	–37
15 Kip Selbach	1895	LF	–0	–37	–37
16 Frank Robinson	1957	LF	–4	–33	–37
17 Clyde Milan	1911	CF	–2	–35	–37
18 George Sisler	1917	1B	–18	–19	–37
19 Dom DiMaggio	1942	CF	6	–43	–37
20 Rogers Hornsby	1924	2B	–2	–34	–36
21 Wally Moses	1938	RF	–7	–29	–36
22 Sam Crawford	1913	RF	–17	–19	–35
23 Jesse Burkett	1898	LF	0	–36	–35
24 Brady Anderson	1996	CF	–6	–29	–35
25 Aurelio Rodriguez	1971	3B	–1	–33	–35

Best Single-Season Runs Performances

Three men dominate the run scoring list: Babe Ruth, Mickey Mantle, and Rickey Henderson. Together they account for one fourth of the best run scoring seasons in history, including 9 of the 10 best. The complete list of top seasons is given in Appendix L.5.

Table 10.7   Top 100 Seasons: Adjusted Runs per 550 NFPs
            58 Different Players with Average Age = 28.0

Era	Seasons	Expected	Era	Seasons	Expected
1876–1900	7	9.9	1947–68	16	16.5
1901–19	14	13.4	1969–92	29	26.8
1920–46	18	19.4	1993–2003	16	14.0

No. of Seasons	Players with Multiple Top 100 Seasons
10	Rickey Henderson
8	*Mickey Mantle*
7	*Babe Ruth*
6	Barry Bonds
4	*Ty Cobb*
3	*Ted Williams, Eddie Collins*
2	Jose Canseco, Eric Davis, Tommy Leach, *Paul Molitor, Joe Morgan,* Alex Rodriguez, Sammy Sosa, *Robin Yount*

Notes: Hall of Fame players are listed in italics.

See the guide to the top 100 seasons tables on page 103.

10. Mickey Mantle, 1957   **113.8 Adjusted Runs/550 NFPs**
In 1957, Mantle had the highest single-season OBP and OPS of his career.

9. Mickey Mantle, 1958   **114.7 Adjusted Runs/550 NFPs**
In 1958, Mantle led the American League in walks for the fourth time; he subsequently led twice more. Five of these 6 years rank among the 25 best, with 1957 (10th), 1954 (13th), 1961 (8th), and 1962 (15th) being the others. In run scoring, and as a slugger, Mantle became a second Babe Ruth.

8. Mickey Mantle, 1961   **115.6 Adjusted Runs/550 NFPs**
Roger Maris batted cleanup for the Yankees behind Mickey Mantle and hit 61 home runs. Mantle hit 54 home runs himself and led the league in walks. The strong combination led to Mantle's best season for run scoring.

7. Babe Ruth, 1928   **115.7 Adjusted Runs/550 NFPs**
Babe Ruth's 1928 season was close to his previous year. With 4 fewer at-bats, Ruth matched his 2B, 3B, and BB totals from 1927, but had 19 fewer hits and 6 fewer home

runs. In spite of this slight slippage, Ruth scored 5 more runs than in 1927, which ranks as 18th best. This illustrates both how random effects are part of the game, and how tight the competition is.

6. Rickey Henderson, 1981   116.1 Adjusted Runs/550 NFPs

In his third season in the majors, 22-year-old Rickey Henderson forged the first of 10 seasons among the best 100. Whereas, Ruth and Mantle primarily hit third in the lineup, Henderson broke new ground as a leadoff hitter. Coupling a high OBP with high stolen bases and, in later years, a fair number of home runs, Rickey set a new standard for leadoff hitters. His runs scored achievements are the evidence of his success.

5. Rickey Henderson, 1984   116.4 Adjusted Runs/550 NFPs

Henderson's averages in 1984 are fairly close to those in 1981. Although his OBP was down 10 points, he hit 10 more home runs.

4. Jeff Bagwell, 1994   117.0 Adjusted Runs/550 NFPs

In this list dominated by Henderson, Ruth, and Mantle, Bagwell is the lone interloper.

3. Babe Ruth, 1920   117.9 Adjusted Runs/550 NFPs

Ruth is among the top players in runs scored, ranking third on the raw runs total list. Many might attribute this to Lou Gehrig, who hit behind Ruth for many years. Interestingly, 2 of the 3 of Ruth's top 10 seasons occurred before Gehrig joined the Yankees. Perhaps Ruth's prowess in 1920 and 1921 is due to the fact that these were 2 of his 3 best seasons for adjusted slugging average, with high DPT rates.

2. Rickey Henderson, 1990   128.5 Adjusted Runs/550 NFPs

Henderson had his best season for both OBP and slugging average and stole 65 bases to lead the Oakland A's, who went to the World Series for the third straight season. This year came close to matching his 1985 season and gave Henderson his fourth season among the top 6.

1. Rickey Henderson, 1985   133.8 Adjusted Runs/550 NFPs

In 1985, Henderson smashed Babe Ruth's old mark of 118.7 by more than 14 runs. Compared to his 1984 season, Henderson increased his OBP by 20 points, struck 8 more home runs, and stole 14 more bases, while playing for a Yankee team that was superior to his '84 Athletics club.

Best Single-Season RBI Performances

Table 10.8 summarizes the top 100 seasons for RBIs. A complete list of top seasons is given in Appendix L.6.

Table 10.8   Top 100 Seasons—Adjusted RBIs per 550 NFPs
74 Different Players with Average Age = 28.8

Era	Seasons	Expected	Era	Seasons	Expected
1876–1900	15	9.6	1947–68	14	16.6
1901–19	16	13.5	1969–92	24	26.9
1920–46	19	19.5	1993–2003	12	14.0

No. of Seasons	Players with Multiple Top 100 Seasons
6	Babe Ruth
3	*Ty Cobb*, George Foster, *Lou Gehrig*, Boog Powell, *Sam Thompson*
2	*Cap Anson, Frank Baker, Gavy Cravath, Joe DiMaggio*, Jim Gentile, Juan Gonzalez, Dave Orr, *Al Simmons, Willie Stargell, Honus Wagner*, Heinie Zimmerman

Notes: Hall of Fame players are listed in italics.

See the guide to the top 100 seasons tables on page 103.

Players separated by at most 0.1 RBIs/550 NFPs are given tied ranks (see the guide at the top of page 104).

10. Gavy Cravath, 1913   121.1 Adjusted RBIs/550 NFPs
Gavy Cravath was a premier home run hitter of the deadball era. In 1913, he won his first home run title with 19, and knocked in 33 more runs than his nearest competitor.

8T. Jim Gentile, 1961   122.1 Adjusted RBIs/550 NFPs
Roger Maris and Mickey Mantle are the American League players best remembered for their 1961 season, when they hit 61 and 54 home runs, and drove in 142 and 128 runs, respectively. However, Jim Gentile hit 141 RBIs in 102 fewer NFPs than Maris in this standout season.

8T. George Brett, 1980   122.2 Adjusted RBIs/550 NFPs
Although never leading the league in RBIs, Brett came within 4 in this 1980 season in which he missed 45 games owing to a variety of injuries.

7. Manny Ramirez, 1999   122.5 Adjusted RBIs/550 NFPs
Manny Ramirez was chasing Hack Wilson's record of 191 RBIs in 1999, before an injury shelved those ambitions. Still, Ramirez bettered Wilson's in both adjusted RBI average and adjusted RBI total.

6. Sam Thompson, 1887   123.0 Adjusted RBIs/550 NFPs
Sam Thompson, the best RBI man of the 19th century, is the only player to place 2

seasons in the top 10. His raw total of 166 RBIs easily outpaced fellow Hall of Fame runners-up Roger Connor (104), Cap Anson (102), and teammate Dan Brouthers (101).

5. Sam Thompson, 1895   123.7 Adjusted RBIs/550 NFPs
In his last of 3 seasons leading the league in RBIs, 35-year-old Sam Thompson hit 165 RBIs to win by 31 RBIs.

3T. Cap Anson, 1886   124.5 Adjusted RBIs/550 NFPs
In 125 games, Anson knocked in 147 RBIs, 52 more than runner-up teammate Fred Pfeffer had.

3T. Juan Gonzalez, 2001   124.6 Adjusted RBIs/550 NFPs
Bouncing back in Cleveland from a subpar 2000 season with Detroit, Gonzalez reached the 140 RBI mark for the third time. In 2001, Gonzalez hit one fewer RBI than Bret Boone in 90 fewer at-bats.

2. Jeff Bagwell, 1994   125.8 Adjusted RBIs/550 NFPs
In 110 games, Bagwell hit 116 RBIs in 465 NFPs, a pace unequaled in the 20th century.

1. Oyster Burns, 1890   132.9 Adjusted RBIs/550 NFPs
The 19th century was the heyday for outstanding RBI performances, with 4 of the top 6 seasons coming before 1901. In this all-time best year, Oyster Burns topped both Cap Anson and Sam Thompson, 2 other top 10 RBI men, by more than 20 RBIs.

Best Productive Career Runs Scored Performances (8000 NFPs)

The top 10 players for productive career runs scored are certainly among the greatest offensive players in baseball history. All placed among the 50 for at least 2 of 4 events: OBP, DPTs, home runs, and SBs, as shown below. Complete lists of the top 100 players for career runs scored and adjusted Runs/550 NFPs are given in Appendix M.5. Here are the top 10:

10. Stan Musial, 1941–63   90.5 Adjusted Runs/550 NFPs
(Adj OBP = .410, Rank = 15; Adj DPTs/500 = 41.3, Rank = 1; Adj HRs/500 = 22.2, Rank = 130; Adj SBs/550 = 12.5, Rank = 545)
This countdown is comprised of one first baseman and 9 outfielders (many of whom moved to first in the later stage of their careers). Stan Musial played more than 1000 games at both positions.

9. Hank Aaron, 1954–76   91.4 Adjusted Runs/550 NFPs
(Adj OBP = .378, Rank = 103; Adj DPTs/500 = 34.9, Rank = 35; Adj HRs/500 = 27.6, Rank = 40; Adj SBs/550 = 22.7, Rank = 252)
Hank Aaron was a model of consistency in hitting. He does not show up prominently in any of the single-season lists. Over the course of a career, however, Aaron's value is more clearly seen. Aaron led the league in scoring 3 times.

8. Willie Mays, 1951–73   92.3 Adjusted Runs/550 NFPs

(Adj OBP = .391, Rank = 58; Adj DPTs/500 = 36.6, Rank = 17; Adj HRs/500 = 28.7, Rank = 32; Adj SBs/550 = 48.7, Rank = 34)

Like Hank Aaron, the impact that Mays has on baseball is seen more clearly in the career lists than in the single-season lists. Mays led the league in scoring twice.

7. Ted Williams, 1939–60   93.0 Adjusted Runs/550 NFPs

(Adj OBP = .448, Rank = 1; Adj DPTs/500 = 35.8, Rank = 22; Adj HRs/500 = 38.7, Rank = 3; Adj SBs/550 = 3.5, Rank = 1019)

In the first half of his career, Williams routinely led the American League in runs scored, winning 6 of the 7 years he played between 1940 and 1949.

6. Ty Cobb, 1905–28   93.6 Adjusted Runs/550 NFPs

(Adj OBP = .406, Rank = 17; Adj DPTs/500 = 37.7, Rank = 8; Adj HRs/500 = 21.9, Rank = 140; Adj SBs/550 = 63.3, Rank = 9)

Cobb, with an aggressive style of play, which included 892 stolen bases, places sixth in the career run scored list. He led the American League in runs scored 5 times in 8 seasons between 1909 and 1916.

5. Lou Gehrig, 1923–39   94.2 Adjusted Runs/550 NFPs

(Adj OBP = .412, Rank = 13; Adj DPTs/500 = 37.1, Rank = 12; Adj HRs/500 = 33.7, Rank = 6; Adj SBs/550 = 9.9, Rank = 663)

It may be surprising that Gehrig finished fifth, just 2 spots behind Babe Ruth. For most of their careers as teammates, Ruth hit third, Gehrig hit cleanup. Thus, Ruth was a frequent beneficiary of Gehrig's batting ability. Gehrig led the American League in scoring 4 times, between 1931 and 1936.

4. Barry Bonds, 1986–   94.9 Adjusted Runs/550 NFPs

(Adj OBP = .429, Rank = 4; Adj DPTs/500 = 33.4, Rank = 73; Adj HRs/500 = 35.7, Rank = 4; Adj SBs/550 = 33.1, Rank = 108)

Barry Bonds pushed his career adjusted runs total 4.1 runs higher after his 8000th NFP, the only top 10 player to gain more than 0.3 runs in late career. This surge moved him up 9 spots into fourth. Bonds led the National League in runs scored only once.

3. Babe Ruth, 1914–35   100.9 Adjusted Runs/550 NFPs

(Adj OBP = .439, Rank = 2; Adj DPTs/500 = 34.2, Rank = 50; Adj HRs/500 = 49.8, Rank = 1; Adj SBs/550 = 10.3, Rank = 639)

Ruth, Mantle, and Henderson, who dominated the single-season runs lists, also hold the top career spots. Ruth led the American League in runs scored 8 times in 10 years from 1919 to 1928.

2. Mickey Mantle, 1951–68   103.8 Adjusted Runs/550 NFPs

(Adj OBP = .416, Rank = 10; Adj DPTs/500 = 29.6, Rank = 325; Adj HRs/500 = 31.9, Rank = 12; Adj SBs/550 = 28.5, Rank = 156)

In claiming second place in this prestigious list, Mantle provides one of the reasons why was so popular in his heyday. Mantle led the American League in runs scored 6 times between 1954 and 1961.

1. Rickey Henderson, 1979–   **105.9 Adjusted Runs/550 NFPs**

(Adj OBP = .411, Rank = 14; Adj DPTs/500 = 31.0, Rank = 223; Adj HRs/500 = 13.4, Rank = 434; Adj SBs/550 = 78.3, Rank = 1)

Whereas the other batters in this runs scored top 10 regularly batted in the third or fourth spots in the lineup, Henderson showed how valuable a leadoff hitter can be. Henderson hit for a good average with power and has stolen more than 1300 bases, propelling him to the top. He led the American League in runs scored 5 times between 1981 and 1990.

Best Productive Career RBI Performances (9000 NFPs)

Complete lists of the top 100 players for career RBIs and adjusted RBIs/550 NFPs are given in Appendix M.6. The top 10 are given below. Players separated by at most 0.1 RBIs/550 NFPs are given tied ranks.

10. Cap Anson, 1876–97   **95.0 Adjusted RBIs/550 NFPs**

Anson's National League career started at age 24 and continued until age 45. Early National League seasons consisted of many fewer games than today. If we consider Anson's productive career to go through age 37 (a typical age for accumulating 9000 NFPs), Anson would have 99.9 adjusted RBIs/550 NFP, boosting his ranking from tenth to second. Between 1880 and 1891, Anson won 8 RBI titles.

9. Willie Stargell, 1962–82   **95.2 Adjusted RBIs/550 NFPs**

Willie Stargell placed among the top 5 RBI men only 4 times, winning once in 1973. After 1974, however, Stargell missed at least 36 games each season. The reduced playing time kept him off the top 5 lists, although Stargell continued to drive in runs at a high rate.

8. Hank Greenberg, 1930–47   **95.9 Adjusted RBIs/550 NFPs**

Hank Greenberg was the big RBI man on powerful Detroit Tigers teams, who won 4 pennants and 2 World Series in his 9 seasons as a regular with them. Greenberg placed among the top 5 RBI men in 7 of those seasons, winning 4 times.

7. Gavy Cravath, 1908–20   **96.1 Adjusted RBIs/550 NFPs**

Gavy Cravath had a short career, playing mainly for the Phillies in the Baker Bowl, which boosted run scoring. Cravath's exploits weren't just a Baker Bowl phenomenon. After adjusting that effect out, Cravath ranks seventh on this list. He won RBI titles in 1913 and 1915.

6. Sam Thompson, 1885–98, 1906   **96.8 Adjusted RBIs/550 NFPs**

Sam Thompson was the premier RBI man of the 19th century, edging out Cap Anson. In *Total Baseball's* "RBIs per Game" list, Thompson ranks first. He led the National League in RBIs 3 times.

5. Juan Gonzalez, 1989–   **97.0 Adjusted RBIs/550 NFPs**

Juan Gonzalez is a modern RBI machine. Gonzalez has placed among the top 5 for

RBIs 6 times, winning once. Gonzalez's performance has been erratic of late, with down years in 2000 and 2002. These subpar years have dropped Gonzalez from a second place spot between Ruth and Gehrig.

4. Mark McGwire, 1986–2001   97.5 Adjusted RBIs/550 NFPs

Known for his booming home runs, McGwire places fourth on the all-time RBI list in spite of winning the RBI crown only once, in 1999.

3. Joe DiMaggio, 1936–51   98.0 Adjusted RBIs/550 NFPs

Joe DiMaggio ranks as the third best RBI man in baseball history. Being a right-handed hitter in Yankee Stadium cost DiMaggio quite a few home runs. As park effect estimation continues to improve, it will be useful to obtain separate runs factors for right- and left-handed hitters. When that day comes and given the asymmetry of Yankee Stadium, I would not be surprised to see DiMaggio supplant Ruth as the best RBI producer in the game's history. DiMaggio won 2 American League RBI crowns.

2. Lou Gehrig, 1923–39   98.5 Adjusted RBIs/550 NFPs

Gehrig and Ruth are the only 2 players to appear in the top 10 for both runs scored and RBIs. With Gehrig hitting behind Ruth, this was Gehrig's event to win. Somehow Ruth still managed to slip past him. Between 1927 and 1934, Gehrig won 5 RBI titles in 8 seasons.

1. Babe Ruth, 1914–35   103.4 Adjusted RBIs/550 NFPs

It is hard to keep Ruth of the top spot in the most important career lists, and RBIs is not an exception. Interestingly, handedness-specific park factors for runs might allow DiMaggio to slip past him. Ruth won 6 RBI titles between 1919 and 1928.

CHAPTER 11

The Count

Adjusting Walk
and Strikeout Totals

The dramatic strikeout and the anticlimactic base on balls—both events are cut from the same baseball leather. While singles, doubles, triples, and home runs involve hitting the ball, strikeouts and walks are the primary outcomes when the plate appearance ends without the final pitch being struck.

In 1876, when 9 balls were needed for a walk and 4 strikes for a strikeout, only 4% of NFPs ended without the final pitch being struck. In 2000, that rate was at an all-time high of 27%.

The rise is strongly linked to that of the home run. A big swing, intended to muscle a home run, more often leads to a strikeout. Home run hitters also claim more free passes, since pitchers tend to throw more pitches off the plate to them.

These linkages can be seen in Table 11.1, which shows the expected number of adjusted strikeouts and walks a player will have per adjusted home run hit. Since 1920, a player hitting zero home runs can expect to strike out 56 times per 550 NFPs, while drawing 39 to 45 walks. An additional 1.03 to 1.26 strikeouts and 0.53 to 0.87 walks

Table 11.1 Expected Strikeouts and Walks Based on Home Runs Hit

	Adj. SOs/550 NFPs	Adj. BBs/550 NFPs
1893–19	$64 + 0.49 \times$ Adj. HR	$51 + 0.00 \times$ Adj. HR
1920–62	$56 + 1.07 \times$ Adj. HR	$45 + 0.53 \times$ Adj. HR
1963–68	$56 + 1.07 \times$ Adj. HR	$39 + 0.87 \times$ Adj. HR
1969–76	$56 + 1.26 \times$ Adj. HR	$39 + 0.87 \times$ Adj. HR
1977–92	$56 + 1.26 \times$ Adj. HR	$44 + 0.57 \times$ Adj. HR
1993–2003	$56 + 1.03 \times$ Adj. HR	$44 + 0.71 \times$ Adj. HR

Notes: Results obtained using *multiple changepoint regression* for 1893–2003. *Changeyears* considered were 1901, '20, '47, '63, '69, '77, and '93.

are expected per home run hit. Notably, more than one additional strikeout, but less than one additional walk, is expected per home run.

Classifying Batters by Walk and Strikeout Rates

In 1941, Ted Williams hit 37 home runs, struck out 27 times, and walked 147 times with 456 at-bats (606 NFPs, including 3 HBPs), yielding adjusted totals of 41.5, 50.2, and 127.8, respectively. Using Table 11.1, his expected number of adjusted strikeouts was 106.1 (= 606/550 × 56 + 1.07 × 40.2) and adjusted walks was 71.8.

Williams' adjusted walk and strikeout totals can be compared to his expected totals using 3 ratios:

BB ratio = Player Adjusted BBs/Expected BBs,
SO ratio = Player Adjusted SOs/Expected SOs, and
BB-to-SO relative rate = BB ratio/SO ratio.

Players can be classified by whether these ratios exceed 1 or not:

	Ratio < 1	Ratio > 1
BB ratio	Impatient batter	Patient batter
SO ratio	Tough K victim	Easy K victim
BB-to-SO rel. rate	Eagle-eyed batter	Extended plate batter

For Williams' 1941 season, his BB ratio was 1.78 and his SO ratio was 0.47, giving him an outstanding BB-to-SO relative rate of 3.76. Thus, in 1941, Williams was a "patient, tough K victim, eagle-eyed batter."

In Tables 11.2–11.5, the 50 most extreme career performances in each category are listed.

Table 11.2   Top 50 Patient and Impatient Batters

BB ratio	Patient Batters
2.1	Max Bishop
2.0	John McGraw, Eddie Stanky
1.9	Topsy Hartsel, Roy Thomas, Billy Hamilton
1.8	Ferris Fain
1.7	Rickey Henderson, Billy North, Mike Hargrove, Eddie Yost, Miller Huggins, Joe Morgan, Dave Magadan, Gene Tenace, Roy Cullenbine,
1.6	Cupid Childs, Willie Randolph, Lu Blue, Steve Braun, Ted Williams, Roger Bresnahan, Donie Bush, Gavy Cravath, Barry Bonds
1.55	Tony Phillips, Babe Ruth, Earl Torgeson, Bud Harrelson, Jim Gilliam, Mel Ott, John Kruk, Elmer Valo, Ken Singleton, Wade Boggs, Gary Pettis, Mickey Tettleton, Greg Gross
1.5	Elbie Fletcher, Bob O'Farrell, Augie Galan, Jimmy Sheckard, Stan Hack, Frank Thomas, Butch Wynegar, Mickey Mantle, Jack Clark, Gus Suhr, Brett Butler, Dwayne Murphy

Note: Patient Batter = BB ratio > 1.

BB ratio	Impatient Batters
0.30	Shawon Dunston
0.35	Don Kolloway, Don Mueller, Damaso Garcia
0.40	Buck Weaver, Ozzie Guillen, George Stovall, Gee Walker, Art Fletcher, Jesus Alou, Vic Power, Mariano Duncan
0.45	Garret Anderson, Everett Scott, Luis Salazar, Ken Reitz, Red Dooin, Sandy Alomar Jr., Hal Chase, Tony Armas, Pete Suder, Tommy Corcoran, Doug Flynn, Rube Oldring
0.50	Eric McNair, George Bell, Joe Dugan, Hobe Ferris, Hy Myers, Enos Cabell, Dante Bichette, Manny Sanguillen, Willie Davis, Aurelio Rodriguez, Carlos Baerga, Vinny Castilla, Mark Grudzielanek, Glenn Wright, Heinie Zimmerman, Andre Dawson, Ivan Rodriguez, Bobby Richardson, Bill Buckner, Rafael Ramirez, Stuffy McInnis, Joe Pepitone, Juan Gonzalez
0.55	Tony Kubek, Carl Reynolds, Walter Holke

Note: Impatient Batter = BB ratio < 1.

Table 11.3   Top 50 Tough and Easy K Victims

SO ratio	Tough K Victims
0.30	Tony Gwynn
0.35	Nellie Fox, Joe Sewell, Gregg Jefferies
0.40	Tommy Holmes, Bill Buckner
0.45	Fernando Vina, Don Mattingly, Vic Power, Tris Speaker, Felix Millan, Eric Young, Bobby Richardson, Don Mueller, Mark Grace, Dale Mitchell
0.50	Rich Dauer, Mike Scioscia, Glenn Beckert, Frank McCormick, Lloyd Waner, Stuffy McInnis, Joe Jackson, Yogi Berra
	Joe DiMaggio, Nomar Garciaparra, Mike Greenwell, Johnny Ray, Ozzie Smith
0.55	Jim Gilliam, Rip Radcliff, Jason Kendall, Smoky Burgess, Gary Sheffield, Frankie Frisch, Edd Roush, Lance Johnson, Bill Madlock, Jesus Alou, Ernie Lombardi, Dave Cash, Andy High, Larry Doyle, Bill Dickey, Cesar Tovar, Red Schoendienst
0.60	Charlie Gehringer, Wade Boggs, Darrin Fletcher, Ted Simmons

Note: Tough K Victim = SO ratio < 1.

SO Ratio	Easy K Victims
1.95	Gary Pettis
1.90	Jose Hernandez
1.85	
1.80	
1.75	Bernie Friberg, Vince DiMaggio
1.70	Ron LeFlore
1.65	Rob Deer,
1.60	Andy Seminick
1.55	Gorman Thomas, Donn Clendenon, Woody English, Cesar Geronimo, Juan Samuel, Pete Incaviglia, Omar Moreno
1.50	Jim Hegan, Wally Post, Ray Lankford, Alex Gonzalez, Woody Held, Eddie Bressoud, Rick Monday
1.45	Rabbit Warstler, Frank O'Rourke, Dean Palmer, Eddie Joost, Dick Stuart, Jerry Priddy, Dolph Camilli, Connie Ryan, Dode Paskert, Vince Coleman, Dick Green, George Kelly, Tommie Agee, Frankie Hayes
1.40	Bob O'Farrell, Reggie Sanders, Hack Wilson, Reggie Jackson, Gavy Cravath, Tony Armas, Mariano Duncan, Bobby Bonds, Jimmy Dykes, Andres Galarraga, Frankie Crosetti, Jim Landis, Del Rice, Billy North, Gus Zernial

Note: Easy K Victim = SO ratio > 1.

Table 11.4 Top 50 Eagle-Eyed Batters

Rank	Player	Years	BB ratio	SO ratio	BB-to-SO Rel. Rate
1	Joe Sewell	1920–33	1.14	0.39	2.95
2	Jim Gilliam	1953–66	1.58	0.55	2.86
3	Tony Gwynn	1982–2001	0.90	0.32	2.85
4	Tris Speaker	1907–28	1.27	0.46	2.75
5	Mike Scioscia	1980–92	1.35	0.50	2.71
6	Wade Boggs	1982–99	1.56	0.60	2.60
7	Mark Grace	1988–2003	1.28	0.49	2.59
8	Greg Gross	1973–89	1.55	0.64	2.43
9	Ted Williams	1939–60	1.63	0.67	2.42
10	Willie Randolph	1975–92	1.67	0.69	2.41
11	Ozzie Smith	1978–96	1.29	0.54	2.41
12	Joe Morgan	1963–84	1.76	0.73	2.41
13	Barry Bonds	1986–2003	1.60	0.67	2.39
14	Eddie Collins	1906–30	1.45	0.62	2.35
15	Mike Hargrove	1974–85	1.77	0.76	2.34
16	Mickey Cochrane	1925–37	1.38	0.61	2.27
17	Elmer Valo	1940–61	1.56	0.70	2.25
18	Ferris Fain	1947–55	1.82	0.81	2.25
19	Arky Vaughan	1932–48	1.46	0.65	2.24
20	Eric Young	1992–2003	1.08	0.48	2.23
21	Gary Sheffield	1988–2003	1.26	0.57	2.20
22	Brian Giles	1995–2003	1.47	0.67	2.17
23	Tommy Holmes	1942–52	0.89	0.41	2.17
24	Gregg Jefferies	1987–2000	0.85	0.39	2.16
25	Ron Hunt	1963–74	1.25	0.62	2.03

BB-to-SO Ratio	Second 25 Players
2.00	Jackie Robinson, Nellie Fox, Stan Musial, Matt Lawton, Dave Magadan
1.95	John Olerud, Ken Oberkfell, Joe Jackson
1.90	Butch Wynegar, Rusty Staub, Rick Ferrell, Andy High, Lenny Dykstra, Tim Raines, Frank Thomas, Rickey Henderson
1.85	Charlie Gehringer, Richie Ashburn, Alvin Davis, Toby Harrah, Eddie Stanky, Jody Reed
1.80	Paul Waner, Johnny Temple, Augie Galan

Table 11.5 Top 50 Extended-Plate Batters

Rank	Player	Years	BB ratio	SO ratio	BB-to-SO Rel. Rate
1	Shawon Dunston	1985–2002	0.34	1.17	0.29
2	Mariano Duncan	1985–97	0.44	1.42	0.31
3	Tony Armas	1976–89	0.47	1.43	0.33
4	Gee Walker	1931–45	0.42	1.16	0.36
5	Pete Suder	1941–55	0.47	1.21	0.39
6	Luis Salazar	1980–92	0.46	1.17	0.39
7	Jose Hernandez	1991–2003	0.75	1.90	0.39
8	Joe Dugan	1917–31	0.50	1.27	0.40
9	Don Kolloway	1940–53	0.38	0.94	0.40
10	Glenn Wright	1924–35	0.53	1.29	0.41
11	Buck Weaver	1912–20	0.40	0.96	0.41
12	Doc Lavan	1913–24	0.60	1.41	0.42
13	Andres Galarraga	1985–2003	0.61	1.41	0.43
14	Dick Stuart	1958–69	0.64	1.48	0.44
15	Juan Samuel	1983–98	0.69	1.56	0.44
16	Aurelio Rodriguez	1967–83	0.52	1.16	0.45
17	Bill Robinson	1966–83	0.57	1.24	0.46
18	Mookie Wilson	1980–91	0.61	1.31	0.46
19	Gus Zernial	1949–59	0.65	1.40	0.46
20	Hy Myers	1909–25	0.51	1.09	0.47
21	George Kelly	1915–32	0.68	1.46	0.47
22	Lee May	1965–82	0.57	1.22	0.47
23	Bob Meusel	1920–30	0.62	1.33	0.47
24	Garry Templeton	1976–91	0.56	1.20	0.47
25	Wally Post	1949–64	0.72	1.54	0.47

BB-to-SO Ratio	Second 25 Players
0.47	Walter Holke, Dante Bichette, Ken Reitz
0.48	Pete Incaviglia, Shano Collins, Walt Dropo
0.49	Tom Paciorek, Willie Wilson, Greg Gagne
0.50	Eric McNair, Art Fletcher, Jim Hegan, Willie McGee, Alex Gonzalez
0.51	Vince DiMaggio, Enos Cabell, Jeffrey Leonard, Benito Santiago
0.52	Claudell Washington, Donn Clendenon, Dave Kingman, Damaso Garcia, Bill Skowron
0.53	Matt Williams, Ron LeFlore

Best Single-Season Bases on Balls Performances

The 100 best seasons for walks in baseball history are summarized in Table 11.6. A complete list of top seasons is given in Appendix L.7. The top 10 seasons are counted down below.

Table 11.6   Top 100 Seasons—Adjusted Bases on Balls per 550 NFPs
45 Different Players with Average Age = 29.9

Era	Seasons	Expected	Era	Seasons	Expected
1876–1900	7	9.8	1947–68	15	16.6
1901–19	14	13.4	1969–92	17	26.8
1920–46	33↑	19.5	1993–2003	14	14.0

No. of Seasons	Players with Multiple Top 100 Seasons
11	*Babe Ruth*
7	Barry Bonds, *Ted Williams*
6	Max Bishop
5	*Mickey Mantle, Mel Ott*
4	Roy Thomas
3	Jack Clark, Topsy Hartsel, Gene Tenace, Jimmy Wynn
2	Dolph Camilli, Rickey Henderson, Billy Lush, John McGraw, Jimmy Sheckard, Gary Sheffield, Eddie Stanky, Frank Thomas, *Arky Vaughan*

Notes: Hall of Fame players are listed in italics. The symbol ↑ means the number of seasons is significantly higher than expected.

See the guide to the top 100 seasons tables on page 103.

10. Mark McGwire, 1998   129.0 Adjusted BBs/550 NFPs
In the season that Mark McGwire broke Roger Maris's single-season home run record, he also set a new National League record for most walks, with 162.

9. Mickey Mantle, 1962   131.7 Adjusted BBs/550 NFPs
The year following his 1961 campaign, when Mantle and Maris combined for 115 home runs, Mantle posted his best season for bases on balls.

8. Ted Williams, 1954   133.1 Adjusted BBs/550 NFPs
Ted Williams' best season for walks cost him the 1954 batting crown. Williams' had 136 walks, but only 386 at-bats. According to the rules at the time, a batter needed 400 at-bats to qualify for the title, or to consider his shortage as all outs. Although Williams hit .345, the title was awarded to Bobby Avila, who hit .341. Under current rules, the minimum playing time is measured in plate appearances, not at-bats. With such rules, Williams would have won the batting crown.

7. Candy Nelson, 1884   **133.3 Adjusted BBs/550 NFPs**

In 1884, the number of balls needed to draw a walk was lowered from 8 to 6. Nelson exploited the new rule to double the best previous bases on balls mark—74 to 37. He also walked twice as often as the runner-up, Billy Geer, who drew 38. No other champion has enjoyed as high a ratio gap—Ruth came the closest in 1923 with a 1.73 ratio (170 to 98).

6. Jack Clark, 1987   **133.7 Adjusted BBs/550 NFPs**

Toward the end of his career, Jack Clark developed into one of the best batters at drawing a walk in baseball history. His best season, 1987, was the first of 3 straight years among the top 100.

5. Babe Ruth, 1920   **135.1 Adjusted BBs/550 NFPs**

Of Babe Ruth's 11 seasons in the top 100, this season, his first as a New York Yankee, ranks as his best. Perhaps having Lou Gehrig hitting behind him regularly from 1925 on reduced the number of walks Ruth may otherwise have received.

4. John McGraw, 1899   **138.3 Adjusted BBs/550 NFPs**

John McGraw was one of the best players at drawing a walk at the turn of the 20th century. Of his 3 top 100 seasons, this was the best.

3. Barry Bonds, 2003   **144.3 Adjusted BBs/550 NFPs**

Current baseball fans have been treated to history in the making, with Barry Bonds fashioning the best 3 seasons for drawing walks.

2. Barry Bonds, 2001   **151.3 Adjusted BBs/550 NFPs**

Just as McGwire drew a large number of walks while breaking Roger Maris's home run record, Bonds did as well in breaking McGwire's home run record. He also broke the record for most walks with 177. (Previous record holder—Ruth, with 170 in 1923.)

1. Barry Bonds, 2002   **173.6 Adjusted BBs/550 NFPs**

On the heels of Bonds' 73-home run season in 2001, pitchers pitched around Bonds in critical situations, giving Bonds another record-breaking season for walks.

Best Single-Season Strikeout Performances

The players with the lowest SO totals tend to be singles hitters who exercise a great deal of bat control and hit for high averages. Three such players—Fox, Gwynn, and Sewell—account for 27 of the top 62 positions. A complete list of top seasons is given in Appendix L.8. The top 11 are given below. Players separated by at most 0.1 SOs/550 NFPs are given tied ranks (see the guide at the top of page 104).

Table 11.7 Top 100 Seasons—Adjusted Strikeouts per 550 NFPs
58 Different Players with Average Age = 30.2

Era	Seasons	Expected	Era	Seasons	Expected
1876–1900	5	6.9	1947–68	25	18.5
1901–19	4	7.0	1969–92	19↓	30.0
1920–46	19	21.8	1993–2003	28↑	15.7

No. of Seasons	Players with Multiple Top 100 Seasons
11	*Nellie Fox*, Tony Gwynn
6	*Joe Sewell*
3	Gregg Jefferies, *Ozzie Smith*
2	*Lou Boudreau*, Bill Buckner, Mark Grace, Ozzie Guillen, Lance Johnson, Stuffy McInnis, Don Mueller, Juan Pierre, Vic Power, Bobby Richardson, Red Schoendienst, John Ward, Eric Young

Notes: Hall of Fame players are listed in italics. The symbol ↑ (↓) means the number of seasons is significantly higher (lower) than expected.

See the guide to the top 100 seasons tables on page 103.

10T. Tony Gwynn, 1991   14.8 Adjusted SOs/550 NFPs

The first of Tony Gwynn's 5 seasons among the top 11.

10T. Charlie Hollocher, 1922   14.8 Adjusted SOs/550 NFPs

Charlie is the youngest hitter among the top 10, at age 26. His career was a short one, with this being his final qualifying season.

9. Tony Gwynn, 1998   13.8 Adjusted SOs/550 NFPs

In his last qualifying season in 1998, Gwynn, fanned 18 times in 496 NFPs, while smacking 16 home runs (12.4 adjusted).

8. Ozzie Smith, 1993   13.6 Adjusted SOs/550 NFPs

In the last full year of his career, Ozzie had his best season for making contact.

7. Don Mueller, 1956   13.4 Adjusted SOs/550 NFPs

Like his peers in the top 10, Mueller demonstrates that players must learn how to avoid strikeouts. His stellar season, at the "young" age of 29, was the next-to-last qualifying season for him.

6. Joe Sewell, 1929   13.2 Adjusted SOs/550 NFPs

The top 6 positions on the list are shared between Joe Sewell and Tony Gwynn. In 1929, Sewell struck out 4 times in 626 NFPs, while working pitchers for 48 walks and hitting 7 home runs (13.2 adjusted).

5. Tony Gwynn, 1996   13.0 Adjusted SOs/550 NFPs

In 1996, Gwynn struck out 17 times in 490 NFPs. There are 2 main reasons why Gwynn's season edged out Sewell's 1929 campaign. First, the strikeout rate of regulars was 2.6 times higher in 1996. Second, a stronger transformation adjustment was needed for SOs before 1947.

4. Tony Gwynn, 1992   **12.5 Adjusted SOs/550 NFPs**

Gwynn had 16 SOs in 546 NFPs, while netting 6 home runs and 46 bases on balls.

3. Tony Gwynn, 1995   **10.0 Adjusted SOs/550 NFPs**

Tony Gwynn ranked among the top 52 single-season performances in lowest strike-outs in all 10 of his final qualifying seasons, from 1989 to 1998, with 9 among the top 25. This is a remarkable performance by a remarkable hitter. Gwynn's best season was 1995, when he struck out 15 times in 570 NFPs, while hitting 9 home runs and walking 35 times.

2. Joe Sewell, 1933   **8.7 Adjusted SOs/550 NFPs**

In his final season, Joe Sewell struck out 4 times in 595 NFPs, hit 2 homers, and netted 71 walks.

1. Joe Sewell, 1932   **6.8 Adjusted SOs/550 NFPs**

This season was truly remarkable. In 1932, Joe Sewell struck out an anemic 3 times in 559 NFPs while claiming 56 bases on balls. More significantly, Sewell hit 11 home runs (13.3 adjusted).

Personal Note: Tony Gwynn's 1997 season is 19th best. I met Gwynn on July 28, 1997, the night he attained his final "productive career" at-bat for batting average. Prior to the game, I told him that after my statistical adjustments, he had edged out Ty Cobb for the best career BA in history. In his first at-bat, Gwynn backed out twice on the pitcher before striking out. I worried that I had jinxed him. The perfection of these top performances is so exacting that that SO cost him 6 spots on the list.

Best Productive Career Bases on Balls Performances (9000 NFPs)

Complete lists of the top 100 players for career walks and adjusted BBs/550 NFPs are given in Appendix M.7. The top 11 are given below. Players separated by at most 0.1 BBs/550 NFPs are given tied ranks.

10T. Yank Robinson, 1882–92   **94.6 Adjusted BBs/550 NFPs**

Robinson is the first of 5 players from the 19th century or deadball era in the list of players with the highest career walk rates. While the 18 players who place in the top 100 is slightly below the fraction of qualifying players (23%) from these two eras, their best players crowd the top spots.

10T. Eddie Stanky, 1943–1953   **94.6 Adjusted BBs/550 NFPs**

Eddie Stanky had only 7 seasons in which he accumulated at least 400 NFPs. In each case, he placed among the top 5 players in bases on balls for the season, finishing on top 3 times.

10T. Bill Joyce, 1890–98   94.7 Adjusted BBs/550 NFPs

Of the 5 early era players in this list, Joyce had the strongest batting numbers. His 70 home runs in 3310 at-bats top those of the other 4 players, who hit a total of 67 home runs in more than 18,000 at-bats.

8. John McGraw, 1891–1906   98.9 Adjusted BBs/550 NFPs

John McGraw did not have great power. He was all about getting on base, though. By combining a strong batting average with an exceptional base on balls rate, McGraw holds the best adjusted on-base percentage of the early eras fivesome.

7. Gene Tenace, 1969–83   99.6 Adjusted BBs/550 NFPs

One might expect catchers to pepper the list of premier walkers, since they have the closest looks at how umpires call the strike zone. However, Gene Tenace is the only catcher among the top 10.

6. Roy Thomas, 1899–1911   100.2 Adjusted BBs/550 NFPs

Roy Thomas had the longest career of the 5 early players—with 5926 at-bats and 1024 walks. Thomas had the weakest power of the group but regularly paced the National League in walks, winning 6 times in 7 seasons between 1900 and 1907.

5. Topsy Hartsel, 1898–1911   100.6 Adjusted BBs/550 NFPs

Topsy Hartsel was the American League counterpart to Roy Thomas. In his final 10 seasons, Hartsel played with the Philadelphia Athletics, the cross-town rivals to Thomas's Phillies. Hartsel won 5 walk titles between 1902 and 1908.

4. Ted Williams, 1939–60   102.9 Adjusted BBs/550 NFPs

One of the real strengths of Williams' game was to know the strike zone. By waiting for favorable pitches to hit, Williams racked up some of the best averages produced in baseball history. His lofty walk average attests to how often pitchers chose not to give him something to hit.

3. Barry Bonds, 1986–   103.4 Adjusted BBs/550 NFPs

Through 2000, Barry Bonds had already attained a career's worth of NFPs—with 9059. With a solid reputation for having among the best walk rates in baseball history, Bonds ranked 13th on this adjusted list. Then, he took the free pass to unheard of levels in 2001–2003, catapulting him into the third spot.

2. Babe Ruth, 1914–35   103.6 Adjusted BBs/550 NFPs

Many writers have described Ruth as "swinging from his heels," as he tried to crush home runs. Ruth also has among the highest adjusted strikeout rates. However, Ruth had a fair dose of plate discipline. With Gehrig hitting behind him, a base on balls was certainly of value to the Yankees. Ruth took his share, good enough for second place on the all-time list.

1. Max Bishop, 1924–35   104.5 Adjusted BBs/550 NFPs

Max Bishop's nickname, "Camera Eye," is certainly apt. As an underaverage hitter with little power, pitchers would not have feared pitching to Bishop. However, as the leadoff hitter for the Philadelphia Athletics, with Mickey Cochrane, Al Simmons, and Jimmie Foxx hitting behind him, Bishop didn't allow pitchers to get away with missing the plate. Walks were such a part of his game that in 5 times as a regular Bishop had more walks than hits.

Best Productive Career Strikeout Performances (9000 NFPs) (3000 NFPs–Minimum to Consider)

List of the 100 players for highest career strikeouts and lowest adjusted SOs/550 NFPs are given in Appendix M.8. The top 11 are given below. Players separated by at most 0.1 SOs/550 NFPs are given tied ranks.

10T. Eric Young, 1992–   **29.5 Adjusted SOs/550 NFPs**
(Adj BA = .271, Rank = 530; Adj HRs/500 = 3.8, Rank = 1030; Adj BBs/550 = 50.1, Rank = 542)
Of the 11 batters with the lowest strikeout rates, 6 are second basemen, including Eric Young.

10T. Glenn Beckert, 1965–75   **29.5 Adjusted SOs/550 NFPs**
(Adj BA = .278, Rank = 362; Adj HRs/500 = 2.2, Rank = 1094; Adj BBs/550 = 28.1, Rank = 1071)
Glenn Beckert was a contact hitter who has one of the best adjusted career batting averages for second basemen but with very little power and an unimpressive base on balls rate, features that favor being among the best at avoiding strikeouts.

9. Bill Buckner, 1969–90   **29.3 Adjusted SOs/550 NFPs**
(Adj BA = .287, Rank = 208; Adj HRs/500 = 9.6, Rank = 663; Adj BBs/550 = 26.1, Rank = 1094)
According to *Baseball: The Biographical Encyclopedia*:

> Buckner was a lefthanded contact hitter who rarely struck out, but who produced only middle infielder offensive statistics while playing a primary hitting position.

8. Felix Millan, 1966–77   **28.6 Adjusted SOs/550 NFPs**
(Adj BA = .276, Rank = 410; Adj HRs/500 = 2.2, Rank = 1090; Adj BBs/550 = 29.5, Rank = 1047)
Felix Millan was a good-hitting second baseman who played with the Atlanta Braves and New York Mets. *Baseball: The Biographical Encyclopedia* says of Millan: "Felix Millan concentrated on making contact at the plate, using a distinctive batting stance and choking up higher on the bat than any player in the modern era."

7. Bobby Richardson, 1955–66   **28.5 Adjusted SOs/550 NFPs**
(Adj BA = .273, Rank = 494; Adj HRs/500 = 2.1, Rank = 1097; Adj BBs/550 = 23.5, Rank = 1119)
Like Beckert and Millan, Bobby Richardson was a singles hitter who had between 5000 and 6000 lifetime at-bats, and played partly during the 1960s. All have nearly identical career HRs/500 rates.

6. Tommy Holmes, 1942–52   28.1 Adjusted SOs/550 NFPs

(Adj BA = .295, Rank = 97; Adj HRs/500 = 11.1, Rank = 569; Adj BBs/550 = 45.4, Rank = 679)

Tommy Holmes was a Boston Braves outfielder who had a relatively short career. His greatest season came in 1945, when he led the National League in hits, doubles, home runs (with 28), and slugging average, while striking out only 9 times. Holmes has the best adjusted home run rate among the top 10 players for low strikeouts.

5. Fernando Vina, 1993–   27.5 Adjusted SOs/550 NFPs

(Adj BA = .275, Rank = 445; Adj HRs/500 = 2.6, Rank = 1075; Adj BBs/550 = 30.8, Rank = 1034)

Fernando Vina, a second baseman, is currently active.

4. Gregg Jefferies, 1987–2000   26.7 Adjusted SOs/550 NFPs

(Adj BA = .284, Rank = 255; Adj HRs/500 = 9.8, Rank = 649; Adj BBs/550 = 42.6, Rank = 752)

Gregg Jefferies played at least 100 games at first base, left field, second base, and third base over his career. Like most of the other players on this list, Jefferies hit for a good average but did not hit for power.

3. Joe Sewell, 1920–33   25.0 Adjusted SOs/550 NFPs

(Adj BA =.275, Rank = 448; Adj HRs/500 = 7.3, Rank = 826; Adj BBs/550 = 55.9, Rank = 394)

Sewell's strikeout rate dropped at every milestone NFP count throughout his career. Sewell ended his career with 7 strikeouts over 2 seasons with 1154 NFPs. These 2 seasons, 1932 and 1933, as mentioned earlier, were the best 2 seasons ever for avoiding strikeouts.

2. Nellie Fox, 1947–65   22.0 Adjusted SOs/550 NFPs

(Adj BA=.289, Rank = 175; Adj HRs/500 = 1.7, Rank = 1108; Adj BBs/550 = 35.0, Rank = 951)

The sixth second baseman in this list, Nellie Fox fits the classic profile of a player with few strikeouts; he hit for a high average but without much power. In fact, Fox holds the record for leading the league in singles 8 times. He also had the fewest strikeouts in the league 11 times, leading to his second-place finish.

1. Tony Gwynn, 1982–2001   19.7 Adjusted SOs/550 NFPs

(Adj BA = .338, Rank = 1; Adj HRs/500 = 5.9, Rank = 898; Adj BBs/550 = 43.5, Rank = 726)

Prior to Gwynn, Sewell and Fox were the players most associated with not striking out. In the modern game, strikeouts are more common and the casual fan may miss the fact that Gwynn was even better at making contact. Gwynn, who also has the best adjusted career batting average in history, can certainly lay claim to be the best contact hitter in baseball history.

CHAPTER 12

Stealing the Show

Adjusting Stolen
Base Totals

My research for this book occasionally involved visits to the University of North Carolina library. One day, I was looking for a book on the history of base stealing. I must confess to having felt rather sheepish, however, walking out of the library with a book whose title blared "*Stolen!*" Even worse, months later I received an overdue notice and, where the book title normally appears, the word, *Stolen!*, confronted me.

Stolen!, written by Russell Roberts, is devoted to the history of base stealing. Through text and stories, Roberts describes the players and events responsible for shaping the bathtub-shaped raw stolen base average curves—high, then low, then high again—shown in Chapter 3. Stolen bases were in their heyday at the outset of the game's history through most of the deadball era. Between 1901 and 1917, at least three quarters of the non-catcher regulars had double-digit stolen base totals. Although stolen bases were in decline before the demise of the deadball era, the decline really steepened at that juncture, particularly in the National League.

The decline continued into the first half of the lively ball era and remained low from the 1930s through the 1950s. Among the ballplayers in these 3 decades, Jackie Robinson and Willie Mays won a combined 6 stolen base titles—but their winning totals ranged only from 27 to 40. Both had reputations as being speedy, serious threats on the basepaths. Thus, their low totals clearly reflect the fact that they played in an era when managers did not greatly encourage stolen bases.

A trio of players—Luis Aparicio of the Chicago White Sox, Maury Wills of the Los Angeles Dodgers, and Lou Brock of the St. Louis Cardinals—was largely responsible for resurrecting the stolen base as an important offensive weapon in the 1950s to 1970s. Rickey Henderson, who played principally with the Oakland A's and New York Yankees, later took the stolen base to new heights by stealing a record 130 bases in 1982. Although the league stolen base averages are higher than they were in the doldrums days of the 1930s through mid-1950s, they will probably never rival those early days of base thievery.

Of the 9 basic offensive events examined in this book, only stolen bases are not adjusted for a ballpark effect. Most likely, there are factors that render one park better than another for accumulating stolen bases, such as the characteristics of the sliding area and the type of grass (artificial or natural) between the bases. Stolen bases are thought to be more important in low-scoring parks. Because base stealing is an elective decision in a team's offensive arsenal, managerial decision is perhaps the most significant factor impacting the ballpark effect. In today's game, team totals are largely attributable to only a few players. Thus, home and away data, which are not yet readily available, are needed to obtain good park effect estimates.

Speed or Power?

Table 12.1 shows the raw averages of regular players by era across baseball history for 4 events. Triples and stolen bases depend on speed. Triples have been in steady decline since the deadball era. Stolen bases declined greatly at the end of the deadball era, but have rebounded somewhat in recent years. Home runs and strikeouts—both power-associated events—have both generally increased over time. Although stolen bases and home runs moved in dramatically opposite directions at the end of the deadball era, in today's game, home runs are at all-time highs, while stolen bases are at historically moderate levels.

Table 12.1   Speed Events versus Power Events over Baseball History

First Year	1876	1901	1920	1947	1963	1969	1977	1993
Last Year	1900	1919	1946	1962	1968	1976	1992	2003
3Bs/500 ABs	8.7	7.7	6.6	4.6	3.9	3.5	3.5	3.0
SBs/550 NFPs	26.0	20.8	7.6	5.2	7.0	9.3	12.0	10.3
HRs/500 ABs	3.5	2.6	8.0	13.8	13.3	12.2	12.8	16.7
SOs/550 NFPs	35	44	38	56	76	69	73	87

The Difficulty in Cross-Era Evaluation of Base-Stealing Ability

The stolen base is the most difficult basic offensive event to adjust for. The key complication is the non-normality of stolen base data, especially since players have failed to steal a single base in more than 10% of *regular player-seasons* since 1947. Appendix E describes the major analytical issues.

The distribution of stolen base averages also differs by league. Since 1963, different *tranformation powers* are used for the National League and the American League. Why? During the 1960s, the National League had a more skewed distribution and required a more severe transformation power (0.15 versus 0.20).

The situation flip-flopped in the 1970s, though, with the Designated Hitter rule. Since then, the National League has been the base stealer's league. With lower run scoring, National League managers often manufacture runs through stolen bases; the

American League relies more on Orioles manager Earl Weaver's famed "three-run homer." The American League stolen base rate from 1977 to 1992 was 25% less than for the National League (9.7 versus 12.9 per 550 NFPs; see Table 3.4).

Best Single-Season Stolen Base Performances

The top 100 seasons for stolen bases are summarized in Table 12.2. The complete list of seasons is given in Appendix L.9.

Table 12.2   Top 100 Seasons—Adjusted Stolen Bases per 550 NFPs
57 Different Players with Average Age = 27.3

Era	Seasons	Expected	Era	Seasons	Expected
1876–1900	10	9.0	1947–68	22	16.7
1901–19	16	13.5	1969–92	20	27.0
1920–46	23	19.7	1993–2003	9	14.1

No. of Seasons	Players with Multiple Top 100 Seasons
6	*Luis Aparicio*, Rickey Henderson
5	Max Carey, George Case
4	Bert Campaneris, *Ty Cobb*, Vince Coleman, *Billy Hamilton*, Maury Wills
3	*Eddie Collins*, *Kiki Cuyler*
2	*Lou Brock*, Tom Goodwin, Kenny Lofton, *Jackie Robinson*, Jimmy Sheckard, *George Sisler*

Notes: Hall of Fame players are listed in italics.

See the guide to the top 100 seasons tables on page 103.

9T. Luis Aparicio, 1959   **94.2 Adjusted SBs/550 NFPs**
Chicago White Sox shortstop Luis Aparicio helped revitalize the stolen base with 56 in 1959, leading the "Go-Go Sox" to the American League pennant. The 56 stolen bases nearly doubled his league-leading 1958 total and was the third highest total since 1920, behind Chapman's 1931 and Case's 1943 seasons, who both pilfered 61 bases. From 1956 to 1964, Aparicio won 9 straight stolen base titles.

9T. Luis Aparicio, 1964   **94.3 Adjusted SBs/550 NFPs**
In his final year as stolen base champion, Aparicio posted his best mark, barely topping his 1959 performance.

8. Otis Nixon, 1991   **95.0 Adjusted SBs/550 NFPs**
In 1991, Nixon stole 72 bases for the Atlanta Braves in only 450 net-facing pitchers.

7. George Case, 1939   **95.9 Adjusted SBs/550 NFPs**
Washington Senator George Case was the most significant base stealer after the dead-ball era and base stealing rise in the late 1950s. From 1939 to 1943, Case won 5 con-

secutive stolen base crowns. Unfortunately, base stealing took a heavy toll on his body. Russell Roberts in *Stolen!* writes:

> Case was considered the fastest player in baseball; some even said he was the fastest ever to play the game. Clyde Milan declared Case "faster than Ty Cobb, Eddie Collins, [and] Max Carey." Senators owner Clark Griffith thought that Case was the swiftest player he had ever seen, and predicted that he would ultimately beat Cobb's single-season record of 96 stolen bases.

6. Sam Rice, 1920   96.5 Adjusted SBs/550 NFPs

The stolen base average declined steadily during the latter half of the deadball era. Bucking that trend was Sam Rice's total of 63 stolen bases—a total that was not exceeded until Wills' 104 stolen bases in 1962. In sharp contrast with the other top 10 finishers, this was the only stolen base crown that Rice garnered.

5. George Case, 1944   97.0 Adjusted SBs/550 NFPs

In 1944, George Case lost his 5-year stranglehold on most stolen bases in the American League to Snuffy Stirnweiss. However, Stirnweiss needed 40% more NFPs to gain 7 more stolen bases than Case—56 to 49. Only Case and Luis Aparicio placed 2 seasons among the 10 best.

4. Rickey Henderson, 1982   106.2 Adjusted SBs/550 NFPs

Rickey Henderson's 130 stolen bases in 1982 set the modern stolen base record, surpassing the 118 steals that Lou Brock obtained in 1974. Henderson stole 76 more bases than the second highest finisher, Damaso Garcia. From 1980 to 1991, Henderson won 11 of 12 American League stolen base crowns.

3. Maury Wills, 1962   107.2 Adjusted SBs/550 NFPs

In 1962, Maury Will's raw total of 104 stolen bases set a new 20th century record, surpassing Cobb's 1915 total. Will's total was more than 3 times higher than the second highest—32 stolen bases by Dodger teammate Willie Davis.

2. Max Carey, 1918   112.3 Adjusted SBs/550 NFPs

Pittsburgh Pirate Max Carey led the National League in stolen bases 10 times. Although his 58 stolen bases was not his highest raw total, it was a standout season given the rapid decline occurring in stolen bases throughout the decade.

1. Ty Cobb, 1915   116.3 Adjusted SBs/550 NFPs

In the deadball era when the number of players with significant stolen base totals was relatively high, Cobb's raw 96 stolen bases were nearly double that of the Fritz Maisel's second-place total of 51. Between 1907 and 1917, Cobb won 6 stolen base titles.

Best Productive Career Stolen Base Performances (5000 NFPs)

Complete lists of the top 100 players for career stolen bases and adjusted SBs/550 NFPs are given in Appendix M.9. The top 11 are given below. Players separated by at most 0.1 SBs/550 NFPs are given tied ranks (see the guide at the top of page 104).

10T. Lou Brock, 1961–79   62.5 Adjusted SBs/550 NFPs

Lou Brock won 8 stolen base crowns in 9 seasons from 1966 to 1974. His final 4 titles, including his best season in 1974, all came after his 5000th NFP. Consequently, Brock's milestone peak occurred on his 9000th NFP and his improvement lifted his rate by 1.5 adjusted SBs/550 NFPs.

10T. Billy Hamilton, 1888–1901   62.6 Adjusted SBs/550 NFPs

Billy Hamilton was the greatest base stealer of the 19th century. Four times Hamilton stole 100 or more bases in a season, leading the league each time. He held the lifetime career stolen base total before Lou Brock surpassed him.

9. Ty Cobb, 1905–28   63.3 Adjusted SBs/550 NFPs

Ty Cobb is well known for his base stealing exploits, especially with spikes flying. Perhaps the fear factor Cobb introduced helped raise his stolen base rate. Cobb won 6 stolen base titles in his career.

8. Tom Goodwin, 1991–   65.8 Adjusted SBs/550 NFPs

In his 7 years as a regular, Tom Goodwin finished among the top 3 stealers on 5 occasions.

7. Bert Campaneris, 1964–83   66.0 Adjusted SBs/550 NFPs

Bert Campaneris was the fleet-footed shortstop on the Athletics, over the years when they moved from Kansas City to Oakland. Between 1965 and 1972, Campaneris won 6 American League stolen base crowns. His highest seasonal total was 62 in 1968, but Campaneris receives a boost from his era of play.

6. Otis Nixon, 1983–99   69.4 Adjusted SBs/550 NFPs

Otis Nixon had a suitcase-carrying career, playing for 9 different teams over 17 years. While never winning a stolen base title, Nixon stole bases with a consistency that netted him sixth place on the career list.

5. Maury Wills, 1959–72   71.4 Adjusted SBs/550 NFPs

Maury Wills furthered the revitalization of the stolen base on the heels of Aparicio's exploits. Wills won 6 stolen base titles in his first 6 full seasons, with 1962 ranking third best in history.

4. Vince Coleman, 1985–97   73.0 Adjusted SBs/550 NFPs

Vince Coleman had a relatively brief career of 5883 NFPs. He burst on the scene immediately, though, winning the stolen base crown in each of his first 6 seasons, all with the St. Louis Cardinals.

3. George Case, 1937–47   74.9 Adjusted SBs/550 NFPs

George Case, principally a Washington Senator, was the most significant base stealer after the end of the deadball era and before the rise of the base stealer in the late 1950s. From 1939 to 1943, Case won 5 consecutive stolen base crowns. Unfortunately, base stealing took a heavy toll on his body. Russell Roberts in *Stolen!* writes:

Case was considered the fastest player in baseball; some even said he was the fastest ever to play the game. Clyde Milan declared Case "faster than Ty Cobb, Eddie Collins, [and] Max Carey." Senators owner Clark Griffith thought that Case was the swiftest player he had ever seen, and predicted that he would ultimately beat Cobb's single-season record of 96 stolen bases.

2. Luis Aparicio, 1956–73   **75.1 Adjusted SBs/550 NFPs**

Luis Aparicio topped the American League in stolen bases in each of his first 9 seasons. In the first 3 years, Aparicio's total ranged from 21 to 29. In the next 6 stolen base championship years, he averaged 48 stolen bases, bringing the stolen base back into prominence as an offensive weapon in baseball.

1. Rickey Henderson, 1979–   **78.3 Adjusted SBs/550 NFPs**

Rickey Henderson holds the record for both most stolen bases in one season (130, in 1982) and for a career. He has also won a record 12 stolen base titles. Further work is needed in solidifying the cross-era comparisons of base stealers. Clearly, though, Henderson is among the greatest in the game's history.

CHAPTER 13

Putting It All Together

First, a Look at
Traditional Measures

So far in this book, we have looked at the performance of players for 9 offensive events. To get an overall view of a player's offensive capabilities, however, we need to combine the information somehow. In the next chapter, I will present my approach, called *Event-Specific Batting Runs* (ESBRs).

Three Derived Offensive Events and a Basic One

Batting Runs is the principal formula that Thorn and Palmer use to rate a player batting performance. However, Pete Palmer also provided a simplified way to closely approximate Batting Runs by taking the sum of 2 averages that are commonly available to baseball fans — *on-base percentage* (OBP) and *slugging average* (SLG), where:

$$\text{On-base percentage} = (H + BB + HBP)/(AB + BB + HBP)$$

$$\text{Slugging average} = (1B + 2 \times 2B + 3 \times 3B + 4 \times HR)/AB.$$

The sum of the two averages is called *on-base-plus-slugging* (OPS).

These three derived offensive events — OBP, SLG, and OPS — are traditional summaries of offensive baseball performance. Since each of the basic offensive events has been separately adjusted for park and era effects, adjusted OPS as calculated in this book is very close to ESBRs per 550 NFPs. Thus, in this chapter, the 10 best single-season and career performances are given for OBP and SLG; in the next chapter, the OPS values for the 10 best players for ESBRs/550 NFPs are indicated.

A 10th basic offensive event, hit-by-pitch (HBP), is part of the formulas for on-base percentage and ESBRs. This is a relatively minor event in baseball. In recent seasons, regular players have gotten hit by pitches about twice per year. There are a handful of players, however, who have a great knack for getting hit. For example, Ron Hunt was hit 50 times in 1971. These occurrences certainly had an impact on his offen-

Table 13.1   Top 100 Seasons—Adjusted Hit-by-Pitches per 550 NFPs
                    59 Different Players with Average Age = 29.1

No. of Seasons	Players with Multiple Top 100 Seasons
7	Don Baylor
6	Ron Hunt, Minnie Minoso
5	*Hughie Jennings*, Tommy Tucker
4	Frankie Crosetti
3	Dan McGann
2	Craig Biggio, Steve Evans, *Carlton Fisk*, Art Fletcher, Bill Freehan, Andres Galarraga, Bucky Harris, Buck Herzog, Jason Kendall, Chet Lemon, Curt Welch

Note: Hall of Fame players are listed in italics.

Table 13.2   Top 10 Single-Season Performances for Hit-by-Pitch

Rank	Player	Year	Adj. HBPs/550 NFPs
1	Ron Hunt	1971	34.6
2	Don Baylor	1987	27.5
3	Ron Hunt	1973	25.2
4	Hughie Jennings	1896	23.0
5	Ron Hunt	1972	22.3
6	Don Baylor	1985	20.9
7	Don Baylor	1986	20.6
8	Don Baylor	1984	19.7
9	Ron Hunt	1968	18.3
10	Hughie Jennings	1897	18.1

Table 13.3   Top 10 Productive Career Performances for Hit-by-Pitch

Rank	Player	Year	Adj. HBP/550 NFPs
1	Ron Hunt	1963–74	18.1
2	Don Baylor	1970–88	13.4
3	Hughie Jennings	1891–1909, 1912, 1918	12.9
4	Minnie Minoso	1949–64, 1976, 1980	11.0
5	Dan McGann	1896–1908	10.6
6	Frankie Crosetti	1932–48	10.5
7	Tommy Tucker	1887–99	10.4
8	Fernando Vina	1993–	10.3
9	Jason Kendall	1996–	10.1
10	Kid Elberfeld	1898–1911, 1914	10.0

sive output that year. Tables 13.1–13.3 give a snapshot of the leading seasons and careers for being hit by a pitch.

Best Single Seasons for On-Base Percentage

Now, we consider the best seasons for on-base percentage (OBP). A complete list of top seasons is given in Appendix L.10. A countdown of the top 10 seasons is given below. Players separated by at most 0.0002 are given tied ranks (see the guide at the top of page 104).

Table 13.4   Top 100 Seasons—Adjusted On-Base Percentage
45 Different Players with Average Age = 29.6

Era	Seasons	Expected	Era	Seasons	Expected
1876–1900	7	9.9	1947–68	20	16.5
1901–19	5↓	13.4	1969–92	20	26.8
1920–46	21	19.4	1993–2003	27↑	14.0

No. of Seasons	Players with Multiple Top 100 Seasons
11	*Ted Williams*
10	*Babe Ruth*
7	Barry Bonds
6	*Mickey Mantle*, Frank Thomas
4	Wade Boggs
3	Jeff Bagwell, *Lou Gehrig, Billy Hamilton, Rogers Hornsby*
2	*George Brett*, Jason Giambi, Tony Gwynn, Edgar Martinez, John McGraw, Mark McGwire, *Joe Morgan*, John Olerud, *Carl Yastrzemski*

Notes: Hall of Fame players are listed in italics. The symbol ↑ (↓) means the number of seasons is significantly higher (lower) than expected.

See the guide to the top 100 seasons tables on page 103.

10. Babe Ruth, 1920   .495 Adjusted OBP
(Adj BA = .327, Rank = 312; Adj BBs/550 = 135.1, Rank = 5)
In his first season as a Yankee, Ruth more than doubled the old home run mark (59 vs. 29), set by himself a year earlier, and claimed the 5th best season for walks and the 10th best for OBP.

9. Ted Williams, 1954   .497 Adjusted OBP
(Adj BA = .330, Rank = 246; Adj BBs/550 = 133.1, Rank = 8)
This list is dominated by players with exceedingly high walk averages, since there is much more spread among the best seasons for bases on balls averages than for batting averages. The 10th and 200th best adjusted bases on balls averages differ by 57 points (.235 vs. .178), compared to 33 points (.364 vs. .331) for batting averages.

8. Babe Ruth, 1923 .498 Adjusted OBP
(Adj BA = .344, Rank = 75; Adj BBs/550 = 124.8, Rank = 16)

In his first season in Yankee Stadium, Ruth fashioned a marvelous season. It is the first of 5 on this list in which both the batting and walk averages placed among the top 100.

7. Mickey Mantle, 1957 .503 Adjusted OBP
(Adj BA = .357, Rank = 18; Adj BBs/550 = 123.3, Rank = 19)

In a very balanced year that ranks among the top 20 for both batting average and walk average, Mantle was narrowly beaten by Red Sox rival Ted Williams for the best adjusted OBP for the season. Both are among the best seasons ever mounted.

5T. John McGraw, 1899 .504 Adjusted OBP
(Adj BA = .328, Rank = 290; Adj BBs/550 = 138.3, Rank = 4)

The only non-slugger among the top 10, John McGraw combined his skills of hitting for high average and drawing a walk, fashioning a season that has stood the test of time well.

5T. Ted Williams, 1957 .504 Adjusted OBP
(Adj BA = .366, Rank = 8; Adj BBs/550 = 114.4, Rank = 36)

Ted Williams and Barry Bonds both crack this prestigious list 3 times, achieving the third at age 38.

3T. Ted Williams, 1941 .512 Adjusted OBP
(Adj BA = .370, Rank = 6; Adj BBs/550 = 116.0, Rank = 28)

Until Barry Bonds' amazing 2001–2003 seasons, this season set the standard for getting on base. In a season in which Joe DiMaggio set a record for hitting in 56 straight games and was on-base in 74 straight games, Williams had a 69 consecutive game on-base streak of his own, noted Herm Krabbenhoft in *The Baseball Research Journal*.

3T. Barry Bonds, 2001 .512 Adjusted OBP
(Adj BA = .320, Rank = 535; Adj BBs/550 = 151.3, Rank = 2)

This is the first season since 1957 to crack the top 10. Bonds achieved this position by setting a new record for the best walk average, exceeding the old mark (set a century earlier by John McGraw) by 25 points.

2. Barry Bonds, 2003 .518 Adjusted OBP
(Adj BA = .334, Rank = 186; Adj BBs/550 = 144.3, Rank = 3)

In the twilight of his career, Bonds has established the best 3 seasons for OBP in baseball history.

1. Barry Bonds, 2002 .574 Adjusted OBP
(Adj BA = .365, Rank = 9; Adj BBs/550 = 173.6, Rank = 1)

Bonds smashed the mark he set for walks per 550 NFPs in 2001 by 22. In addition, he won his first batting title, with the seventh best adjusted all-time batting average. This picture-perfect season for OBP may never be broken.

Best Single-Seasons for Slugging Average

Slugging average is the second component of OPS, and the component that has a greater influence on which players have the highest OPS rankings. As we will soon see (values in small type on pages 181–82), one of the 10 best seasons for OPS had a 1st-ranked OBP season as a component. However, the lowest slugging average component to rank among the top 10 for OPS is 26th. Thus, this list deserves special scrutiny. The complete list of top 100 seasons is given in Appendix L.11.

Table 13.5   Top 100 Seasons—Adjusted Slugging Average
53 Different Players with Average Age = 28.5

Era	Seasons	Expected	Era	Seasons	Expected
1876–1900	10	9.9	1947–68	18	16.5
1901–19	15	13.4	1969–92	10↓	26.8
1920–46	30↑	19.4	1993–2003	17	14.0

No. of Seasons	Players with Multiple Top 100 Seasons
11	*Babe Ruth*
7	*Ted Williams*
6	Barry Bonds
5	*Rogers Hornsby*
4	*Joe DiMaggio*
3	*Ty Cobb, Ed Delahanty, Lou Gehrig, Mickey Mantle*
2	Dick Allen, Albert Belle, *Jimmie Foxx, Nap Lajoie, Willie Mays*, Mark McGwire, *Frank Robinson, Willie Stargell*, Harry Stovey, *Honus Wagner*

Notes: Hall of Fame players are listed in italics. The symbol ↑ (↓) means the number of seasons is significantly higher (lower) than expected.

See the guide to the top 100 seasons tables on page 103.

9T. Ed Delahanty, 1893   .726 Adjusted Slugging Average
In 1893, the pitcher's box was moved from 45 feet to 60 feet, 6 inches from home plate. Big Ed Delahanty responded to the change with delight, achieving one of the best seasons ever produced. He won the home run title with 19 in a bad park for homers. Given the low league home run rate in 1893, his adjusted home run total places ninth.

9T. Jeff Bagwell, 1994   .726 Adjusted Slugging Average
Bagwell's only year in the top 100 slugging seasons was a monster year, ranking fourth in TPR per 150 games.

8. Rogers Hornsby, 1922   .728 Adjusted Slugging Average
The third of 6 straight seasons in which Hornsby led the National League in both batting and slugging, he hit a career high 42 home runs, while driving in 152.

7. Babe Ruth, 1923   .739 Adjusted Slugging Average

While Hornsby was dominating the National League, Ruth was enthroned in the American League. Over a 5-year period from 1919 to 1923, Ruth placed 4 seasons among the top 7 all-time bests.

6. Barry Bonds, 2003   .750 Adjusted Slugging Average

Barry Bonds has 3 consecutive seasons among the top 6, as does one other player—Babe Ruth.

5. Babe Ruth, 1921   .768 Adjusted Slugging Average

In 1921, Ruth produced 171 RBIs while scoring 177 runs, both career highs. In so doing, he capped the greatest-ever 3-year stretch for a player.

4. Babe Ruth, 1919   .769 Adjusted Slugging Average

Interestingly, Ruth's adjusted slugging average for 1919 beat that of his 1920 and 1921 seasons, even though the raw 1919 slugging average was 190 points shy. This major change reflects how significant the shift for Ruth was from the most difficult home run park in the American League (Fenway) to the best home run park (Polo Grounds).

3. Babe Ruth, 1920   .801 Adjusted Slugging Average

The year 1920 was the one in which Babe Ruth personally outhomered each of the non-Yankee American League teams. Consequently, it is no surprise at all that it would rank among the best slugging years of all time.

2. Barry Bonds, 2002   .817 Adjusted Slugging Average

In 2002, Bonds had a lower home run rate than in 2001 but countered it with a higher batting average. However, given the criticality of home run hitting in the slugging average, the 2002 season landed on the short side.

1. Barry Bonds, 2001   .829 Adjusted Slugging Average

At age 36, Barry Bonds took his game to a new level, hitting 73 home runs and setting a new slugging average record, both raw and adjusted. In so doing, he ended Ruth's 78-year tenure of holding down the top 4 spots.

Best Productive Careers for On-Base Percentage (9000 NFPs)

Complete lists of the top 100 players for career times on-base and adjusted OBP are given in Appendix M.10. The top 10 are listed below.

10. Mickey Mantle, 1951–68   .416 Adjusted OBP
(Adj BA = .302, Rank = 52; Adj BBs/550 = 92.0, Rank = 14)

Five of the top 10 players for OBP also hold top 10 rankings in slugging average. They are Bonds, Hornsby, Mantle, Ruth, and Williams. They model one secret to success in making this list: Be a great slugger with a high batting average, thereby causing pitchers to nibble at the plate. Accept the walks when the pitchers don't give you anything to hit. Voila!

9. Roy Thomas, 1899–1911   .418 Adjusted OBP

(Adj BA = .279, Rank = 354; Adj BBs/550 = 100.2, Rank = 6)

There were 2 great base on balls masters at the turn of the 20th century. Roy Thomas was the National League master, winning 7 titles between 1900 and 1907.

8. Mel Ott, 1926–47   .418 Adjusted OBP

(Adj BA = .288, Rank = 179; Adj BBs/550 = 93.3, Rank = 12)

Mel Ott is well known for his home run prowess. However, his ability to draw a walk was a vital part of his placement among baseball's elites. Over his career, Ott won 6 walk titles, and ranked among the top three 16 times.

7. Topsy Hartsel, 1898–1911   .419 Adjusted OBP

(Adj BA = .276, Rank = 419; Adj BBs/550 = 100.6, Rank = 5)

Topsy Hartsel was the American League walk master at the turn of the 20th century. Between 1902 and 1908, he won 5 titles.

6. Billy Hamilton, 1888–1901   .423 Adjusted OBP

(Adj BA = .308, Rank = 27; Adj BBs/550 = 88.6, Rank = 22)

Billy Hamilton shows great balance, ranking in the 20s for both batting and walk average. As one of the premier stolen base threats in history, getting on base was a key part of Hamilton's strategy.

5. John McGraw, 1891–1906   .427 Adjusted OBP

(Adj BA = .292, Rank = 139; Adj BBs/550 = 98.9, Rank = 8)

As a smaller player without much power, John McGraw's game was all about getting on base. After becoming manager of the New York Giants at age 29, he had only 90 additional NFPs. Instead, his Giants became the best at drawing walks. From 1903 to 1908, McGraw's first 6 full seasons as manager, the team averaged 101 walks more than the other teams in the league (484 compared to 383), until the league began to catch on.

4. Barry Bonds, 1986–   .429 Adjusted OBP

(Adj BA = .294, Rank = 107; Adj BBs/550 = 103.4, Rank = 3)

Barry Bonds was in 16th place in career OBP through the 2000 season, with 9059 NFPs already under his belt. Then, Bonds crafted the best 3 OBP seasons in baseball history, catapulting himself into fourth place. The key to this meteoric late career rise was his 3 off-the-chart walk averages.

3. Rogers Hornsby, 1915–37   .430 Adjusted OBP

(Adj BA = .327, Rank = 4; Adj BBs/550 = 75.0, Rank = 86)

Rogers Hornsby is tied for fourth place in batting average with Stan Musial. However, Hornsby's walk rate is superior, placing him 3rd, while Musial ranks 15th.

2. Babe Ruth, 1914–35   .439 Adjusted OBP

(Adj BA = .309, Rank = 25; Adj BBs/550 = 103.6, Rank = 2)

Babe Ruth and Ted Williams are the only players to rank among the top 25 in both adjusted batting average and walk average. The stratospheric walk averages are the real key to setting them apart from the other hitters.

1. Ted Williams, 1939–60   **.448 Adjusted OBP**

(Adj BA = .322, Rank = 9; Adj BBs/550 = 102.9, Rank = 4)

Ted Williams finally wins something! On many of these top 10 lists, Williams can't escape the Babe's shadow. As the only player who ranks among the top 10 in both batting and walk average, Williams certainly earns the crown.

Best Productive Careers for Slugging Average (8000 ABs)

Complete lists of the top 100 players for career total bases and adjusted slugging average are given in Appendix M.11. Here are the top 10:

10. Stan Musial, 1941–63   **.553 Adjusted Slugging Average**

(Adj BA = .327, Rank = 5; Adj DPTs/500 = 41.3, Rank = 1; Adj HRs/500 = 22.2, Rank = 130)

Slugging average can be broken down into essentially 3 components: batting average, DPTs, and especially home runs, which net 4 total bases each. Stan Musial earned his top 10 place by having his batting averages and doubles-plus-triples among the top 5, while hitting a respectable number of home runss, with 475 lifetime dingers.

9. Mickey Mantle, 1951–68   **.554 Adjusted Slugging Average**

(Adj BA = .302, Rank = 52; Adj DPTs/500 = 29.6, Rank = 325; Adj HRs/500 = 31.9, Rank = 12)

Mickey Mantle's batting and doubles-plus-triples averages are less striking than those of Musial and Mays. However, Mantle's strength was his home run hitting, which was able to make up the difference.

8. Mark McGwire, 1986–2001   **.556 Adjusted Slugging Average**

(Adj BA = .263, Rank = 736; Adj DPTs/500 = 21.7, Rank = 1079; Adj HRs/500 = 41.5, Rank = 2)

Mark McGwire is an example of how significant home runs are to slugging average. Both McGwire's batting average and his doubles-plus-triples rate are well below average. However, his home run rate is second only to Babe Ruth's. As a result, McGwire places eighth in this prestigious list.

7. Willie Mays, 1951–73   **.566 Adjusted Slugging Average**

(Adj BA = .308, Rank = 29; Adj DPTs/500 = 36.6, Rank = 17; Adj HRs/500 = 28.7, Rank = 32)

Willie Mays shows consistency as an offensive threat, with all 3 components ranking among the 32 best. Three players yet to come will equal or better this mark of consistency.

6. Joe DiMaggio, 1936–51   **.582 Adjusted Slugging Average**

(Adj BA = .309, Rank = 24; Adj DPTs/500 = 35.1, Rank = 27; Adj HRs/500 = 31.5, Rank = 14)

Joe DiMaggio, like Musial and Mays, ranks among the top 30 for both batting average and doubles-plus-triples. By also placing 14th in home runs, DiMaggio claims 6th place, with a 16-point slugging edge over Mays.

4T. Barry Bonds, 1986–   **.584 Adjusted Slugging Average**

(Adj BA = .294, Rank = 107; Adj DPTs/500 = 33.4, Rank = 73; Adj HRs/500 = 35.7, Rank = 4)

Bonds edged out Joe DiMaggio for adjusted slugging average. Although batting 15 points less, Bonds hit more than 4 extra home runs per 500 at-bats.

4T. Lou Gehrig, 1923–39   .584 Adjusted Slugging Average

(Adj BA = .307, Rank = 33; Adj DPTs/500 = 37.1, Rank = 12; HRs/500 = 33.7, Rank = 6)

Lou Gehrig and Barry Bonds are in a virtual dead heat for adjusted slugging average. Gehrig batted 13 points higher than Bonds, with 4 extra DPTs/500, while Bonds hit 2 extra home runs.

3. Rogers Hornsby, 1915–37   .597 Adjusted Slugging Average

(Adj BA = .327, Rank = 4; Adj DPTs/500 = 36.6, Rank = 16; Adj HRs/500 = 31.1, Rank = 17)

Hornsby has no weakness in his offensive game, with all 3 components of slugging ranking among the top 17. Rogers Hornsby's home run rate is close to that of DiMaggio's, not Gehrig's. However, Hornsby's batting average is 18 points better than DiMaggio's. Thus, Hornsby is able to offset the decreased home runs with extra hits, and slip past Gehrig.

2. Ted Williams, 1939–60   .628 Adjusted Slugging Average

(Adj BA = .322, Rank = 9; Adj DPTs/500 = 35.8, Rank = 22; Adj HRs/500 = 38.7, Rank = 3)

Ted Williams tops Hornsby by a considerable gap—243 total bases over 8000 at-batss. Hornsby ranks somewhat better than Williams in batting average and doubles-plus-triples average. However, Williams hit 7.6 more HRs/500 ABs.

1. Babe Ruth, 1914–35   .673 Adjusted Slugging Average

(Adj BA = .309, Rank = 25; Adj DPTs/500 = 34.2, Rank = 50; Adj HRs/500 = 49.8, Rank = 1)

Talk about gaps! Ruth slugged 45 points higher than Williams, an edge of 364 total bases over 8000 at-bats. How did Ruth do it? Home runs, home runs, home runs. Ruth's 11 HRs/500 advantage over Williams easily overcomes Williams' 6.5 hits/500 ABs edge.

CHAPTER 14

Fantasy League
Baseball's Best Batters

"Starting for the National League," the huge speakers blared, "leading off and playing second base, Johnny Evers; centerfield, Wee Willie Keeler; left field, Jim Delahanty; right field, Hack Wilson; first base, Frank Chance; third base, Harry Steinfeldt; catching, Roger Bresnahan; shortstop, Joe Tinker . . . and pitching, Christy Mathewson!"

These words were written in 1952 by Frank O'Rourke in a short story entitled "The Heavenly World Series." How baseball players from different eras would perform if they played on the same field has long captured the baseball fan's imagination. This is the ultimate fantasy league!

In the first two chapters of this book, the ground rules and adjustment procedures for such a comparison were provided. In subsequent chapters, the four adjustments were explained further and applied to the nine basic offensive events. Now it is time to combine these results together and give an overarching view of the best offensive players in the history of the game.

In *Baseball's All-Time Best Hitters*, I formally defined three terms: best hitters, best batters, and best players. The *best hitters* are those "players with the best chance to get a hit in a given at-bat." The *best batters* are those players who are the best at the plate overall. The *best players* are those players who are the best overall. The first two terms, then, are limited in the scope of baseball play considered.

To identify the best players, we would have to look at their running and fielding abilities, as well as their offensive performance. Whereas adjusted stolen base totals were obtained in the last chapter, caught stealing data are not available throughout baseball history. Furthermore, the situations under which bases are stolen—the number of outs, the lineup positions of the upcoming batters, and the base that is stolen—render some stolen bases better than others. In addition, the average number of bases that a player advances on a single or double varies from player to player, which would have an impact on their value.

The fielding abilities of players are considered only in the next chapter, in which a player's batting performance is adjusted to account for his fielding position. However, this adjustment is a generalized one for players at the given position; it does not account for a player's individual defensive ability.

The focus of *Baseball's All-Time Best Hitters* was the identification of the *best hitters* across baseball history, whereas the goal of this book is identifying the *best batters*.

Batting Evaluation Methods

Runs are the currency of baseball. The goal of major league teams is to win games, and games are won when teams score more runs than their opponents. Thus, it is useful to compare players by how many runs they "produce" for their teams. Many baseball researchers have done this by assigning a run value to each offensive event. Jim Albert and Jay Bennett (in Chapters 6 and 7 of *Curve Ball*) and Pete Palmer and John Thorn (in a chapter titled "Sabermetrics" in *Total Baseball*, Seventh Edition) provide excellent reviews of the historical developments in measuring offensive performance. I will now briefly describe five methods, including my own, that are based on linear regression.

Lindsey's Method

George Lindsey pioneered the business of assigning run values to various offensive events in baseball. Lindsey estimated the run value of the 4 kinds of base hits: 0.45 runs per single, 0.82 per double, 1.06 per triple, and 1.42 per home run. Let's apply this method to Babe Ruth's 1920 season. In 1920, Ruth hit 73 singles, 36 doubles, 9 triples, and 54 home runs. These hits were "worth":

$$\underline{\text{Singles}} \quad \underline{\text{Doubles}} \quad \underline{\text{Triples}} \quad \underline{\text{Home runs}}$$
$$73 \times 0.45 + 36 \times 0.82 + 9 \times 1.06 + 54 \times 1.42 = 148.6 \text{ runs.}$$

Although home runs constituted 31% of Ruth's hits, they produced 52% of his run value for the team.

Palmer's Batting Runs

In *The Hidden Game of Baseball*, John Thorn and Pete Palmer expanded on Lindsey's work. Their formula, known as Batting Runs, made two significant improvements.

First, they gave credit to walks and hit-by-pitches, whose value was assessed at 0.33 runs each. Thus, Ruth's 150 walks and 3 hit-by-pitches in 1920 contributed an additional 50.5 runs.

Second, Thorn and Palmer charged a run value fee for each out, either at the plate or on the basepaths, and centered it so that a player who produces runs at an average rate will wind up at zero—players who produce runs above the average rate will have positive runs totals; those who produce runs at a below-average rate will have negative runs totals. Specifically, run credits are removed for failing to reach base on a plate appearance (measured as at-bats minus hits); being caught stealing or making some other out-on-base, such as being picked off; or being thrown out trying to reach the next base.

The run values for Batting Runs were obtained primarily using a computer simulation method supported by baseball data. The Batting Runs approach is also called Linear Weights because the overall run value of a player is obtained by adding or subtracting the run values of the different events.

To compare players from different eras who played in different ballparks, Thorn and Palmer give an adjusted statistic, Batting Runs+ (BR+), that normalizes Batting Runs to the league average and adjusts for the ballpark effect for runs.

Albert and Bennett's LSLR Method

Linear regression methods are a standard statistical method for building a "linear" formula. In *Curve Ball*, Jim Albert and Jay Bennett built such a model, which they called LSLR (for least-squares linear regression). To develop the model, they used the different offensive events as predictor variables to "explain" the single-season runs totals for each team from 1954 to 1999.

Event-Specific Batting Runs

I used essentially the same strategy as Albert and Bennett, but applied it to the 1310 major league teams from 1947 to 2003. The run values obtained for this method are shown in Formula 14.1.

The run value for batting outs from the regression model above is –0.111. To make this approach comparable to the Batting Runs method, however, we need to assess how many runs to expect per batting out. In this book, player averages have been standardizing to the National League data from 1977 to 1992. For these seasons, teams averaged 650 runs scored and 4005 batting outs, which equals .162 runs per batting out. Adding this fee to .111 yields a total fee of .273 runs per batting out.

The approach used here follows the tradition of the Batting Runs method, with three principal differences: (1) run values of the component offensive events differ slightly; (2) the factors SB, CS, and OOB have not been used; and (3) each component has been adjusted for its own ballpark effect, rather than using a single ballpark effect for runs.

The third difference is the most significant one. For example, a park may be favorable for runs by being a great home run park, while being an underaverage park for hits. In such a park, a home run hitter might do quite well, while a singles hitter may be disadvantaged. By adjusting each offensive event for its own park effect, we avoid such problems. Recall also that home run hitting itself is adjusted for batter handedness. Thus, for example, between 1933 and 1973 left-handed Yankee bombers were much more likely to belt home runs than their right-handed counterparts in

Yankee Stadium (see Figure 6.8). Because of the park adjustment difference from Batting Runs+, I have called my formula *Event-Specific Batting Runs* (ESBRs). The formula is:

Formula 14.1   Event-Specific Batting Runs

$$\text{ESBRs} = 0.52 \times 1B + 0.80 \times 2B + 1.11 \times 3B + 1.52 \times HR + .32 \times (BB + HBP) - 0.273 \times (AB - H),$$

where fully adjusted totals are used for all offensive events.

D'Esopo and Lefkowitz's Scoring Index

One problem with linear regression models is that they look at correlations, not causation. For example, the estimated run value for triples may not be the intrinsic run value of a triple. Players with more triples tend to be faster around the basepaths, so perhaps part of the run value accounts for their running aggressiveness when teammates knock them in, thereby giving their team additional runs.

The D'Esopo and Lefkowitz scoring index model (DLSI) took a more detailed approach to understanding run production, as described in *Curve Ball*. The DLSI model uses offensive event run values based on the 1959 National League season.

None of the formulas include a term for strikeouts, as distinct from any other out. In my regression estimation, I did see evidence of a significant negative effect for strikeouts for the years 1920–46. However, because this effect did not apply to the standardizing period, 1977–92 in the National League, I did not include it in my formula.

Other formulas for run production have also been developed, most notably, Runs Created, by Bill James. His method is not a linear method and relies somewhat more on subjective judgments, however, than those presented here.

Table 14.1   Run Values for Five Batting Evaluation Methods

Method	1B	2B	3B	HR	BB/HBP	Outs	SB	CS	OOB
Lindsey	.45*	.82	1.06	1.42					
Batting Runs	.47	.78	1.09	1.40	.33	−.25	.30	−.60	−.50
LSLR	.52	.67	1.18	1.50	.36		.16		
DLSI	.53	.73	.99	1.58	.37	−.29			
ESBR	.52	.80	1.11	1.52	.32	−.273			
Average	.50	.76	1.09	1.48	.34	−.27	.23		

Sources: Lindsey—Lindsey (1963) (*Curve Ball* gives a corrected value for 1B of .45, original value was .41); Batting Runs—*Total Baseball,* Seventh Edition; LSLR, DLSI—*Curve Ball;* Average = average of the 5 methods.

Table 14.1 provides the run values for offensive events from each of the 5 methods mentioned earlier. Overall, there is very good agreement in the run value of the different hits. The ESBR method has slightly higher run values compared to the Batting Runs method for each of the hits, but also has a larger negative run effect for an out to offset them.

The 10 best single-seasons and productive careers for ESBRs/550 NFPs will now be unveiled. After that, another measure called *Career Batter Rating* will be developed. That rating combines the rate of performance with the length of a player's productive career, which provides the overall ranking of the *best batters*.

Best Single-Seasons for Event-Specific Batting Runs

Table 14.2 shows a summary of the top 100 seasons for ESBRs/550 NFPs. The complete list is given in Appendix M.12. The top 10 are listed below. Players separated by at most 0.1 ESBRs/550 NFPs are given tied ranks (see the guide at the top of page 104).

Table 14.2   Top 100 Seasons—Adjusted Event-Specific Batting Runs per 550 NFPs
49 Different Players with Average Age = 28.7

Era	Seasons	Expected	Era	Seasons	Expected
1876–1900	7	9.9	1947–68	17	16.5
1901–19	11	13.4	1969–92	10↓	26.8
1920–46	34↑	19.4	1993–2003	21	14.0

No. of Seasons	Players with Multiple Top 100 Seasons
12	*Babe Ruth*
8	*Rogers Hornsby, Ted Williams*
7	Barry Bonds
5	*Lou Gehrig*
4	*Mickey Mantle*
3	*Ty Cobb, Ed Delahanty*
2	George Brett, Joe DiMaggio, Jimmie Foxx, Jason Giambi, *Nap Lajoie*, Mark McGwire, Manny Ramirez, *Frank Robinson, Honus Wagner*

Notes: Hall of Fame players are listed in italics. The symbol ↑ (↓) means the number of seasons is significantly higher (lower) than expected.

See the guide to the top 100 seasons tables on page 103.

10. Babe Ruth, 1919   87.4 Adjusted ESBRs/550 NFPs
(Adj OBP = .442, Rank = 71; Adj SLG = .769, Rank = 4; Adj OPS = 1.212, Rank = 9)
This season furthered the transition of Ruth from pitcher to outfielder. His 29 HRs in 1919 set a new record. The significance of his accomplishment was obscured, however, since it was hard to homer in his home park, Fenway. Of his 29 smashes, only 9 were at Fenway.

9. Ted Williams, 1941   92.1 Adjusted ESBRs/550 NFPs
(Adj OBP = .512, Rank = 4; Adj SLG = .708, Rank = 15; Adj OPS = 1.220, Rank = 7)

In this storied season, a 22-year-old Williams combined the fourth best year for OBP with a stellar slugging average. Still, because of DiMaggio's 56-game hitting streak, Williams did not win the MVP award.

7T. Babe Ruth, 1923   92.6 Adjusted ESBRs/550 NFPs
(Adj OBP = .498, Rank = 8; Adj SLG = .739, Rank = 7; Adj OPS = 1.237, Rank = 6)

This is the first of 5 seasons, where both the adjusted OBP and SLG ranked among the top 10. Ruth has 2; Bonds has 3.

7T. Ted Williams, 1957   92.6 Adjusted ESBRs/550 NFPs
(Adj OBP = .504, Rank = 5; Adj SLG = .713, Rank = 13; Adj OPS = 1.216, Rank = 8)

What a season Williams had in 1957 . . . and he did it at age 38! This season was one of the biggest reasons that Williams was able to say in his book, *My Turn At Bat* (page 120): "If in the end I didn't make it as the greatest hitter who ever lived—that long-ago boyhood dream—I kind of enjoy thinking that I might have become the greatest old hitter who ever lived."

6. Babe Ruth, 1921   92.8 Adjusted ESBRs/550 NFPs
(Adj OBP = .471, Rank = 22; Adj SLG = .768, Rank = 5; Adj OPS = 1.239, Rank = 5)

Of Ruth's 12 seasons among the top 100, 4 are in the top 10. All occurred in a 5-year stretch, 1919–23, when Ruth was 24–28 years old.

5. Rogers Hornsby, 1924   93.7 Adjusted ESBRs/550 NFPs
(Adj OBP = .495, Rank = 11; Adj SLG = .689, Rank = 26; Adj OPS = 1.183, Rank = 10)

In his crowning season, Hornsby hit for the highest adjusted average in history and hit with power, propelling it into fifth best overall.

4. Barry Bonds, 2003   97.8 Adjusted ESBRs/550 NFPs
(Adj OBP = .518, Rank = 2; Adj SLG = .750, Rank = 6; Adj OPS = 1.268, Rank = 4)

The first of 3 consecutive years among the top 4 in baseball history.

3. Babe Ruth, 1920   101.5 Adjusted ESBRs/550 NFPs
(Adj OBP = .495, Rank = 10; Adj SLG = .801, Rank = 3; Adj OPS = 1.296, Rank = 3)

In his first season as a Yankee, Ruth smashed the home run record he set the previous year by 25 home runs! Perhaps no other player-season was as momentous. Ruth's 1920 season sealed the coffin of the deadball era and began baseball's love of the home run, which continues to this day.

2. Barry Bonds, 2001   107.7 Adjusted ESBRs/550 NFPs
(Adj OBP = .512, Rank = 3; Adj SLG = .829, Rank = 1; Adj OPS = 1.340, Rank = 2)

Barry Bonds set 3 major new records—home runs with 73, slugging average at .863, and walks with 177. This potent combination led to a new record for adjusted ESBRs, breaking Ruth's 81-year-old mark.

1. Barry Bonds, 2002   116.1 Adjusted ESBRs/550 NFPs
(Adj OBP = .574, Rank = 1; Adj SLG = .817, Rank = 2; Adj OPS = 1.391, Rank = 1)

In the twilight years of his career, Bonds has fashioned the greatest 2 years in baseball history! In so doing, he has moved alongside Ruth and Williams, and displaced Williams from his perch as greatest *old* hitter.

Best Productive Careers for Event-Specific Batting Runs (9000 NFPs)

The ranking for ESBRs/550 is very similar to that for adjusted OPS, as can be seen below. Since adjusted OBP and SLG are based on 9000 NFPS and 8000 ABs, their sum does not exactly equal adjusted OPS. Complete lists of the top 100 players for career ESBRs and adjusted ESBRs/550 NFPs are given in Appendix M.12. Here are the top 10:

10. Willie Mays, 1951–1973   46.7 ESBRs/550 NFPs
(Adj OBP = .391, Rank = 58; Adj SLG = .566, Rank = 7; Adj OPS = .960, Rank =10)

Willie Mays is often ranked among the 3 greatest ballplayers. Such rankings take his great fielding, base stealing, and longevity, none of which is accounted for here. Still, one may wonder why Mays doesn't rank higher. His greatest liability is his walk rate. It ranks 176th, dragging his adjusted OBP rank down to 58th place.

9. Jimmie Foxx, 1925–45   47.1 ESBRs/550 NFPs
(Adj OBP = .394, Rank = 44; Adj SLG = .550, Rank = 13; Adj OPS = .947, Rank = 12)

Starting in 1929, Foxx became the most significant competitor to Ruth and Gehrig's stranglehold of the top spots for adjusted OPS. Between 1929 and 1938, Gehrig, Foxx, and an aging Ruth, placed 8, 7, and 5 seasons among the best 25 for the American League, with Al Simmons (2), Hank Greenberg (2), and Joe DiMaggio (1) accounting for the other 5 seasons.

8. Ty Cobb, 1905–1928   48.1 ESBRs/550 NFPs
(Adj OBP = .406, Rank = 17; Adj SLG = .550, Rank = 14; Adj OPS = .958, Rank = 9)

Ty Cobb was the greatest player of the deadball era and its leading slugger, winning 8 slugging titles. His low raw total of HRs, 117, was attributable to his era. His adjusted HR total, 418, ranks as the 29th highest.

7. Stan Musial, 1941–63   49.9 ESBRs/550 NFPs
(Adj OBP = .410, Rank = 15; Adj SLG = .553, Rank = 10; Adj OPS = .961, Rank = 7)

All of the top 7 players finished among the top 15 batters in both OBP and SLG. Musial relied on a high batting average and topping the career DPT list rather than exceptional home run hitting to claim the seventh spot.

6. Mickey Mantle, 1951–68   52.3 ESBRs/550 NFPs
(Adj OBP = .416, Rank = 10; Adj SLG = .554, Rank = 9; Adj OPS = .974, Rank = 6)

Mickey Mantle is one of 3 Yankees to rank among the top 6 players, and Joe DiMaggio barely misses the top 10 list, ranking 12th. Given such dominant players, it is not that surprising that the Yankees have been the dominant team in baseball history.

5. Lou Gehrig, 1923–39   55.6 ESBRs/550 NFPs
(Adj OBP = .412, Rank = 13; Adj SLG = .584, Rank = 5; Adj OPS = .998, Rank = 5)

There is great consensus among baseball aficionados that Lou Gehrig is the greatest first baseman in baseball history. Gehrig, a left-hander, did not exploit the favorable right field wall of Yankee Stadium. Over his career, Gehrig hit only 9 more home runs at home than he did on the road.

4. Barry Bonds, 1986–   57.4 ESBRs/550 NFPs
(Adj OBP = .429, Rank = 4; Adj SLG = .584, Rank = 4; Adj OPS = 1.020, Rank = 4)

The 2001–2003 seasons, which rank as the 3 of the best 4 single-seasons in baseball history for ESBRs/550, have allowed Bonds to rocket up the list of the all-time greats.

3. Rogers Hornsby, 1915–37   60.1 ESBRs/550 NFPs
(Adj OBP = .430, Rank = 3; Adj SLG = .597, Rank = 3; Adj OPS = 1.040, Rank = 3)

Hornsby combined top 3 placements in both OBP and SLG to claim third place. That Hornsby was a second baseman adds to his accomplishment—all other top 10 members are first basemen or outfielders.

2. Ted Williams, 1939–60   70.4 ESBRs/550 NFPs
(Adj OBP = .448, Rank = 1; Adj SLG = .628, Rank = 2; Adj OPS = 1.070, Rank = 2)

The largest gap in this list is that between Hornsby and Williams. In fact the gap is larger than that between Hornsby and the seventh place batter, Stan Musial.

1. Babe Ruth, 1914–35   74.9 ESBRs/550 NFPs
(Adj OBP = .439, Rank = 2; Adj SLG = .673, Rank = 1; Adj OPS = 1.120, Rank = 1)

It is certainly no surprise that Babe Ruth ends up on top. Ruth was a huge statistical outlier in his time. Some of that was reduced owing to era effects. Still, Ruth's separation from his peers was unmatched by any other ballplayer. Ruth and Williams split the top two positions on the two components of OPS. Ruth's edge in slugging exceeded Williams's margin in OBP, giving Ruth the overall victory.

Formula 14.2 Career Batter Rating (CBR)

Career Batter Rating

= productive career ESBRs/550 NFPs × career fullness score,

where a player's *productive career ESBRs/550 NFPs* is obtained by multiplying his single-season ESBRs per 550 NFPs by the fraction of his productive career NFPs obtained that season and adding up all player-seasons through the 9000th NFP (or whole career if less than 9000 NFPs), and the *career fullness score* is 1 if the player had at least 9000 NFPs, and NFPs/9000 if he had less.

If the productive career ESBRs/550 NFPs is less than zero, a career fullness score of 1 is used. Consequently, players with negative scores and short careers do not gain an advantage.

Career Batter Rating

Throughout this book so far, the rate of offensive performance has been emphasized. Batting average is a rate measure since it gives the number of hits per at-bat. When evaluating a player's entire career, though, some account of longevity should be made. For overall batting, this might be done by looking at the total adjusted hits over a player's career. Thus, while Tony Gwynn has the highest adjusted batting average, Pete Rose holds the mark for the most adjusted hits.

For overall offensive performance, ESBRs per 550 NFPs is the rate statistic used here to rank players. In this chapter, another rating, called the *Career Batter Rating*, is presented. From this rating, the ranking of the 100 best batters is made.

Total Baseball's Batting Runs mixes performance rate and longevity since it compares the player's rate of run production to that of an average player and sums that over the player's career. Since underaverage seasons cause the Batting Runs total to drop, however, additional years of play do not necessarily help a player move up the list.

Since the productive career length for ESBRs is 9000 NFPs, a player with at least this total has had a "full career." Remember, these were the *longtime players* defined in Chapter 4. The longevity adjustment down-adjusts players with shorter careers to account for the fraction of a full career missed. Consequently, active players with less than 9000 NFPs who maintain their performance level will rise in the CBR list with additional playing time.

Explanation of the Career Batter Rating

For a player, ESBRs/550 NFPs gives the number of extra runs that the player produces above that provided by an average player per 550 NFPs, which is basically one season of play. As a prospective general manager for a team, you would want not only a high rate of performance, but also a player who provides ample playing time.

For a player with a "full career" (at least 9000 NFPs), CBR equals ESBRs/550 NFPs.

Table 14.3 The 100 Best Batters

Rank	Player	Years	Primary Team	Pos	ESBRs /550	CBR
1	Babe Ruth	1914–35	NY–A	RF	74.9	74.9
2	Ted Williams	1939–60	Bos–A	LF	70.4	70.4
3	Rogers Hornsby	1915–37	StL–N	2B	60.1	60.1
4	**Barry Bonds**	1986–2003	SF–N	LF	57.4	57.4
5	Lou Gehrig	1923–39	NY–A	1B	55.6	55.6
6	Mickey Mantle	1951–68	NY–A	CF	52.3	52.3
7	Stan Musial	1941–63	StL–N	RF	49.9	49.9
8	Ty Cobb	1905–28	Det–A	CF	48.1	48.1
9	Jimmie Foxx	1925–45	Phi–A	1B	47.1	47.1
10	Willie Mays	1951–73	SF–N	CF	46.7	46.7
11	Mel Ott	1926–47	NY–N	RF	45.5	45.5
12	Honus Wagner	1897–1917	Pit–N	SS	45.3	45.3
13	Frank Robinson	1956–76	Cin–N	RF	43.7	43.7
14	Tris Speaker	1907–28	Cle–A	CF	41.2	41.2
15	Hank Aaron	1954–76	Atl–N	RF	40.7	40.7
16	**Frank Thomas**	1990–2003	Chi–A	1B	45.0	40.3
17	Mike Schmidt	1972–89	Phi–N	3B	39.1	39.1
18	Joe DiMaggio	1936–51	NY–A	CF	45.4	38.6
19	**Jeff Bagwell**	1991–2003	Hou–N	1B	40.6	38.5
20	Roger Connor	1880–97	NY–N	1B	38.1	37.4
21	Dan Brouthers	1879–1904	–N	1B	43.9	37.4
22	Mark McGwire	1986–2001	Oak–A	1B	44.2	37.2
23	Reggie Jackson	1967–87	Oak–A	RF	37.1	37.1
24	Willie McCovey	1959–80	SF–N	1B	36.4	36.4
25	Eddie Mathews	1952–68	Mil–N	3B	36.2	36.2
26	Nap Lajoie	1896–1916	Cle–A	2B	36.2	36.2
27	**Edgar Martinez**	1987–2003	Sea–A	DH	40.0	35.7
28	Harmon Killebrew	1954–75	Min–A	3B	35.4	35.4
29	Ed Delahanty	1888–1903	Phi–N	LF	36.7	34.0
30	George Brett	1973–93	KC–A	3B	33.6	33.6
31	Willie Stargell	1962–82	Pit–N	LF	33.6	33.4
32	Johnny Mize	1936–53	StL–N	1B	40.8	33.3
33	Sam Crawford	1899–1917	Det–A	RF	33.1	33.1
34	Dick Allen	1963–77	Phi–N	1B	41.0	33.0
35	Eddie Murray	1977–97	Bal–A	1B	32.8	32.8
36	**Gary Sheffield**	1988–2003	–N	RF	37.0	32.6
37	Rickey Henderson	1979–2002	Oak–A	LF	32.4	32.4
38	Harry Heilmann	1914–32	Det–A	RF	33.4	32.2
39	Carl Yastrzemski	1961–83	Bos–A	LF	31.9	31.9
40	Jesse Burkett	1890–1905	Cle–N	LF	31.2	31.2
41	Wade Boggs	1982–99	Bos–A	3B	31.2	31.2
42	Paul Waner	1926–45	Pit–N	RF	30.6	30.6
43	Duke Snider	1947–64	Bkn–N	CF	33.6	30.4
44	**Fred McGriff**	1986–2003	–N	1B	30.4	30.4
45	Al Kaline	1953–74	Det–A	RF	29.6	29.6
46	Jack Clark	1975–92	SF–N	RF	32.6	29.5
47	Harry Stovey	1880–93	Phi–a	LF	38.6	29.3
48	**Ken Griffey Jr.**	1989–2003	Sea–A	CF	32.3	29.0
49	Rod Carew	1967–85	Min–A	2B	28.9	28.9
50	Tony Gwynn	1982–2001	SD–N	RF	28.8	28.8

Table 14.3 *(continued)*

Rank	Player	Years	Primary Team	Pos	ESBRs /550	CBR
51	**Manny Ramirez**	1993–2003	Cle–A	RF	44.0	28.7
52	Joe Morgan	1963–84	Cin–N	2B	28.6	28.6
53	Eddie Collins	1906–30	Phi–A	2B	28.2	28.2
54	Joe Jackson	1908–20	Cle–A	LF	45.3	28.0
55	Will Clark	1986–2000	SF–N	1B	30.8	28.0
56	Hank Greenberg	1930–47	Det–A	1B	40.8	27.5
57	Dave Winfield	1973–95	NY–A	RF	27.5	27.5
58	Zack Wheat	1909–27	Bkn–N	LF	27.3	27.3
59	**Jim Thome**	1991–2003	Cle–A	1B	38.4	27.2
60	Al Simmons	1924–44	Phi–A	LF	27.2	27.2
61	**Rafael Palmeiro**	1986–2003	Tex–A	1B	27.1	27.1
62	Goose Goslin	1921–38	Was–A	LF	26.9	26.9
63	**Mike Piazza**	1992–2003	LA–N	C	40.3	26.7
64	Mike Tiernan	1887–99	NY–N	RF	35.9	26.7
65	Billy Williams	1959–76	Chi–N	LF	26.6	26.6
66	Ken Singleton	1970–84	Bal–A	RF	28.1	26.5
67	Frank Howard	1958–73	Was–A	LF	32.3	26.2
68	Cap Anson	1876–97	Chi–N	1B	26.1	26.1
69	Reggie Smith	1966–82	Bos–A	RF	29.2	25.8
70	Billy Hamilton	1888–1901	Phi–N	CF	30.6	25.7
71	Boog Powell	1961–77	Bal–A	1B	29.6	25.4
72	Sherry Magee	1904–19	Phi–N	LF	27.5	25.3
73	**John Olerud**	1989–2003	Tor–A	1B	27.4	25.2
74	Joe Medwick	1932–48	StL–N	LF	27.4	24.6
75	Keith Hernandez	1974–90	StL–N	1B	26.2	24.6
76	Norm Cash	1958–74	Det–A	1B	28.3	24.6
77	Arky Vaughan	1932–48	Pit–N	SS	29.1	24.6
78	Ralph Kiner	1946–55	Pit–N	LF	35.3	24.5
79	Bob Johnson	1933–45	Phi–A	LF	27.5	24.5
80	**Larry Walker**	1989–2003	Col–N	RF	30.1	24.4
81	Orlando Cepeda	1958–74	SF–N	1B	25.3	24.2
82	**Jason Giambi**	1995–2003	Oak–A	1B	40.2	24.1
83	Charlie Gehringer	1924–42	Det–A	2B	24.1	24.1
84	Hack Wilson	1923–34	Chi–N	CF	39.6	24.0
85	Joe Kelley	1891–1908	Bal–N	LF	26.5	23.6
86	Jack Fournier	1912–27	–N	1B	36.0	23.6
87	Fred Clarke	1894–1915	Pit–N	LF	23.5	23.5
88	Albert Belle	1989–2000	Cle–A	LF	32.1	23.5
89	Babe Herman	1926–45	Bkn–N	RF	34.2	23.3
90	Elmer Flick	1898–1910	Phi–N	RF	33.1	23.2
91	Pete Browning	1882–94	Lou–a	CF	39.0	23.1
92	**Chipper Jones**	1993–2003	Atl–N	3B	34.5	23.0
93	Tim Raines	1979–2002	Mon–N	LF	23.0	23.0
94	Dolph Camilli	1933–45	Phi–N	1B	32.5	22.8
95	Cy Williams	1912–30	Phi–N	CF	27.2	22.8
96	Roberto Clemente	1955–72	Pit–N	RF	22.4	22.4
97	Chuck Klein	1928–44	Phi–N	RF	28.3	22.3
98	**Alex Rodriguez**	1994–2003	Sea–A	SS	35.7	22.3
99	Bill Terry	1923–36	NY–N	1B	28.7	22.3
100	Paul Molitor	1978–98	Mil–A	DH	22.3	22.3

For a player who provides less service, you will have to find one or more additional players to fill out the theoretical full career. One can expect to find only an average player, whose ESBRs/550 NFPs would be 0. Thus, the player's value to you is equal to ESBRs/550 NFPs times his career fullness score, which is his CBR.

The 28% of players with 4000 or more NFPs who have negative ESBRs/550 NFPs are ranked only by their rate of performance, not by factoring in longevity as well. Some baseball researchers would prefer a lower baseline than the average player. For them, the term *replacement player* is used for the player who fills in for the more superior player whose career is shortened. It is not very clear, however, what standard should be used for the replacement player and whether such a player should stand in for thousands of NFPs.

In many respects, Table 14.3 represents the climax of this book. It gives a recapitulation of Table 1.1 along with the player's career period, his principal team, and primary position. It also provides the Career Batter Rating, upon which the ranking is based.

Babe Ruth and Ted Williams are the 2 best batters, according to CBR. Rogers Hornsby claims third, edging out Barry Bonds and Lou Gehrig.

What about the active players? Through 2003, Barry Bonds ranks as the fourth best batter. Although he has already had a "full career," his performance after his 9000th NFP has pushed his CBR even higher. In his remaining seasons, Bonds could slip past Hornsby, but he is unlikely to overtake either Ruth or Williams, Frank Thomas, and Jeff Bagwell are the other active players who rank among the 25 best batters.

Eddie Mathews currently ranks 25th, with a CBR of 36.2. Thus, active players with ESBRs/550 above 36.2 are on target for a top 25 CBR if they maintain their performance level through a full career. Six players currently are on target for the top 25: Edgar Martinez, Gary Sheffield, Manny Ramirez, Jim Thome, Mike Piazza, and Jason Giambi.

CHAPTER 15

The Players Take the Field

Accounting for Player Position

As fans know, it is more difficult to acquire a good hitting shortstop than a first basemen. This is one of the reasons why Alex Rodriguez is so highly valued in baseball today. Indeed, 27 first basemen placed in the 100 best batters list compared to only 3 shortstops, with A-Rod ranking 98th. Perhaps a player's batting ability ought to be evaluated in the context of what position he holds in the field.

In this chapter, the 25 best batters are given separately for each position, along with any Hall of Famer who ranks below the 25th spot. Then, an additional rating, *Position-Adjusted Career Batter Rating*, is provided. This rating adjusts for the fact that good batters are harder to find for some positions than others. Rather than being better than the average animal, Yogi Bear's goal was to be "better than the average bear." For the position-adjusted CBR (CBR+), A-Rod ranks 34th. More significantly, A-Rod is on pace to rank seventh on this list, which would place him between Mickey Mantle and Lou Gehrig. Interestingly, Mike Piazza (currently 26th for CBR+) is on pace for a nearly identical final placement.

Top Batters by Position

Tables 15.1–15.9 rank the top 25 batters at each position, and list all Hall of Fame players regardless of their rank. A guide to the tables is given below, using the designated hitters table as an example.

Table 15.1   Top Batting Designated Hitters

DH Rank	Player	Years	Primary Team	ESBRs/ 550	CBR	Overall Rank
1	**Edgar Martinez**	1987–2003	Sea–A	40.0	35.7	27
2	*Paul Molitor*	1978–98	Mil–A	22.3	22.3	100
3	**Harold Baines**	1980–2001	Chi–A	19.6	19.6	138
4	Don Baylor	1970–88	Cal–A	18.1	18.1	165
5	Hal McRae	1968–87	KC–A	18.6	16.4	210
6	Andre Thornton	1973–87	Cle–A	19.0	13.1	291
7	Cliff Johnson	1972–86	–A	19.0	10.5	373

Notes: Seven designated hitters have at least 4000 NFPs. Hall of Famers are in italics; active players or those retired less than 5 years are in bold.

Table 14.4 shows that Edgar Martinez is the top offensive designated hitter in baseball history, with a CBR of 35.7. His ESBRs/550 NFPs of 40.0 is also the highest, indicating that he has had the highest rate of offensive performance among all designated hitters. The fact that the two ratings are not the same indicates that Martinez has not yet had a "full career," which many players never achieve. Cliff Johnson exemplifies a player with a shorter career. His rate of offensive performance, 19.0 ESBRs/550 NFPs is tied for fourth highest among designated hitters. However, his Career Batter Rating is seventh.

Table 15.2 Top Batting Catchers

C Rank	Player	Years	Primary Team	ESBRs/ 550	CBR	Overall Rank
1	**Mike Piazza**	1992–2003	LA–N	40.3	26.7	63
2	Joe Torre	1960–77	Mil–N	21.5	20.9	119
3	*Gabby Hartnett*	1922–41	Chi–N	25.8	20.6	125
4	*Johnny Bench*	1967–83	Cin–N	20.4	19.4	142
5	Gene Tenace	1969–83	Oak–A	30.2	18.3	161
6	*Mickey Cochrane*	1925–37	Phi–A	27.1	18.2	163
7	*Ernie Lombardi*	1931–47	Cin–N	25.6	18.0	168
8	Ted Simmons	1968–88	StL–N	18.0	18.0	169
9	*Carlton Fisk*	1969–93	Chi–A	16.6	16.6	202
10	*Buck Ewing*	1880–97	NY–N	25.8	16.5	206
11	*Yogi Berra*	1946–65	NY–A	17.8	16.4	209
12	*Gary Carter*	1974–92	Mon–N	15.5	15.3	238
13	*Bill Dickey*	1928–46	NY–A	19.6	15.3	241
14	Wally Schang	1913–31	–A	17.0	11.9	328
15	*Roger Bresnahan*	1897–15	NY–N	20.0	11.7	335
16	Thurman Munson	1969–79	NY–A	17.9	11.6	337
17	Mickey Tettleton	1984–97	Det–A	18.3	11.5	339
18	Darrell Porter	1971–87	KC–A	15.3	11.1	356
19	Charlie Bennett	1878–93	Det–N	23.0	11.0	358
20	*Roy Campanella*	1948–57	Bkn–N	20.1	10.6	367
21	Bill Freehan	1961–76	Det–A	12.0	9.1	407
22	**Ivan Rodriguez**	1991–2003	Tex–A	12.3	9.0	411
23	Walker Cooper	1940–57	StL–N	15.2	8.5	433
24	Smoky Burgess	1949–67	Pit–N	14.0	7.7	462
25	Jack Clements	1884–1900	Phi–N	14.7	7.7	465
54	*Rick Ferrell*	1929–47	Was–A	0.6	0.5	800
75	*Ray Schalk*	1912–29	Chi–A	–6.8	–6.8	984

Notes: Ninety-four catchers have at least 4000 NFPs. Hall of Famers are in italics; active players or those retired less than 5 years are in bold.

Table 15.3 Top Batting First Basemen

1B Rank	Player	Years	Primary Team	ESBRs/ 550	CBR	Overall Rank
1	*Lou Gehrig*	1923–39	NY–A	55.6	55.6	5
2	*Jimmie Foxx*	1925–45	Phi–A	47.1	47.1	9
3	**Frank Thomas**	1990–2003	Chi–A	45.0	40.3	16
4	**Jeff Bagwell**	1991–2003	Hou–N	40.6	38.5	19
5	*Roger Connor*	1880–97	NY–N	38.1	37.4	20
6	*Dan Brouthers*	1879–1904	–N	43.9	37.4	21
7	**Mark McGwire**	1986–2001	Oak–A	44.2	37.2	22
8	*Willie McCovey*	1959–80	SF–N	36.4	36.4	24
9	*Harmon Killebrew*	1954–75	Min–A	35.4	35.4	28
10	*Johnny Mize*	1936–53	StL–N	40.8	33.3	32
11	Dick Allen	1963–77	Phi–N	41.0	33.0	34
12	*Eddie Murray*	1977–97	Bal–A	32.8	32.8	35
13	**Fred McGriff**	1986–2003	–N	30.4	30.4	44
14	**Will Clark**	1986–2000	SF–N	30.8	28.0	55
15	*Hank Greenberg*	1930–47	Det–A	40.8	27.5	56
16	**Jim Thome**	1991–2003	Cle–A	38.4	27.2	59
17	**Rafael Palmeiro**	1986–2003	Tex–A	27.1	27.1	61
18	*Cap Anson*	1876–97	Chi–N	26.1	26.1	68
19	Boog Powell	1961–77	Bal–A	29.6	25.4	71
20	**John Olerud**	1989–2003	Tor–A	27.4	25.2	73
21	Keith Hernandez	1974–90	StL–N	26.2	24.6	75
22	Norm Cash	1958–74	Det–A	28.3	24.6	76
23	*Orlando Cepeda*	1958–74	SF–N	25.3	24.2	81
24	**Jason Giambi**	1995–2003	Oak–A	40.2	24.1	82
25	Jack Fournier	1912–27	–N	36.0	23.6	86
27	*Bill Terry*	1923–36	NY–N	28.7	22.3	99
30	*Tony Perez*	1964–86	Cin–N	19.4	19.4	140
32	*Jake Beckley*	1888–1907	Pit–N	19.2	9.2	146
33	*Jim Bottomley*	1922–37	StL–N	20.8	18.9	151
45	*George Sisler*	1915–30	StL–A	16.7	16.3	212
53	*Frank Chance*	1898–1914	Chi–N	27.5	15.2	243
84	*George Kelly*	1915–32	NY–N	12.5	8.9	415

Notes: One hundred and forty-five first basemen have at least 4000 NFPs. Hall of Famers are in italics; active players or those retired less than 5 years are in bold.

Table 15.4   Top Batting Second Basemen

1B Rank	Player	Years	Primary Team	ESBRs/ 550	CBR	Overall Rank
1	*Rogers Hornsby*	1915–37	StL–N	60.1	60.1	3
2	*Nap Lajoie*	1896–1916	Cle–A	36.2	36.2	26
3	*Rod Carew*	1967–85	Min–A	28.9	28.9	49
4	*Joe Morgan*	1963–84	Cin–N	28.6	28.6	52
5	*Eddie Collins*	1906–30	Phi–A	28.2	28.2	53
6	*Charlie Gehringer*	1924–42	Det–A	24.1	24.1	83
7	Bobby Grich	1970–86	Cal–A	23.7	21.2	115
8	**Roberto Alomar**	1988–2003	–A	19.9	19.9	134
9	*Jackie Robinson*	1947–56	Bkn–N	29.2	18.4	158
10	**Craig Biggio**	1988–2003	Hou–N	17.5	17.5	175
11	George Grantham	1922–34	Pit–N	27.1	17.3	181
12	Larry Doyle	1907–20	NY–N	21.4	17.1	188
13	Lou Whitaker	1977–95	Det–A	16.6	16.6	203
14	*Tony Lazzeri*	1926–39	NY–A	19.3	15.4	234
15	Joe Gordon	1938–50	NY–A	21.0	15.2	244
16	**Jeff Kent**	1992–2003	SF–N	19.9	14.8	252
17	Danny Murphy	1900–15	Phi–A	22.1	14.2	270
18	Ryne Sandberg	1981–97	Chi–N	13.4	13.4	286
19	Cupid Childs	1888–1901	Cle–N	18.1	13.4	288
20	Hardy Richardson	1879–92	Buf–N	18.8	12.6	309
21	**Tony Phillips**	1982–99	Oak–A	12.1	12.1	318
22	*Frankie Frisch*	1919–37	NY–N	11.8	11.8	330
23	Jimmy Williams	1899–1909	NY–A	17.2	11.5	345
24	*Bobby Doerr*	1937–51	Bos–A	12.5	11.0	359
25	Willie Randolph	1975–92	NY–A	10.4	10.4	375
27	*Billy Herman*	1931–47	Chi–N	11.0	10.4	377
28	*Bid McPhee*	1882–99	Cin–N	9.6	9.6	397
46	*Johnny Evers*	1902–29	Chi–N	7.2	5.6	555
68	*Nellie Fox*	1947–65	Chi–A	2.1	2.1	731
82	*Red Schoendienst*	1945–63	StL–N	–2.1	–2.1	877
126	*Bill Mazeroski*	1956–72	Pit–N	–10.0	–10.0	1049

Notes: One hundred and forty-six second basemen have at least 4000 NFPs. Hall of Famers are in italics; active players or those retired less than 5 year are in bold.

Table 15.5 Top Batting Third Basemen

3B Rank	Player	Years	Primary Team	ESBRs/ 550	CBR	Overall Rank
1	*Mike Schmidt*	1972–89	Phi–N	39.1	39.1	17
2	*Eddie Mathews*	1952–68	Mil–N	36.2	36.2	25
3	*George Brett*	1973–93	KC–A	33.6	33.6	30
4	**Wade Boggs**	1982–99	Bos–A	31.2	31.2	41
5	**Chipper Jones**	1993–2003	Atl–N	34.5	23.0	92
6	Ron Santo	1960–74	Chi–N	21.7	21.7	104
7	Bob Elliott	1939–53	Pit–N	21.4	19.4	143
8	*Frank Baker*	1908–22	Phi–A	26.7	19.3	144
9	**Bobby Bonilla**	1986–2001	Pit–N	20.9	18.9	149
10	Darrell Evans	1969–89	SF–N	18.7	18.7	154
11	Denny Lyons	1885–97	Phi–a	32.5	18.0	166
12	Bill Joyce	1890–98	Was–N	39.3	18.0	167
13	Ron Cey	1971–87	LA–N	18.9	17.3	180
14	Stan Hack	1932–47	Chi–N	18.1	16.9	193
15	Bill Madlock	1973–87	Pit–N	20.8	16.8	195
16	Sal Bando	1966–81	Oak–A	18.0	16.3	215
17	Tommy Leach	1898–1918	Pit–N	16.0	15.7	228
18	Ken Boyer	1955–69	StL–N	17.1	15.5	231
19	Al Rosen	1947–56	Cle–A	31.4	15.1	246
20	John McGraw	1891–1906	Bal–N	27.1	14.8	255
21	Toby Harrah	1969–86	Tex–A	15.3	14.7	257
22	**Robin Ventura**	1989–2003	Chi–A	14.5	12.9	297
23	*Brooks Robinson*	1955–77	Bal–A	12.7	12.7	305
24	Richie Hebner	1968–85	Pit–N	16.0	12.2	314
25	Eddie Yost	1944–62	Was–A	12.0	12.0	321
39	*George Kell*	1943–57	Det–A	11.0	9.0	412
42	*Jimmy Collins*	1895–08	Bos–N	10.9	8.9	418
55	*Pie Traynor*	1920–37	Pit–N	6.5	5.8	543
60	*Freddie Lindstrom*	1924–36	NY–N	7.0	4.6	594

Notes: One hundred and forty third basemen have at least 4000 NFPs. Hall of Famers are in italics; active players or those retired less than 5 year are in bold.

Table 15.6   Top Batting Shortstops

SS Rank	Player	Years	Primary Team	ESBRs/ 550	CBR	Overall Rank
1	*Honus Wagner*	1897–17	Pit–N	45.3	45.3	12
2	*Arky Vaughan*	1932–48	Pit–N	29.1	24.6	77
3	**Alex Rodriguez**	1994–2003	Sea–A	35.7	22.3	98
4	*George Davis*	1890–1909	NY–N	20.2	20.2	130
5	*Ernie Banks*	1953–71	Chi–N	18.9	18.9	150
6	**Cal Ripken Jr.**	1981–2001	Bal–A	17.7	17.7	171
7	*Joe Cronin*	1926–45	Bos–A	17.4	16.7	198
8	*Robin Yount*	1974–93	Mil–A	16.3	16.3	213
9	Ed McKean	1887–99	Cle–N	18.5	15.6	230
10	**Barry Larkin**	1986–2003	Cin–N	16.1	15.3	242
11	Bill Dahlen	1891–1911	Chi–N	15.1	15.1	247
12	Vern Stephens	1941–55	StL–A	18.3	14.7	258
13	*Luke Appling*	1930–50	Chi–A	13.7	13.7	280
14	**Julio Franco**	1982–2003	Cle–A	13.6	13.2	289
15	Alan Trammell	1977–96	Det–A	13.1	13.1	292
16	*Lou Boudreau*	1938–52	Cle–A	17.1	13.0	293
17	**Derek Jeter**	1995–2003	NY–A	21.4	13.0	295
18	**Nomar Garciaparra**	1996–2003	Bos–N	26.0	11.9	326
19	Jim Fregosi	1961–78	Cal–A	13.3	10.7	363
20	Pee Wee Reese	1940–58	Bkn–N	6.9	6.9	495
21	*Joe Sewell*	1920–33	Cle–A	7.3	6.5	515
22	Sam Wise	1881–93	Bos–N	11.4	6.5	516
23	Johnny Pesky	1942–54	Bos–A	9.7	5.8	540
24	**Tony Fernandez**	1983–2001	Tor–A	5.5	5.3	563
25	*Bobby Wallace*	1894–1918	StL–A	5.2	5.2	564
33	*Hughie Jennings*	1891–1918	Bal–N	6.6	4.0	622
42	*Travis Jackson*	1922–36	NY–N	2.7	1.9	739
43	*Dave Bancroft*	1915–30	Phi–N	2.1	1.9	740
45	*Joe Tinker*	1902–16	Chi–N	2.2	1.7	750
52	*Phil Rizzuto*	1941–56	NY–A	–0.1	–0.1	825
66	*Maury Wills*	1959–72	LA–N	–3.7	–3.7	910
67	*Ozzie Smith*	1978–96	StL–N	–4.0	–4.0	915
68	*John Ward*	1878–94	NY–N	–5.0	–5.0	937
87	*Rabbit Maranville*	1912–35	Bos–N	–7.2	–7.2	998
90	*Luis Aparicio*	1956–73	Chi–A	–7.6	–7.6	1010

Notes: One hundred and thirty-eight shortstops have at least 4000 NFPs. Hall of Famers are in italics; active players or those retired less than 5 years are in bold.

Table 15.7   Top Batting Left Fielders

LF Rank	Player	Years	Primary Team	ESBRs/ 550	CBR	Overall Rank
1	*Ted Williams*	1939–60	Bos–A	70.4	70.4	2
2	**Barry Bonds**	1986–2003	SF–N	57.4	57.4	4
3	*Ed Delahanty*	1888–1903	Phi–N	36.7	34.0	29
4	*Willie Stargell*	1962–82	Pit–N	33.6	33.4	31
5	**Rickey Henderson**	1979–2003	Oak–A	32.4	32.4	37
6	*Carl Yastrzemski*	1961–83	Bos–A	31.9	31.9	39
7	*Jesse Burkett*	1890–1905	Cle–N	31.2	31.2	40
8	Harry Stovey	1880–93	Phi–a	38.6	29.3	47
9	Joe Jackson	1908–20	Cle–A	45.3	28.0	54
10	*Zack Wheat*	1909–27	Bkn–N	27.3	27.3	58
11	*Al Simmons*	1924–44	Phi–A	27.2	27.2	60
12	*Goose Goslin*	1921–38	Was–A	26.9	26.9	62
13	*Billy Williams*	1959–76	Chi–N	26.6	26.6	65
14	Frank Howard	1958–73	Was–A	32.3	26.2	67
15	Sherry Magee	1904–19	Phi–N	27.5	25.3	72
16	*Joe Medwick*	1932–48	StL–N	27.4	24.6	74
17	*Ralph Kiner*	1946–55	Pit–N	35.3	24.5	78
18	Bob Johnson	1933–45	Phi–A	27.5	24.5	79
19	*Joe Kelley*	1891–1908	Bal–N	26.5	23.6	85
20	*Fred Clarke*	1894–1915	Pit–N	23.5	23.5	87
21	**Albert Belle**	1989–2000	Cle–A	32.1	23.5	88
22	**Tim Raines**	1979–2002	Mon–N	23.0	23.0	93
23	Minnie Minoso	1949–80	Chi–A	25.9	21.9	103
24	Jim Rice	1974–89	Bos–A	21.0	20.9	118
25	Greg Luzinski	1970–84	Phi–N	24.3	20.0	132
35	*Jim O'Rourke*	1876–1904	NY–N	19.2	17.0	190
41	*Chick Hafey*	1924–37	StL–N	29.0	16.2	219
48	*Heinie Manush*	1923–39	Was–A	16.2	14.8	253
60	*Lou Brock*	1961–79	StL–N	11.6	11.6	336

Notes: One hundred and fifty-four left fielders have at least 4000 NFPs. Hall of Famers are in italics; active players or those retired less than 5 years are in bold.

Table 15.8 Top Batting Center Fielders

CF Rank	Player	Years	Primary Team	ESBRs/ 550	CBR	Overall Rank
1	*Mickey Mantle*	1951–68	NY–A	52.3	52.3	6
2	*Ty Cobb*	1905–28	Det–A	48.1	48.1	8
3	*Willie Mays*	1951–73	SF–N	46.7	46.7	10
4	*Tris Speaker*	1907–28	Cle–A	41.2	41.2	14
5	*Joe DiMaggio*	1936–51	NY–A	45.4	38.6	18
6	*Duke Snider*	1947–64	Bkn–N	33.6	30.4	43
7	**Ken Griffey Jr.**	1989–2003	Sea–A	32.3	29.0	48
8	*Billy Hamilton*	1888–1901	Phi–N	30.6	25.7	70
9	*Hack Wilson*	1923–34	Chi–N	39.6	24.0	84
10	Pete Browning	1882–94	Lou–a	39.0	23.1	91
11	Cy Williams	1912–30	Phi–N	27.2	22.8	95
12	Jimmy Wynn	1963–77	Hou–N	25.0	22.0	101
13	**Bernie Williams**	1991–2003	NY–A	26.5	21.6	106
14	*Edd Roush*	1913–31	Cin–N	24.6	21.6	108
15	*Larry Doby*	1947–59	Cle–A	30.8	21.4	111
16	Jimmy Ryan	1885–1903	Chi–N	21.2	21.2	116
17	Wally Berger	1930–40	Bos–N	33.2	20.8	120
18	Fred Lynn	1974–90	Bos–A	23.6	20.5	126
19	*Earl Averill*	1929–41	Cle–A	25.4	20.2	131
20	Al Oliver	1968–85	Pit–N	18.8	18.8	153
21	**Chili Davis**	1981–99	Cal–A	18.7	18.7	155
22	**Ellis Burks**	1987–2003	Bos–A	20.4	18.2	162
23	George Van Haltren	1887–1903	NY–N	17.8	17.7	172
24	*Kirby Puckett*	1984–95	Min–A	20.3	17.5	177
25	Rick Monday	1966–84	Chi–N	22.0	17.3	179
28	*Max Carey*	1910–29	Pit–N	17.1	17.1	186
30	*Hugh Duffy*	1888–1906	Bos–N	19.0	16.3	214
32	*Richie Ashburn*	1948–62	Phi–N	15.5	15.5	233
43	*Earle Combs*	1924–35	NY–A	17.2	12.3	313
145	*Lloyd Waner*	1927–45	Pit–N	–1.7	–1.7	863

Notes: One hundred and sixty-seven center fielders have at least 4000 NFPs. Hall of Famers are in italics; active players or those retired less than 5 years are in bold.

Table 15.9   Top Batting Right Fielders

RF Rank	Player	Years	Primary Team	ESBRs/ 550	CBR	Overall Rank
1	*Babe Ruth*	1914–35	NY–A	74.9	74.9	1
2	*Stan Musial*	1941–63	StL–N	49.9	49.9	7
3	*Mel Ott*	1926–47	NY–N	45.5	45.5	11
4	*Frank Robinson*	1956–76	Cin–N	43.7	43.7	13
5	*Hank Aaron*	1954–76	Atl–N	40.7	40.7	15
6	*Reggie Jackson*	1967–87	Oak–A	37.1	37.1	23
7	*Sam Crawford*	1899–1917	Det–A	33.1	33.1	33
8	**Gary Sheffield**	1988–2003	–N	37.0	32.6	36
9	*Harry Heilmann*	1914–32	Det–A	33.4	32.2	38
10	*Paul Waner*	1926–45	Pit–N	30.6	30.6	42
11	*Al Kaline*	1953–74	Det–A	29.6	29.6	45
12	Jack Clark	1975–92	SF–N	32.6	29.5	46
13	**Tony Gwynn**	1982–2001	SD–N	28.8	28.8	50
14	**Manny Ramirez**	1993–2003	Cle–A	44.0	28.7	51
15	*Dave Winfield*	1973–95	NY–A	27.5	27.5	57
16	Mike Tiernan	1887–99	NY–N	35.9	26.7	64
17	Ken Singleton	1970–84	Bal–A	28.1	26.5	66
18	Reggie Smith	1966–82	Bos–A	29.2	25.8	69
19	**Larry Walker**	1989–2003	Col–N	30.1	24.4	80
20	Babe Herman	1926–45	Bkn–N	34.2	23.3	89
21	*Elmer Flick*	1898–1910	Phi–N	33.1	23.2	90
22	*Roberto Clemente*	1955–72	Pit–N	22.4	22.4	96
23	*Chuck Klein*	1928–44	Phi–N	28.3	22.3	97
24	**Jose Canseco**	1985–2001	Oak–A	24.6	22.0	102
25	Bill Nicholson	1936–53	Chi–N	30.4	21.6	105
32	*Kiki Cuyler*	1921–38	Chi–N	23.6	20.7	121
34	*Sam Thompson*	1885–1906	Phi–N	28.6	20.6	123
37	*Enos Slaughter*	1938–59	StL–N	20.3	20.3	128
49	*Harry Hooper*	1909–25	Bos–A	16.1	16.1	220
52	*King Kelly*	1878–93	Chi–N	21.4	15.4	237
55	*Ross Youngs*	1917–26	NY–N	25.4	14.7	256
57	*Willie Keeler*	1892–1910	NY–A	14.3	14.3	266
79	*Sam Rice*	1915–34	Was–A	10.1	10.1	382
108	*Tommy McCarthy*	1884–96	StL–a	7.6	4.9	585

Notes: One hundred and forty-nine right fielders have at least 4000 NFPs. Hall of Famers are in italics; active players or those retired less than 5 years are in bold.

Position-Adjusted Career Batter Rating

In this book, the primary focus has been on determining the *best batters*. The ultimate challenge, though, is to identify the *best players* overall. Such a ranking would require that the fielding ability of players be assessed as well, which I haven't attempted here. There is a way, however, to calibrate the offensive ability of players in the context of the average defensive demands of the position that they played.

The batting ability of players certainly varies by fielding position. Positions with greater defensive demands are manned by players with reduced offensive production. In fact, some may regard this as a law of baseball:

> *The offensive ability at a given position is inversely related to the defensive demands of the position.*

This "law" is a baseball version of the economic law that, under free market conditions, claims that the price of an item is a result of the natural trade-off between the opposing forces of supply and demand.

If a general manager could easily acquire a better batting shortstop with defensive skills equal to those of his current one, he would. Why can't he convert one of the many good-hitting outfielders from the farm system into a shortstop, generally one of the weakest hitting regulars? Well . . . he would lose too much on defense.

Table 15.10 shows the average difference of the ESBRs per 550 NFPs for players at each position compared to the overall average for regular players for 10 different

Table 15.10   Positional Adjustment to Event-Specific Batting Runs per 550 NFPs

Era	Min N	1B	LF	RF	DH	CF	3B	C	2B	SS
1876–92	198	8.5	3.3	1.0	—	5.8	−4.9	−2.0	−6.8	−6.7
1893–1910	231	0.5	8.5	5.6	—	5.8	−5.7	−9.5	−5.3	−6.8
1911–19	147	2.6	4.9	7.5	—	8.5	−3.6	−11.2	−4.4	−12.1
1920–30	166	6.4	9.9	10.7	—	5.2	−10.2	−5.5	−4.4	−16.1
1931–46	251	10.2	7.3	8.5	—	1.1	−5.8	−2.7	−9.5	−12.0
1947–62	248	5.4	10.0	4.7	—	3.1	0.5	−4.1	−10.9	−11.0
1963–72	213	8.5	10.0	9.6	—	2.8	0.6	−4.1	−12.9	−16.4
1973–81	217	8.7	7.5	7.8	4.0	0.0	1.2	−2.0	−9.2	−19.1
1982–92	292	9.9	5.1	4.9	5.2	−0.5	1.3	−6.2	−6.0	−14.0
1993–2003	336	10.4	6.4	7.3	9.0	−2.6	−1.7	−7.3	−6.8	−11.8
1876–1946 Avg.		6.0	7.0	6.8	—	4.9	−6.0	−5.4	−6.3	−10.4
1947–2003 Avg.		8.7	7.6	6.7	6.3	0.4	0.3	−5.0	−8.8	−14.0

Notes: The positional adjustment is the difference of the average ESBRs/550 NFPs for players at the position compared to all regulars in the era.

Positions are listed in decreasing order of the adjustment for 1947–2003.

Min N gives the smallest sample size for any adjustment, except for C and DH.

Highest two positional adjustments in era are in bold, lowest two are underlined.

eras. This table enables us to assess changes in the defensive demands of positions over time and to adjust for the batting exploits of players based on the position they anchored in the field.

The first era, 1876–92, shows substantial departure from the next era, with first basemen and catchers having much higher positional adjustments, while left fielders have a much lower adjustment. Disregarding this initial era, several key shifts can be seen. The catcher position shows an offensive rise in 1920 but a decline in 1982. Meanwhile, second base is the counterbalancing position to catcher, with the offense of second basemen declining in 1931 but shifting upward in 1982.

The average positional adjustments for 1876–1946 and 1947–2003, shown in Table 15.10, highlight the main changes. The offense of first basemen was about 3 points lower prior to 1947. Third base has been a much more potent position offensively since 1947, with the average positional adjustment rising from –6.1 to 0.3. By contrast, the offensive productivity of shortstops and centerfielders has declined.

Interestingly, the designated hitters do not have the highest positional adjustments in Table 15.10; since 1973, first basemen have. Sometimes players with crippled knees became their team's designated hitters. Now, with star players such as Frank Thomas and Edgar Martinez anchored as their team's designated hitters, the positional adjustment has risen to just below that of first basemen. Because the defensive demands of designated hitters are less than those of first basemen, though, the positional adjustment of first basemen will be used for designated hitters. Formulas 15.1 and 15.2 show how to use Table 15.10 to obtain position-adjusted single-season and career ratings.

In 1997 Mike Piazza posted an outstanding mark of 65.9 ESBRs/550 NFPs—good for 58th place on the all-time single season list. His accomplishment is even more remarkable when one considers that Piazza is a catcher. Piazza's position-adjusted mark in 1997 (using Formula 15.1) was 73.2, which is 27th on the position-adjusted list (Appendix L.14).

Formula 15.1   **Single-season position-adjusted ESBRs/550 NFPs**

Single-season position-adjusted ESBRs/550 NFPs (ESBRs+/550 NFPs)

= ESBRs/550 NFPs − positional adjustment to ESBRs/550 NFPs,
where the last term above is obtained from Table 15.10. For DHs, the position with the greatest downward adjustment (1B in all eras) is used.

The top 100 players for position-adjusted Career Batter Rating are shown in Table 15.11. Shortstops, second-basemen, and catchers move up in this list compared to their placement in CBR. Meanwhile, the rankings of first basemen, left fielders, and right fielders drop. After position is adjusting for, Rogers Hornsby slips past Ted Williams into second place, Honus Wagner jumps from 12th into 5th place, while Joe Morgan skyrockets from 52nd to 12th.

Complete Listing of All Qualifying Players

Appendix N gives adjusted values for all basic offensive events, as well as OBP, SLG, CBR, and rankings for both CBR and CBR+ for all 1140 players with at least 4000 NFPs in their careers.

Table 15.11 The 100 Best Position-Adjusted Batters

Rank	Player	Years	Primary Team	Pos	ESBRs+/ 550	CBR+
1	Babe Ruth	1914–35	NY–A	RF	66.2	66.2
2	Rogers Hornsby	1915–37	StL–N	2B	65.5	65.5
3	Ted Williams	1939–60	Bos–A	LF	61.3	61.3
4	**Barry Bonds**	1986–2003	SF–N	LF	51.8	51.8
5	Honus Wagner	1897–1917	Pit–N	SS	50.2	50.2
6	Mickey Mantle	1951–68	NY–A	CF	48.6	48.6
7	Lou Gehrig	1923–39	NY–A	1B	47.1	47.1
8	Willie Mays	1951–73	SF–N	CF	43.7	43.7
9	Stan Musial	1941–63	StL–N	RF	42.8	42.8
10	Ty Cobb	1905–28	Det–A	CF	40.9	40.9
11	Nap Lajoie	1896–1916	Cle–A	2B	40.6	40.6
12	Joe Morgan	1963–84	Cin–N	2B	39.7	39.7
13	Jimmie Foxx	1925–45	Phi–A	1B	38.5	38.5
14	Mel Ott	1926–47	NY–N	RF	38.1	38.1
15	Mike Schmidt	1972–89	Phi–N	3B	37.3	37.3
16	Joe DiMaggio	1936–51	NY–A	CF	43.0	36.6
17	Eddie Mathews	1952–68	Mil–N	3B	35.7	35.7
18	Frank Robinson	1956–76	Cin–N	RF	35.3	35.3
19	Tris Speaker	1907–28	Cle–A	CF	34.1	34.1
20	Hank Aaron	1954–76	Atl–N	RF	33.9	33.9
21	Arky Vaughan	1932–48	Pit–N	SS	39.8	33.6
22	Eddie Collins	1906–30	Phi–A	2B	32.7	32.7
23	Roger Connor	1880–97	NY–N	1B	33.1	32.5
24	**Frank Thomas**	1990–2003	Chi–A	1B	35.7	32.0
25	Charlie Gehringer	1924–42	Det–A	2B	31.8	31.8
26	**Mike Piazza**	1992–2003	LA–N	C	47.6	31.6
27	Dan Brouthers	1879–1904	–N	1B	37.0	31.5
28	Cal Ripken Jr.	1981–2001	Bal–A	SS	31.4	31.4
29	Rod Carew	1967–85	Min–A	2B	31.0	31.0
30	George Brett	1973–93	KC–A	3B	30.8	30.8
31	**Ken Griffey Jr.**	1989–2003	Sea–A	CF	34.3	30.8
32	Wade Boggs	1982–99	Bos–A	3B	30.1	30.1
33	**Edgar Martinez**	1987–2003	Sea–A	DH	33.5	29.9
34	**Alex Rodriguez**	1994–2003	Sea–A	SS	47.4	29.6
35	Harmon Killebrew	1954–75	Min–A	3B	29.6	29.6
36	Bobby Grich	1970–86	Cal–A	2B	32.8	29.4
37	Reggie Jackson	1967–87	Oak–A	RF	29.4	29.4
38	**Gary Sheffield**	1988–2003	–N	RF	32.9	29.0
39	Dick Allen	1963–77	Phi–N	1B	35.7	28.8
40	Mark McGwire	1986–2001	Oak–A	1B	34.1	28.7
41	**Jeff Bagwell**	1991–2003	Hou–N	1B	30.3	28.7
42	Ed Delahanty	1888–1903	Phi–N	LF	31.0	28.7
43	Joe Cronin	1926–45	Bos–A	SS	29.2	28.2
44	Alan Trammell	1977–96	Det–A	SS	28.0	28.0
45	Willie McCovey	1959–80	SF–N	1B	27.9	27.9
46	Rickey Henderson	1979–2002	Oak–A	LF	27.9	27.9
47	Robin Yount	1974–93	Mil–A	SS	27.6	27.6
48	**Barry Larkin**	1986–2003	Cin–N	SS	28.7	27.3
49	Duke Snider	1947–64	Bkn–N	CF	29.8	27.0
50	Sam Crawford	1899–1917	Det–A	RF	26.8	26.8

Table 15.11 *(continued)*

Rank	Player	Years	Primary Team	Pos	ESBRs+/550	CBR+
51	Johnny Mize	1936–53	StL–N	1B	32.3	26.4
52	**Roberto Alomar**	1988–2003	–A	2B	26.4	26.4
53	Harry Stovey	1880–93	Phi–a	LF	33.5	25.4
54	Luke Appling	1930–50	Chi–A	SS	25.0	25.0
55	George Davis	1890–1909	NY–N	SS	24.9	24.9
56	Willie Stargell	1962–82	Pit–N	LF	24.4	24.2
57	**Craig Biggio**	1988–2003	Hou–N	2B	24.1	24.1
58	Al Kaline	1953–74	Det–A	RF	23.9	23.9
59	**Manny Ramirez**	1993–2003	Cle–A	RF	36.8	23.9
60	Joe Jackson	1908–20	Cle–A	LF	38.4	23.7
61	Mike Tiernan	1887–99	NY–N	RF	31.9	23.7
62	Tony Gwynn	1982–2001	SD–N	RF	23.7	23.7
63	Eddie Murray	1977–97	Bal–A	1B	23.6	23.6
64	Jesse Burkett	1890–1905	Cle–N	LF	23.6	23.6
65	Gabby Hartnett	1922–41	Chi–N	C	29.7	23.6
66	**Bernie Williams**	1991–2003	NY–A	CF	28.9	23.6
67	Lou Whitaker	1977–95	Det–A	2B	23.3	23.3
68	Harry Heilmann	1914–32	Det–A	RF	24.1	23.2
69	**Chipper Jones**	1993–2003	Atl–N	3B	34.5	23.0
70	Jack Clark	1975–92	SF–N	RF	25.3	22.9
71	Carl Yastrzemski	1961–83	Bos–A	LF	22.7	22.7
72	Frank Baker	1908–22	Phi–A	3B	31.2	22.6
73	**Jim Thome**	1991–2003	Cle–A	1B	31.7	22.4
74	Joe Gordon	1938–50	NY–A	2B	31.0	22.4
75	Vern Stephens	1941–55	StL–A	SS	27.8	22.2
76	Stan Hack	1932–47	Chi–N	3B	23.7	22.1
77	Paul Molitor	1978–98	Mil–A	DH	21.9	21.9
78	Lou Boudreau	1938–52	Cle–A	SS	28.7	21.9
79	Ernie Banks	1953–71	Chi–N	SS	21.8	21.8
80	Billy Hamilton	1888–1901	Phi–N	CF	25.9	21.7
81	Bill Dahlen	1891–1911	Chi–N	SS	21.7	21.7
82	Johnny Bench	1967–83	Cin–N	C	22.6	21.5
83	Tony Lazzeri	1926–39	NY–A	2B	26.7	21.3
84	Toby Harrah	1969–86	Tex–A	3B	22.2	21.3
85	Paul Waner	1926–45	Pit–N	RF	21.2	21.2
86	Hank Greenberg	1930–47	Det–A	1B	31.6	21.2
87	Ed McKean	1887–99	Cle–N	SS	25.2	21.2
88	Pete Browning	1882–94	Lou–a	CF	35.8	21.2
89	Dave Winfield	1973–95	NY–A	RF	21.1	21.1
90	Ron Santo	1960–74	Chi–N	3B	21.0	21.0
91	Mickey Cochrane	1925–37	Phi–A	C	31.2	21.0
92	Reggie Smith	1966–82	Bos–A	RF	23.7	20.9
93	Denny Lyons	1885–97	Phi–a	3B	37.4	20.8
94	Larry Doyle	1907–20	NY–N	2B	26.0	20.8
95	Al Simmons	1924–44	Phi–A	LF	20.7	20.7
96	Jackie Robinson	1947–56	Bkn–N	2B	32.8	20.7
97	Joe Torre	1960–77	Mil–N	C	21.3	20.7
98	Hack Wilson	1923–34	Chi–N	CF	33.9	20.6
99	Carlton Fisk	1969–93	Chi–A	C	20.5	20.5
100	Jim Fregosi	1961–78	Cal–A	SS	25.3	20.4

CHAPTER 16

Final Score

Updates for the 2004 Season

Ichiro and Barry: Chasing for Marks They Already Own?

History Through 2003

One of the highlights of the 2004 season was Ichiro's quest to break the single-season hits mark of 257 set in 1920 by George Sisler. Meanwhile, Barry Bonds' assault of the single-season on-base mark received much less attention. Not surprisingly, Bonds was chasing Ruth's long shadow, since Ruth was on base 379 times in 1923.

In the early 1960s, the baseball season was lengthened from 154 to 162 games. As a consequence, players since then have had a certain advantage in single-season count records. On the other hand, players from the 1920s and 1930s enjoyed the highest seasons for batting average since the turn of the 20th century. Adjusted count totals, presented in the left-side columns of Appendix L, account for the differences in league averages over time, and thus render an advantage to recent players. Bearing this in mind, both Ichiro and Bonds already hold the adjusted marks in their respective categories.

Ichiro had 246.6 adjusted hits in 2001, which easily outdistanced the previous mark of 236.8 set by Don Mattingly in 1986. Moreover, each of Ichiro's first three seasons ranks among the top 29 of all-time. The bias toward 162-game seasons is readily apparent, with only 3 of the top 20 seasons having occurred before then.

Adjusted averages (shown in the right-side columns in Appendix L), which account for the playing time, is one way to adjust for season length. For adjusted batting average, 10 of the top 20 seasons were of the 162-game variety, with Ichiro's 2001 campaign placing 20th. Meanwhile, Sisler's 1920 season ranked 24th for adjusted hits but only 88th for adjusted batting average, through 2003.

In 2002, Barry Bonds set the adjusted times on base mark, beating the mark set in 1988 by Wade Boggs, with Ruth's 1923 season placing third. Interestingly, 8 of the top 20 seasons occurred prior to the current 162-game format, with Ted Williams and Babe Ruth accounting for 6 of them. When looking at adjusted on-base percentage, Barry Bonds' 2002 season still ranks first, followed by his 2003 and 2001 seasons.

The 2004 Season

Ichiro broke Sisler's unadjusted total by 5, with 262 hits. He smashed his own adjusted hits mark by 18, by racking up 264.4 adjusted hits. For adjusted batting average, Ichiro's 2004 campaign ranks fourth, with a .376 mark.

Bonds fell three short of Ruth's times-on-base mark, getting on base 376 times, including a record 232 bases on balls. Bonds topped his 2002 adjusted times on base total by 16, with 360.3. Bonds's 2004 adjusted on-base percentage is .599, easily outpacing the previous mark of .574, set by Bonds in 2002. To achieve this mark, Bonds had the 30th highest adjusted batting average (.353) and highest adjusted bases on balls rate (200.1 per 550 NFPs) in history.

With the 2004 season in the books, Ichiro and Bonds hold the top 2 adjusted totals for hits and times-on-base in a season in baseball history, with Ichiro holding the raw mark for hits as well.

Triples Time

In 2004, Tampa Bay's Carl Crawford and Anaheim's Chone Figgins both ran their way into the top 10 single seasons for adjusted triples, with 21.7 (7th) and 21.1 (10th), respectively. Per 500 at-bats, Figgins's season places 10th at 18.3, while Crawford's ranks 16th at 17.3

Climbing the Ladder of Success

The Career Batter Rating weights a player's productive career ESBRs/550 NFPs with his career fullness score. Consequently, players will tend to climb up the CBR list with more playing time if they have had less than a full career. Table 16.1 lists the 31 players who were active in 2004 and are currently on target for a final CBR in the top 100. To achieve their targets, players need to maintain their established performance level (given by ESBRs/550 NFPs) and complete a full career of 9000 NFPs. Many of the players will fail to achieve a full career due to injuries or early retirement. Table 16.2 shows the average number of NFPs by age for the 112 players who attained a full career through the 2003 season.

Barry Bonds, with a terrific 2004 season, slipped past Rogers Hornsby into third place for CBR. Albert Pujols, at 24 years old, is in the early stages of an outstanding baseball career. He is currently on target to become the eighth best batter in baseball history, which would rank him next to Ty Cobb. Nine additional active players—Frank Thomas, Manny Ramirez, Jeff Bagwell, Jim Thome, Mike Piazza, Jason Giambi, Vladimir Guerrero, Gary Sheffield, and Brian Giles—are seeking top 25 career rankings, with Thomas and Bagwell already there.

Table 16.1 Career Batting Rating Levels and Targets through 2004 for Players Active in 2004

Player	Age	CFS	ESBRs/ 550	CBR	2004 Rank	Target Rank	Player to Pass
Barry Bonds	39	1.00	60.7	60.7	3	3	Rogers Hornsby
Albert Pujols	24	.30	49.8	14.9	250	8	Ty Cobb
Frank Thomas	36	.93	44.9	41.7	14	13	Frank Robinson
Manny Ramirez	32	.72	43.9	31.7	40	13	Frank Robinson
Jeff Bagwell	37	1.00	38.6	38.6	18	18	Joe DiMaggio
Jim Thome	33	.78	38.3	29.7	45	20	Roger Connor
Mike Piazza	35	.72	38.1	27.5	56	20	Roger Connor
Jason Giambi	33	.64	37.6	23.9	85	20	Roger Connor
Vladimir Guerrero	28	.54	37.3	20.2	130	22	Mark McGwire
Gary Sheffield	35	.96	36.7	35.1	29	24	Willie McCovey
Brian Giles	33	.55	36.4	19.9	133	24	Willie McCovey
Edgar Martinez	41	.95	37.5	35.8	27	27	Harmon Killebrew
Alex Rodriguez	28	.70	34.7	24.4	80	29	Ed Delahanty
Todd Helton	30	.53	34.5	18.2	162	29	Ed Delahanty
Chipper Jones	29	.73	33.0	24.1	82	34	Dick Allen
Carlos Delgado	32	.66	33.0	21.8	104	34	Dick Allen
Bobby Abreu	30	.55	32.9	18.0	167	35	Eddie Murray
Ken Griffey, Jr.	34	.94	31.6	29.6	45	40	Jesse Burkett
Larry Walker	37	.84	30.4	25.7	70	43	Duke Snider
Fred McGriff	40	1.00	30.4	30.4	44	44	Al Kaline
Jim Edmonds	34	.65	29.3	19.1	148	47	Harry Stovey
John Olerud	35	.97	27.4	25.9	69	58	Zach Wheat
Rafael Palmeiro	39	1.00	27.1	27.1	61	61	Goose Goslin
Scott Rolen	29	.56	25.7	14.5	261	70	Billy Hamilton
Ryan Klesko	33	.61	25.5	15.7	226	71	Boog Powell
Nomar Garciaparra	30	.50	25.1	12.5	310	74	Joe Medwick
Bernie Williams	35	.89	25.1	22.2	101	74	Joe Medwick
Tim Salmon	35	.75	25.0	18.7	154	74	Joe Medwick
Juan Gonzalez	34	.79	24.8	19.5	139	74	Joe Medwick
Ichiro Suzuki	30	.33	24.7	8.0	453	74	Joe Medwick
Moises Alou	37	.73	24.2	17.6	173	81	Orlando Cepeda

Notes: Players who are on target to attain a "full career" using the NFP targets by age are in bold.

Age = age as of June 30, 2004; CFS = career fullness score. ESBRs/550 NFPs and CBR are given through the 2004 season. Target Rank = CBR ranking of player if they maintain their career ESBRs/550 NFPs through a full career. Player to Pass = the retired player that they would just outrank if they achieve their target rank.

Table 16.2 Benchmark NFP Totals by Player Age to Attain a Full Career

Age	28	29	30	31	32	33	34	35	36	37
NFPs	3900	4500	5100	5800	6400	6900	7500	8100	8600	9100
CFS	.44	.50	.57	.64	.71	.77	.84	.90	.96	1.00

Notes: CFS = career fullness score.

Player	Age	CFS	ESBRs/ 550	CBR+	2004 Rank	Target Rank	Player to Pass
Barry Bonds	39	1.00	55.0	55.0	4	4	Honus Wagner
Alex Rodriguez	28	.70	45.3	31.8	25	8	Willie Mays
Albert Pujols	24	.30	44.4	13.3	244	8	Willie Mays
Mike Piazza	35	.72	44.0	31.7	26	8	Willie Mays
Nomar Garciaparra	30	.50	36.8	18.4	130	16	Joe DiMaggio
Manny Ramirez	32	.72	36.7	26.6	51	16	Joe DiMaggio
Frank Thomas	36	.93	35.5	33.1	22	18	Frank Robinson
Ken Griffey, Jr.	34	.94	33.6	31.5	27	21	Arky Vaughan
Chipper Jones	32	.73	33.1	24.2	56	22	Eddie Collins
Gary Shefffield	35	.96	32.3	31.0	29	24	Charlie Gehringer
Brian Giles	33	.55	32.3	17.7	144	24	Charlie Gehringer
Derek Jeter	30	.68	32.1	22.0	77	24	Charlie Gehringer
Jim Edmonds	34	.65	31.3	20.4	100	29	Rod Carew
Jim Thome	33	.78	31.3	24.3	56	29	Rod Carew
Edgar Martinez	41	.95	29.4	29.4	36	36	Bobby Grich
Vladimir Guerrero	28	.54	30.0	16.2	172	33	Harmon Killebrew
Jeff Bagwell	36	1.00	28.3	28.3	43	43	Joe Cronin
Barry Larkin	40	.99	28.2	28.0	44	43	Joe Cronin
Jason Giambi	33	.64	28.1	17.8	142	44	Alan Trammell
Bernie Williams	35	.89	27.5	24.4	56	48	Duke Snider
Scott Rolen	29	.56	27.4	15.5	187	48	Duke Snider
Jorge Posada	32	.44	26.7	11.8	285	51	Johnny Mize
Roberto Alomar	36	1.00	26.4	26.4	52	52	Harry Stovey
Jeff Kent	36	.81	25.7	20.8	93	53	Harry Stovey
Bobby Abreu	30	.55	25.6	14.0	224	53	Harry Stovey
Todd Helton	30	.53	24.2	12.8	258	56	Willie Stargell
Craig Biggio	38	1.00	24.1	24.1	57	57	Al Kaline
Larry Walker	37	.84	24.1	20.3	102	57	Al Kaline
Carlos Delgado	32	.66	22.9	15.1	195	70	Jack Clark
Javy Lopez	33	.55	22.3	12.3	270	75	Vern Stephens
Miguel Tejada	28	.52	21.7	11.2	306	80	Billy Hamilton
Ivan Rodriguez	32	.79	21.1	16.7	162	89	Dave Winfield

Notes: who are on target to attain a "full career" using the NFP targets by age are in bold.

Age = age as of June 30, 2004; CFS = career fullness score. ESBRs+/550 NFPs and CBR+ are given through the 2004 season. Target Rank = CBR+ ranking of player if they maintain their career ESBRs+/550 NFPs through a full career. Player to Pass = the retired player that they would just outrank if they achieve their target rank.

Interestingly, Nomar Garciaparra, Bernie Williams, Tim Salmon, Juan Gonzalez, and Ichiro Suzuki are all trying to take 74th place away from Joe Medwick. However, all are behind the average pace to attain a full career. In Ichiro's case, it is attributable to his seasons in the Japanese League prior to joining the Seattle Mariners. With an appropriate statistical adjustment for those seasons, they could be incorporated into Ichiro's career record, providing a better picture of his place in baseball history.

Table 16.3 lists the 32 players who were active in 2004 and are currently on target for a final position-adjusted CBR in the top 100. Four are targeting top 10 finishes for position-adjusted CBR—Barry Bonds ranks fourth, while Alex Rodriguez, Albert Pujols, and Mike Piazza would all like to attain the batting value of Willie Mays. Unfortunately, both A-Rod and Piazza are transitioning to positions for which greater offensive production is the norm and are thus likely to fall off their targets. On the positive side, both have already earned rankings among the top 26. Eight additional players—Nomar Garciaparra, Manny Ramirez, Frank Thomas, Ken Griffey Jr., Chipper Jones, Gary Sheffield, Brian Giles, and Derek Jeter—are all on target for placement among the top 25.

CHAPTER 17

Post-Game Report
Conclusions

The primary goal of this book has been to identify the *best batters*. The two players at the top of my method—Babe Ruth and Ted Williams—will surprise few aficionados of the game. In a recent article that appeared in *Math Horizons* entitled "Who is the Greatest Hitter of Them All?" Joseph A. Gallian compares several evaluation methods and reaches the same conclusion. A wonderful cartoon, reprinted from that article, illustrates the melee for third place, though.

It is important to bear in mind the limitations of the Event-Specific Batting Runs and Career Batter Rating formulas. They identify the *best batters* across baseball history, not the *best players* overall. As such, only batting has been rated—neither fielding nor base-running ability has been assessed.

Cartoon courtesy of Chuck Slack.

Three overall ratings have been introduced:

1. *Event-Specific Batting Runs/550 NFPs* is a rate statistic, giving the number of batting runs produced in 550 NFPs, which is a typical seasonal total for a regular player.
2. *Career Batter Rating* is a lifetime achievement rating that downweights players with less than a full career (defined as 9000 NFPs).
3. *Position-Adjusted Career Batter Rating* adjusts the player's offensive performance for the average level achieved by other players at that position in his era.

Either of the last two ratings is more suitable when judging a player's credentials for the Hall of Fame. The first formula is a rate measure; the latter two represent a blend between a rate measure and a quantity measure, with the quantity capped at 9000 NFPs.

Total Baseball's Total Player Rating (TPR) is similarly a mixed rating, since under-average seasons cause TPR to decline. On the other hand, Bill James' Win Shares is a pure quantity measure. In his overall ranking of players, presented in *The New Bill James Historical Baseball Abstract*, however, James mixes the player's Win Shares with rate measures. Thus, the most significant ratings for Palmer, James, and myself all are mixtures of rate and quantity measures.

All of the single-season and productive career performance rankings have been based on rate statistics. Readers can use the adjusted number of hits, home runs, and so forth as quantity measures for particular events. These are given in Appendices L and M.

Comparison with Other Methods

Table 17.1 contrasts the Career Batter Ranking with Palmer's Adjusted Batting Wins from the *Baseball Encyclopedia* and the Batting portion of Bill James's Win Shares. All three methods rank Babe Ruth at the top. We will calibrate them by giving Ruth a score of 100 and the other players scores that are relative to that. This is done for the other two methods by obtaining the Adjusted Batting Wins or Batting Win Shares per 9000 NFPs and then applying the longevity adjustment as in the Career Batter Rating. For example, Ruth has 135.2 Adjusted Batting Wins and 10,504 career NFPs. This corresponds to 115.8 Adjusted Batting Wins per 9000 NFPs. Through 2003, Barry Bonds has 91.9 Adjusted Batting Wins per 9000 NFPs, which is 79% of Ruth's mark. Thus, Bonds receives a score of 79.

In agreement with the Math Horizons cartoon, all three methods rank Babe Ruth first and Ted Williams second. They also all rank Bonds, Cobb, Gehrig, Hornsby, and Mantle in the top 10. CBR and Adjusted Batting Wins bot give Musial and Foxx top 10 placements, while CBR and Win Shares both include Mays. Thomas, Speaker, and Wagner made only one of the lists.

Table 17.1   Comparison of Three Best Batter Evaluations

	Career Batter Rating		Adjusted Batting Wins		Batting Win Shares	
Rank	Player	Score	Player	Score	Player	Score
1	Babe Ruth	100	Babe Ruth	100	Babe Ruth	100
2	Ted Williams	94	Ted Williams	82	Ted Williams	89
3	Rogers Hornsby	80	Barry Bonds	79	Mickey Mantle	89
4	Barry Bonds	77	Lou Gehrig	76	Ty Cobb	87
5	Lou Gehrig	74	Rogers Hornsby	74	Barry Bonds	85
6	Mickey Mantle	70	Mickey Mantle	71	Rogers Hornsby	83
7	Stan Musial	67	Ty Cobb	63	Lou Gehrig	82
8	Ty Cobb	64	Stan Musial	57	Honus Wagner	77
9	Jimmie Foxx	63	Jimmie Foxx	57	Tris Speaker	76
10	Willie Mays	62	Frank Thomas	56	Willie Mays	75

The Win Shares method has the lowest gap between Ruth and the other players, while the Adjusted Batting Wins approach has the greatest.

Table 17.2 shows a composite rating of the three methods, obtained by averaging the player's 3 scores. The 10 players are all members of the CBR top 10. While the three methods disagreed on the third place batter, the composite rating gives Barry Bonds the nod (even though the Win Shares method goes through the 2001 season, missing Bonds' superlative 2002 and 2003 seasons).

Table 17.2   Top 10 Batters Based on Composite Rating

1	Babe Ruth	100	6	Mickey Mantle	77
2	Ted Williams	88	7	Ty Cobb	71
3	Barry Bonds	80	8	Stan Musial	66
4	Rogers Hornsby	79	9	Willie Mays	64
5	Lou Gehrig	77	10	Jimmie Foxx	63

Baseball and Statistics

Ranking baseball players over history is a difficult enterprise and can sometimes be based on subjective judgments. Since major league baseball now extends more than 125 years, however, no single observer has seen all of the players. Thus, such rankings require that judgments from many sources be pooled together somehow.

Baseball is a game steeped in statistics, which record the play-by-play achievements of players. I believe that these statistics have become the major source of our collective wisdom of players' abilities. The mathematical field of statistics provides tools for the evaluation of data. Which tools are used depends heavily on the assumptions one employs. The primary assumption at the core of my work is:

After adjusting for the ballpark effect, a pth percentile player in one year is equal in ability to a pth percentile player from another year for each basic offensive event.

When comparing players, there is no escaping making assumptions. The use of unadjusted averages to compare players is tantamount to assuming that the unadjusted averages are based on equal conditions. Since the batters, pitchers, managers, equipment, ballparks, and rules have all changed over time, such an assumption is quite strong indeed.

In *Baseball's All-Time Best Hitters*, I made the case that at least some of the shifts in batting average seen in different ballparks and different seasons are due to the conditions of play, not differences in players' abilities. For those who accept that argument, well-considered adjusted averages would provide a fairer means of comparison than raw, unadjusted averages.

Unfortunately, there are no baseball gods that declare that such adjustments will be easy to make or understand. In this book, I have attempted to keep the adjustments as simple as possible, while not forsaking accuracy for simplicity. Each decision that affected the adjustment was done to render the comparison fairer in my judgment, and I believed it important to describe those decisions to the reader.

Where Do We Go from Here?

I believe that the primary assumption that underlies this book goes a long way toward being able to compare players fairly over baseball history. Below is my subjective score between 1 and 10 on how fair various approaches are for ranking the batting ability of individual players over baseball history.

Progressive Steps in Identifying the Best Batters		Score
	Past	
1	Batting average	3
2	Mean-adjusted batting average	4
3	Linear weights; OPS; Runs Created	6
4	Park adjustment for runs	7
	Present	
5	Transformations and individual event park adjustments	8
	Future	
6	Improved estimation of park effects	8.2
7	Changing ability of an "average player" over history	9.0
8	Game-by-game analysis, weather conditions, etc.	9.2
9	Play-by-play analysis	9.9

Step 1: Batting Average

Historically, the first method for comparing batting ability was the batting average. Before 1920, home runs were an especially rare event. Thus, the top hitters for average tended to be among the game's best overall, even though players' abilities to garner extra-base hits certainly differed.

Step 2: Mean-Adjusted Batting Average

Since at least the late 1960s, some fans and reporters have recognized that a player's batting average should be looked at in the context of the league batting average. In the year my love affair with baseball began—1969—*Street and Smith's Baseball* described such an adjustment. They speculated about the impact that lowering the pitcher's mound from 15 inches to 10 inches above the level of home plate would have on batting averages.

Step 3: Linear Weights; OPS; Runs Created

In the 1980s, Pete Palmer developed the Linear Weights method, and Bill James created his Runs Created formula. Both methods incorporated walks into the system and rated the hit by the number of bases the hitter reached.

Step 4: Park Adjustment for Runs

Bill James and Pete Palmer also both recognized that ballparks have an important impact on the offensive production of players. In his Win Shares system, James uses three different park adjustments: for runs, for home runs, and for offense other than home runs. Unfortunately, James did not publish these park effects, so they cannot be directly compared to those developed in this book. In his Linear Weights system, Palmer adjusted the offensive data by the park effect for runs.

Step 5: Transformations and Individual Event Park Adjustment

This book gives separate ballpark effect adjustments for individual offensive events that comprise an overall batter rating. It also uses standard deviations and statistical transformations to handle changes in the distribution of player performance over time, which reduces era biases present in methods that are simply mean adjusted. Moreover, they also allow for fair comparisons of individual offensive events, extending the work done in *Baseball's All-Time Best Hitters* for batting average and bases on balls.

Step 6: Improved Park Effect Estimates

With time, additional home/road data will become available, yielding further improvements in the park adjustments. As the inside-the-park home run data become more complete for the 19th century and deadball eras, these different kinds of home runs may be analyzed differently.

Step 7: Improved Talent Pool Modeling

Perhaps the next major statistical advance will be the incorporation of a model that estimates how the talent pool may have improved or declined on a year-by-year basis. The standard deviation adjustment is really just an initial attempt to deal with talent pool issues. The primary assumption that a 90th percentile player in say, 1901, would be a 90th percentile player today is not likely to be true for each offensive event that we have considered. With a more statistically sophisticated model for talent changes over time than the one presented here, I suspect that Babe Ruth's home run exploits will not look quite as dramatic as they do here. I don't know if that will be enough to unseat his largely unchallenged claim to the top spot. The most recent entrants to the top 10—Barry Bonds and Willie Mays—are likely to benefit from such an improvement.

Step 8: Game-by-Game Analysis

All the previous steps require only that player and ballpark data be summed up across entire seasons. How will game-by-game data help? I'll suggest three benefits.

First, single-season ballpark effects are a mixture of random variation and effects due to conditions at game time, such as weather and visibility. I suspect that some of the short-lived ballpark effects that I have identified are weather related. Chicago, with its famed "wind blowing out" days and Montreal, with its frigid days, seem especially worthy of further investigation.

Second, player declines may occur mid-season owing to injury, illness, or aging. For example, in a personal correspondence, researcher David Stephan has suggested that Lou Gehrig's decline due to amyotrophic lateral sclerosis began on August 14, 1937.

Third and finally, some games (more common in the 19th century and deadball eras than today) are so unusual as to be best treated as statistical outliers and removed from the data for the purposes of player evaluation.

One such game occurred on June 9, 1901 in Cincinnati between the New York Giants and the Cincinnati Reds. Fourteen doubles were struck in that game, with 10 hit by the Giants. In 1901, an average of 2.79 doubles were hit per game in the National League. Under a standard statistical model for such data (a Poisson model), 14 or more doubles should occur only once in 700,000 non–extra-inning games. Something was clearly strange here!

According to the *Cincinnati Enquirer*, the game was "forfeited to New York in the last half of the ninth after two were out because there was not enough space to play on." The space problem was the huge standing room only crowd in the outfield. The *Cincinnati Enquirer* continued: "On an open ground, many of the flies would have been easy outs. Good fielding was simply out of the question, and the man who knocked the ball into the crowd was a lucky mortal."

If this game is discounted, the Giants' (who had 31 hits in 57 at-bats) raw 1901 batting average would drop 3 points, from .253 to .250.

Step 9: Play-by-Play Analysis

Finally, we come down to play-by-play data, with any additional relevant data, such as injury information on the player. Since this represents all the data we will ever have, when we have properly analyzed it, we should converge on the final answer to our quest. Thus, I have given a 9.9 to this final step, since there will probably still be subjective differences of opinion that cannot be reconciled.

Game-by-game level data improves our baseball microscope by a factor of 162 from our current basic data unit—the season. Play-by-play data will further improve our vision only by a factor of about 4. Still, I expect the play-by-play data to play a larger role in reshaping the ranking of players, because it allows us to look at individual batting situations. Here are a couple of examples.

In today's game, a relief pitcher is often called in to face the team's main star in the latter innings, with the pitcher having the same handedness as the batting star. If this happens routinely, batters ahead of the superstar have a relative advantage by facing more tired pitchers, while opposite-handed batters who hit afterward have a handedness edge.

The impact of lineup position one one's offensive statistics needs to be studied further. We have seen how runs and RBIs are affected by the player's position in the lineup. Linear Weights methods, such as Event-Specific Batting Runs and CBR, are supposed to show run productivity regardless of lineup position. However, that's not entirely true.

Table 17.3 Offensive Averages Under Different Situations, National League 1984–92

Situation	National League, 1984–92					
	AB	Pct	BA	OBP	SLG	OPS
Bases empty	38,049	58	.247	.307	.369	.676
Runner on first	11,375	17	.270	.320	.398	.718
Runners/Scor. Pos.	16,376	25	.253	.341	.375	.716

Source: Averages drawn from the Elias Baseball Analysts from 1985 to 1993.

Table 17.3 shows how various offensive events are affected by whether the bases are empty or not. If there is a runner on first, the batting average is up 23 points but the on-base percentage is up only 13 points, since the walk rate drops. On the other hand, when runners are in scoring position, the batting average is up only 6 points, but the on-base percentage is up a whopping 34 points because the walk rate jumps. The jump is no doubt greatly influenced by walks that are given when first base is open in order to "keep the double play in order" or to allow a force out at second base. Interestingly, in both situations when players are on base, the on base-plus-slugging average is up about 40 points, though.

These results indicate how player averages depend to some degree on the situation that exists when he strides to the plate. In a preliminary investigation, I found that National League leadoff hitters during the 1980s batted with the bases empty about 65–70% of the time, compared to 55% for cleanup hitters. A 10% gap in bases empty situations would give cleanup hitters an advantage of 4 OPS points (40 OPS points × 10%) over leadoff hitters. A "lineup position" adjustment of that size would lead to ranking changes of roughly 10–25 positions for OPS, except at the extreme ends—an appreciable, but modest, effect.

Concluding Remark

I am happy to contribute another voice toward the ongoing goal of identifying the *best batters* in baseball history. I believe that the baseball research community is, in its ratings, converging on who the best batters and best pitchers are. To more closely approach the "holy grail" list of *best players*, we will need to improve considerably in our assessment of fielding ability and how to rate its importance compared to offensive and pitching ability. Although there is still much in the evaluation of player performance to argue about, our arguments thus far have borne a good deal of fruit.

APPENDICES

On previous page: Milwaukee Braves Celebrate Their World Championship, 1957. (National Baseball Hall of Fame Library, Cooperstown, NY.)

The Piecewise Linear Regression Method

Overview of Regression Methods

Three principal statistical methods are used in this book to model baseball data over time: *piecewise linear regression, moving averages,* and *multiple changepoint regression.* There are several reasons to model data. First, models extract key features from data and present a simplified view of them. Second, models can allow firmer, more precise conclusions to be made than when each data point is considered by itself—so long as the assumptions on which the models are based are reasonable. Finally, models may generate insights into factors that caused the data to be as they are.

The table below lists the appendix in which each method is presented and identifies the two characteristics that determine which method is best to use in a given situation. The first characteristic is whether the data are expected to change gradually over time or stay constant except for jump or drop points. The second characteristic is whether the method smoothes data from nearby years using a constant number of years or flexibly uses the data to determine when key shifts occurred in time. While the moving average method is a standard statistical approach, statisticians differ in their implementation of piecewise linear regression and multiple changepoint regression. The methods presented here were developed by the author.

Regression Method	Appendix	Jumps?	Equal No. of Years?
Piecewise linear	A	No	No
Moving average	B	No	Yes
Multiple changepoint	C	Yes	No

For the piecewise linear regression method, described in this appendix, changes over time are modeled using joined line segments whose slopes change at various years. The centerpiece of the method is identifying the years when the slopes change.

Let's look at how the method works for the American League home run average from 1901 to 2002.

Perfect Fit Model

To characterize the 103 years of American League home run averages perfectly, we need a complete listing of the data. The first 5 years, 1901–1905, are shown in Table A.1.

Table A.1 American League Home Runs, 1901–1905

	Year				
	1901	1902	1903	1904	1905
At-bats	38,138	38,005	37,434	41,479	40,622
Home runs	228	258	184	156	156
AL HR avg	.0060	.0068	.0049	.0038	.0038
AL HRs/500 ABs	3.0	3.4	2.4	1.9	1.9
Change		0.4	−1.0	−0.5	0.0

Notes: American League HR avg = home runs/at-bats. Change is the difference in HRs/500 AB from the previous year.

Equivalent information is given by listing: (1) the 5 HRs/500 ABs or (2) the HRs/500 ABs for 1901 and the four changes from one year to the next. The average for 1901 can be called the *intercept*, while the four changes are *slopes* (as explained in the box that follows).

Stats Time **Definition of intercept and slope**

Let's look at the top left panel of Figure A.1. The "*y*-variable" is American League HRs/500 AB and the "*x*-variable" is the year. If the "*x*-variable" were redefined as the year minus 1901, then the *intercept* is the American League HRs/500 ABs in 1901, since it is the *y*-value when the *x*-value is zero.

The *slope* is the change in the *y*-variable per unit change in the *x*-variable. For us, the slopes are the changes in American League HRs/500 ABs from one year to the next, since the difference in consecutive years is 1.

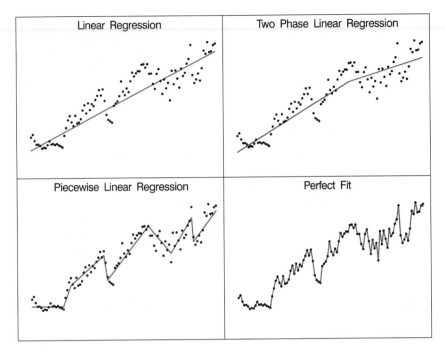

Figure A.1 Four Regression Models for the American League Home Run Data, 1901–2003

For the 103 seasons, perfect characterization of the data needs either the 103 averages or the first year and 101 successive changes. In either case, no compression of the data has occurred. Graphically, these 101 slopes correspond to 101 line segments that could be drawn starting from the American League home run average in 1901 and linking up all the other points in the 103-year time sequence—a "connect the dots" approach, as shown in the lower right panel of Figure A.1. We will call this the "perfect fit model."

In a 1970s TV game show called *Name That Tune*, contestants would try to identify songs from a limited number of notes. The contestant who claimed to be able to identify the song after hearing the fewest number of notes was awarded the opportunity; 4–6 notes was often the going rate. In model fitting, we want to do something similar. We want to understand 103 years of American League home run data without having to stare at all 103 numbers.

Constant Average Model

At the opposite extreme from the perfect fit model is the "constant average model," which summarizes the data using one number—the average value. For 1901 to 1905, the average number of American League home runs per 500 ABs is 2.5. For 1901 to 2003, the average is 10.2. Figure A.1, though, shows that the data tended to rise over the years. Consequently, the constant average model describes the data inadequately.

Linear Regression

Linear regression is a popular method for modeling how one variable changes as a function of another—in our case, how the HRs/500 ABs number changes over time. The linear regression model is just one step away from the constant average model described earlier.

It makes a very bold claim: to name the "tune" of the data in 2 notes—using a linear function. The linear regression model is:

$$\text{AL HRs per 500 ABs} = 1.0 + 0.15 \times (\text{year} - 1901).$$

The two numbers computed in the model, 1.0 and 0.15, use standard equations available in many statistics books and statistical software packages.

The first number, 1.0, the intercept, is the model's guess at the home runs per 500 ABs for 1901. The second number, 0.15, is the slope. The estimated HRs/500 ABs for $2003 = 1.0 + 0.15 \times (2003 - 1901) = 17.3$. The regression fit is shown in the top left panel of Figure A.1.

The model has an *r-square* (r^2) value of .899, indicating that 89.9% of the variability in HRs/500 ABs can be "explained" by the linear regression model. Since a perfect fit has an r^2 value of 1, the linear regression fit fell 10.1% short. On the other hand, the constant model has an r^2 value of 0, so the extra "note"—the slope—goes a long way in accurately describing how home runs have changed over the years.

The linear regression model presented here is a weighted linear regression, as explained in the following Stats Fact.

Two-Phase Linear Regression

An improved fit can be obtained from a regression model with a change of slope somewhere. Looking at the top right panel of Figure A.1 suggests that the home runs per 500 ABs did not rise so steeply after the 1950s. Let's put a slope change in at 1961, the year the American League was expanded to 10 teams. The new model is:

$$\text{AL HRs/500 ABs} = 0.5 + 0.18 \times (\text{year} - 1901), \text{ for year} \leq 1960$$
$$= 11.2 + 0.09 \times (\text{year} - 1960), \text{ for year} > 1960.$$

Such a model is called a *two-phase linear regression* model. For this model (shown in Figure A.1c), $r^2 = .910$, an increase of .011 over the linear regression r^2 value, .899.

The r^2 value can rise only as slope changes are added to the model. Consequently, statistical measures other than r^2 are used to decide whether the addition of slope changes produces a "better" model, balancing off an improved fit with greater model complexity.

The two-phase linear regression model is an extension of the weighted linear regression model obtained by adding a single slope change. Slope changes can be added until the improvement in model fit does not outweigh the additional complexity of the model. Such a procedure is called a forward selection procedure.

Stats Time   Weighting in regression

The simplest regression model, appropriately called *simple linear regression*, assumes that all of the yearly averages, which are actually only estimates of the true average ability of players in that season, are equally precise. Throughout this book, a more sophisticated variant of this method, called *weighted linear regression*, is generally used.

Weighted linear regression uses different weights for the data points depending on how precisely they are estimated. The home run average is given by:

HR average = HRs/ABs.

Such averages can be assumed to arise from a *binomial distribution*. It then follows that the estimated variance for this average is:

HR average variance = [HR avg $\times$ (1 – HR avg)]/ABs.

In statistics, the *precision* of an estimate is defined to be 1 divided by the variance, so

HR average precision = ABs/[HR avg $\times$ (1 – HR avg)].

Thus, precision is based on two factors: the number of ABs and the HR average. Both change over time, resulting in different precisions.

The HR average precision is the *weight* used for the linear regression formula in the text. For example, in 1920 the American League hit 369 HRs in 41,949 ABs (HR average = .0088). Thus,

HR average precision = 41,949/[.0088 $\times$ (1 – .0088)] = 4.81 $\times$ 10^6.

In 1960, the American League hit 1086 HRs in 41,838 ABs, so HR avg = .0260 and the weight is 1.65 $\times$ 10^6. Had a simple linear regression model been used in the text, the formula would have been:

AL HRs per 500 ABs = 1.9 + .14 $\times$ (year – 1901).

Piecewise Linear Regression

The *piecewise linear regression* method involves a step-by-step procedure with stopping criteria (see "Stats Time: Backward elimination and SLS"). Rather than working forward from the constant average model, however, it works backward from the perfect fit model. The perfect fit model is not a statistical model, but a mathematical one, with the same number of variables as data points. Statistical models require the possibility of "modeling error" (a deviation of the data from the fit) as a way to judge the adequacy of simpler versus more complex fits.

In order for the step-by-step *backward elimination procedure* to work at all, one of the slopes needs to be dropped—so which one? With no statistically clear choice, I have chosen the final one—the slope between 2002 and 2003. By construction of the starting model, all years from 1901 to 2001 are perfectly fit, with no error. Removal of the final slope produces the crucial modeling error needed to jump-start the procedure, unless the data points for 2001, 2002, and 2003 lie on exactly the same line. In such a case, another slope should be removed to begin the procedure.

At each step, the procedure removes the slope change causing the smallest reduction in the r^2 value. If 50 slopes are removed from the American League home run regression fit, an r^2 value of .9987 is obtained.

Stats Time   Backward elimination and SLS

The piecewise linear regression uses a backward elimination procedure. The critical issue is when to stop the procedure. At each step, the year with the least significant slope change is considered for removal. A test statistic is calculated and a p-value obtained to assess how important the slope change is. The procedure stops at the first step that produces a p-value below a number called the SLS value.

The critical question regarding use of the backward elimination procedure is when to stop. The answer involves the *significance-level-to-stay* (SLS) value. The SLS establishes a "line in the sand" for the procedure.

At each step of the procedure, a test statistic is calculated and a number between 0 and 1, known as the p-value, is produced. A low p-value means that something highly unusual has happened given some underlying assumption. In our situation, this assumption is that the slope change is not needed. When a low enough p-value is obtained, we reject that assumption and conclude that the slope change is necessary.

For classical statistical problems, the p-value is the probability that a result such as that seen or a "more extreme" result would occur, given the validity of the assumption. Most often in statistical testing, p-values less than .05 are considered to be "unusual."

Step-by-step procedures are statistically quite complicated, and p-values generated from these procedures do not have this strong interpretation. What is known is that the standard "line in the sand," .05, is too high. In the absence of a crystal clear choice, the following four-step rule yields good model fits:

1. Consider SLS values no greater than .005.
2. Choose the SLS value to be equal to the first p-value that is at most one fourth of the previous low p-value (which we'll call SLS+).
3. If more than four consecutive p-values past the one chosen in step 2 exceed it, start from that step forward to obtain the SLS value.
4. If no SLS value satisfying steps 1–3 exists, take SLS = .0001.

With the SLS so chosen, the backward elimination procedure stops at the step at which the p-value is less than or equal to the SLS.

For American League home runs, SLS = .0001, and SLS+ = .0031, yielding a piecewise linear regression fit which has 9 slopes, with r^2 = .971. Note the improvement in fit of this model over the two simpler models in Figure A.1. Table A.2 provides a comparison of the models.

Table A.2   Modeling the American League Home Runs per 500 At-Bats, 1901–2003

Method	r^2	No. of slopes
Perfect fit	1.000	102
50-Slope linear regression	.999	50
Piecewise linear regression	.971	9
Two-phase linear regression	.910	2
Linear regression	.899	1
Constant average	.000	0

Note from Table A.2 that the piecewise linear regression achieves a very high r^2 with only 10 "notes" (9 slopes + 1 intercept). Table A.3 shows regression estimates for the different models for 6 arbitrarily selected years. The model becomes more complex as the number of slopes increases. The numbers in bold show the only instances in which the less complex model (to the left of the number) was closer to the actual value.

Table A.3   Regression Model Estimates of American League Home Runs per 500 At-Bats for Selected Years

	Number of Slopes for Model				Actual
Year	1	2	9	50	Value
1901	1.0	**0.5**	1.8	3.0	3.0
1920	3.8	3.9	**3.4**	4.3	4.4
1940	6.9	7.4	9.6	10.4	10.3
1960	9.9	11.0	12.6	13.2	13.0
1980	12.9	12.9	11.8	11.8	11.8
2000	15.9	**14.7**	17.6	16.9	17.1

Moving Average Smoothing of Data

A *moving average* is used in this book to smooth the seasonal standard deviations (SDs) for each offensive event. For the National League, we have 128 standard deviations, one for each year from 1876 to 2003. The numbers form a *time series*.

The moving average is the second of three methods presented in this book for modeling time series data. It differs from the other two (piecewise linear regression and multiple changepoint regression) in that the number of years included in each average is constant, except for *end effects* that apply to the first and last years of the time series.

Many financial reports on stock market prices use moving averages to provide simpler summary views of trends over time. The *moving average* estimate of the SD for a given year is the average of a certain fixed number of years just below and above the given year plus the year itself.

The critical question is: how many years? If the number of years is too small, the random component will not get smoothed out. If the number is too large, the real trend will get partly smoothed away. Moreover, no single number is likely to perfectly separate the random and true components of variation from each other.

In this book, a 5-year moving average is used. Why use 5 years? Given the definition of a moving average given earlier, an odd number of years is needed. Dramatic changes such as league expansion, a shift in the style of play, or rule alterations can affect the spread of performance fairly quickly, pushing the choice toward a small number of years. Although some baseball analysts use three years, I believe that a 5-year moving average, which produces SD estimates that shift direction much less often (as explained further later), is a better choice.

How to Calculate Moving Averages

Table B.1 gives the raw standard deviations (first row) of the mean-adjusted regular players' home run averages for the National League for 1993–2000, on square root transformed data. Below it are the 3- and 5-year moving averages of the SDs. The 3-year moving average for 1995, .0521, is obtained from averaging SDs from 1994, 1995, and 1996. The 5-year moving average is obtained by averaging the SDs from 1993–97. Note that the 3- and 5-year moving averages are more stable than the raw SDs themselves. In four cases, the raw SDs change by at least .0020 from one year to the next, with the greatest being a drop of .0051 from 1999 to 2000. For the 3-year moving averages, the largest change is .0022, while the greatest 5-year change is only .0009.

Table B.1 Moving Averages for National League Home Run Standard Deviations

	1993	1994	1995	1996	1997	1998	1999	2000
Raw SD	.0540	.0545	.0510	.0507	.0534	.0513	.0517	.0466
3-Year	.0547	.0532	.0521	.0517	.0518	.0521	.0499	.0495
5-Year	.0541	.0532	.0527	.0522	.0516	.0507	.0506	.0499

What Size Moving Average Should Be Used?

The total number of direction changes in the year-to-year trends is helpful in choosing the number of years for the moving average. Frequent direction changes in the true standard deviation are unlikely.

In Table B.1, the raw SD rose from 1993 to 1994, then fell in 1995—that's one direction change. Other direction changes occurred in 1997, 1998, 1999, and 2000— that's 5 altogether. The 3-year moving average has only two direction changes, while the 5-year moving average has none. Over the 128-year history, the raw SD values have 79 direction changes, the 3-year moving average has 51, and the 5-year moving average has 34 (not counting direction changes when the transformation power shifted, that is, in 1901, 1920, 1931, and 1947).

Frequent direction changes can occur when the SDs hover around some value, as they did from 1970 to 1980. Ignoring those years, the direction changes were 70 for the raw SD, 43 for the 3-year moving average, and only 25 for the 5-year moving average.

End Effects

Sometimes, the full number of years is unavailable for averaging. For example, for a 5-year moving average of the current season, only 3 years are available—the current season and previous 2 years, so these 3 numbers are averaged. Similarly, the moving averages of the second-to-last and second years are based on only 4 years. These *end effects* occur at the both ends of a time series.

When the *transformation power* shifts from one year to the next (see Appendix E), SDs are no longer comparable. Thus additional end effects occur around shift years.

The Multiple Changepoint Regression Procedure

The multiple changepoint regression procedure—used to obtain park effects—can be applied to either linear regression or *logistic regression*, depending on whether the data being fit can take on many different values or only two. For level 3 or level 4 data, where both home and road counts are available (see Appendix D), it was applied to logistic regression. For level 1 or 2 data (and for the determination of the minimum number of NFPs for regular players), the multiple changepoint regression procedure was applied to linear regression.

Different park effect levels could be estimated for each season. Like all data, however, baseball data are composed of both real effects and random variation, both "signal" and "noise."

Park effects calculated using a formula or a statistical model are merely estimates of some true but unknown park effect. This is very much akin to Plato's famous "Allegory in the Cave."

We earth dwellers observe merely the shadows of reality, not reality itself. There's good news for us earth dwellers, though. As data are accumulated, a powerful statistical law claims that the estimates becomes closer to the true value with higher probability—that is, we get more signal and less noise. Let's look at the 1999 and 2000 Atlanta Braves seasons.

Stats Time   Logistic regression model

A *logistic regression model* is quite similar to a linear regression model. The primary difference is that the dependent variable for a linear regression model can take on many possible values (such as the number of home runs hit in a season), whereas the dependent variable for a logistic regression can take on only two values (such as whether a home run is hit at home or on the road).

A Demonstration of How Estimates Improve with More Data

In 1999, the Braves and their opponents hit 161 home runs at Turner Field and 178 home runs at the opponents' parks. The percentage of home runs hit at the Braves' home park, then, was $161/(161 + 178) = 47.5\%$. Using binomial theory, the 95% *confidence interval* (95% CI) for the true rate is $47.5\% \pm 5.3\%$, that is, between 42.2% and 52.8%. (The 95% CI gives the range of values which includes the true, but unknown, rate with a probability of 95%.) Consequently, even though more home runs were hit away from Turner Field in 1999, we cannot conclude that home runs were truly harder to hit there in 1999 because the 95% confidence interval includes values on both sides of 50%.

In 2000, the home and road totals were 166 and 178, giving a 48.3% home percentage. (*Note:* for both years, the home run totals were from 81 home and 81 road games.) Again, the 95% confidence interval, 43.0% to 53.6%, includes values on both sides of 50%.

Should we combine the data from the 2 years? The answer is yes only if we believe that the true park effect level was the same (or very similar) in both years. Since the 2000 park effect estimate is contained within the 1999 confidence interval and vice versa, we might expect the true effect levels to be the same. A standard way to test such an assumption is to perform a *chi-square* (χ^2) test. The data for the 2 years are given in the 2×2 table (that is, 2 rows and 2 columns) below, along with row and column totals.

Atlanta Braves/Opponents Actual Home Run Totals

	Home	Road	Total
1999	161	178	339
2000	166	178	344
Total	327	356	683

These 2 years look quite similar. The number of road home runs is the same, while the home run totals at home rose by 5 in 2000.

An "expected" results table could be obtained from the row and column totals above. To get the expected number for a given cell, simply multiply the corresponding row and column totals and divide by the grand total. For example, the expected total of home runs at home in 1999 was $162.30 = 327 \times 339/683$.

Atlanta Braves/Opponents "Expected" Home Run Totals

	Home	Road	Total
1999	162.30	176.70	339
2000	164.70	179.30	344
Total	327	356	683

Now we are ready for the χ^2 test. For each of the 4 cells of the actual home run totals table, we subtract the corresponding "expected" home run total and square the result. For the home-1999 cell of the tables, we get:

$$(161 - 162.30)^2 = (1.30)^2 = 1.69.$$

The result is exactly the same for all 4 cells of the table, as it is for all 2×2 tables. Then, divide this number by each of the 4 "expected" totals and add the results together:

$$1.69/162.30 + 1.69/176.70 + 1.69/164.70 + 1.69/179.30 = 0.04.$$

This value, 0.04, is called the χ^2 value. In usual statistical practice, a χ^2 value greater than 3.84 is taken as evidence that the processes generating the 2 rows of data are different. Thus, we do not have statistical evidence that the park effects for Turner Field were different for 1999 and 2000. In fact, our result is less than 1, which is the average χ^2 value expected by chance alone.

Table C.1   Actual Atlanta Braves/Opponents Home Runs, 1997–2003

| Year | Home Runs | | | Home Pct | 95% CI | Spread |
	Home	Road	Total			
1997	131	154	285	46.0	(40.2, 51.8)	11.6
1998	162	170	332	48.8	(43.4, 54.2)	10.8
1999	161	178	339	47.5	(42.2, 52.8)	10.6
2000	166	178	344	48.3	(43.0, 53.6)	10.6
2001	164	163	327	50.2	(44.8, 55.6)	10.8
2002	146	141	287	50.9	(45.1, 56.7)	11.6
2003	179	203	382	46.9	(41.9, 51.9)	10.0
1997-2003	1109	1187	2296	48.3	(46.3, 50.3)	4.0

Notes: Home Pct = home HRs / (home HRs + road HRs).

95% CI = Home Pct $\pm$ 1.96 $\times$ (Home Pct $\times$ (100 – Home Pct) / Total)$^{0.5}$, where 1.96 is the normal distribution multiplier that yields the 95% confidence interval.

Spread = upper value of 95% CI – lower value of 95% CI.

Table C.1 shows the actual home runs for Braves players and their opponents from 1997, when the Braves moved into Turner Field, through 2003. Note that the percentage of home runs hit at Turner Field ranged from 46.0% in 1997 to 50.9% in 2002. The single-season spreads for the 95% confidence intervals range from 10.0% to 11.6%.

Using the χ^2 method for successive years, no statistically identifiable change in the park effect occurred between 1997 and 2003. When we combine the seasons together, the percentage of home runs hit at Turner Field is estimated to be 48.3%, with a 95% confidence interval of 46.3% to 50.3%—a spread of only 4.0%. Combining data in this way improves the accuracy of a park effect estimate, assuming that the true park effect remained constant.

Tracking the Backward Elimination Procedure

The *multiple changepoint regression* model is the third and final method for modeling time series data. This method models a time series to be constant over time except at specific changeyears, in which the model jumps or drops to a new level. The number and location of the changeyears are determined in a flexible way by the method.

The χ^2 analysis presented in the previous section is at the core of the *backward elimination* procedure used to determine changeyears for each baseball franchise. The procedure is illustrated for the estimation of home run park effects for the Braves franchise.

Each home run hit in Braves' games was either hit at or away from the Braves' home stadium. Whether the home run was hit at home or not is the dependent variable for the model. Our independent variables are the years 1894–2003. (Mathematically, we define 109 variables, starting with 1895, taking on the value 0 before the given year and 1 for the year and all subsequent years.) The data are *normalized* to adjust for raw data when the number of home and road games differs in a given season, as described in Appendix D.

At each step, the backward elimination procedure finds 2 two consecutive years or groups of years that are the most similar to each other (using the χ^2 value described earlier) and, if they are not too different, combines them. This process could be continued so that eventually data from all years are combined into a single park effect estimate. This is undesirable, however. Since the Braves were in 5 parks in 3 different cities, at a minimum, separate estimates are needed for the different parks.

Thus, we "force" selected changeyears into the model. For all teams, including the Braves, any year in which the team moved into a new ballpark is forced into the model. For nonforced years, however, the backward elimination procedure is allowed to drop out potential changeyears until statistical criteria indicate that the process should stop. The years remaining in the model are the changeyears. The procedure is described at several noteworthy steps.

Step 0. All 110 years are in the model. This model, called a *full model*, has a *likelihood ratio chi-square (LR χ^2)* value of 1097.1. A "no-change" model is a model with no changeyears—that is, one park effect estimate is used to fit all years. Over the 110-year period, the expected value of the *LR χ^2* is 109—that is, 1 less than the number of years. Consequently, the *LR χ^2* value of 1097.1 strongly suggests that the "no change" assumption is false and that significant changeyears exist. Let's begin our search for them!

Step 1. 1900 is removed as a potential changeyear. The new model, called a *reduced model*, also has an $LR \chi^2$ value of 1097.1, indicating that the reduced model fits the data as well as the full model.

Step 10. In steps 2–10, these 9 years were removed: 1967, 1980, 1994, 1976, 1949, 2002, 1948, 1952, and 1984. At this point, the $LR \chi^2$ value for the reduced model has declined by only 0.2 from the initial one. Mathematically, the $LR \chi^2$ value can decline only as the backward elimination procedure progresses.

Step 16. The year 2000 is removed from the model. The decline in the $LR \chi^2$ value is .04, the same as the χ^2 value we calculated earlier.

Step 55. Half of the 109 potential changeyears have been eliminated. At this point, the $LR \chi^2$ value is 1081.5. The difference in value from the full model, $1097.1 - 1081.5 = 15.6$, is called the *residual χ^2.*

This method works quite well in separating where the changes in the home run park effect levels are occurring from where they are not—that is, extracting the signal from the noise.

Step 90. The residual χ^2, which rises from one step to the next, has finally topped 109—the number of potential changeyears. This is a notable event because, under a "no change" model, the residual χ^2 has an expected value of 109.

In our case, 19 potential changeyears are left in the model, including the 4 forced years for the ballpark changes. Is this the step at which to stop? No, for two reasons.

First, under an assumed "no change" model, a residual χ^2 value of 109 is the expected value. However, owing to random variation, the actual value will differ from one data set to another. Statisticians generally don't like to claim that an effect exists unless there is reasonably strong evidence in favor of it. In other words, statisticians tend to be biased toward the default assumption of a "no change" model. Consequently, a statistician is more likely to stop the procedure at a residual χ^2 value of 126 since, under a "no-change" model, 95% of the time that's as high as the residual χ^2 value would get.

Second, home run hitting does not perfectly follow the assumptions of the χ^2 test. The test assumes that each count (home runs in our case) is independent of every other count. On some days, though, perhaps days when the wind is blowing out, the conditions for hitting home runs deviate from the park average. Since several home runs can be hit in a single day, independence doesn't hold perfectly. The effect of this dependence is to make the home run totals even more variable, driving up the χ^2 test value.

Consequently, a flexible approach is used to separate (it is hoped) "true" changeyears from years whose jumps or drops are due only to random variation. At each step, one potential changeyear, which has an associated *p*-value, is eliminated. These *p*-values tend to decline as the procedure goes forward. Strong evidence of a true changeyear exists when the *p*-value drops dramatically from those preceding it. Thus, the following rule has been adopted:

When the p-value for removal of a given year is both less than .005 and is at most one fourth of the minimum p-value from the previous steps of the backward elimi-

nation procedure, the procedure stops and all years remaining in the model are accepted as changeyears.

Step 95. Based on this rule,, this is the final step. The final model has an $LR \chi^2$ value of 934.5, leaving $1097.1 - 934.5 = 162.6$ as the residual χ^2 value.

Exception to the rule. The final year removed by the procedure was 1929. Although it fell slightly short of the statistical bar for convincing evidence of a changeyear, we do have considerable baseball evidence. In 1928, the fence distances in Braves Field were dramatically shortened, resulting in a huge increase in home runs. To reduce this effect, the park dimensions were enlarged on July 24, 1928. Consequently, 1929 is included as a changeyear.

Model Park Effects for Home Runs for the Braves Franchise

The changeyears for the home run park effects for the Braves franchise are shown in Table C.2, along with a possible explanation for the change and χ^2 values. Larger χ^2 values are indicative of having greater statistical evidence that the park effect truly changed in that year. The evidence is weakest for a change in park effect in 1929, while the evidence is strongest for changes in 1928, 1942, 1946, 1959, and 1983. Of the 14 changeyears, 4 were attributable to the Braves moving into new parks, 6 coincided with changes in fence distances, and 4 lack obvious explanations.

Table C.2   Park Changeyears for the Atlanta Braves Franchise

Years	Estimated Home Pct	Change	χ^2 value
1894–1902	73.5	South End Grounds II	—
1903–12	63.5		16.2
1913–14	41.3		22.7
1915–27	27.8	Braves Field	10.5 F
1928	56.9	Fences shortened considerably	46.9
1929–35	42.6	Fences lengthened	10.6
1936–40	33.1	LC, CF moved out, RF in	16.1
1942–45	58.9	CF moved in 25 feet	89.1
1946–52	39.4	Fence height raised 12 feet	64.8
1953–58	38.1	County Stadium—Milwaukee	0.5 F
1959–65	50.1		56.4
1966–76	58.0	Atlanta/Fulton Co. Stadium	31.9 F
1977–82	64.6		17.9
1983–96	53.8	Fence height raised 4 feet	50.2
1997–2003	48.3	Turner Field	17.1 F

Note: F = Forced into the model; dashed lines reflect different parks.

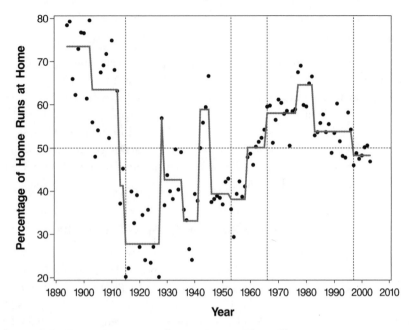

Figure C.1   Braves Percentage of Home Runs at Home Plot

Graphical Presentation of the Home Run Park Effects

A graphical view of the home run data for the Braves franchise is shown in Figure C.1. The dots show the percent of normalized home runs hit at the Braves home field year-by-year, by both the Braves and their opponents.

The solid line consisting of joined line segments shows the multiple changepoint regression model. The horizontal line segments indicate years for which the ballpark effect is modeled as constant, with the value indicating the composite average. The near vertical line segments show the changeyear locations. The vertical lines indicate the years when the team moved into a new ballpark. Note that the year-by-year values tend to deviate more from the averages in the early years of the Braves history. This is because fewer home runs were hit then, making the park effect estimates less stable.

How to Estimate Ballpark Effects

Ballparks are one of the most fascinating aspects of major league baseball. Park dimensions are not standardized, as they are for most other professional sports. Hence the need for "ground rules," such as the ground rule for the beer garden in the right field corner of Sportsman's Park in St. Louis. Until the 1888 World Series, balls hit into the seats there were still in play; later, they were automatic home runs. Even if park dimensions were standardized today—and there is little or no interest to do so—differences of altitude, wind conditions, temperature, and playing surface would yield different results for different parks.

As a consequence of ballpark differences, use of raw counts—such as the number of home runs a player hits—is an unfair way to compare player abilities. No baseball gods have declared, though, that it will be easy to estimate park effects well—and it isn't. In this appendix, a method is presented for estimating park effects for each of the basic offensive events across major league history (except for stolen bases), which is step 3 of the 7-step procedure for player evaluation game plan outlined in Chapter 2.

Many different aspects of park effect estimation are dealt with. They are:

1. Levels of data available for estimating park effects
2. Estimating park effects for level 3 or 4 data
   a. Normalization
   b. Determining franchise changeyears
   c. Obtaining changeyears for a given offensive event
   d. The odds ratio for left- versus right-handed home runs
3. Estimating park effects for level 1 or 2 data
4. Shrinkage of ballpark effect estimates
5. The effect of shrinkage and the need for squeezing

Levels of Data Available for Estimating Park Effect

The precision with which ballpark effects can be estimated is limited by the availability of data. Suppose we wanted to compare Fenway Park to Yankee Stadium. The best data to have are the batting records of the Red Sox and Yankees at Fenway Park and, separately, at Yankee Stadium. More generally, a park effect for Fenway Park is best estimated by having the composite batting record of the Red Sox and their opponents separated into Red Sox home and road games. In this book, data with four levels of precision are used. They are:

Level 4. Home-Road Data with NFPs. This is the highest level. Park effects are identified by contrasting the home and road offensive event totals. Since games can stop early because of rain or continue into extra innings because of a tie, the number of NFPs scales the raw totals to account for batting opportunities. Level 4 data are available for all events from 1969 to 2003. These data were provided by Pete Palmer and Retrosheet (*www.retrosheet.org*).

Level 3. Home-Road Data without NFPs. This level is inferior to level 4 data since the number of events cannot be scaled by the number of NFPs. Level 3 data are available for home runs in *SABR Presents the Home Run Encyclopedia*, edited by Bob McConnell and David Vincent. David Vincent has provided additional data through the 2003 season, and separate home and road data for left- and right-handed hitters. Level 3 data for runs is given in *Total Baseball*, Fourth Edition, through 1994. Pete Palmer provided updated data through the 2003 season.

Level 2. Team Batting and Pitching Data. For years prior to 1969, home and road split data are not available except for runs and home runs. Team data, which are a mixture of home and road data, can be used to estimate park effects. For batting average, bases on balls, and strikeouts, data are available for both what the batters produced and what the pitchers gave up.

Level 1. Team Batting Data. For years prior to 1969, team data on the number of doubles and triples yielded by pitchers are not available. For these events, park effects are developed using only the team batting data, which have the lowest level of precision.

Estimating Park Effects for Level 3 or 4 Data

Step A. Normalization of Ballpark Effect Estimates

The first step in obtaining good park effect estimates for level 3 or 4 data is *normalization*, which involves adjusting for the number of home and road games played (or at-bats or NFPs for level 4 data). Table D.1 shows the home runs totals for five 19th century parks.

Team	Years	HRs		Games		Avg. No. of Games	Norm. HRs		Park Pct
		Hm	Rd	Hm	Rd		Hm	Rd	
Pit–U	1884	1	0	5	14	9.5	1.9	0	100
Chi–N	1884	197	28	57	56	56.5	195.3	28.2	87
NY–N	1876	9	1	33	24	28.5	7.8	1.2	87
Phi–N	1883–4	2	72	107	105	106.0	2.0	72.7	3
Har–N	1876	0	4	32	37	34.5	0	3.7	0

Notes: Norm. Home HRs = Home HRs × Avg. No. of Games/Home Games.

Norm. Road HRs = Road HRs × Avg. No. of Games/Road Games.

Park Pct = 100 × Norm. Home HRs/(Norm. Home HRs + Norm. Road HRs).

In 1876, the New York Mutuals (third row of Table D.1) and their opponents hit 9 home runs in 33 games at the Union Grounds, the Mutuals' home field, and a single home run in 24 games at the road parks. If the number of home and road games were evenly divided, there would have been 28.5 of each. In 28.5 games, the teams would have hit an expected $9 \times 28.5/33 = 7.8$ *normalized* home home runs and 1.2 normalized road home runs for a *park percentage* of 87%, according to Definitions D.1.

Step B. Determining Franchise Changeyears

Level 3 data are available for home runs and runs throughout baseball history. The modeling approach we will use, called *multiple changepoint regression*, estimates park effects as constant over some range of years before jumping or falling to a new level. A change in the park effect makes sense whenever a team moves into a new ballpark or makes a dramatic change in the park design, such as fence distances or heights. Key elements of multiple changepoint regression model are the years in which the park effect changes, called *changepoint years* or *changeyears* for short, and the park effects for the years between changeyears, which we will call *park effect levels*.

Definitions D.1   **Normalization, park percentage**

Normalized home OEs = Home OEs × NF,

where NF = Average no. of ABs /Home ABs for level 4 data, and

NF = Average no. of games /Home games for level 3 data.

Park percentage = 100 × Normalized home OEs/(Normalized home OEs + normalized road OEs)

where OE stands for offensive event and NF for normalization factor.

The multiple changepoint regression model is illustrated for home runs for the Braves franchise from 1894 to 2003 in Appendix C.

If multiple changepoint regression models are used for different offensive events for the same franchise, different sets of changeyears are obtained. To obtain a single set of changeyears for a franchise, the following 6-step procedure is used (at each step, changepoints obtained from a prior step are forced in the model):

1. Take as changeyears any year in which the team moved into a new ballpark.
2. Run the multiple changepoint regression model for home runs to get additional changeyears.
3. Run the multiple changepoint regression model for the right–left odds ratio data for home runs. Take as additional changeyears any remaining years in the model that are at least 4 years away from the forced changeyears, or where a documented park change has occurred.
4. Run the multiple changepoint regression model (with SLS = .0025) for batting average, doubles-plus-triples, triples, runs, bases on balls, and strikeouts between 1969 and 2003. Identify as additional changeyears any years:
   a. that remain in the models for at least two events,
   b. have p-values < .0001 and that are at least 2 years away from existing changeyears, or
   c. have p-value < .0010 for the BA, DPT, or R regression models and that are at least 4 years away from existing changeyears.
5. Run the multiple changepoint regression model for runs. Take as additional changeyears those that remain after the backward elimination procedure stops that are at least 4 years away from changeyears identified from the previous steps.
6. Add additional changeyears between 1876 and 1968 if they are more than 15 years apart. Choose the new changeyears in the middle (one-half year past the middle for an odd gap of years), unless a documented ballpark change can be found within 3 years of the middle. If so, use that year instead.

At steps 2, 4, and 5, see if there is a documented ballpark change within 2 years of the changeyear identified. If so, try substituting the year with the documented ballpark change. If the resulting likelihood ratio χ^2 for the model is within 12 units of that for the substituted changeyear, switch to the documented ballpark changeyear. Philip Lowrey's book, *Green Cathedrals*, and *Total Baseball*, Fifth Edition are used as the documenting references.

Step C. Obtaining Changeyears for a Given Offensive Event
Starting with the set of changeyears for a given franchise, a backward elimination procedure reduces the set to include only changeyears that show substantial change for the offensive event under study. The criterion by which a final set of changeyears for a given event is retained is the *significance-level-to-stay* (SLS) for the procedure.

The best choice of SLS balances over- and underfitting of data. For home runs and runs, which use logistic regression, an SLS of 0.10 seems best; for the other events, which use linear regression, SLS = 0.15.

Step D. The Odds Ratio for Left- versus Right-Handed Home Runs

Home runs have a strong tendency to be hit to the "pull" field, that is, left field for right-handed batters and right field for left-handed batters. Thus parks, especially asymmetrical ones, may favor batters with a given handedness. One way to measure the favoritism is to separately estimate the odds of hitting a home run in the home park for right- and left-handed batters and then look at the ratio of these two odds—which is appropriately called the *odds ratio* (OR).

Estimating Park Effects for Level 1 or Level 2 Data

We have seen how park effects can be estimated when we have home and road data. Such methods can be used for data from 1969 to the present, and for home runs and runs across baseball history. For other offensive events, however, such data are not yet generally available.

In Chapter 4 of *Baseball's All-Time Best Hitters*, a method to obtain park effect estimates for batting average was introduced. The basic plan was to regress the year-by-year team batting average on the team winning percentage. Changeyears, based on ballpark transitions and a few selected other years, were used to yield estimates over various time periods. The underlying principle behind the method was this:

Definitions D.2   Odds ratio, log odds ratio

As a formula, the RHB-to-LHB odds ratio is

$$OR = \frac{\text{RHB home odds}}{\text{LHB home odds}} = \frac{(\text{RHB home HRs / RHB road HRs})}{(\text{LHB home HRs / LHB road HRs})}.$$

The *log odds ratio* (LOR) is the base 2 logarithm of the odds ratio. Log odds ratios are useful for graphs, since there is numerical symmetry around the central value, zero.

OR > 1	Odds higher for RHB	LOR > 0
OR = 1	Odds same for RHB and LHB	LOR = 0
OR < 1	Odds higher for LHB	LOR < 0

Example: An OR of 2 (LOR = 1) means that the odds of a right-handed batter hitting a home run are twice the odds for a left-handed batter.

Average teams should hit for an average batting average. If an average team—a team that wins half of its ballgames—consistently hits above the league average, it is due to a favorable ballpark effect for hitters. The difference between the team's average and the league's average is the size of the park effect.

The caliber of a team is measured by its winning percentage. Above-average teams are expected to hit better than average, because of the superior ability—but how much better? Linear regression provides the answers. A team that wins 60% of its games— a .600 team—on average hits 7.7 points above the league average. Since the effect is assumed to be linear, a .550 team is expected to hit 3.85 points better than average— halfway between an average team and a .600 team—while a .400 team, on average, hits 7.7 points below average.

Table D.2 shows the expected differences between a .600 team and an average team for 7 different offensive events. The numbers are per 500 ABs or 550 NFPs. Using the "Batter" column, we see that players from .600 teams average 3.8 more hits per 500 ABs, including 1.1 more doubles, 0.2 more triples, and 1.5 more home runs. In 550 NFPs, these batters get 2.2 more walks, 3.5 fewer strikeouts, and score 5.9 more runs.

Although superior teams bat better, their pitchers also keep their opponents' averages down. The "Pitcher" column shows the average effect for a .600 team. Opposing teams get 4.5 fewer hits per 500 ABs, with 0.6 fewer homers. The pitchers yield 2.0 fewer walks, strike out 6.9 more batters, and give up 7.5 fewer runs per 550 NFPs.

The expected differences for batters and pitchers are opposite in direction, and fairly similar in magnitude. Thus, they basically cancel each other out, as is shown

Table D.2   Expected Changes in Events for a .600 Team

| Event | Standard Avg. | Expected Changes* | | | r^2 | RMSE Reduction |
		Batter	Pitcher	Both		
BA	127.5	+3.8	−4.5	−0.3	.01	20%
DPT	25.0	+1.3				
T	3.5	+0.2				
HR	10.5	+1.5	−0.6	+0.5	.04	30%
R	66.6	+5.9	−7.5	−0.8	.04	10%
BB	47.8	+2.2	−2.0	+0.1	.00	33%
SO	88.6	−3.5	+6.9	+1.7	.05	27%

Notes: The expected changes were determined using a weighted linear regression, with winning percentage as the independent variable and the normalized event averages for all teams as the dependent variable, 1893–1968.

Standard Avg. and expected changes are given per 500 ABs for BA, DPT, T, and HR, and per 550 NFPs for R, BB, and SO.

r^2 is the percent of variance explained by the regression model which includes both batter and pitcher data.

RMSE reduction is the % reduction in the root-mean-squared error of the "Both" model compared to the "Batter" model.

in the "Both" column. For example, batters on .600 teams get 3.8 more hits per 500 ABs, while their pitchers yield 4.4 fewer hits. The net effect is for the combined hit total of both teams to be 0.3 hits lower.

Some .600 teams have great hitters and average pitchers, while others have mediocre hitters and superb pitchers. Combining batter and pitcher data improves park effect estimation by reducing this source of variability. The "RMSE Reduction" column shows the reduction in the root-mean-square error of the park effect estimates obtained from the combined data, compared to the batter-only data. The improvement ranges from 10% for runs to 33% for walks. The r^2 values show the proportion of variability in the combined average "explained" by the team's winning percentage — very little, with .04 being the highest.

The results for home runs and runs shown in Table D.1 are for illustration only, since they will be estimated using level 3 data. For batting average and walks, the effect of team winning percentage on the combined data is minimal, so none will be applied. For doubles and triples, winning percentage adjustments based on the batter's expected changes is used. For strikeouts, substantial differences were found for the combined batter and pitcher data over time. The periods and effects are: 1893–1923, +0.2; 1924–35, +5.1; 1936–55, +2.5; and 1956–1968, +0.6. We will use these period-specific effects in estimating the ballpark effects for strikeouts.

Shrinkage of Ballpark Effect Estimates

Multiple changepoint regression analysis smoothes out much of the random variation seen in ballpark data from season to season. By pooling data over several seasons, the park effects stabilize. However, 19th century teams frequently changed ballparks or became defunct. They also played fewer games per season. Consequently, a statistical technique called *shrinkage* is needed to improve the estimated ballpark effects.

The parks presented earlier in Table D.1 are 5 of the 8 most extreme parks for home runs in baseball history (with park percentages farthest from 50%). Four were used by their teams for a single season only. These results raise an interesting question. Were these older parks really the most extreme, or do they only appear so owing to limited data?

Baseball fans know that it is harder to bat .400 for an entire season than for the first 2 weeks. This is because small amounts of data produce wild spreads in averages that settle down with additional play. In a 1977 *Scientific American* article, statisticians Bradley Efron and Carl Morris showed how the concept of shrinkage can statistically help averages "settle down." They shrunk the batting averages of all players who had 45 at-bats on April 26, 1970, toward (but not to) the league average. They obtained new estimates that better predicted the players' final batting averages than those based on only 45 at-bats.

A similar approach is useful for improving park percentage estimates. The most extreme home run parks in baseball history, based on raw data (see Table D.1), are Pittsburgh's Exposition Park and Hartford's Hartford Ball Club Grounds, with park percentages of 100% and 0%, respectively. The park percentages are based 4 or fewer home runs, though.

Many other park percentages also rely on small amounts of data. In the case of the 1883–4 Philadelphia Quakers, only 2 home runs were hit by both the Quakers and their opponents at Recreation Park in Philadelphia compared with 72 at the road parks. Park percentages depend more heavily on the smaller home run total. So let's focus on the home total for Recreation Park — 2, in 107 games.

Counts of "rare" events are often assumed to follow a Poisson distribution. The 2 home runs hit at Philadelphia's Recreation Park in 107 games are an historical fact. If we were able to resurrect the players, however, the home runs total from an additional 107 games is likely to be different. Suppose that the "true" long-term rate for hitting home runs at Recreation Park is 5 per 107 games. Then, assuming that the Poisson distribution holds, the probability of hitting 2 or fewer home runs in 107 games is 12%, a plausible outcome.

Thus, a discrepancy of 3 home runs (from 2 to 5) between the true and observed counts is not that surprising. Given that Recreation Park shows up as one of the worst home run parks adds further weight to the suspicion that the "observed" home run total is below the expected rate. Although other choices could be defended statistically, park percentages will be shrunk toward the average park percentage, 50%, by adding 3 home runs to both the normalized home and road home run totals.

Shrinking the parks presented in Table D.1 yields the adjusted park percentages shown in Table D.3. The two ballparks whose unadjusted park percentages are based on the most home runs — Lake Front Park II in Chicago and Recreation Park in Philadelphia — now emerge as the most extreme of the five ballparks. In fact, after shrinkage they are the most extreme across baseball history.

Interestingly, additional home run data exist for the other 3 ballparks, since other teams used them. Union Grounds in Brooklyn was home to 3 different National Asso-

---

Definitions D.3 **Shrinkage factor, adjusted park percentage**

Level 3 or 4 Data

Adjusted park percentage = 100 × (Normalized home OEs + SF)/(Normalized home OEs + normalized road OEs + 2 × SF),

where OE stands for offensive event and SF for the shrinkage factor, which is the number of events to be added to both the home and road totals.

Level 1 or 2 Data

Adjusted offensive event average = (raw event average × total ABs + 4000 × league event average) / (total ABs + 4000)

Note: For R, BB, and SO, NFPs are used rather than ABs.

Table D.3 Shrinkage of Park Percentages for Selected Parks

Team	Park	Total HRs	Park Pct	Adj Park Pct	HRs	Pct
Chi–N	Lake Front Park II	223.5	87	86	—	—
NY–N	Union Grounds	9.8	87	72	107.1	56
Pit–U	Exposition Park I	1.9	100	62	58.3	50
Har–N	Hartford Ball Club Gds	3.7	0	31	13.3	13
Phi–N	Recreation Park	74.7	3	6	—	—

Note: Adj Park Pct. = 100 × (Norm. Home HRs + 3)/(Norm. Home HRs + Norm. Road HRs + 6).

ciation teams from 1871 to 1875 and the Brooklyn Hartfords in the National League in 1877. Altogether, 107.1 normalized home runs were hit, with a raw park percentage of 56%. Additional home run data gives Exposition Park I a park percentage of 50% (58.3 normalized home runs) and the Hartford Ball Club Grounds a park percentage of 13% (13.3 home runs). These data lends support to the idea that park percentages should be shrunk.

Shrinkage factors are needed for the other offensive events as well. Unfortunately, the determination of the appropriate factors is not straightforward. Regarding runs, shrinkage factors of between 200 and 750 runs seem reasonable, using a statistical method that is beyond the scope of this book. Since average annual home and road run totals in the 20th century generally exceed 600, the more conservative total of 200 runs, which corresponds to roughly one third of a season, was used.

Table D.4 shows how much shrinkage reduces the standard deviations of the estimated park effects for home runs and runs in different time periods. Shrinkage affects the earliest time period (1876–92) the most, with the home run SD declining 20%, while the runs SD declined by 19%. By contrast, the shrinkage has a small overall effect post-1919, with the home run and run SDs declining at most 1% and 5%, respectively.

Table D.4 Effect of Shrinkage on Park Effect Standard Deviations of Level 3 Data

Years	Team-Years	Home Run SD/500 AB			Run SD/550 NFPs		
		Raw	Shrunk	Ratio	Raw	Shrunk	Ratio
1876–92	241	3.30	2.65	.80	3.30	2.67	.81
1893–1919	412	2.49	2.43	.97	2.13	1.98	.93
1920–62	694	1.72	1.71	.99	2.43	2.34	.96
1963–92	728	1.01	1.01	1.00	2.44	2.37	.97
1993–2003	320	0.70	0.70	1.00	3.44	3.28	.95
1993–2003*	309	0.55	0.54	1.00	2.26	2.13	.95

Notes: Ratio = shrunk SD/raw SD.

Standardizing averages: HRs 10.5/500 ABs; runs 66.6/550 NFPs.

*Col-N not included.

Table D.4 shows that the variation in park effect estimates for home runs has progressively declined over the years. The story for runs is less clear. From 1993 to the present, the shrunken SD, which is the highest of any period, is strongly dependent on the extreme park effects seen at Coors Field in Colorado. When the Colorado data are excluded, the shrunken SD drops 35%, to one of the smallest values.

The Effect of Shrinking and the Need for Squeezing

Level 4 data, which yield the most accurate park effect estimates, are currently available only for 1969 to the present. Decisions regarding shrinking and squeezing were earlier in the development of this book, on data from 1974 to 2002. Table D.5 compares the park effect estimates obtained from level 4 data against the best level data available across baseball history for each event. Park effect estimates are constructed to have an overall average equal to the league average.

Two key features of the comparison of lower level data to level 4 data are the Pearson r-value and the SD ratio shown in Table D.5. Since the means of the park effects have been calibrated, if the Pearson r-value and SD ratio are both 1, that would indicate that the park effects from the 2 data levels agree. If the values differ from 1, remedies are available to make park effects estimates prior to 1969 closer to those obtained from level 4 data. These remedies, which are used in this book for ballpark estimation, will now be described for each offensive event and summarized in Table D.6.

Home Runs: The Pearson r-value and SD ratio are both very close to 1, indicating that level 3 and level 4 data produce nearly identical park effect estimates. Given that result, and since only level 3 data are available by batter handedness, we will use level 3 data throughout baseball history.

Table D.5   Comparison of Park Effect Estimates by Data Quality

Event	Pearson r	Lower Level Data SD*		Level 4 Data SD	SD Ratio
		Raw	Shrunk		
HR	.994	0.82	0.82	0.80	.98
R	.993	2.30	2.22	1.99	.90
BA	.643	1.94	1.80	1.90	1.05
DPT	.875	1.66	1.58	1.36	.86
3B	.805	0.64	0.60	0.42	.70
BB	.176	2.04	1.91	0.77	.40
SO	.457	3.46	3.21	1.99	.62

Notes: Comparison based on all team seasons from 1974–2002 except Colorado (all years), 1974 (Cin–N, Pit–N, SF–N), and 1974–5 (Cle–A).

* Level 1 data (DPT, T), level 2 data (BA, SO, BB), level 3 data (HR, R).

SD per 500 ABs or 550 NFPs.

SD Ratio = Level 4 data SD/lower level data shrunken SD.

Runs: The Pearson *r*-value is near 1 but the level 4 data SD is 10% smaller than that for level 3 data. This occurs since parks where more runs are scored have greater NFPs per game. Level 3 data will be used throughout baseball history, but squeezed to account for the association between runs and at-bats. By not switching to level 4 data, we don't have to force a changeyear at 1969.

RBIs: Park effect estimates for runs will serve as estimates for RBIs.

Offensive events other than home runs, runs, and RBIs: Pearson *r*-values are all substantially below 1. Thus, we will use level 4 data for 1969–2003 and the next best level available for 1876–1968. In cases where teams have changeyears between 1970 and 1972, we shift the level data used at the changeyears. These exceptions are: 1970 for Cal–A, Cin–N and Cle–A; 1971 for NY–N, Phi–N and Pit–N, and 1972 for Hou–N and Tex–A. For three teams, park effect estimates using data from 1969 and later were also applied to estimate earlier years: Oak–A, for 1968, and Atl–N and StL–N, for 1966–68.

Batting average: Since the SD ratio is close to 1, no squeezing is done.

Doubles-plus-triples: Pearson's *r*-value is impressively high, given that only level 1 data were compared to level 4 data. Fourteen percent squeezing is needed.

Triples: Like DPTs, the Pearson *r*-value is high. Thirty percent squeezing is needed.

Bases on Balls: Since the Pearson *r*-value and the SD ratio are both quite low, level 2 data park effect estimation is not reliable for bases on balls. Consequently, all parks will be considered "average" prior to 1969. Level 4 data will be used for 1969–2003.

Strikeouts: The Pearson *r*-value is a moderate .457, and 38% squeezing is needed. Given these values, park effect estimates prior to 1969 are only moderately reliable.

Stolen bases: Although park differences are likely to exist, only level 1 data are available throughout baseball history. Given the great variability in player stolen base totals, such data are unlikely to provide good park estimates. Thus, no park effect estimation was attempted.

There is a difference between shrinking and squeezing. When data are shrunk, park estimates based on fewer data are shrunk more than park estimates that have more data to stabilize them. Squeezing shifts all estimates equally toward the average park effect. The correlation of level 3 data park estimates for runs with at-bats, which does not smooth out with additional data, demonstrates that both types of adjustments to the raw SD estimates are needed.

Summary of Park Estimation Analyses

Based on this comparative analysis, the following table summarizes the approach used to produce park effect estimates:

Table D.6 Summary of the Data Level Used for Park Estimation before and after 1969 by Event along with Shrinkage, Squeezing, and Modeling Details

Event	Data Level 1876–1968	Data Level 1969–2003	Shrinkage Factor	Squeezing Factor	Regression Model
BA	2	4	4000 ABs	1.00	Linear
DPT	1	4	4000 ABs	.86	Linear
3B	1	4	4000 ABs	.70	Linear
HR	3	3	3 HRs	1.00	Logistic
Runs	3	3	200 Runs	.90	Logistic
BB	—	4	4000 NFPs	—	Linear
SO	2	4	4000 NFPs	.62	Linear

Notes: Squeezing Factor = SD ratio from Table 4.7. Weight = Team AB / [Event Avg × (1 − Event Avg) × (Standardizing Event Avg / League Event Avg)^2].

Transformations of Offensive Event Averages

We want to develop a method to indicate how much each player's performance compares to the average performance in his and other eras. There are some notable obstacles to developing this method, though. First, the spread of mean-adjusted averages—as measured by the standard deviation—is not constant over baseball history. For 7 of the 9 basic offensive events, the spread was greater early in baseball history, while for the other 2 events—triples and stolen bases—the spread is greater in the modern game. Second, the distributions of all basic offensive events are positively *skewed*, that is, the best performances tend to be farther away from the average performances than the worst performances. This makes sense, since players who perform well are kept in the lineup, while players who don't are benched.

These two factors—unequal spread over time and positive skewness—conspire together to complicate the comparison of players from different eras. Two causes come to mind to account for large spreads in performance: (1) a weak league, in which top players greatly outperform poor players, or (2) a style of play accentuating differences in ability.

The dominance of players such as Cobb, Jackson, Speaker, Lajoie, and Collins over their deadball era peers is an example of the first cause. The base stealing of Maury Wills in the early 1960s exemplifies the second cause—the gap between his stolen base totals and the league average is partly accounted for by his greater number of attempts, and thus not exactly commensurate with his stealing ability. The home run hitting of Babe Ruth seems to have been a combination of both causes—weaker league talent and Ruth's style of hitting, which was conducive to home runs.

A player's ability relative to that of his peers will be measured by the number of standard deviations above or below the mean that his offensive event average is—but only after the skewness in the distribution has been nearly eliminated by using a statistical procedure known as a power transformation.

> *Stats Time*   Transforming data to obtain an approximately normal
>   distribution
>
> There is a large class of transformations called *power transformations*. For power
> transformations, we produce a transformed variable Y by the formula:
>
> $$Y = X^b,$$
>
> where X is the raw data and b is the power. If $b = 1$, the variable X is not trans-
> formed at all, since Y = X. If $b = 1/2$, Y is the square root of X. If $b = 1/3$, Y is the
> cube root of X. If b is very close to 0 (it actually involves the limit as b goes to 0,
> a concept from calculus), Y is the natural logarithm of X. For positively skewed
> raw data, the skewness typically declines as b declines below 1 and, in my expe-
> rience, nears zero for some value of b between 0 and 1.
>
> When the skewness is near zero, the distribution of values tends to be sym-
> metric; that is, it looks the same when reflected in the mirror as it does when one
> looks straight at it. Symmetric distributions, such as the normal distribution, have
> mathematical beauty. Many kinds of rankings, such as IQ scores, are based on
> the normal distribution.
>
> In comparing baseball players, we would like to use a distribution as close to
> a normal distribution as possible. We will look at power transformations with the
> choices of b of 0, .05, .10, .15, .20, 25, 1/3, 1/2, 3/4, and 1, and choose the most-
> normal-like distribution by use of the *normality score* developed by Anderson and
> Darling. The normality score is a non-negative number. The closer it is to 0, the
> more normal-like the distribution.

A First Attempt at Transforming Offensive Event Averages

Table E.1 shows the normality scores for the original data for the 8 eras identified in
Chapter 3. We will take a normality score of 2 or greater—shown in bold in the table—
as a measure of a substantial departure from normality. Note that only the batting average, runs, and doubles-plus-triples distributions are consistently normal-like.

The bottom row of Table E.1 shows the *geometric mean* of the normality scores for
the basic events across the eight eras. The geometric mean—obtained by multiplying
the 8 normality scores in a given column together and raising the result to the 1/8th
power—is often used when summarizing non-negative data where some values are many
times larger than other values. The 9 basic events besides HBPs are ordered from most-
normal-like to least normal-like based on the geometric means of the normality scores.

Table E.2 shows the normality scores after the best power transformation for each
event was used. In 6 cases, the square root power transformation ($b = 1/2$) yielded the
most normal-like distribution. For runs, doubles-plus-triples, and triples, $b = 0.75$
proved best.

248   APPENDIX E

Table E.1 Normality Scores for Original Data

	BA	R	DPT	RBI	SO	BB	3B	HR	SB
1885–1900	1.1	2.4	3.7	3.8	7.0	11.3	10.2	27.2	18.2
1901–19	2.3	1.3	5.0	6.3	4.4	10.3	11.9	81.0	26.4
1920–46	1.1	1.8	0.9	11.3	28.1	15.0	12.5	107.5	116.2
1947–62	0.6	0.9	0.8	7.0	6.7	12.4	10.0	26.4	114.8
1963–68	0.5	0.5	0.5	2.5	3.3	4.2	9.1	10.2	69.8
1969–76	0.3	0.2	1.2	3.6	8.8	9.6	20.3	18.0	109.1
1977–92	0.9	1.1	1.6	6.1	12.1	15.8	46.7	35.9	213.9
1993–2003	0.7	0.4	1.8	4.8	5.7	13.2	59.9	22.9	146.5
Geo. Mean	0.8	0.8	1.5	5.2	7.6	10.8	17.3	31.4	79.1

Note: Scores of 2 or more, shown in bold, indicate substantial non-normality.

Table E.2 Normality Scores for Transformed Data

	BA	R	DPT	RBI	SO	BB	3B	HR	SB
1885–1900	0.3	1.0	1.2	0.4	0.4	0.7	2.6	18.1	1.3
1901–19	1.3	0.3	1.3	1.1	0.4	0.4	1.9	47.3	1.7
1920–46	0.6	0.3	1.0	1.5	1.7	0.8	1.4	8.6	12.2
1947–61	0.2	0.3	0.2	2.2	0.7	1.1	2.1	1.0	14.6
1963–68	0.3	0.3	0.2	1.2	0.2	0.4	2.3	1.1	8.3
1969–76	0.5	0.4	0.3	2.1	0.5	1.1	5.8	3.4	14.1
1977–92	0.2	0.4	0.5	4.3	0.4	0.8	14.6	7.9	25.4
1993–2003	0.3	0.4	0.7	2.5	0.6	0.5	23.3	2.1	14.7
Geo. Mean	0.4	0.4	0.5	1.6	0.5	0.7	4.0	5.1	8.0

Notes: Scores of 2 or more, shown in bold, indicate substantial non-normality.

The 0.75 power was used for runs, doubles-plus-triples and triples; the square root transformation was used for all other events.

Notice how dramatically the normality scores have declined. For 5 of the first 6 events in the table—batting average, runs, doubles-plus-triples, strikeouts, and walks— all normality scores are now less than 2. The scores for RBIs are somewhat higher, but acceptable. The normality scores for triples, home runs, and stolen bases are all dramatically improved, but are still less than ideal. We'll take additional steps to further lower their normality scores, but first I'll explain why improvements seen with the square root transformation are not unexpected.

Stats Time   Using a square-root transformation for
                Poisson-distributed data

Suppose that we want to compare two players who consistently have about 500 at-bats per year and whose home run hitting abilities are constant over a number of seasons. Then, statistically, comparing the number of home runs hit per year is equivalent to comparing the number of home runs per 500 at-bats.

Home runs are, by and large, "rare" events, believed to be modeled well by a *Poisson distribution*. For a Poisson distribution, the variance is equal to the mean. For example, if one players' long-term ability is to hit 20 home runs a year, the variance of his yearly totals is 20. If a second player hits 5 home runs a year, his variance is only 5. Thus, the higher the average number of home runs, the higher the variance. Most standard statistical tools for detecting differences between means assume that the variances are the same. A square root transformation is often applied to Poisson-distributed data, since it renders the variance of the transformed data nearly constant, regardless of the value of the mean.

The distributions that we are considering, though, are the averages from different players, who have different abilities. Consequently, the square root transformation is not guaranteed to work, but it is a leading candidate for consideration.

A Problem: Player-Seasons with Zero Averages

The normality scores in Table E.2 for triples, home runs, and stolen bases are higher than those for the other events. Why is that so? These happen to be the only offensive events in which some regular players have zero seasonal averages. When a significant percentage of players have zero averages, the distribution has a "spike" at zero, and an approximately normal distribution is not obtainable with a simple power transformation. Table E.3 shows the percents of *player-seasons* with zero triples, home runs, or stolen bases by era of play.

As Table E.3 shows, zero home runs were hit in 23% of regular player-seasons in the deadball era (1901–19), which in Table E.2 had the highest normality score for home runs. This raises a question. Were 23% of players completely unable to hit home runs or were home runs sufficiently rare during this era that the probability of hitting zero home runs is appreciable?

Let's look at player performance in back-to-back years from that era. Eighty-two players were regulars in both 1904 and 1905. Of these players, 32 failed to hit a home run in one of the two seasons. Only 4 players, however, failed to get a home run in both seasons. Later in the era, from 1916 to 1917, 26 of 82 players failed to hit a home run in one of the seasons, but only 7 failed in both seasons. Every one of these 7 players hit home runs during his career, with an average of 16 home runs each.

Table E.3 Percentage of Regular Player-Seasons with Zero Averages

Era	No. of Player-Seasons	Percentage 3B	Percentage HR	Percentage SB
1885–1900	1546	0.4	13	0
1901–19	2304	1	24	0
1920–46	3283	2	9	5
1947–62	2068	6	2	13
1963–68	962	7	2	12
1969–76	1558	9	4	12
1977–92	3586	12	4	10
1993–2001	2812	16	1	11

Note: A player-season occurs whenever a player has enough NFPs to be a regular. Mickey Cochrane was a regular every year from 1925 to 1935, so he contributed 11 player-seasons to the 1920–46 era.

A Remedy for the Zero Average Player-Seasons: The Rare Events Correction

Based on the evidence in the preceding section, we can conclude that a zero home run player-season does not identify players who are unable to hit home runs, but rather is an occasional seasonal total when home runs are rare. As a result, it is reasonable to improve the normality of the distribution by adding a small amount, called the *rare event correction* (REC), to the raw averages prior to the transformation.

Recall from Formula 2.1 that the mean-adjusted event average included an REC term. A different REC value is used depending whether or not the player had at least one home run.

Case 1: Player had at least one home run.

$$REC = 0.5/(\text{Average no. of ABs for regular players}).$$

The rationale is that we are essentially giving each player half a home run per year. Because an average is a rate statistic, we are dividing by at-bats. The reason for using the same number of at-bats—the average number for a regular player for the season— is that we preserve the ranking of players as it was before the REC was used. Since the average number of at-bats for regular players is about 500 each season, REC is about .001.

Case 2: Player had zero home runs.

$$REC = 0.5/\text{Player ABs}.$$

The rationale is that if we use the REC formula given in case 1, all players with zero home runs wind up with the same mean-adjusted average, leaving the "spike" in the distribution of averages. This spike is particularly noticeable in seasons when many players fail to hit any home runs. Using the player's own at-bats in the REC formula smoothes this spike somewhat, yielding an improved normality score. With the revised formula, a player with zero home runs in 300 at-bats now has a REC of .0017 (= 0.5/300), while a player with zero home runs in 600 at-bats has a REC of .0008. This adjustment makes some sense since the latter player has demonstrated a greater inability to hit home runs. Consequently, we will add this amount to the raw home run average before applying the transformation.

Table E.4 Normality Scores after the Rare Events Correction Is Used

Years	3B	HR	SB
1885–1900	0.3	**2.3**	1.0
1901–1919	0.5	**15.8**	**2.4**
1920–46	1.7	**11.9**	0.9
1947–62	1.8	1.2	**2.6**
1963–68	0.9	0.9	1.8
1969–76	1.5	**2.5**	**3.4**
1977–92	**3.9**	**5.4**	**7.5**
1993–2003	**8.3**	**2.1**	**6.1**
Geo. Mean	1.5	**3.3**	**2.5**

Notes: Scores of 2 or more, shown in bold, indicate substantial non-normality.

Square root transformations ($b = 1/2$) are used for triples and home runs; $b = .20$ is used for stolen bases.

Table E.4 shows the normality scores for the triple, home run, and stolen base averages after the REC correction. Comparison with Table E.2 shows that nearly all of the scores have been improved.

For the fully adjusted event averages, the REC will be subtracted away. Thus, players who hit zero home runs in a season, will wind up with zero home runs. Why, then, was it added in to begin with? There are two main reasons: (1) to help determine the best power transformation and (2) to obtain a more appropriate standardizing mean and standard deviation to be used in the fully adjusted event average formula.

Final Approach: Using Different Transformation Powers over Time

Unfortunately, the normality scores in Table E.4 are still quite high for some eras. Of greatest concern are the scores above 10 for home runs in the eras 1901–19 and 1920–46. Something more can and should be done. For a given event, different transformation powers will be used for different eras.

Table E.5 shows normality scores for these final transformations. Overall, our transformations have worked quite well—the geometric mean of normality scores are below 2 for all events except home runs, and the highest normality score in any era is 7.8.

Table E.5 Normality Scores with Shifting Transformations

	BA	R	DPT	RBI	SO	BB	3B	HR	SB
1885–1900	0.3	<u>0.4</u>	0.5	0.4	0.4	0.7	0.3	**<u>3.1</u>**	0.2
1901–19	1.3	0.3	<u>0.3</u>	1.1	0.6	0.4	0.5	**<u>6.2</u>**	<u>0.6</u>
1920–46	0.6	0.3	1.0	1.5	<u>0.3</u>	0.8	1.7	<u>1.6</u>	<u>1.2</u>
1947–62	0.2	0.3	0.2	**<u>2.2</u>**	0.7	1.1	1.8	1.2	**<u>2.6</u>**
1963–68	0.3	0.3	0.2	1.3	0.2	0.4	<u>0.9</u>	0.9	0.6
1969–76	0.5	0.4	0.3	**2.1**	0.5	1.1	2.6	**2.5**	<u>1.3</u>
1977–92	0.2	0.4	0.5	**3.4**	0.4	0.8	**7.0**	**5.4**	**<u>5.1</u>**
1993–2003	0.3	0.4	0.7	**2.3**	0.6	0.5	**6.3**	**2.1**	7.8
Geo. Mean	0.4	0.3	0.4	1.5	0.4	0.7	1.6	**2.4**	1.4

Notes: Scores of 2 or more, shown in bold, indicate substantial non-normality.

Underlines show where shifts in the transformation power occur, for example, in 1901 for runs.

Illustrating the Transformation Steps

Figure E.1 illustrates the effect of the transformation steps that have just been described. The top left panel shows the distribution of the raw home run average (HRs/AB) for all 3283 regular player-seasons between 1920 and 1946, with the best fitting normal distribution (black curve) overlaid on it. Although not visible on the graph, player-seasons—principally those of Babe Ruth—occur as far out as the right-hand edge. The normality score is 107.5, indicating that the distribution of the raw data is quite far from that of a normal distribution.

The top right panel shows the same data after a square root transformation has been applied. The normality score is much closer to zero, indicating a great improvement in the normality of the transformed data. There is a big spike at zero, the first histogram bin. These are the 283 player-seasons where the batter failed to hit a single home run.

The bottom right panel shows the data after the rare events correction has been applied. Notice that there is no longer a gap between the player-seasons with zero home runs and the rest of the player-seasons. However, the normality score is even higher than before that correction, and there is still an extended right-hand tail to the distribution. This is improved by using a more extreme transformation—the fourth root of the rare events corrected data, as shown in the bottom right panel. In this panel, the left-hand tail has been lengthened and the right-hand tail shortened, giving a more normal-like distribution.

Use of the fourth root compared to the square root can be staggering, as evidenced in Table 2.7. For Babe Ruth, it means crediting him with 64 adjusted home runs rather than 79 in 1920, and 58 home runs rather than 80 in 1927. The biggest discrepancy involves Ruth's 1919 season, where the fifth root transformation gives Ruth 62 adjusted home runs rather than a whopping 103 home runs if one used a square root trans-

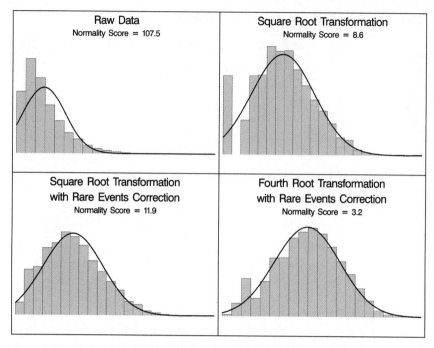

Figure E.1   Illustration of Transformation Steps for Home Runs, 1920–46

formation! Because a square root transformation for home runs is applied in this book to all player-seasons after 1946, the adjusted home runs for Mark McGwire in 1998 (59 HRs) and Barry Bonds in 2001 (74 HRs) do not change with the adoption of the "variable transformation powers" approach.

Discussion of the Different Transformation Powers

Table E.6 shows the powers needed to transform the averages of regular players to an approximate normal distribution. For example, for strikeouts, a 0.33 power normalizes the data for the years 1876–1946, while a 0.50 power normalizes the data for the years 1947–2001.

Much can be understood about baseball performance data by inspecting this table. First, a single power suffices for fitting batting average and bases on balls over baseball history, suggesting that the basic significance of these two events has not changed very much. Second, the power for three other events—runs, doubles-plus-triples, and RBIs—climbed from 0.50 to 0.75, implying that the performances have become less positively skewed over time. Since 0.75 is the highest transformation power used, this suggests that baseball requires greater clustering of these events than the others. Third, home runs have undergone interesting changes over time. Clustering diminished in the deadball era and became progressively tighter through the lively ball era. Since 1947, the transformation power has remained stable. Fourth, triples and stolen bases—

Table E.6   Transformation Powers over Baseball History

Event	Initial Year								
	1876	1901	1920	1931	1947	1963	1969	1977	1993
BA	0.50								
R	0.50	0.75							
DPT	0.50		0.75						
SO	0.33				0.50				
RBI	0.50					0.75			
BB	0.50								
3B	0.50						0.33		
HR	0.33	0.20	0.25	0.33	0.50				
SB (NL)	0.33		0.25	0.20		0.15		0.33	
SB (AL)	0.33		0.25	0.20					0.25

Note: For blank cells in the table, the previous number in the row gives the transformation power.

two events that depend heavily on speed—became less clustered over time, although stolen bases have tightened again in recent years.

Explaining the Poorer Transformations: Home Runs, RBIs, and Stolen Bases

Home runs, RBIs, and stolen bases are the only events in Table E.5 for which at least three eras have normality scores of 2 or more. To understand why, we need to talk about the *moments* of a distribution. Each distribution has an infinite set of moments, providing its fingerprint. For a normal distribution, the first moment—the mean— can have any value. The second moment—the standard deviation—can have any positive value. At this point, the flexibility ends. For a normal distribution, scaled versions of the third and fourth moments—the *skewness* and *kurtosis*, respectively—should both be zero. Table E.7 shows the skewness and kurtosis values for home runs, RBIs, and stolen basess.

For home runs, skewness values fall in a tight range around zero. Excluding the 1920–30 era, kurtosis values also range between –0.27 and –0.54. While not near zero, they are close to each other. As such, the transformed distributions are fairly comparable. The distinctive 1920–30 era is largely attributable to the influence of Babe Ruth and Lou Gehrig. Consequently, some strain exists in comparing this era to the others.

For RBIs, skewness values fall in a tight range around zero. Except for the 1885–1900 era, kurtosis values clustered between –0.29 and –0.52. These eras are thus similar to each other, even though the kurtosis is not near zero. The 1885–1900 era, with its kurtosis of almost 0, is different, making comparisons with this era more tenuous.

For stolen bases, a divide exists across the eras. The first three eras look similar. The 1931–46 era is transitional, with a distinct kurtosis value. For eras starting on or after 1947, the skewness values hover around 0.2, while the kurtosis values range from –0.27 to –0.57. Thus, post–World War II stolen base distributions are distinctly different from those of earlier eras, rendering comparisons to them somewhat suspect.

Table E.7   Skewness and Kurtosis Values for Home Runs, RBIs, and Stolen Bases

Years	HR			RBI			SB*		
	Power	Skew	Kurt	Power	Skew	Kurt	Power	Skew	Kurt
1885–1900	.33	–.04	–.38	.50	.06	–.01	.33	–.04	.11
1901–19	.20	.12	–.48	.50	.01	–.36	.33	–.06	.24
1920–30	.25	.10	–.16	.50	.08	–.29	.25	.05	.16
1931–46	.33	.03	–.52	.50	.05	–.44	.20	.03	–.17
1947–62	.50	.06	–.43	.50	–.01	–.48	.20	.21	–.33
1963–68	.50	–.02	–.46	.75	.07	–.52	.15	.21	–.27
1969–76	.50	–.02	–.54	.75	.11	–.42	.15	.17	–.48
1977–92	.50	–.04	–.51	.75	.05	–.44	.33	.28	–.52
1993–2003	.50	.01	–.27	.75	.06	–.42	.33	.30	–.57

* The values for SB from 1963 to 2002 apply to the National League only.

How to Adjust for Doubles and Triples

In Chapter 8, doubles-plus-triples was adopted as a basic offensive event. Two different methods for calculating them were proposed: the DPT method and the separate-events method. In this appendix, these two methods are compared.

Calculation of Separate-Events and Doubles-plus-Triples Methods of Adjustment

Step 3 of the game plan for leveling the playing field for player comparison (Chapter 2) calls for the following park adjustment:

Park-adjusted average = mean-adjusted average ÷ park factor.

Data from Table 8.1 are used to show how the two methods give different results. For the purposes of this illustration, several simplifications will be made. First, the raw averages will be considered to be the mean-adjusted averages. Second, the park factors for Exposition Park for 1900–1908 are obtained by contrasting the extra-base hit averages of the Pirates to that of the league as a whole.

The first column of Table F.1 shows the averages for the National League for 1900–08. The "Pirates" column is obtained using data from the "Total" line of Table 8.1 (e.g., 3B Avg. = .0185 = 833/45,113). The averages for Wagner, Clarke, and Leach were obtained similarly.

Table F.1   Raw Extra-Base Hit Averages for Selected Pirates

	NL	Pirates	Wagner	Clarke	Leach
2B Average	.0333	.0350	.0700	.0424	.0285
3B Average	.0135	.0185	.0290	.0301	.0272
DPT Average	.0467	.0534	.0990	.0725	.0557

Separate-Events Method Calculation

If doubles and triples are considered to be separate events, the park factor is the ratio of the Pirate team park effect average to the league park effect average. Thus, Honus Wagner's park-adjusted double average is:

$$.0700 \div (.0350/.0333) = .0666.$$

Similarly, Wagner's adjusted 3B average is $.0290 \div (.0185/.0135) = .0212$, so his DPT average is: $.0878 = .0666 + .0212$.

DPT Method Calculation

If doubles and triples are considered to be parts of a combined event, the adjusted averages are calculated in a different, slightly more complicated way. First, Wagner's DPT average is calculated as:

$$.0990 \div (.0534/.0467) = .0866.$$

Then, a his triples average is based on the odds that he gets a triple compared to an idealized "average hitter" with the same park effects, adjusted to the league triple odds. Using the data from Table F.1 for Honus Wagner, the components are:

Wagner's triple odds   = $.0290/.0700 = .414$
"Average Pirate" triple odds = $.0185/.0350 = .529$
League average triple odds = $.0135/.0333 = .405$

Wagner's park-adjusted triple odds = $.414 \div .529 / .405 = .317$,
where the ratio $.405 / .529$ is the park factor.

Then, to calculate the proportion of DPTs that are triples, one takes the park-adjusted triples odds divided by one plus the odds, that is

$$.317 / (1 + .317) = .241.$$

Finally, Wagner's adjusted triples average is $.241 \times .0866 = .0209$. Wagner's adjusted doubles average is obtained by subtraction as $.0657 = .0866 - .0209$, as shown in Table F.2.

Table F.2   Adjusted Averages for Selected Pirates

	Separate-Events Method			DPT Method		
	Wagner	Clarke	Leach	Wagner	Clarke	Leach
2B Avg.	.0666	.0403	.0271	.0657	.0413	.0283
3B Avg.	.0212	.0220	.0198	.0209	.0221	.0204
DPT Avg.	.0878	.0623	.0469	.0866	.0634	.0487

Comparison of Separate-Events and Doubles-plus-Triples
Methods of Adjustment

Compared to the separate-events method, the DPT method led to a lower adjusted DPT average for Wagner but higher DPT averages for Clarke and Leach. This is because Clarke and Leach had higher proportions of their doubles-plus-triples in triples than the "average" Pittsburgh hitter, while Wagner did not. Tommy Leach's raw DPT average was 56% (= .0557/.0990) of that for Honus Wagner. The DPT method preserves that ratio (56% = .0487/.0866), while the separate-events method does not (53% = .0469/.0878).

Exposition Park was more favorable to triples (up 37%) than to doubles (up 5%) compared to the average park. Consequently, the separate-events method down-adjusted triples more, hitting Leach harder than Wagner. The DPT method down-adjusted DPTs the same for Leach and Wagner and reshaped the triples fraction at Exposition Park to that of an average National League park using odds ratios. Because we found a sharper distinction between singles and doubles than between doubles and triples (see Chapter 8), the DPT method is the best method.

Predicting Runs and RBIs from the Batting Record

Using linear regression, weights were found for various factors in order to predict runs, RBIs, and runs-plus-RBIs for regular players from 1893 to 2003, divided into 3 eras, as shown in Table 10.2. In addition to the offensive events used in CHI (1B, 2B, 3B, and HR), walks, stolen bases, Team OBP edge, league error difference, and catcher-on-firsts were used. The final three factors are explained further in Formula G.1.

Table G.1 shows the weights for predicting the number of runs, RBIs, or runs-plus-RBIs that a player will get per factor. In looking at the weights, we should keep in mind how regression models work. In our context, they do not simply reflect the inherent value of a given event; they also account for differences for lineup placement. An obvious example of this occurs with runs scored per home run. In baseball, one run is scored per home run, but the regression models credit only .89 to .90 runs per home run. Why? Run scoring for other events, such as singles or walks, depends on one's position in the lineup. An overall valuation of .29 to .34 runs is given per single, however, regardless of one's lineup position. Players who hit home runs more frequently tend to be placed in the cleanup or fifth position in the lineup. These players will tend to score fewer runs per single than the leadoff, second place, and perhaps other lineup-position batters. The regression model compensates for all such lineup-position complications by giving a run valuation for home runs of less than 1.

A second example of a paradoxical regression model weight is the −0.22 weight for stolen bases from 1947 to 2003. This weight does not mean that base stealing is bad for RBI production, but that base stealers tend to be in the leadoff or second positions in the lineup. Why not leave it out of the RBI model entirely, then? Although a stolen base is not an offensive event that can generate an RBI, it can lead to a run scored. By including it in the RBI model, we take advantage of the lineup information provided by the number of stolen bases, and preserve the property that sum of the weights from the runs and RBIs models equals the weight for the runs-plus-RBIs% model.

Table G.1 Weights for Predicting Runs and RBIs

	Runs		
	1893–1919 (N = 2967)	1920–1946 (N = 3283)	1947–2003 (N = 10,986)
1B	.338	.304	.288
2B	.34	.42	.40
3B	.59	.72	1.04
HR	.89	.89	.90
BB + HBP	.31	.25	.21
SB	.29	.38	.37
Team OBP edge	.36	.45	.38
League errors diff.	.94	—	—
Catcher-on-firsts	−.07	−.08	−.04
r^2	.983	.984	.987
Root MSE	9.3	9.6	7.7

	RBIs		
	1893–1919	1920–1946	1947–2003
1B	.288	.264	.258
2B	1.02	.66	.54
3B	.87	.76	.31
HR	2.00	2.01	1.90
BB + HBP	−.10	−.02	.01
SB	−.08	−.25	−.22
Team OBP edge	.37	.36	.29
League errors diff.	.60	—	—
Catcher-on-firsts	.02	.03	.01
r^2	.958	.969	.980
Root MSE	12.0	12.5	9.2

	Runs-Plus-RBIs		
	1893–1919	1920–1946	1947–2002
1B	.626	.568	.546
2B	1.36	1.08	.94
3B	1.46	1.48	1.35
HR	2.89	2.90	2.79
BB + HPB	.21	.23	.23
SB	.20	.13	.15
Team OBP edge	.73	.82	.67
League errors diff.	1.53	—	—
Catcher-on-firsts	−.05	−.05	−.03
r^2	.991	.993	.994
Root MSE	12.2	12.1	10.3

Players with high home runs totals tend not to have extreme RPRBI%. The Additional Scoring Rating (ASR), described in Formula G.2, is a modified version of RPRBI%, which substantially reduces the correlation between RPRBI% SD and career home runs. A further discussion of this issue is presented in Chapter 10.

Model Building Notes

1. Shifts in weights were explored for the changes of other eras, as identified in Chapter 3, that is, at 1901, 1920, 1947, 1963, 1969, and 1993. Only 1920 and 1947 yielded appreciable shifts in formula weights, so separate models were constructed for these major epochs.

2. The models can be built in a forward manner adding one variable at a time, with the r^2 value rising with each step. Recall that the r^2 value is a number between 0 and 1 that indicated the percentage of variation in the data that is explained by the model. The following chart shows the forward steps for 1947–2003:

Expected Runs		Expected RBIs		Expected RPRBIs	
Step/Factor	r^2	Step/Factor	r^2	Step/Factor	r^2
1. DPT	.934	1. DPT	.887	1. DPT	.931
2. BB + HBP	.963	2. HR	.968	2. HR	.975
3. 1B	.971	3. 1B	.977	3. 1B	.990
4. HR	.979	4. SB	.978	4. Team OBP edge	.992
5. SB	.984	5. Team OBP edge	.980	5. BB + HBP	.993
6. Team OBP edge	.986	6. 3B	.980	6. S B	.994
7. COF	.986	7. COF	.980	7. COF	.994
8. 3B	.987	8. BB + HBP	.980	8. 3B	.994

Note: Below the underlines, each factor led to a gain of at most .002.

The table above shows that doubles-plus-triples is the single factor most closely associated with runs, RBIs and RPRBIs, and that the r^2 values are quite high with that one factor. Adding in home runs and singles to RBIs and RPRBIs further improves the models; additional factors beyond them only modestly increase the r^2 values. For run scoring, BB + HBP and stolen bases also lead to sizable gains in model fit. Three factors, *team OBP edge*, *catcher-on-firsts* (COF), and triples (a factor that distinguishes the impact of a triple from that of a double since DPT is already in the model) have statistically significant but only modest impact on model fitting.

Other baseball researchers have suggested that I include a slugging edge term in the models. I haven't for two reasons. First, it is highly correlated with team OBP edge ($r = .75$), making it difficult to sort out their separate effects. Second, it would have a very modest effect on the model, even less than team OBP edge. These results should be heartening, because they suggest that the effects of one's particular teammates is not very strong on the runs and RBI totals that a player accrues.

Formula G.1 **RPRBI%**

The formula for RPRBI% for player-seasons between 1947 and 2003 is:

$$RPRBI\% = 100 \times (\text{Actual RPRBIs} - \text{Expected RPRBIs}) / \text{Expected RPRBIs},$$

where

Expected RPRBIs = .546 × 1B + .94 × 2B + 1.35 × 3B + 2.79 × HR + .23 × (BB + HBP) + .15 × SB + .67 × Team OBP edge − .03 × Catcher-on-firsts.

and

"Team OBP edge" gives the difference in the player's team OBP and .322 (the average team OBP in the National League from 1977 to 1992, the standardizing years used throughout this book), multiplied by the number of NFPs for the player, and

"Catcher-on-firsts" is the number of singles plus walks plus HBPs if the principal position for the player is catcher and 0 otherwise.

Notes:
1. The "team OBP edge" factor adjusts for the additional of fewer runs and RBIs that a player can expect to have, based on being on a team with a better or poorer on-base percentage than the standardizing years.
2. Since catchers are typically slower players, they score fewer expected runs and have fewer expected RPRBIs than other position players (see Table 10.2). No striking differences were seen between the other fielding positions.
3. The weights for the formula come from Table 10.2. The weights for other eras and for *Run%* and *RBI%* are obtained similarly by using the appropriate weights.
4. "League errors difference" (used only for Run % for 1893–1919) is the difference in the number of league errors per NFP and .053 (the average rate of league errors from 1893 to 1919), multiplied by the number of NFPs for the player.

Formula G.2   **Additional Scoring Rating (ASR)**

Additional Scoring Rating = $(|RPRBI\%/100 - 1|^{0.5})/\{(.193 - .00365 \times HRs^{0.5}) \times 1.52\}$

If the RPRBI% is less than 100, then multiply the ASR by −1 to undo the effect of the absolute value operation on the sign.

Rationale for the ASR formula:
1. Since home runs tend to compress the values toward the mean (see Table 10.3), this effect can be best estimated by looking at the absolute value of the difference between the RPRBI%/100 and 1.
2. The square root scale is a better scale to use when comparing the absolute differences in step 1 with home runs. Then, the equation $|RPRBI\%/100 - 1|^{0.5} = .193 - .00365 \times HRs^{0.5}$ was obtained using linear regression. By dividing the term on the left by the term on the right, we adjust out the effect of home runs. The r^2 value for this regression, .069, is rather low. It is highly significant, however, and has a significant impact in identifying which players deviate most from their expected totals.
3. To undo the effect that the absolute value function had on the sign of the number, we multiply all RPRBI % values below 100 by −1.
4. Dividing by 1.52 scales the resulting score to have an SD of 1.

Regular Player
Event Averages

This appendix will be found online at http://pup.princeton.edu/schell/apph.pdf.

Event Performance Spreads

This appendix will be found online at http://pup.princeton.edu/schell/appi.pdf.

Event Park Effects

Guide to the tables

The tables in this appendix give the Adjusted Park Indices (APIs) for seven basic offensive events (see Chapter 6). The park effect indices for RBIs are the same as those for runs; no park indices were attempted for stolen bases. For bases on balls, a park effect index of 100 was used for all parks prior to the more precise home and away data level 4 data.

Level 4 data, the highest quality data, are available for the years from 1969 to 2003. For a few teams, the change to the more precise API estimates was made in nearby years, where a more natural break in ballpark or identified potential changeyear was identified. A dotted line indicates where the switch in estimation approach occurred for each franchise. Since level 3 data were used throughout baseball history for home runs and runs, it is sometimes the case that a new API does not occur at the switchpoint for those events. See Appendix D for details.

Adjusted park indices for home runs are given separately by the handedness of the batter. They are denoted as HR-R for right-handed batters and HR-L for left-handed batters.

A blank space indicates that no change occurred for that particular event from the previous changeyear.

Changes in ballpark for a given franchise are indicated by alternating the use of gray scale.

Adjusted Park Indices (APIs) that rank roughly among the top 25% of seasons are shown in bold. APIs that tank roughly among the lowest 25% of seasons are underlined. The remaining APIs place among the middle 50%. The breaks are as follows:

Event	Bottom 25%	Middle 50%	Top 25%
R	≤ 95	96–104	≥105
BA	≤ 97	98–102	≥103
DPT	≤ 91	92–108	≥109
2B	≤ 90	91–109	≥110
3B	≤ 85	86–114	≥115
HRR	≤ 75	76–124	≥125
HRL	≤ 75	76–124	≥125
BB	≤ 97	98–103	≥103
SO	≤ 95	96–104	≥105

AMERICAN LEAGUE TEAMS

California-Anaheim Angels, 1961–2003

Years	R	BA	DPT	2B	3B	HR–R	HR–L	BB	SO
1961	117	97	96	103	64	196	157	100	118
1962–1965	90	97	97	98	95	58	59	100	98
1966–1969	96	98	86	81	115	105	95	100	101
1970–1979	89	96	82	84	69	82	74	97	104
1980–1997	99	99	89	93		111	120		100
1998–2001							91		
2002–2003	92		100			80			

St. Louis Browns–Baltimore Orioles, 1901–2003

Years	R	BA	DPT	2B	3B	HR–R	HR–L	BB	SO
1901	96	97	104	108	88	94	110	100	108
1902–1908	95	97	83	83	82	94	118	100	96
1909–1919	95	98	94	95	92	70	140	100	102
1920–1928	110	102	101	100	95	111	246	100	96
1929–1941			107	110			139		103
1942–1953									109
1954–1957	89	93	92	94	100	64	53	100	103
1958–1963		94			75	77	85		
1964–1968	99	97	110	116		102			
1969–1973	92	99	94	94	88	88		96	98
1974–1979		93			59				105
1980–1991	96	97	88			104	107	102	
1992–1995	104	101	93	94	70	110	115	100	100
1996–2003	93	97	81	82			97		

Boston Red Sox, 1901–2003

Years	R	BA	DPT	2B	3B	HR–R	HR–L	BB	SO
1901–1911	101	98	95	88	125	163	144	100	101
1912–1922	95	95	107	111	89	40	40	100	93
1923–1933	99					72	60		105
1934–1936	106	97	102	103		92	26		97
1937–1938		106				133			
1939–1949			113	119			75		
1950–1955	117					159	100		102
1956–1964	109		122	129		123	83		
1965–1968	114						101		
1969–1984		108	129	133	104			104	99
1985–2003	105	106	118	120			100	82	99

Chicago White Sox, 1901–2003

Years	R	BA	DPT	2B	3B	HR–R	HR–L	BB	SO
1901	91	93	79	82	97	56	114	100	105
1902–1909					60	26	33		92
1910–1918	95	95	82	75	111	72	52	100	101
1919–1927		99	101	104	94				91
1928–1933			88	88		104	71		
1934–1935	108				69	160	129		
1936–1949	97				93	92	83		
1950–1963			97		109				
1964–1968	88	94	87			71	64		
1969–1973	108	101	103	99	98	119	105	102	98
1974–1982	101				137	84	79		
1983–1985	106					105	122	108	104
1986–1990	100					82	73	97	
1991–1999	94	99	94	93	98	99	83	99	96
2000–2003	104					132	113		

Cleveland Indians, 1901–2003

Years	R	BA	DPT	2B	3B	HR–R	HR–L	BB	SO
1901–1909	97	102	123	126	109	66	72	100	104
1910–1917	107	105	122	129	91	63	65	100	104
1918–1929	103					32	86		86
1930–1931	111	109				67	151		
1932–1936	104	101	114	114	116	52	132	100	94
1937–1946	91	96					89		111
1947–1953	89	97	87	85	83	108	105	100	107
1954–1969	98				95	57			
1970–1975	108	101	92		58	158	145	104	100
1976–1990	102				80	111	81	99	95
1991	97				106	58	43		
1992–1993						98	110		
1994–2003	101	101	101	103	79	94	105	100	100

Detroit Tigers, 1901–2003

Years	R	BA	DPT	2B	3B	HR–R	HR–L	BB	SO
1901–1908	103	104	91	88	104	90	53	100	91
1909–1911	111	110	119	123		204	103		
1912–1922	102	105	109	107	123	88	59	100	86
1923–1931						153			101
1932–1935	97	101				96			
1936					77	140	94		
1937	113						150		
1938–1946	110	98	91	93	88	144	139	100	110
1947–1960	103	102	103	105		115			101
1961–1968			91	87	109				
1969–1976	106	100	100	102	107			99	105
1977–1981				94				104	98
1982–1999	99	96	88	87	92	114	120		103
2000–2003	93	99	96	89	152	60	86	98	90

Kansas City Royals, 1969–2003

Years	R	BA	DPT	2B	3B	HR–R	HR–L	BB	SO
1969–1972	100	102	119	114	160	55	87	105	97
1973–1994	103	103	124	119	155	80	69	95	87
1995–2000			103	95		102	108		
2001–2003	121	109		108	107	125		101	

Washington Senators–Minnesota Twins, 1901–2003

Years	R	BA	DPT	2B	3B	HR–R	HR–L	BB	SO
1901–1903	104	103	114	117	102	213	118	100	88
1904–1910	95	100	96	95	102	50	58	100	107
1911–1913	97	96	80	81	94	104	202	100	115
1914–1920			87				30	42	
1921–1929	94				120				99
1930–1941		101	102	96	136	49			84
1942–1950					116	34			94
1951–1955					138		55		
1956–1960	104					122	75		105
1961–1968	106	102	109	109	109	114	110	100	103
1969–1981		103	101	95	138		94	99	100
1982–2003	106	102	115	113	130	95	106	101	104

Baltimore Orioles–New York Yankees, 1901–2003

Years	R	BA	DPT	2B	3B	HR–R	HR–L	BB	SO
1901–1902	110	108	110	101	152	87	158	100	98
1903	101	98	93	90	82	69	111	100	93
1904	113	104			112	229	335		
1905–1912						141	143		
1913–1922	101	96	87	90	70	183	168	100	109
1923–1924	99	101	83	79	105	161	165	100	116
1925–1932	91					104	126		
1933–1936	86	95				78			
1937–1944	94						168		104
1945	110	98			124	166	247		
1946–1949	96		94	88		66	157		
1950–1960	90						124		
1961–1968	93			79	80	75			95
1969–1973		94	98	93	134	48		100	100
1974–1975	95	97	103	104	94	85	101	105	107
1976–1984	96	99	93	94	113	64	124	97	99
1985–2003					75	95	111		

Philadelphia–Kansas City–Oakland Athletics, 1901–2003

Years	R	BA	DPT	2B	3B	HR–R	HR–L	BB	SO
1901–1908	105	99	124	135	<u>78</u>	109	106	100	121
1909–1911	<u>94</u>	101	118	115	129	<u>41</u>	126	100	96
1912–1914		106	98	98	100	161			
1915–1922	105	100				271			109
1923–1934	102				<u>80</u>	133			
1935–1942					99		<u>63</u>		101
1943–1950	99								<u>91</u>
1951–1954	111								
1955–1958	106	101	112	109	129	148	98	100	<u>95</u>
1959–1961		105				98			
1962–1964	113					146	121		
1965	97				166	<u>50</u>			100
1966–1967		99	123		151		<u>35</u>		
1968–1995	<u>90</u>	<u>94</u>	<u>81</u>	<u>83</u>	<u>70</u>	97	81	101	103
1996–2003	97	98	96	97	<u>84</u>	95	98	99	

Seattle Mariners, 1977–2003

Years	R	BA	DPT	2B	3B	HR–R	HR–L	BB	SO
1977–1989	105	100	101	103	88	137	136	104	105
1990–1999	101		111	114		100	108		
2000–2003	<u>90</u>	<u>93</u>	<u>83</u>	<u>84</u>	<u>77</u>	80	100	107	105

Tampa Bay Devil Rays, 1998–2003

Years	R	BA	DPT	2B	3B	HR–R	HR–L	BB	SO
1998	101	100	105	104	110	93	107	98	101

Washington Senators–Texas Rangers, 1961–2003

Years	R	BA	DPT	2B	3B	HR–R	HR–L	BB	SO
1961	<u>95</u>	<u>97</u>	109	107	118	<u>69</u>	<u>49</u>	100	98
1962–1967	101	98	92	<u>89</u>	104	110	89	100	97
1968–1971	<u>92</u>					89			
1972–1984	97	101	96	97	<u>75</u>	84	91	<u>97</u>	105
1985–1993	101				105	106	106		
1994	<u>93</u>	104	105	102	134	<u>65</u>	86	100	<u>95</u>
1995–2003	110					104	118		

Toronto Blue Jays, 1977–2003

Years	R	BA	DPT	2B	3B	HR–R	HR–L	BB	SO
1977–1988	106	101	118	116	135	105	108	102	100
1989–2003	102	100	110	110	106	109	99	102	100

NATIONAL LEAGUE TEAMS

Arizona Diamondbacks, 1998–2003

Years	R	BA	DPT	2B	3B	HR–R	HR–L	BB	SO
1998–2003	106	105	114	109	161	105	101	99	95

Boston–Milwaukee–Atlanta Braves, 1876–2003

Years	R	BA	DPT	2B	3B	HR–R	HR–L	BB	SO
1876–1887	97	102	101	100	104	83	67	100	112
1888–1890	108	99	95	100	98	81	105	100	108
1891–1893					53	165	169		
1894–1902	111	98	87	91	67	285	173	100	98
1903–1909	101					190	90		
1910–1912	120	106	106	114			169		
1913–1914	98	99				59	98		
1915–1927	91	98	87	85	94	44	41	100	96
1928	101			106		151	82		
1929–1935	88	94		85		101	44		
1936–1940			74	74	70	71	25		
1941		99	103	111			79		
1942–1945	104					128	141		
1946–1952	91					54	92		
1953–1958	84	97	94	97	79	64	66	100	95
1959–1965	94	101				102	97		
1966–1976	108	105	90	95	65	129	150	100	93
1977–1982	113					172			
1983–1991			100	102	85	115	125		
1992–1996	102	102				96			
1997–2003	98	100	97	96	100	92	96	100	98

Chicago Cubs, 1876–2003

Years	R	BA	DPT	2B	3B	HR–R	HR–L	BB	SO
1876	123	111	128	133	99	58	137	100	80
1877	101	102	108	110					
1878–1882	105	103	127	137	75	77	78	100	104
1883	113	103	132	139	92	85	280	100	90
1884		110	100	102		413			
1885–1888	118	103	106	101	128	218	200	100	111
1889–1891	106	98	79	76	93				
1892	90	98	98	94	114	86	28	100	105
1893–1898	108	100	102	97	106	74	117		106
1899–1907	97	93	91		78		59		
1908–1915		96	111	114	101	95	132		
1916	121	99	107	114	74	125	216	100	109
1917–1922	101						81		
1923–1925		96	92	95		205	113		
1926–1937	98	98	104	109		94			
1938–1952		101		102	110		63		
1953–1960	101	96				109	85		
1961–1968	109	101				138	126		97
1969–1983	115	106	104	105	99			101	95
1984–1985	121		97	95		165	218	110	100
1986–1999	106	103				124	107	101	
2000–2003	93	96			66	110	78		108

Cincinnati Reds, 1890–2003

Years	R	BA	DPT	2B	3B	HR–R	HR–L	BB	SO
1890–1893	100	95	87	81	112	120	137	100	92
1894	101	99	114	115	76	162	108	100	82
1895–1899	109				113	21	27		
1900–1901	92					106	108		109
1902–1906	117	104	117	113	139	89	92	100	88
1907–1911	95		86	76		39	52		
1912–1919	99	103	95	91	130	46	51	100	87
1920–1933	93	97				29	26		
1934–1937						55	37		106
1938–1945		93			70	85	72		99

(continued)

Cincinnati Reds, 1890–2003 (*continued*)

Years	R	BA	DPT	2B	3B	HR–R	HR–L	BB	SO
1946–1950	100	<u>97</u>	104	111			149		
1951–1952						<u>66</u>	95		
1953–1959	109	106				113	152		<u>91</u>
1960–1964	102	99				93	106		103
1965–1969	113	107	127	131	112	117	148		
1970–1983	99	99	115	113	113	100	98	99	97
1984–1992	108	103	108		87	121	125	107	
1993–2002	102	100				104	106		
2003	99	100	94	103	<u>30</u>	122	122	<u>95</u>	101

Colorado Rockies, 1993–2003

Years	R	BA	DPT	2B	3B	HR–R	HR–L	BB	SO
1993–1994	130	115	124	108	272	133	82	106	<u>89</u>
1995–2003	141	120	119	115	156	161	147	99	<u>86</u>

Florida Marlins, 1993–2003

Years	R	BA	DPT	2B	3B	HR–R	HR–L	BB	SO
1993–2003	<u>95</u>	<u>97</u>	97	93	129	89	83	104	105

Houston Astros, 1962–2003

Years	R	BA	DPT	2B	3B	HR–R	HR–L	BB	SO
1962–1964	<u>90</u>	<u>93</u>	<u>84</u>	<u>79</u>	106	85	<u>44</u>	100	101
1965	<u>86</u>	99	96	93	108	<u>47</u>	<u>31</u>	100	96
1966–1971	<u>94</u>		115	117		<u>63</u>	<u>68</u>		105
1972–1976		<u>96</u>	102	104	96	86		101	103
1977–1984	<u>87</u>			93	142	<u>50</u>	<u>52</u>		
1985–1991	<u>92</u>			102	101	<u>68</u>	<u>70</u>	<u>97</u>	
1992–1999						83			112
2000–2003	108	103	106	103	142	111	119	<u>97</u>	101

Brooklyn–Los Angeles Dodgers, 1890–2003

Years	R	BA	DPT	2B	3B	HR–R	HR–L	BB	SO
1890	98	101	105	106	97	94	72	100	90
1891–1892	99	104	113	115	104	86	92	100	99
1893–1896	86	96	99	98					
1897	103								85
1898–1901	104	102	106	97	101	82	85	100	91
1902–1912	94	95	94						106
1913–1921	104	99	93	91	104	92	108	100	98
1922–1935	95								115
1936–1946	104		115	114	120				104
1947–1957			98	101	83	123			110
1958	109	96	81	77	95	157	39	100	118
1959–1961							124		
1962–1968	84	95	84	84	85	67	54	100	105
1969–1982	93	99	77	80	54	106	89	95	102
1983–1993						91			99
1994–2003	86	93							102

Seattle Pilots–Milwaukee Brewers, 1969–2003

Years	R	BA	DPT	2B	3B	HR–R	HR–L	BB	SO
1969	101	100	92	92	98	125	120	102	101
1970–1979	100	100	92	92	98	92	85	102	101
1980–1984	88	95						94	
1985–1997	102	101	101	101				102	
1998–2000	99	99	91	92	82	88	89	99	89
2001–2003	100	99	99	100	92	108	122	98	101

Montreal Expos, 1969–2003

Years	R	BA	DPT	2B	3B	HR–R	HR–L	BB	SO
1969–1976	106	102	93	92	101	108	133	101	101
1977–1999	99	99	110	111	113	85	91	106	100
2000–2002	103				87	111	108	97	
2003	124	106				144	159		

New York Mets, 1962–2003

Years	R	BA	DPT	2B	3B	HR–R	HR–L	BB	SO
1962–1963	109	98	90	87	101	134	194	100	99
1964–1970	99	93	89	90	79	112	99	100	105
1971–2003	94	97	92	93	84	91		98	105

Philadelphia Phillies, 1883–2003

Years	R	BA	DPT	2B	3B	HR–R	HR–L	BB	SO
1883–1884	97	106	111	114	88	11	27	100	86
1885–1886		90	91	93		86			99
1887	95	101	118	124	90	100	141	100	106
1888–1890	111					54			95
1891–1894	97	108							
1895–1896	102	110	127	136	92	85	187	100	97
1897–1910	97	102	119	129		53	74		
1911–1921	110				61	228	178		107
1922–1925	128	109							
1926–1937	120		111	120		131	156		
1938–1952	98	99	93	94	92	96	56	100	99
1953–1957			108	106	118	112			
1958–1970							76		107
1971–1978	104	100	112	111	116	118	110	104	104
1979–1998						99			
1999–2003	96	95	106			83			114

Pittsburgh Pirates, 1887–2003

Years	R	BA	DPT	2B	3B	HR–R	HR–L	BB	SO
1887–1890	87	102	107	111	87	18	19	100	91
1891–1892	95	96	92	84	137	110	109	100	103
1893–1900						50	71		
1901–1908	100	104	105	97					
1909–1920	100	96	95	90	129	61	57	100	97
1921–1931	103	101	103		156				83
1932–1946		105	112	103		52	75		88
1947–1953	109	102	93	89	113	146	63		103
1954–1958	97		109	101	146	50			95
1959–1970		107				64	77		
1971–1974	95	100	106	106	107	72	80	102	100
1975–2000	101					98	106		
2001–2003	102	102	103	106	75	89	92	97	92

San Diego Padres, 1969–2003

Years	R	BA	DPT	2B	3B	HR–R	HR–L	BB	SO
1969–1981	90	97	95	95	94	81	64	94	97
1982–1997	96		89	88		121	113	98	107
1998–2003	86	93	82	81		86	84		

New York–San Francisco Giants, 1883–2003

Years	R	BA	DPT	2B	3B	HR–R	HR–L	BB	SO
1883	100	100	84	76	132	254	200	100	93
1884–1885				81		58	61		
1886		80			102				
1887–1888	95	94							114
1889–1890	98	96	117	115	124	58	61	100	115
1891–1894	96	96	93	94	85	162	105	100	117
1895–1903						67			
1904–1910	100	104	104	108		198	197		
1911–1925	95	102	99	102	87	127	126	100	97
1926–1935		99	76	75	69	194			
1936–1944	101					235	189		
1945–1957					97	136	166		
1958–1959	96	99	108	112	85	101	89	100	105
1960	84	98	105	84	125	53	65	100	99
1961–1968	98		80		70	99	125		
1969–1974	104	100	104	102	98			104	100
1975–1977				162			76		108
1978–1981	92	96	92	94	78	65		99	
1982–1999						100	96		104
2000–2003	89	97	100	96	138	76	66	95	97

St. Louis Cardinals, 1892–2003

Years	R	BA	DPT	2B	3B	HR–R	HR–L	BB	SO
1892	96	100	86	88	76	205	214	100	97
1893–1894	103	91	83	76	111	76	86	100	104
1895–1899		101	89	86		173	192		89
1900–1908	97					116	104		
1909–1919						73			99
1920–1923	94	105	120	122	109	73	98	100	101
1924–1928	103	102				111	151		
1929–1937						84	109		112
1938–1941	110				124	111	159		104
1942–1953	102					73	100		95
1954–1957					96		138		
1958–1962	114		110	110		93			
1963–1965		107			129	133			
1966–1991	100	101	110	105	136	81	79	97	93
1992–1997	97	98	103		83	93	101		99
1998–2003			94	96				104	

19th-Century National League Franchises

Years	R	BA	DPT	2B	3B	HR–R	HR–L	BB	SO
Buffalo Bisons, 1879–85									
1879–1883	103	106	101	99	111	50	43	100	102
1884–1885	109	112	109	107	116	86	112	100	88
Cincinnati Reds, 1876–80									
1876	96	102	89	89	89	75	73	100	120
1877–1879	90	104	103	98	120	168	161		96
1880	103	100	93	91	106	236	103	100	100
Cleveland Spiders, 1889–1899									
1889–1890	97	95	74	68	98	68	56	100	91
1891–1899	104	102	100	103	87	39	42	100	96
Hartford Dark Blues									
1876	102	94	101	104	86	49	55	100	116
1877	85	97	87	86	91	46	174	100	89
Louisville Colonels, 1892–99									
1892	89	97	81	81	81	38	47	100	96
1893–1895	91	96	93	91	98	61	60	100	108
1896–1899	99					198	188		

(continued)

19th-Century National League Franchises (*continued*)

Years	R	BA	DPT	2B	3B	HR–R	HR–L	BB	SO
Providence Grays, 1878–85									
1878–1883	93	97	86	87	94	121	26	100	100
1884–1885		89			59	48			
St. Louis Brown Stockings, 1876–77									
1876	77	88	82	77	109	68	129	100	115
1877	100								
Troy Trojans, 1879–82									
1879	98	101	100	102	88	108	93	100	93
1880–1881	108	100	92	93	88	200	250	100	93
1882	96	101	97	92	117	66	81	100	93
Other 19th Century Teams									
1892–9, Bal	102	106	105	106	103	52	43	100	95
1879–84, Cle	96	91	102	104	91	53	38	100	104
1881–8, Det	101	102	100	95	118	76	149	100	101
1878, Ind	85	96	96	99	84	67	129	100	101
1887–9, Ind	106	105	114	125	69	190	156	100	90
1886, KC	116	105	115	120	95	55	64	100	98
1876–7, Lou	117	94	89	90	85	249	177	100	121
1878, Mil–N	113	98	98	96	107	52	100	100	101
1876, NY–N	89	100	76	73	92	224	128	100	77
1876, Phi–N	109	108	120	114	150	74	103	100	68
1885–6, StL	92	93	102	109	68	67	45	100	101
1879, Syr	91	98	75	73	80	91	78	100	95
1886–9, Was	93	93	84	82	95	101	67	100	100
1892–9, Was	101	103	110	109	118	128	123	100	107
1880–2, Wor	113	102	101	97	123	121	168	100	97

AMERICAN ASSOCIATION TEAMS

Years	R	BA	DPT	2B	3B	HR–R	HR–L	BB	SO
Baltimore Orioles, 1882–1891									
1882	110	98	87	86	93	68	113	100	94
1883–1885		95	96	96	99				113
1886–1890	92								
1890	107	97	94	93	97	59	124	100	101
1891	101	100	95	90	118	29	125	100	97

Years	R	BA	DPT	2B	3B	HR–R	HR–L	BB	SO
Brooklyn Bridegrooms, 1884–1890									
1884–1888	101	98	98	101	88	126	120	100	86
1889	90	98	92	92	92	125	128	100	87
1890	101	99	109	110	105	63	82	100	90
Cincinnati Reds, 1882–1889, 1891									
1882–1883	99	96	92	88	110	228	154	100	84
1884–1889	104	101	81	73	121	163	151	100	90
1891	112	95	96	95	100	161	161	100	97
Columbus Senators (1883–84) and Solons (1889–1891)									
1883–1884	88	98	90	80	139	127	91	100	115
1889–1891	87	92	98	97	104	58	66	100	112
Louisville Colonels, 1882–1891									
1882–1884	85	101	102	102	102	28	58	100	96
1885–1887	109					149			112
1888–1891	95	107				47			100
New York Mets, 1883–1887									
1883	105	92	92	91	95	60	87	100	119
1884–1885	86	102	102	106	83	62	50	100	101
1886	105	98	74	69	94	87	68	100	100
1887	86		102	104					
Philadelphia Athletics, 1882–1891									
1882	112	101	93	99	69	209	169	100	95
1883–1890	103	104	127	133	99	89	67	100	100
1891	103	102	117	113	138	83	66	100	105
Pittsburgh Alleghanies, 1882–1886									
1882–1883	97	107	118	116	128	83	99	100	102
1884–1885	103	96	101	93	107	25	66	100	101
1886	86		108						
St. Louis Browns, 1882–1891									
1882–1884	108	98	96	103	61	86	177	100	87
1885	85								
1886–1888	110					135			
1889–1891	119					230			109
Other Teams									
1891, Bos	94	102	96	94	106	168	125	100	101
1887–8 Cle	101	104	96	95	104	61	57	100	104
1884, Ind	101	102	109	110	105	146	39	100	107

(*continued*)

Years	R	BA	DPT	2B	3B	HR–R	HR–L	BB	SO
Other Teams (*continued*)									
1888, KC	**116**	**104**	103	103	104	95	**200**	100	96
1889, KC	**114**	102	<u>91</u>	<u>89</u>	103	<u>54</u>	<u>71</u>	100	102
1891, Mil	**113**	99	**113**	119	86	187	**144**	100	100
1884, Ric	102	100	99	95	116	94	**141**	100	109
1890, Roc	<u>88</u>	<u>95</u>	<u>85</u>	<u>83</u>	94	<u>54</u>	78	100	98
1890, Syr	<u>88</u>	**104**	101	103	93	<u>43</u>	<u>29</u>	100	93
1884, Tol	105	<u>97</u>	116	123	<u>82</u>	<u>52</u>	81	100	109
1890, Tol	102	98	105	97	148	120	**238**	100	104
1884, Was	<u>92</u>	99	97	98	91	<u>34</u>	**126**	100	106
1891, Was	100	**107**	108	106	**115**	77	95	100	98

Union Association, 1884

Years	R	BA	DPT	2B	3B	HR–R	HR–L	BB	SO
Alt–U	105	**105**	98	98	97	93	<u>66</u>	100	<u>94</u>
Bal–U	**113**	102	<u>90</u>	93	<u>75</u>	209	85	100	102
Bos–U	97	<u>94</u>	101	104	89	<u>62</u>	<u>58</u>	100	119
CP–U	97	<u>94</u>	99	100	94	<u>39</u>	100	100	110
Cin–U	107	102	<u>84</u>	<u>69</u>	156	168	227	100	<u>88</u>
KC–U	<u>88</u>	98	102	105	86	106	88	100	96
Mil–U	100	<u>94</u>	105	109	<u>84</u>	100	100	100	110
Phi–U	97	**107**	117	112	141	<u>60</u>	140	100	<u>94</u>
StL–U	99	**105**	127	136	<u>84</u>	76	<u>54</u>	100	<u>87</u>
StP–U	100	98	103	104	96	100	100	100	100
Was–U	97	99	<u>79</u>	<u>79</u>	<u>82</u>	103	**130**	100	100
Wil–U	102	<u>97</u>	95	<u>90</u>	118	209	100	100	106

Players League, 1890

Years	R	BA	DPT	2B	3B	HR–R	HR–L	BB	SO
Bos–P	106	102	108	**114**	<u>79</u>	269	97	100	105
Bro–P	108	101	<u>89</u>	<u>88</u>	93	77	107	100	98
Buf–P	<u>95</u>	103	101	104	87	<u>63</u>	<u>50</u>	100	<u>95</u>
Chi–P	101	<u>93</u>	96	96	96	123	<u>72</u>	100	112
Cle–P	<u>91</u>	**105**	113	115	106	<u>67</u>	87	100	<u>91</u>
NY–P	**112**	98	99	99	97	97	**141**	100	107
Phi–P	102	100	97	93	117	<u>63</u>	108	100	<u>94</u>
Pit–P	<u>88</u>	<u>97</u>	97	91	126	84	**162**	100	98

Federal League, 1914–15

Years	R	BA	DPT	2B	3B	HR–R	HR–L	BB	SO
1914, Bal	98	103	101	104	88	**216**	<u>75</u>	100	102
1915, Bal	**116**		107	**111**			214		
1914–5, Bro	101	**104**	**109**	109	111	95	113	100	100
1914–5, Buf	103	<u>95</u>	<u>87</u>	<u>90</u>	96	117	<u>72</u>	100	**108**
1914–5, Chi	<u>87</u>	<u>94</u>	97	97	<u>78</u>	<u>51</u>	127	100	102
1914–5, KC	<u>94</u>	99	**110**	108	99	**244**	<u>75</u>	100	<u>95</u>
1914–5, Pit	98	102	84	<u>88</u>	119	<u>40</u>	<u>53</u>	100	<u>89</u>
1914–5, StL	**107**	99	95	96	100	<u>55</u>	182	100	103
1914, Ind	**114**	**105**	107	106	113	<u>43</u>	82	100	102
1915, New	<u>91</u>	99	106	106	107	<u>42</u>	<u>37</u>	100	99

Home Run Park Effects

Guide to the tables

Home run park effects are shown for the 30 active franchises, presented in alphabetical order of current team name for each league. The changeyears for the home run park effects for each franchise have been obtained using the multiple changepoint regression procedure presented in Appendix C.

Home runs at **home** gives the number of home runs hit at home games by both the team and their opponents. The totals have been normalized for the number of games played (see Appendix D) and rounded to the nearest home run. The road home runs have been similarly normalized.

Home percentage

All – the percentage of home runs hit at the home park. This equals home HRs divided by total HRs.

RHB – the percentage of HRs hit by right-handed batters that were hit at the home park

LHB – the percentage of HRs hit by left-handed batters that were hit at the home park

The **hand OR** gives a number followed by either "R" or "L." A hand OR of 1 means that the odds that a right-handed batter hits a home run in the park is equal to that of a left-handed batter. All other hand ORs are greater than 1, with the letter indicating which handedness has the greater odds. For example, the hand OR = 2.1L for Yankee Stadium for 1950–68, meaning that a LHB is 2.1 times as likely to hit a home run at the home park than a right-handed batter.

Change – provides an explanation, where known, for the shift in the park effect.

Each new ballpark for a particular franchise is shown by a shift in the shading.

AMERICAN LEAGUE TEAMS

California – Anaheim Angels, 1961–2003

Years	Home Runs			Home Percentage			Hand	Change
	Total	Home	Road	All	RHB	LHB	OR	
1961	367	245	123	67	69	63	1.3R	Wrigley Field
1962–65	855	303	552	36	35	36	1.0	Dodger Stadium
1966–69	918	462	456	50	51	49	1.1R	Anaheim Stadium
1970–79	2159	945	1214	44	45	42	1.1R	
1980–97	5240	2812	2428	54	53	55	1.1L	
1998–2001	1436	735	701	51	53	49	1.2R	Stadium redesign
2002–03	661	291	370	44	44	44	1.0	

St. Louis Browns – Baltimore Orioles, 1901–2003

Years	Home Runs			Home Percentage			Hand	Change
	Total	Home	Road	All	RHB	LHB	OR	
1901	58	29	29	50	48	53	1.2L	Lloyd Street Grounds
1902–08	262	134	128	51	48	55	1.3L	Sportsman's Park II
1909–19	394	201	193	51	40	60	2.3L	Sportsman's Park III
1920–28	1338	915	423	68	56	76	2.5L	Sportsman's Park V
1929–53	4626	2572	2054	56	52	60	1.3L	RF fence raised 22 ft
1954–57	660	238	421	36	38	33	1.3R	Memorial Stadium
1958–63	1520	649	871	43	43	43	1.0	Power alleys short. 25 ft
1964–68	1326	661	665	50	50	49	1.1R	
1969–79	2817	1301	1516	46	47	45	1.0	
1980–91	3702	1904	1798	51	51	52	1.0	CF shortened 5 ft
1992–95	1174	634	541	54	54	54	1.0	Camden Yards
1996–2003	3049	1546	1503	51	52	49	1.1R	

Boston Red Sox, 1901–2003

Years	Home Runs			Home Percentage			Hand OR	Change
	Total	Home	Road	All	RHB	LHB		
1901–11	618	388	230	62	64	61	1.2R	Huntington Ave Grounds
1912–22	483	127	356	26	27	26	1.0	Fenway Park
1923–33	1086	415	671	38	41	36	1.2R	
1934–36	422	170	252	40	48	17	4.6R	Green Monster
1937–38	392	219	173	56	61	20	6.2R	
1939–49	2013	1048	965	52	58	42	1.9R	
1950–58	1428	848	580	59	63	50	1.7R	
1956–64	2596	1330	1266	51	55	45	1.5R	
1965–84	5858	3176	2683	54	56	50	1.3R	
1985–2003	5752	2745	3007	48	50	45	1.2R	

Chicago White Sox, 1901–2003

Years	Home Runs			Home Percentage			Hand OR	Change
	Total	Home	Road	All	RHB	LHB		
1901	59	24	35	41	35	32	2.6L	South Side Park
1902–09	194	36	158	19	17	21	1.3L	
1910–27	1072	395	677	37	41	32	1.4R	Comiskey Park I
1928–33	710	328	382	46	51	40	1.5R	
1934–35	390	242	148	62	64	58	1.3R	Foul lines shortened 20 ft
1936–63	4979	2317	2662	46	48	45	1.1R	Foul lines length. 12 ft ('37)
1964–68	1009	399	610	40	41	38	1.1R	
1969–73	1204	644	560	54	55	51	1.1R	Foul lines shortened 17 ft
1974–82	1984	887	1097	45	45	44	1.1R	Fence raised 2.5 ft
1983–85	919	486	433	53	51	55	1.2L	Power alleys shortened 8 ft
1986–90	1346	584	762	43	45	42	1.1R	Power alleys lengthened 8 ft
1991–1999	2841	1362	1479	48	50	45	1.2R	Comiskey Park II
2000–2003	1595	889	706	56	57	53	1.2R	

Cleveland Indians, 1901–2003

Years	Home Runs Total	Home	Road	Home Percentage All	RHB	LHB	Hand OR	Change
1901–09	318	125	193	39	38	40	1.1L	League Park I
1910–17	238	89	149	37	37	38	1.0	League Park II
1918–29	918	341	577	37	22	46	3.0L	
1930–31	292	151	141	52	38	62	2.7L	
1932–36	785	378	407	48	34	58	2.6L	Some games in Municipal
1937–46	1499	588	911	39	32	47	1.9L	
1947–69	6161	3194	2967	52	52	51	1.0	All games in Municipal
1970–75	1712	1056	656	62	63	60	1.1R	Power alleys short. to 385 ft
1976–90	3693	1852	1840	50	53	45	1.4R	Fence height raised
1991	190	62	128	33	35	27	1.5R	Power alleys length to 395 ft
1992–3	609	308	301	51	49	53	1.1L	Fence distances shortened
1994–2003	3598	1796	1803	50	48	51	1.1L	Jacobs Field

Detroit Tigers, 1901–2003

Years	Home Runs Total	Home	Road	Home Percentage All	RHB	LHB	Hand OR	Change
1901–08	249	101	148	40	47	32	1.9R	Bennett Park
1909–11	155	96	59	62	72	51	2.5R	
1912–22	618	255	363	41	46	36	1.5R	Navin Field
1923–31	1098	561	538	51	62	37	2.8R	
1932–35	657	278	380	42	49	33	1.9R	
1936–37	446	259	187	58	60	54	1.2R	Right field shortened 42 ft
1938–46	1563	942	621	60	61	59	1.1R	Tiger Stadium
1947–81	9617	5394	4223	56	54	59	1.3L	
1982–1999	6274	3397	2876	54	54	55	1.0	
2000–2003	1308	551	757	42	37	46	1.5L	Comerica Park

Kansas City Royals, 1969–2003

Years	Home Runs			Home Percentage			Hand OR	Change
	Total	Home	Road	All	RHB	LHB		
1969–72	795	313	482	39	34	46	1.6L	Municipal Stadium
1973–89	4958	2105	2853	42	44	40	1.2R	Royals Stadium
1995–2000	1976	1000	976	51	51	51	1.0	Power alleys shortened 10 ft
2001–2003	1065	580	485	54	56	55	1.1R	

Washington Senators – Minnesota Twins, 1901–2003

Years	Home Runs			Home Percentage			Hand OR	Change
	Total	Home	Road	All	RHB	LHB		
1901–03	243	167	75	69	72	55	2.1R	American League Park I
1904–10	198	63	135	32	31	34	1.2L	American League Park II
1911–13	153	94	58	61	51	72	2.4L	Griffith Stadium
1914–29	1029	259	770	25	21	29	1.5L	
1930–41	1577	473	1105	30	31	28	1.1R	
1942–50	1029	262	767	25	24	27	1.2L	
1951–55	810	220	590	27	23	34	1.7L	
1956–60	1383	727	656	53	56	42	1.7R	Left field short.; CF f. lower
1961–68	2512	1352	1160	54	54	53	1.1R	Metropolitan Stadium
1969–81	2949	1506	1443	51	53	48	1.2L	
1982–2003	6841	3405	3437	50	48	52	1.1L	Metrodome

Baltimore Orioles – New York Yankees, 1901–2003

Years	Home Runs			Home Percentage			Hand OR	Change
	Total	Home	Road	All	RHB	LHB		
1901–02	109	59	50	54	46	65	2.2L	Oriole Park
1903	37	16	21	44	37	54	2.0L	Hilltop Park
1904	57	49	9	85	79	90	2.5L	
1905–12	325	196	128	61	60	61	1.0	
1913–22	928	616	313	66	68	65	1.1R	Polo Grounds
1923–24	329	213	116	65	64	65	1.0	Yankee Stadium
1925–32	1702	920	782	54	51	56	1.2L	
1933–36	877	451	426	51	41	59	2.1L	
1937–44	1799	984	815	55	44	65	2.4L	
1945	159	116	43	73	66	77	1.7L	Outlier year

(continued)

Baltimore Orioles – New York Yankees, 1901–2003 *(continued)*

Years	Home Runs			Home Percentage			Hand OR	Change
	Total	Home	Road	All	RHB	LHB		
1946–49	858	454	404	53	42	63	2.4L	
1950–68	5190	2425	2765	47	38	56	2.1L	
1969–73	1105	503	602	46	32	58	3.0L	
1974–75	419	201	218	48	46	50	1.2L	Shea Stadium
1976–84	2296	1100	1197	48	38	56	2.0L	Yankee Stadium
1985–2003	6236	3157	3079	51	49	53	1.2L	Left field shorten. 7–19 ft

Philadelphia – Kansas City – Oakland Athletics, 1901–2003

Years	Home Runs			Home Percentage			Hand OR	Change
	Total	Home	Road	All	RHB	LHB		
1901–08	375	196	179	52	52	52	1.0	Columbia Park
1909–11	109	38	71	35	25	49	2.9L	Shibe Park
1912–14	138	80	58	58	65	52	1.7R	
1915–22	723	532	192	74	79	61	2.3R	
1923–34	2064	1202	863	58	59	56	1.1R	
1935–54	3670	1882	1788	51	58	37	2.3R	RF fence raised 22 ft
1955–58	1203	711	493	59	62	52	1.5R	Municipal Stadium
1959–61	765	369	396	48	49	47	1.1L	LF fence raised 20 ft
1962–64	953	561	391	59	61	57	1.2R	Right CF shortened by 23 ft
1965	271	115	156	42	35	51	1.9L	Left field lengthened 39 ft
1966–67	372	101	271	27	30	24	1.4R	RF fence raised 35 ft
1968–95	7692	3627	4065	47	49	44	1.2R	Oakland/Alameda Stadium
1996–2003	2970	1469	1501	49	50	49	1.1R	

Seattle Mariners, 1977–2003

Years	Home Runs			Home Percentage			Hand OR	Change
	Total	Home	Road	All	RHB	LHB		
1977–89	3681	2150	1531	58	58	58	1.0	Kingdome
1990–99	3440	1749	1690	51	50	52	1.1L	LF out; RF field in
2000–2003	1336	615	721	46	44	50	1.3L	Safeco Field

Tampa Bay Devil Rays, 1998–2003

Years	Home Runs			Home Percentage			Hand OR	Change
	Total	Home	Road	All	RHB	LHB		
1998–2003	1968	978	990	50	48	52	1.2L	Tropicana Field

Washington Senators – Texas Rangers, 1961–2003

Years	Home Runs			Home Percentage			Hand OR	Change
	Total	Home	Road	All	RHB	LHB		
1961	249	89	160	36	40	30	1.5R	Griffith Stadium
1962–67	1698	867	831	51	53	48	1.2R	R.F.K. Stadium
1968–71	1021	469	552	46	47	44	1.1R	
1972–84	2915	1347	1567	46	45	48	1.1L	Arlington Stadium
1985–93	2654	1367	1287	52	52	51	1.0	
1994	286	118	169	41	38	46	1.4L	Ballpark at Arlington
1995–2003	3530	1864	1666	53	51	54	1.1L	

Toronto Blue Jays, 1977–2003

Years	Home Runs			Home Percentage			Hand OR	Change
	Total	Home	Road	All	RHB	LHB		
1977–88	3325	1715	1610	52	51	52	1.0	Exhibition Stadium
1989–2003	4920	2524	2396	51	52	50	1.1R	Skydome

NATIONAL LEAGUE TEAMS

Arizona Diamondbacks, 1998–2003

Years	Home Runs			Home Percentage			Hand OR	Change
	Total	Home	Road	All	RHB	LHB		
1998–2003	2148	1091	1057	51	51	50	1.0	Bank One Ballpark

Boston – Milwaukee – Atlanta Braves, 1876–2003

Years	Home Runs			Home Percentage			Hand OR	Change
	Total	Home	Road	All	RHB	LHB		
1876–87	444	189	256	43	45	39	1.3R	South End Grounds I
1888–90	233	108	125	46	44	52	1.4L	South End Ground II
1891–93	309	201	108	65	64	65	1.1L	
1894–1902	845	621	224	73	78	65	1.9R	South End Grounds III
1903–09	331	197	133	60	68	47	2.4R	
1910–12	259	177	82	68	70	66	1.2R	
1913–14	143	59	84	41	35	49	1.8L	
1915–27	885	246	639	28	28	27	1.1R	Braves Field
1928	152	87	66	57	63	44	2.1R	fences shorten. considerably
1929–35	967	412	555	43	50	28	2.5R	fences lengthened
1936–40	636	205	431	32	42	18	3.3R	LF, CF moved out, RF in
1941	122	46	76	38	32	43	1.6L	
1942–45	615	363	253	59	57	60	1.1L	CF moved in 25 ft
1946–52	1417	558	859	39	33	48	1.8L	fence height raised 12 ft
1953–58	1754	668	1085	38	38	39	1.0	County Stadium
1959–65	2204	1104	1100	50	51	49	1.1R	
1966–76	2955	1714	1240	58	57	60	1.1L	Atlanta/Fulton Co. Stadium
1977–82	1497	967	530	65	65	64	1.0	
1983–91	2320	1267	1053	54	54	56	1.1L	fence height raised 4 ft
1992–96	1302	681	621	52	49	56	1.3L	
1997–2003	2296	1108	1188	48	48	49	1.1L	Turner Field

Chicago Cubs, 1876–2003

Years	Home Runs			Home Percentage			Hand OR	Change
	Total	Home	Road	All	RHB	LHB		
1876	14	4	9	31	27	53	3.0L	23rd Street Grounds
1877	7	4	3	59	35	76	6.0L	
1878–82	81	35	46	44	42	41	1.0	Lake Front Park I
1883	34	17	17	50	44	71	3.1L	Lake Front Park II
1884	224	195	28	87	90	83	1.8R	
1885–88	462	345	117	75	75	74	1.0	West Side Park
1889–91	367	255	112	69	69	66	1.1R	
1892	59	20	40	33	45	08	9.7R	South Side Park II
1893–98	427	201	226	47	43	54	1.6L	West Side Grounds
1899–1907	303	116	187	38	39	35	1.2R	
1908–15	531	285	247	54	48	58	1.5L	

(continued)

Chicago Cubs, 1876–2003 *(continued)*

Years	Home Runs			Home Percentage			Hand OR	Change
	Total	Home	Road	All	RHB	LHB		
1916	78	55	22	71	66	75	1.5L	Wrigley Field
1917–22	416	211	205	51	55	44	1.6R	
1923–25	518	340	179	66	71	53	2.2R	LF shortened by 18 ft
1926–37	1966	982	984	50	47	54	1.3L	LF lengthened by 23 ft
1938–52	2525	1125	1399	45	49	37	1.6R	
1953–60	2399	1197	1202	50	52	45	1.3R	
1961–83	5838	3384	2453	58	59	56	1.1R	
1984–85	541	359	183	66	64	72	1.4L	
1986–99	4202	2285	1917	54	56	52	1.2R	
2000–2003	1454	715	739	49	52	43	1.4R	

Cincinnati Reds, 1890–2003

Years	Home Runs			Home Percentage			Hand OR	Change
	Total	Home	Road	All	RHB	LHB		
1890–93	296	166	130	56	55	60	1.2R	League Park I
1894	146	88	58	60	64	52	1.6R	League Park II
1895–1899	244	41	203	17	14	19	1.4L	
1900–01	148	78	70	53	52	52	1.0	Grandstand burned down
1902–06	189	88	101	47	46	47	1.1L	Palace of the Fans
1907–11	200	54	145	27	25	31	1.3L	
1912–19	375	114	261	30	29	32	1.1L	Crosley Field
1920–33	1160	227	933	20	20	18	1.1R	
1934–37	500	148	351	30	34	25	1.5R	
1938–45	1084	468	616	43	44	41	1.2R	distances reduced by 20 ft
1946–50	994	529	465	53	47	62	1.8L	RF shortened 14 ft
1951–52	422	177	245	42	38	48	1.5L	RF lengthened 14 ft
1953–59	2325	1341	984	58	54	62	1.4L	RF shortened 14 ft
1960–64	1376	682	694	50	48	52	1.2L	
1965–69	1372	779	593	57	54	61	1.3L	
1970–83	3438	1715	1722	50	50	50	1.0R	Riverfront Stadium
1984–1992	2365	1314	1051	56	55	56	1.0	Fence lowered 4 ft
1993–2002	3314	1694	1620	51	51	51	1.0	
2003	391	215	176	55	56	55	1.0	Great American Ballpark

Colorado Rockies, 1993–2003

Years	Home Runs			Home Percentage			Hand OR	Change
	Total	Home	Road	All	RHB	LHB		
1993–94	568	307	261	54	58	44	1.7R	Mile High Stadium
1995–2003	3640	2247	1393	62	63	60	1.1R	Coors Field

Florida Marlins, 1993–2003

Years	Home Runs			Home Percentage			Hand OR	Change
	Total	Home	Road	All	RHB	LHB		
1993–2003	3078	1421	1657	46	47	45	1.1R	Pro Player Stadium

Houston Astros, 1962–2003

Years	Home Runs			Home Percentage			Hand OR	Change
	Total	Home	Road	All	RHB	LHB		
1962–64	551	216	335	39	45	29	2.1R	Colt Stadium
1965	220	57	163	26	30	21	1.6R	Astrodome
1966–71	1210	462	748	38	38	39	1.1L	
1972–76	1026	457	569	45	46	41	1.2R	Fences shortened 10–12 ft
1977–84	1269	411	858	32	32	33	1.0	Fences lengthened 10–12 ft
1985–91	1597	623	974	39	39	38	1.1R	Fences shortened 10–12 ft
1992–99	2074	915	1159	44	45	42	1.1R	Fences shortened 5 ft
2000–2003	1582	840	742	53	53	55	1.1L	Enron Field

Brooklyn – Los Angeles Dodgers, 1890–2003

Years	Home Runs			Home Percentage			Hand OR	Change
	Total	Home	Road	All	RHB	LHB		
1890	71	31	40	44	48	39	1.4R	Washington Park II
1891–97	494	231	263	47	46	48	1.1L	Eastern Park
1898–1901	713	322	390	45	44	45	1.1R	Washington Park III
1913–21	528	271	257	51	47	56	1.4L	Ebbets Field
1922–35	1991	1006	984	51	48	53	1.2L	
1936–46	1527	751	776	49	48	50	1.1L	
1947–57	3382	1851	1532	55	56	52	1.2R	
1958	345	193	152	56	63	24	5.4R	Memorial Coliseum
1959–61	909	550	359	61	63	56	1.3R	
1962–68	1347	502	845	37	39	34	1.3R	Dodger Stadium
1969–82	3214	1607	1607	50	52	46	1.2R	Power alleys 10 ft shorter
1983–93	2376	1098	1278	46	47	45	1.1R	Powers alleys longer
1994–2003	3103	1493	1609	48	48	48	1.0	

Seattle Pilots – Milwaukee Brewers, 1969–2003

| Years | Home Runs | | | Home Percentage | | | Hand | |
	Total	Home	Road	All	RHB	LHB	OR	Change
1969	297	166	131	56	56	55	1.1R	Sick's Stadium, Seattle
1970–97	7537	3540	3997	47	48	46	1.1R	County Stadium
1998–2000	1069	500	569	47	47	47	1.0	Switch to NL
2001–2003	1159	618	541	53	52	55	1.1L	Miller Park

Montreal Expos, 1969–2003

| Years | Home Runs | | | Home Percentage | | | Hand | |
	Total	Home	Road	All	RHB	LHB	OR	Change
1969–76	1805	985	819	55	52	58	1.3L	Parc Jarry
1977–99	5526	2555	2971	46	46	47	1.1L	Olympic Stadium
2000–2002	1007	525	482	52	53	52	1.0	
2003	325	197	128	61	60	63	1.1L	Some games in Puerto Rico

New York Mets, 1962–2003

| Years | Home Runs | | | Home Percentage | | | Hand | |
	Total	Home	Road	All	RHB	LHB	OR	Change
1962–63	590	368	221	62	58	69	1.6L	Polo Grounds
1964–70	1609	851	758	53	53	52	1.0	Shea Stadium
1971–2003	8171	3934	4238	48	47	49	1.1L	

Philadelphia Phillies, 1883–2003

| Years | Home Runs | | | Home Percentage | | | Hand | |
	Total	Home	Road	All	RHB	LHB	OR	Change
1883–84	75	2	73	03	04	00	—	Recreation Park
1885–86	93	38	55	41	45	32	1.7R	
1887	95	47	48	49	50	52	1.1L	Philadelphia Baseball Gds
1888–94	501	244	257	49	34	61	3.1L	
1895–96	183	104	79	57	45	68	2.6L	Baker Bowl
1897–1910	574	212	362	37	33	42	1.4L	
1911–25	1819	1287	532	71	74	67	1.4R	
1926–37	2347	1428	919	61	58	63	1.2L	LF lengthened by 6 ft
1938–52	2408	1073	1336	45	49	35	1.8R	Shibe Park
1953–57	1330	643	688	48	54	34	2.3R	
1958–70	3218	1574	1644	49	53	42	1.5R	
1971–78	1956	1070	886	55	55	55	1.0	Veteran's Stadium
1979–1998	4895	2464	2431	50	50	52	1.1L	
1999–2003	1678	805	873	48	45	52	1.3L	

Pittsburgh Pirates, 1887–2003

Years	Home Runs			Home Percentage			Hand OR	Change
	Total	Home	Road	All	RHB	LHB		
1887–90	245	32	213	13	13	12	1.1R	Recreation Park
1891–1892	122	65	58	53	53	53	1.0	Exposition Park
1893–1908	698	252	446	36	32	41	1.4L	
1909–31	1886	674	1212	36	37	35	1.1R	Forbes Field
1932–46	1859	693	1165	37	33	42	1.5L	
1947–53	1881	1035	845	55	61	38	2.5R	LF shortened by 30 ft
1954–58	1193	397	796	33	32	36	1.2L	LF lengthened by 30 ft
1959–70	2653	1052	1601	40	38	43	1.2L	Backstop shortened by 9 ft
1971–74	933	396	537	42	41	44	1.1L	Three Rivers Stadium
1975–2000	6331	3189	3142	50	49	52	1.1L	Fences shortened 5–10 ft
2001–2003	974	460	514	47	47	48	1.0	

San Diego Padres, 1969–2003

Years	Home Runs			Home Percentage			Hand OR	Change
	Total	Home	Road	All	RHB	LHB		
1969–81	2656	1133	1523	43	44	38	1.3R	Qualcomm Stadium
1982–97	4092	2230	1862	54	55	53	1.1R	Fence lowered 10 ft
1998–2003	2029	926	1103	46	46	45	1.0	

New York – San Francisco Giants, 1883–2003

Years	Home Runs			Home Percentage			Hand OR	Change
	Total	Home	Road	All	RHB	LHB		
1883	43	35	8	81	82	79	1.3R	Polo Grounds I
1884–88	278	98	180	35	35	36	1.0	
1889–90	128	45	83	35	34	35	1.1L	Polo Grounds III
1891–94	318	191	127	60	64	56	1.4R	Polo Grounds IV
1895–1903	448	194	254	43	39	48	1.5L	
1904–10	367	258	108	71	70	70	1.0	
1911–25	1544	875	669	57	57	56	1.0	Polo Grounds V
1926–35	1996	1263	733	63	69	57	1.7R	
1936–44	1750	1252	498	72	75	69	1.7R	
1945–57	3757	2294	1463	61	59	65	1.3L	
1958–59	642	316	326	49	50	46	1.2R	Seals Stadium
1960	236	81	155	34	32	38	1.3L	Candlestick Park
1961–74	3997	2073	1924	52	50	56	1.3L	Fences distances shortened

(continued)

New York – San Francisco Giants, 1883–2003 (*continued*)

Years	Home Runs			Home Percentage			Hand OR	Change
	Total	Home	Road	All	RHB	LHB		
1975–77	577	267	311	46	50	42	1.4R	Fence height raised 4 ft
1978–81	760	305	456	40	39	43	1.2L	
1982–99	5146	2552	2593	50	50	49	1.0	Fences distance shortened
2000–2003	1387	573	814	41	43	39	1.2R	Pacific Bell Park

St. Louis Cardinals, 1892–2003

Years	Home Runs			Home Percentage			Hand OR	Change
	Total	Home	Road	All	RHB	LHB		
1892	93	66	27	71	71	75	1.2L	Sportsman's Park I
1893–94	151	66	85	44	42	45	1.1L	Robison Field
1895–1899	397	263	134	66	65	68	1.1L	
1900–08	403	218	185	54	54	53	1.0	
1909–19	584	262	322	45	41	50	1.4L	
1920–23	507	226	281	45	41	49	1.4L	Sportsman's Park III
1924–28	851	486	365	57	53	62	1.5L	
1929–37	1482	722	760	49	45	52	1.3L	22 ft higher screen in RF
1938–41	697	408	289	58	53	64	1.5L	CF fence lowered 10 ft
1942–53	2192	976	1216	45	40	50	1.5L	
1954–57	1168	588	580	50	44	58	1.8L	
1958–62	1314	691	623	53	48	59	1.6L	
1963–65	769	460	309	60	58	62	1.2L	
1966–91	4790	2113	2677	44	44	44	1.0	Busch Stadium
1992–2003	3826	1872	1954	49	48	50	1.0	Power alleys, CF shortened

Best Individual Seasons

Table L.1   Single-Season Batting Average Top 100

Adjusted Hits			Adjusted BA		
1	**Ichiro Suzuki, 2001**	246.6	1	Rogers Hornsby, 1924	.379
2	Don Mattingly, 1986	236.8	2	Rod Carew, 1977	.377
3	Rod Carew, 1977	232.4	3	**Tony Gwynn, 1994**	.376
4	Wade Boggs, 1985	231.4	4	George Brett, 1980	.375
5	Kirby Puckett, 1988	230.4	5	Nap Lajoie, 1901	.372
6	**Darrin Erstad, 2000**	229.8	6	Ted Williams, 1941	.370
7	Tommy Davis, 1962	226.6	7	Tip O'Neill, 1887	.366
8	Pete Rose, 1973	224.6	8	Ted Williams, 1957	.366
9	Tony Oliva, 1964	223.3	9	**Barry Bonds, 2002**	.365
10	Stan Musial, 1946	222.6	10	Stan Musial, 1948	.364
11	Joe Torre, 1971	222.4	11	Rod Carew, 1974	.361
12	Stan Musial, 1948	222.2	12	Nap Lajoie, 1904	.361
13	Matty Alou, 1969	221.5	13	**Tony Gwynn, 1997**	.361
14	Willie Wilson, 1980	220.7	14	George Sisler, 1922	.361
15	**Lance Johnson, 1996**	219.4	15	Tony Gwynn, 1987	.360
16	Kirby Puckett, 1986	219.0	16	**Mike Piazza, 1997**	.359
17	Joe Medwick, 1937	218.3	17	Tony Gwynn, 1984	.359
18	Cecil Cooper, 1980	218.2	18	Mickey Mantle, 1957	.357
19	Tony Gwynn, 1984	217.6	19	Stan Musial, 1946	.357
20	Rod Carew, 1974	216.5	20	**Ichiro Suzuki, 2001**	.356
21	**Ichiro Suzuki, 2003**	216.5	21	Norm Cash, 1961	.356
22	Al Simmons, 1925	216.4	22	Honus Wagner, 1908	.355
23	Willie McGee, 1985	216.4	23	**Tony Gwynn, 1995**	.355
24	George Sisler, 1920	216.3	24	Rod Carew, 1975	.355
25	George Brett, 1976	215.7	25	Wade Boggs, 1988	.355
26	Tony Gwynn, 1986	215.2	26	Nap Lajoie, 1910	.354
27	**Paul Molitor, 1991**	215.0	27	Wade Boggs, 1985	.354
28	Hank Aaron, 1959	214.4	28	**Jeff Bagwell, 1994**	.354
29	**Ichiro Suzuki, 2002**	213.9	29	Willie McGee, 1985	.354
30	Rogers Hornsby, 1922	213.9	30	Heinie Zimmerman, 1912	.352
31	Stan Musial, 1943	213.9	31	George Stone, 1906	.352
32	Tony Gwynn, 1997	213.8	32	Ty Cobb, 1909	.352
33	Richie Ashburn, 1951	213.6	33	Tris Speaker, 1916	.351
34	Tommy Holmes, 1945	213.3	34	Tony Gwynn, 1989	.351
35	Pete Rose, 1976	213.1	35	**John Olerud, 1993**	.351
36	Cal Ripken Jr., 1991	213.0	36	Will Clark, 1989	.351
37	Bobby Richardson, 1962	213.0	37	Joe Torre, 1971	.351
38	Steve Sax, 1986	212.9	38	Cecil Cooper, 1980	.351
39	Tony Gwynn, 1987	212.2	39	Kirby Puckett, 1988	.351
40	Tony Gwynn, 1989	212.1	40	Hugh Duffy, 1894	.351
41	**Vernon Wells, 2003**	211.9	41	Ty Cobb, 1912	.350
42	Paul Waner, 1927	211.9	42	Cy Seymour, 1905	.350
43	Heinie Manush, 1928	211.5	43	Don Mattingly, 1986	.350
44	Kirby Puckett, 1989	211.5	44	Ty Cobb, 1917	.350
45	George Sisler, 1922	211.3	45	Elston Howard, 1961	.349
46	Don Mattingly, 1985	211.3	46	**Albert Pujols, 2003**	.349
47	Bill Terry, 1930	211.2	47	Joe DiMaggio, 1939	.349
48	Cal Ripken Jr., 1983	210.8	48	Harvey Kuenn, 1959	.349
49	Robin Yount, 1982	210.8	49	Ty Cobb, 1910	.348
50	Tony Fernandez, 1986	210.7	50	Honus Wagner, 1909	.348

Table L.1 *(continued)*

Adjusted Hits			Adjusted BA		
51	**Derek Jeter, 1999**	210.2	51	Wade Boggs, 1987	.348
52	Richie Ashburn, 1958	210.1	52	Harry Walker, 1947	.348
53	Felipe Alou, 1968	210.0	53	Al Simmons, 1931	.348
54	Ralph Garr, 1971	209.9	54	Tommy Tucker, 1889	.347
55	**Bret Boone, 2001**	209.7	55	Harry Heilmann, 1923	.347
56	Billy Herman, 1935	209.5	56	Rogers Hornsby, 1928	.347
57	Alex Johnson, 1970	209.5	57	Rod Carew, 1973	.347
58	Nap Lajoie, 1910	209.5	58	Ed Delahanty, 1899	.347
59	Paul Molitor, 1996	209.3	59	Stan Musial, 1943	.347
60	Ron LeFlore, 1977	208.9	60	Bobby Murcer, 1971	.346
61	Felipe Alou, 1966	208.6	61	Paul Molitor, 1987	.346
62	**Alfonso Soriano, 2002**	208.5	62	Rogers Hornsby, 1925	.346
63	Kirby Puckett, 1992	208.4	63	Ty Cobb, 1918	.346
64	Dave Parker, 1977	208.3	64	**Tony Gwynn, 1993**	.346
65	**Alex Rodriguez, 1998**	207.8	65	Luke Appling, 1936	.345
66	Vada Pinson, 1963	207.8	66	Rogers Hornsby, 1921	.345
67	Freddie Lindstrom, 1928	207.7	67	Roberto Clemente, 1967	.345
68	Dave Cash, 1975	207.6	68	Rogers Hornsby, 1920	.345
69	Pete Rose, 1968	207.4	69	Joe Medwick, 1937	.345
70	Pete Rose, 1969	207.3	70	**Nomar Garciaparra, 2000**	.345
71	Dick Wakefield, 1943	207.2	71	Ty Cobb, 1913	.344
72	Wade Boggs, 1988	207.2	72	King Kelly, 1886	.344
73	Lefty O'Doul, 1929	207.2	73	Alan Trammell, 1987	.344
74	Nap Lajoie, 1906	206.5	74	Edgar Martinez, 1992	.344
75	Bill Terry, 1932	206.5	75	Babe Ruth, 1923	.344
76	Garry Templeton, 1979	206.4	76	Roger Connor, 1885	.344
77	Cecil Cooper, 1982	206.3	77	Tris Speaker, 1912	.344
78	Will Clark, 1989	206.3	78	Arky Vaughan, 1935	.344
79	**Albert Pujols, 2003**	206.1	79	Dixie Walker, 1944	.344
80	Lou Whitaker, 1983	206.0	80	Wade Boggs, 1986	.344
81	Pete Rose, 1975	205.9	81	**John Olerud, 1998**	.343
82	Don Mattingly, 1984	205.9	82	Rogers Hornsby, 1922	.343
83	Steve Garvey, 1975	205.7	83	Willie Keeler, 1897	.343
84	Ty Cobb, 1917	205.7	84	Honus Wagner, 1907	.343
85	Maury Wills, 1962	205.7	85	Nap Lajoie, 1906	.343
86	Keith Hernandez, 1979	205.7	86	Ty Cobb, 1922	.343
87	Jim Rice, 1978	205.6	87	Dan Brouthers, 1889	.343
88	Heinie Manush, 1933	205.6	88	George Sisler, 1920	.343
89	Steve Sax, 1989	205.6	89	Pete Browning, 1885	.343
90	**Craig Biggio, 1998**	205.5	90	Carney Lansford, 1989	.343
91	Alan Trammell, 1987	205.4	91	Jake Daubert, 1913	.343
92	Frank McCormick, 1938	205.4	92	Cleon Jones, 1969	.342
93	Cesar Tovar, 1971	205.2	93	**Edgar Martinez, 1995**	.342
94	Lou Brock, 1967	205.2	94	Joe DiMaggio, 1941	.342
95	George Kell, 1950	205.1	95	Pete Browning, 1887	.342
96	Paul Molitor, 1993	205.0	96	Edd Roush, 1917	.342
97	Snuffy Stirnweiss, 1944	204.9	97	Hal Chase, 1916	.342
98	Cecil Cooper, 1983	204.9	98	Carl Yastrzemski, 1967	.342
99	Carlos Baerga, 1992	204.9	99	Richie Ashburn, 1958	.342
100	**Miguel Tejada, 2002**	204.6	100	Goose Goslin, 1928	.342

Note: Seasons from the power era, 1993-2003, are shown in bold.

Table L.2   Single-Season Doubles-Plus-Triples Top 100

Adjusted DPTs		Adjusted DPTs per 500 ABs	
1 Lou Brock, 1968	65.0	1 Carl Yastrzemski, 1965	49.6
2 Joe Medwick, 1936	61.9	2 Lou Brock, 1968	49.3
3 Zoilo Versalles, 1965	61.5	3 Paul Molitor, 1987	49.1
4 Stan Musial, 1946	61.1	4 Honus Wagner, 1904	49.0
5 Robin Yount, 1982	59.4	5 Stan Musial, 1946	49.0
6 Stan Musial, 1943	59.3	6 **Craig Biggio, 1994**	48.9
7 Ryne Sandberg, 1984	58.8	7 Joe Medwick, 1936	48.7
8 Robin Yount, 1980	58.6	8 Honus Wagner, 1900	48.6
9 Hal McRae, 1977	57.6	9 Jay Johnstone, 1976	48.4
10 Don Mattingly, 1986	57.5	10 Fred Lynn, 1975	48.3
11 Stan Musial, 1948	57.3	11 Tip O'Neill, 1887	48.3
12 Floyd Robinson, 1962	57.3	12 Stan Musial, 1943	48.0
13 Keith Hernandez, 1979	57.2	13 George Brett, 1978	48.0
14 George Kell, 1950	56.9	14 Tris Speaker, 1922	48.0
15 Tony Oliva, 1964	56.4	15 Robin Yount, 1980	48.0
16 Wade Boggs, 1989	55.9	16 **Geoff Jenkins, 1999**	48.0
17 Bill Terry, 1931	55.5	17 Edd Roush, 1923	47.9
18 Wes Parker, 1970	55.4	18 **Eric Hinske, 2003**	47.8
19 Jack Clark, 1978	55.3	19 Floyd Robinson, 1962	47.8
20 Dick Groat, 1963	55.1	20 Ival Goodman, 1939	47.5
21 Billy Herman, 1936	55.0	21 Babe Ruth, 1923	47.3
22 Juan Samuel, 1984	54.9	22 Harvey Kuenn, 1959	47.0
23 Snuffy Stirnweiss, 1945	54.9	23 **John Olerud, 1993**	47.0
24 Vada Pinson, 1959	54.8	24 Stan Musial, 1948	46.9
25 Frank Robinson, 1962	54.8	25 Keith Hernandez, 1979	46.9
26 George Brett, 1979	54.7	26 **Edgar Martinez, 1996**	46.8
27 Paul Waner, 1928	54.6	27 Robin Yount, 1982	46.8
28 Hank Greenberg, 1934	54.6	28 Jack Clark, 1978	46.7
29 Charlie Gehringer, 1936	54.5	29 Ty Cobb, 1908	46.5
30 Stan Musial, 1953	54.3	30 Chief Zimmer, 1892	46.3
31 Hank Aaron, 1959	54.1	31 Lou Gehrig, 1926	46.3
32 Joe Medwick, 1937	54.1	32 Ryne Sandberg, 1984	46.2
33 Ty Cobb, 1908	54.0	33 Zoilo Versalles, 1965	46.2
34 Cal Ripken Jr., 1991	54.0	34 Willie Stargell, 1973	46.2
35 **Garret Anderson, 2002**	53.9	35 Stan Musial, 1944	46.1
36 Ty Cobb, 1917	53.7	36 Hank Greenberg, 1934	46.1
37 Vada Pinson, 1963	53.6	37 **Chuck Knoblauch, 1994**	46.0
38 Cesar Tovar, 1970	53.5	38 Jim Gleeson, 1940	45.8
39 Alvin Dark, 1951	53.2	39 Stan Musial, 1953	45.8
40 Hy Myers, 1920	53.2	40 Hy Myers, 1920	45.7
41 Lou Gehrig, 1927	53.2	41 Honus Wagner, 1907	45.7
42 Andy Van Slyke, 1992	53.1	42 Ty Cobb, 1917	45.7
43 Rod Carew, 1977	53.0	43 **Edgar Martinez, 1995**	45.7
44 Paul Waner, 1932	53.0	44 **Tony Gwynn, 1993**	45.6
45 Lou Gehrig, 1926	53.0	45 **Albert Belle, 1995**	45.6
46 Rafael Palmeiro, 1991	53.0	46 Joe DiMaggio, 1941	45.6
47 Tommy Henrich, 1948	52.9	47 Lou Gehrig, 1927	45.5
48 Harvey Kuenn, 1959	52.7	48 Ed Delahanty, 1892	45.5
49 Don Mattingly, 1985	52.7	49 Edgar Martinez, 1992	45.5
50 Joe Rudi, 1974	52.7	50 Bill Terry, 1931	45.4

Table L.2   *(continued)*

Adjusted DPTs			Adjusted DPTs per 500 ABs		
51	Rogers Hornsby, 1920	52.6	51	John Anderson, 1898	45.4
52	**Steve Finley, 1996**	52.6	52	**Lance Berkman, 2001**	45.4
53	Willie Davis, 1971	52.5	53	Paul Waner, 1928	45.4
54	Joe Jackson, 1916	52.4	54	Dick Allen, 1967	45.4
55	Stan Musial, 1944	52.4	55	Honus Wagner, 1908	45.4
56	Snuffy Stirnweiss, 1944	52.4	56	Lou Boudreau, 1947	45.3
57	**Lance Berkman, 2001**	52.4	57	**Kevin Millar, 2002**	45.3
58	Ruben Sierra, 1989	52.3	58	**Bobby Abreu, 2002**	45.2
59	Earl Webb, 1931	52.2	59	**Mark Grace, 1995**	45.1
60	Billy Herman, 1935	52.1	60	Wes Parker, 1970	45.1
61	Kiki Cuyler, 1925	51.9	61	Steve Evans, 1914	45.1
62	Steve Sax, 1986	51.8	62	Jake Beckley, 1890	45.0
63	**John Olerud, 1993**	51.8	63	Wade Boggs, 1989	45.0
64	**Bobby Abreu, 2002**	51.8	64	Frank Robinson, 1962	45.0
65	Stan Spence, 1946	51.6	65	Hal McRae, 1977	45.0
66	Joe Rudi, 1972	51.6	66	Tommy Henrich, 1948	44.9
67	Pete Rose, 1974	51.6	67	**Larry Walker, 1998**	44.7
68	Paul Waner, 1936	51.5	68	Dave Orr, 1885	44.7
69	Al Kaline, 1961	51.5	69	Cesar Cedeno, 1972	44.7
70	Honus Wagner, 1908	51.5	70	Honus Wagner, 1909	44.7
71	Willie Mays, 1957	51.5	71	Stan Spence, 1946	44.7
72	Red Rolfe, 1939	51.4	72	**Kevin Millar, 2001**	44.6
73	Al Oliver, 1974	51.4	73	Tris Speaker, 1914	44.6
74	**Nomar Garciaparra, 2002**	51.3	74	Hank Greenberg, 1940	44.6
75	Honus Wagner, 1900	51.3	75	Rogers Hornsby, 1920	44.6
76	Hank Greenberg, 1940	51.2	76	Joe Cronin, 1938	44.6
77	Johnny Ray, 1988	51.1	77	Roy White, 1969	44.5
78	Sam Crawford, 1907	51.1	78	Ray Grimes, 1922	44.5
79	Hank Aaron, 1956	51.1	79	Bruce Campbell, 1937	44.5
80	Dave Parker, 1979	51.0	80	Frank Thomas, 1992	44.5
81	Barney McCosky, 1940	51.0	81	Tony Gonzalez, 1963	44.5
82	Vic Power, 1958	51.0	82	Lenny Dykstra, 1987	44.5
83	Fred Lynn, 1975	51.0	83	Nap Lajoie, 1904	44.4
84	Tris Speaker, 1914	51.0	84	Ben Chapman, 1936	44.4
85	Frank Thomas, 1992	51.0	85	Joe Rudi, 1974	44.4
86	Lee Maye, 1964	51.0	86	Hal McRae, 1975	44.4
87	Mickey Vernon, 1946	50.9	87	George Kell, 1950	44.4
88	Tris Speaker, 1923	50.9	88	Gene Freese, 1960	44.4
89	Robin Yount, 1983	50.8	89	Earl Webb, 1931	44.3
90	**Shawn Green, 2003**	50.8	90	Tris Speaker, 1923	44.3
91	Joe Vosmik, 1935	50.7	91	Pete Reiser, 1941	44.3
92	Paul Waner, 1927	50.7	92	Joe Jackson, 1916	44.3
93	George Sisler, 1920	50.7	93	Phil Garner, 1976	44.3
94	Mickey Vernon, 1953	50.6	94	Carl Furillo, 1953	44.2
95	Tommy Holmes, 1945	50.6	95	**Jason Giambi, 2001**	44.2
96	Edd Roush, 1923	50.5	96	Minnie Minoso, 1951	44.1
97	Steve Garvey, 1975	50.5	97	Lou Whitaker, 1993	44.1
98	Alvin Dark, 1953	50.3	98	Paul Waner, 1936	44.1
99	Felipe Alou, 1968	50.3	99	Willie Mays, 1957	44.0
100	Dick Allen, 1964	50.3	100	Brian Harper, 1990	44.0

Note: Seasons from the power era, 1993-2003, are shown in bold

Table L.3   Single-Season Triples Top 100

Adjusted Triples		Adjusted Triples per 500 ABs	
1 Dale Mitchell, 1949	29.3	1 Dale Mitchell, 1949	22.9
2 **Lance Johnson, 1996**	25.4	2 Chief Wilson, 1912	21.7
3 Chief Wilson, 1912	25.2	3 Tom Long, 1915	21.5
4 Willie Mays, 1957	23.7	4 Willie Mays, 1957	20.2
5 **Cristian Guzman, 2000**	22.0	5 Harry Davis, 1897	20.1
6 Tom Long, 1915	21.8	6 Walt Wilmot, 1889	20.1
7 Snuffy Stirnweiss, 1945	21.5	7 Ival Goodman, 1939	19.4
8 Dave Orr, 1886	21.2	8 **Lance Johnson, 1996**	18.6
9 Ralph Garr, 1974	20.2	9 Dave Orr, 1886	18.6
10 Bill Terry, 1931	20.1	10 Earle Combs, 1933	18.2
11 Barney McCosky, 1940	19.6	11 Perry Werden, 1893	17.5
12 Ryne Sandberg, 1984	19.3	12 **Cristian Guzman, 2000**	17.4
13 Willie Wilson, 1985	19.3	13 Heinie Reitz, 1894	17.4
14 Jim Rivera, 1953	18.7	14 Tommy Leach, 1902	17.3
15 Tony Fernandez, 1990	18.7	15 Snuffy Stirnweiss, 1945	17.0
16 Willie Davis, 1970	18.4	16 Jeff Heath, 1938	16.9
17 Ival Goodman, 1939	18.2	17 Larry Doyle, 1911	16.8
18 Johnny Callison, 1965	18.1	18 Ralph Garr, 1974	16.6
19 Juan Samuel, 1984	17.9	19 Barney McCosky, 1940	16.6
20 Minnie Minoso, 1954	17.9	20 Mickey Rivers, 1974	16.6
21 Tommy Leach, 1902	17.8	21 Jim Rivera, 1953	16.5
22 Enos Slaughter, 1942	17.7	22 Bill Terry, 1931	16.4
23 Larry Doyle, 1911	17.6	23 Dave Collins, 1984	16.4
24 Paul Molitor, 1979	17.5	24 Ed Delahanty, 1892	16.4
25 George Brett, 1979	17.5	25 **Kenny Lofton, 1995**	16.2
26 Perry Werden, 1893	17.5	26 Hank Edwards, 1946	16.0
27 Brett Butler, 1986	17.5	27 Willie Wilson, 1985	15.9
28 Walt Wilmot, 1889	17.4	28 Bill Bruton, 1956	15.8
29 George Davis, 1893	17.3	29 George Davis, 1893	15.8
30 Bobby Thomson, 1952	17.3	30 Minnie Minoso, 1954	15.7
31 Harry Davis, 1897	17.2	31 Sam Thompson, 1894	15.7
32 Jim Gilliam, 1953	17.2	32 **Lance Johnson, 1993**	15.7
33 Vada Pinson, 1963	17.1	33 Les Mann, 1915	15.6
34 Mickey Rivers, 1975	17.1	34 John Anderson, 1898	15.6
35 Sam Crawford, 1902	17.1	35 Harry Walker, 1947	15.6
36 Jeff Heath, 1938	17.0	36 Harry Stovey, 1891	15.5
37 **Lance Johnson, 1993**	17.0	37 Willie Davis, 1970	15.5
38 Stan Musial, 1948	16.9	38 Sam Crawford, 1902	15.4
39 Roger Metzger, 1973	16.9	39 Tommy McCraw, 1968	15.3
40 Harry Stovey, 1891	16.9	40 John Stone, 1935	15.3
41 Brett Butler, 1985	16.7	41 Vic Saier, 1913	15.3
42 Bill Bruton, 1956	16.6	42 Ryne Sandberg, 1984	15.2
43 Stan Musial, 1943	16.5	43 Ted Kluszewski, 1952	15.1
44 Mike Devereaux, 1992	16.4	44 Pete Reiser, 1941	15.1
45 Jim Bottomley, 1928	16.3	45 Jorge Orta, 1973	15.0
46 Joe Jackson, 1912	16.3	46 Enos Slaughter, 1942	15.0
47 Lou Brock, 1968	16.3	47 Paul Molitor, 1979	15.0
48 John Anderson, 1898	16.2	48 Earle Combs, 1930	15.0
49 Lance Johnson, 1992	16.2	49 Luis Polonia, 1987	14.9
50 **Lance Johnson, 1994**	16.2	50 Minnie Minoso, 1951	14.9

Table L.3   (*continued*)

Adjusted Triples		Adjusted Triples per 500 ABs	
51 Pete Reiser, 1941	16.2	51 Brett Butler, 1986	14.9
52 Kiki Cuyler, 1925	16.1	52 Tony Fernandez, 1990	14.7
53 Jeff Heath, 1941	16.1	53 **David Dellucci, 1998**	14.7
54 Devon White, 1989	16.1	54 Johnny Callison, 1965	14.6
55 Willie McGee, 1985	16.1	55 Roger Metzger, 1973	14.6
56 Stan Musial, 1946	16.0	56 Tom McCreery, 1896	14.4
57 Garry Templeton, 1979	16.0	57 Edd Roush, 1924	14.4
58 Harry Walker, 1947	16.0	58 Dale Long, 1955	14.4
59 George Stone, 1906	15.9	59 Mariano Duncan, 1990	14.3
60 Earle Combs, 1930	15.9	60 Lance Johnson, 1992	14.3
61 **Delino DeShields, 1997**	15.9	61 **Cristian Guzman, 2001**	14.3
62 Jim Rice, 1978	15.9	62 Joe Jackson, 1912	14.3
63 **Joey Cora, 1993**	15.9	63 Harry Stovey, 1888	14.2
64 Vic Saier, 1913	15.8	64 Roberto Clemente, 1968	14.2
65 Joe Medwick, 1934	15.8	65 Bobby Thomson, 1952	14.2
66 Minnie Minoso, 1951	15.8	66 Jim Gilliam, 1953	14.2
67 Billy Herman, 1939	15.6	67 Jim Bottomley, 1928	14.2
68 Zoilo Versalles, 1963	15.6	68 Dave Orr, 1885	14.2
69 Ed Delahanty, 1892	15.6	69 Brett Butler, 1985	14.1
70 Earle Combs, 1927	15.6	70 Mike Tiernan, 1895	14.1
71 Ty Cobb, 1917	15.6	71 Johnny Lindell, 1943	14.1
72 **Kenny Lofton, 1995**	15.6	72 Tris Speaker, 1913	14.0
73 Heinie Reitz, 1894	15.5	73 Sam Crawford, 1903	14.0
74 Jim Fregosi, 1963	15.5	74 Paul Blair, 1967	14.0
75 Wally Pipp, 1924	15.5	75 Roger Connor, 1886	13.9
76 Mickey Rivers, 1974	15.5	76 **Delino DeShields, 1997**	13.9
77 Larry Herndon, 1982	15.5	77 John Reilly, 1890	13.9
78 Wally Moses, 1945	15.4	78 Stan Musial, 1948	13.9
79 Paul Blair, 1967	15.4	79 Mickey Rivers, 1975	13.9
80 Sam Crawford, 1903	15.4	80 Grover Gilmore, 1915	13.8
81 John Reilly, 1890	15.4	81 Bud Stewart, 1948	13.8
82 Sam Crawford, 1914	15.4	82 Carl Reynolds, 1931	13.8
83 **Chuck Knoblauch, 1996**	15.4	83 Jeff Heath, 1941	13.8
84 Ruben Sierra, 1989	15.3	84 George Stone, 1906	13.7
85 **Adam Kennedy, 2000**	15.3	85 Joey Cora, 1993	13.7
86 Joe Vosmik, 1935	15.2	86 Charlie Keller, 1940	13.7
87 Earle Combs, 1933	15.2	87 Jim Fogarty, 1889	13.7
88 Chuck Hinton, 1963	15.2	88 Earl Averill, 1938	13.7
89 Dick Allen, 1965	15.2	89 Gino Cimoli, 1962	13.6
90 Harry Stovey, 1888	15.1	90 **Mark McLemore, 2001**	13.6
91 Ted Kluszewski, 1952	15.0	91 Wally Moses, 1945	13.6
92 Gino Cimoli, 1962	15.0	92 George Brett, 1979	13.6
93 Brady Anderson, 1992	15.0	93 Harry Stovey, 1884	13.6
94 Elmer Flick, 1906	15.0	94 **Vince Coleman, 1994**	13.5
95 Ty Cobb, 1908	15.0	95 Elmer Flick, 1905	13.5
96 Lance Johnson, 1991	15.0	96 Kiko Garcia, 1979	13.4
97 Paul Molitor, 1991	14.9	97 Pete Runnels, 1954	13.4
98 **Jose Offerman, 1998**	14.9	98 Chuck Hinton, 1963	13.4
99 Garry Templeton, 1977	14.9	99 Ed McKean, 1893	13.4
100 Jim Fregosi, 1968	14.8	100 Stan Musial, 1943	13.3

Note: Seasons from the power era, 1993-2003, are shown in bold.

Table L.4   Single-Season Home Runs Top 100

Adjusted HRs		Adjusted Home Runs per 500 ABs	
1 Barry Bonds, 2001	70.0	1 Barry Bonds, 2001	73.5
2 Ed Delahanty, 1893	63.7	2 Babe Ruth, 1920	63.7
3 Buck Freeman, 1899	63.5	3 Babe Ruth, 1919	61.8
4 Mark McGwire, 1998	62.7	4 Mark McGwire, 1998	61.6
5 Babe Ruth, 1927	62.4	5 Barry Bonds, 2002	61.4
6 Rogers Hornsby, 1922	62.0	6 Barry Bonds, 2003	60.3
7 Babe Ruth, 1921	60.4	7 Babe Ruth, 1927	57.7
8 Babe Ruth, 1920	58.4	8 Babe Ruth, 1921	56.0
9 Bill Nicholson, 1943	55.6	9 Buck Freeman, 1899	54.0
10 Ted Williams, 1949	54.9	10 Babe Ruth, 1926	53.7
11 Lou Gehrig, 1927	54.6	11 Ed Delahanty, 1893	53.5
12 Babe Ruth, 1928	54.0	12 Tim Jordan, 1906	51.8
13 Joe DiMaggio, 1948	53.9	13 Willie Stargell, 1971	50.8
14 Babe Ruth, 1919	53.4	14 Babe Ruth, 1928	50.4
15 Babe Ruth, 1926	53.2	15 Mark McGwire, 1999	50.1
16 Mark McGwire, 1999	52.2	16 Rogers Hornsby, 1922	49.8
17 Kevin Mitchell, 1989	52.1	17 Jim Thome, 2002	49.4
18 Willie Stargell, 1971	51.9	18 Dave Kingman, 1976	49.1
19 Tris Speaker, 1912	51.7	19 Roy Sievers, 1954	49.0
20 Mike Schmidt, 1980	51.4	20 Jeff Bagwell, 1994	48.7
21 Babe Ruth, 1924	51.3	21 Ted Williams, 1949	48.5
22 Frank Howard, 1968	51.2	22 Babe Ruth, 1924	48.5
23 Lou Gehrig, 1931	50.8	23 Kevin Mitchell, 1989	48.0
24 Harry Stovey, 1889	50.7	24 Ted Williams, 1942	47.5
25 Ed McKean, 1898	50.7	25 Babe Ruth, 1923	47.2
26 Alex Rodriguez, 2002	50.4	26 Mike Schmidt, 1980	46.9
27 Roy Sievers, 1954	50.3	27 Mark McGwire, 1996	46.8
28 Jimmie Foxx, 1932	50.3	28 Lou Gehrig, 1927	46.8
29 Cecil Fielder, 1990	50.2	29 Babe Ruth, 1922	46.7
30 Sammy Sosa, 1998	50.0	30 Ted Williams, 1957	46.3
31 Ted Williams, 1942	49.6	31 Mark McGwire, 1992	46.3
32 Barry Bonds, 2002	49.5	32 Fred Dunlap, 1884	46.3
33 Roger Maris, 1961	49.4	33 Barry Bonds, 2000	46.2
34 Babe Ruth, 1923	49.3	34 Babe Ruth, 1931	45.9
35 Babe Ruth, 1931	49.0	35 Harry Stovey, 1885	45.8
36 Jimmie Foxx, 1933	48.7	36 Charlie Hickman, 1906	45.8
37 Bill Nicholson, 1944	48.0	37 Bill Nicholson, 1943	45.7
38 Willie Mays, 1964	47.8	38 Harry Stovey, 1889	45.6
39 Ralph Kiner, 1949	47.8	39 Boog Powell, 1964	45.6
40 Joe DiMaggio, 1937	47.7	40 Ted Williams, 1941	45.5
41 Willie Mays, 1965	47.7	41 Joe DiMaggio, 1948	45.4
42 Al Rosen, 1953	47.6	42 Eddie Mathews, 1954	45.4
43 Jim Thome, 2002	47.4	43 Mickey Mantle, 1961	45.3
44 Reggie Jackson, 1969	47.1	44 Tris Speaker, 1912	44.6
45 Frank Robinson, 1966	47.1	45 Ted Williams, 1954	44.6
46 Barry Bonds, 2003	47.1	46 Ted Williams, 1947	44.6
47 Ted Williams, 1947	47.0	47 Jim Gentile, 1961	44.0
48 Carl Yastrzemski, 1967	47.0	48 Cecil Fielder, 1990	43.8
49 Tim Jordan, 1906	46.6	49 Ralph Kiner, 1949	43.6
50 Mickey Mantle, 1961	46.6	50 Dick Allen, 1974	43.0

Table L.4 *(continued)*

Adjusted HRs		Adjusted Home Runs per 500 ABs	
51 Dave Kingman, 1976	46.5	51 Jimmie Foxx, 1932	43.0
52 **Ken Griffey Jr, 1998**	46.4	52 Babe Ruth, 1929	43.0
53 Hank Aaron, 1957	46.4	53 **Matt Williams, 1994**	43.0
54 Mike Tiernan, 1890	46.3	54 Reggie Jackson, 1969	42.9
55 Eddie Mathews, 1953	45.6	55 Frank Howard, 1968	42.8
56 Harry Stovey, 1883	45.6	56 Willie Mays, 1965	42.8
57 Honus Wagner, 1908	45.5	57 **Barry Bonds, 1994**	42.7
58 Frank Howard, 1969	45.3	58 Jimmie Foxx, 1933	42.5
59 Ken Griffey Jr, 1997	45.2	59 Joe Adcock, 1956	42.3
60 **Alex Rodriguez, 2001**	45.1	60 Mickey Mantle, 1956	42.1
61 Darryl Strawberry, 1988	45.1	61 Barry Bonds, 1992	42.0
62 Barry Bonds, 1993	45.1	62 Ed McKean, 1898	41.9
63 Hack Wilson, 1930	45.1	63 Mike Tiernan, 1890	41.9
64 Mickey Mantle, 1956	44.9	64 Tim Jordan, 1908	41.9
65 Glenn Davis, 1989	44.9	65 Roger Maris, 1961	41.8
66 George Foster, 1977	44.8	66 **Barry Bonds, 1993**	41.8
67 Harmon Killebrew, 1967	44.8	67 Darryl Strawberry, 1988	41.5
68 Jimmy Wynn, 1967	44.8	68 Willie Mays, 1964	41.4
69 **Sammy Sosa, 2001**	44.7	69 Rogers Hornsby, 1925	41.2
70 Ralph Kiner, 1947	44.7	70 Bill Nicholson, 1944	41.2
71 Joe Medwick, 1937	44.7	71 Babe Ruth, 1932	41.2
72 Ival Goodman, 1938	44.6	72 Cy Williams, 1923	41.1
73 **Greg Vaughn, 1998**	44.6	73 Lou Gehrig, 1931	41.1
74 Harry Stovey, 1885	44.6	74 Frank Howard, 1963	41.0
75 **Barry Bonds, 2000**	44.3	75 **Jim Thome, 2001**	41.0
76 Jim Rice, 1978	44.1	76 Harmon Killebrew, 1967	41.0
77 Jose Canseco, 1988	44.1	77 Frank Robinson, 1966	40.9
78 Hank Aaron, 1963	44.1	78 Willie Stargell, 1973	40.9
79 Cy Williams, 1923	44.0	79 Dave Kingman, 1975	40.8
80 Gus Zernial, 1953	43.7	80 Oyster Burns, 1890	40.7
81 Mike Schmidt, 1976	43.7	81 Carl Yastrzemski, 1967	40.6
82 Lou Gehrig, 1934	43.4	82 Jose Canseco, 1990	40.6
83 Reggie Jackson, 1975	43.3	83 Tommy Leach, 1902	40.4
84 Lou Gehrig, 1936	43.3	84 **Alex Rodriguez, 2002**	40.4
85 Mark McGwire, 1992	43.3	85 Hank Aaron, 1971	40.4
86 Eddie Mathews, 1954	43.2	86 Gorman Thomas, 1978	40.0
87 Tim Jordan, 1908	43.1	87 Honus Wagner, 1908	40.0
88 **Jim Thome, 2001**	43.1	88 Mike Schmidt, 1984	39.8
89 Harry Davis, 1906	43.1	89 Willie Stargell, 1968	39.7
90 Ben Oglivie, 1980	43.0	90 Al Rosen, 1953	39.7
91 Rudy York, 1943	43.0	91 Hank Sauer, 1948	39.7
92 **Sammy Sosa, 1999**	42.9	92 Willie McCovey, 1968	39.7
93 Babe Ruth, 1929	42.9	93 **Javy Lopez, 2003**	39.6
94 Jim Gentile, 1961	42.8	94 Bo Jackson, 1990	39.6
95 Johnny Mize, 1947	42.8	95 Ralph Kiner, 1947	39.6
96 Willie Mays, 1962	42.8	96 Gavy Cravath, 1915	39.5
97 Hank Sauer, 1952	42.8	97 Babe Ruth, 1933	39.5
98 Hack Wilson, 1927	42.7	98 Eddie Mathews, 1953	39.4
99 Willie Stargell, 1973	42.7	99 Reggie Jackson, 1976	39.4
100 Gorman Thomas, 1979	42.6	100 Gus Zernial, 1953	39.3

Note: Seasons from the power era, 1993-2003, are shown in bold.

Table L.5   Single-Season Runs Top 100

Adjusted Runs		Adjusted Runs per 550 NFPs	
1 Rickey Henderson, 1985	157.9	1 Rickey Henderson, 1985	133.8
2 **Craig Biggio, 1997**	142.7	2 Rickey Henderson, 1990	128.5
3 Babe Ruth, 1928	142.2	3 Babe Ruth, 1920	117.9
4 Paul Molitor, 1982	142.0	4 **Jeff Bagwell, 1994**	117.0
5 Babe Ruth, 1921	141.7	5 Rickey Henderson, 1984	116.4
6 Lou Gehrig, 1936	139.3	6 Rickey Henderson, 1981	116.1
7 Rickey Henderson, 1990	137.8	7 Babe Ruth, 1928	115.7
8 **Sammy Sosa, 2001**	137.1	8 Mickey Mantle, 1961	115.6
9 Babe Ruth, 1927	136.2	9 Mickey Mantle, 1958	114.7
10 Pete Rose, 1976	136.1	10 Mickey Mantle, 1957	113.8
11 Mickey Mantle, 1958	135.6	11 Babe Ruth, 1921	113.1
12 Ted Williams, 1946	135.1	12 Paul Molitor, 1987	111.8
13 Lou Gehrig, 1931	135.1	13 Mickey Mantle, 1954	111.4
14 Robin Yount, 1982	134.8	14 Joe Morgan, 1976	111.1
15 Ty Cobb, 1915	134.7	15 Mickey Mantle, 1962	111.0
16 Mickey Mantle, 1961	134.5	16 Rickey Henderson, 1988	110.9
17 Jose Canseco, 1988	133.9	17 Dave Henderson, 1988	110.8
18 Roger Maris, 1961	133.1	18 Babe Ruth, 1927	110.7
19 Babe Ruth, 1923	132.8	19 Ted Williams, 1946	110.6
20 Paul Molitor, 1991	132.7	20 Eddie Collins, 1914	110.5
21 Ted Williams, 1949	132.7	21 Fred Dunlap, 1884	110.4
22 Rickey Henderson, 1986	132.6	22 Don Buford, 1971	110.4
23 Wade Boggs, 1988	132.5	23 Tom Brown, 1891	109.6
24 Tom Brown, 1891	132.2	24 John McGraw, 1899	109.6
25 Tim Raines, 1983	131.9	25 **Barry Bonds, 2003**	109.5
26 Zoilo Versalles, 1965	131.5	26 Robin Yount, 1980	109.1
27 Ted Williams, 1942	131.2	27 Nap Lajoie, 1901	108.7
28 Snuffy Stirnweiss, 1944	131.2	28 **Barry Bonds, 2002**	108.2
29 Babe Ruth, 1920	131.0	29 **Sammy Sosa, 2001**	107.8
30 Frank Robinson, 1966	130.8	30 Babe Ruth, 1926	107.8
31 Mickey Mantle, 1954	130.7	31 **Barry Bonds, 2000**	107.6
32 **Lenny Dykstra, 1993**	130.5	32 Ted Williams, 1942	107.5
33 Lou Brock, 1971	130.5	33 Ted Williams, 1941	107.5
34 Hank Aaron, 1963	130.1	34 Robin Yount, 1982	107.5
35 Ron LeFlore, 1978	129.9	35 Rickey Henderson, 1991	107.4
36 Reggie Jackson, 1969	129.5	36 Ty Cobb, 1915	107.2
37 Willie Wilson, 1980	129.1	37 Lou Gehrig, 1936	107.0
38 Albert Pujols, 2003	129.0	38 Eric Davis, 1986	107.0
39 Stan Musial, 1948	128.8	39 Mickey Mantle, 1960	107.0
40 Rickey Henderson, 1988	128.8	40 Frank Robinson, 1966	106.9
41 **Jeff Bagwell, 1999**	128.8	41 Mickey Mantle, 1953	106.8
42 Lou Gehrig, 1927	128.5	42 Bobby Murcer, 1972	106.7
43 Mickey Mantle, 1957	128.3	43 Tommy Leach, 1909	106.5
44 Joe DiMaggio, 1937	128.1	44 **Craig Biggio, 1997**	106.5
45 **Alex Rodriguez, 2000**	127.6	45 **Alex Rodriguez, 2000**	106.2
46 **Ichiro Suzuki, 2001**	127.3	46 Paul Molitor, 1982	106.1
47 Bobby Bonds, 1973	127.3	47 Roger Maris, 1961	106.0
48 Tommy Leach, 1909	126.9	48 **Frank Thomas, 1994**	105.8
49 Maury Wills, 1962	126.7	49 Davy Jones, 1907	105.6
50 Chuck Klein, 1932	126.6	50 Jose Canseco, 1988	105.5

Table L.5 (*continued*)

Adjusted Runs		Adjusted Runs per 550 NFPs	
51 Robin Yount, 1980	126.6	51 Reggie Jackson, 1969	105.5
52 Eddie Collins, 1914	126.4	52 Pete Reiser, 1941	105.4
53 Rickey Henderson, 1989	126.2	53 Willie Mays, 1959	105.3
54 Bobby Murcer, 1972	126.1	54 Ty Cobb, 1909	105.1
55 **Roberto Alomar, 1999**	126.1	55 Babe Ruth, 1923	105.0
56 Lou Gehrig, 1933	126.0	56 Mickey Mantle, 1956	104.8
57 Babe Ruth, 1926	125.8	57 Jimmy Wynn, 1972	104.6
58 Tommy Henrich, 1948	125.8	58 Pepper Martin, 1935	104.6
59 **Jeff Bagwell, 2000**	125.5	59 Hub Collins, 1890	104.6
60 Rickey Henderson, 1984	125.5	60 **Manny Ramirez, 1999**	104.5
61 **Alfonso Soriano, 2002**	125.3	61 Eddie Collins, 1913	104.5
62 Joe Morgan, 1972	125.2	62 **Albert Pujols, 2003**	104.3
63 Rod Carew, 1977	125.0	63 Rickey Henderson, 1986	104.3
64 Stan Musial, 1946	124.7	64 Tommy Leach, 1913	104.0
65 Mickey Mantle, 1960	124.3	65 **Rickey Henderson, 1993**	104.0
66 Johnny Mize, 1947	124.2	66 Donie Bush, 1909	103.9
67 **Barry Bonds, 1993**	124.2	67 **Roberto Alomar, 1999**	103.7
68 Paul Waner, 1928	123.4	68 Rickey Henderson, 1982	103.6
69 **Derek Jeter, 1999**	123.4	69 Rickey Henderson, 1989	103.6
70 Babe Ruth, 1931	123.4	70 Tommy Henrich, 1948	103.6
71 Mickey Mantle, 1956	123.3	71 Al Kaline, 1967	103.5
72 Rickey Henderson, 1982	123.2	72 King Kelly, 1886	103.3
73 **Barry Bonds, 2001**	123.1	73 Eric Davis, 1987	103.3
74 Dick Allen, 1964	123.1	74 Barry Bonds, 1992	103.3
75 Jimmy Wynn, 1972	123.1	75 Fred Clarke, 1902	103.1
76 **Alex Rodriguez, 1996**	123.0	76 Ty Cobb, 1916	103.0
77 Willie Mays, 1959	123.0	77 Al Simmons, 1930	102.9
78 Babe Ruth, 1924	122.9	78 Johnny Mize, 1947	102.9
79 Rocky Colavito, 1961	122.9	79 Joe Rudi, 1972	102.5
80 Hank Aaron, 1957	122.9	80 Jimmie Foxx, 1939	102.5
81 Mel Ott, 1942	122.5	81 **Barry Bonds, 1993**	102.4
82 **Sammy Sosa, 2002**	122.3	82 Wade Boggs, 1988	102.4
83 Augie Galan, 1935	122.3	83 Dick Allen, 1966	102.4
84 Lou Gehrig, 1926	122.2	84 Ken Griffey Sr., 1976	102.4
85 Rogers Hornsby, 1927	122.2	85 Babe Ruth, 1931	102.3
86 Jose Canseco, 1991	122.2	86 Joe Morgan, 1972	102.3
87 Derek Jeter, 1998	121.9	87 **Barry Bonds, 2001**	102.3
88 Rogers Hornsby, 1922	121.9	88 Eddie Collins, 1912	102.3
89 Cal Ripken Jr., 1983	121.9	89 Stan Musial, 1948	102.3
90 Pepper Martin, 1933	121.8	90 Rogers Hornsby, 1927	102.1
91 Dale Murphy, 1983	121.8	91 Joe DiMaggio, 1937	102.1
92 Lou Gehrig, 1928	121.8	92 Frank Chance, 1906	102.1
93 **Rafael Furcal, 2003**	121.4	93 Jose Canseco, 1991	102.0
94 **Mark McGwire, 1998**	121.2	94 Mel Ott, 1942	101.9
95 Vada Pinson, 1959	121.2	95 **Alex Rodriguez, 1996**	101.9
96 Willie Mays, 1963	121.1	96 Ty Cobb, 1918	101.8
97 **Ray Durham, 1998**	121.0	97 Jim McTamany, 1890	101.8
98 Lonnie Smith, 1982	120.9	98 George Gore, 1890	101.6
99 **Derek Jeter, 2002**	120.9	99 Tim Raines, 1983	101.6
100 George Burns, 1920	120.8	100 **Sammy Sosa, 2002**	101.6

Note: Seasons from the power era, 1993-2003, are shown in bold.

Table L.6   Single-Season RBIs Top 100

Adjusted RBIs		Adjusted RBIs per 550 NFPs	
1 Lou Gehrig, 1931	149.5	1 Oyster Burns, 1890	132.9
2 Lou Gehrig, 1927	148.3	2 Jeff Bagwell, 1994	125.8
3 Don Mattingly, 1985	145.3	3 Juan Gonzalez, 2001	124.6
4 Joe Medwick, 1937	144.5	4 Cap Anson, 1886	124.5
5 Sammy Sosa, 2001	143.7	5 Sam Thompson, 1895	123.7
6 Babe Ruth, 1921	142.9	6 Sam Thompson, 1887	123.0
7 Hank Greenberg, 1935	142.7	7 Manny Ramirez, 1999	122.5
8 George Foster, 1977	141.2	8 George Brett, 1980	122.2
9 Manny Ramirez, 1999	140.6	9 Jim Gentile, 1961	122.1
10 Al Rosen, 1953	140.2	10 Gavy Cravath, 1913	121.1
11 Albert Belle, 1998	139.8	11 Babe Ruth, 1929	120.1
12 Babe Ruth, 1927	139.7	12 Lee May, 1976	119.8
13 Rogers Hornsby, 1922	139.3	13 Ty Cobb, 1907	118.8
14 Tommy Davis, 1962	139.2	14 Kevin Mitchell, 1989	118.7
15 Joe Torre, 1971	138.8	15 Willie Stargell, 1971	118.2
16 Lou Gehrig, 1934	138.3	16 Sam Thompson, 1894	118.2
17 Bret Boone, 2001	138.1	17 Joe Medwick, 1937	117.5
18 Cecil Fielder, 1990	137.7	18 Lou Gehrig, 1927	117.2
19 Ty Cobb, 1907	136.9	19 Dick Allen, 1972	116.9
20 Hank Greenberg, 1937	136.8	20 Sherry Magee, 1910	116.9
21 Hack Wilson, 1930	136.7	21 Ty Cobb, 1908	116.9
22 Kevin Mitchell, 1989	136.6	22 Dave Kingman, 1984	116.7
23 Sammy Sosa, 1998	136.2	23 Gavvy Cravath, 1915	115.9
24 Harmon Killebrew, 1969	136.1	24 Cap Anson, 1885	115.7
25 Joe DiMaggio, 1948	136.1	25 George Kelly, 1924	115.7
26 Don Baylor, 1979	136.1	26 Mickey Mantle, 1964	115.1
27 Jimmie Foxx, 1933	135.3	27 George Davis, 1897	115.1
28 Joe DiMaggio, 1937	135.2	28 Boog Powell, 1966	114.7
29 Dan Brouthers, 1892	135.2	29 Babe Ruth, 1926	114.2
30 Ted Williams, 1949	135.2	30 George Foster, 1977	114.1
31 Juan Gonzalez, 1998	134.8	31 Babe Ruth, 1921	114.1
32 Vern Stephens, 1949	134.8	32 Boog Powell, 1969	114.0
33 Hank Aaron, 1963	134.7	33 Babe Ruth, 1919	114.0
34 Carlos Delgado, 2003	134.3	34 Heinie Zimmerman, 1917	113.9
35 Bill Nicholson, 1943	133.9	35 Honus Wagner, 1908	113.6
36 Jim Rice, 1978	133.8	36 Babe Ruth, 1927	113.5
37 Jose Canseco, 1988	133.6	37 Cecil Fielder, 1990	113.4
38 Babe Ruth, 1926	133.3	38 Willie Stargell, 1972	113.4
39 Ken Williams, 1922	132.9	39 Heinie Zimmerman, 1913	113.2
40 Sherry Magee, 1910	132.9	40 Sammy Sosa, 2001	113.1
41 Jimmie Foxx, 1932	132.7	41 Bret Boone, 2001	113.0
42 Babe Ruth, 1931	132.7	42 Hack Wilson, 1932	112.8
43 Roger Maris, 1961	132.7	43 Juan Gonzalez, 1998	112.7
44 Mark McGwire, 1998	132.2	44 Don Mattingly, 1985	112.5
45 Ty Cobb, 1908	132.0	45 Sam Crawford, 1910	112.5
46 Jim Gentile, 1961	131.7	46 Jim Gentile, 1960	112.4
47 Jimmie Foxx, 1938	131.4	47 Reggie Jackson, 1973	112.4
48 Enos Slaughter, 1946	131.3	48 Mike Donlin, 1908	112.1
49 Juan Gonzalez, 2001	131.1	49 Al Rosen, 1953	112.1
50 Sam Thompson, 1887	131.1	50 George Foster, 1981	112.1

Table L.6 *(continued)*

Adjusted RBIs		Adjusted RBIs per 550 NFPs	
51 Lou Gehrig, 1930	130.6	51 Boog Powell, 1964	112.0
52 **Ken Griffey Jr, 1997**	130.4	52 Joe Kelley, 1898	112.0
53 Johnny Bench, 1970	130.3	53 Henry Larkin, 1892	111.9
54 Frank Robinson, 1966	130.3	54 Willie McCovey, 1968	111.9
55 Johnny Bench, 1974	130.1	55 Joe DiMaggio, 1948	111.9
56 Frank Howard, 1970	130.0	56 Dave Orr, 1890	111.7
57 Ted Williams, 1942	130.0	57 Hank Aaron, 1971	111.7
58 Cecil Fielder, 1991	130.0	58 Lou Gehrig, 1931	111.7
59 Lou Gehrig, 1937	129.6	59 Frank Baker, 1913	111.6
60 Honus Wagner, 1908	129.5	60 **Javy Lopez, 2003**	111.3
61 **Ken Griffey Jr, 1998**	129.4	61 Joe Adcock, 1956	111.3
62 Frank Howard, 1968	129.4	62 **Albert Belle, 1998**	111.3
63 Gavvy Cravath, 1915	129.3	63 Frank Howard, 1962	111.2
64 Frank Baker, 1913	129.2	64 Joe DiMaggio, 1940	111.2
65 **Manny Ramirez, 1998**	129.2	65 Honus Wagner, 1909	111.2
66 George Kelly, 1924	129.2	66 Al Simmons, 1929	111.2
67 Willie Stargell, 1971	129.1	67 Rogers Hornsby, 1922	111.2
68 Sam Thompson, 1895	129.1	68 Hank Greenberg, 1935	111.2
69 Dick Allen, 1972	128.8	69 **Jeff Kent, 1998**	111.1
70 Jeff Burroughs, 1974	128.8	70 Jimmie Foxx, 1933	111.1
71 Gavy Cravath, 1913	128.3	71 Fred Whitfield, 1965	111.0
72 **Edgar Martinez, 2000**	128.3	72 John Mayberry, 1972	110.9
73 **Tino Martinez, 1997**	128.2	73 Nap Lajoie, 1904	110.8
74 Sam Crawford, 1910	128.1	74 Frank Baker, 1912	110.5
75 Cecil Cooper, 1983	128.0	75 Lou Gehrig, 1934	110.3
76 Hank Aaron, 1957	128.0	76 Roger Connor, 1889	110.1
77 Oyster Burns, 1890	127.3	77 Babe Ruth, 1931	110.1
78 Frank Baker, 1912	127.2	78 George Foster, 1976	110.0
79 Reggie Jackson, 1973	127.1	79 Ty Cobb, 1909	109.9
80 Dave Kingman, 1984	127.1	80 Duke Farrell, 1891	109.9
81 Johnny Bench, 1972	127.1	81 Larry Hisle, 1978	109.9
82 Carl Yastrzemski, 1967	127.0	82 Ken Williams, 1922	109.8
83 Ed Delahanty, 1899	127.0	83 **Kirby Puckett, 1994**	109.7
84 Yogi Berra, 1954	127.0	84 Frank Robinson, 1971	109.7
85 Cecil Fielder, 1992	126.6	85 Joe Rudi, 1976	109.5
86 Mike Donlin, 1908	126.6	86 Luke Easter, 1952	109.5
87 Cap Anson, 1886	126.6	87 Ken Harrelson, 1968	109.5
88 Hal McRae, 1982	126.0	88 **Jay Buhner, 1995**	109.5
89 Rocky Colavito, 1961	125.8	89 Wally Berger, 1933	109.4
90 Nap Lajoie, 1898	125.7	90 Tommy Davis, 1962	109.3
91 Joe Medwick, 1936	125.6	91 Johnny Bench, 1972	109.2
92 Boog Powell, 1969	125.6	92 Ed Delahanty, 1899	109.1
93 **Jeff Bagwell, 1997**	125.4	93 Spud Johnson, 1890	109.1
94 Babe Ruth, 1929	125.4	94 Gary Carter, 1986	109.0
95 Ty Cobb, 1909	125.3	95 Jeff Burroughs, 1974	109.0
96 **Mark McGwire, 1999**	125.3	96 Mark McGwire, 1992	109.0
97 **Alex Rodriguez, 2002**	125.3	97 Joe Torre, 1971	108.9
98 Lou Gehrig, 1932	125.3	98 Al Simmons, 1930	108.9
99 **Barry Bonds, 2001**	125.2	99 Dave Orr, 1885	108.8
100 Lou Gehrig, 1933	125.2	100 **Edgar Martinez, 2001**	108.8

Note: Seasons from the power era, 1993-2003, are shown in bold.

Table L.7   Single-Season Bases on Balls Top 100

Adjusted BBs		Adjusted BBs per 550 NFPs	
1 Barry Bonds, 2002	192.5	1 Barry Bonds, 2002	173.6
2 Barry Bonds, 2001	182.1	2 Barry Bonds, 2001	151.3
3 Mark McGwire, 1998	158.8	3 Barry Bonds, 2003	144.3
4 Babe Ruth, 1923	157.9	4 John McGraw, 1899	138.3
5 Eddie Mathews, 1963	151.1	5 Babe Ruth, 1920	135.1
6 Barry Bonds, 1996	150.4	6 Jack Clark, 1987	133.7
7 Babe Ruth, 1920	150.1	7 Candy Nelson, 1884	133.3
8 Ted Williams, 1947	144.9	8 Ted Williams, 1954	133.1
9 Barry Bonds, 2003	143.8	9 Mickey Mantle, 1962	131.7
10 Ted Williams, 1946	143.6	10 Mark McGwire, 1998	129.0
11 Babe Ruth, 1921	143.4	11 Yank Robinson, 1888	128.7
12 Jimmy Wynn, 1969	141.7	12 Jack Crooks, 1892	127.9
13 Eddie Stanky, 1945	141.0	13 Toby Harrah, 1985	127.5
14 Mel Ott, 1932	139.5	14 Jack Clark, 1989	126.2
15 Topsy Hartsel, 1907	139.2	15 Topsy Hartsel, 1907	124.9
16 Mickey Mantle, 1957	139.0	16 Babe Ruth, 1923	124.8
17 Barry Bonds, 1997	138.9	17 Eddie Mathews, 1963	123.7
18 Ted Williams, 1942	138.4	18 Barry Bonds, 1996	123.7
19 Gary Sheffield, 1996	138.2	19 Mickey Mantle, 1957	123.3
20 Topsy Hartsel, 1905	138.1	20 Roy Thomas, 1902	121.0
21 Jeff Bagwell, 1999	137.7	21 Jimmy Wynn, 1969	120.7
22 Harmon Killebrew, 1967	136.8	22 Topsy Hartsel, 1908	119.1
23 Yank Robinson, 1888	136.4	23 Jimmy Wynn, 1976	118.7
24 Jimmy Sheckard, 1911	136.3	24 Max Bishop, 1927	118.5
25 Jeff Bagwell, 1996	136.0	25 Ted Williams, 1946	117.6
26 Babe Ruth, 1927	135.8	26 John McGraw, 1897	117.5
27 Jack Crooks, 1892	135.6	27 Barry Bonds, 1992	116.3
28 Ted Williams, 1951	135.5	28 Ted Williams, 1941	116.0
29 Frank Thomas, 1991	135.1	29 Miller Huggins, 1913	115.7
30 John McGraw, 1899	135.1	30 Max Bishop, 1930	115.7
31 Jack Clark, 1989	134.9	31 Ted Williams, 1947	115.2
32 Jack Clark, 1987	134.9	32 Topsy Hartsel, 1905	115.1
33 Arky Vaughan, 1936	134.1	33 Rickey Henderson, 1996	114.5
34 Roy Thomas, 1902	134.0	34 Mel Ott, 1932	114.5
35 Babe Ruth, 1924	133.5	35 Babe Ruth, 1921	114.5
36 Babe Ruth, 1928	133.5	36 Ted Williams, 1957	114.4
37 Wade Boggs, 1988	132.0	37 Bob O'Farrell, 1922	114.0
38 Jason Giambi, 2003	131.7	38 Mel Ott, 1939	113.7
39 Dolph Camilli, 1936	131.6	39 Gene Tenace, 1977	113.7
40 Babe Ruth, 1926	130.3	40 Ted Williams, 1942	113.5
41 Harmon Killebrew, 1969	130.0	41 Gary Sheffield, 1996	113.3
42 Barry Bonds, 1993	130.0	42 Willie Mays, 1971	112.3
43 Lenny Dykstra, 1993	129.8	43 Mickey Mantle, 1967	112.2
44 Rickey Henderson, 1989	129.8	44 Roy Cullenbine, 1947	112.0
45 Barry Bonds, 1998	129.6	45 Max Bishop, 1926	111.7
46 Jason Giambi, 2001	129.6	46 Babe Ruth, 1926	111.6
47 Brian Giles, 2002	129.6	47 Brian Giles, 2002	111.5
48 Roy Thomas, 1900	128.9	48 Dolph Camilli, 1936	111.5
49 Babe Ruth, 1930	128.9	49 Barry Bonds, 1997	111.5
50 Elbie Fletcher, 1940	128.7	50 Babe Ruth, 1932	111.3

Table L.7   *(continued)*

Adjusted BBs		Adjusted BBs per 550 NFPs	
51 Ted Williams, 1949	128.1	51 Mickey Mantle, 1968	111.2
52 Barry Bonds, 1992	128.0	52 Joe Morgan, 1966	110.9
53 Ted Williams, 1941	127.8	53 Elbie Fletcher, 1940	110.9
54 Roy Thomas, 1899	127.3	54 Max Bishop, 1933	110.8
55 John Mayberry, 1973	126.9	55 Roy Thomas, 1901	110.7
56 Eddie Yost, 1959	126.9	56 Harmon Killebrew, 1967	110.5
57 Mickey Mantle, 1958	126.6	57 Ted Williams, 1951	110.4
58 Ted Williams, 1954	126.6	58 Babe Ruth, 1927	110.3
59 Donie Bush, 1912	126.2	59 John Mayberry, 1973	110.1
60 Mel Ott, 1936	126.1	60 Donie Bush, 1912	110.0
61 Eddie Yost, 1956	125.7	61 Eddie Stanky, 1945	109.7
62 Richie Ashburn, 1960	125.6	62 Wes Westrum, 1951	109.6
63 Jimmy Sheckard, 1912	125.6	63 Arky Vaughan, 1935	109.5
64 Lou Gehrig, 1935	125.3	64 George Gore, 1886	109.3
65 **Rickey Henderson, 1996**	124.9	65 Roy Thomas, 1904	109.2
66 Candy Nelson, 1884	124.8	66 Billy Lush, 1903	109.1
67 Eddie Stanky, 1950	124.6	67 Jimmy Sheckard, 1911	108.8
68 Jimmy Wynn, 1976	124.3	68 Babe Ruth, 1924	108.8
69 Ralph Kiner, 1951	123.5	69 Babe Ruth, 1934	108.8
70 **Jason Giambi, 2000**	123.4	70 Babe Ruth, 1928	108.6
71 Mike Schmidt, 1983	123.3	71 Eddie Stanky, 1946	108.5
72 Frank Howard, 1970	123.2	72 Mel Ott, 1943	108.5
73 Darrell Porter, 1979	122.9	73 Rogers Hornsby, 1928	108.4
74 Carl Yastrzemski, 1968	122.9	74 Jimmy Wynn, 1975	108.4
75 John McGraw, 1898	122.8	75 Johnny Evers, 1910	108.4
76 **Jeff Bagwell, 1997**	122.8	76 Jack Clark, 1988	108.2
77 Eddie Stanky, 1946	122.7	77 Babe Ruth, 1930	108.2
78 Roy Cullenbine, 1947	122.4	78 Billy Lush, 1902	107.7
79 **Tony Phillips, 1993**	122.3	79 **Jim Thome, 2002**	107.7
80 Dolph Camilli, 1938	122.0	80 **Jason Giambi, 2001**	107.6
81 Joe Morgan, 1975	121.6	81 Elmer Valo, 1952	107.4
82 Hack Wilson, 1930	121.6	82 Mel Ott, 1944	107.4
83 Fred McGriff, 1989	121.4	83 Max Bishop, 1929	107.4
84 Willie Randolph, 1980	121.4	84 **Gary Sheffield, 1997**	107.3
85 Mel Ott, 1938	121.1	85 Roy Thomas, 1900	107.3
86 **Frank Thomas, 1995**	120.9	86 **Frank Thomas, 1994**	107.3
87 Max Bishop, 1930	120.9	87 **Barry Bonds, 1993**	107.2
88 Bob Elliott, 1948	120.9	88 Mickey Mantle, 1958	107.1
89 Richie Ashburn, 1954	120.8	89 Willie McCovey, 1973	107.0
90 Eddie Yost, 1952	120.6	90 Babe Ruth, 1919	106.9
91 Rogers Hornsby, 1924	120.4	91 Dolph Camilli, 1938	106.9
92 John Mayberry, 1975	120.3	92 Max Bishop, 1932	106.9
93 Jack Clark, 1988	120.2	93 Mel Ott, 1936	106.7
94 Billy Hamilton, 1900	120.1	94 Arky Vaughan, 1936	106.7
95 Arky Vaughan, 1935	120.1	95 Rickey Henderson, 1989	106.5
96 Eddie Yost, 1953	120.0	96 Frank Thomas, 1991	106.4
97 Eddie Yost, 1954	120.0	97 Jimmy Sheckard, 1912	106.2
98 Mel Ott, 1930	119.9	98 Gene Tenace, 1978	106.1
99 Harmon Killebrew, 1970	119.8	99 John Kruk, 1988	106.1
100 Topsy Hartsel, 1908	119.8	100 Gene Tenace, 1974	106.1

Note: Seasons from the power era, 1993-2003, are shown in bold.

Table L.8   Single-Season Strikeouts Top 100

Most Adjusted SOs		Fewest Adjusted SOs per 550 NFPs	
1 Gary Alexander, 1978	187.6	1 Joe Sewell, 1932	6.8
2 Dave Nicholson, 1963	182.6	2 Joe Sewell, 1933	8.7
3 Jack McCandless, 1915	181.2	3 Tony Gwynn, 1995	10.0
4 Reggie Jackson, 1983	176.2	4 Tony Gwynn, 1992	12.5
5 Boze Berger, 1935	169.3	5 Tony Gwynn, 1996	13.0
6 Jimmy Smith, 1915	165.3	6 Joe Sewell, 1929	13.2
7 Tom Daly, 1893	165.0	7 Don Mueller, 1956	13.4
8 Benji Gil, 1995	164.7	8 Ozzie Smith, 1993	13.6
9 Gus Williams, 1914	164.4	9 Tony Gwynn, 1998	13.8
10 Byron Browne, 1966	164.4	10 Charlie Hollocher, 1922	14.8
11 Steve Balboni, 1984	164.4	11 Tony Gwynn, 1991	14.8
12 Vince DiMaggio, 1938	162.6	12 Nellie Fox, 1964	15.5
13 Gorman Thomas, 1979	162.2	13 Tony Gwynn, 1993	15.8
14 Tom Brown, 1894	160.9	14 Joe Sewell, 1925	15.8
15 Bo Jackson, 1988	160.8	15 Nellie Fox, 1962	15.9
16 Sam Chapman, 1938	160.5	16 Tim Foli, 1979	16.1
17 Danny Walton, 1970	160.1	17 Dave Cash, 1976	16.4
18 Bo Jackson, 1989	159.8	18 Dan Brouthers, 1889	16.4
19 Bobby Darwin, 1972	159.4	19 Tony Gwynn, 1997	16.5
20 Pat Seerey, 1945	157.7	20 Felix Fermin, 1993	16.6
21 Melvin Nieves, 1996	157.2	21 Tony Gwynn, 1990	17.1
22 Gorman Thomas, 1978	157.0	22 Nellie Fox, 1961	17.1
23 Mike Schmidt, 1973	156.6	23 Jack Doyle, 1894	17.3
24 Reggie Jackson, 1971	156.4	24 Red Schoendienst, 1957	17.4
25 Pete Incaviglia, 1988	155.9	25 Tony Gwynn, 1994	17.5
26 Howie Goss, 1963	155.7	26 Nellie Fox, 1958	17.7
27 Jimmy Dykes, 1922	155.3	27 Jack Glasscock, 1890	17.7
28 Rob Deer, 1993	154.8	28 Stuffy McInnis, 1924	18.1
29 Jimmie Foxx, 1936	154.2	29 Ozzie Guillen, 1997	18.2
30 Ray Powell, 1919	153.9	30 Barry Larkin, 1988	18.4
31 Don Lock, 1966	153.8	31 Don Mueller, 1955	18.6
32 Wes Westrum, 1951	153.7	32 John Ward, 1893	18.6
33 Dave Kingman, 1975	153.6	33 Tony Gwynn, 1984	18.9
34 Jose Hernandez, 2003	153.5	34 Nellie Fox, 1957	19.0
35 Vince DiMaggio, 1943	152.7	35 Nellie Fox, 1959	19.1
36 Pancho Herrera, 1961	152.7	36 Mark Grace, 2000	19.1
37 Adolfo Phillips, 1966	152.4	37 Gus Getz, 1915	19.2
38 Frank Parkinson, 1922	152.1	38 Nellie Fox, 1960	19.3
39 Rob Deer, 1986	151.9	39 Juan Pierre, 2001	19.6
40 Reggie Jackson, 1970	151.3	40 Doc Cramer, 1943	19.7
41 Vince DiMaggio, 1945	151.3	41 Gary DiSarcina, 1997	19.7
42 Gorman Thomas, 1980	150.3	42 Nellie Fox, 1956	19.8
43 Rob Deer, 1991	150.1	43 Bob Bailor, 1978	19.8
44 Hack Wilson, 1928	150.1	44 Gregg Jefferies, 1997	19.8
45 Ray Lankford, 2000	150.0	45 Tris Speaker, 1915	19.9
46 Dave Kingman, 1976	149.9	46 Rich Dauer, 1980	19.9
47 Reggie Jackson, 1968	149.7	47 John Ward, 1889	20.1
48 Babe Ruth, 1922	148.9	48 Bill Sweeney, 1914	20.1
49 Butch Hobson, 1977	148.8	49 Bill Buckner, 1980	20.1
50 Dave Kingman, 1982	148.8	50 Tony Gwynn, 1989	20.2

Table L.8 *(continued)*

Most Adjusted SOs		Fewest Adjusted SOs per 550 NFPs	
51 Andres Galarraga, 1990	148.7	51 Nellie Fox, 1963	20.3
52 **Jose Hernandez, 2002**	148.7	52 Dale Mitchell, 1952	20.3
53 Jerry Martin, 1982	148.3	53 Stuffy McInnis, 1922	20.3
54 Ron Kittle, 1983	148.0	54 Joe Sewell, 1931	20.3
55 Tom Brown, 1893	147.9	55 **Eric Young, 1999**	20.3
56 Mike Schmidt, 1975	147.6	56 Nellie Fox, 1954	20.6
57 Jimmie Foxx, 1941	146.9	57 Johnny Evers, 1913	20.6
58 Dale Murphy, 1978	146.5	58 Joe Sewell, 1926	20.7
59 Tony Armas, 1981	146.4	59 Emil Verban, 1947	20.7
60 Chet Ross, 1940	146.3	60 Tommy Holmes, 1945	20.8
61 Rob Deer, 1989	146.0	61 Ozzie Smith, 1984	21.0
62 Rob Deer, 1992	145.7	62 Matty Alou, 1970	21.0
63 Tom Brown, 1890	145.7	63 Glenn Beckert, 1968	21.0
64 Dave Kingman, 1978	145.1	64 Harvey Kuenn, 1954	21.1
65 Rob Deer, 1987	145.1	65 Bill Buckner, 1986	21.2
66 Wally Post, 1956	144.5	66 **Gregg Jefferies, 1995**	21.2
67 Vince DiMaggio, 1937	144.4	67 **Gregg Jefferies, 1998**	21.4
68 Reggie Jackson, 1978	144.2	68 Frankie Frisch, 1934	21.4
69 Ed McDonald, 1912	144.0	69 Johnny Ray, 1985	21.4
70 **Ron Karkovice, 1993**	143.5	70 **Eric Young, 1996**	21.5
71 Darryl Strawberry, 1983	143.3	71 Joe DiMaggio, 1941	21.5
72 Reggie Jackson, 1982	143.3	72 Vic Power, 1958	21.6
73 Gus Zernial, 1950	143.2	73 Vic Power, 1961	21.7
74 George Treadway, 1893	143.1	74 Mike Scioscia, 1987	21.7
75 George Kelly, 1920	142.9	75 **Fernando Vina, 2001**	21.8
76 Aaron Ward, 1920	142.7	76 **Juan Pierre, 2003**	21.9
77 Red Shannon, 1919	142.5	77 **Paul Lo Duca, 2002**	22.0
78 Tom McCreery, 1896	142.5	78 **Randall Simon, 2002**	22.0
79 Bo Jackson, 1990	142.4	79 Bobby Richardson, 1963	22.0
80 Gus Zernial, 1955	141.9	80 Pie Traynor, 1929	22.2
81 Bruce Campbell, 1932	141.7	81 Felix Millan, 1974	22.3
82 Jim Thome, 2001	141.6	82 **Jason Kendall, 2002**	22.4
83 John Morrill, 1887	141.5	83 Freddy Leach, 1931	22.4
84 Ralph Kiner, 1946	141.3	84 Lou Boudreau, 1948	22.5
85 **Ray Lankford, 2001**	141.1	85 Charlie Gehringer, 1936	22.5
86 Grover Gilmore, 1914	140.9	86 Mark Grace, 1993	22.5
87 Pat Seerey, 1946	140.8	87 Bobby Richardson, 1966	22.7
88 Bill Joyce, 1890	140.6	88 Billy Goodman, 1953	22.7
89 **Jose Hernandez, 2001**	140.5	89 Lou Boudreau, 1946	22.7
90 Ron Kittle, 1984	140.5	90 **Lance Johnson, 1996**	22.7
91 Steve Balboni, 1985	140.3	91 **Ozzie Guillen, 1996**	22.7
92 Larry Hisle, 1970	140.2	92 Nellie Fox, 1955	22.7
93 Larry Doby, 1953	140.0	93 Red Schoendienst, 1956	22.8
94 **Jim Thome, 1999**	140.0	94 Mickey Cochrane, 1929	22.8
95 Eddie Mathews, 1952	139.9	95 **David Eckstein, 2002**	22.9
96 Pete Incaviglia, 1986	139.8	96 **Lance Johnson, 1995**	22.9
97 **Ruben Rivera, 1999**	139.7	97 Ozzie Smith, 1986	23.1
98 Hank Greenberg, 1933	139.6	98 George Brett, 1977	23.1
99 Leroy Stanton, 1974	139.5	99 **Joey Cora, 1996**	23.1
100 Pancho Herrera, 1960	139.2	100 Sam Rice, 1929	23.1

Table L.9   Single-Season Stolen Bases Top 100

Adjusted SBs		Adjusted SBs per 550 NFPs	
1 Ty Cobb, 1915	146.2	1 Ty Cobb, 1915	116.3
2 Maury Wills, 1962	145.7	2 Max Carey, 1918	112.3
3 Rickey Henderson, 1982	126.3	3 Maury Wills, 1962	107.2
4 **Juan Pierre, 2003**	120.5	4 Rickey Henderson, 1982	106.2
5 Sam Rice, 1920	117.1	5 George Case, 1944	97.0
6 Maury Wills, 1965	116.5	6 Sam Rice, 1920	96.5
7 Luis Aparicio, 1959	114.4	7 George Case, 1939	95.9
8 Ben Chapman, 1931	110.3	8 Otis Nixon, 1991	95.0
9 Max Carey, 1918	109.0	9 Luis Aparicio, 1964	94.3
10 Jackie Robinson, 1949	108.8	10 Luis Aparicio, 1959	94.2
11 Luis Aparicio, 1964	108.0	11 Frank Chance, 1903	93.1
12 Vince Coleman, 1985	107.0	12 Maury Wills, 1965	92.3
13 George Sisler, 1922	105.9	13 George Sisler, 1922	91.3
14 Rickey Henderson, 1980	105.3	14 Rickey Henderson, 1983	91.2
15 Kiki Cuyler, 1930	105.0	15 **Juan Pierre, 2003**	91.1
16 Snuffy Stirnweiss, 1944	104.9	16 Billy Hamilton, 1891	90.2
17 Benny Kauff, 1914	104.4	17 Bill Bruton, 1954	89.8
18 Billy Hamilton, 1891	104.4	18 Ben Chapman, 1931	89.2
19 George Case, 1943	104.0	19 Eddie Collins, 1923	89.1
20 Lou Brock, 1974	103.6	20 Benny Kauff, 1914	88.2
21 Rickey Henderson, 1983	102.8	21 Jackie Robinson, 1949	87.1
22 George Case, 1939	102.2	22 George Case, 1943	87.1
23 Luis Aparicio, 1960	100.0	23 **Roger Cedeno, 1999**	87.1
24 Bill Bruton, 1954	99.8	24 George Case, 1942	86.5
25 **Kenny Lofton, 1996**	99.4	25 Pete Reiser, 1946	86.2
26 Max Carey, 1922	98.1	26 Vince Coleman, 1985	85.8
27 Lou Brock, 1966	97.9	27 Luis Aparicio, 1960	85.4
28 Vince Coleman, 1987	97.2	28 Ty Cobb, 1916	85.4
29 Sam Jethroe, 1950	97.1	29 Billy Hamilton, 1898	84.9
30 Luis Aparicio, 1961	96.8	30 Kiki Cuyler, 1928	84.1
31 Vince Coleman, 1986	96.8	31 Sam Jethroe, 1950	83.6
32 Ty Cobb, 1916	96.6	32 Jim Rivera, 1955	83.5
33 Rickey Henderson, 1988	96.5	33 **Tom Goodwin, 1996**	83.5
34 Max Carey, 1916	96.3	34 Jim Fogarty, 1889	83.1
35 Wally Moses, 1943	96.2	35 Rickey Henderson, 1988	83.0
36 Eddie Collins, 1923	96.1	36 **Luis Castillo, 2000**	82.4
37 Bert Campaneris, 1967	95.5	37 Eric Davis, 1986	82.2
38 Frankie Frisch, 1927	95.1	38 John McGraw, 1899	82.2
39 Willie Mays, 1956	95.1	39 Richie Ashburn, 1948	82.1
40 Rickey Henderson, 1986	94.2	40 Lou Brock, 1974	81.6
41 Clyde Milan, 1912	93.0	41 Bert Campaneris, 1967	81.6
42 Johnny Mostil, 1925	92.9	42 Kiki Cuyler, 1929	81.4
43 **Luis Castillo, 2000**	92.5	43 Rickey Henderson, 1980	81.3
44 Luis Aparicio, 1963	91.9	44 Honus Wagner, 1907	81.1
45 Jackie Robinson, 1947	91.6	45 Harry Stovey, 1890	81.1
46 George Case, 1944	91.0	46 Max Carey, 1925	81.0
47 George Case, 1941	90.7	47 Willie Mays, 1956	80.8
48 Ty Cobb, 1909	90.2	48 Wally Moses, 1943	80.8
49 Max Carey, 1925	90.1	49 Snuffy Stirnweiss, 1944	80.5
50 Lou Brock, 1968	89.9	50 Vince Coleman, 1986	80.4

Table L.9 *(continued)*

Adjusted SBs		Adjusted SBs per 550 NFPs	
51 Ty Cobb, 1911	89.6	51 Luis Aparicio, 1961	80.2
52 George Case, 1940	89.6	52 Vince Coleman, 1990	80.0
53 Frank Chance, 1903	89.5	53 Kiki Cuyler, 1930	79.8
54 Tommy Harper, 1969	89.1	54 Max Carey, 1916	79.7
55 **Brian Hunter, 1997**	89.0	55 Lou Brock, 1966	79.6
56 Billy Hamilton, 1895	88.9	56 Luis Aparicio, 1963	79.1
57 Willie Wilson, 1980	88.7	57 Ty Cobb, 1909	79.1
58 **Tony Womack, 1999**	88.6	58 Billy Hamilton, 1895	78.9
59 Maury Wills, 1964	88.5	59 Dave Collins, 1984	78.7
60 Willie Wilson, 1979	88.1	60 **Dave Roberts, 2002**	78.7
61 George Case, 1942	88.1	61 Billy Hamilton, 1890	78.6
62 Bob Dillinger, 1947	87.5	62 George Sisler, 1918	78.5
63 Omar Moreno, 1979	87.5	63 Maury Wills, 1960	78.5
64 Lou Brock, 1971	87.1	64 Frankie Frisch, 1927	78.4
65 Lou Brock, 1965	87.0	65 Rudy Law, 1983	78.1
66 Marquis Grissom, 1992	86.9	66 Pepper Martin, 1934	78.0
67 Eddie Collins, 1924	86.6	67 Dave Fultz, 1905	77.8
68 Jim Fogarty, 1889	86.3	68 Willie Wilson, 1979	77.8
69 Lou Brock, 1973	86.2	69 Ron LeFlore, 1980	77.6
70 Bob Dillinger, 1948	86.0	70 Tommy Harper, 1969	77.4
71 Kiki Cuyler, 1929	85.9	71 Danny Hoffman, 1905	76.8
72 **Tony Womack, 1998**	85.8	72 Vince Coleman, 1987	76.8
73 **Tom Goodwin, 1996**	85.7	73 Ty Cobb, 1911	76.7
74 Fritz Maisel, 1914	85.6	74 Max Carey, 1920	76.5
75 Bert Campaneris, 1965	85.4	75 Clyde Milan, 1912	76.4
76 Johnny Barrett, 1944	85.3	76 Ed Andrews, 1886	76.3
77 Kiki Cuyler, 1928	85.2	77 Jimmy Sheckard, 1903	76.3
78 Max Carey, 1924	85.1	78 Bob Dillinger, 1947	76.3
79 Eddie Collins, 1910	85.0	79 Billy Werber, 1937	76.0
80 Ron LeFlore, 1979	84.9	80 Luis Aparicio, 1958	75.9
81 Rickey Henderson, 1985	84.6	81 Max Carey, 1922	75.7
82 Frankie Frisch, 1921	84.5	82 Bert Campaneris, 1966	75.6
83 Ron LeFlore, 1978	84.5	83 **Kenny Lofton, 1996**	75.6
84 Max Carey, 1923	84.4	84 **Kenny Lofton, 1994**	75.6
85 Lyn Lary, 1936	84.0	85 Marquis Grissom, 1991	75.5
86 Billy Hamilton, 1890	84.0	86 **Tom Goodwin, 2000**	75.4
87 Harry Stovey, 1890	83.6	87 Fritz Maisel, 1914	75.2
88 Ben Chapman, 1932	83.5	88 Jackie Robinson, 1947	74.9
89 Don Buford, 1966	83.5	89 Bert Campaneris, 1965	74.8
90 Honus Wagner, 1907	83.4	90 George Case, 1946	74.4
91 Bob Bescher, 1911	83.4	91 Rickey Henderson, 1986	74.1
92 Billy Werber, 1934	83.1	92 Eddie Collins, 1910	73.5
93 Bert Campaneris, 1966	82.9	93 Eddie Collins, 1924	73.5
94 **Kenny Lofton, 1993**	82.8	94 Charlie Dexter, 1898	73.4
95 Bert Campaneris, 1968	82.8	95 Jimmy Sheckard, 1899	73.3
96 Jimmy Sheckard, 1903	82.7	96 **Tony Womack, 1999**	73.0
97 Joe Morgan, 1973	82.6	97 Gee Walker, 1932	72.9
98 Ron LeFlore, 1980	82.4	98 Bert Campaneris, 1969	72.7
99 Willie Mays, 1957	82.3	99 Maury Wills, 1964	72.5
100 **Carl Crawford, 2003**	82.2	100 Rickey Henderson, 1984	72.5

Note: Seasons from the power era, 1993-2003, are shown in bold.

Table L.10 Single-Season On-Base Percentage Top 100

Adjusted Times on Base		Adjusted OBP	
1 Barry Bonds, 2002	344.6	1 Barry Bonds, 2002	.574
2 Wade Boggs, 1988	341.6	2 Barry Bonds, 2003	.518
3 Babe Ruth, 1923	340.2	3 Barry Bonds, 2001	.512
4 Barry Bonds, 2001	338.9	4 Ted Williams, 1941	.512
5 Wade Boggs, 1985	334.6	5 Ted Williams, 1957	.504
6 Rogers Hornsby, 1924	325.7	6 John McGraw, 1899	.504
7 Babe Ruth, 1921	323.2	7 Mickey Mantle, 1957	.503
8 Ted Williams, 1947	321.9	8 Babe Ruth, 1923	.498
9 Ted Williams, 1942	318.3	9 Ted Williams, 1954	.497
10 Lenny Dykstra, 1993	317.8	10 Babe Ruth, 1920	.495
11 Jeff Bagwell, 1996	316.2	11 Rogers Hornsby, 1924	.495
12 Wade Boggs, 1989	314.8	12 Mickey Mantle, 1962	.492
13 Frank Thomas, 1991	314.3	13 Ted Williams, 1942	.479
14 Jason Giambi, 2001	312.8	14 Arky Vaughan, 1935	.478
15 Ted Williams, 1946	312.2	15 Jason Giambi, 2001	.477
16 Ted Williams, 1949	311.7	16 Ted Williams, 1947	.476
17 Ty Cobb, 1915	311.5	17 Wade Boggs, 1988	.476
18 Richie Ashburn, 1958	310.9	18 Rogers Hornsby, 1928	.475
19 Jeff Bagwell, 1999	310.4	19 Frank Thomas, 1994	.474
20 Mark McGwire, 1998	310.4	20 Ted Williams, 1946	.473
21 Mel Ott, 1932	309.6	21 Norm Cash, 1961	.472
22 Frank Thomas, 1992	308.5	22 Babe Ruth, 1921	.471
23 Lou Gehrig, 1936	308.4	23 Babe Ruth, 1926	.470
24 Arky Vaughan, 1936	308.2	24 Barry Bonds, 1992	.463
25 Mickey Mantle, 1957	308.2	25 Mark McGwire, 1998	.462
26 Barry Bonds, 1993	308.0	26 Babe Ruth, 1924	.462
27 Lou Gehrig, 1937	308.0	27 Billy Hamilton, 1898	.462
28 Norm Cash, 1961	307.9	28 John Olerud, 1993	.460
29 Babe Ruth, 1924	307.5	29 Barry Bonds, 1993	.459
30 Pete Rose, 1976	306.8	30 Barry Bonds, 1996	.459
31 Rod Carew, 1977	306.6	31 Jason Giambi, 2000	.458
32 Carlos Delgado, 2000	306.6	32 Ted Williams, 1948	.456
33 Barry Bonds, 1996	306.5	33 Joe Morgan, 1975	.456
34 John Olerud, 1993	304.8	34 Ty Cobb, 1915	.456
35 Sammy Sosa, 2001	303.7	35 Gary Sheffield, 1996	.456
36 Wade Boggs, 1986	303.4	36 Edgar Martinez, 1995	.455
37 Babe Ruth, 1927	302.7	37 Rogers Hornsby, 1925	.455
38 Gary Sheffield, 1996	302.2	38 King Kelly, 1886	.455
39 Babe Ruth, 1920	302.1	39 Babe Ruth, 1932	.454
40 Ken Singleton, 1975	301.8	40 Babe Ruth, 1931	.454
41 Woody English, 1930	301.7	41 Frank Thomas, 1991	.452
42 Derek Jeter, 1999	300.9	42 Jack Clark, 1987	.452
43 Ted Williams, 1941	300.8	43 Wade Boggs, 1987	.452
44 Augie Galan, 1935	300.8	44 Ken Singleton, 1977	.451
45 Rickey Henderson, 1980	300.5	45 George Brett, 1980	.450
46 Pete Rose, 1975	300.4	46 Frank Thomas, 1997	.450
47 Jimmie Foxx, 1932	300.3	47 Joe Morgan, 1976	.450
48 Tony Phillips, 1993	300.3	48 Eddie Collins, 1915	.449
49 Pete Rose, 1979	300.2	49 Joe Cunningham, 1959	.449
50 Carl Yastrzemski, 1970	300.0	50 Jeff Bagwell, 1994	.449

Table L.10 *(continued)*

Adjusted Times on Base		Adjusted OBP	
51 Lou Gehrig, 1927	299.9	51 Willie McCovey, 1969	.448
52 Stan Musial, 1948	299.6	52 Frank Chance, 1905	.448
53 Arky Vaughan, 1935	299.4	53 Babe Ruth, 1927	.448
54 Lou Gehrig, 1931	298.7	54 Rickey Henderson, 1990	.447
55 **Barry Bonds, 1998**	298.6	55 Babe Ruth, 1930	.447
56 Eddie Mathews, 1963	298.3	56 Ted Williams, 1949	.447
57 Cupid Childs, 1892	297.8	57 John McGraw, 1898	.447
58 Babe Ruth, 1931	297.5	58 Ted Williams, 1958	.446
59 Hack Wilson, 1930	297.5	59 Jeff Bagwell, 1996	.445
60 Stan Musial, 1949	297.2	60 Carl Yastrzemski, 1968	.445
61 Frank Robinson, 1966	297.2	61 **Carlos Delgado, 2000**	.445
62 **Barry Bonds, 1997**	296.8	62 Lou Gehrig, 1937	.445
63 Pete Rose, 1969	296.6	63 Ted Williams, 1951	.445
64 Ross Youngs, 1920	296.4	64 Rod Carew, 1977	.444
65 Wade Boggs, 1987	296.4	65 **Edgar Martinez, 1997**	.444
66 Ted Williams, 1951	296.3	66 Frank Thomas, 1992	.444
67 Eddie Murray, 1984	295.6	67 Wade Boggs, 1986	.444
68 Brett Butler, 1991	295.6	68 Toby Harrah, 1985	.443
69 Carl Yastrzemski, 1968	295.3	69 George Brett, 1985	.443
70 Rod Carew, 1974	295.2	70 Wade Boggs, 1985	.442
71 Babe Ruth, 1926	295.1	71 Babe Ruth, 1919	.442
72 Paul Molitor, 1991	294.6	72 Lou Gehrig, 1935	.442
73 Lou Gehrig, 1935	294.6	73 **Tony Gwynn, 1994**	.442
74 Hank Aaron, 1963	294.6	74 **Mark McGwire, 1996**	.442
75 Harmon Killebrew, 1967	294.5	75 **John Olerud, 1998**	.442
76 Carl Yastrzemski, 1967	294.4	76 **Jim Thome, 2002**	.441
77 Wade Boggs, 1983	294.2	77 Ted Williams, 1956	.441
78 Pete Rose, 1973	294.1	78 **Brian Giles, 2002**	.441
79 Tony Gwynn, 1987	294.0	79 Billy Hamilton, 1894	.441
80 **Edgar Martinez, 1997**	293.9	80 **Frank Thomas, 1995**	.440
81 **Luis Gonzalez, 2001**	293.7	81 Wally Moon, 1961	.440
82 Rogers Hornsby, 1927	293.5	82 **Barry Bonds, 1997**	.440
83 Ken Singleton, 1977	293.4	83 **Jeff Bagwell, 1999**	.440
84 Billy Hamilton, 1894	293.3	84 Bobby Murcer, 1971	.439
85 Topsy Hartsel, 1905	293.2	85 Mickey Mantle, 1958	.439
86 **Jason Giambi, 2000**	293.2	86 Lou Gehrig, 1936	.439
87 George Brett, 1985	293.1	87 Topsy Hartsel, 1907	.439
88 Rogers Hornsby, 1921	292.8	88 Mickey Mantle, 1961	.439
89 Mike Hargrove, 1980	292.7	89 Frank Robinson, 1966	.439
90 Lou Gehrig, 1934	292.6	90 Carl Yastrzemski, 1970	.439
91 **Todd Helton, 2003**	292.4	91 Richie Ashburn, 1955	.438
92 **Jason Giambi, 2002**	292.1	92 Mickey Mantle, 1956	.438
93 Jack Fournier, 1924	291.9	93 Tony Gwynn, 1987	.438
94 Babe Ruth, 1928	291.7	94 Billy Hamilton, 1896	.438
95 **Jeff Bagwell, 1997**	291.7	95 Cupid Childs, 1892	.438
96 Rogers Hornsby, 1922	291.5	96 Mickey Mantle, 1964	.438
97 Joe Torre, 1971	291.5	97 Mickey Cochrane, 1933	.438
98 Roy Thomas, 1899	291.5	98 Mel Ott, 1936	.437
99 Carl Yastrzemski, 1963	291.2	99 **Sammy Sosa, 2001**	.437
100 Richie Ashburn, 1954	291.1	100 **Frank Thomas, 1996**	.437

Table L.11 Single-Season Slugging Average Top 100

Adjusted Total Bases		Adjusted Slugging Average	
1 Rogers Hornsby, 1922	453.5	1 **Barry Bonds, 2001**	.829
2 Ed Delahanty, 1893	432.1	2 **Barry Bonds, 2002**	.817
3 Stan Musial, 1948	424.3	3 Babe Ruth, 1920	.801
4 Lou Gehrig, 1927	416.6	4 Babe Ruth, 1919	.769
5 Babe Ruth, 1921	414.8	5 Babe Ruth, 1921	.768
6 Joe Medwick, 1937	412.8	6 **Barry Bonds, 2003**	.750
7 Tris Speaker, 1912	408.3	7 Babe Ruth, 1923	.739
8 Buck Freeman, 1899	408.1	8 Rogers Hornsby, 1922	.728
9 Honus Wagner, 1908	401.6	9 **Jeff Bagwell, 1994**	.726
10 Bill Nicholson, 1943	396.7	10 Ed Delahanty, 1893	.726
11 **Barry Bonds, 2001**	394.5	11 Babe Ruth, 1927	.716
12 Joe DiMaggio, 1937	393.9	12 Lou Gehrig, 1927	.713
13 Jim Rice, 1978	390.4	13 Ted Williams, 1957	.713
14 Lou Gehrig, 1931	390.2	14 Babe Ruth, 1926	.711
15 Joe DiMaggio, 1948	387.3	15 Ted Williams, 1941	.708
16 Rogers Hornsby, 1921	387.1	16 Honus Wagner, 1908	.707
17 Ted Williams, 1949	386.8	17 Fred Dunlap, 1884	.707
18 Babe Ruth, 1927	386.7	18 Tris Speaker, 1912	.704
19 Babe Ruth, 1923	385.8	19 Tip O'Neill, 1887	.703
20 Jimmie Foxx, 1932	382.9	20 **Mark McGwire, 1998**	.699
21 Al Rosen, 1953	380.4	21 Ted Williams, 1947	.696
22 Jimmie Foxx, 1933	380.2	22 Stan Musial, 1948	.694
23 Carl Yastrzemski, 1967	379.8	23 Buck Freeman, 1899	.694
24 Frank Robinson, 1966	377.7	24 Ted Williams, 1942	.693
25 Hank Aaron, 1963	375.4	25 Babe Ruth, 1924	.691
26 Hank Aaron, 1957	374.9	26 Rogers Hornsby, 1924	.689
27 Frank Howard, 1968	373.5	27 Ted Williams, 1949	.683
28 **Albert Belle, 1998**	372.7	28 Kevin Mitchell, 1989	.683
29 Stan Musial, 1946	372.7	29 Rogers Hornsby, 1925	.676
30 Hank Aaron, 1959	371.3	30 George Brett, 1980	.668
31 Kevin Mitchell, 1989	370.7	31 Nap Lajoie, 1901	.668
32 Ed Delahanty, 1899	370.4	32 Tim Jordan, 1906	.665
33 Ty Cobb, 1909	369.4	33 **Barry Bonds, 1993**	.665
34 Tommy Holmes, 1945	369.3	34 Jimmie Foxx, 1933	.663
35 Rogers Hornsby, 1924	369.1	35 Ted Williams, 1954	.661
36 Hank Greenberg, 1935	368.8	36 Babe Ruth, 1931	.660
37 Jimmy Williams, 1899	368.4	37 Harry Lumley, 1906	.657
38 Ted Williams, 1947	367.4	38 Barry Bonds, 1992	.657
39 Don Mattingly, 1986	367.4	39 Carl Yastrzemski, 1967	.656
40 Babe Ruth, 1920	366.8	40 Harry Stovey, 1889	.656
41 Stan Musial, 1949	365.9	41 Frank Robinson, 1966	.656
42 Lou Gehrig, 1934	365.9	42 Ed Delahanty, 1896	.655
43 Babe Ruth, 1924	365.8	43 Willie Stargell, 1971	.655
44 Willie Mays, 1962	365.2	44 Jimmie Foxx, 1932	.654
45 Stan Musial, 1943	364.9	45 Rogers Hornsby, 1921	.654
46 Harry Stovey, 1889	364.7	46 Babe Ruth, 1928	.653
47 Tony Oliva, 1964	364.6	47 **Frank Thomas, 1994**	.653
48 Ty Cobb, 1917	364.6	48 Mickey Mantle, 1956	.653
49 **Sammy Sosa, 2001**	364.3	49 Bill Nicholson, 1943	.652
50 Al Simmons, 1925	364.1	50 Joe Medwick, 1937	.652

Table L.11   (continued)

Adjusted Total Bases		Adjusted Slugging Average	
51 Sam Crawford, 1908	363.7	51 Joe DiMaggio, 1948	.652
52 Tip O'Neill, 1887	363.5	52 Harry Stovey, 1885	.650
53 Nap Lajoie, 1901	363.2	53 Mickey Mantle, 1961	.650
54 Chuck Klein, 1933	363.0	54 Babe Ruth, 1922	.649
55 Chuck Klein, 1932	362.9	55 Mickey Mantle, 1957	.647
56 Cal Ripken Jr., 1991	362.6	56 Rogers Hornsby, 1923	.646
57 Sam Crawford, 1913	362.4	57 Joe DiMaggio, 1941	.646
58 Robin Yount, 1982	362.4	58 Dick Allen, 1972	.645
59 Frank Robinson, 1962	362.3	59 Ty Cobb, 1909	.645
60 Ted Williams, 1942	361.7	60 Mike Tiernan, 1890	.643
61 Jose Canseco, 1988	361.0	61 **Albert Belle, 1994**	.642
62 Willie Mays, 1963	360.4	62 Ted Williams, 1946	.641
63 **Albert Pujols, 2003**	360.3	63 **Jim Thome, 2002**	.640
64 **Alex Rodriguez, 2001**	360.0	64 Reggie Jackson, 1969	.639
65 **Alex Rodriguez, 2002**	359.6	65 Willie Stargell, 1973	.638
66 Willie Mays, 1964	358.9	66 **Barry Bonds, 2000**	.638
67 **Alfonso Soriano, 2002**	358.7	67 Ed Delahanty, 1899	.638
68 **Barry Bonds, 1993**	358.6	68 Edd Roush, 1918	.636
69 Lou Gehrig, 1930	358.5	69 Jim Gentile, 1961	.636
70 Tommy Davis, 1962	357.7	70 Al Rosen, 1953	.635
71 George Foster, 1977	357.5	71 Willie Mays, 1965	.635
72 Ripper Collins, 1934	356.6	72 Wally Berger, 1933	.634
73 **Sammy Sosa, 1998**	356.5	73 Joe DiMaggio, 1937	.634
74 Joe Medwick, 1936	356.5	74 Mike Schmidt, 1980	.634
75 **Bret Boone, 2001**	356.4	75 **Jason Giambi, 2001**	.632
76 Joe Medwick, 1935	356.1	76 Lou Gehrig, 1934	.632
77 Rogers Hornsby, 1929	356.0	77 Heinie Zimmerman, 1912	.632
78 **Mark McGwire, 1998**	355.6	78 **Sammy Sosa, 2001**	.631
79 Lou Gehrig, 1933	355.5	79 Charlie Hickman, 1906	.631
80 Mike Tiernan, 1890	355.3	80 Lou Gehrig, 1931	.630
81 Don Mattingly, 1985	354.8	81 **Manny Ramirez, 2000**	.629
82 Ty Cobb, 1907	354.5	82 Joe DiMaggio, 1939	.628
83 Rogers Hornsby, 1920	354.3	83 Goose Goslin, 1928	.627
84 Lou Gehrig, 1936	354.3	84 **Javy Lopez, 2003**	.626
85 Willie Mays, 1965	354.2	85 Nap Lajoie, 1904	.625
86 Bill Terry, 1932	354.1	86 Frank Howard, 1968	.625
87 Joe Torre, 1971	353.8	87 Hank Aaron, 1971	.624
88 George Sisler, 1920	353.4	88 **Mark McGwire, 1996**	.623
89 **Luis Gonzalez, 2001**	352.9	89 Dick Allen, 1974	.623
90 Ruben Sierra, 1989	352.9	90 Ty Cobb, 1910	.621
91 Cy Seymour, 1905	352.6	91 Tommy Leach, 1902	.621
92 Kirby Puckett, 1988	352.5	92 Willie Mays, 1964	.621
93 Babe Ruth, 1931	352.5	93 **Albert Belle, 1995**	.621
94 **Ken Griffey Jr, 1997**	352.4	94 Frank Robinson, 1967	.621
95 Babe Ruth, 1926	352.1	95 Ty Cobb, 1917	.620
96 **Alex Rodriguez, 1998**	352.1	96 Boog Powell, 1964	.620
97 Heinie Zimmerman, 1912	351.8	97 **Mike Piazza, 1997**	.620
98 Dave Orr, 1886	351.6	98 Dave Orr, 1885	.619
99 Andres Galarraga, 1988	351.3	99 Honus Wagner, 1909	.619
100 Reggie Jackson, 1969	350.9	100 Babe Ruth, 1929	.617

Note: Seasons from the power era, 1993-2003, are shown in bold.

Table L.12   Single-Season On-Base-Plus-Slugging Average Top 100

Adjusted OPS Units		Adjusted OPS	
1 **Barry Bonds, 2001**	888.1	1 **Barry Bonds, 2002**	1.391
2 Babe Ruth, 1921	850.5	2 **Barry Bonds, 2001**	1.340
3 Babe Ruth, 1923	844.7	3 Babe Ruth, 1920	1.296
4 **Barry Bonds, 2002**	834.9	4 **Barry Bonds, 2003**	1.268
5 Rogers Hornsby, 1922	801.6	5 Babe Ruth, 1921	1.239
6 Lou Gehrig, 1927	796.0	6 Babe Ruth, 1923	1.237
7 Ted Williams, 1947	792.1	7 Ted Williams, 1941	1.220
8 Babe Ruth, 1920	790.8	8 Ted Williams, 1957	1.216
9 Ted Williams, 1949	787.7	9 Babe Ruth, 1919	1.212
10 Babe Ruth, 1927	786.6	10 Rogers Hornsby, 1924	1.183
11 **Mark McGwire, 1998**	779.4	11 Babe Ruth, 1926	1.181
12 Ted Williams, 1942	779.1	12 **Jeff Bagwell, 1994**	1.175
13 Rogers Hornsby, 1924	779.1	13 Ted Williams, 1947	1.172
14 Stan Musial, 1948	777.6	14 Ted Williams, 1942	1.171
15 Babe Ruth, 1924	767.7	15 Babe Ruth, 1927	1.164
16 Tris Speaker, 1912	761.4	16 **Mark McGwire, 1998**	1.161
17 Lou Gehrig, 1931	758.4	17 Ted Williams, 1954	1.158
18 **Barry Bonds, 1993**	754.0	18 Babe Ruth, 1924	1.154
19 Jimmie Foxx, 1932	752.9	19 Mickey Mantle, 1957	1.149
20 **Sammy Sosa, 2001**	742.2	20 Lou Gehrig, 1927	1.144
21 Babe Ruth, 1926	741.7	21 Rogers Hornsby, 1922	1.144
22 Frank Robinson, 1966	741.3	22 Tris Speaker, 1912	1.136
23 Lou Gehrig, 1936	738.2	23 Tip O'Neill, 1887	1.134
24 Rogers Hornsby, 1921	737.6	24 Honus Wagner, 1908	1.132
25 Carl Yastrzemski, 1967	737.4	25 Ted Williams, 1949	1.131
26 Ted Williams, 1946	735.3	26 Rogers Hornsby, 1925	1.131
27 Babe Ruth, 1928	731.0	27 Fred Dunlap, 1884	1.130
28 Babe Ruth, 1931	729.6	28 Stan Musial, 1948	1.130
29 **Jason Giambi, 2001**	727.5	29 **Frank Thomas, 1994**	1.126
30 Hank Aaron, 1963	724.7	30 **Barry Bonds, 1993**	1.125
31 Jimmie Foxx, 1933	723.0	31 Barry Bonds, 1992	1.120
32 Stan Musial, 1949	723.0	32 George Brett, 1980	1.118
33 Lou Gehrig, 1934	721.6	33 Babe Ruth, 1931	1.115
34 Honus Wagner, 1908	720.0	34 Ted Williams, 1946	1.113
35 Ted Williams, 1941	717.2	35 **Jason Giambi, 2001**	1.109
36 Al Rosen, 1953	716.6	36 Ed Delahanty, 1893	1.096
37 **Carlos Delgado, 2000**	711.5	37 Frank Robinson, 1966	1.095
38 Joe Medwick, 1937	711.0	38 Carl Yastrzemski, 1967	1.092
39 Hack Wilson, 1930	710.5	39 Mickey Mantle, 1956	1.091
40 Lou Gehrig, 1930	709.0	40 Mickey Mantle, 1961	1.089
41 Bill Nicholson, 1943	708.4	41 Jimmie Foxx, 1932	1.089
42 Luis Gonzalez, 2001	708.3	42 Kevin Mitchell, 1989	1.088
43 Mel Ott, 1932	705.6	43 Jimmie Foxx, 1933	1.088
44 Stan Musial, 1946	704.6	44 Babe Ruth, 1928	1.087
45 Mickey Mantle, 1957	704.6	45 Rogers Hornsby, 1921	1.084
46 Frank Robinson, 1962	704.1	46 Nap Lajoie, 1901	1.083
47 Ed Delahanty, 1893	702.7	47 Mickey Mantle, 1962	1.083
48 Norm Cash, 1961	700.8	48 **Jim Thome, 2002**	1.081
49 Rogers Hornsby, 1929	696.6	49 Dick Allen, 1972	1.078
50 **Albert Belle, 1998**	696.4	50 Norm Cash, 1961	1.074

Table L.12   (continued)

Adjusted OPS Units		Adjusted OPS	
51 Jeff Bagwell, 1996	696.4	51 Rogers Hornsby, 1923	1.073
52 Stan Musial, 1943	695.5	52 Ted Williams, 1948	1.072
53 Jim Rice, 1978	695.2	53 Sammy Sosa, 2001	1.069
54 Harmon Killebrew, 1967	694.8	54 Arky Vaughan, 1935	1.066
55 Albert Pujols, 2003	694.6	55 Rogers Hornsby, 1928	1.065
56 Lou Gehrig, 1937	694.6	56 Mark McGwire, 1996	1.065
57 Tommy Holmes, 1945	693.9	57 Joe DiMaggio, 1941	1.064
58 Jose Canseco, 1988	693.8	58 Manny Ramirez, 2000	1.063
59 Joe DiMaggio, 1937	692.8	59 Lou Gehrig, 1934	1.063
60 Jeff Bagwell, 1997	692.2	60 Ty Cobb, 1909	1.063
61 Lou Gehrig, 1932	691.8	61 Joe Morgan, 1976	1.062
62 Rogers Hornsby, 1920	691.1	62 Barry Bonds, 2000	1.062
63 Rogers Hornsby, 1927	691.0	63 Albert Belle, 1994	1.062
64 Reggie Jackson, 1969	690.1	64 Babe Ruth, 1922	1.060
65 Lou Gehrig, 1928	689.9	65 Ed Delahanty, 1896	1.060
66 Kevin Mitchell, 1989	689.6	66 Jim Gentile, 1961	1.056
67 Barry Bonds, 1998	688.8	67 Rickey Henderson, 1990	1.054
68 Chuck Klein, 1933	688.2	68 Willie Stargell, 1971	1.053
69 Willie Mays, 1964	688.0	69 Harry Lumley, 1906	1.053
70 Frank Thomas, 1991	687.9	70 Honus Wagner, 1909	1.052
71 Chuck Klein, 1932	687.4	71 Ty Cobb, 1910	1.052
72 Frank Thomas, 1992	686.7	72 Frank Robinson, 1967	1.052
73 Barry Bonds, 1996	686.5	73 Lou Gehrig, 1936	1.051
74 Gary Sheffield, 1996	686.3	74 Babe Ruth, 1930	1.051
75 Alex Rodriguez, 2002	686.3	75 Ed Delahanty, 1899	1.050
76 Don Mattingly, 1986	686.2	76 Mike Piazza, 1997	1.050
77 Alex Rodriguez, 2001	685.9	77 Al Rosen, 1953	1.050
78 Mel Ott, 1934	685.7	78 Willie McCovey, 1969	1.049
79 Jack Fournier, 1924	684.9	79 Babe Ruth, 1932	1.048
80 Mickey Mantle, 1956	684.8	80 Reggie Jackson, 1969	1.045
81 Lou Gehrig, 1933	684.3	81 Lou Gehrig, 1928	1.045
82 Willie Mays, 1962	684.3	82 Willie Mays, 1965	1.045
83 Joe Torre, 1971	683.9	83 Joe Medwick, 1937	1.044
84 Rogers Hornsby, 1925	683.7	84 Jason Giambi, 2000	1.042
85 Barry Bonds, 2003	683.3	85 Lou Gehrig, 1930	1.041
86 Rod Carew, 1977	682.9	86 Lou Gehrig, 1931	1.040
87 John Mayberry, 1975	682.5	87 Roger Connor, 1888	1.040
88 George Brett, 1985	682.4	88 Harry Stovey, 1885	1.040
89 Mickey Mantle, 1961	681.3	89 Joe DiMaggio, 1939	1.038
90 Babe Ruth, 1930	680.6	90 Pedro Guerrero, 1985	1.037
91 Jeff Bagwell, 1999	680.5	91 Albert Pujols, 2003	1.036
92 Bill Nicholson, 1944	680.2	92 Goose Goslin, 1928	1.035
93 Hank Greenberg, 1935	679.9	93 Gary Sheffield, 1996	1.035
94 Ed Delahanty, 1899	679.1	94 Bill Nicholson, 1943	1.034
95 Wade Boggs, 1988	679.0	95 Nap Lajoie, 1904	1.034
96 Carl Yastrzemski, 1970	678.5	96 Ty Cobb, 1917	1.033
97 John Olerud, 1993	678.5	97 Carlos Delgado, 2000	1.033
98 Willie Mays, 1963	678.3	98 Bill Joyce, 1894	1.032
99 Ty Cobb, 1909	678.1	99 Boog Powell, 1964	1.031
100 Barry Bonds, 1992	678.0	100 Joe Jackson, 1913	1.031

Note: Seasons from the power era, 1993-2003, are shown in bold.

Table L.13   Single-Season Event-Specific Batting Runs Top 100

ESBRs			ESBRs per 550 NFP		
1	Barry Bonds, 2001	129.7	1	Barry Bonds, 2002	116.1
2	Barry Bonds, 2002	128.8	2	Barry Bonds, 2001	107.7
3	Babe Ruth, 1923	117.2	3	Babe Ruth, 1920	101.5
4	Babe Ruth, 1921	116.2	4	Barry Bonds, 2003	97.8
5	Babe Ruth, 1920	112.8	5	Rogers Hornsby, 1924	93.7
6	Rogers Hornsby, 1924	106.8	6	Babe Ruth, 1921	92.8
7	Ted Williams, 1947	103.1	7	Ted Williams, 1957	92.6
8	Ted Williams, 1942	102.5	8	Babe Ruth, 1923	92.6
9	Rogers Hornsby, 1922	101.6	9	Ted Williams, 1941	92.1
10	Ted Williams, 1941	101.4	10	Babe Ruth, 1919	87.4
11	Babe Ruth, 1927	100.0	11	Jeff Bagwell, 1994	85.6
12	Lou Gehrig, 1927	98.6	12	Ted Williams, 1942	84.0
13	Mark McGwire, 1998	98.5	13	Babe Ruth, 1926	83.8
14	Stan Musial, 1948	98.1	14	Fred Dunlap, 1884	83.1
15	Babe Ruth, 1926	97.8	15	Mickey Mantle, 1957	82.4
16	Babe Ruth, 1924	97.8	16	Ted Williams, 1947	81.9
17	Barry Bonds, 2003	97.4	17	Ted Williams, 1954	81.9
18	Ted Williams, 1949	97.3	18	Babe Ruth, 1927	81.2
19	Tris Speaker, 1912	95.6	19	Rogers Hornsby, 1922	81.1
20	Barry Bonds, 1993	93.2	20	Rogers Hornsby, 1925	80.6
21	Mickey Mantle, 1957	92.9	21	Mark McGwire, 1998	80.1
22	Ted Williams, 1957	91.6	22	Babe Ruth, 1924	79.7
23	Honus Wagner, 1908	90.4	23	Tip O'Neill, 1887	79.6
24	Ted Williams, 1946	90.3	24	Honus Wagner, 1908	79.3
25	Babe Ruth, 1931	90.1	25	Tris Speaker, 1912	78.7
26	Jason Giambi, 2001	89.9	26	George Brett, 1980	78.3
27	Jimmie Foxx, 1932	89.2	27	Lou Gehrig, 1927	77.9
28	Frank Robinson, 1966	89.0	28	Stan Musial, 1948	77.8
29	Carl Yastrzemski, 1967	88.3	29	Barry Bonds, 1993	76.9
30	Rogers Hornsby, 1921	86.9	30	Frank Thomas, 1994	76.4
31	Rogers Hornsby, 1925	86.3	31	Barry Bonds, 1992	75.2
32	Babe Ruth, 1919	85.7	32	Babe Ruth, 1931	74.8
33	Jimmie Foxx, 1933	85.1	33	Jason Giambi, 2001	74.7
34	Sammy Sosa, 2001	85.0	34	Ted Williams, 1946	73.9
35	Norm Cash, 1961	84.6	35	Ted Williams, 1949	73.3
36	Babe Ruth, 1928	83.8	36	Frank Robinson, 1966	72.7
37	Tip O'Neill, 1887	82.8	37	Mickey Mantle, 1962	72.6
38	Barry Bonds, 1992	82.8	38	Rogers Hornsby, 1921	72.5
39	Lou Gehrig, 1936	82.5	39	Arky Vaughan, 1935	72.5
40	Lou Gehrig, 1934	82.3	40	Carl Yastrzemski, 1967	72.1
41	Mickey Mantle, 1956	82.1	41	Nap Lajoie, 1901	72.0
42	Ed Delahanty, 1893	81.7	42	Rogers Hornsby, 1928	70.4
43	Lou Gehrig, 1931	80.8	43	Jimmie Foxx, 1932	70.0
44	Mickey Mantle, 1961	80.2	44	Jimmie Foxx, 1933	69.8
45	Al Rosen, 1953	79.8	45	Mickey Mantle, 1956	69.8
46	Arky Vaughan, 1935	79.4	46	Norm Cash, 1961	69.7
47	Kevin Mitchell, 1989	78.4	47	Rogers Hornsby, 1923	69.2
48	Ty Cobb, 1909	77.9	48	Mickey Mantle, 1961	68.9
49	Ted Williams, 1954	77.9	49	Ed Delahanty, 1893	68.9
50	Ted Williams, 1948	77.7	50	Ty Cobb, 1909	68.3

Table L.13   *(continued)*

ESBRs		ESBRs per 550 NFP	
51 Joe Medwick, 1937	77.6	51 **Jim Thome, 2002**	68.3
52 **Carlos Delgado, 2000**	77.6	52 Dick Allen, 1972	68.2
53 Lou Gehrig, 1930	77.0	53 Babe Ruth, 1928	68.2
54 **Albert Pujols, 2003**	76.4	54 Kevin Mitchell, 1989	68.1
55 Babe Ruth, 1930	76.3	55 Ted Williams, 1948	67.0
56 Nap Lajoie, 1901	76.0	56 **Sammy Sosa, 2001**	66.9
57 Rogers Hornsby, 1928	76.0	57 Joe Morgan, 1976	66.3
58 Lou Gehrig, 1928	75.8	58 **Mike Piazza, 1997**	65.9
59 Ed Delahanty, 1899	75.7	59 Ty Cobb, 1910	65.8
60 **Gary Sheffield, 1996**	75.6	60 Honus Wagner, 1909	65.8
61 **Jim Thome, 2002**	75.4	61 Lou Gehrig, 1934	65.6
62 **Jason Giambi, 2000**	75.3	62 Rickey Henderson, 1990	65.4
63 **Mike Piazza, 1997**	75.2	63 **Manny Ramirez, 2000**	65.4
64 Dick Allen, 1972	75.2	64 **Albert Belle, 1994**	65.2
65 **Barry Bonds, 1996**	75.0	65 Joe DiMaggio, 1941	65.1
66 **John Olerud, 1993**	74.9	66 Ed Delahanty, 1899	65.0
67 Stan Musial, 1949	74.8	67 Frank Robinson, 1967	65.0
68 George Brett, 1985	74.5	68 **Mark McGwire, 1996**	64.5
69 Stan Musial, 1946	74.5	69 Ed Delahanty, 1896	64.2
70 Rogers Hornsby, 1920	74.3	70 Roger Connor, 1888	64.1
71 Rogers Hornsby, 1927	73.9	71 Babe Ruth, 1932	64.1
72 Bill Nicholson, 1943	73.6	72 Babe Ruth, 1930	64.0
73 Joe DiMaggio, 1941	73.5	73 Willie McCovey, 1969	63.9
74 Willie Mays, 1965	73.4	74 Harry Lumley, 1906	63.8
75 Hank Aaron, 1963	73.4	75 Al Rosen, 1953	63.8
76 **Jeff Bagwell, 1994**	73.0	76 Willie Mays, 1965	63.7
77 Lou Gehrig, 1937	72.7	77 Lou Gehrig, 1936	63.4
78 Ty Cobb, 1917	72.6	78 **Barry Bonds, 2000**	63.3
79 George Brett, 1980	72.4	79 Nap Lajoie, 1904	63.3
80 Frank Robinson, 1962	72.2	80 Babe Ruth, 1922	63.2
81 Fred Dunlap, 1884	72.2	81 Joe Medwick, 1937	63.1
82 Hack Wilson, 1930	72.2	82 **Jason Giambi, 2000**	63.1
83 Reggie Jackson, 1969	72.1	83 Lou Gehrig, 1928	63.1
84 Harmon Killebrew, 1967	71.6	84 Harry Stovey, 1885	63.0
85 Willie McCovey, 1969	71.6	85 Pedro Guerrero, 1985	63.0
86 Stan Musial, 1943	71.4	86 Jim Gentile, 1961	62.8
87 Frank Thomas, 1991	71.3	87 Rogers Hornsby, 1920	62.7
88 Rod Carew, 1977	71.2	88 George Brett, 1985	62.5
89 George Stone, 1906	71.1	89 Willie Stargell, 1971	62.2
90 Rogers Hornsby, 1929	71.1	90 **Gary Sheffield, 1996**	61.9
91 Mel Ott, 1932	71.0	91 **Albert Pujols, 2003**	61.8
92 Chuck Klein, 1933	71.0	92 Lou Gehrig, 1930	61.8
93 Tris Speaker, 1923	71.0	93 Goose Goslin, 1928	61.8
94 **Frank Thomas, 1994**	70.9	94 Rogers Hornsby, 1927	61.7
95 Joe Morgan, 1976	70.8	95 Joe DiMaggio, 1939	61.7
96 **Albert Belle, 1998**	70.7	96 **Manny Ramirez, 2002**	61.7
97 Will Clark, 1989	70.3	97 **Barry Bonds, 1996**	61.7
98 Jack Fournier, 1924	70.3	98 **John Olerud, 1993**	61.3
99 Rickey Henderson, 1990	70.2	99 Ty Cobb, 1917	61.2
100 Joe DiMaggio, 1937	70.1	100 George Stone, 1906	61.1

Note: Seasons from the power era, 1993-2003, are shown in bold.

Table L.14   Single-Season Position-Adjusted Event-Specific Batting Runs Top 100

Position-Adjusted ESBRs		Position-Adjusted ESBRs per 550 NFP	
1 Barry Bonds, 2001	122.0	1 Barry Bonds, 2002	109.8
2 Barry Bonds, 2002	121.7	2 Barry Bonds, 2001	101.4
3 Rogers Hornsby, 1924	111.8	3 Rogers Hornsby, 1924	98.1
4 Rogers Hornsby, 1922	107.2	4 Barry Bonds, 2003	91.4
5 Babe Ruth, 1921	103.9	5 Babe Ruth, 1920	90.8
6 Babe Ruth, 1923	103.6	6 Fred Dunlap, 1884	89.9
7 Babe Ruth, 1920	100.9	7 Honus Wagner, 1908	86.1
8 Honus Wagner, 1908	98.1	8 Rogers Hornsby, 1922	85.6
9 Ted Williams, 1942	93.5	9 Rogers Hornsby, 1925	85.0
10 Ted Williams, 1941	93.3	10 Ted Williams, 1941	84.7
11 Arky Vaughan, 1935	92.6	11 Arky Vaughan, 1935	84.4
12 Rogers Hornsby, 1921	92.2	12 Babe Ruth, 1921	82.9
13 Stan Musial, 1948	92.1	13 Ted Williams, 1957	82.7
14 Barry Bonds, 2003	91.1	14 Babe Ruth, 1919	82.5
15 Rogers Hornsby, 1925	91.0	15 Babe Ruth, 1923	81.9
16 Ted Williams, 1947	90.6	16 Mickey Mantle, 1957	79.3
17 Lou Gehrig, 1927	90.4	17 Nap Lajoie, 1901	77.3
18 Mickey Mantle, 1957	89.4	18 George Brett, 1980	77.1
19 Babe Ruth, 1927	86.8	19 Rogers Hornsby, 1921	76.9
20 Babe Ruth, 1926	86.2	20 Ted Williams, 1942	76.7
21 Mark McGwire, 1998	85.7	21 Tip O'Neill, 1887	76.4
22 Barry Bonds, 1993	85.5	22 Joe Morgan, 1976	75.6
23 Tris Speaker, 1912	85.3	23 Jeff Bagwell, 1994	75.2
24 Babe Ruth, 1924	84.6	24 Rogers Hornsby, 1928	74.8
25 Ted Williams, 1949	84.1	25 Babe Ruth, 1926	73.9
26 Mike Piazza, 1997	83.6	26 Rogers Hornsby, 1923	73.6
27 Ted Williams, 1957	81.8	27 Mike Piazza, 1997	73.2
28 Nap Lajoie, 1901	81.6	28 Stan Musial, 1948	73.1
29 Ted Williams, 1946	81.4	29 Honus Wagner, 1909	72.5
30 Babe Ruth, 1919	80.8	30 Ted Williams, 1947	72.0
31 Rogers Hornsby, 1928	80.8	31 Ted Williams, 1954	71.9
32 Joe Morgan, 1976	80.7	32 Lou Gehrig, 1927	71.5
33 Babe Ruth, 1931	79.9	33 Babe Ruth, 1927	70.5
34 Rogers Hornsby, 1920	79.6	34 Barry Bonds, 1993	70.5
35 Tip O'Neill, 1887	79.4	35 Tris Speaker, 1912	70.2
36 Al Rosen, 1953	79.2	36 Barry Bonds, 1992	70.2
37 Rogers Hornsby, 1927	79.2	37 Rogers Hornsby, 1917	69.9
38 Mickey Mantle, 1956	78.4	38 Mark McGwire, 1998	69.7
39 Fred Dunlap, 1884	78.1	39 Mickey Mantle, 1962	69.5
40 Norm Cash, 1961	78.1	40 Babe Ruth, 1924	68.9
41 Jason Giambi, 2001	77.4	41 Nap Lajoie, 1904	68.6
42 Frank Robinson, 1966	77.3	42 Rogers Hornsby, 1920	67.1
43 Alex Rodriguez, 2001	77.2	43 Mickey Mantle, 1956	66.6
44 Barry Bonds, 1992	77.2	44 Ted Williams, 1946	66.6
45 Robin Yount, 1982	76.9	45 Honus Wagner, 1904	66.5
46 Rogers Hornsby, 1929	76.7	46 Babe Ruth, 1931	66.3
47 Mickey Mantle, 1961	76.6	47 Rogers Hornsby, 1927	66.2
48 Alex Rodriguez, 2002	76.5	48 Frank Thomas, 1994	66.0
49 Jimmie Foxx, 1932	76.2	49 Mickey Mantle, 1961	65.8
50 Carl Yastrzemski, 1967	76.1	50 Honus Wagner, 1911	64.6

Table L.14   *(continued)*

Position-Adjusted ESBRs		Position-Adjusted ESBRs per 550 NFP	
51 Sammy Sosa, 2001	75.7	51 Jason Giambi, 2001	64.3
52 Mel Ott, 1938	74.7	52 Norm Cash, 1961	64.3
53 Honus Wagner, 1909	74.4	53 Heinie Zimmerman, 1912	64.1
54 **Alex Rodriguez, 2000**	74.3	54 Joe DiMaggio, 1941	64.0
55 Cal Ripken Jr., 1991	74.1	55 Bill Joyce, 1894	63.7
56 Nap Lajoie, 1904	73.3	56 Ted Williams, 1949	63.4
57 George Brett, 1985	73.0	57 Al Rosen, 1953	63.3
58 Rogers Hornsby, 1917	72.7	58 Mel Ott, 1938	63.2
59 **Derek Jeter, 1999**	72.7	59 Frank Robinson, 1966	63.2
60 Jimmie Foxx, 1933	72.6	60 Kevin Mitchell, 1989	63.1
61 Kevin Mitchell, 1989	72.6	61 Ty Cobb, 1909	62.8
62 Joe DiMaggio, 1941	72.3	62 Carl Yastrzemski, 1967	62.1
63 Ed Delahanty, 1893	71.6	63 **Alex Rodriguez, 2000**	61.9
64 Ty Cobb, 1909	71.6	64 Bill Joyce, 1896	61.8
65 George Brett, 1980	71.2	65 Joe Morgan, 1975	61.8
66 Joe Morgan, 1975	71.1	66 Ed Lennox, 1914	61.7
67 Lou Boudreau, 1948	71.1	67 Honus Wagner, 1907	61.6
68 Jimmy Williams, 1899	70.7	68 Robin Yount, 1982	61.3
69 Babe Ruth, 1928	70.6	69 George Brett, 1985	61.2
70 **Alex Rodriguez, 2003**	70.2	70 Rogers Hornsby, 1929	61.1
71 Willie Mays, 1965	70.1	71 Willie Mays, 1965	60.8
72 Heinie Zimmerman, 1912	70.0	72 Joe DiMaggio, 1939	60.6
73 Nap Lajoie, 1910	69.7	73 Ed Delahanty, 1893	60.4
74 Lou Gehrig, 1934	69.4	74 Art Wilson, 1914	60.3
75 Lou Gehrig, 1936	69.2	75 Rickey Henderson, 1990	60.3
76 Lou Gehrig, 1930	68.9	76 Ty Cobb, 1910	60.0
77 Joe DiMaggio, 1937	68.7	77 Jimmie Foxx, 1932	59.8
78 Stan Musial, 1949	68.6	78 Dick Allen, 1972	59.7
79 Joe Medwick, 1937	68.6	79 Jimmie Foxx, 1933	59.6
80 **Albert Pujols, 2003**	68.5	80 **Sammy Sosa, 2001**	59.6
81 Ted Williams, 1954	68.4	81 **Mike Piazza, 1995**	59.5
82 Lou Gehrig, 1928	68.0	82 Lou Boudreau, 1948	59.2
83 Jackie Robinson, 1949	67.6	83 **Javy Lopez, 2003**	59.1
84 **Barry Bonds, 1996**	67.2	84 **Albert Belle, 1994**	58.9
85 Bill Joyce, 1896	67.2	85 **Alex Rodriguez, 2001**	58.7
86 Lou Gehrig, 1931	67.1	86 Nap Lajoie, 1910	58.4
87 Honus Wagner, 1904	66.8	87 **Alex Rodriguez, 2002**	58.4
88 **Gary Sheffield, 1996**	66.7	88 Harry Lumley, 1906	58.3
89 Arky Vaughan, 1936	66.7	89 Honus Wagner, 1905	58.3
90 Eddie Collins, 1915	66.5	90 **Manny Ramirez, 2000**	58.1
91 **Alex Rodriguez, 1996**	66.5	91 Mickey Mantle, 1964	57.9
92 Frank Robinson, 1962	66.3	92 **Jim Thome, 2002**	57.9
93 **Chipper Jones, 1999**	66.2	93 Pedro Guerrero, 1985	57.9
94 Willie Mays, 1964	66.1	94 Cal Ripken Jr., 1991	57.6
95 Alan Trammell, 1987	66.1	95 Babe Ruth, 1928	57.4
96 Ted Williams, 1948	66.1	96 Jim Gentile, 1961	57.4
97 Wade Boggs, 1988	65.9	97 Bill Dahlen, 1896	57.3
98 Joe Torre, 1971	65.9	98 Eddie Mathews, 1954	57.3
99 Wade Boggs, 1987	65.8	99 Ted Williams, 1948	57.0
100 Ed Delahanty, 1899	65.8	100 **Barry Bonds, 2000**	56.9

Best Careers

Table M.1   Career Batting Average Top 100

Adjusted Hits		Adjusted Batting Average	
1 Pete Rose	4195	1 Tony Gwynn	.338
2 Ty Cobb	3745	2 Ty Cobb	.336
3 Hank Aaron	3699	3 Rod Carew	.332
4 Stan Musial	3494	4 Rogers Hornsby	.327
5 Carl Yastrzemski	3380	5 Stan Musial	.327
6 Honus Wagner	3279	6 Nap Lajoie	.324
7 Paul Molitor	3271	7 Joe Jackson	.324
8 Eddie Murray	3262	8 Honus Wagner	.324
9 Willie Mays	3256	9 Ted Williams	.322
10 Tris Speaker	3193	10 Wade Boggs	.322
11 Cal Ripken Jr.	3176	11 Pete Browning	.321
12 Robin Yount	3147	12 Tris Speaker	.319
13 Tony Gwynn	3130	13 **Mike Piazza**	.313
14 Dave Winfield	3109	14 Dan Brouthers	.312
15 George Brett	3108	15 Tip O'Neill	.312
16 Rickey Henderson	3072	16 Kirby Puckett	.312
17 Eddie Collins	3063	17 Tony Oliva	.312
18 Rod Carew	3059	18 **Vladimir Guerrero**	.311
19 Nap Lajoie	3025	19 Mike Donlin	.311
20 Al Kaline	3021	20 Willie Keeler	.311
21 Brooks Robinson	2977	21 **Edgar Martinez**	.311
22 Lou Brock	2974	22 Hank Aaron	.310
23 Frank Robinson	2954	23 **Derek Jeter**	.309
24 Wade Boggs	2906	24 Joe DiMaggio	.309
25 Roberto Clemente	2891	25 Babe Ruth	.309
26 Paul Waner	2858	26 Eddie Collins	.309
27 Harold Baines	2829	27 Billy Hamilton	.308
28 Sam Crawford	2823	28 Jesse Burkett	.308
29 Cap Anson	2764	29 Willie Mays	.308
30 Zack Wheat	2759	30 Cap Anson	.308
31 Andre Dawson	2750	31 Dale Mitchell	.308
32 Luis Aparicio	2738	32 Don Mattingly	.307
33 Vada Pinson	2737	33 Lou Gehrig	.307
34 Jake Beckley	2736	34 Paul Waner	.306
35 Rusty Staub	2719	35 Bill Terry	.306
36 Sam Rice	2715	36 Pete Rose	.306
37 **Rafael Palmeiro**	2712	37 George Brett	.306
38 Al Oliver	2709	38 Roberto Clemente	.306
39 Dave Parker	2693	39 Joe Medwick	.306
40 Mel Ott	2693	40 George Sisler	.305
41 Tony Perez	2691	41 **Nomar Garciaparra**	.305
42 Rogers Hornsby	2667	42 Zack Wheat	.305
43 Billy Williams	2665	43 Ed Delahanty	.304
44 Reggie Jackson	2655	44 Paul Molitor	.304
45 Bill Buckner	2652	45 **Manny Ramirez**	.303
46 Willie Keeler	2649	46 Al Simmons	.303
47 Nellie Fox	2644	47 Al Kaline	.303
48 **Roberto Alomar**	2641	48 Frank Robinson	.302
49 Al Simmons	2619	49 **Frank Thomas**	.302
50 Luke Appling	2600	50 Edd Roush	.302

Adjusted Hits		Adjusted Batting Average	
51 Tim Raines	2599	51 Jackie Robinson	.302
52 Steve Garvey	2596	52 Mickey Mantle	.302
53 Frankie Frisch	2579	53 Matty Alou	.301
54 Jesse Burkett	2579	54 Pedro Guerrero	.301
55 Willie Davis	2577	55 **Bobby Abreu**	.301
56 Babe Ruth	2572	56 Harry Heilmann	.301
57 **Barry Bonds**	2568	57 **Roberto Alomar**	.301
58 Ernie Banks	2560	58 Bill Madlock	.301
59 George Davis	2558	59 Tommy Davis	.301
60 Charlie Gehringer	2555	60 Will Clark	.301
61 Max Carey	2538	61 Al Oliver	.300
62 Doc Cramer	2525	62 Riggs Stephenson	.300
63 Joe Morgan	2518	63 Richie Ashburn	.300
64 George Sisler	2513	64 Sam Thompson	.299
65 Fred Clarke	2510	65 Johnny Mize	.299
66 Richie Ashburn	2509	66 Barney McCosky	.299
67 Buddy Bell	2503	67 Thurman Munson	.299
68 Ted Williams	2482	68 John Kruk	.299
69 Lave Cross	2478	69 Manny Mota	.298
70 Goose Goslin	2459	70 George Kell	.298
71 Rabbit Maranville	2457	71 **Todd Helton**	.298
72 Lou Gehrig	2453	72 **Bernie Williams**	.298
73 Ozzie Smith	2451	73 Roger Connor	.298
74 Ted Simmons	2450	74 Cecil Cooper	.298
75 Mickey Mantle	2439	75 Frank Chance	.297
76 **Fred McGriff**	2434	76 Ralph Garr	.297
77 Mickey Vernon	2433	77 **Alex Rodriguez**	.297
78 **Craig Biggio**	2428	78 Steve Garvey	.297
79 Jimmie Foxx	2389	79 Harvey Kuenn	.297
80 Lou Whitaker	2384	80 **Chipper Jones**	.297
81 Harry Hooper	2382	81 Ginger Beaumont	.297
82 Alan Trammell	2375	82 Frank McCormick	.297
83 Brett Butler	2373	83 Eddie Murray	.297
84 Dwight Evans	2371	84 Sam Crawford	.297
85 Chili Davis	2370	85 Mickey Rivers	.297
86 Mark Grace	2363	86 Elmer Flick	.297
87 Bill Dahlen	2360	87 Hugh Duffy	.297
88 Red Schoendienst	2360	88 Arky Vaughan	.296
89 Jim Rice	2358	89 Minnie Minoso	.296
90 Bert Campaneris	2346	90 **Jason Giambi**	.296
91 Harry Heilmann	2344	91 Heinie Zimmerman	.296
92 Ryne Sandberg	2337	92 Jim O'Rourke	.296
93 George Van Haltren	2335	93 Keith Hernandez	.295
94 Joe Medwick	2334	94 Ernie Lombardi	.295
95 Jimmy Ryan	2328	95 Tim Raines	.295
96 Orlando Cepeda	2324	96 **Julio Franco**	.295
97 **Julio Franco**	2322	97 Tommy Holmes	.295
98 Carlton Fisk	2321	98 **Gary Sheffield**	.295
99 Roger Connor	2321	99 Hal Morris	.295
100 Dave Concepcion	2320	100 Sam Rice	.295

Table M.2 Career Doubles-Plus-Triples Top 100

Adjusted DPTs		Adjusted DPTs/500 ABs	
1 Pete Rose	862	1 Stan Musial	41.3
2 Ty Cobb	832	2 Honus Wagner	41.2
3 Stan Musial	814	3 Dan Brouthers	39.3
4 Honus Wagner	792	4 Tris Speaker	39.1
5 Hank Aaron	783	5 Nap Lajoie	38.2
6 Tris Speaker	782	6 Joe Jackson	38.0
7 George Brett	735	7 George Brett	37.7
8 Willie Mays	732	8 Ty Cobb	37.7
9 Robin Yount	731	9 Joe Medwick	37.6
10 Paul Molitor	698	10 Babe Herman	37.3
11 Carl Yastrzemski	694	11 Hal McRae	37.2
12 Sam Crawford	689	12 Lou Gehrig	37.1
13 Nap Lajoie	673	13 Paul Waner	37.0
14 Cal Ripken Jr.	666	14 Roger Connor	36.9
15 Paul Waner	645	15 Sam Crawford	36.8
16 Lou Brock	644	16 Rogers Hornsby	36.6
17 Dave Winfield	642	17 Willie Mays	36.6
18 Frank Robinson	640	18 Sherry Magee	36.5
19 Jake Beckley	640	19 Ed Delahanty	36.2
20 Al Kaline	638	20 Hank Greenberg	36.1
21 Tony Gwynn	637	21 John Reilly	35.9
22 Vada Pinson	637	22 Ted Williams	35.8
23 Eddie Murray	620	23 **Edgar Martinez**	35.5
24 Brooks Robinson	620	24 **Bobby Abreu**	35.5
25 Al Oliver	619	25 Cesar Cedeno	35.3
26 Roberto Clemente	616	26 **Nomar Garciaparra**	35.2
27 Willie Davis	615	27 Joe DiMaggio	35.1
28 Rod Carew	605	28 **Todd Helton**	35.1
29 Rickey Henderson	599	29 Joe Rudi	35.1
30 Dave Parker	598	30 Chet Lemon	35.1
31 Zack Wheat	591	31 Wade Boggs	35.1
32 Rogers Hornsby	590	32 Harry Stovey	35.0
33 Reggie Jackson	589	33 Keith Hernandez	35.0
34 Wade Boggs	589	34 Dave Parker	35.0
35 Rusty Staub	586	35 Hank Aaron	34.9
36 Mickey Vernon	584	36 Rod Carew	34.9
37 George Davis	584	37 Tommy Henrich	34.8
38 Andre Dawson	580	38 Jake Beckley	34.7
39 **Barry Bonds**	574	39 Gavy Cravath	34.7
40 Tony Perez	569	40 Pete Browning	34.6
41 Lou Gehrig	567	41 Minnie Minoso	34.6
42 Roger Connor	567	42 Al Oliver	34.6
43 Bill Buckner	562	43 Buck Freeman	34.5
44 Cap Anson	561	44 Don Mattingly	34.5
45 Eddie Collins	559	45 Joe Kelley	34.5
46 Billy Williams	559	46 Vada Pinson	34.4
47 **Rafael Palmeiro**	557	47 Robin Yount	34.4
48 Sam Rice	556	48 Tony Gwynn	34.3
49 Joe Medwick	552	49 Tony Oliva	34.3
50 Bill Dahlen	551	50 Babe Ruth	34.2

Table M.2 *(continued)*

Adjusted DPTs		Adjusted DPTs/500 ABs	
51 Fred Clarke	549	51 Buck Ewing	34.2
52 **Roberto Alomar**	549	52 Dick Allen	34.2
53 Joe Morgan	547	53 Charlie Hickman	34.0
54 Steve Garvey	546	54 Harry Davis	34.0
55 Charlie Gehringer	543	55 Lou Brock	34.0
56 Ed Delahanty	543	56 Ed Konetchy	34.0
57 Mel Ott	541	57 Bob Meusel	33.9
58 Jimmy Ryan	534	58 Edd Roush	33.9
59 Ted Simmons	534	59 Reggie Jackson	33.8
60 Luis Aparicio	534	60 Harry Heilmann	33.8
61 Harold Baines	533	61 Albert Belle	33.8
62 Ted Williams	532	62 Chick Hafey	33.8
63 Al Simmons	531	63 Frank Robinson	33.7
64 Sherry Magee	528	64 Willie Davis	33.7
65 Harry Heilmann	527	65 Lenny Dykstra	33.6
66 Bobby Wallace	527	66 Joe Cronin	33.6
67 Max Carey	525	67 Bill Terry	33.6
68 Mark Grace	523	68 Lou Boudreau	33.6
69 Dan Brouthers	522	69 **Larry Walker**	33.6
70 Tim Raines	522	70 Mickey Vernon	33.4
71 Goose Goslin	520	71 George Davis	33.4
72 Babe Ruth	519	72 **Jeff Kent**	33.4
73 **Craig Biggio**	517	73 **Barry Bonds**	33.4
74 Dwight Evans	517	74 Jimmy Ryan	33.3
75 Ernie Banks	516	75 Sam Thompson	33.3
76 Hal McRae	513	76 Carl Yastrzemski	33.3
77 Ed Konetchy	511	77 Oyster Burns	33.3
78 Buddy Bell	509	78 Tip O'Neill	33.3
79 Lou Whitaker	509	79 Bill Joyce	33.2
80 Cesar Cedeno	501	80 Jim O'Rourke	33.2
81 Rabbit Maranville	501	81 Pepper Martin	33.2
82 Enos Slaughter	497	82 Mark Grace	33.1
83 Nellie Fox	496	83 Johnny Callison	33.1
84 Billy Herman	494	84 Will Clark	33.1
85 Joe Cronin	493	85 Wally Moses	33.1
86 Willie Stargell	492	86 Jimmy Collins	33.1
87 Joe Judge	491	87 Paul Molitor	33.0
88 Alan Trammell	491	88 Harvey Kuenn	33.0
89 Heinie Manush	488	89 Jackie Robinson	33.0
90 Jose Cruz	488	90 Jeff Heath	33.0
91 Harry Hooper	487	91 Bobby Wallace	32.9
92 Wally Moses	486	92 Bobby Veach	32.9
93 Jim O'Rourke	483	93 Pete Rose	32.9
94 Lave Cross	483	94 Ray Lankford	32.9
95 George Sisler	483	95 **Rusty Greer**	32.9
96 Frankie Frisch	483	96 Elmer Flick	32.9
97 Luke Appling	482	97 Zack Wheat	32.9
98 Keith Hernandez	482	98 Ben Chapman	32.8
99 Ryne Sandberg	480	99 Cecil Cooper	32.8
100 Joe DiMaggio	479	100 Del Pratt	32.8

Table M.3   Career Triples Top 100

Adjusted Triples		Adjusted 3Bs/500 ABs	
1 Sam Crawford	187	1 Lance Johnson	13.2
2 Ty Cobb	170	2 Stan Musial	11.1
3 Willie Davis	158	3 Buck Ewing	11.0
4 Brett Butler	157	4 Joe Jackson	10.6
5 Stan Musial	144	5 Sam Crawford	10.4
6 Willie Mays	144	6 Brett Butler	10.4
7 Robin Yount	144	7 Willie Mays	10.2
8 Willie Wilson	141	8 Bill Bruton	10.1
9 Vada Pinson	141	9 Jeff Heath	9.5
10 Roberto Clemente	139	10 Luis Polonia	9.4
11 Lance Johnson	138	11 Elmer Flick	9.4
12 Paul Molitor	132	12 Earle Combs	9.4
13 Honus Wagner	130	13 Roger Connor	9.4
14 Pete Rose	129	14 Willie Wilson	9.3
15 Lou Brock	128	15 Larry Herndon	9.3
16 Tris Speaker	128	16 Mickey Rivers	9.3
17 Roger Connor	125	17 Ival Goodman	9.2
18 George Brett	122	18 Minnie Minoso	9.0
19 Enos Slaughter	122	19 Juan Samuel	9.0
20 Tim Raines	121	20 Carl Reynolds	8.9
21 **Steve Finley**	117	21 Brady Anderson	8.9
22 Jake Beckley	116	22 George Brett	8.8
23 Rod Carew	116	23 Jose Offerman	8.8
24 Fred Clarke	115	24 **Kenny Lofton**	8.8
25 **Kenny Lofton**	111	25 **Steve Finley**	8.8
26 Sherry Magee	109	26 Roger Metzger	8.8
27 Dan Brouthers	108	27 Buck Freeman	8.7
28 Paul Waner	107	28 Jim Fregosi	8.7
29 Juan Samuel	106	29 Bill Joyce	8.7
30 Earle Combs	106	30 Vada Pinson	8.7
31 Joe Jackson	106	31 Ty Cobb	8.6
32 Bill Bruton	106	32 Sherry Magee	8.6
33 Nellie Fox	105	33 Willie Davis	8.6
34 Ed Konetchy	105	34 Johnny Callison	8.5
35 Edd Roush	104	35 Garry Templeton	8.5
36 Buck Ewing	104	36 Edd Roush	8.5
37 Elmer Flick	103	37 Lou Gehrig	8.4
38 Goose Goslin	102	38 Mookie Wilson	8.4
39 Kiki Cuyler	101	39 Andy Van Slyke	8.3
40 Joe Kelley	101	40 Omar Moreno	8.3
41 Lou Gehrig	101	41 Gary Pettis	8.3
42 Luis Aparicio	101	42 Dick Allen	8.3
43 George Sisler	100	43 Dan Brouthers	8.3
44 Rogers Hornsby	100	44 Goose Goslin	8.3
45 Al Simmons	100	45 Enos Slaughter	8.3
46 Tony Fernandez	99	46 Vince Coleman	8.2
47 Harry Stovey	98	47 Jim Bottomley	8.2
48 Ed Delahanty	98	48 Rogers Hornsby	8.2
49 Bert Campaneris	98	49 Les Mann	8.2
50 Eddie Collins	98	50 Lou Brock	8.1

Table M.3 *(continued)*

Adjusted Triples		Adjusted 3Bs/500 ABs	
51 Hank Aaron	98	51 Joe Kelley	8.1
52 Sam Rice	98	52 Joe Morgan	8.1
53 Garry Templeton	97	53 Harry Stovey	8.0
54 **Roberto Alomar**	97	54 Tony Fernandez	8.0
55 Dave Winfield	97	55 Willie McGee	8.0
56 Wally Pipp	96	56 Harry Davis	8.0
57 Jim Bottomley	96	57 Johnny Hopp	7.9
58 Joe DiMaggio	96	58 Dale Mitchell	7.9
59 Joe Morgan	96	59 Oyster Burns	7.9
60 Brady Anderson	95	60 Tim Raines	7.9
61 Andre Dawson	95	61 Chick Stahl	7.8
62 Rabbit Maranville	94	62 Kiki Cuyler	7.8
63 Tony Gwynn	93	63 **Johnny Damon**	7.8
64 Larry Bowa	92	64 **Ray Durham**	7.8
65 Heinie Manush	92	65 Charlie Keller	7.7
66 Jim Fregosi	91	66 Luis Alicea	7.7
67 Luis Polonia	91	67 Bill Terry	7.7
68 Willie McGee	91	68 Delino DeShields	7.7
69 Zack Wheat	91	69 **Fernando Vina**	7.7
70 Tommy Leach	91	70 Sam Mertes	7.6
71 Jesse Burkett	91	71 Gavy Cravath	7.6
72 Richie Ashburn	90	72 Joe DiMaggio	7.6
73 Mickey Vernon	90	73 Lou Finney	7.6
74 Jake Daubert	89	74 Chief Wilson	7.6
75 Bill Terry	89	75 Snuffy Stirnweiss	7.6
76 Andy Van Slyke	89	76 **Nomar Garciaparra**	7.6
77 Delino DeShields	89	77 Dave Martinez	7.5
78 George Davis	88	78 George Sisler	7.5
79 Rickey Henderson	88	79 Tris Speaker	7.5
80 Harry Hooper	88	80 Dick McAuliffe	7.5
81 Devon White	88	81 Babe Herman	7.5
82 Vince Coleman	87	82 Gary Redus	7.5
83 Mike Tiernan	87	83 Wally Pipp	7.5
84 Nap Lajoie	86	84 Frank Schulte	7.5
85 George Van Haltren	86	85 Mike Tiernan	7.5
86 Joe Judge	86	86 Paul Waner	7.5
87 Harry Davis	86	87 Zoilo Versalles	7.4
88 Jeff Heath	86	88 Ed Konetchy	7.4
89 **Barry Larkin**	86	89 Tony Gwynn	7.4
90 Joe Medwick	85	90 Nap Lajoie	7.4
91 Mickey Rivers	85	91 Barney McCosky	7.4
92 Arky Vaughan	85	92 Harold Reynolds	7.4
93 Earl Averill	85	93 Red Murray	7.4
94 Bid McPhee	84	94 Roberto Clemente	7.4
95 Billy Williams	84	95 Al Bumbry	7.3
96 Wally Moses	84	96 Phil Garner	7.3
97 Jimmie Foxx	84	97 Craig Reynolds	7.3
98 Johnny Callison	84	98 John Reilly	7.3
99 Alfredo Griffin	83	99 Johnny Mize	7.3
100 **Barry Bonds**	83	100 John Stone	7.3

Table M.4   Career Home Runs Top 100

Adjusted Home Runs		Adjusted HRs/500 ABs	
1 Babe Ruth	805	1 Babe Ruth	49.8
2 Hank Aaron	676	2 Mark McGwire	41.5
3 **Barry Bonds**	622	3 Ted Williams	38.7
4 Ted Williams	588	4 **Barry Bonds**	35.7
5 Willie Mays	587	5 Mike Schmidt	34.7
6 Reggie Jackson	570	6 Lou Gehrig	33.7
7 Mike Schmidt	555	7 Harmon Killebrew	33.5
8 Frank Robinson	542	8 Jimmie Foxx	33.3
9 Mel Ott	533	9 Dave Kingman	33.1
10 Harmon Killebrew	522	10 Reggie Jackson	32.0
11 Lou Gehrig	516	11 Bill Nicholson	32.0
12 Mark McGwire	513	12 Mickey Mantle	31.9
13 Jimmie Foxx	513	13 Ralph Kiner	31.5
14 Mickey Mantle	501	14 Joe DiMaggio	31.5
15 Rogers Hornsby	498	15 Willie Stargell	31.5
16 Willie Stargell	495	16 Hack Wilson	31.4
17 Eddie Mathews	486	17 Rogers Hornsby	31.1
18 Willie McCovey	484	18 Darryl Strawberry	30.9
19 Dave Winfield	474	19 Willie McCovey	30.9
20 Eddie Murray	466	20 Glenn Davis	30.4
21 Dave Kingman	442	21 Wally Berger	30.4
22 Stan Musial	440	22 Eddie Mathews	30.2
23 Andre Dawson	439	23 Harry Stovey	30.0
24 Carl Yastrzemski	433	24 Frank Howard	29.5
25 Joe DiMaggio	429	25 Mel Ott	29.4
26 **Fred McGriff**	427	26 Hank Sauer	29.1
27 **Rafael Palmeiro**	421	27 Charlie Hickman	29.0
28 Sam Crawford	420	28 Hank Greenberg	29.0
29 Ty Cobb	418	29 **Jim Thome**	29.0
30 Ernie Banks	414	30 Jose Canseco	28.8
31 **Sammy Sosa**	410	31 **Manny Ramirez**	28.7
32 Jose Canseco	406	32 Willie Mays	28.7
33 Honus Wagner	403	33 **Alex Rodriguez**	28.5
34 Darrell Evans	387	34 Cy Williams	28.4
35 Goose Goslin	386	35 Gorman Thomas	28.4
36 Cy Williams	385	36 **Mike Piazza**	28.2
37 Johnny Bench	383	37 Rob Deer	27.9
38 Frank Howard	383	38 Johnny Mize	27.9
39 **Ken Griffey Jr**	381	39 **Juan Gonzalez**	27.9
40 Al Simmons	376	40 Hank Aaron	27.6
41 Billy Williams	375	41 Vince DiMaggio	27.6
42 Tony Perez	369	42 Kevin Mitchell	27.5
43 Harry Stovey	369	43 Dick Allen	27.5
44 George Foster	367	44 **Carlos Delgado**	27.2
45 Dale Murphy	364	45 **Sammy Sosa**	27.2
46 Jack Clark	361	46 Albert Belle	27.1
47 Graig Nettles	361	47 Gus Zernial	27.1
48 Lee May	360	48 Frank Robinson	27.1
49 Johnny Mize	359	49 Dolph Camilli	26.9
50 **Juan Gonzalez**	358	50 **Ken Griffey Jr**	26.9

Adjusted Home Runs		Adjusted HRs/500 ABs	
51 **Jeff Bagwell**	358	51 John Mayberry	26.8
52 Carlton Fisk	358	52 Joe Gordon	26.7
53 Bill Nicholson	355	53 Buck Freeman	26.6
54 Orlando Cepeda	355	54 Dick Stuart	26.5
55 Gary Carter	354	55 Jack Clark	26.4
56 Don Baylor	351	56 Gavy Cravath	26.3
57 Cal Ripken Jr.	349	57 Al Rosen	26.2
58 George Brett	349	58 Bill Joyce	26.2
59 Boog Powell	348	59 George Foster	26.2
60 Dick Allen	348	60 Boog Powell	26.0
61 Dwight Evans	347	61 Jay Buhner	25.8
62 Duke Snider	343	62 Johnny Bench	25.7
63 Jim Rice	342	63 Mo Vaughn	25.6
64 Nap Lajoie	341	64 Roy Sievers	25.5
65 Ed Delahanty	340	65 Gene Tenace	25.4
66 Harry Heilmann	339	66 Cecil Fielder	25.3
67 Dave Parker	339	67 Chick Hafey	25.3
68 Harold Baines	338	68 Chuck Klein	25.2
69 Al Kaline	337	69 **Fred McGriff**	25.2
70 Bobby Bonds	337	70 **Jeff Bagwell**	25.2
71 Tris Speaker	335	71 Charlie Keller	25.1
72 Darryl Strawberry	335	72 Rudy York	25.0
73 Andres Galarraga	332	73 Jack Fournier	24.8
74 Roger Connor	330	74 Jeff Heath	24.7
75 Matt Williams	330	75 Jimmy Wynn	24.7
76 Jimmy Wynn	329	76 Larry Doby	24.7
77 Ralph Kiner	328	77 Rocky Colavito	24.6
78 Chuck Klein	327	78 Mike Tiernan	24.6
79 Roy Sievers	325	79 **Frank Thomas**	24.6
80 **Frank Thomas**	325	80 Greg Vaughn	24.4
81 **Gary Sheffield**	323	81 Lee May	24.4
82 Joe Carter	323	82 **Jason Giambi**	24.4
83 Rocky Colavito	320	83 Duke Snider	24.2
84 Reggie Smith	320	84 Ripper Collins	24.2
85 Joe Adcock	317	85 Bob Horner	24.1
86 Albert Belle	317	86 **Gary Sheffield**	24.0
87 Yogi Berra	316	87 Joe Adcock	24.0
88 Bob Johnson	314	88 Bobby Bonds	23.9
89 Wally Berger	313	89 Babe Herman	23.9
90 Gary Gaetti	312	90 Danny Tartabull	23.9
91 Ron Cey	311	91 Socks Seybold	23.7
92 Willie Horton	306	92 Dale Murphy	23.7
93 Joe Gordon	305	93 Goose Goslin	23.7
94 Norm Cash	304	94 Ernie Lombardi	23.6
95 Gabby Hartnett	303	95 Matt Williams	23.6
96 **Jim Thome**	302	96 Cliff Johnson	23.6
97 **Mike Piazza**	302	97 Gary Carter	23.6
98 Hank Greenberg	301	98 Eric Davis	23.6
99 Zack Wheat	301	99 Gabby Hartnett	23.5
100 Chili Davis	300	100 Hal Trosky	23.5

Table M.5 Career Runs Top 100

Adjusted Runs		Adjusted Runs/550 NFPs	
1 Rickey Henderson	2343	1 Rickey Henderson	105.9
2 Hank Aaron	2151	2 Mickey Mantle	103.8
3 Pete Rose	2149	3 Babe Ruth	100.9
4 Ty Cobb	2075	4 **Barry Bonds**	94.9
5 Willie Mays	2015	5 Lou Gehrig	94.2
6 Babe Ruth	1879	6 Ty Cobb	93.6
7 **Barry Bonds**	1877	7 Ted Williams	93.0
8 Stan Musial	1838	8 Willie Mays	92.3
9 Frank Robinson	1825	9 Hank Aaron	91.4
10 Carl Yastrzemski	1746	10 Stan Musial	90.5
11 Tris Speaker	1735	11 Joe DiMaggio	90.3
12 Eddie Collins	1735	12 **Alex Rodriguez**	89.7
13 Mel Ott	1733	13 Billy Hamilton	88.3
14 Mickey Mantle	1732	14 Rogers Hornsby	88.2
15 Paul Molitor	1720	15 Frank Robinson	87.9
16 Dave Winfield	1682	16 Eddie Collins	87.4
17 Joe Morgan	1680	17 **Derek Jeter**	87.2
18 Robin Yount	1634	18 Joe Morgan	86.9
19 Reggie Jackson	1632	19 Eddie Mathews	86.7
20 Honus Wagner	1619	20 Willie Keeler	86.6
21 Al Kaline	1608	21 Earle Combs	86.4
22 Lou Gehrig	1608	22 Bobby Bonds	86.4
23 Ted Williams	1603	23 Reggie Jackson	86.3
24 Lou Brock	1595	24 **Kenny Lofton**	86.1
25 Eddie Murray	1593	25 Harry Stovey	86.1
26 Cal Ripken Jr.	1554	26 Mel Ott	85.9
27 Tim Raines	1545	27 Dick Allen	85.8
28 George Brett	1545	28 George Gore	85.5
29 Eddie Mathews	1515	29 Paul Molitor	85.5
30 Mike Schmidt	1485	30 Tommy Henrich	85.2
31 Max Carey	1461	31 Tris Speaker	85.0
32 Paul Waner	1458	32 Tim Raines	84.9
33 Rogers Hornsby	1456	33 Pepper Martin	84.7
34 Rod Carew	1442	34 **Jeff Bagwell**	84.6
35 Charlie Gehringer	1438	35 Mike Schmidt	84.4
36 **Craig Biggio**	1427	36 John McGraw	84.3
37 Jimmie Foxx	1423	37 Jackie Robinson	84.2
38 Wade Boggs	1417	38 Frank Chance	84.1
39 **Rafael Palmeiro**	1410	39 Honus Wagner	83.8
40 Willie Keeler	1408	40 Jimmie Foxx	83.7
41 Nap Lajoie	1406	41 Jack Smith	83.6
42 Roberto Clemente	1405	42 Charlie Keller	83.5
43 Fred Clarke	1403	43 Mike Griffin	83.5
44 **Roberto Alomar**	1400	44 Billy North	83.4
45 Dwight Evans	1396	45 Red Rolfe	83.3
46 Harry Hooper	1365	46 Ray Chapman	83.0
47 Frankie Frisch	1357	47 Ron LeFlore	83.0
48 Tony Gwynn	1357	48 Lonnie Smith	82.8
49 Sam Crawford	1352	49 Tommy Leach	82.8
50 Andre Dawson	1350	50 Don Buford	82.5

Adjusted Runs		Adjusted Runs/550 NFPs	
51 Brett Butler	1349	51 **Jim Edmonds**	82.5
52 Billy Williams	1348	52 King Kelly	82.1
53 Lou Whitaker	1347	53 Mark McGwire	81.8
54 Jesse Burkett	1344	54 Nap Lajoie	81.6
55 Vada Pinson	1340	55 Lenny Dykstra	81.6
56 Luis Aparicio	1340	56 **Nomar Garciaparra**	81.6
57 Sam Rice	1328	57 Larry Doby	81.4
58 Darrell Evans	1326	58 Ross Youngs	81.3
59 Tommy Leach	1305	59 George Burns	81.3
60 **Jeff Bagwell**	1303	60 Fred Clarke	81.1
61 Bill Dahlen	1290	61 Joe Jackson	81.1
62 George Davis	1286	62 **Craig Biggio**	81.1
63 Brooks Robinson	1279	63 Lou Brock	80.7
64 Bert Campaneris	1278	64 Kirk Gibson	80.7
65 Harmon Killebrew	1271	65 **Manny Ramirez**	80.7
66 Willie Davis	1271	66 Mike Tiernan	80.6
67 Jake Beckley	1269	67 Pete Rose	80.3
68 Don Baylor	1266	68 Donie Bush	80.3
69 Ozzie Smith	1259	69 Arky Vaughan	80.3
70 Bobby Bonds	1258	70 Roger Maris	80.3
71 Joe DiMaggio	1257	71 Paul Waner	80.2
72 **Fred McGriff**	1254	72 **Frank Thomas**	80.1
73 Tony Perez	1252	73 **Chipper Jones**	80.1
74 Dave Parker	1247	74 Brett Butler	80.1
75 Tony Phillips	1247	75 Al Bumbry	80.1
76 Pee Wee Reese	1247	76 Roy Thomas	80.0
77 Ernie Banks	1245	77 Jimmy Wynn	79.9
78 Willie Randolph	1244	78 Stan Hack	79.9
79 Richie Ashburn	1244	79 **Jim Thome**	79.9
80 Ryne Sandberg	1239	80 Bob Bescher	79.8
81 Goose Goslin	1238	81 Davey Lopes	79.8
82 George Van Haltren	1235	82 Charlie Gehringer	79.7
83 Willie McCovey	1230	83 Hank Greenberg	79.7
84 Carlton Fisk	1226	84 Eric Davis	79.6
85 Nellie Fox	1226	85 Minnie Minoso	79.6
86 Zack Wheat	1225	86 Dave Winfield	79.6
87 Al Simmons	1223	87 **Ken Griffey Jr**	79.5
88 Graig Nettles	1220	88 Eddie Stanky	79.5
89 Donie Bush	1219	89 **Bernie Williams**	79.5
90 Cap Anson	1218	90 Kiki Cuyler	79.4
91 Willie Stargell	1217	91 Davy Jones	79.4
92 Billy Hamilton	1212	92 Ed Delahanty	79.4
93 Bid McPhee	1208	93 Johnny Pesky	79.3
94 **Sammy Sosa**	1207	94 Dom DiMaggio	79.3
95 Jimmy Sheckard	1206	95 Jesse Burkett	79.3
96 Rusty Staub	1204	96 Max Carey	79.2
97 Stan Hack	1203	97 Gary Redus	79.1
98 Ed Delahanty	1203	98 Duke Snider	79.1
99 Jimmy Ryan	1202	99 **Sammy Sosa**	79.1
100 George Burns	1200	100 Al Kaline	79.0

Table M.6 Career RBIs Top 100

Adjusted RBIs		Adjusted RBIs/550 NFPs	
1 Hank Aaron	2224	1 Babe Ruth	103.4
2 Ty Cobb	1981	2 Lou Gehrig	98.5
3 Babe Ruth	1940	3 Joe DiMaggio	98.0
4 Eddie Murray	1875	4 Mark McGwire	97.5
5 Honus Wagner	1863	5 **Juan Gonzalez**	97.0
6 Dave Winfield	1832	6 Sam Thompson	96.8
7 Willie Mays	1827	7 Gavy Cravath	96.1
8 Stan Musial	1811	8 Hank Greenberg	95.9
9 Frank Robinson	1788	9 Willie Stargell	95.2
10 Reggie Jackson	1778	10 Cap Anson	95.0
11 Carl Yastrzemski	1769	11 Honus Wagner	94.8
12 Mel Ott	1740	12 **Mike Piazza**	94.3
13 Cap Anson	1707	13 Nap Lajoie	93.9
14 Lou Gehrig	1683	14 Johnny Mize	93.8
15 Nap Lajoie	1683	15 Albert Belle	93.6
16 Sam Crawford	1675	16 **Manny Ramirez**	92.6
17 **Barry Bonds**	1647	17 Hack Wilson	92.2
18 Tony Perez	1618	18 Ted Williams	92.0
19 Ted Williams	1616	19 Jose Canseco	91.5
20 Mike Schmidt	1577	20 Reggie Jackson	91.1
21 Cal Ripken Jr.	1571	21 Yogi Berra	91.0
22 Harmon Killebrew	1569	22 Frank Baker	90.9
23 Tris Speaker	1567	23 Boog Powell	90.9
24 Andre Dawson	1566	24 Dave Kingman	90.8
25 Jimmie Foxx	1553	25 Jimmie Foxx	90.5
26 Willie Stargell	1548	26 Rogers Hornsby	90.5
27 Al Kaline	1545	27 Dick Stuart	90.0
28 Willie McCovey	1544	28 Hank Aaron	89.9
29 George Brett	1534	29 Harmon Killebrew	89.7
30 Rogers Hornsby	1524	30 Ty Cobb	89.5
31 Ernie Banks	1520	31 Sherry Magee	89.5
32 Mickey Mantle	1519	32 Sam Crawford	89.4
33 Harold Baines	1516	33 George Foster	89.4
34 Al Simmons	1498	34 Heinie Zimmerman	89.3
35 Rusty Staub	1494	35 Joe Medwick	89.3
36 **Rafael Palmeiro**	1493	36 Kevin Mitchell	89.1
37 Jake Beckley	1491	37 Darryl Strawberry	89.0
38 Dave Parker	1483	38 Willie McCovey	88.9
39 Brooks Robinson	1426	39 Al Simmons	88.6
40 **Fred McGriff**	1423	40 Harry Heilmann	88.6
41 Eddie Mathews	1422	41 Bobby Veach	88.2
42 Billy Williams	1416	42 Bob Meusel	88.1
43 George Davis	1404	43 Frank Howard	87.7
44 Harry Heilmann	1399	44 Charlie Keller	87.7
45 Eddie Collins	1394	45 Johnny Bench	87.6
46 Ted Simmons	1391	46 Mel Ott	87.6
47 Yogi Berra	1374	47 Cecil Fielder	87.5
48 Goose Goslin	1369	48 Roy Campanella	87.5
49 Robin Yount	1368	49 Dick Allen	87.5
50 Joe DiMaggio	1364	50 Mike Schmidt	87.3

Table M.6 (*continued*)

Adjusted RBIs		Adjusted RBIs/550 NFPs	
51 Johnny Bench	1364	51 Al Rosen	86.9
52 Jim Rice	1354	52 Ed Delahanty	86.8
53 Steve Garvey	1353	53 Mickey Mantle	86.7
54 Sherry Magee	1348	54 Charlie Hickman	86.7
55 Mark McGwire	1344	55 Bob Horner	86.3
56 Graig Nettles	1342	56 Buck Freeman	86.2
57 Darrell Evans	1342	57 Rudy York	86.1
58 Joe Carter	1341	58 Frank McCormick	86.0
59 Jose Canseco	1339	59 Dan Brouthers	86.0
60 Al Oliver	1330	60 Lee May	85.7
61 Pete Rose	1329	61 **Frank Thomas**	85.7
62 Ed Delahanty	1316	62 Dave Winfield	85.3
63 Joe Medwick	1315	63 Walker Cooper	85.2
64 Orlando Cepeda	1314	64 Jeff Heath	85.1
65 Zack Wheat	1304	65 Frank Robinson	85.1
66 Roberto Clemente	1304	66 Gus Zernial	84.9
67 Chili Davis	1303	67 Vic Wertz	84.9
68 Dwight Evans	1297	68 Ernie Lombardi	84.8
69 **Jeff Bagwell**	1295	69 Irish Meusel	84.8
70 **Sammy Sosa**	1290	70 Willie Mays	84.7
71 Don Baylor	1287	71 Pedro Guerrero	84.5
72 Mickey Vernon	1277	72 **Sammy Sosa**	84.5
73 Boog Powell	1274	73 Tony Perez	84.5
74 Carlton Fisk	1273	74 **Carlos Delgado**	84.1
75 Lave Cross	1273	75 Wally Berger	83.9
76 Lee May	1270	76 **Ken Griffey Jr**	83.9
77 Ron Santo	1269	77 Orlando Cepeda	83.9
78 George Foster	1258	78 Eddie Murray	83.6
79 **Frank Thomas**	1256	79 Jim Bottomley	83.5
80 Johnny Mize	1254	80 Vern Stephens	83.5
81 Gary Carter	1246	81 **Jeff Bagwell**	83.5
82 Andres Galarraga	1246	82 **Alex Rodriguez**	83.3
83 Jim Bottomley	1242	83 **Barry Bonds**	83.3
84 Enos Slaughter	1237	84 Sam Mertes	83.2
85 **Ken Griffey Jr**	1234	85 Rocky Colavito	83.2
86 Gary Gaetti	1224	86 **Moises Alou**	83.1
87 **Juan Gonzalez**	1223	87 Jim Rice	83.1
88 Roger Connor	1218	88 **Jeff Kent**	83.0
89 Dave Kingman	1212	89 Gabby Hartnett	83.0
90 Paul Waner	1208	90 Joe Adcock	82.9
91 Bobby Wallace	1204	91 Del Ennis	82.8
92 Dale Murphy	1203	92 Hank Sauer	82.8
93 Dan Brouthers	1196	93 Cliff Johnson	82.8
94 Jack Clark	1195	94 Glenn Davis	82.7
95 Joe Cronin	1193	95 Hal Trosky	82.6
96 Bill Dahlen	1193	96 Duffy Lewis	82.6
97 Duke Snider	1192	97 Matt Williams	82.6
98 Joe Torre	1190	98 Dave Parker	82.5
99 Del Ennis	1187	99 Danny Tartabull	82.4
100 Willie Horton	1183	100 George Kelly	82.3

Table M.7 Career Bases on Balls Top 100

Adjusted Bases on Balls		Adjusted BBs/550 NFPs	
1 Rickey Henderson	2156	1 Max Bishop	104.5
2 **Barry Bonds**	2045	2 Babe Ruth	103.6
3 Babe Ruth	1978	3 **Barry Bonds**	103.4
4 Mel Ott	1891	4 Ted Williams	102.9
5 Joe Morgan	1852	5 Topsy Hartsel	100.6
6 Carl Yastrzemski	1827	6 Roy Thomas	100.2
7 Ted Williams	1813	7 Gene Tenace	99.6
8 Mickey Mantle	1648	8 John McGraw	98.9
9 Pete Rose	1590	9 Bill Joyce	94.7
10 Darrell Evans	1573	10 Eddie Stanky	94.6
11 Stan Musial	1554	11 Yank Robinson	94.6
12 Eddie Mathews	1531	12 Mel Ott	93.3
13 Eddie Collins	1529	13 Roy Cullenbine	92.3
14 Harmon Killebrew	1528	14 Mickey Mantle	92.0
15 Willie Mays	1510	15 Joe Morgan	91.2
16 Frank Robinson	1472	16 Mark McGwire	90.8
17 Mike Schmidt	1460	17 Rickey Henderson	89.8
18 Eddie Yost	1445	18 **Frank Thomas**	89.4
19 Hank Aaron	1441	19 **Jim Thome**	89.3
20 Lou Gehrig	1401	20 Ferris Fain	89.1
21 Dwight Evans	1399	21 Miller Huggins	89.1
22 Tris Speaker	1398	22 Billy Hamilton	88.6
23 Wade Boggs	1398	23 Eddie Yost	87.7
24 Reggie Jackson	1379	24 Dolph Camilli	87.1
25 Willie McCovey	1363	25 Harmon Killebrew	87.1
26 Eddie Murray	1342	26 Mickey Tettleton	86.9
27 Jimmie Foxx	1330	27 Jack Clark	86.9
28 **Frank Thomas**	1311	28 Jimmy Wynn	85.5
29 Ty Cobb	1301	29 Eddie Mathews	85.2
30 Tim Raines	1288	30 **Brian Giles**	85.1
31 Rusty Staub	1287	31 Charlie Keller	85.1
32 Jack Clark	1285	32 Joe Cunningham	84.3
33 **Fred McGriff**	1278	33 Mike Hargrove	83.2
34 Willie Randolph	1274	34 Cupid Childs	83.1
35 Ken Singleton	1263	35 Earl Torgeson	82.7
36 Rogers Hornsby	1263	36 Mike Schmidt	82.2
37 **Jeff Bagwell**	1261	37 Ken Singleton	82.0
38 Tony Phillips	1257	38 Roger Bresnahan	81.9
39 Mark McGwire	1252	39 George Grantham	81.8
40 Jimmy Sheckard	1239	40 Lu Blue	81.6
41 Max Carey	1238	41 Darrell Evans	81.5
42 Dave Winfield	1229	42 **Jeff Bagwell**	81.3
43 Paul Waner	1229	43 Lou Gehrig	81.3
44 Jimmy Wynn	1228	44 Ralph Kiner	81.2
45 Donie Bush	1226	45 Dwayne Murphy	81.0
46 Al Kaline	1223	46 Gavy Cravath	81.0
47 Brian Downing	1222	47 Hack Wilson	80.9
48 Billy Hamilton	1215	48 George Gore	80.8
49 Richie Ashburn	1195	49 Jason Thompson	80.8
50 Cap Anson	1194	50 **Jason Giambi**	80.7

Adjusted Bases on Balls		Adjusted BBs/550 NFPs	
51 Toby Harrah	1184	51 Dave Magadan	80.5
52 **Rafael Palmeiro**	1177	52 Donie Bush	80.3
53 Lou Whitaker	1175	53 Elbie Fletcher	80.0
54 Ron Santo	1170	54 Willie McCovey	79.6
55 Roy Thomas	1168	55 Augie Galan	79.5
56 Chili Davis	1161	56 Darren Daulton	79.4
57 Brett Butler	1155	57 Ned Williamson	78.9
58 Harry Hooper	1155	58 Gus Suhr	78.6
59 Bill Dahlen	1154	59 Darrell Porter	78.5
60 Luke Appling	1147	60 John Kruk	78.4
61 Jesse Burkett	1146	61 Johnny Briggs	78.4
62 Roger Connor	1141	62 Charlie Bennett	78.3
63 George Brett	1138	63 John Mayberry	78.0
64 Pee Wee Reese	1138	64 Bob O'Farrell	78.0
65 **Edgar Martinez**	1137	65 Andre Thornton	77.9
66 Stan Hack	1132	66 **Edgar Martinez**	77.8
67 **John Olerud**	1129	67 Jimmie Foxx	77.6
68 Bobby Grich	1126	68 Harlond Clift	77.6
69 Cal Ripken Jr.	1107	69 Jimmy Sheckard	77.2
70 Ozzie Smith	1101	70 Tony Phillips	77.0
71 Ron Fairly	1094	71 **Bobby Abreu**	76.8
72 Graig Nettles	1088	72 Ed Bailey	76.8
73 Billy Williams	1088	73 Bobby Grich	76.8
74 Honus Wagner	1087	74 Eddie Joost	76.7
75 Charlie Gehringer	1086	75 Elmer Valo	76.6
76 Bid McPhee	1086	76 Billy North	76.5
77 Keith Hernandez	1086	77 Paul Radford	76.3
78 Jim Gilliam	1081	78 Steve Braun	76.2
79 Max Bishop	1078	79 Willie Randolph	75.6
80 George Burns	1077	80 Alvin Davis	75.6
81 Paul Molitor	1073	81 Toby Harrah	75.5
82 **Gary Sheffield**	1071	82 Carl Yastrzemski	75.4
83 Miller Huggins	1070	83 **John Olerud**	75.1
84 Dummy Hoy	1050	84 Wade Boggs	75.0
85 Mark Grace	1045	85 Arky Vaughan	75.0
86 Lu Blue	1044	86 Rogers Hornsby	75.0
87 Topsy Hartsel	1042	87 **Tim Salmon**	74.8
88 Arky Vaughan	1037	88 **Chipper Jones**	74.5
89 **Jim Thome**	1035	89 Lee Mazzilli	74.5
90 Rod Carew	1034	90 David Justice	74.3
91 Norm Cash	1023	91 **Gary Sheffield**	74.2
92 Harold Baines	1022	92 Stan Hack	74.2
93 Sal Bando	1016	93 Ross Youngs	73.9
94 Fielder Jones	1010	94 Dwight Evans	73.7
95 Cupid Childs	1008	95 Norm Siebern	73.6
96 Ron Cey	1008	96 Mickey Cochrane	73.6
97 Dave Bancroft	1007	97 Wally Schang	73.6
98 **Craig Biggio**	1005	98 Jack Graney	73.5
99 Augie Galan	1004	99 Davy Jones	73.3
100 Dolph Camilli	1002	100 Brian Downing	73.2

Table M.8   Career Strikeouts Top 100

Adjusted Strikeouts			Adjusted SOs/550 NFPs	
1	Reggie Jackson	2692	1	Tony Gwynn	19.7
2	Babe Ruth	2277	2	Nellie Fox	22.0
3	Jimmie Foxx	2117	3	Joe Sewell	25.0
4	Willie Stargell	1929	4	Gregg Jefferies	26.7
5	Mickey Mantle	1916	5	**Fernando Vina**	27.5
6	Tony Perez	1890	6	Tommy Holmes	28.1
7	Mike Schmidt	1882	7	Bobby Richardson	28.5
8	Andres Galarraga	1843	8	Felix Millan	28.6
9	Lou Brock	1803	9	Bill Buckner	29.3
10	Dale Murphy	1799	10	Glenn Beckert	29.5
11	Dave Kingman	1799	11	**Eric Young**	29.5
12	Bobby Bonds	1771	12	Vic Power	30.0
13	Harmon Killebrew	1745	13	Don Mueller	30.2
14	Dwight Evans	1734	14	Lloyd Waner	30.5
15	Eddie Mathews	1708	15	Rich Dauer	31.1
16	Jose Canseco	1703	16	Ozzie Smith	31.1
17	**Sammy Sosa**	1686	17	Dale Mitchell	31.4
18	Dave Winfield	1685	18	Mark Grace	32.0
19	Willie Mays	1663	19	Jim Gilliam	32.8
20	Mel Ott	1642	20	Stuffy McInnis	32.9
21	**Fred McGriff**	1633	21	Mike Scioscia	33.0
22	Frank Robinson	1617	22	Don Mattingly	33.0
23	Jimmy Dykes	1586	23	Johnny Ray	33.4
24	Willie McCovey	1578	24	Tris Speaker	33.5
25	Lee May	1570	25	Lance Johnson	33.8
26	Rickey Henderson	1567	26	Johnny Evers	34.4
27	Chili Davis	1561	27	Dave Cash	34.7
28	Rick Monday	1561	28	**Jason Kendall**	35.3
29	Hank Aaron	1547	29	Jesus Alou	35.6
30	Dave Parker	1546	30	Rip Radcliff	35.7
31	Greg Luzinski	1521	31	Red Schoendienst	35.8
32	Dick Allen	1514	32	Cesar Tovar	36.0
33	Duke Snider	1509	33	Greg Gross	36.6
34	Andre Dawson	1495	34	Lenny Harris	36.8
35	Rabbit Maranville	1492	35	Tommy Helms	36.9
36	Lance Parrish	1491	36	Wade Boggs	37.1
37	Jim Rice	1487	37	Joey Cora	37.5
38	George Scott	1484	38	Horace Clarke	37.7
39	Frank Howard	1480	39	Ken Oberkfell	37.7
40	George Foster	1470	40	Jack Glasscock	37.8
41	Eddie Murray	1469	41	Frank McCormick	38.0
42	Gary Gaetti	1469	42	Frankie Frisch	38.0
43	Darrell Evans	1441	43	Andy High	38.0
44	Carl Yastrzemski	1436	44	Matty Alou	38.0
45	Lou Gehrig	1430	45	Harvey Kuenn	38.1
46	Tony Lazzeri	1429	46	Doc Cramer	38.2
47	Bob Johnson	1421	47	Ozzie Guillen	38.3
48	Gil Hodges	1417	48	Ron Hunt	38.5
49	Al Simmons	1417	49	George Kell	38.6
50	Carlton Fisk	1410	50	Ossie Vitt	38.6

Adjusted Strikeouts		Adjusted SOs/550 NFPs	
51 Jack Clark	1409	51 Mike Greenwell	38.6
52 Jimmy Wynn	1408	52 Sam Rice	38.7
53 Gorman Thomas	1408	53 Smoky Burgess	39.0
54 Kiki Cuyler	1394	54 Lave Cross	39.4
55 Dolph Camilli	1391	55 **Nomar Garciaparra**	39.5
56 Mark McGwire	1385	56 Joe Jackson	39.5
57 Rogers Hornsby	1378	57 Tim Foli	39.6
58 **Jim Thome**	1372	58 Larry Bowa	40.2
59 Ron Santo	1366	59 Dick Groat	40.3
60 Juan Samuel	1355	60 Manny Sanguillen	40.3
61 Tony Phillips	1354	61 Lou Finney	40.3
62 Robin Yount	1353	62 Doggie Miller	40.9
63 Tom Brown	1353	63 Willie Randolph	41.0
64 Harold Baines	1350	64 Clyde Milan	41.1
65 Bobby Grich	1347	65 Jody Reed	41.1
66 Willie Horton	1345	66 George Brett	41.1
67 Mickey Vernon	1344	67 Cap Anson	41.2
68 George Kelly	1344	68 Cookie Rojas	41.2
69 Larry Parrish	1344	69 Eddie Collins	41.4
70 Johnny Bench	1343	70 Luis Aparicio	41.4
71 Ernie Banks	1339	71 Johnny Temple	41.4
72 Devon White	1333	72 Dan Brouthers	41.5
73 Max Carey	1324	73 George Cutshaw	41.5
74 Greg Vaughn	1322	74 Yogi Berra	41.6
75 Roberto Clemente	1321	75 Edd Roush	41.6
76 Cy Williams	1321	76 **Omar Vizquel**	41.7
77 Ray Lankford	1317	77 Eddie Waitkus	41.7
78 Claudell Washington	1312	78 Larry Doyle	41.8
79 Larry Doby	1312	79 Darrin Fletcher	42.1
80 Rudy York	1307	80 Ted Sizemore	42.1
81 Joe Cronin	1300	81 Bill Madlock	42.1
82 Eric Davis	1299	82 Tim McCarver	42.3
83 Ken Singleton	1294	83 Bucky Dent	42.4
84 Deron Johnson	1294	84 Billy Southworth	42.5
85 Hank Greenberg	1290	85 Johnny Pesky	42.7
86 Ron Cey	1290	86 Tommy McCarthy	42.7
87 Frankie Crosetti	1289	87 Harold Reynolds	42.8
88 Pee Wee Reese	1287	88 **Barry Larkin**	42.8
89 **Jay Bell**	1284	89 Charlie Gehringer	43.0
90 Eddie Yost	1277	90 Jim Gantner	43.2
91 Ron Gant	1271	91 Steve Sax	43.3
92 Dave Concepcion	1268	92 Lou Bierbauer	43.3
93 Joe Carter	1264	93 Pete Rose	43.6
94 Eddie Joost	1262	94 Bill Dickey	43.7
95 Darryl Strawberry	1261	95 **Matt Lawton**	44.1
96 Mo Vaughn	1258	96 Joe Orsulak	44.3
97 Graig Nettles	1257	97 Cupid Childs	44.4
98 Joe Adcock	1251	98 Arky Vaughan	44.4
99 Pete Rose	1248	99 Paul Waner	44.5
100 Tim Wallach	1242	100 Buddy Bell	44.6

Table M.9   Career Stolen Bases Top 100

Adjusted Stolen Bases		Adjusted SBs/550 NFPs	
1 Rickey Henderson	1557	1 Rickey Henderson	78.3
2 Lou Brock	1193	2 Luis Aparicio	75.1
3 Max Carey	1129	3 George Case	74.9
4 Ty Cobb	1119	4 Vince Coleman	73.0
5 Luis Aparicio	1042	5 Maury Wills	71.4
6 Bert Campaneris	922	6 Otis Nixon	69.4
7 Eddie Collins	918	7 Bert Campaneris	66.0
8 Maury Wills	896	8 **Tom Goodwin**	65.8
9 Joe Morgan	837	9 Ty Cobb	63.3
10 Tim Raines	827	10 Billy Hamilton	62.6
11 Frankie Frisch	823	11 Lou Brock	62.5
12 Willie Wilson	773	12 Kiki Cuyler	62.1
13 Vince Coleman	768	13 Max Carey	61.2
14 Kiki Cuyler	747	14 Willie Wilson	58.4
15 George Case	744	15 **Kenny Lofton**	57.2
16 Billy Hamilton	743	16 Tim Raines	56.3
17 Willie Mays	720	17 Ron LeFlore	56.3
18 Otis Nixon	709	18 Ben Chapman	54.8
19 **Kenny Lofton**	683	19 **Tony Womack**	54.7
20 Honus Wagner	680	20 Jackie Robinson	54.2
21 Paul Molitor	665	21 Gary Pettis	54.0
22 Willie Davis	645	22 Omar Moreno	53.1
23 Pee Wee Reese	619	23 **Eric Young**	52.2
24 Brett Butler	617	24 Julio Cruz	52.1
25 Ben Chapman	614	25 Billy North	52.1
26 Bobby Bonds	612	26 George Sisler	51.6
27 Cesar Cedeno	610	27 Cesar Cedeno	51.6
28 Davey Lopes	601	28 Frankie Frisch	51.4
29 **Roberto Alomar**	601	29 Billy Werber	50.9
30 Tommy Harper	601	30 Pepper Martin	50.2
31 George Sisler	599	31 Bob Bescher	50.0
32 Sam Rice	589	32 Joe Morgan	49.9
33 Ozzie Smith	579	33 Minnie Minoso	49.5
34 Eric Young	579	34 Willie Mays	48.7
35 Richie Ashburn	578	35 Frank Chance	48.6
36 Minnie Minoso	571	36 Freddie Patek	48.0
37 **Barry Bonds**	562	37 Tommy Harper	47.7
38 Vada Pinson	552	38 Delino DeShields	47.5
39 Delino DeShields	550	39 Davey Lopes	46.8
40 Jackie Robinson	546	40 Eddie Collins	45.8
41 Chuck Knoblauch	537	41 Bill Bruton	45.6
42 Bill Bruton	518	42 Dave Collins	45.2
43 Billy Werber	513	43 Honus Wagner	44.9
44 Gee Walker	512	44 Sam Mertes	44.3
45 Freddie Patek	507	45 Gary Redus	44.1
46 Marquis Grissom	503	46 Gee Walker	44.1
47 Omar Moreno	499	47 Bobby Bonds	43.8
48 Ron LeFlore	495	48 **Marquis Grissom**	43.4
49 Tom Goodwin	492	49 Willie Davis	43.1
50 Rod Carew	492	50 Chuck Knoblauch	42.3

Adjusted Stolen Bases		Adjusted SBs/550 NFPs	
51 Jose Cardenal	490	51 Luis Polonia	42.2
52 Amos Otis	483	52 Pee Wee Reese	41.6
53 George Burns	478	53 John McGraw	41.6
54 Jim Gilliam	473	54 Jose Cardenal	41.0
55 Arlie Latham	470	55 Frank Taveras	40.9
56 **Craig Biggio**	467	56 George Burns	40.8
57 Steve Sax	465	57 Lance Johnson	40.4
58 Bob Bescher	459	58 Clyde Milan	40.3
59 Clyde Milan	459	59 Sam Rice	40.2
60 Hank Aaron	456	60 Johnny Hopp	40.1
61 Tom Brown	455	61 Stan Hack	39.7
62 Tony Taylor	450	62 Jackie Jensen	39.6
63 Stan Hack	449	63 Pat Kelly	38.8
64 Frank Chance	440	64 Jack Smith	38.7
65 Devon White	440	65 Lonnie Smith	38.7
66 Dave Collins	431	66 Snuffy Stirnweiss	38.5
67 Billy North	431	67 Richie Ashburn	38.4
68 **Tony Womack**	427	68 Jim Gilliam	38.3
69 George Davis	426	69 Brett Butler	38.3
70 **Barry Larkin**	424	70 Paul Molitor	38.2
71 Brady Anderson	423	71 **Roberto Alomar**	38.1
72 **Omar Vizquel**	419	72 Don Buford	37.8
73 Jackie Jensen	415	73 Jim Landis	37.4
74 Phil Rizzuto	414	74 Lyn Lary	37.2
75 Julio Cruz	412	75 Eric Davis	37.1
76 Pepper Martin	411	76 Sandy Alomar Sr.	36.8
77 Gary Pettis	408	77 Amos Otis	36.6
78 Frank Robinson	407	78 Darren Lewis	36.6
79 Mickey Mantle	405	79 Tommie Agee	36.4
80 Juan Samuel	400	80 **Mike Cameron**	36.3
81 Lance Johnson	400	81 Jack Doyle	36.3
82 Robin Yount	400	82 Phil Rizzuto	36.2
83 Luis Polonia	396	83 **Edgar Renteria**	36.1
84 Luke Appling	395	84 **Johnny Damon**	36.0
85 Larry Bowa	394	85 Bip Roberts	35.8
86 Sam Mertes	391	86 Damaso Garcia	35.6
87 Joe Kuhel	384	87 Juan Samuel	35.4
88 Don Baylor	379	88 Red Murray	35.3
89 Sherry Magee	377	89 Earl Torgeson	34.9
90 Lonnie Smith	375	90 Cesar Tovar	34.8
91 Jimmy Wynn	375	91 Don Baylor	34.8
92 **Mark McLemore**	374	92 Sherry Magee	34.8
93 Jimmy Sheckard	374	93 Johnny Temple	34.7
94 Dave Concepcion	374	94 Chuck Hinton	34.6
95 Earl Torgeson	373	95 Mickey Rivers	34.5
96 John Ward	371	96 Arlie Latham	34.5
97 Lloyd Moseby	370	97 Steve Sax	34.3
98 John McGraw	370	98 Cliff Heathcote	34.2
99 Jack Doyle	370	99 Al Bumbry	33.9
100 Willie Randolph	368	100 Bobby Tolan	33.9

Table M.10   Career Adjusted On-Base Percentage Top 100

Adjusted Times On-Base		Adjusted On-Base Percentage	
1 Pete Rose	5886	1 Ted Williams	.448
2 Rickey Henderson	5301	2 Babe Ruth	.439
3 Carl Yastrzemski	5241	3 Rogers Hornsby	.430
4 Hank Aaron	5169	4 **Barry Bonds**	.429
5 Ty Cobb	5107	5 John McGraw	.427
6 Stan Musial	5103	6 Billy Hamilton	.423
7 Willie Mays	4806	7 Topsy Hartsel	.419
8 **Barry Bonds**	4667	8 Mel Ott	.418
9 Tris Speaker	4658	9 Roy Thomas	.418
10 Mel Ott	4653	10 Mickey Mantle	.416
11 Eddie Collins	4638	11 Wade Boggs	.416
12 Eddie Murray	4622	12 **Frank Thomas**	.415
13 Frank Robinson	4597	13 Lou Gehrig	.412
14 Babe Ruth	4588	14 Rickey Henderson	.411
15 Honus Wagner	4437	15 Stan Musial	.410
16 Joe Morgan	4408	16 **Edgar Martinez**	.409
17 Paul Molitor	4382	17 Ty Cobb	.406
18 Dave Winfield	4362	18 Dan Brouthers	.406
19 Ted Williams	4337	19 Tris Speaker	.406
20 Cal Ripken Jr.	4332	20 Joe Cunningham	.405
21 Wade Boggs	4323	21 George Gore	.405
22 Al Kaline	4288	22 Eddie Collins	.402
23 George Brett	4274	23 Ross Youngs	.402
24 Robin Yount	4163	24 Mike Hargrove	.402
25 Paul Waner	4125	25 **Jeff Bagwell**	.402
26 Reggie Jackson	4115	26 **Jason Giambi**	.401
27 Rod Carew	4115	27 Arky Vaughan	.401
28 Mickey Mantle	4097	28 Pete Browning	.400
29 Rusty Staub	4074	29 Gavy Cravath	.400
30 Cap Anson	3976	30 Frank Robinson	.399
31 Rogers Hornsby	3974	31 **Brian Giles**	.399
32 **Rafael Palmeiro**	3942	32 John Kruk	.399
33 Tony Gwynn	3933	33 Bill Joyce	.399
34 Tim Raines	3925	34 Rod Carew	.398
35 Lou Gehrig	3903	35 Cap Anson	.398
36 Harold Baines	3863	36 Joe Morgan	.397
37 Brooks Robinson	3856	37 Jesse Burkett	.396
38 Max Carey	3837	38 Ferris Fain	.396
39 Eddie Mathews	3835	39 **Bobby Abreu**	.396
40 Darrell Evans	3833	40 Gene Tenace	.396
41 Dwight Evans	3817	41 Honus Wagner	.395
42 Lou Brock	3811	42 Frank Chance	.394
43 Billy Williams	3788	43 Roger Connor	.394
44 Jesse Burkett	3762	44 Jimmie Foxx	.394
45 Luke Appling	3761	45 Jackie Robinson	.394
46 Mike Schmidt	3759	46 Roy Cullenbine	.393
47 Richie Ashburn	3746	47 Dave Magadan	.393
48 Sam Crawford	3739	48 Ken Singleton	.393
49 **Fred McGriff**	3739	49 **Manny Ramirez**	.393
50 Jimmie Foxx	3734	50 Joe Jackson	.393

Adjusted Times On-Base		Adjusted On-Base Percentage	
51 Nap Lajoie	3732	51 **Gary Sheffield**	.393
52 Charlie Gehringer	3700	52 Paul Waner	.393
53 Harmon Killebrew	3684	53 **Jim Thome**	.392
54 Tony Perez	3657	54 Tony Gwynn	.392
55 **Roberto Alomar**	3645	55 Hack Wilson	.392
56 Willie McCovey	3638	56 Elmer Flick	.392
57 Harry Hooper	3586	57 Cupid Childs	.391
58 Ozzie Smith	3586	58 Willie Mays	.391
59 Bill Dahlen	3584	59 **Chipper Jones**	.391
60 George Davis	3582	60 Max Bishop	.391
61 Lou Whitaker	3576	61 **John Olerud**	.391
62 **Craig Biggio**	3574	62 Carl Yastrzemski	.391
63 Zack Wheat	3570	63 Charlie Keller	.390
64 Fred Clarke	3566	64 Eddie Stanky	.390
65 Roberto Clemente	3566	65 Richie Ashburn	.390
66 Brett Butler	3562	66 Roger Bresnahan	.390
67 Chili Davis	3544	67 George Grantham	.389
68 Willie Randolph	3529	68 Keith Hernandez	.389
69 Jake Beckley	3514	69 Miller Huggins	.389
70 Roger Connor	3483	70 Dick Allen	.388
71 Rabbit Maranville	3483	71 Stan Hack	.387
72 Sam Rice	3471	72 Eddie Mathews	.387
73 Frankie Frisch	3464	73 Mark McGwire	.387
74 Luis Aparicio	3446	74 Riggs Stephenson	.387
75 Brian Downing	3443	75 Yank Robinson	.386
76 Andre Dawson	3436	76 Jack Clark	.386
77 Mark Grace	3431	77 Jack Fournier	.386
78 **Jeff Bagwell**	3425	78 **Todd Helton**	.385
79 Ron Santo	3424	79 Dolph Camilli	.385
80 Dave Parker	3422	80 Mickey Cochrane	.384
81 Ernie Banks	3410	81 Augie Galan	.384
82 Goose Goslin	3401	82 Tim Raines	.384
83 Graig Nettles	3391	83 Heinie Groh	.384
84 Nellie Fox	3388	84 Alvin Davis	.383
85 Buddy Bell	3380	85 Willie McCovey	.383
86 Vada Pinson	3375	86 Tip O'Neill	.383
87 Willie Keeler	3371	87 Fielder Jones	.383
88 Eddie Yost	3362	88 Johnny Mize	.383
89 Ted Simmons	3352	89 Harmon Killebrew	.382
90 **Frank Thomas**	3350	90 Brett Butler	.382
91 Jimmy Sheckard	3335	91 Mike Schmidt	.381
92 Ken Singleton	3331	92 George Brett	.381
93 Bid McPhee	3330	93 Will Clark	.381
94 Al Oliver	3328	94 **Mike Piazza**	.381
95 Tony Phillips	3316	95 **Bernie Williams**	.380
96 Keith Hernandez	3297	96 Bobby Grich	.380
97 Pee Wee Reese	3293	97 Eddie Murray	.380
98 Mickey Vernon	3293	98 Willie Randolph	.380
99 Enos Slaughter	3287	99 Denny Lyons	.380
100 Carlton Fisk	3287	100 King Kelly	.380

Table M.11 Career Adjusted Slugging Average Top 100

Adjusted Total Bases		Adjusted Slugging Average	
1 Hank Aaron	6607	1 Babe Ruth	.673
2 Ty Cobb	6001	2 Ted Williams	.628
3 Willie Mays	5892	3 Rogers Hornsby	.597
4 Stan Musial	5772	4 **Barry Bonds**	.584
5 Pete Rose	5660	5 Lou Gehrig	.584
6 Babe Ruth	5583	6 Joe DiMaggio	.582
7 Carl Yastrzemski	5436	7 Willie Mays	.566
8 Honus Wagner	5411	8 Mark McGwire	.556
9 Eddie Murray	5327	9 Mickey Mantle	.554
10 Frank Robinson	5295	10 Stan Musial	.553
11 Dave Winfield	5271	11 Joe Jackson	.552
12 Tris Speaker	5108	12 Honus Wagner	.551
13 **Barry Bonds**	5092	13 Jimmie Foxx	.550
14 Reggie Jackson	5014	14 Ty Cobb	.550
15 George Brett	5012	15 Harry Stovey	.548
16 Sam Crawford	4959	16 Hank Greenberg	.546
17 Cal Ripken Jr.	4953	17 Hank Aaron	.546
18 Mel Ott	4885	18 Charlie Hickman	.543
19 Rogers Hornsby	4851	19 **Manny Ramirez**	.542
20 Ted Williams	4837	20 Johnny Mize	.539
21 Nap Lajoie	4807	21 Dick Allen	.538
22 Al Kaline	4745	22 Frank Robinson	.535
23 Andre Dawson	4741	23 Wally Berger	.534
24 Robin Yount	4738	24 Reggie Jackson	.533
25 Paul Molitor	4691	25 **Mike Piazza**	.533
26 Lou Gehrig	4669	26 Willie Stargell	.532
27 **Rafael Palmeiro**	4579	27 Nap Lajoie	.531
28 Rickey Henderson	4514	28 Dan Brouthers	.531
29 Mickey Mantle	4476	29 Mike Schmidt	.530
30 Jimmie Foxx	4464	30 Hack Wilson	.530
31 Roberto Clemente	4452	31 Gavy Cravath	.528
32 Tony Perez	4443	32 **Alex Rodriguez**	.527
33 Billy Williams	4434	33 Buck Freeman	.527
34 Brooks Robinson	4426	34 Mel Ott	.526
35 Harold Baines	4425	35 Ed Delahanty	.526
36 Ernie Banks	4391	36 Sam Crawford	.525
37 Mike Schmidt	4386	37 Babe Herman	.525
38 Dave Parker	4382	38 Albert Belle	.522
39 Al Simmons	4378	39 **Vladimir Guerrero**	.519
40 Zack Wheat	4343	40 Mike Tiernan	.519
41 Jake Beckley	4313	41 Bill Nicholson	.518
42 Paul Waner	4280	42 Frank Howard	.517
43 Eddie Collins	4266	43 Kevin Mitchell	.517
44 Eddie Mathews	4260	44 Jeff Heath	.517
45 Goose Goslin	4238	45 **Frank Thomas**	.515
46 Willie Stargell	4216	46 **Juan Gonzalez**	.515
47 Rusty Staub	4209	47 Roger Connor	.514
48 Lou Brock	4206	48 Chick Hafey	.513
49 Tony Gwynn	4183	49 Ralph Kiner	.512
50 **Fred McGriff**	4176	50 Tris Speaker	.512

Adjusted Total Bases		Adjusted Slugging Average	
51 Vada Pinson	4168	51 Jack Fournier	.512
52 Willie McCovey	4153	52 Darryl Strawberry	.511
53 Al Oliver	4098	53 Willie McCovey	.510
54 Harmon Killebrew	4052	54 **Jeff Bagwell**	.510
55 Joe Morgan	4047	55 **Ken Griffey Jr**	.509
56 Rod Carew	4033	56 Al Simmons	.509
57 Steve Garvey	4012	57 Harry Heilmann	.509
58 Dwight Evans	4009	58 **Jim Thome**	.509
59 Roger Connor	4004	59 Bill Joyce	.508
60 Joe DiMaggio	3971	60 Pete Browning	.507
61 Harry Heilmann	3964	61 Charlie Keller	.507
62 Charlie Gehringer	3962	62 Duke Snider	.507
63 George Davis	3953	63 Joe Medwick	.506
64 Willie Davis	3949	64 Eddie Mathews	.505
65 Ed Delahanty	3944	65 **Jason Giambi**	.505
66 Cap Anson	3923	66 **Carlos Delgado**	.504
67 Carlton Fisk	3900	67 Sam Thompson	.504
68 Orlando Cepeda	3887	68 Glenn Davis	.503
69 Jim Rice	3880	69 Oyster Burns	.502
70 Fred Clarke	3868	70 Socks Seybold	.502
71 Joe Medwick	3867	71 Chuck Klein	.502
72 Jesse Burkett	3866	72 George Brett	.501
73 Wade Boggs	3836	73 Frank Baker	.501
74 Ted Simmons	3826	74 Mike Donlin	.500
75 Darrell Evans	3818	75 **Brian Giles**	.500
76 Mickey Vernon	3797	76 Al Rosen	.499
77 Bill Buckner	3782	77 Harmon Killebrew	.499
78 Graig Nettles	3767	78 **Gary Sheffield**	.498
79 Chili Davis	3766	79 Larry Doby	.497
80 Max Carey	3759	80 Buck Ewing	.496
81 Bill Dahlen	3751	81 Goose Goslin	.495
82 **Roberto Alomar**	3731	82 Reggie Smith	.494
83 Jimmy Ryan	3724	83 Eddie Murray	.494
84 Tim Raines	3718	84 Cy Williams	.493
85 Harry Hooper	3715	85 Pedro Guerrero	.493
86 Sam Rice	3711	86 Dolph Camilli	.492
87 Frankie Frisch	3693	87 **Edgar Martinez**	.492
88 George Sisler	3692	88 **Nomar Garciaparra**	.491
89 Don Baylor	3681	89 Orlando Cepeda	.490
90 Andres Galarraga	3679	90 Ken Williams	.490
91 Gary Gaetti	3679	91 Denny Lyons	.490
92 Joe Carter	3669	92 Andre Dawson	.490
93 **Sammy Sosa**	3661	93 Dave Winfield	.489
94 Buddy Bell	3640	94 Ripper Collins	.489
95 **Jeff Bagwell**	3633	95 Jose Canseco	.489
96 Duke Snider	3630	96 **Larry Walker**	.489
97 Ryne Sandberg	3628	97 Ernie Lombardi	.488
98 Johnny Bench	3608	98 George Foster	.488
99 **Ken Griffey Jr**	3604	99 Elmer Flick	.487
100 Dale Murphy	3596	100 Tip O'Neill	.487

Table M.12   Career Adjusted On-Base-Plus-Slugging Top 100

Adjusted OPS Units		Adjusted OPS	
1 Hank Aaron	12559	1 Babe Ruth	1.120
2 Pete Rose	12225	2 Ted Williams	1.071
3 Ty Cobb	11820	3 Rogers Hornsby	1.043
4 Stan Musial	11717	4 **Barry Bonds**	1.017
5 Willie Mays	11535	5 Lou Gehrig	.998
6 Carl Yastrzemski	11532	6 Mickey Mantle	.974
7 Babe Ruth	11527	7 Stan Musial	.961
8 **Barry Bonds**	11064	8 Willie Mays	.960
9 Frank Robinson	10762	9 Ty Cobb	.958
10 Rickey Henderson	10728	10 Mel Ott	.957
11 Eddie Murray	10596	11 Honus Wagner	.950
12 Mel Ott	10559	12 Jimmie Foxx	.947
13 Tris Speaker	10506	13 Joe Jackson	.945
14 Honus Wagner	10458	14 Joe DiMaggio	.942
15 Ted Williams	10354	15 Dan Brouthers	.940
16 Dave Winfield	10234	16 Mark McGwire	.939
17 Reggie Jackson	9873	17 Gavy Cravath	.939
18 George Brett	9867	18 Frank Robinson	.937
19 Cal Ripken Jr.	9782	19 Hack Wilson	.933
20 Al Kaline	9638	20 Harry Stovey	.932
21 Rogers Hornsby	9606	21 **Manny Ramirez**	.929
22 Eddie Collins	9582	22 Dick Allen	.929
23 Paul Molitor	9561	23 Hank Aaron	.926
24 Mickey Mantle	9497	24 **Frank Thomas**	.926
25 Lou Gehrig	9420	25 Johnny Mize	.921
26 Robin Yount	9344	26 Roger Connor	.916
27 Joe Morgan	9284	27 Tris Speaker	.916
28 Sam Crawford	9174	28 Pete Browning	.916
29 **Rafael Palmeiro**	9113	29 Hank Greenberg	.916
30 Paul Waner	8981	30 Mike Schmidt	.913
31 Mike Schmidt	8959	31 **Mike Piazza**	.912
32 Jimmie Foxx	8944	32 **Jeff Bagwell**	.908
33 Nap Lajoie	8892	33 Reggie Jackson	.907
34 Rusty Staub	8874	34 Jack Fournier	.906
35 Eddie Mathews	8874	35 Ed Delahanty	.904
36 Wade Boggs	8761	36 **Jason Giambi**	.903
37 Harold Baines	8753	37 Babe Herman	.902
38 Billy Williams	8752	38 Eddie Mathews	.901
39 Brooks Robinson	8647	39 Nap Lajoie	.900
40 Rod Carew	8604	40 Bill Joyce	.899
41 **Fred McGriff**	8551	41 Willie McCovey	.899
42 Tony Perez	8542	42 Wally Berger	.899
43 Harmon Killebrew	8523	43 Sam Crawford	.897
44 Willie McCovey	8521	44 Mike Tiernan	.897
45 Andre Dawson	8510	45 **Jim Thome**	.895
46 Tony Gwynn	8480	46 **Edgar Martinez**	.893
47 Dwight Evans	8474	47 **Brian Giles**	.893
48 Cap Anson	8422	48 Willie Stargell	.891
49 Lou Brock	8358	49 Charlie Keller	.890
50 Roberto Clemente	8346	50 **Alex Rodriguez**	.889

Adjusted OPS Units		Adjusted OPS	
51 Darrell Evans	8334	51 Elmer Flick	.888
52 Zack Wheat	8304	52 Harmon Killebrew	.887
53 Ernie Banks	8202	53 **Gary Sheffield**	.887
54 Tim Raines	8196	54 George Brett	.885
55 Jake Beckley	8183	55 **Vladimir Guerrero**	.884
56 Charlie Gehringer	8170	56 Duke Snider	.883
57 Jesse Burkett	8168	57 Dolph Camilli	.883
58 Dave Parker	8150	58 Socks Seybold	.882
59 Max Carey	8119	59 Ralph Kiner	.881
60 Goose Goslin	8099	60 Harry Heilmann	.881
61 Roger Connor	8095	61 Mike Donlin	.881
62 George Davis	7976	62 Kevin Mitchell	.880
63 Willie Stargell	7969	63 Charlie Hickman	.879
64 Fred Clarke	7913	64 Buck Freeman	.879
65 Al Simmons	7904	65 Frank Howard	.877
66 Bill Dahlen	7843	66 Eddie Murray	.875
67 Vada Pinson	7820	67 Jack Clark	.875
68 Chili Davis	7820	68 Darryl Strawberry	.874
69 Harry Hooper	7813	69 Pedro Guerrero	.874
70 **Roberto Alomar**	7804	70 **Chipper Jones**	.874
71 **Jeff Bagwell**	7745	71 Albert Belle	.874
72 Al Oliver	7708	72 Chick Hafey	.874
73 Harry Heilmann	7652	73 **Carlos Delgado**	.872
74 Graig Nettles	7631	74 Tip O'Neill	.872
75 Lou Whitaker	7630	75 Bill Nicholson	.870
76 Carlton Fisk	7626	76 Paul Waner	.870
77 Ted Simmons	7580	77 Chuck Klein	.867
78 Luke Appling	7572	78 **Ken Griffey Jr**	.867
79 **Craig Biggio**	7571	79 **Todd Helton**	.865
80 Ed Delahanty	7542	80 Denny Lyons	.865
81 Ron Santo	7529	81 Jeff Heath	.864
82 Frankie Frisch	7515	82 Cy Williams	.863
83 Sam Rice	7484	83 Carl Yastrzemski	.863
84 Mickey Vernon	7465	84 Bill Terry	.862
85 **Frank Thomas**	7462	85 Oyster Burns	.862
86 Jimmy Ryan	7390	86 Jesse Burkett	.861
87 Steve Garvey	7380	87 Sam Thompson	.860
88 Buddy Bell	7376	88 **Fred McGriff**	.859
89 Don Baylor	7360	89 Reggie Smith	.858
90 Jim Rice	7314	90 Will Clark	.857
91 Brian Downing	7313	91 Buck Ewing	.857
92 Richie Ashburn	7287	92 Joe Medwick	.857
93 Orlando Cepeda	7248	93 Boog Powell	.857
94 Luis Aparicio	7228	94 George Grantham	.857
95 Willie Davis	7227	95 Al Rosen	.856
96 Joe DiMaggio	7213	96 Rickey Henderson	.855
97 Mark Grace	7209	97 Ripper Collins	.855
98 Duke Snider	7199	98 Arky Vaughan	.855
99 Dan Brouthers	7195	99 Larry Doby	.854
100 Enos Slaughter	7192	100 Zack Wheat	.854

Table M.13 Career Event-Specific Batting Runs Top 100

Event-Specific Batting Runs		ESBRs/550 NFPs	
1 Babe Ruth	1366	1 Babe Ruth	74.9
2 Ted Williams	1213	2 Ted Williams	70.4
3 **Barry Bonds**	1135	3 Rogers Hornsby	60.1
4 Stan Musial	1003	4 **Barry Bonds**	57.4
5 Rogers Hornsby	996	5 Lou Gehrig	55.6
6 Ty Cobb	988	6 Mickey Mantle	52.3
7 Hank Aaron	954	7 Stan Musial	49.9
8 Willie Mays	944	8 Ty Cobb	48.1
9 Lou Gehrig	931	9 Jimmie Foxx	47.1
10 Mickey Mantle	905	10 Willie Mays	46.7
11 Mel Ott	882	11 Mel Ott	45.5
12 Frank Robinson	881	12 Joe DiMaggio	45.4
13 Tris Speaker	811	13 Honus Wagner	45.3
14 Honus Wagner	789	14 Joe Jackson	45.3
15 Jimmie Foxx	770	15 **Frank Thomas**	45.0
16 Mike Schmidt	670	16 Mark McGwire	44.2
17 **Frank Thomas**	659	17 **Manny Ramirez**	44.0
18 Carl Yastrzemski	650	18 Dan Brouthers	43.9
19 Reggie Jackson	633	19 Frank Robinson	43.7
20 Joe DiMaggio	632	20 Tris Speaker	41.2
21 **Jeff Bagwell**	630	21 Gavy Cravath	41.1
22 Roger Connor	613	22 Dick Allen	41.0
23 Dan Brouthers	611	23 Hank Greenberg	40.8
24 Eddie Mathews	609	24 Johnny Mize	40.8
25 Mark McGwire	609	25 Hank Aaron	40.7
26 George Brett	605	26 **Jeff Bagwell**	40.6
27 Rickey Henderson	604	27 **Mike Piazza**	40.3
28 Willie McCovey	596	28 **Jason Giambi**	40.2
29 Sam Crawford	590	29 **Edgar Martinez**	40.0
30 Eddie Collins	586	30 Hack Wilson	39.6
31 **Edgar Martinez**	584	31 Bill Joyce	39.3
32 Harmon Killebrew	582	32 Mike Schmidt	39.1
33 Eddie Murray	581	33 Pete Browning	39.0
34 Al Kaline	578	34 **Brian Giles**	38.6
35 Nap Lajoie	563	35 Harry Stovey	38.6
36 Ed Delahanty	557	36 **Jim Thome**	38.4
37 Joe Morgan	547	37 Roger Connor	38.1
38 Dave Winfield	547	38 Charlie Keller	37.6
39 Willie Stargell	546	39 Reggie Jackson	37.1
40 Johnny Mize	545	40 **Gary Sheffield**	37.0
41 Dick Allen	540	41 Ed Delahanty	36.7
42 **Gary Sheffield**	534	42 Willie McCovey	36.4
43 **Fred McGriff**	534	43 Eddie Mathews	36.2
44 Wade Boggs	528	44 Nap Lajoie	36.2
45 **Rafael Palmeiro**	528	45 Jack Fournier	36.0
46 Harry Heilmann	527	46 Mike Tiernan	35.9
47 Paul Waner	527	47 **Vladimir Guerrero**	35.7
48 Jesse Burkett	526	48 **Alex Rodriguez**	35.7
49 Tony Gwynn	518	49 Harmon Killebrew	35.4
50 Rod Carew	510	50 Ralph Kiner	35.3

Event-Specific Batting Runs		ESBRs/550 NFPs	
51 Duke Snider	498	51 **Chipper Jones**	34.5
52 Jack Clark	482	52 Babe Herman	34.2
53 Harry Stovey	479	53 George Brett	33.6
54 Billy Williams	478	54 **Carlos Delgado**	33.6
55 **Ken Griffey Jr**	475	55 Willie Stargell	33.6
56 Pete Rose	471	56 Duke Snider	33.6
57 **Manny Ramirez**	469	57 Harry Heilmann	33.4
58 Joe Jackson	458	58 Wally Berger	33.2
59 Will Clark	458	59 Elmer Flick	33.1
60 Zack Wheat	456	60 Sam Crawford	33.1
61 Goose Goslin	451	61 **Todd Helton**	32.9
62 Hank Greenberg	450	62 Eddie Murray	32.8
63 Cap Anson	450	63 Jack Clark	32.6
64 **Jim Thome**	445	64 Dolph Camilli	32.5
65 **Mike Piazza**	437	65 Denny Lyons	32.5
66 Mike Tiernan	437	66 Mike Donlin	32.4
67 Al Simmons	434	67 Kevin Mitchell	32.4
68 Ken Singleton	433	68 Rickey Henderson	32.4
69 Frank Howard	429	69 Frank Howard	32.3
70 Paul Molitor	425	70 **Ken Griffey Jr**	32.3
71 Reggie Smith	423	71 Pedro Guerrero	32.2
72 Billy Hamilton	420	72 Tip O'Neill	32.2
73 Boog Powell	416	73 Albert Belle	32.1
74 Sherry Magee	414	74 Carl Yastrzemski	31.9
75 **John Olerud**	412	75 **Bobby Abreu**	31.8
76 Charlie Gehringer	412	76 Al Rosen	31.4
77 Roberto Clemente	412	77 Jesse Burkett	31.2
78 Fred Clarke	410	78 Wade Boggs	31.2
79 Tim Raines	406	79 Darryl Strawberry	30.8
80 Dwight Evans	403	80 Will Clark	30.8
81 Joe Medwick	403	81 Larry Doby	30.8
82 Keith Hernandez	403	82 Billy Hamilton	30.6
83 Norm Cash	403	83 Paul Waner	30.6
84 Arky Vaughan	402	84 Bill Nicholson	30.4
85 Ralph Kiner	401	85 **Fred McGriff**	30.4
86 Rusty Staub	401	86 Socks Seybold	30.3
87 Bob Johnson	400	87 Jeff Heath	30.2
88 **Larry Walker**	398	88 Gene Tenace	30.2
89 Orlando Cepeda	397	89 **Larry Walker**	30.1
90 **Jason Giambi**	395	90 Boog Powell	29.6
91 Hack Wilson	392	91 Roy Cullenbine	29.6
92 Joe Kelley	386	92 Al Kaline	29.6
93 Jack Fournier	386	93 Buck Freeman	29.3
94 Albert Belle	384	94 Reggie Smith	29.2
95 Babe Herman	381	95 Jackie Robinson	29.2
96 Elmer Flick	379	96 Charlie Hickman	29.1
97 Pete Browning	377	97 Arky Vaughan	29.1
98 **Chipper Jones**	377	98 Chick Hafey	29.0
99 Dolph Camilli	374	99 Rod Carew	28.9
100 Cy Williams	374	100 Tony Gwynn	28.8

Table M.14   Career Position-Adjusted Event-Specific Batting Runs Top 100

Position-Adjusted ESBRs		Position-Adjusted ESBRs/550 NFPs	
1 Babe Ruth	1200	1 Babe Ruth	66.2
2 Rogers Hornsby	1085	2 Rogers Hornsby	65.5
3 Ted Williams	1051	3 Ted Williams	61.3
4 **Barry Bonds**	1024	4 **Barry Bonds**	51.8
5 Honus Wagner	916	5 Honus Wagner	50.2
6 Willie Mays	878	6 Mickey Mantle	48.6
7 Stan Musial	838	7 **Mike Piazza**	47.6
8 Mickey Mantle	833	8 **Alex Rodriguez**	47.4
9 Ty Cobb	825	9 Lou Gehrig	47.1
10 Lou Gehrig	780	10 Bill Joyce	43.8
11 Hank Aaron	775	11 Willie Mays	43.7
12 Joe Morgan	756	12 Joe DiMaggio	43.0
13 Mel Ott	728	13 Stan Musial	42.8
14 Frank Robinson	712	14 Ty Cobb	40.9
15 Eddie Collins	682	15 Nap Lajoie	40.6
16 Tris Speaker	667	16 Arky Vaughan	39.8
17 Nap Lajoie	645	17 Joe Morgan	39.7
18 Mike Schmidt	637	18 Jimmie Foxx	38.5
19 Jimmie Foxx	620	19 Joe Jackson	38.4
20 Joe DiMaggio	599	20 Mel Ott	38.1
21 Eddie Mathews	594	21 **Nomar Garciaparra**	37.7
22 Charlie Gehringer	557	22 Denny Lyons	37.4
23 Arky Vaughan	550	23 Mike Schmidt	37.3
24 Cal Ripken Jr.	549	24 Dan Brouthers	37.0
25 Roger Connor	531	25 **Manny Ramirez**	36.8
26 George Brett	526	26 Pete Browning	35.8
27 **Frank Thomas**	523	27 Dick Allen	35.7
28 Rod Carew	520	28 Eddie Mathews	35.7
29 **Mike Piazza**	517	29 **Frank Thomas**	35.7
30 Wade Boggs	516	30 Frank Robinson	35.3
31 Dan Brouthers	515	31 **Brian Giles**	34.9
32 Robin Yount	512	32 **Chipper Jones**	34.5
33 **Ken Griffey Jr**	504	33 **Ken Griffey Jr**	34.3
34 **Edgar Martinez**	489	34 Mark McGwire	34.1
35 Reggie Jackson	485	35 Tris Speaker	34.1
36 **Alex Rodriguez**	485	36 Hack Wilson	33.9
37 Harmon Killebrew	482	37 Hank Aaron	33.9
38 Bobby Grich	481	38 Harry Stovey	33.5
39 Rickey Henderson	480	39 **Edgar Martinez**	33.5
40 **Gary Sheffield**	474	40 Gavy Cravath	33.4
41 Dick Allen	471	41 **Derek Jeter**	33.2
42 Mark McGwire	470	42 Roger Connor	33.1
43 Sam Crawford	470	43 John McGraw	33.1
44 **Jeff Bagwell**	470	44 **Gary Sheffield**	32.9
45 Ed Delahanty	469	45 Bobby Grich	32.8
46 Joe Cronin	461	46 Jackie Robinson	32.8
47 Al Kaline	451	47 Eddie Collins	32.7
48 Luke Appling	451	48 Johnny Mize	32.3
49 Alan Trammell	450	49 Mike Tiernan	31.9
50 Willie McCovey	448	50 Charlie Gehringer	31.8

Position-Adjusted ESBRs		Position-Adjusted ESBRs/550 NFPs	
51 **Barry Larkin**	446	51 **Jim Thome**	31.7
52 Carl Yastrzemski	443	52 Hank Greenberg	31.6
53 Duke Snider	442	53 Cal Ripken Jr.	31.4
54 **Roberto Alomar**	435	54 Frank Baker	31.2
55 Johnny Mize	432	55 Mickey Cochrane	31.2
56 Tony Gwynn	420	56 Joe Gordon	31.0
57 Harry Stovey	416	57 Rod Carew	31.0
58 Lou Whitaker	415	58 Ed Delahanty	31.0
59 George Davis	409	59 Al Rosen	30.9
60 Dave Winfield	404	60 George Brett	30.8
61 **Craig Biggio**	397	61 Jack Fournier	30.7
62 Willie Stargell	397	62 **Jason Giambi**	30.7
63 Jesse Burkett	394	63 **Jeff Bagwell**	30.3
64 **Manny Ramirez**	391	64 Wade Boggs	30.1
65 Joe Jackson	388	65 Duke Snider	29.8
66 Mike Tiernan	388	66 Wally Berger	29.8
67 Gabby Hartnett	387	67 Charlie Keller	29.7
68 **Bernie Williams**	386	68 Gabby Hartnett	29.7
69 Harry Heilmann	380	69 Harmon Killebrew	29.6
70 **Chipper Jones**	377	70 Reggie Jackson	29.4
71 Jack Clark	375	71 Joe Cronin	29.2
72 Paul Molitor	370	72 Tip O'Neill	29.2
73 Frank Baker	370	73 **Bernie Williams**	28.9
74 Eddie Murray	368	74 **Jim Edmonds**	28.7
75 **Jim Thome**	367	75 Fred Dunlap	28.7
76 Joe Gordon	366	76 **Barry Larkin**	28.7
77 Vern Stephens	364	77 Lou Boudreau	28.7
78 Stan Hack	361	78 Oyster Burns	28.4
79 Lou Boudreau	358	79 **Vladimir Guerrero**	28.4
80 Pete Rose	357	80 Ernie Lombardi	28.3
81 Billy Hamilton	356	81 George Grantham	28.2
82 Bill Dahlen	354	82 Alan Trammell	28.0
83 Johnny Bench	352	83 Gene Tenace	27.9
84 **Fred McGriff**	351	84 Willie McCovey	27.9
85 Paul Waner	350	85 Rickey Henderson	27.9
86 Tony Lazzeri	349	86 Vern Stephens	27.8
87 Toby Harrah	349	87 Kevin Mitchell	27.8
88 Hank Greenberg	348	88 Frank Chance	27.7
89 Ed McKean	347	89 Larry Doby	27.7
90 Pete Browning	346	90 Robin Yount	27.6
91 Cap Anson	345	91 Elmer Flick	27.6
92 Mickey Cochrane	343	92 Sam Crawford	26.8
93 Reggie Smith	342	93 Tony Lazzeri	26.7
94 Denny Lyons	340	94 Pedro Guerrero	26.7
95 Larry Doyle	340	95 Charlie Hickman	26.6
96 Jackie Robinson	339	96 **Roberto Alomar**	26.4
97 Ernie Banks	339	97 Roger Bresnahan	26.3
98 Joe Torre	339	98 Ralph Kiner	26.2
99 **Rafael Palmeiro**	337	99 Larry Doyle	26.0
100 Hack Wilson	337	100 Buck Ewing	26.0

Adjusted Career Offensive Averages

	BA	DPT	T	HR	R	RBI	BB	SO	SB	OBP	SLG	CBR	Rank	Rank+
Hank Aaron	.310	35	7	28	91	90	57	61	23	.378	.546	40.7	15	20
Bobby Abreu	.301	35	6	13	75	66	77	82	33	.396	.461	14.9	251	296
Jerry Adair	.265	25	3	5	49	48	25	64	9	.299	.353	−10	1053	833
Bobby Adams	.263	29	6	4	67	34	47	81	22	.327	.358	−2.1	875	830
Sparky Adams	.260	21	2	1	67	31	48	48	31	.330	.315	−9.8	1046	933
Joe Adcock	.275	26	3	24	61	83	45	95	3	.335	.476	15.4	236	341
Tommie Agee	.267	29	3	16	75	59	44	110	36	.330	.429	4.8	589	660
Edgarda Alfonzo	.282	27	2	11	68	62	54	48	7	.353	.405	6.9	493	374
Luis Alicea	.250	27	8	3	58	43	59	66	13	.335	.341	−2.8	893	751
Dick Allen	.293	34	8	27	86	87	71	115	18	.388	.538	33.0	34	39
Ethan Allen	.270	28	3	8	63	52	29	72	22	.312	.379	−3.5	906	1069
Gene Alley	.251	25	5	8	60	47	42	81	16	.313	.360	−6.2	968	589
Bob Allison	.259	29	5	22	75	73	73	97	19	.360	.457	14.3	267	363
Roberto Alomar	.301	32	6	9	79	56	54	52	38	.370	.428	19.9	134	52
Sandy Alomar Sr.	.256	19	2	1	66	32	31	53	37	.298	.306	−19	1116	1044
Sandy Alomar Jr.	.267	27	2	10	53	59	23	49	5	.301	.381	−5.1	942	806
Felipe Alou	.287	32	4	13	70	61	31	52	18	.331	.435	9.5	399	644
Jesus Alou	.283	25	3	4	56	49	18	36	8	.311	.363	−6.3	969	1133
Matty Alou	.301	27	4	3	71	41	29	38	28	.343	.379	3.0	684	886
Moises Alou	.293	30	4	18	71	83	50	55	11	.358	.468	15.5	232	301
Brady Anderson	.251	32	9	12	70	47	66	75	32	.347	.399	8.5	434	489
Garret Anderson	.292	32	4	13	59	74	24	57	10	.323	.442	6.6	507	623
John Anderson	.278	33	6	13	62	81	34		20	.328	.433	6.7	501	669
Cap Anson	.308	32	4	10	69	95	65	41	4	.398	.438	26.1	68	108
Luis Aparicio	.269	26	6	3	69	38	34	41	75	.314	.349	−7.6	1010	507
Luke Appling	.295	28	5	4	64	55	62	56	21	.371	.382	13.7	280	54
Tony Armas	.251	24	4	23	59	81	27	123	3	.290	.446	1.9	742	873
Richie Ashburn	.300	27	6	1	72	32	68	46	38	.390	.369	15.5	233	269
Alan Ashby	.247	24	1	13	48	64	56	77	1	.326	.376	0.2	818	727
Bob Aspromonte	.257	21	3	7	48	57	43	54	5	.320	.347	−6.6	977	1060

	BA	DPT	T	HR	R	RBI	BB	SO	SB	OBP	SLG	CBR	Rank	Rank+
Brad Ausmus	.249	23	4	4	54	42	47	67	13	.316	.329	−9.3	1040	935
Jimmy Austin	.250	24	3	5	61	42	56	89	15	.330	.335	−5.4	947	882
Earl Averill	.284	30	7	21	75	72	54	75	10	.355	.482	20.2	131	130
Bobby Avila	.280	26	4	8	75	48	52	58	25	.346	.389	4.9	584	312
Carlos Baerga	.286	26	3	10	65	67	26	49	9	.324	.403	2.9	692	571
Jeff Bagwell	.293	32	3	25	85	84	81	75	17	**.402**	**.510**	**38.5**	**19**	**41**
Bob Bailey	.255	25	4	16	61	61	68	89	15	.350	.405	8.5	435	493
Ed Bailey	.249	21	2	16	54	68	77	88	5	.360	.391	5.1	576	480
Harold Baines	.287	29	5	18	62	76	51	68	6	.353	.453	19.6	138	291
Dusty Baker	.276	28	2	17	68	71	54	69	14	.350	.433	13.6	281	403
Frank Baker	.292	32	6	23	74	**91**	42	48	13	.350	**.501**	19.3	144	**71**
Dave Bancroft	.259	26	3	5	68	40	69	67	9	.360	.345	1.9	740	196
Sal Bando	.263	29	4	18	71	75	68	65	9	.360	.432	16.3	215	187
Ernie Banks	.276	28	5	23	69	82	43	70	11	.337	.473	18.9	150	**78**
Jesse Barfield	.256	25	4	23	71	69	57	117	11	.337	.449	8.9	413	530
Jack Barry	.249	22	2	7	65	60	50		9	.325	.338	−6.1	965	763
Shad Barry	.263	24	3	7	62	55	43		8	.327	.359	−3.4	904	1082
Dick Bartell	.261	30	4	6	65	41	53	75	17	.345	.361	1.5	758	271
Kevin Bass	.275	29	5	13	65	65	37	65	16	.328	.421	4.7	591	739
Johnny Bates	.279	31	5	13	70	60	65		15	.369	.431	9.7	395	529
Earl Battey	.274	25	2	11	50	59	56	68	4	.351	.395	4.5	601	510
Hank Bauer	.274	29	5	18	78	66	43	81	15	.330	.452	9.4	403	508
Don Baylor	.265	28	3	22	77	77	49	63	**35**	.347	.452	18.1	165	365
Ginger Beaumont	**.297**	26	4	14	79	62	46		17	.360	.441	12.8	298	379
Glenn Beckert	.278	24	3	2	67	37	28	**29**	11	.318	.344	−7.8	1013	679
Jake Beckley	.289	**35**	7	16	70	81	37	73	6	.343	.468	19.2	146	168
Mark Belanger	.236	21	4	2	61	34	50	75	23	.309	.295	−17	1112	844
Buddy Bell	.281	30	5	10	64	60	47	**45**	6	.344	.409	9.9	388	415
Derek Bell	.271	25	2	11	65	67	40	86	22	.327	.392	2.1	733	919
Albert Belle	.286	**34**	3	27	74	**94**	53	70	12	.356	**.522**	23.5	88	126
George Bell	.277	27	4	19	66	82	28	63	10	.317	.453	8.0	453	629
Gus Bell	.269	29	6	12	61	67	35	67	6	.317	.407	2.5	708	895
Jay Bell	.259	29	6	10	68	51	55	85	8	.335	.384	3.7	641	222
Johnny Bench	.266	28	2	26	71	88	57	86	9	.343	.471	19.4	142	**81**
Juan Beniquez	.273	25	4	7	65	49	39	62	16	.328	.374	0.2	816	910
Charlie Bennett	.258	31	4	22	54	66	**78**	118	1	.372	.460	11.0	358	272
Wally Berger	.284	31	4	**30**	75	84	50	112	8	.357	**.534**	20.8	120	125
Tony Bernazard	.261	29	4	9	66	48	57	81	21	.341	.379	2.0	734	575
Yogi Berra	.282	27	3	21	77	**91**	40	**42**	5	.334	.464	16.4	209	111
Ken Berry	.270	26	3	7	57	46	36	71	11	.320	.367	−2.8	894	1050
Bob Bescher	.255	28	4	11	**80**	41	69	88	**50**	.354	.385	5.0	580	778
Dante Bichette	.275	29	2	14	60	73	27	78	18	.312	.422	3.5	650	937
Lou Bierbauer	.258	25	3	9	52	66	26	**43**	4	.295	.367	−9.6	1043	970
Carson Bigbee	.269	24	4	7	71	37	52	46	29	.346	.364	1.0	777	1038
Craig Biggio	.285	30	4	11	**81**	49	57	62	30	.367	.414	17.5	175	**57**
Max Bishop	.247	23	2	8	76	29	**104**	85	4	**.391**	.342	8.5	436	263
Paul Blair	.261	32	7	11	70	55	37	76	24	.313	.401	0.6	793	902
Don Blasingame	.255	23	6	1	65	28	53	49	24	.328	.319	−8.6	1024	749
Jeff Blauser	.256	26	4	12	68	50	60	92	7	.343	.387	4.0	621	330
Ossie Bluege	.248	21	3	8	57	56	52	81	22	.324	.344	−4.6	928	652

For table explanations see page 379.   *(continued)*

	BA	DPT	T	HR	R	RBI	BB	SO	SB	OBP	SLG	CBR	Rank	Rank+
Lu Blue	.256	27	5	7	74	46	**82**	75	19	.368	.365	7.8	459	724
Bruce Bochte	.284	28	3	8	58	60	62	64	7	.366	.394	8.7	424	657
Ping Bodie	.268	31	5	19	53	75	45		5	.331	.455	6.3	526	666
Wade Boggs	**.322**	**35**	4	5	77	47	**75**	**37**	3	**.416**	.426	**31.2**	**41**	**32**
Frank Bolling	.251	25	4	8	61	49	41	59	11	.309	.354	−7.6	1006	698
Barry Bonds	.294	**33**	5	**36**	**95**	**83**	**103**	61	33	**.429**	**.584**	**57.4**	**4**	**4**
Bobby Bonds	.268	29	5	**24**	**86**	71	62	**122**	**44**	.354	.478	21.2	114	224
Bobby Bonilla	.276	32	5	18	70	75	60	71	4	.356	.456	18.9	149	176
Zeke Bonura	.280	30	2	18	68	80	49	51	4	.345	.453	8.1	448	638
Bob Boone	.253	23	2	7	44	55	46	46	4	.317	.341	−7.8	1015	978
Bret Boone	.268	28	3	16	66	72	39	81	10	.322	.422	5.1	573	346
Ray Boone	.269	24	5	16	64	73	56	68	6	.342	.420	7.4	473	369
Mike Bordick	.257	24	4	5	52	47	41	59	13	.316	.341	−7.6	1007	696
Jim Bottomley	.276	32	8	21	69	**84**	50	80	6	.349	.471	18.9	151	285
Lou Boudreau	.290	**34**	4	9	68	63	56	45	10	.363	.419	13.0	293	77
Larry Bowa	.259	21	6	1	61	33	30	**40**	31	.299	.320	−17	1107	817
Clete Boyer	.245	24	4	13	57	57	40	84	9	.302	.377	−5.7	953	1023
Ken Boyer	.282	26	5	17	70	72	51	75	23	.351	.442	15.5	231	204
Jack Boyle	.241	21	3	7	53	53	39	81	3	.297	.331	−14	1094	1118
Bill Bradley	.268	29	5	12	70	59	37		10	.326	.407	2.7	697	516
Phil Bradley	.288	30	7	8	72	45	56	86	26	.369	.412	7.9	457	539
Jackie Brandt	.267	30	5	12	70	63	44	77	14	.326	.410	2.7	698	835
Kitty Bransfield	.268	29	4	7	56	77	28		10	.310	.378	−4.7	930	1016
Steve Braun	.271	26	2	7	61	50	**76**	60	9	.375	.371	5.7	547	665
Roger Bresnahan	.274	31	4	10	69	63	**82**		16	**.390**	.403	11.7	335	186
Eddie Bressoud	.251	31	5	10	58	48	50	100	3	.321	.383	−0.4	837	531
Rube Bressler	.273	27	7	9	61	68	65	69	8	.368	.394	6.1	532	716
George Brett	**.306**	38	9	18	78	77	57	**41**	20	**.381**	**.501**	**33.6**	30	30
Al Bridwell	.258	17	2	1	54	46	69		8	.355	.300	−4.4	924	736
Johnny Briggs	.258	29	6	19	72	61	78	90	13	.365	.440	10.6	371	486
Ed Brinkman	.231	23	4	4	46	39	36	71	7	.284	.308	−22	1134	1013
Lou Brock	.291	**34**	8	9	81	46	41	89	**63**	.346	.420	11.6	336	703
Steve Brodie	.278	24	4	7	56	68	39	52	12	.334	.376	2.0	735	947
Hubie Brooks	.272	27	4	13	57	72	33	84	6	.320	.412	3.4	662	643
Tom Brookens	.248	29	6	7	59	53	37	80	17	.301	.361	−9.0	1033	1101
Scott Brosius	.252	25	2	13	62	59	42	76	11	.312	.384	−1.2	854	853
Dan Brouthers	**.312**	**39**	8	21	79	**86**	68	**41**	6	**.406**	**.531**	**37.4**	21	26
George Browne	.273	24	4	8	73	44	38		14	.328	.376	−0.3	835	1045
Pete Browning	**.321**	**35**	4	18	72	59	58		10	**.400**	**.507**	23.1	91	87
Tom Brown	.259	26	5	13	75	36	56	136	34	.339	.393	5.1	569	765
Tom Brunansky	.244	25	3	21	58	67	60	87	9	.330	.423	6.9	492	676
Bill Bruton	.269	30	**10**	6	77	45	38	80	**46**	.322	.380	−0.4	838	975
Bill Buckner	.287	31	3	10	61	65	26	**29**	17	.323	.413	4.8	587	988
Steve Buechele	.244	24	3	14	55	60	48	89	3	.315	.380	−1.7	864	943
Don Buford	.280	27	6	10	**83**	47	69	61	**38**	.374	.401	9.7	394	393
Jay Buhner	.250	23	3	**26**	67	81	68	114	1	.345	.455	12.2	315	423
Al Bumbry	.286	29	7	5	80	39	48	74	**34**	.351	.389	5.1	572	627
Jack Burdock	.250	22	3	7	61	54	43	82	1	.321	.338	−11	1071	1007
Smoky Burgess	.284	29	3	12	50	71	53	**39**	4	.353	.418	7.7	462	342
Jesse Burkett	**.308**	29	6	15	**79**	48	66	81	12	**.396**	.461	**31.2**	40	63

	BA	DPT	T	HR	R	RBI	BB	SO	SB	OBP	SLG	CBR	Rank	Rank+
Ellis Burks	.278	29	6	20	76	71	53	82	20	.350	.461	18.2	162	184
Rick Burleson	.265	26	2	4	60	40	42	50	12	.324	.347	−5.4	948	470
Jeromy Burnitz	.246	27	4	22	71	72	64	103	10	.336	.436	7.2	476	654
George Burns	.274	30	4	9	81	45	73	74	41	.378	.393	12.8	299	494
George Burns	.282	31	3	16	65	73	29	72	13	.327	.446	9.5	400	544
Oyster Burns	.288	33	8	22	68	81	52	67	8	.359	**.502**	16.5	208	170
Tom Burns	.264	27	3	8	56	68	42	82	6	.328	.373	−2.1	874	733
Jeff Burroughs	.260	25	2	21	61	76	72	104	2	.359	.440	13.5	285	440
Jim Busby	.261	25	3	6	63	51	31	73	34	.303	.354	−8.5	1022	1113
Donie Bush	.246	20	2	3	80	32	80	66	25	.359	.305	−2.4	884	391
Brett Butler	.290	27	**10**	3	80	33	68	50	38	**.382**	.378	14.6	259	200
Bobby Byrne	.257	25	3	4	68	37	49	52	10	.328	.335	−6.2	967	925
Enos Cabell	.279	27	5	6	69	55	24	65	26	.314	.381	−2.7	892	1059
Johnny Callison	.265	33	9	18	69	63	52	79	13	.339	.447	11.8	332	598
Mike Cameron	.249	29	7	14	71	62	61	116	36	.334	.407	3.6	647	584
Dolph Camilli	.262	28	7	27	75	78	87	121	13	**.385**	**.492**	22.8	94	183
Ken Caminiti	.271	28	2	17	67	72	56	78	8	.346	.428	11.0	357	304
Bert Campaneris	.271	30	6	4	77	39	36	67	66	.321	.362	−4.0	918	235
Roy Campanella	.269	23	2	23	66	**88**	58	78	7	.350	.457	10.6	367	253
Bruce Campbell	.268	31	7	13	65	66	50	100	11	.336	.423	6.5	513	772
Jose Canseco	.265	26	2	29	78	**92**	59	116	23	.347	**.489**	22.0	102	190
Jose Cardenal	.276	30	4	9	67	56	43	61	**41**	.333	.397	4.5	600	878
Leo Cardenas	.257	28	4	8	49	52	41	87	7	.315	.364	−5.1	938	422
Rod Carew	**.332**	35	7	5	78	55	55	57	30	**.398**	.443	28.9	49	29
Max Carey	.277	28	4	13	79	43	65	69	**61**	.372	.417	17.1	186	310
Hick Carpenter	.266	23	2	6	61	42	27		6	.309	.352	−10	1050	1030
Chico Carrasquel	.257	23	2	5	57	48	44	70	9	.318	.339	−6.7	981	709
Cliff Carroll	.258	23	3	10	69	49	51	71	12	.332	.365	−0.2	833	974
Gary Carter	.263	25	2	**24**	66	77	52	63	4	.338	.450	15.3	238	119
Joe Carter	.257	29	4	20	67	82	31	77	24	.303	.437	4.5	599	887
Rico Carty	.294	29	2	16	61	76	58	61	4	.370	.451	16.4	211	344
George Case	.271	24	2	5	76	35	38	55	**75**	.323	.352	−4.0	916	1098
Doc Casey	.256	24	3	5	63	44	38		14	.314	.338	−10	1047	990
Dave Cash	.279	27	5	3	67	40	39	**35**	16	.332	.357	−1.8	866	552
Norm Cash	.277	24	3	23	74	78	72	78	10	.377	.468	**24.6**	76	141
Vinny Castilla	.258	22	2	16	54	65	29	68	3	.299	.400	−2.2	880	851
Danny Cater	.291	28	4	7	61	65	28	46	6	.329	.397	2.3	723	977
Phil Cavarretta	.282	32	7	11	69	66	58	72	13	.361	.422	13.9	276	448
Cesar Cedeno	.286	**35**	4	16	77	69	45	68	**52**	.350	.457	17.1	185	194
Orlando Cepeda	.293	31	2	23	74	**84**	39	79	23	.351	**.490**	24.2	81	157
Rick Cerone	.244	25	2	7	45	51	41	58	1	.304	.340	−12	1076	1055
Ron Cey	.259	27	2	22	66	77	67	85	2	.355	.446	17.3	180	174
Chris Chambliss	.278	33	4	11	61	65	43	66	4	.337	.414	8.2	447	864
Frank Chance	**.297**	32	6	11	84	75	68		49	**.394**	.440	15.2	243	188
Ben Chapman	.276	33	6	10	73	62	56	73	**55**	.349	.411	10.0	385	490
Ray Chapman	.268	28	6	12	83	53	59	96	30	.348	.407	5.1	570	311
Sam Chapman	.255	24	4	18	67	69	45	104	9	.314	.415	3.1	677	798
Hal Chase	.287	31	4	14	70	77	24	79	22	.321	.442	8.1	450	500
Cupid Childs	.280	26	5	7	73	51	**83**	44	9	**.391**	.382	13.4	288	145
Jeff Cirillo	.282	30	3	6	61	54	48	53	9	.347	.386	4.6	596	549

For table explanations see page 379.   *(continued)*

	BA	DPT	T	HR	R	RBI	BB	SO	SB	OBP	SLG	CBR	Rank	Rank+
Fred Clarke	.293	32	7	14	81	59	56		24	.372	.451	23.5	87	191
Horace Clarke	.270	22	3	2	63	34	37	38	28	.320	.331	–8.7	1028	735
Jack Clark	.268	29	4	26	77	81	87	95	7	.386	.487	29.5	46	75
Will Clark	.301	33	5	17	76	77	61	72	6	.381	.479	28.0	55	122
Royce Clayton	.249	24	5	5	57	45	39	82	24	.304	.340	–11	1069	840
Jack Clements	.271	29	3	20	53	73	44	84	0	.334	.453	7.7	465	337
Roberto Clemente	.306	33	7	14	76	71	35	72	11	.353	.471	22.4	96	203
Donn Clendenon	.270	28	6	18	66	76	45	120	19	.334	.446	7.4	472	684
Harlond Clift	.251	26	4	18	71	56	78	94	12	.358	.414	12.0	322	167
Ty Cobb	.336	38	9	22	94	90	56	52	63	.406	.550	48.1	8	10
Mickey Cochrane	.287	29	4	16	77	63	74	45	9	.384	.449	18.2	163	90
Rocky Colavito	.271	27	2	25	71	83	68	69	3	.362	.475	21.3	112	207
Vince Coleman	.262	23	8	2	77	30	44	86	73	.323	.337	–7.2	999	1119
Dave Collins	.273	25	6	3	67	36	49	70	45	.343	.352	0.2	814	1014
Eddie Collins	.309	30	6	9	87	68	73	41	46	.402	.432	28.2	53	22
Jimmy Collins	.281	33	5	12	68	72	40		7	.340	.425	8.9	418	251
Ripper Collins	.275	28	6	24	75	81	56	84	5	.357	.489	11.8	331	473
Shano Collins	.260	32	6	8	59	62	27	77	14	.301	.382	–5.8	956	1125
Earle Combs	.290	32	9	9	86	48	55	52	14	.361	.426	12.3	313	375
Charlie Comiskey	.267	24	4	8	63	56	24		19	.304	.371	–7.2	997	1129
Dave Concepcion	.266	25	3	7	59	56	43	74	30	.325	.361	–2.8	895	210
Jeff Conine	.282	28	3	13	58	72	47	73	6	.345	.421	8.3	444	647
Roger Connor	.298	37	9	21	77	76	71	63	5	.394	.514	37.4	20	23
Wid Conroy	.254	27	5	10	60	52	46		24	.323	.379	–1.6	860	814
Duff Cooley	.272	26	5	8	65	49	41		11	.331	.385	1.2	772	1004
Cecil Cooper	.298	33	4	17	71	78	32	66	11	.340	.468	16.5	205	404
Walker Cooper	.279	28	3	21	60	85	32	65	4	.322	.470	8.5	433	326
Joey Cora	.271	26	7	2	76	32	47	38	20	.336	.349	–1.2	852	699
Tommy Corcoran	.247	24	4	7	56	63	25	68	12	.283	.347	–17	1106	1094
Wil Cordero	.266	29	3	11	61	58	37	76	7	.318	.392	0.6	788	822
Pop Corkhill	.260	23	4	11	56	59	27		3	.302	.378	–6.4	975	1099
Bill Coughlin	.252	23	2	5	62	56	37		15	.312	.334	–11	1073	1026
Al Cowens	.268	30	6	8	62	63	37	65	18	.321	.391	0.5	797	1022
Billy Cox	.255	27	3	8	59	44	37	49	15	.306	.362	–7.0	990	994
Doc Cramer	.277	23	4	3	66	40	28	38	6	.315	.351	–6.6	978	1067
Del Crandall	.250	21	1	17	58	65	42	61	6	.310	.393	–0.8	847	737
Gavy Cravath	.286	35	8	26	70	96	81	107	3	.400	.528	20.7	122	156
Sam Crawford	.297	37	10	23	74	89	48		11	.363	.525	33.1	33	50
Hughie Critz	.246	21	5	6	66	42	28	54	17	.287	.336	–17	1109	1105
Warren Cromartie	.279	32	4	9	59	51	42	57	7	.338	.404	3.5	649	861
Joe Cronin	.273	34	6	15	65	76	61	82	11	.355	.434	16.7	198	43
Frankie Crosetti	.233	22	4	12	68	44	54	99	20	.320	.352	–4.0	917	522
Lave Cross	.274	27	4	10	61	74	31	39	7	.317	.392	–0.6	843	585
Monte Cross	.230	24	3	9	50	50	63		18	.326	.337	–7.0	988	875
Jose Cruz	.287	31	5	13	69	71	56	66	28	.360	.438	18.3	160	260
Julio Cruz	.237	19	4	2	67	31	60	67	52	.323	.293	–14	1091	1032
Tony Cuccinello	.265	28	2	13	57	70	53	74	7	.342	.402	5.6	549	270
Roy Cullenbine	.272	28	3	19	70	69	92	75	6	.393	.450	15.6	229	297
Joe Cunningham	.287	31	3	7	67	56	84	59	5	.405	.394	10.2	380	437
Chad Curtis	.258	25	3	9	70	47	58	71	33	.338	.366	1.3	767	823

	BA	DPT	T	HR	R	RBI	BB	SO	SB	OBP	SLG	CBR	Rank	Rank+
George Cutshaw	.259	25	4	8	58	67	33	41	27	.307	.365	−7.1	996	958
Kiki Cuyler	.290	32	8	15	79	66	54	97	62	.371	.456	20.7	121	208
Bill Dahlen	.264	33	7	16	73	65	63	97	21	.354	.425	15.1	247	**80**
Babe Dahlgren	.250	23	3	15	53	66	45	86	3	.314	.395	0.4	802	1080
Abner Dalrymple	.280	29	5	9	74	50	44	79	3	.348	.405	3.7	638	729
Tom Daly	.262	29	4	13	67	63	63	123	20	.350	.404	7.5	471	320
Johnny Damon	.272	29	8	6	75	43	47	46	36	.335	.379	1.8	747	688
Alvin Dark	.282	32	4	7	71	51	29	55	15	.324	.391	1.7	751	386
Jake Daubert	.295	26	6	14	73	51	47	59	13	.362	.435	17.0	189	233
Rich Dauer	.260	27	0	5	58	48	41	31	2	.318	.345	−7.4	1004	854
Darren Daulton	.243	28	3	17	62	71	79	85	7	.355	.411	6.4	521	389
Vic Davalillo	.292	28	5	3	69	44	27	53	29	.328	.380	0.5	801	999
Jim Davenport	.258	27	4	8	63	52	46	80	4	.324	.366	−2.5	888	897
Alvin Davis	.281	27	2	15	58	72	76	58	2	**.383**	.427	12.6	307	467
Chili Davis	.274	28	4	18	69	73	65	87	12	.359	.437	18.7	155	257
Eric Davis	.266	24	3	**24**	80	80	65	117	37	.354	.461	14.5	261	245
George Davis	.288	33	7	16	72	80	54	61	25	.360	.452	20.2	130	**55**
Glenn Davis	.265	25	2	30	69	83	49	76	4	.341	**.503**	11.4	347	485
Harry Davis	.274	34	8	21	72	78	51		16	.348	.479	17.2	183	166
Spud Davis	.278	25	2	13	39	67	52	72	1	.354	.408	6.1	533	434
Tommy Davis	**.301**	26	3	10	60	78	28	54	21	.338	.417	8.7	425	816
Willie Davis	.282	34	9	11	74	63	26	58	43	.319	.433	7.3	475	583
Andre Dawson	.281	30	6	23	74	82	32	77	25	.329	**.490**	19.6	137	153
Doug DeCinces	.262	31	4	19	65	74	54	79	9	.338	.445	10.1	384	373
Rob Deer	.222	21	2	28	68	70	69	150	8	.323	.436	4.9	583	726
Ivan DeJesus	.246	24	5	3	61	34	51	77	22	.319	.319	−11	1067	648
Ed Delahanty	**.304**	36	7	23	79	87	53	73	21	.376	**.526**	**34.0**	29	42
Jim Delahanty	.278	30	4	10	62	68	54		10	.358	.406	6.4	519	429
Carlos Delgado	.275	31	2	27	73	84	73	99	2	.375	**.504**	20.2	129	220
Frank Demaree	.284	25	3	13	67	71	47	62	9	.350	.416	6.2	527	626
Rick Dempsey	.237	27	2	10	53	47	63	76	4	.327	.351	−3.7	911	842
Jerry Denny	.260	28	4	16	58	67	28	105	3	.302	.422	0.4	803	655
Bucky Dent	.247	23	2	5	49	47	38	42	3	.302	.328	−14	1096	725
Delino DeShields	.265	26	8	5	69	44	62	78	47	.349	.364	3.1	681	460
Mike Devereaux	.253	28	6	12	62	60	38	78	16	.306	.393	−2.0	873	959
Art Devlin	.267	26	4	4	65	64	67		27	.364	.349	3.2	675	541
Bill Dickey	.290	28	4	16	63	82	48	**44**	4	.353	.449	15.3	241	146
Dom DiMaggio	.281	29	4	9	79	47	54	79	26	.351	.397	8.0	454	513
Joe DiMaggio	**.309**	35	8	31	90	98	47	48	4	.369	**.582**	38.6	18	16
Vince DiMaggio	.244	29	2	28	63	76	53	150	27	.319	.471	6.7	503	535
Larry Doby	.281	29	5	25	81	82	66	115	15	.366	**.497**	21.4	111	113
Bobby Doerr	.270	29	5	17	67	78	48	72	9	.331	.438	11.0	359	107
Mike Donlin	**.311**	32	7	18	76	74	48		20	.376	**.500**	15.1	248	279
Patsy Donovan	.279	21	2	3	71	43	35	51	25	.329	.343	−4.7	931	1093
Red Dooin	.244	22	2	5	46	54	23		9	.279	.321	−22	1133	1115
Mickey Doolan	.232	26	4	5	45	55	34	87	7	.282	.322	−20	1128	1111
Bill Doran	.270	25	4	9	71	48	67	53	21	.361	.382	6.5	512	327
Patsy Dougherty	.287	26	5	8	77	55	54		25	.368	.398	7.1	481	705
Taylor Douthit	.259	23	2	6	67	40	60	77	14	.349	.345	0.0	822	993
Tommy Dowd	.253	23	4	5	61	35	37	79	20	.305	.337	−12	1083	1132

                                          (*continued*)

	BA	DPT	T	HR	R	RBI	BB	SO	SB	OBP	SLG	CBR	Rank	Rank+
Brian Downing	.269	27	2	16	70	62	73	68	6	.375	.421	19.9	133	197
Jack Doyle	.277	29	3	7	64	75	41		36	.335	.385	2.5	712	701
Larry Doyle	.286	31	7	16	76	71	54	42	20	.362	.455	17.1	188	**93**
Dan Driessen	.266	27	2	15	66	67	67	69	19	.359	.413	10.1	383	595
Walt Dropo	.263	23	2	17	53	78	33	96	1	.307	.414	1.4	763	952
Hugh Duffy	**.297**	29	4	13	79	78	49	53	29	.360	.439	16.3	214	286
Joe Dugan	.256	25	2	8	57	51	25	83	2	.294	.358	−11	1068	893
Mariano Duncan	.263	28	5	8	66	51	22	95	20	.296	.375	−7.9	1016	877
Fred Dunlap	.285	29	3	18	73	47	58	72	4	.371	.455	10.4	376	231
Shawon Dunston	.264	29	6	10	61	55	17	80	20	.290	.393	−6.4	973	677
Leon Durham	.270	33	6	18	67	68	60	94	14	.351	.455	8.6	429	580
Ray Durham	.271	32	8	7	78	43	51	71	33	.340	.395	4.6	598	441
Leo Durocher	.231	20	3	4	50	50	41	83	6	.292	.303	−21	1132	1086
Jimmy Dykes	.254	28	4	10	57	55	55	96	5	.338	.371	2.7	696	383
Lenny Dykstra	.284	**34**	5	8	**82**	41	67	47	32	.374	.408	10.0	387	323
Damian Easley	.248	27	3	10	59	49	44	73	17	.314	.367	−3.3	903	769
Mike Easler	.289	28	3	15	61	69	45	96	3	.351	.446	7.9	456	588
Jim Edmonds	.285	31	3	20	**83**	73	62	99	8	.365	.476	15.7	227	159
Johnny Edwards	.244	27	3	8	47	58	53	70	3	.320	.354	−5.5	949	923
Jim Eisenreich	.284	29	5	6	58	56	41	52	17	.338	.387	2.3	720	884
Kid Elberfeld	.267	26	3	5	65	62	58		15	.359	.351	2.3	719	528
Bob Elliott	.279	32	6	17	70	79	62	71	12	.359	.454	19.4	143	123
Bones Ely	.243	21	2	7	49	57	29		5	.285	.332	−18	1115	1120
Woody English	.260	24	4	6	71	39	69	96	12	.362	.349	2.1	732	380
Del Ennis	.277	30	6	19	65	**83**	39	73	8	.330	.454	12.6	308	564
Darrin Erstad	.281	27	5	8	72	50	40	60	26	.335	.390	2.5	709	839
Darrell Evans	.251	23	3	22	70	70	**82**	74	9	.363	.430	18.7	154	206
Dwight Evans	.264	29	5	20	74	69	**74**	91	8	.366	.451	21.5	109	205
Carl Everett	.269	28	4	17	69	73	46	92	18	.335	.435	5.9	536	554
Hoot Evers	.268	29	5	13	66	67	43	81	17	.325	.414	3.6	646	845
Johnny Evers	.276	24	3	4	74	50	68	**34**	26	.370	.353	5.6	555	368
Buck Ewing	.289	**34**	**11**	20	78	77	46	63	21	.354	**.496**	16.5	206	161
Ferris Fain	.284	31	3	8	63	61	**89**	53	16	**.396**	.399	12.6	306	350
Ron Fairly	.268	27	3	15	63	71	73	60	5	.369	.415	15.7	226	421
Bibb Falk	.280	29	3	16	61	75	44	70	5	.338	.441	8.0	455	719
Duke Farrell	.262	28	5	10	55	73	44	70	3	.324	.390	1.2	771	519
Tony Fernandez	.285	30	8	4	63	48	42	45	24	.343	.383	5.3	563	173
Rick Ferrell	.260	24	2	4	45	49	67	45	4	.349	.335	0.5	800	686
Hobe Ferris	.248	30	5	15	52	71	26		2	.287	.408	−5.5	951	869
Cecil Fielder	.254	20	1	**25**	64	88	61	107	0	.338	.448	10.5	374	622
Steve Finley	.271	30	**9**	12	74	57	43	57	27	.330	.417	7.8	461	370
Lou Finney	.263	25	8	5	59	46	31	**40**	8	.304	.357	−8.3	1019	1137
Carlton Fisk	.267	28	5	21	73	72	48	79	14	.340	.452	16.6	202	**100**
Max Flack	.266	25	4	10	74	39	56	46	19	.348	.385	3.7	640	962
Ira Flagstead	.264	28	3	12	65	47	55	76	11	.343	.396	4.1	620	786
Art Fletcher	.269	27	4	7	65	72	21	58	9	.310	.375	−4.2	920	555
Darrin Fletcher	.261	25	1	12	42	67	32	**42**	0	.308	.387	−2.0	872	710
Elbie Fletcher	.262	27	4	13	68	59	**80**	82	7	.375	.406	11.3	349	566
Scott Fletcher	.260	26	4	2	60	43	48	50	14	.329	.335	−5.6	952	672
Elmer Flick	**.297**	**33**	**9**	18	79	71	66		26	**.392**	**.487**	23.2	**90**	112

	BA	DPT	T	HR	R	RBI	BB	SO	SB	OBP	SLG	CBR	Rank	Rank+
Curt Flood	.287	26	3	6	66	51	38	53	15	.342	.380	3.4	658	790
Doug Flynn	.238	20	5	1	40	40	22	48	4	.269	.296	−29	1139	1139
Tim Foli	.249	23	2	2	49	44	24	40	11	.287	.312	−21	1130	975
Dan Ford	.269	32	5	15	73	68	38	95	11	.327	.430	4.5	602	744
Hod Ford	.237	23	3	4	45	49	42	82	2	.302	.312	−17	1113	1027
Eddie Foster	.262	24	3	3	64	45	47	49	13	.328	.335	−6.2	966	913
George Foster	.275	25	4	**26**	71	**89**	48	104	7	.343	**.488**	19.8	135	223
Jack Fournier	.290	31	6	**25**	72	81	64	76	15	**.386**	**.512**	23.6	86	105
Dave Foutz	.271	28	5	11	65	80	37	62	13	.323	.402	1.7	749	850
Nellie Fox	.289	29	6	2	70	41	35	**22**	19	.338	.365	2.1	731	248
Pete Fox	.276	28	5	7	69	54	31	75	32	.319	.385	0.2	817	1061
Jimmie Foxx	.294	28	6	**33**	84	**91**	78	118	10	**.394**	**.550**	47.1	9	13
Julio Franco	**.295**	28	5	8	72	61	51	64	27	.362	.401	13.2	289	163
Tito Francona	.276	29	4	10	62	62	51	73	13	.346	.401	5.9	537	804
Bill Freehan	.270	27	3	15	58	63	50	59	5	.344	.418	9.1	407	303
Buck Freeman	.281	35	9	27	63	86	43		3	.346	**.527**	14.8	254	259
Jim Fregosi	.278	32	9	11	68	57	53	82	15	.349	.421	10.7	363	**99**
Lonny Frey	.264	28	5	9	73	48	69	79	26	.361	.384	6.9	494	218
Bernie Friberg	.248	22	3	6	52	47	65	109	8	.344	.334	−3.3	902	712
Frankie Frisch	.285	28	6	12	79	65	48	**38**	**51**	.351	.416	11.8	330	128
Travis Fryman	.270	29	5	13	61	69	43	91	11	.328	.412	5.6	554	410
Tito Fuentes	.268	25	4	4	57	42	29	57	15	.310	.351	−8.6	1026	764
Shorty Fuller	.237	20	3	1	60	34	57	56	14	.316	.291	−15	1103	1074
Carl Furillo	.292	30	5	12	65	76	38	51	12	.344	.429	10.6	369	462
Gary Gaetti	.253	25	3	18	59	70	36	83	12	.305	.415	1.6	754	797
Greg Gagne	.251	28	5	8	59	48	32	90	17	.298	.367	−8.4	1020	662
Augie Galan	.275	30	5	13	76	64	80	58	31	**.384**	.423	16.9	192	267
Andres Galarraga	.276	27	2	21	67	77	35	115	10	.329	.455	14.5	260	594
Oscar Gamble	.266	26	4	21	70	71	66	61	8	.359	.451	11.9	324	456
Chick Gandil	.277	29	5	7	56	77	33	59	10	.324	.388	0.8	784	900
Jim Gantner	.275	25	3	3	58	44	32	**43**	17	.323	.351	−4.9	935	870
Ron Gant	.252	26	5	22	76	70	57	96	24	.330	.444	10.2	379	464
Damaso Garcia	.280	25	3	3	62	39	18	45	**36**	.308	.357	−8.1	1018	915
Nomar Garciaparra	**.305**	35	8	17	82	75	35	**39**	17	.352	**.491**	11.9	326	152
Larry Gardner	.276	28	6	9	62	73	51	57	7	.345	.398	6.7	502	305
Phil Garner	.262	32	7	10	65	63	46	71	22	.328	.401	3.3	669	498
Ralph Garr	**.297**	29	7	7	72	41	26	53	27	.333	.412	4.5	603	889
Steve Garvey	**.297**	32	5	16	71	80	30	63	9	.337	.460	16.3	217	428
Charlie Gehringer	.292	31	6	16	80	66	59	**43**	24	.367	.458	24.1	83	24
Lou Gehrig	**.307**	37	8	**34**	94	**99**	81	82	10	**.412**	**.584**	55.6	5	7
Wally Gerber	.237	18	2	2	47	42	46	77	3	.304	.290	−19	1122	987
Cesar Geronimo	.258	27	6	7	61	53	47	103	15	.326	.369	−1.1	850	948
Jason Giambi	**.296**	30	2	24	76	81	81	74	2	**.401**	**.505**	24.1	82	129
George Gibson	.244	26	3	10	41	55	41		0	.304	.359	−8.5	1021	819
Kirk Gibson	.270	28	6	19	81	70	60	102	32	.355	.451	14.4	264	331
Brian Giles	.290	33	6	22	78	77	**85**	53	13	**.399**	**.500**	18.1	164	165
Bernard Gilkey	.269	31	3	12	68	60	56	73	15	.346	.410	5.5	556	717
Jim Gilliam	.263	29	6	4	74	37	73	**33**	38	.365	.350	5.0	579	345
Joe Girardi	.255	24	3	2	48	45	33	65	7	.302	.323	−15	1100	1062
Dan Gladden	.272	27	5	7	74	47	38	66	29	.327	.379	0.4	804	960

For table explanations see page 379.   (*continued*)

	BA	DPT	T	HR	R	RBI	BB	SO	SB	OBP	SLG	CBR	Rank	Rank+
Doug Glanville	.275	22	5	5	64	37	25	51	30	.307	.355	−7.7	1011	1039
Jack Glasscock	.284	27	3	5	64	57	43	**38**	15	.348	.375	3.4	665	377
Kid Gleason	.249	21	2	4	57	53	39		14	.307	.317	−15	1104	1083
Alex Gonzalez	.237	27	4	9	53	46	38	101	16	.292	.351	−12	1082	874
Juan Gonzalez	.285	29	3	**28**	74	97	34	88	4	.332	**.515**	19.5	139	202
Luis Gonzalez	.278	32	5	16	68	71	58	54	12	.357	.448	17.2	184	281
Tony Gonzalez	.286	30	6	10	66	60	48	68	17	.356	.413	8.5	431	568
Billy Goodman	.288	30	4	2	62	46	49	46	10	.349	.363	3.7	643	542
Ival Goodman	.273	31	9	20	75	66	52	81	16	.352	.473	10.6	372	501
Tom Goodwin	.257	18	6	1	72	29	45	74	**66**	.317	.313	−12	1079	1091
Joe Gordon	.263	27	3	27	73	78	54	92	19	.336	.482	15.2	244	**73**
Sid Gordon	.277	27	4	22	68	74	65	57	4	.362	.472	16.3	216	254
George Gore	.290	28	5	11	86	51	81	60	6	**.405**	.421	17.1	187	237
Goose Goslin	.287	31	8	24	71	78	51	70	20	.353	**.495**	26.9	**62**	138
Mark Grace	.294	**33**	3	8	65	62	63	**32**	6	.376	.415	19.4	141	372
Jack Graney	.248	28	5	10	69	48	**74**	82	7	.352	.370	3.5	651	859
George Grantham	.272	31	5	19	75	60	**82**	101	23	**.389**	.456	17.3	181	139
Dick Green	.250	25	3	9	56	56	41	98	7	.310	.362	−6.0	962	704
Hank Greenberg	.290	**36**	5	29	80	96	69	117	11	.378	**.546**	27.5	**56**	**85**
Mike Greenwell	.291	30	5	13	64	71	48	**39**	13	.357	.441	10.7	366	449
Shawn Green	.279	33	4	20	75	71	50	80	20	.346	.471	12.9	296	405
Rusty Greer	.288	**33**	4	10	68	62	61	58	7	.366	.419	8.6	428	557
Bobby Grich	.271	30	6	17	74	59	**77**	92	15	**.380**	.439	21.2	115	**35**
Alfredo Griffin	.250	25	7	1	56	38	26	52	24	.288	.317	−20	1127	1003
Ken Griffey Sr.	.294	31	7	10	77	59	50	66	21	.360	.422	14.2	269	402
Ken Griffey Jr.	.288	27	4	27	80	84	59	73	20	.364	**.509**	29.0	**48**	**31**
Mike Griffin	.279	31	5	10	**83**	48	67	65	22	.369	.411	12.7	303	411
Tommy Griffith	.267	27	4	13	59	70	45	55	4	.332	.408	3.4	663	971
Charlie Grimm	.264	27	4	9	52	64	43	60	4	.327	.378	−0.1	828	1058
Marquis Grissom	.267	25	5	11	69	54	33	67	**43**	.312	.391	−0.6	844	787
Dick Groat	.276	29	3	2	54	48	35	**40**	2	.325	.352	−4.7	929	461
Heinie Groh	.280	31	4	7	75	50	69	56	14	**.384**	.393	11.9	325	160
Greg Gross	.284	23	6	1	58	40	66	**37**	6	.370	.348	3.4	660	836
Jerry Grote	.257	24	3	5	43	49	48	71	4	.327	.341	−5.7	954	944
Johnny Groth	.272	30	4	8	57	58	45	64	7	.328	.385	1.6	753	866
Johnny Grubb	.276	30	4	12	64	55	66	70	6	.369	.419	9.4	404	489
Mark Grudzielanek	.282	28	4	4	64	41	24	57	16	.317	.367	−3.2	900	636
Pedro Guerrero	**.301**	29	4	21	69	85	57	79	10	.378	**.493**	21.6	107	140
Vladimir Guerrero	**.311**	29	5	23	74	79	47	52	24	.370	**.519**	16.6	201	241
Ozzie Guillen	.261	25	6	1	55	43	18	**38**	22	.285	.329	−19	1118	1024
Frankie Gustine	.255	27	3	6	58	53	39	81	17	.309	.353	−7.9	1017	896
Don Gutteridge	.249	28	6	8	68	45	37	86	28	.299	.362	−9.3	1039	907
Tony Gwynn	**.338**	34	7	6	75	60	44	20	25	.392	.451	28.8	50	62
Mule Haas	.265	27	3	7	66	47	47	69	1	.328	.368	−0.3	834	1000
Stan Hack	.288	28	5	7	80	41	**74**	57	**40**	.387	.393	16.9	193	**76**
Chick Hafey	.285	**34**	4	25	74	80	47	96	16	.354	**.513**	16.2	219	268
Odell Hale	.262	29	4	15	60	64	41	77	16	.315	.421	2.5	711	532
Tom Haller	.261	28	4	15	59	64	65	74	4	.355	.416	6.6	508	396
Bill Hallman	.253	24	3	6	58	56	38	79	5	.307	.342	−11	1054	1015
Mel Hall	.276	31	4	14	67	73	33	69	5	.321	.431	3.9	631	770

	BA	DPT	T	HR	R	RBI	BB	SO	SB	OBP	SLG	CBR	Rank	Rank+
Billy Hamilton	**.308**	25	4	8	88	42	89	61	63	**.423**	.411	**25.7**	70	79
Darryl Hamilton	.281	24	5	4	68	42	50	46	23	.346	.361	1.9	738	754
Granny Hamner	.256	28	4	7	59	59	29	58	8	.295	.364	–9.7	1045	825
Ned Hanlon	.261	22	4	7	70	48	62	66	22	.352	.353	0.7	786	1002
Ron Hansen	.244	24	2	11	52	59	61	75	2	.330	.364	–0.3	836	452
Mike Hargrove	.288	28	3	7	65	56	**83**	49	4	**.402**	.393	16.1	221	356
Tommy Harper	.257	25	3	11	76	44	60	86	48	.341	.378	3.4	654	917
Toby Harrah	.264	26	3	13	72	58	76	57	25	.371	.400	14.7	257	83
Bud Harrelson	.243	22	6	1	57	30	64	69	21	.333	.302	–9.5	1041	596
Bucky Harris	.252	25	3	4	66	48	49	73	31	.328	.332	–6.0	961	924
Lenny Harris	.266	22	3	3	57	43	35	37	20	.315	.337	–9.1	1038	1097
Jim Ray Hart	.281	27	4	23	70	78	54	75	5	.358	.481	11.7	334	321
Gabby Hartnett	.274	30	4	24	60	**83**	63	95	4	.365	.481	20.6	125	**64**
Topsy Hartsel	.276	27	6	13	78	36	**101**		22	**.419**	.416	17.4	178	274
Roy Hartzell	.258	21	3	5	56	50	55		10	.337	.339	–3.1	899	957
Billy Hatcher	.263	26	4	6	67	45	31	52	26	.311	.358	–6.5	976	1081
Grady Hatton	.250	23	3	10	59	57	66	74	12	.339	.360	1.2	770	707
Charlie Hayes	.255	23	2	11	49	64	39	79	5	.308	.370	–5.0	936	991
Frankie Hayes	.246	23	2	16	52	62	55	107	6	.321	.393	1.6	755	670
Jackie Hayes	.242	23	2	4	51	51	35	62	7	.290	.315	–19	1117	1089
Von Hayes	.268	29	4	13	69	63	65	70	26	.356	.411	9.0	410	545
Cliff Heathcote	.253	25	3	9	67	50	49	79	34	.327	.366	–2.3	881	1114
Jeff Heath	.285	33	10	25	74	**85**	53	100	13	.352	**.517**	18.6	157	230
Mike Heath	.257	26	4	9	55	56	34	73	11	.306	.372	–5.7	955	906
Richie Hebner	.272	28	5	17	68	71	53	64	4	.349	.436	12.2	314	348
Jim Hegan	.228	25	5	10	56	54	39	105	4	.280	.347	–15	1102	1109
Harry Heilmann	**.301**	**34**	6	22	72	89	54	74	7	.372	**.509**	**32.2**	38	68
Woodie Held	.245	24	3	18	61	66	59	115	5	.332	.410	4.0	627	481
Tommy Helms	.267	25	2	4	44	52	26	**37**	7	.304	**.345**	–11	1066	892
Todd Helton	**.298**	**35**	3	19	72	73	69	56	5	**.385**	.485	14.9	249	332
Charlie Hemphill	.270	23	4	9	62	52	62		18	.360	.378	4.0	624	818
Rollie Hemsley	.242	26	5	5	48	49	33	73	6	.287	.332	–17	1108	1126
Dave Henderson	.262	31	2	17	69	67	45	100	9	.324	.427	5.1	574	563
Ken Henderson	.257	28	3	13	62	61	62	85	16	.343	.400	5.0	582	771
Rickey Henderson	.294	31	6	13	106	47	90	62	78	**.411**	.442	**32.4**	37	46
George Hendrick	.277	27	2	20	67	80	41	77	7	.334	.453	12.7	302	378
Tommy Henrich	.273	**35**	6	19	85	76	62	66	8	.356	.467	13.9	277	355
Babe Herman	.293	**37**	8	24	70	81	55	91	20	.369	**.525**	23.3	89	150
Billy Herman	.290	32	5	5	74	54	51	54	13	.360	.395	10.4	377	118
Jose Hernandez	.243	22	5	12	60	57	39	132	6	.298	.371	–7.3	1002	826
Keith Hernandez	**.295**	**35**	5	12	76	71	71	68	10	**.389**	.441	24.6	75	181
Larry Herndon	.276	28	9	10	62	57	38	84	13	.328	.409	3.4	661	782
Tom Herr	.270	26	4	3	62	52	58	54	19	.351	.345	0.9	778	562
Buck Herzog	.256	25	4	5	68	48	45	52	29	.329	.345	–4.3	922	743
Charlie Hickman	.286	**34**	7	**29**	60	87	29		2	.332	**.543**	13.6	283	265
Jim Hickman	.252	26	3	16	61	65	61	101	4	.338	.408	4.2	613	776
Bobby Higginson	.270	29	4	14	65	60	60	64	15	.349	.418	7.5	470	628
Pinky Higgins	.273	27	3	13	58	69	53	75	10	.343	.407	8.6	427	236
Andy High	.255	25	4	9	61	50	56	38	4	.338	.367	0.3	810	567
Glenallen Hill	.265	26	3	21	67	73	36	101	16	.314	.448	4.3	610	766

  (*continued*)

	BA	DPT	T	HR	R	RBI	BB	SO	SB	OBP	SLG	CBR	Rank	Rank+
Paul Hines	.292	32	4	14	69	62	48	55	5	.364	.444	13.7	279	367
Chuck Hinton	.275	29	7	11	66	56	51	85	**35**	.343	.415	5.3	561	761
Larry Hisle	.273	29	4	20	77	79	54	111	22	.349	.456	10.0	386	475
Don Hoak	.255	30	4	9	63	54	61	70	18	.341	.375	1.9	741	756
Dick Hoblitzel	.275	29	5	12	64	72	43	53	9	.335	.415	5.1	568	618
Gil Hodges	.267	26	3	21	70	79	63	97	12	.352	.447	16.6	204	280
Solly Hofman	.275	27	4	9	68	69	54		18	.348	.391	4.0	626	744
Walter Holke	.266	22	3	7	52	60	27	75	8	.307	.356	−8.9	1032	1127
Bug Holliday	.294	30	4	20	71	74	48	74	16	.356	.482	11.4	348	401
Tommy Holmes	**.295**	32	5	11	68	58	45	28	9	.355	.435	10.6	370	424
Harry Hooper	.272	28	6	14	76	48	64	62	19	.360	.423	16.1	220	432
Johnny Hopp	.287	31	8	8	77	52	51	74	**40**	.354	.410	6.8	498	624
Bob Horner	.271	24	1	**24**	71	86	50	73	2	.341	.466	8.7	423	488
Rogers Hornsby	**.327**	37	8	**31**	88	**91**	75	82	10	**.430**	**.597**	60.1	3	2
Joe Hornung	.260	25	5	10	66	63	26	87	7	.302	.378	−7.5	1005	1106
Willie Horton	.278	26	4	21	60	82	42	93	3	.337	.461	15.4	235	459
Elston Howard	.280	29	6	15	60	73	34	81	2	.326	.439	7.0	489	447
Frank Howard	.283	26	3	**29**	68	88	58	111	1	.361	**.517**	**26.2**	67	120
Roy Howell	.261	28	4	11	55	59	44	97	2	.324	.389	0.6	791	932
Dummy Hoy	.271	25	4	9	71	39	70	52	26	.369	.382	11.6	338	524
Kent Hrbek	.278	25	2	21	65	79	65	60	5	.366	.456	18.4	159	324
Glenn Hubbard	.238	27	3	7	56	47	60	74	4	.327	.342	−5.1	941	805
Miller Huggins	.264	20	2	3	77	29	89	81	20	**.389**	.327	6.3	523	343
John Hummel	.262	28	7	15	56	60	46		6	.326	.420	3.3	668	633
Todd Hundley	.234	22	1	22	60	72	57	108	2	.315	.415	2.2	727	558
Ron Hunt	.276	27	3	4	69	36	53	**39**	12	.368	.355	5.4	559	244
Pete Incaviglia	.246	25	3	22	61	74	42	130	6	.309	.434	3.0	689	858
Arthur Irwin	.250	22	2	2	54	49	55	85	4	.333	.309	−11	1072	1011
Charlie Irwin	.249	24	2	8	58	57	45		12	.316	.351	−6.7	980	903
Frank Isbell	.260	28	5	8	63	66	33		30	.312	.375	−5.1	939	982
Joe Jackson	**.324**	38	11	22	81	82	53	40	12	**.393**	**.552**	28.0	54	60
Reggie Jackson	.277	**34**	4	**32**	86	**91**	68	129	25	.370	**.533**	37.1	23	36
Travis Jackson	.263	28	5	13	63	71	39	92	13	.319	.407	1.9	739	290
Baby Doll Jacobson	.280	30	6	17	63	69	34	81	10	.327	.451	8.5	437	597
Brook Jacoby	.269	27	4	11	55	56	49	81	3	.336	.393	3.0	686	720
Charlie Jamieson	.271	23	4	4	68	36	55	62	16	.346	.346	0.5	798	1079
Julian Javier	.254	25	4	7	63	46	30	76	26	.298	.351	−12	1077	847
Stan Javier	.269	26	5	4	73	45	54	71	31	.342	.355	0.7	787	949
Gregg Jefferies	.284	28	3	10	65	57	43	27	22	.342	.404	5.9	539	651
Hughie Jennings	.277	29	5	7	73	73	38		24	.338	.386	4.0	622	463
Jackie Jensen	.270	29	5	17	69	78	61	66	**40**	.351	.437	11.5	344	408
Derek Jeter	**.309**	26	7	9	87	52	50	74	27	.376	.425	13.0	295	103
Alex Johnson	.291	26	4	8	63	60	28	71	22	.331	.399	2.8	693	985
Bob Johnson	.276	30	5	23	74	78	67	97	15	.364	.482	**24.5**	79	131
Cliff Johnson	.254	25	1	**24**	63	83	69	91	2	.355	.447	10.5	373	518
Davey Johnson	.269	31	2	12	60	64	55	70	7	.344	.407	6.1	531	295
Deron Johnson	.244	25	3	19	59	76	50	109	2	.315	.414	2.7	701	986
Doc Johnston	.253	26	5	7	62	55	38	74	18	.311	.357	−7.0	989	1107
Howard Johnson	.252	28	2	23	74	74	68	96	25	.348	.449	10.9	362	335
Jay Johnstone	.268	29	5	10	62	57	45	72	9	.330	.398	2.7	699	891

	BA	DPT	T	HR	R	RBI	BB	SO	SB	OBP	SLG	CBR	Rank	Rank+
Jimmy Johnston	.276	24	4	5	71	41	49	53	20	.347	.363	1.2	774	640
Lance Johnson	.286	26	13	2	69	42	32	34	40	.327	.377	0.2	813	794
Roy Johnson	.270	31	6	12	66	52	52	80	32	.340	.419	5.9	538	781
Andrew Jones	.261	26	4	21	73	72	48	88	19	.327	.446	6.5	517	465
Chipper Jones	.297	29	4	21	80	76	75	60	15	.391	.486	23.0	92	69
Cleon Jones	.286	29	4	11	68	64	44	81	20	.348	.419	6.5	511	708
Davy Jones	.266	21	3	4	79	42	73		19	.372	.341	2.3	721	920
Fielder Jones	.278	23	3	8	78	48	73		21	.383	.376	11.2	353	511
Ruppert Jones	.250	30	5	14	69	62	60	93	21	.334	.403	3.4	655	692
Tom Jones	.262	24	2	3	50	57	35		10	.315	.330	−11	1070	1116
Willie Jones	.252	24	2	14	61	64	61	64	11	.336	.387	3.7	642	650
Eddie Joost	.238	24	3	13	68	47	77	104	13	.344	.369	4.0	623	278
Brian Jordan	.280	28	5	15	69	76	33	69	15	.327	.433	5.8	542	731
Bill Joyce	.267	33	9	26	78	68	95	110	20	.399	.508	18.0	167	104
Wally Joyner	.286	30	2	11	62	70	56	52	8	.360	.418	14.0	273	576
Joe Judge	.276	32	7	13	66	60	59	64	19	.356	.424	15.3	239	360
Billy Jurges	.249	22	4	5	56	51	48	75	6	.321	.330	−8.9	1031	748
David Justice	.271	25	3	22	71	76	74	75	6	.370	.456	17.8	170	262
Al Kaline	.303	32	5	17	79	77	59	53	25	.377	.478	29.6	45	58
Willie Kamm	.255	28	4	6	55	59	64	72	18	.342	.353	0.9	780	453
Eric Karros	.269	27	2	19	60	77	42	78	6	.326	.436	8.1	451	857
Willie Keeler	.311	25	5	7	87	44	39		26	.365	.406	14.3	266	388
Charlie Keller	.281	30	8	25	83	88	85	93	11	.390	.507	19.2	147	193
Joe Kelley	.284	34	8	16	74	74	68		25	.377	.464	23.6	85	149
George Kell	.298	32	4	6	62	62	38	39	12	.346	.406	9.0	412	347
George Kelly	.266	29	3	21	63	82	39	115	6	.323	.458	8.9	415	574
King Kelly	.292	32	4	12	82	78	61	69	21	.380	.436	15.4	237	180
Pat Kelly	.268	28	5	9	70	46	64	91	39	.356	.388	5.5	557	815
Roberto Kelly	.285	27	4	11	69	57	33	82	31	.332	.413	4.6	597	611
Ken Keltner	.270	29	5	20	62	73	39	69	7	.320	.457	8.9	416	283
Steve Kemp	.275	26	3	13	66	71	69	77	8	.369	.413	8.9	419	556
Jason Kendall	.293	27	4	5	65	43	44	35	21	.357	.386	5.7	546	364
Bob Kennedy	.251	26	4	8	54	54	32	77	12	.292	.354	−11	1063	1124
Terry Kennedy	.267	27	1	11	49	65	38	84	1	.320	.389	0.4	809	631
Jeff Kent	.283	33	4	19	72	83	43	80	9	.342	.468	14.8	252	114
Don Kessinger	.249	23	5	1	57	35	45	55	16	.313	.312	−14	1093	646
Harmon Killebrew	.261	22	1	34	77	90	87	97	2	.382	.499	35.4	28	34
Ralph Kiner	.269	24	3	32	78	81	81	94	4	.376	.512	24.5	78	134
Jeff King	.250	26	2	15	64	75	51	60	10	.321	.398	1.5	760	926
Dave Kingman	.237	21	3	33	67	91	46	135	12	.306	.481	10.6	368	605
Malachi Kittridge	.220	19	2	6	36	43	45		1	.286	.295	−24	1137	1136
Chuck Klein	.284	30	5	25	76	79	54	76	16	.359	.502	22.3	97	185
Ryan Klesko	.276	31	4	21	71	81	65	79	12	.362	.475	14.3	265	361
Johnny Kling	.273	29	4	10	57	71	39		8	.328	.400	1.9	743	487
Ted Kluszewski	.287	26	3	17	65	79	40	48	5	.340	.448	11.4	346	446
Otto Knabe	.247	24	3	3	62	45	56	46	7	.328	.317	−9.1	1037	992
Ray Knight	.273	30	3	9	52	64	37	62	2	.328	.395	2.0	737	880
Chuck Knoblauch	.279	28	7	5	76	37	57	46	42	.359	.373	7.4	474	299
Mark Koenig	.254	23	3	7	62	49	29	52	6	.296	.346	−13	1087	871
Don Kolloway	.265	26	3	5	58	49	18	59	24	.288	.352	−13	1086	1063

For table explanations see page 379.   *(continued)*

	BA	DPT	T	HR	R	RBI	BB	SO	SB	OBP	SLG	CBR	Rank	Rank+
Ed Konetchy	.277	34	7	17	65	74	50	77	11	.350	.458	17.5	176	195
Ed Kranepool	.267	26	3	11	52	59	45	57	3	.329	.389	1.8	748	1028
Mike Kreevich	.265	28	7	7	63	48	42	66	27	.319	.374	−1.2	853	942
Red Kress	.258	26	3	13	54	64	43	85	7	.315	.391	0.2	819	560
John Kruk	.299	28	4	11	68	69	78	77	7	.399	.432	13.9	275	357
Tony Kubek	.269	29	4	4	66	46	25	62	10	.303	.359	−8.6	1025	809
Bill Kuehne	.243	28	6	10	51	50	24		7	.280	.372	−14	1090	1084
Harvey Kuenn	.297	33	5	5	66	47	42	38	18	.351	.398	8.3	442	371
Joe Kuhel	.260	28	4	14	67	58	54	70	24	.334	.401	7.0	488	967
Candy LaChance	.261	26	4	12	57	67	29		10	.306	.394	−2.5	887	964
Lee Lacy	.287	29	5	10	73	51	42	74	22	.343	.413	5.6	548	609
Nap Lajoie	.324	38	7	23	82	94	36		16	.374	.531	36.2	26	11
Jim Landis	.249	28	6	9	69	51	63	94	37	.342	.371	2.1	728	852
Ken Landreaux	.266	30	6	12	66	60	38	55	20	.321	.410	2.0	736	755
Ray Lankford	.268	33	6	17	75	68	67	114	29	.359	.448	14.2	268	219
Carney Lansford	.293	28	4	9	72	61	39	54	23	.348	.411	9.9	391	390
Mike Lansing	.257	28	2	7	57	45	35	59	17	.306	.358	−7.6	1009	904
Frank LaPorte	.276	32	5	8	60	75	40		4	.334	.398	2.4	716	581
Barry Larkin	.288	30	6	10	76	54	55	43	29	.360	.418	15.3	242	48
Henry Larkin	.290	32	6	19	69	79	54		3	.365	.479	15.8	224	277
Lyn Lary	.243	25	3	6	67	44	66	85	37	.335	.338	−2.4	882	540
Arlie Latham	.266	24	3	5	76	31	49	76	35	.337	.350	−1.7	865	683
Cookie Lavagetto	.257	26	3	9	62	64	70	62	24	.355	.370	2.8	695	533
Doc Lavan	.241	23	3	4	47	57	30	89	4	.285	.313	−21	1131	1065
Matt Lawton	.257	26	3	9	64	53	66	44	24	.350	.370	3.1	679	881
Vance Law	.256	28	3	9	57	56	53	76	6	.329	.371	−0.1	827	777
Tony Lazzeri	.265	29	7	21	65	79	63	109	23	.349	.456	15.4	234	82
Tommy Leach	.267	28	7	20	83	56	57	78	16	.347	.444	15.7	228	213
Ron LeFlore	.287	27	6	6	83	38	42	110	56	.344	.390	3.6	645	680
Nemo Leibold	.257	22	3	1	70	35	66	76	15	.348	.315	−3.6	908	1104
Chet Lemon	.274	35	5	14	67	60	53	73	9	.356	.437	15.1	245	214
Jeffrey Leonard	.269	27	5	14	63	76	35	98	18	.318	.417	3.0	687	898
Buddy Lewis	.276	27	6	11	69	51	46	55	18	.335	.405	5.4	558	592
Darren Lewis	.243	19	5	2	67	36	47	52	37	.312	.302	−15	1099	1123
Duffy Lewis	.279	30	3	13	59	83	35	85	3	.327	.421	5.1	577	774
Sixto Lezcano	.271	28	4	19	65	68	68	96	6	.365	.448	11.3	350	442
Freddie Lindstrom	.280	29	5	11	73	65	35	58	17	.329	.416	4.6	594	438
Hans Lobert	.274	26	5	11	71	61	46		32	.339	.404	4.4	607	479
Whitey Lockman	.272	25	4	7	65	44	44	51	10	.331	.369	0.4	805	1035
Kenny Lofton	.288	28	9	5	86	40	55	55	57	.359	.394	9.7	393	287
Johnny Logan	.263	26	4	8	62	53	42	60	5	.325	.368	−1.3	855	520
Sherm Lollar	.262	25	1	14	52	68	53	58	5	.339	.398	5.8	541	397
Ernie Lombardi	.295	24	2	24	51	85	40	48	1	.353	.488	18.0	168	106
Herman Long	.263	30	4	15	71	59	43	69	24	.324	.410	4.7	590	313
Davey Lopes	.262	25	6	12	80	48	64	69	47	.351	.394	7.7	464	238
Al Lopez	.249	19	3	8	49	54	51	80	10	.322	.339	−7.3	1001	997
Hector Lopez	.270	27	4	12	65	62	42	86	5	.326	.406	3.1	678	788
Javy Lopez	.277	23	2	22	58	78	33	79	1	.322	.457	6.5	510	340
Bobby Lowe	.260	23	3	9	61	62	37	82	10	.314	.366	−4.6	927	894
Peanuts Lowrey	.265	25	4	5	62	54	43	47	14	.323	.356	−3.5	907	1092

	BA	DPT	T	HR	R	RBI	BB	SO	SB	OBP	SLG	CBR	Rank	Rank+
Fred Luderus	.273	28	3	18	57	73	50	70	0	.346	.442	9.1	408	445
Jerry Lumpe	.267	26	6	3	61	44	42	47	5	.323	.346	−5.4	945	687
Greg Luzinski	.273	29	2	23	64	81	61	113	4	.361	.469	20.0	132	243
Fred Lynn	.279	32	4	20	72	74	61	79	9	.361	.467	20.5	126	109
Denny Lyons	.290	32	3	22	73	73	68	70	6	**.380**	**.490**	18.0	166	
Garry Maddox	.281	32	6	10	63	62	27	68	28	.320	.412	3.2	674	663
Bill Madlock	**.301**	30	4	13	69	64	46	**42**	19	.365	.442	16.8	195	175
Dave Magadan	.288	27	2	4	56	54	**81**	53	1	**.393**	.370	9.0	409	476
Lee Magee	.272	25	4	6	65	43	39	50	20	.325	.364	−2.7	890	1052
Sherry Magee	.290	**36**	9	18	76	89	54	64	**35**	.368	.483	**25.3**	72	116
Candy Maldonado	.257	30	3	17	60	75	46	97	5	.324	.422	3.7	637	792
Frank Malzone	.268	24	2	9	56	64	30	48	4	.308	.371	−4.8	933	1017
Gus Mancuso	.249	22	1	8	40	57	53	58	1	.324	.340	−6.8	985	983
Rick Manning	.256	24	5	5	62	41	46	64	24	.320	.344	−6.7	983	1053
Les Mann	.272	30	8	14	73	61	42	91	11	.335	.431	5.8	544	741
Mickey Mantle	**.302**	30	5	**32**	**104**	87	**92**	107	28	**.416**	**.554**	**52.3**	6	6
Heinie Manush	.294	33	6	14	72	68	33	53	14	.341	.450	14.8	253	444
Rabbit Maranville	.247	26	5	7	60	48	50	75	20	.320	.349	−7.2	998	504
Marty Marion	.255	25	3	5	52	56	40	82	8	.311	.339	−9.7	1044	785
Roger Maris	.263	26	4	23	**80**	80	61	76	6	.348	.462	12.8	300	395
Willard Marshall	.269	25	4	14	64	68	49	46	3	.334	.408	4.3	611	742
Al Martin	.269	28	6	11	70	51	44	89	25	.328	.406	3.0	685	890
Dave Martinez	.270	25	8	6	63	45	46	68	20	.333	.369	0.8	783	936
Edgar Martinez	**.311**	**36**	2	18	74	73	78	64	6	**.409**	**.492**	**35.7**	27	37
Pepper Martin	.276	**33**	7	12	**85**	57	54	89	**50**	.353	.431	7.2	477	483
Tino Martinez	.266	26	2	17	63	79	49	62	3	.333	.427	8.7	420	831
Eddie Mathews	.269	27	5	**30**	87	80	**85**	94	11	**.387**	**.505**	**36.2**	25	17
Gary Matthews	.276	27	5	16	71	64	63	80	16	.360	.429	15.7	225	358
Don Mattingly	**.307**	**34**	2	13	71	77	42	**33**	2	.361	.456	18.6	156	328
John Mayberry	.253	21	2	**27**	63	77	**78**	77	4	.366	.459	16.7	199	325
Carlos May	.278	27	3	10	65	63	58	71	17	.359	.402	6.8	496	730
Dave May	.255	24	3	13	65	59	45	72	14	.320	.390	0.6	790	981
Lee Maye	.276	32	5	11	69	55	37	62	15	.328	.413	3.1	682	888
Lee May	.269	27	2	**24**	66	**86**	34	106	5	.319	.467	12.4	312	590
Milt May	.264	22	1	11	43	62	42	55	1	.322	.378	−0.5	839	803
Willie Mays	**.308**	**37**	10	**29**	**92**	85	67	67	**49**	**.391**	**.566**	**46.7**	10	8
Bill Mazeroski	.252	25	3	10	52	58	31	52	4	.296	.362	−10	1049	752
Lee Mazzilli	.259	27	3	12	66	54	**74**	75	24	.363	.390	6.3	524	586
Jimmy McAleer	.242	19	2	5	55	48	46	96	17	.308	.317	−14	1089	1138
Dick McAuliffe	.253	28	8	12	70	54	68	75	14	.348	.395	7.0	487	147
Bake McBride	.294	28	6	9	72	57	33	68	28	.344	.415	5.0	578	685
George McBride	.232	20	2	3	50	49	42		4	.296	.297	−21	1129	1103
Jack McCarthy	.275	27	4	4	57	59	39		8	.331	.358	−2.4	885	1100
Tim McCarver	.269	28	5	9	54	59	51	**42**	11	.342	.387	3.8	635	537
Tommy McCarthy	.279	24	3	8	71	57	53	**43**	25	.351	.381	4.9	585	718
Frank McCormick	**.297**	30	2	17	65	**86**	35	**38**	4	.344	.464	13.4	287	492
Barney McCosky	**.299**	31	7	4	69	41	50	54	14	.361	.399	7.0	486	591
Willie McCovey	.272	28	5	**31**	75	89	80	89	4	**.383**	**.510**	**36.4**	24	45
Tommy McCraw	.259	29	6	9	67	55	41	70	34	.319	.385	0.0	823	1078
Gil McDougald	.275	27	5	14	73	60	52	83	14	.344	.421	7.6	466	300

For table explanations see page 379.   *(continued)*

	BA	DPT	T	HR	R	RBI	BB	SO	SB	OBP	SLG	CBR	Rank	Rank+
Dan McGann	.271	28	6	14	71	72	47		22	.346	.420	8.4	439	416
Willie McGee	.293	29	8	5	68	57	30	80	30	.332	.390	3.4	659	753
John McGraw	.292	23	4	6	84	40	99		42	.427	.378	14.8	255	137
Fred McGriff	.282	26	2	25	72	78	72	90	7	.377	.483	**30.4**	**44**	101
Deacon McGuire	.261	28	3	10	46	61	47	70	2	.329	.379	0.9	781	503
Mark McGwire	.263	22	1	**41**	82	98	**91**	101	2	.387	**.556**	37.2	22	40
Stuffy McInnis	.286	24	3	5	56	74	27	**33**	7	.323	.369	−2.0	871	1031
Matty McIntyre	.269	27	5	3	70	46	68		7	.368	.352	2.5	707	966
Ed McKean	.280	30	7	18	64	70	48	49	9	.345	.459	15.6	230	86
Mark McLemore	.253	23	5	2	65	40	64	66	30	.338	.320	−4.9	934	940
Marty McManus	.259	28	5	15	63	63	50	85	17	.328	.411	5.4	560	289
Roy McMillan	.237	22	3	4	51	42	49	65	9	.311	.311	−14	1097	939
Ken McMullen	.261	24	3	15	59	63	49	80	4	.327	.402	3.2	673	697
Eric McNair	.249	22	2	11	54	59	26	70	13	.287	.361	−12	1075	901
Bid McPhee	.266	29	6	10	73	45	64	68	16	.356	.390	9.6	397	178
George McQuinn	.264	29	4	14	64	63	54	86	5	.335	.414	6.8	497	862
Brian McRae	.255	28	6	8	64	46	46	71	26	.320	.371	−1.9	869	863
Hal McRae	.286	37	4	14	63	74	47	60	16	.355	.448	16.4	210	398
Kevin McReynolds	.269	30	4	20	67	76	48	61	9	.334	.453	9.9	390	439
Joe Medwick	**.306**	38	7	20	77	89	31	68	7	.349	**.506**	24.6	74	133
Ski Melillo	.235	20	4	4	48	44	31	65	13	.280	.305	−23	1136	1134
Bill Melton	.257	25	1	19	61	73	57	88	5	.339	.424	6.0	535	599
Denis Menke	.252	28	4	10	59	59	69	81	8	.352	.375	4.2	615	302
Orlando Merced	.270	29	4	10	63	65	58	70	9	.348	.395	4.5	604	832
Fred Merkle	.270	30	4	14	64	74	45	89	19	.335	.422	6.6	509	582
Sam Mertes	.268	32	8	17	68	**83**	56		**44**	.348	.446	8.7	422	553
Roger Metzger	.236	22	9	1	57	33	43	60	15	.297	.302	−20	1126	912
Bob Meusel	.275	**34**	6	22	66	**88**	36	107	24	.324	.485	11.5	343	577
Irish Meusel	.283	30	6	18	68	**85**	34	52	13	.332	.461	8.7	421	642
Cass Michaels	.257	23	5	8	54	54	52	74	20	.328	.358	−0.7	845	593
Clyde Milan	.280	25	4	5	68	48	50	**41**	**40**	.350	.369	4.4	605	969
Felix Millan	.276	26	5	2	62	38	29	**29**	13	.322	.349	−5.8	958	630
Bing Miller	.278	30	5	15	64	69	31	62	19	.327	.436	7.7	463	813
Doggie Miller	.263	24	2	10	61	48	48	**41**	10	.332	.372	0.6	796	734
Dots Miller	.261	28	5	10	62	70	38	74	9	.317	.388	−0.8	848	855
Eddie Miller	.237	27	2	13	51	63	32	76	17	.288	.372	−10	1052	807
Rick Miller	.264	25	5	3	68	44	58	80	15	.345	.346	−0.1	826	909
Don Mincher	.259	28	2	23	65	80	70	78	5	.356	.457	10.9	361	495
Minnie Minoso	**.296**	35	9	13	80	71	53	58	49	.373	.456	21.9	103	234
Dale Mitchell	**.308**	30	8	6	69	50	34	**31**	17	.347	.418	6.4	520	760
Kevin Mitchell	.285	30	4	28	73	89	57	78	3	.363	**.517**	16.8	197	211
Mike Mitchell	.275	29	7	15	64	72	47		16	.340	.437	6.7	504	634
Johnny Mize	**.299**	32	7	28	79	**94**	62	67	4	**.383**	**.539**	33.3	32	51
Paul Molitor	**.304**	**33**	6	10	85	54	51	55	38	.371	.443	22.3	**100**	94
Rick Monday	.266	29	7	20	75	62	70	121	16	.360	.458	17.3	179	177
Raul Mondesi	.273	30	7	19	76	69	41	82	27	.328	.459	9.8	392	550
Don Money	.264	30	3	14	65	59	49	71	14	.333	.415	6.1	529	536
Willie Montanez	.272	27	2	12	56	70	41	70	5	.328	.401	3.4	656	954
Wally Moon	.283	29	6	10	69	63	67	69	23	.373	.415	10.9	360	502
Charlie Moore	.262	30	6	4	55	49	45	61	10	.325	.358	−3.7	909	963

	BA	DPT	T	HR	R	RBI	BB	SO	SB	OBP	SLG	CBR	Rank	Rank+
Jo-Jo Moore	.281	28	4	9	72	46	37	49	10	.336	.398	3.6	644	928
Terry Moore	.267	26	2	12	72	52	44	69	24	.329	.397	2.4	714	762
Jerry Morales	.253	26	4	10	55	62	41	71	6	.311	.376	−3.7	912	1077
Mickey Morandini	.261	26	6	2	58	34	45	66	15	.324	.337	−6.1	964	846
Keith Moreland	.275	25	2	11	53	71	44	57	3	.335	.398	3.5	653	821
Omar Moreno	.250	25	8	4	71	40	40	95	53	.307	.340	−11	1058	1108
Joe Morgan	.274	31	8	16	87	58	**91**	53	50	**.397**	.441	28.6	**52**	**12**
Hal Morris	**.295**	30	3	7	61	58	43	61	6	.351	.406	5.6	551	828
John Morrill	.261	29	4	13	66	68	62	103	1	.356	.405	5.2	565	713
Lloyd Moseby	.256	28	6	12	70	58	53	93	32	.333	.397	3.9	630	635
Wally Moses	.276	**33**	6	10	68	40	48	56	26	.337	.410	8.4	441	758
Manny Mota	**.298**	27	7	5	68	62	41	47	13	.355	.393	4.6	595	801
Mike Mowrey	.256	28	2	4	56	61	58	68	11	.338	.339	−3.3	901	834
Don Mueller	.288	23	4	5	55	58	18	30	3	.313	.368	−4.5	926	1087
Rance Mulliniks	.271	32	2	8	56	54	63	74	4	.356	.390	4.4	606	606
Joe Mulvey	.260	26	4	11	56	63	22	64	7	.293	.385	−7.4	1003	950
Jerry Mumphrey	.288	27	6	7	67	59	49	72	21	.352	.398	6.1	530	573
Thurman Munson	**.299**	27	3	13	69	70	41	57	8	.354	.439	11.6	337	240
Bobby Murcer	.280	28	4	18	72	77	60	65	16	.360	.447	17.5	174	247
Danny Murphy	.287	32	6	20	67	77	40		10	.347	.482	14.2	270	217
Dale Murphy	.260	26	4	**24**	71	74	61	110	13	.345	.452	17.2	182	199
Dwayne Murphy	.251	20	3	20	71	66	**81**	102	16	.365	.415	9.4	401	366
Eddie Murray	**.297**	30	2	23	74	**84**	64	64	9	**.380**	**.494**	32.8	35	67
Red Murray	.269	29	7	14	67	78	37		35	.322	.426	3.8	634	849
Stan Musial	**.327**	**41**	**11**	22	**91**	81	68	46	13	**.410**	**.553**	49.9	7	
Buddy Myer	.275	26	5	6	67	50	61	63	24	.357	.374	7.5	468	172
Hy Myers	.270	27	7	10	59	65	26	74	9	.309	.399	−1.2	851	1070
Billy Nash	.263	28	4	10	61	69	68	77	9	.357	.385	7.1	485	316
Graig Nettles	.254	23	2	21	68	73	59	68	5	.336	.425	11.2	351	352
Bill Nicholson	.261	28	5	**32**	71	81	66	106	5	.355	**.518**	21.6	105	164
Otis Nixon	.263	15	3	1	78	26	54	60	**69**	.335	.303	−8.7	1029	1068
Billy North	.267	23	5	3	83	29	76	84	52	.373	.340	3.4	657	649
Jim Northrup	.276	32	5	13	66	67	47	67	8	.340	.429	7.1	482	656
Ken Oberkfell	.275	28	4	3	55	44	56	38	7	.352	.359	2.2	726	700
Pete O'Brien	.261	25	3	14	55	63	59	50	4	.341	.398	5.1	571	941
Danny O'Connell	.254	28	4	3	60	37	51	64	15	.325	.336	−6.4	974	848
Jack O'Connor	.253	24	3	7	51	65	32	60	8	.298	.350	−12	1074	1057
Ron Oester	.264	26	4	5	55	41	44	83	5	.323	.354	−4.2	921	796
Bob O'Farrell	.248	27	4	10	54	59	78	95	5	.362	.372	3.5	648	509
Jose Offerman	.264	26	9	3	65	38	64	67	22	.351	.347	1.4	766	547
Ben Oglivie	.275	28	3	20	66	76	49	76	14	.343	.456	12.7	304	426
Rube Oldring	.269	29	5	11	69	63	25		14	.306	.403	−0.6	842	1034
Troy O'Leary	.259	29	6	12	58	62	39	70	4	.313	.401	0.6	792	1021
John Olerud	.294	32	2	13	66	69	75	52	1	**.391**	.440	25.2	73	182
Tony Oliva	**.312**	34	5	16	71	78	35	51	18	.359	.481	19.8	136	258
Al Oliver	**.300**	35	5	14	71	77	31	48	10	.346	.462	18.8	153	225
Ivy Olson	.248	21	2	4	59	40	29	45	9	.292	.318	−19	1120	1064
Paul O'Neill	.281	31	2	15	64	77	57	69	12	.355	.434	16.0	222	339
Steve O'Neill	.249	24	2	6	43	55	60	80	1	.334	.335	−4.2	919	694
Tip O'Neill	**.312**	**33**	6	16	71	75	53		4	.383	.487	16.9	194	189

For table explanations see page 379.   *(continued)*

	BA	DPT	T	HR	R	RBI	BB	SO	SB	OBP	SLG	CBR	Rank	Rank+
Frank O'Rourke	.231	22	2	5	56	46	40	92	19	.294	.306	−19	1124	1088
Jim O'Rourke	.296	33	5	11	74	68	52	56	5	.373	.435	17.0	190	221
Joe Orsulak	.274	26	6	6	65	46	37	44	13	.326	.373	−0.5	840	1020
Jorge Orta	.277	29	6	12	62	63	44	67	12	.337	.419	7.0	491	497
Amos Otis	.276	30	5	16	76	68	53	76	37	.348	.434	13.6	282	252
Mel Ott	.288	30	4	29	86	88	93	77	10	.418	.526	45.5	11	14
Marv Owen	.248	21	3	6	50	54	39	71	7	.305	.329	−12	1084	1037
Spike Owen	.246	27	7	4	55	39	56	49	11	.323	.336	−7.1	991	645
Tom Paciorek	.279	33	4	9	59	60	31	91	11	.326	.408	2.5	710	965
Andy Pafko	.277	25	4	18	64	74	41	60	8	.338	.441	11.1	355	435
Mike Pagliarulo	.242	29	3	14	55	61	44	92	4	.307	.387	−3.0	897	980
Dean Palmer	.242	23	2	23	65	74	48	121	7	.311	.431	3.8	636	615
Rafael Palmeiro	.289	32	4	22	73	76	60	54	9	.363	.481	27.1	61	151
Freddy Parent	.267	26	4	7	64	55	45		11	.336	.368	−0.1	829	681
Dave Parker	.291	35	6	18	72	83	37	84	15	.342	.476	20.6	124	229
Wes Parker	.271	32	4	8	68	58	66	71	14	.363	.394	6.2	528	757
Larry Parrish	.261	30	3	18	61	72	40	100	4	.319	.434	6.5	514	664
Lance Parrish	.253	25	3	21	58	73	44	106	4	.315	.430	5.6	550	336
Dode Paskert	.265	28	3	9	70	53	66	99	20	.359	.383	6.6	505	820
Freddie Patek	.243	25	5	4	68	44	48	78	48	.312	.326	−12	1078	604
Roger Peckinpaugh	.252	23	3	9	64	52	55	81	11	.328	.356	−2.1	878	322
Heinie Peitz	.255	29	4	7	50	61	54		2	.332	.364	−0.7	846	612
Tony Pena	.259	24	3	8	51	54	35	65	8	.309	.361	−6.7	982	883
Terry Pendleton	.267	27	4	9	60	67	35	67	12	.314	.380	−2.1	879	961
Joe Pepitone	.266	23	4	18	63	77	30	54	8	.309	.425	2.6	702	955
Tony Perez	.279	30	4	21	69	84	47	97	6	.344	.467	19.4	140	226
Johnny Pesky	.291	27	4	3	79	36	57	43	14	.362	.368	5.8	540	338
Rico Petrocelli	.251	25	2	16	58	69	58	86	2	.330	.403	4.2	612	349
Gary Pettis	.239	23	8	2	74	29	70	114	54	.337	.313	−7.1	992	1047
Fred Pfeffer	.252	25	4	11	60	70	47	75	15	.319	.374	−2.8	896	678
Bill Phillips	.273	32	6	8	52	66	38		0	.331	.394	1.0	776	1043
Dave Philley	.266	28	5	7	59	55	39	66	28	.316	.376	−1.6	859	1051
Tony Phillips	.266	28	6	8	77	45	77	82	17	.369	.377	12.1	318	273
Mike Piazza	.313	25	1	28	77	94	54	64	2	.381	.533	26.7	63	25
Jim Piersall	.269	27	5	7	64	46	40	62	27	.323	.372	−0.9	849	1001
Lou Piniella	.293	31	4	10	58	69	32	51	6	.336	.422	7.1	480	784
George Pinkney	.266	24	2	7	68	52	60		12	.350	.362	2.3	722	559
Vada Pinson	.287	34	9	12	74	63	33	66	34	.334	.440	12.2	317	422
Wally Pipp	.265	30	7	16	66	72	45	78	9	.328	.433	8.1	449	620
Luis Polonia	.292	27	9	2	74	37	37	53	42	.340	.378	2.4	715	911
Darrell Porter	.246	26	4	19	64	69	78	93	5	.359	.419	11.1	356	242
Wally Post	.256	28	3	21	69	79	41	122	6	.314	.442	4.0	625	800
Boog Powell	.277	25	1	26	67	91	71	88	3	.373	.484	25.4	71	142
Vic Power	.283	30	5	8	62	54	21	30	10	.311	.397	−0.1	824	1018
Del Pratt	.279	33	5	13	62	76	39	57	17	.332	.428	8.2	446	282
Jerry Priddy	.259	28	4	9	59	53	54	98	12	.328	.375	1.2	773	455
Kirby Puckett	.312	30	5	12	71	70	31	63	16	.353	.454	17.5	177	154
Terry Puhl	.284	29	5	9	74	48	53	54	23	.358	.405	7.5	469	579
Blondie Purcell	.266	24	3	6	64	53	47	53	8	.337	.356	−2.5	886	989
Joe Quinn	.251	22	2	5	47	50	31	53	8	.297	.327	−16	1105	1117

	BA	DPT	T	HR	R	RBI	BB	SO	SB	OBP	SLG	CBR	Rank	Rank+
Rip Radcliff	.286	26	4	7	60	55	33	36	9	.328	.385	1.4	764	1010
Doug Rader	.255	28	4	16	62	71	50	100	7	.327	.418	4.6	593	619
Paul Radford	.244	23	2	4	65	35	76	82	15	.352	.317	–2.0	870	927
Tim Raines	**.295**	31	8	9	85	50	69	49	56	**.384**	.425	**23.0**	93	135
Manny Ramirez	**.303**	31	2	**29**	81	**93**	70	90	5	**.393**	**.542**	28.7	**51**	**59**
Rafael Ramirez	.260	24	3	5	53	46	25	59	11	.296	.341	–14	1088	829
Joe Randa	.272	29	5	6	52	57	39	56	8	.326	.375	0.0	821	811
Len Randle	.258	25	6	4	63	42	47	68	23	.324	.342	–6.0	960	953
Willie Randolph	.277	26	6	3	76	38	**76**	41	29	**.380**	.353	10.4	375	144
Johnny Rawlings	.236	19	2	5	54	43	42	77	10	.302	.309	–18	1114	1112
Johnny Ray	.290	32	4	5	59	58	35	**33**	9	.336	.391	2.9	690	496
Gary Redus	.253	32	7	12	79	46	65	90	44	.343	.406	4.1	617	789
Jody Reed	.264	28	2	2	57	37	58	41	6	.344	.337	–1.3	856	625
Pee Wee Reese	.264	26	4	7	76	50	67	76	**42**	.355	.364	6.9	495	143
John Reilly	.287	**36**	7	19	72	61	26		10	.328	.486	10.2	381	551
Ken Reitz	.256	26	1	8	40	60	22	66	1	.292	.360	–12	1080	1122
Jerry Remy	.270	20	5	1	67	34	41	49	31	.326	.324	–8.6	1023	876
Edgar Renteria	.283	26	3	5	68	51	42	56	36	.337	.372	1.5	756	433
Carl Reynolds	.275	31	9	13	64	68	29	70	28	.319	.432	4.1	618	827
Craig Reynolds	.258	23	7	6	58	46	27	48	8	.296	.351	–12	1081	728
Harold Reynolds	.259	29	7	2	62	31	48	**43**	33	.326	.340	–5.8	959	856
Del Rice	.230	24	2	11	40	54	46	96	0	.300	.345	–11	1057	1054
Harry Rice	.267	25	5	10	68	58	50	61	12	.339	.388	2.6	706	951
Jim Rice	.288	26	7	22	73	**83**	41	91	9	.345	.475	20.9	118	216
Sam Rice	**.295**	31	6	7	73	56	39	**39**	40	.347	.407	10.1	382	793
Bobby Richardson	.273	26	4	2	64	37	24	**28**	19	.304	.344	–11	1062	837
Danny Richardson	.255	22	2	10	58	58	36	70	10	.307	.361	–7.6	1008	945
Hardy Richardson	.284	32	6	16	75	71	49	77	10	.357	.454	12.6	309	210
Cal Ripken Jr.	.279	31	4	17	73	69	52	52	4	.350	.447	17.7	171	**28**
Claude Ritchey	.265	25	3	6	55	60	59		5	.351	.358	2.1	730	523
Mickey Rivers	**.297**	31	9	5	76	46	25	47	**35**	.332	.404	3.8	632	677
Phil Rizzuto	.270	26	4	5	71	46	46	57	36	.332	.358	–0.1	825	419
Bip Roberts	.291	27	4	3	76	39	47	58	36	.354	.369	3.2	676	693
Bill Robinson	.259	30	4	19	64	76	32	100	11	.304	.442	2.8	694	931
Brooks Robinson	.287	31	5	13	65	70	40	49	4	.338	.433	12.7	305	276
Eddie Robinson	.264	23	2	23	59	77	49	65	2	.330	.455	8.5	430	548
Frank Robinson	**.302**	**34**	4	**27**	88	85	70	74	29	**.399**	**.535**	43.7	**13**	**18**
Jackie Robinson	**.302**	**33**	5	12	84	65	67	45	54	**.394**	.448	18.4	158	**96**
Wilbert Robinson	.256	24	2	7	46	64	32		7	.302	.348	–11	1059	1009
Yank Robinson	.249	27	3	6	63	46	**95**		15	**.386**	.346	5.2	566	427
Alex Rodriguez	**.297**	27	3	**28**	90	83	52	83	25	.365	**.527**	22.3	98	**33**
Aurelio Rodriguez	.242	29	5	9	48	51	25	79	7	.278	.359	–15	1101	1135
Ivan Rodriguez	.291	30	3	14	68	64	29	61	12	.330	.441	9.0	411	212
Billy Rogell	.243	24	4	6	57	47	55	73	15	.320	.335	–7.1	993	661
Cookie Rojas	.266	23	2	5	60	51	34	41	11	.313	.344	–8.7	1030	768
Scott Rolen	.277	32	4	19	74	77	60	84	15	.358	.466	11.7	333	261
Red Rolfe	.269	29	5	7	**83**	43	46	62	8	.329	.380	1.5	757	565
Johnny Roseboro	.252	28	5	10	52	57	59	69	14	.337	.378	1.8	745	603
Al Rosen	.284	27	2	**26**	74	87	64	70	15	.366	**.499**	15.1	246	201
Pete Rose	**.306**	**33**	6	7	80	47	56	**44**	14	.379	.425	21.2	117	117

For table explanations see page 379.

(continued)

	BA	DPT	T	HR	R	RBI	BB	SO	SB	OBP	SLG	CBR	Rank	Rank+
Edd Roush	.302	34	8	17	74	71	40	42	26	.359	.477	21.6	108	169
Jack Rowe	.275	29	5	9	67	74	40	46	1	.335	.395	1.8	744	601
Jerry Royster	.244	24	5	4	62	41	49	68	24	.314	.328	-11	1061	1085
Joe Rudi	.274	35	6	17	68	81	34	85	5	.322	.456	8.0	452	715
Muddy Ruel	.253	20	1	2	47	51	63	60	8	.341	.305	-6.6	979	905
Pete Runnels	.286	28	5	3	63	45	59	62	8	.362	.369	7.2	478	317
Bill Russell	.263	28	6	4	58	46	35	51	18	.315	.349	-7.8	1014	505
Jim Russell	.256	29	5	14	71	56	64	94	20	.345	.405	4.7	592	722
Babe Ruth	.309	34	7	50	101	103	104	119	10	.439	.673	74.9	1	1
Connie Ryan	.244	27	5	8	63	46	59	95	23	.325	.356	-2.7	889	641
Jimmy Ryan	.286	33	5	17	74	57	53	74	12	.359	.458	21.2	116	192
Luis Salazar	.262	22	4	11	56	58	23	82	15	.296	.380	-7.0	986	1076
Tim Salmon	.276	30	3	19	71	70	75	93	7	.376	.457	19.1	148	227
Juan Samuel	.260	31	9	12	71	56	35	113	35	.315	.413	2.4	717	569
Rey Sanchez	.263	21	4	0	51	35	25	45	9	.298	.314	-17	1111	1049
Ryne Sandberg	.280	29	6	15	76	60	45	69	26	.340	.436	13.4	286	121
Reggie Sanders	.261	28	6	20	76	69	52	111	33	.334	.449	9.4	402	534
Manny Sanguillen	.292	27	5	7	59	62	24	40	7	.325	.401	2.3	725	637
Benito Santiago	.262	25	3	13	53	65	31	83	8	.305	.395	-1.8	867	614
Ron Santo	.274	28	5	18	67	76	70	79	5	.371	.440	21.7	104	89
Hank Sauer	.260	22	1	29	68	83	55	98	2	.337	.482	12.5	310	466
Steve Sax	.283	26	5	4	68	40	41	43	34	.339	.365	1.3	769	521
Paul Schaal	.252	25	4	8	62	46	68	63	11	.348	.359	1.6	752	779
Germany Schaefer	.260	25	3	7	68	50	54		21	.339	.361	-0.5	841	780
Ray Schalk	.248	22	2	4	52	57	58	68	15	.332	.321	-6.8	984	795
Wally Schang	.265	28	5	12	62	61	74	94	10	.372	.406	11.9	328	171
Mike Schmidt	.267	27	4	35	84	87	82	104	18	.381	.530	39.1	17	15
Red Schoendienst	.279	28	4	4	71	44	34	36	17	.324	.367	-2.1	877	451
Dick Schofield	.232	20	5	5	54	36	51	74	19	.310	.312	-14	1095	872
Frank Schulte	.275	30	7	19	71	71	45	96	10	.340	.463	14.0	274	385
Fred Schulte	.263	26	3	10	65	57	52	82	11	.332	.380	1.4	761	879
Mike Scioscia	.261	27	2	8	46	51	65	33	3	.353	.368	3.0	688	517
Everett Scott	.243	21	3	5	49	51	23	55	3	.276	.320	-22	1135	1071
George Scott	.269	27	5	18	65	71	46	100	11	.334	.436	11.2	352	602
Emmett Seery	.254	28	6	9	67	36	72	108	16	.358	.376	3.3	671	740
David Segui	.283	28	2	11	62	61	52	59	2	.350	.408	7.0	490	784
Kevin Seitzer	.289	28	4	5	62	49	60	54	12	.369	.385	8.5	438	471
Kip Selbach	.270	32	6	11	67	56	72		18	.372	.409	12.2	316	538
Andy Seminick	.237	21	3	21	56	64	65	130	7	.333	.411	4.4	609	514
Hank Severeid	.267	25	2	6	44	62	39	46	2	.321	.356	-4.4	925	759
Joe Sewell	.275	27	3	7	66	63	56	25	8	.354	.373	6.5	515	132
Luke Sewell	.233	22	3	4	50	54	42	64	10	.293	.305	-19	1121	1131
Socks Seybold	.290	31	4	24	61	81	54		2	.369	.502	13.5	284	307
Cy Seymour	.290	28	4	17	61	77	38		12	.344	.457	11.8	329	381
Howie Shanks	.250	26	5	9	53	60	37	78	15	.304	.366	-7.1	994	976
Jimmy Sheckard	.269	32	6	14	77	55	77		32	.378	.420	19.2	145	284
Earl Sheely	.269	24	1	12	54	73	60	57	3	.353	.393	5.7	545	745
Gary Sheffield	.295	27	2	24	78	80	74	47	20	.393	.498	32.6	36	38
Billy Shindle	.256	26	4	9	63	56	35	69	12	.306	.366	-6.3	970	899
Burt Shotton	.268	23	3	4	73	33	72	82	22	.367	.343	3.3	667	921

	BA	DPT	T	HR	R	RBI	BB	SO	SB	OBP	SLG	CBR	Rank	Rank+
Dick Siebert	.273	28	3	8	53	61	33	45	7	.318	.385	−0.2	832	1102
Norm Siebern	.272	29	4	12	68	64	**74**	84	6	.370	.407	9.6	398	578
Ruben Sierra	.268	32	6	16	65	78	38	68	17	.319	.434	7.1	484	775
Roy Sievers	.263	28	3	**25**	68	81	57	85	3	.340	.475	16.8	196	319
Al Simmons	**.303**	32	7	23	74	**89**	34	82	9	.345	**.509**	27.2	60	95
Ted Simmons	.285	32	3	17	65	80	50	45	2	.352	.447	18.0	169	110
Ken Singleton	.285	27	2	17	66	69	**82**	84	3	**.393**	.444	26.5	66	127
George Sisler	**.305**	31	8	13	72	68	30	49	52	.345	.450	16.3	212	306
Ted Sizemore	.259	22	2	3	57	44	46	**42**	10	.323	.323	−9.1	1036	810
Bob Skinner	.266	29	5	11	70	59	57	84	17	.346	.402	4.8	586	860
Bill Skowron	.287	30	5	19	63	81	32	87	4	.331	.473	12.1	319	425
Jimmy Slagle	.266	21	3	1	71	37	69		19	.364	.321	0.1	820	1048
Don Slaught	.280	32	4	8	47	55	39	65	3	.336	.397	2.9	691	525
Enos Slaughter	.289	32	8	12	72	76	58	55	11	.365	.437	20.3	128	250
Roy Smalley	.254	24	2	13	60	55	67	80	4	.347	.384	5.0	581	249
Al Smith	.274	31	5	13	73	59	55	82	18	.349	.425	9.9	389	515
Elmer Smith	.284	32	6	13	68	57	68		10	.376	.435	13.2	290	353
Germany Smith	.242	25	4	11	50	54	35	80	5	.292	.363	−11	1065	998
Jack Smith	.265	25	4	10	**84**	43	46	79	39	.332	.382	0.9	779	1033
Lonnie Smith	.285	31	5	10	**83**	48	59	80	39	.374	.415	12.0	323	409
Ozzie Smith	.262	24	4	2	66	42	59	**31**	32	.343	.326	−4.0	915	298
Pop Smith	.238	26	4	10	59	42	53		8	.322	.360	−5.2	944	824
Red Smith	.279	32	3	13	63	77	62	86	7	.369	.428	8.9	417	333
Reggie Smith	.286	32	5	23	79	76	60	75	18	.365	**.494**	25.8	69	91
Duke Snider	.289	32	6	**24**	79	80	66	101	27	.376	**.507**	30.4	43	49
J.T. Snow	.259	25	2	13	61	68	61	84	2	.342	.390	4.8	588	956
Frank Snyder	.250	24	2	10	38	67	42	93	2	.312	.365	−6.3	972	812
Sammy Sosa	.271	23	4	**27**	79	85	50	110	28	.338	.485	20.4	127	215
Billy Southworth	.275	27	6	14	71	65	56	**43**	21	.356	.427	7.8	460	668
Tris Speaker	**.319**	39	8	17	85	75	67	**34**	25	**.406**	**.512**	41.2	14	19
Chris Speier	.246	25	4	8	53	50	56	71	6	.325	.352	−3.5	905	294
Daryl Spencer	.240	24	2	11	56	54	61	79	4	.329	.357	−2.1	876	639
Jim Spencer	.254	24	4	15	56	63	42	63	2	.313	.400	0.6	795	1066
Stan Spence	.276	30	6	20	67	73	57	54	4	.352	.465	10.7	364	362
Ed Sprague	.240	25	2	13	51	57	40	86	1	.301	.373	−5.5	950	1005
Chick Stahl	.289	31	8	11	72	60	58		11	.372	.431	11.9	327	412
Eddie Stanky	.262	25	3	3	80	36	**95**	66	12	**.390**	.335	7.1	479	239
Mickey Stanley	.254	29	6	10	67	52	37	58	9	.304	.385	−3.9	914	1041
Mike Stanley	.261	25	1	17	61	68	69	91	2	.356	.416	8.3	443	399
Willie Stargell	.277	32	4	**31**	76	**95**	58	117	3	.359	**.532**	33.4	31	56
Rusty Staub	.281	31	3	15	64	74	65	47	6	.371	.437	21.2	113	264
Harry Steinfeldt	.267	31	5	9	62	72	46		8	.335	.393	3.3	672	458
Terry Steinbach	.270	27	3	12	55	65	37	78	4	.323	.402	2.7	700	471
Casey Stengel	.276	30	6	19	66	68	61	92	12	.367	.461	12.1	320	430
Rennie Stennett	.271	25	5	6	58	52	25	47	11	.307	.363	−7.2	1000	783
Riggs Stephenson	**.300**	32	4	13	68	75	61	61	9	**.387**	.451	14.9	250	288
Vern Stephens	.278	25	2	23	71	**84**	45	82	4	.333	.468	14.7	258	74
Shannon Stewart	.294	31	5	6	74	42	44	49	30	.355	.403	5.6	553	675
Snuffy Stirnweiss	.267	30	8	7	78	35	62	90	**38**	.347	.387	3.9	629	400
Milt Stock	.270	23	2	4	67	60	46	54	13	.336	.345	−3.8	913	721

For table explanations see page 379.

(*continued*)

	BA	DPT	T	HR	R	RBI	BB	SO	SB	OBP	SLG	CBR	Rank	Rank+
John Stone	.277	31	7	14	67	65	46	76	8	.339	.440	7.8	458	653
George Stovall	.267	27	3	6	58	67	21			6	.297	.363	−10	1048	1110
Harry Stovey	.282	**35**	8	**30**	**86**	57	65	97	26	.374	**.548**	**29.3**	**47**	**53**
Darryl Strawberry	.261	28	4	**31**	79	89	72	**111**	21	.363	**.511**	21.5	110	148
Cub Stricker	.244	20	2	5	62	32	54		12	.323	.317	−11	1064	996
Joe Stripp	.272	26	3	6	64	52	40	57	14	.330	.365	−1.6	862	791
Amos Strunk	.272	28	5	6	67	57	58	72	13	.350	.376	3.7	639	930
Dick Stuart	.258	24	3	27	62	**90**	39	126	0	.314	.470	6.3	525	674
Pete Suder	.246	24	3	6	45	53	23	77	4	.276	.335	−19	1119	1090
Gus Suhr	.255	31	7	14	60	70	**79**	78	12	.368	.412	9.7	396	659
Jim Sundberg	.248	24	4	8	48	49	59	80	4	.332	.349	−3.0	898	838
B.J. Surhoff	.277	29	4	9	59	64	38	45	16	.327	.393	3.1	683	714
Ezra Sutton	.279	28	4	8	70	66	43	48	2	.349	.393	2.6	703	600
Bill Sweeney	.269	25	3	4	56	55	58		14	.348	.346	0.4	808	689
Pat Tabler	.279	28	4	4	53	61	49	71	4	.346	.368	1.8	746	984
Jim Tabor	.255	25	3	17	58	76	34	85	20	.301	.412	0.3	812	691
Lee Tannehill	.238	25	2	2	48	59	41		2	.301	.305	−20	1125	1121
Danny Tartabull	.270	29	3	24	67	82	71	117	6	.365	.476	17.0	191	246
Frank Taveras	.253	23	5	0	65	29	33	67	**41**	.302	.312	−17	1110	808
Tony Taylor	.262	26	5	4	67	41	42	72	32	.324	.349	−5.1	943	667
Birdie Tebbetts	.257	23	2	5	40	54	43	60	9	.313	.340	−7.7	1012	995
Patsy Tebeau	.258	26	2	9	52	68	36	75	5	.310	.371	−4.7	932	972
Garry Templeton	.272	29	9	5	61	50	26	75	22	.307	.369	−6.3	971	392
Johnny Temple	.275	24	4	1	62	34	60	**41**	**35**	.356	.339	1.3	768	406
Gene Tenace	.247	25	3	25	71	73	**100**	107	5	**.396**	.456	18.3	161	155
Fred Tenney	.281	26	3	5	72	43	64		11	.370	.366	8.6	426	431
Bill Terry	**.306**	**34**	8	16	79	77	49	73	9	.373	.483	**22.3**	**99**	179
Mickey Tettleton	.242	25	2	22	64	65	87	112	4	.362	.426	11.5	339	266
Tommy Thevenow	.222	15	2	1	41	50	29	60	4	.267	.259	−35	1140	1140
Derrel Thomas	.249	24	6	6	63	41	49	68	19	.320	.342	−7.1	995	865
Frank Thomas	.259	24	2	20	60	72	38	86	3	.316	.433	5.6	552	773
Frank Thomas	**.302**	32	1	25	80	**86**	**89**	65	4	**.415**	**.515**	**40.3**	**16**	**28**
Gorman Thomas	.227	26	1	28	69	79	73	144	8	.332	.451	8.3	445	477
Roy Thomas	.279	17	3	3	80	27	**100**		13	**.418**	.338	12.5	311	413
Jim Thome	.275	27	3	29	80	79	89	118	3	**.392**	**.509**	27.2	59	72
Jason Thompson	.260	23	1	21	61	75	**81**	90	1	.370	.432	12.8	301	478
Milt Thompson	.273	24	5	6	63	46	44	79	29	.334	.364	0.2	815	946
Robby Thompson	.262	30	5	12	73	50	47	97	11	.333	.406	3.8	633	457
Sam Thompson	**.299**	**33**	7	21	77	**97**	41	49	6	.356	**.504**	20.6	123	124
Bobby Thomson	.265	29	6	17	67	76	42	88	9	.323	.438	7.6	467	632
Dickie Thon	.267	26	5	9	58	50	40	73	19	.321	.382	−0.2	831	454
Andre Thornton	.250	26	3	22	67	76	**78**	80	8	.361	.438	13.1	291	491
Mike Tiernan	.293	32	7	25	81	62	63	69	17	.377	**.519**	26.7	64	61
Joe Tinker	.268	29	5	11	62	72	37		22	.319	.403	1.7	750	420
John Titus	.280	30	4	14	71	63	65		6	.372	.432	13.0	294	376
Jack Tobin	.282	27	5	10	68	45	43	49	11	.340	.402	6.0	534	916
Bobby Tolan	.263	25	4	10	68	60	32	73	**34**	.315	.383	−1.5	858	1036
Earl Torgeson	.259	26	4	14	75	65	**83**	84	35	.368	.402	10.7	365	469
Joe Torre	.293	28	4	16	64	75	51	72	3	.365	.447	20.9	119	97
Cesar Tovar	.285	31	6	3	79	40	36	**36**	**35**	.338	.376	2.3	724	885

	BA	DPT	T	HR	R	RBI	BB	SO	SB	OBP	SLG	CBR	Rank	Rank+
Alan Trammell	.288	30	5	9	72	56	51	53	23	.355	.411	13.1	292	**44**
Cecil Travis	.289	28	5	5	59	59	35	57	4	.335	.382	2.5	713	418
Pie Traynor	.285	29	6	9	70	77	37	47	23	.338	.402	5.8	543	228
Tom Tresh	.256	31	5	15	72	64	63	79	11	.346	.419	6.5	518	474
Gus Triandos	.248	22	1	21	48	75	52	90	0	.320	.420	3.3	670	587
Manny Trillo	.258	23	3	5	49	48	39	68	7	.315	.340	−8.6	1027	934
Hal Trosky	.279	29	4	**24**	68	**83**	46	74	4	.339	.485	14.1	271	443
Tommy Tucker	.275	25	3	9	58	60	38	66	11	.335	.383	3.9	628	843
Terry Turner	.256	24	4	4	61	55	42		15	.317	.334	−9.6	1042	1008
Bill Tuttle	.254	24	5	6	62	47	50	62	13	.320	.347	−5.1	940	1072
Del Unser	.261	24	5	8	61	47	44	69	11	.321	.366	−2.4	883	1025
Willie Upshaw	.260	27	5	12	65	56	54	75	16	.336	.400	3.4	664	968
John Valentin	.263	33	3	11	66	58	54	55	9	.338	.404	4.1	619	414
Jose Valentin	.239	28	5	16	69	61	54	100	20	.314	.403	1.1	775	506
Elmer Valo	.276	30	7	8	65	51	77	45	31	.377	.394	11.5	340	482
George Van Haltren	.291	28	6	13	77	54	56	72	22	.366	.424	17.7	172	256
Andy Van Slyke	.273	32	8	14	70	67	57	87	23	.351	.437	11.5	342	308
Arky Vaughan	**.296**	31	7	12	80	65	**75**	44	24	**.401**	.446	**24.6**	77	**21**
Greg Vaughn	.238	23	3	**24**	73	75	64	104	14	.327	.436	8.5	432	658
Mo Vaughn	.279	22	2	**26**	65	79	59	109	5	.360	.479	18.8	152	293
Bobby Veach	.285	**33**	6	16	68	88	43	60	13	.345	.455	14.5	262	387
Randy Velarde	.269	27	4	8	65	43	51	87	14	.339	.380	2.6	704	546
Robin Ventura	.263	25	2	17	62	72	69	69	3	.355	.414	12.9	297	232
Mickey Vernon	.280	**33**	5	13	66	72	46	75	31	.338	.438	14.1	272	468
Zoilo Versalles	.248	31	7	7	65	46	31	80	22	.294	.364	−10	1051	695
Fernando Vina	.275	26	8	3	64	34	31	28	20	.324	.359	−1.9	868	706
Bill Virdon	.257	27	6	6	60	43	38	64	10	.310	.360	−7.0	987	1096
Ossie Vitt	.240	21	3	2	72	44	59	39	8	.322	.301	−13	1085	1075
Jose Vizcaino	.266	21	5	2	56	41	35	58	10	.313	.329	−11	1056	868
Omar Vizquel	.266	23	5	2	63	36	47	42	31	.330	.333	−5.4	946	527
Joe Vosmik	.276	29	6	9	59	65	41	51	3	.331	.402	4.2	614	908
Honus Wagner	**.324**	**41**	7	22	84	95	53	68	**45**	**.395**	**.551**	**45.3**	12	**5**
Leon Wagner	.283	21	2	21	73	77	48	73	14	.350	.458	11.1	354	543
Eddie Waitkus	.279	30	4	4	59	43	40	42	8	.332	.368	0.3	811	1019
Curt Walker	.270	29	7	14	62	62	63	62	16	.358	.424	8.9	414	702
Dixie Walker	.294	32	6	11	69	70	55	47	9	.365	.433	16.5	207	309
Gee Walker	.275	29	4	12	63	67	22	82	**44**	.307	.413	1.4	762	979
Larry Walker	.289	**34**	4	21	77	74	60	76	23	.371	**.489**	**24.4**	80	115
Tilly Walker	.269	28	4	22	66	70	42	98	8	.328	.462	9.1	406	616
Bobby Wallace	.267	**33**	6	9	60	71	56		5	.346	.388	5.2	564	275
Tim Wallach	.259	29	3	17	58	70	39	76	4	.317	.420	5.1	575	607
Bill Wambsganss	.245	22	3	3	62	49	46	71	16	.312	.310	−14	1092	1073
Lloyd Waner	.287	22	5	4	72	35	31	**31**	11	.331	.360	−1.7	863	1006
Paul Waner	**.306**	**37**	7	14	80	63	64	**44**	17	**.393**	.470	**30.6**	42	**84**
Gary Ward	.275	27	5	13	64	64	41	84	14	.330	.415	4.1	616	746
John Ward	.271	22	3	6	72	55	38	46	26	.327	.352	−5.0	937	867
Rabbit Warstler	.217	17	3	2	46	35	48	88	11	.288	.271	−26	1138	1130
Claudell Washington	.277	32	7	12	69	61	36	99	29	.328	.422	6.3	522	750
Bob Watson	.294	29	3	16	65	80	52	68	3	.364	.456	17.6	173	318
Buck Weaver	.271	27	3	12	68	52	20	67	14	.302	.401	−1.6	861	610

For table explanations see page 379.

(continued)

	BA	DPT	T	HR	R	RBI	BB	SO	SB	OBP	SLG	CBR	Rank	Rank+
Walt Weiss	.248	22	4	2	55	35	66	61	13	.341	.309	−6.0	963	621
Curt Welch	.266	29	3	7	74	51	48		25	.339	.374	2.1	729	938
Billy Werber	.256	27	4	11	73	44	62	66	51	.342	.379	3.5	652	450
Don Wert	.251	23	2	7	55	48	49	66	6	.321	.344	−5.8	957	1040
Vic Wertz	.271	28	4	21	63	85	56	89	2	.343	.455	14.4	263	329
Sam West	.270	28	6	9	60	56	51	82	8	.336	.391	4.4	608	690
Zack Wheat	**.305**	**33**	6	17	69	75	43	58	8	.366	.483	**27.3**	**58**	102
Lou Whitaker	.278	30	6	11	76	57	67	61	15	.365	.415	16.6	203	**66**
Bill White	.280	30	6	14	66	69	54	80	20	.355	.430	11.5	341	526
Deacon White	.286	25	3	4	62	72	49	49	1	.363	.368	3.3	666	570
Devon White	.261	30	7	11	73	52	36	92	33	.313	.398	0.6	794	767
Frank White	.252	28	4	11	57	55	28	74	23	.293	.373	−9.1	1035	922
Roy White	.282	31	5	12	75	58	67	53	29	.371	.420	15.9	223	407
Rondell White	.281	28	4	15	66	65	34	75	13	.328	.432	5.3	562	613
Art Whitney	.237	17	2	2	48	44	49		1	.310	.287	−19	1123	1128
Pinky Whitney	.263	25	4	12	52	71	40	74	8	.321	.390	0.4	806	561
Ernie Whitt	.247	24	2	15	53	65	58	64	5	.327	.391	1.4	765	617
Bernie Williams	**.298**	32	7	13	80	70	65	63	18	**.380**	.452	21.6	106	**65**
Billy Williams	.291	31	6	20	74	75	57	57	13	.365	.480	**26.6**	65	158
Cy Williams	.269	25	3	28	66	69	61	96	7	.361	**.493**	22.8	95	162
Jimmy Williams	.268	33	7	18	65	77	56		6	.351	.452	11.5	345	198
Ken Williams	.284	29	5	23	72	80	57	67	27	.361	**.490**	16.7	200	314
Matt Williams	.264	25	4	24	68	83	33	88	5	.311	.461	9.2	405	334
Ned Williamson	.257	28	5	11	64	69	79	93	3	.376	.389	6.6	506	354
Ted Williams	**.322**	36	5	39	93	92	103	63	3	**.448**	**.628**	70.4	2	
Maury Wills	.283	19	5	1	74	34	40	47	**71**	.336	.339	−3.7	910	436
Walt Wilmot	.266	29	6	17	66	64	45	64	29	.327	.438	5.2	567	711
Chief Wilson	.271	28	8	21	58	72	29	94	3	.313	.469	6.8	499	673
Dan Wilson	.259	24	2	7	46	55	32	78	5	.302	.355	−9.0	1034	929
Glenn Wilson	.266	28	3	11	55	63	30	80	4	.308	.394	−1.4	857	1029
Hack Wilson	.276	28	5	**31**	77	**92**	81	124	8	**.392**	**.530**	**24.0**	84	**98**
Jimmie Wilson	.251	23	2	5	51	56	43	62	19	.315	.332	−11	1055	1042
Mookie Wilson	.278	30	8	7	77	45	29	85	34	.319	.394	0.5	799	841
Willie Wilson	.281	26	**9**	2	76	35	29	79	**58**	.325	.364	−2.7	891	1012
Dave Winfield	.287	30	5	23	80	**85**	56	74	19	.361	**.489**	**27.5**	57	88
Ivey Wingo	.250	27	5	11	46	65	41	69	7	.310	.380	−4.4	923	723
Sam Wise	.266	31	6	16	66	66	49	106	10	.337	.433	6.5	516	359
Whitey Witt	.266	22	4	5	68	34	58	73	8	.344	.350	0.4	807	918
Jimmy Wolf	.283	30	5	8	61	51	32		5	.331	.401	2.6	705	738
Tony Womack	.259	22	7	2	66	34	30	57	**55**	.300	.328	−14	1098	1056
George Wood	.270	29	6	15	67	53	52	87	2	.347	.431	8.4	440	512
Gene Woodling	.283	30	6	12	68	68	69	56	8	.372	.427	15.3	240	384
Glenn Wright	.263	27	5	19	64	80	29	99	7	.305	.439	2.4	718	351
Butch Wynegar	.251	23	2	7	51	53	72	50	2	.353	.341	0.8	785	682
Jimmy Wynn	.253	27	3	**25**	80	70	**85**	98	30	.372	.460	22.0	101	136
Johnny Wyrostek	.265	29	5	7	57	53	51	78	9	.336	.374	1.5	759	914
Carl Yastrzemski	.292	**33**	4	19	74	71	**75**	57	17	**.391**	.470	**31.9**	**39**	70
Rudy York	.267	27	3	**25**	65	**86**	59	107	6	.344	.476	16.2	218	315
Eddie Yost	.250	28	3	10	71	38	88	77	13	.371	.365	12.0	321	292
Eric Young	.271	27	4	4	69	37	50	**30**	**52**	.340	.356	0.9	782	572

	BA	DPT	T	HR	R	RBI	BB	SO	SB	OBP	SLG	CBR	Rank	Rank+
Joel Youngblood	.268	29	3	12	64	60	46	82	8	.337	.402	3.1	680	802
Kevin Young	.251	28	2	14	60	67	40	97	14	.309	.395	−0.1	830	1095
Ralph Young	.238	19	1	3	61	36	66	67	10	.331	.295	−11	1060	1046
Ross Youngs	.295	32	7	9	**81**	63	**74**	88	21	**.402**	.427	14.7	256	382
Robin Yount	.292	**34**	7	11	77	63	45	59	19	.350	.442	16.3	213	**47**
Todd Zeile	.259	27	2	13	59	65	59	70	5	.341	.395	6.8	500	499
Gus Zernial	.260	23	2	**27**	63	**85**	39	122	5	.312	.472	7.1	483	732
Chief Zimmer	.256	31	4	10	49	60	45	118	4	.323	.386	0.6	789	608
Heinie Zimmerman	.296	32	6	16	70	89	27	68	10	.334	.465	10.3	378	255
Richie Zisk	.283	27	3	21	65	76	51	93	1	.351	.468	13.8	278	394

Notes: Averages among the best 100 are shown in bold.

DPT = doubles-plus-triples; T = triples; Rank = CBR rank; Rank+ = Position-adjusted CBR rank.

DPTs, Ts, Hrs are per 500 ABs over the productive career length.

Rs, RBIs, BBs, SOs, SBs are per 550 NFPs over the productive career length.

Players whose SO data are available for fewer than 2000 NFPs are not evaluated for SOs.

GLOSSARY

Key locations, including the page where each glossary item is defined in the text, are provided in the parentheses at the end of the entry.

Additional scoring rating (ASR)   A rating that measures whether a player has more runs-plus-RBIs than expected by Formula G.2 (Appendix G; 262).

Adjusted park index (API)   The adjusted park index gives the relative rate of a given offensive event compared to an "average park," which includes the park being rated. Parks with APIs greater than 100 are above average (Chapter 6; 86).

Back transformation   A method that reverses the steps involved in a transformation (Chapter 2; 22).

Backward elimination procedure   A variable selection method used in regression analysis in which the initial model contains all possible variables that are removed one at a time until only significant variables remain (Appendix A; 223–24, 231–33).

Basic offensive event   The generic name given to describe one of the following nine events: batting average, doubles-plus-triples, triples, home runs, runs, RBIs, bases on balls, strikeouts, or stolen bases. These are the events for which the four adjustments are directly applied (Chapter 1; 2).

Best batters   Hitters who are the best overall batters. These batters are determined using the *Event-Specific Batting Runs* formula (Chapter 1; 1).

Best hitters   Hitters with the highest adjusted batting average. Since baseball writers differ in their definition of this term, "best hitters for average" is a less ambiguous alternative (Chapter 1; 1).

Best players   Players who are the best in baseball overall. This list would rank pitchers as well as non-pitchers and incorporate all aspects of play on the field, including base stealing and fielding (Chapter 1; 1).

Binomial distribution   The classic statistical distribution for the situation in which a variable represents the number of events in one of two possible categories (Appendix A; 223).

Career Batter Rating (CBR)   A rating of the 1140 qualifying players, obtained by adjusting Event-Specific Batting Runs for a player's season positions and for longevity (Chapter 14; 185–88).

Career fullness score   A player's career fullness score is 1 if he has had 9000 NFPs, and his total NFPs divided by 9000 if he has had fewer. This factor is used in the career batter rating (Chapter 14; 185).

Career position   The position that a player played the most games at through his 9000th NFP (Chapter 2; 17).

Catchers-on-firsts   A term used to calculate a catcher's run%, RBI%, RPRBI%, and additional scoring rating for a given season. Catchers-on-firsts is the number of singles, walks, and hit-by-pitches that the catcher obtains in the season (Chapter 10; 133, 261–63).

Changepoint year   A year in which the park factor changes for a given franchise. This includes both years that franchises move into new stadiums and years in which statistically significant park effect changes are identified using multiple changepoint regression (Appendix D; 237).

Changeyears   An abbreviated name for changepoint years (Appendix D; 237–39).

Chi-square test   A commonly used statistical test that can be used to determined whether the actual number of individuals in a given group is consistent with the expected number, which can be mathematically calculated based on a specified set of assumptions (Appendix C; 229–30).

Clutch performance   A frequently used, but often poorly defined term. Clutch performance is said to occur if a player performs particularly well under critical situations. Which situations are critical and how performance is scored and contrasted to situations that are less critical is key to clarifying the term (Chapter 10; 138–40).

Derived offensive event   The generic name used to describe one of the events derived from two or more basic offensive events. The key derived offensive events used in this book are: outs, doubles, on-base percentage, slugging average, on-base-plus-slugging, event-specific batting runs, and career batter rating (Chapter 1; 3).

Distribution   A complete layout of the values of a variable (Chapter 2; 13).

Doubles-plus-triples (DPT)   The number of doubles plus the number of triples hit in the stated time period (Chapter 1; 2, 108–11).

Eagle-eyed batter   A batter whose walk rate compared to his expected walk rate given his era and number of home runs exceeds that of his strikeout rate compared to the expected strikeout rate, where the expected rates are given by an equation in Table 11.1 (Chapter 11; 150, 153).

Early player-seasons   Seasons prior to 1947, the year that Jackie Robinson joined the National League and soon after players returned from World War II military duty, are referred to as early player-seasons (Chapter 4; 45).

Easy K victim   A batter who strikes out more often than expected given his era and number of home runs, where the expected number is given by an equation in Table 11.1 (Chapter 11; 150, 152).

End effects   Phenomenon referring to the fact that the full number of data values is unavailable for taking a moving average at the beginning and ending of a time series. Thus, the initial and final values are not estimated as reliably (Appendix B; 226–27).

Era   Baseball averages for all offensive events have undergone changes over its history because of changes in the game. Consequently, it is useful to divide it into eras of play. In Chapter 3, seasons from 1901 to 2003 have been divided into 6 eras and several sub-eras (Chapter 3; 29–32).

Event-Specific Batting Runs (ESBR)   Related to the batting runs formula of *Total Baseball*, this formula assesses the run productivity of players compared to that of an average player. Each of the basic offensive events used in the formula has been adjusted for park effects. By contrast, the only park effect for which batting runs has been adjusted is runs (Chapter 14; 179–84).

Excessive RBI gap   A player whose RBI gap exceeds his run gap by 10 or more has an excessive RBI gap (Chapter 10; 135–38).

Excessive run gap   A player whose run gap exceeds his RBI gap by 10 or more has an excessive run gap (Chapter 10; 135–38).

Extended-plate batter   A batter whose walk rate compared to his expected walk rate given his era and number of home runs falls short of his strikeout rate compared to the expected strikeout rate, where the expected rates are given by an equation in Table 11.1 (Chapter 11; 150, 154).

Full model   A statistical model with all variables under consideration included in the model is referred to as a full model (Appendix C; 231).

Fully adjusted average   The player's average for a basic offensive event after adjustment for hitting feasts and famines, ballpark effect, and talent pool (Chapter 2, Formula 2.4; 22).

Geometric mean   Quantity obtained by multiplying the n data values together and raising the result to the $1/n$th power. The geometric mean is often used when trying to summarize non-negative data when some values are many times larger than other values (Appendix E; 248).

Impatient batter   A batter who walks less often than expected given his era and number of home runs, where the expected number is given by an equation in Table 11.1 (Chapter 11; 150–51).

Inside-the-park (IP)   A hit that stays in the field of play. For inside-the-park home runs, in contrast to other home runs, the batter must run to beat the throw in from the field (Chapter 8; 108).

Intercept   One of two key model parameters in a linear regression (*slope* is the other), the intercept gives the value of the independent variable when the dependent variable is zero (Appendix A; 220).

Kurtosis   A number that provides significant information regarding a data distribution. It is considered to be a measure of how peaked or flat a distribution is (Appendix E; 255).

League errors difference   This is a term used to calculate a player's run%, RBI%, RPRBI%, and additional scoring rating values for a given season, for seasons between 1893 and 1919. The league errors difference is the difference in the number of league errors per NFP and the average rate of league errors from 1893 to 1919 multiplied by the number of NFPs for the player (Chapter 10; 133, 260–61, 263).

Likelihood ratio chi-square (LR χ^2)   A special kind of chi-square that is used to evaluate the statistical significance of potential changeyears (Appendix C; 231–33).

Logistic regression model   A regression model in which the dependent variable has only two possible outcomes. This regression is used to model park effects, where the hits are either at home or on the road (Appendix C; 228).

Log odds ratio (LOR)   The logarithm (base 2, in this book) of the odds ratio. Log odds ratio are especially useful for graphs (such as those in Chapter 6), since there is numerical symmetry around the central value, zero (Appendix D; 239).

Longtime players   Players who attained 8000 at-bats ($N = 110$) or 9000 NFPs ($N = 105$), depending on the event (Chapter 4; 46).

Mean   The average of a set of numbers. The mean is the first moment of a distribution (Chapter 2; 13).

Mean-adjusted average   The player's average for a basic offensive event after adjustment for hitting feasts and famines (Chapter 2, Formula 2.1; 17).

Milestone   Every 1000th chance constitutes a milestone. Milestones are based on either at-bats or *net-facing-pitchers* (Chapter 4; 46).

Modern player-seasons   Seasons beginning in 1947, the year that Jackie Robinson joined the National League and soon after players returned from World War II military duty, are referred to as modern player-seasons (Chapter 4; 45).

Moments   A sequence of numbers, usually infinite, which describes the main features of a distribution. In practice, only the first four moments are considered. The measures derived from these moments are the mean, the standard deviation, the skewness, and the kurtosis (Chapter 2; 24).

Moving average   A method for smoothing time series data by averaging a fixed number of consecutive data points, thereby producing a more stable series of numbers that is believed to more accurately estimate some underlying parameter than the raw data (Appendix B; 226–27).

Multiple changepoint regression   A regression model in which the dependent variable is modeled as a constant over various intervals of the independent variable, but jumps or drops at multiple places known as changepoints. The major use of this model is to identify ballpark effect changes (Appendix C; 228–34).

Net-facing pitcher (NFP)   The number of at-bats plus walks plus hit-by-pitches (Chapter 2; 15).

95% Confidence interval   An interval of numbers which are believed (under certain assumptions) to include the true average with 95% probability (Appendix C; 229).

Normal distribution   The classic, bell-shaped distribution that plays a central role in statistics. In applying the talent pool adjustment, the distribution of a basic offensive event is transformed to be as close as possible to a normal distribution. Then, the standard deviation of the transformed data is a measure of the talent pool (Chapter 2; 13).

Normality score   The normality score is a non-negative number that indicates how close the distribution of a particular set of data matches a normal distribution. The score used throughout this book is more completely referred to as the Anderson–Darling normality score (Appendix E; 248).

Normalization   Normalization involves adjusting raw home and road totals for offensive events to account for differences in playing time, as measured by games, at-bats, or NFPs (Appendix D; 236–37).

Odds ratio (OR)   A standard concept in statistics; park differences in home run hitting ease of right-handed versus left-handed hitters is expressed as an odds ratio (Appendix D; 239).

Offensive event   See *basic offensive event* or *derived offensive event*.

On-base percentage (OBP)   Defined as hits plus walks plus hit-by-pitches divided by at-bats plus walks plus hit-by-pitches (Chapters 7, 13; 101, 168).

On-base-plus-slugging average (OPS)   Defined as on-base percentage plus slugging average (Chapter 13; 168).

***p*th Percentile player**   A player who is better than *p* out of 100 players in accomplishing the offensive event being considered, where *p* is any number between 0 and 100 (Chapter 2; 11-13).

***p*-Value**   A number between 0 and 1 that measures the rarity of a given occurrence under some statistical assumptions. It plays a key role in deciding when to stop the backward elimination procedures that is used in both piecewise linear regression and multiple changepoint regression (Appendix A; 224).

Park-adjusted average   A player's average for a basic offensive event after adjustment for hitting feasts and famines and ballpark effect (Chapter 2, Formula 2.2; 18).

Park factor   The term that the mean-adjusted average is divided by in order to obtain the park-adjusted average (Chapter 6; 86).

Park index   Quantity that gives the relative rate of a given offensive event in that park compared to all other parks (Chapter 6; 86).

Park-neutral home runs (PN HRs)   Home run totals that have been adjusted only for the ballpark effect (Chapter 9, Formula 9.2; 122).

Park percentage   The percentage of time that a given offensive event occurs at a selected home park compared to road parks after the occurrences from both the team whose park is being evaluated and their opponents have been normalized for the number of home and road games (Appendix D, Definition D.1; 237).

Patient batter   A batter who walks more often than expected given his era and number of home runs, where the expected number is given by an equation in Table 11.1 (Chapter 11; 150–51).

Performance spread   The spread of performance in a given season. It is the same as the moving average of the standard deviation of the offensive event for the given season (Chapter 2; 18–19).

Piecewise linear regression   A regression method that models data using a sequence of adjoining line segments (Appendix A; 223–26).

Poisson distribution   The classic distribution that counts the number of times an event occurs in a given period of time (Appendix E; 250).

Position-Adjusted Career Batter Rating   A revised version of the Career Batter Rating that adjusts for the position that the player holds in the field (Chapter 15; 199–203).

Position-Adjusted Event-Specific Batting Runs   A revised version of the Event-Specific Batting Runs that adjusts for the position that the player holds in the field (Chapter 15; 200).

Power transformation   A class of statistical transformations that involves raising the raw data to a given power (Appendix E; 248).

Precision   A term referring to the accuracy of a given average. Formally, it is defined as one divided by the variance (Appendix A; 223).

Productive career length   The milestone of at least 4000 on or past the peak average milestone for which the percent of peak is closest to 99% (Chapter 4; 46–56).

Qualifying player   A player who has a minimum of 4000 NFPs. There are 1140 qualifying players in major league history through 2003, excluding Negro League players (Chapter 2; 16–17).

Rare events correction   A term used in the mean-adjusted average to improve the normality of three offensive events triples, home runs, and stolen bases for which sizable fractions of players had zero seasonal totals for some eras (Appendix E; 251–52).

RBI gap   The absolute value of the RBI% − 100 (Chapter 10; 135).

RBI%   A term comparing a player's actual RBIs to those expected given by Formula G.1. Values above 100 represent above-average performances (Appendix G; 263).

Reduced model   A statistical model in which not all variables under consideration are included (Appendix C; 232).

Regular player   A player is a regular in a given season if he has at least as many NFPs as given in Table 2.2 (Chapter 2; 15–16).

Regular player-season   A season in which a player is a regular. For example, Mickey Cochrane was a regular every year from 1925 to 1935, so he had 11 regular player-seasons in his career (Chapter 2; 15).

Relative batting average   A quantity equal to 100 times the player's batting average divided by the league non-pitcher's batting average (Chapter 2; 13).

Replacement player   A relatively poorly defined term used to describe an average-performing player who could be called up from the bench or the minor leagues to replace a regular player who has stopped playing due to injury, retirement, or a trade (Chapter 14; 188).

Residual chi-square   A chi-square term that is a measure of the variability in certain models, including logistic regression. As terms are dropped from the model, the residual chi-square value increases. A statistical test can be used to compare the residual chi-square from a model to its expected value, thereby allowing the fit of a model to be assessed (Appendix C; 232–33).

RPRBI%   A term comparing a player's actual RPRBIs to those expected given by Formula G.1. Values above 100 represent above average performances (Appendix G; 263–64).

r-Square (r^2)   The Pearson correlation coefficient for a regression model; it represents the fraction of the variability in the data that is accounted for by the model (Appendix A; 222).

Run gap   The absolute value of the run% − 100 (Chapter 10; 135).

Run%   A term comparing a player's actual runs to those expected given by Formula G.1. Values above 100 represent above average performances (Appendix G; 263).

Runs-plus-RBIs (RPRBIs)   The sum of runs and RBIs (Chapter 10; 132).

Shrinkage   A statistical procedure that adjusts a raw average toward a global average. Shrinkage particularly pulls in extreme averages that are based on small sample sizes (Appendix D; 241–46).

Significance-level-to-stay (SLS)   A number between 0 and 1 that gives the maximum p-value for which a variable will be retained in a backward elimination regression (Appendix A; 224, 238–39).

Simple linear regression   Linear regression analysis is divided into two main types: simple linear regression and weighted linear regression. Simple linear regression refers to the situation when the data points all have the same weights (Appendix A; 223).

Skewness   A statistical value that describes an important aspect of the data distribution. It is derived from the third moment of a distribution. If the value is a positive number, the distribution has positive skewness, which indicates that the most extreme averages are more likely to be above the mean, rather than below (Chapter 2; 19).

Slope   One of two key model parameters from a linear regression model (*intercept* is the other), the slope measures how fast the dependent variable changes with a unit change in the independent variable. A piecewise linear regression model has as many slopes are there are line segments in the model (Appendix A; 220).

Slugging average   A standard baseball formula that divides the total number of bases that a player reaches by his hits divided by his at-bats (Chapter 13; 168).

Standard deviation (SD)   A measure of variability of a distribution. This measure plays a central role in statistics and is used to measure the performance spread for the various offensive events. It is based on the second moment of a distribution (Chapter 2; 13).

Standardization   A variable has a distribution, which has a mean and a standard deviation. Standardization of a variable consists of subtracting the mean from the variable value and dividing the result by the standard deviation of the distribution (Chapter 2; 18). (See z-score.)

Standardizing averages   These are the overall park-adjusted averages of regular players for the basic offensive events for the standardizing seasons (Chapter 2; 17).

Standardizing seasons   The standardizing seasons for this book are the 1977–92 National League seasons. These seasons were chosen since they are familiar to many readers and represent arguably the most stable period in baseball history for all of the basic offensive events. These seasons are described in greater detail in Chapter 3 (Chapter 2; 17).

Team OBP edge   A term used to calculate a player's run%, RBI%, RPRBI%, and additional scoring rating values for a given season. The team OBP edge is the difference in a player's team OBP and .319 (the average team OBP for the standardizing seasons, 1977–92 National League) multiplied by the number of NFPs for the player (Chapter 10; 133, 261–63).

Time series   A sequence of numbers that are ordered over time. Typically, the times are uniformly spaced, such as years. Baseball data from consecutive seasons constitutes a time series (Appendix B; 226).

Tough K victim   A batter who strikes out less often than expected given his era and number of home runs, where the expected number is given by an equation in Table 11.1 (Chapter 11; 150, 152).

Transformation, transformation power   A method that modifies the distributional form of a set of data. In this book, basic offensive events are transformed by raising the data to a value between 0 and 1, called the transformation power. The reason for applying the transformation is to produce comparable distributions across baseball history normal distributions in this book (Chapter 2; 19–20).

Two-phase linear regression   A regression fit that is comprised of two line segments that join at a point (Appendix A; 222).

Weight   A factor used in regression analysis to give more influence to some data points than others. Typically, one weights data points by how precise they are, with the precision determined by the reciprocal of the variance of the data point. The term "weight" has also been used to express the number of runs that various hits are worth in the Batting Runs formula (Appendix A; 223).

Weighted linear regression   Linear regression analysis is divided into two main types: simple linear regression and weighted linear regression. Weighted linear regression refers to the situation in which the data points do not all have the same weights (Appendix A; 223).

z-Score   Standardizing a variable value from a normal distribution produces a score called the z-score. The distribution of z-scores has a normal distribution, with a mean of 0 and a standard deviation of 1 (Chapter 2; 13, 21–22).

REFERENCES

Albert, Jim, and Jay Bennett. *Curve Ball: Baseball, Statistics, and the Role of Chance in the Game.* New York: Copernicus Books, 2001.

Efron, Bradley, and Carl Morris. "Stein's Paradox in Statistics." *Scientific American,* May 1977.

Felber, Bill, and Gary Gillette. "The Changing Game." In *Total Baseball,* Seventh Edition (John Thorn, Pete Palmer, and Michael Gershman, eds.). Kingston, NY: Total Sports, 2001.

Gallian, Joseph A. "Who is the Greatest Hitter of Them All?" *Math Horizons,* September 2002.

Gershman, Michael. *Diamonds: The Evolution of the Ballpark.* Boston: Houghton Mifflin, 1993.

Gillette, Gary, and Pete Palmer (eds.). *The Baseball Encyclopedia.* New York: Barnes & Noble Books, 2004.

Gould, Stephen J. *Full House: The Spread of Excellence from Plato to Darwin.* New York: Three Rivers Press, 1996.

Honig, Donald. *The Power Hitters.* New York: Sporting News, 1989.

James, Bill. *The New Bill James Historical Baseball Abstract.* New York: Free Press, 2001.

———. *Win Shares.* Morton Grove, IL: STATS, Inc., 2002.

Krabbenhoft, Herm. "Ted Williams' OPBCG." *The Baseball Research Journal* 32:41–46, 2003.

Lindsey, George. "An Investigation of Strategies in Baseball." *Operations Research* 11:477–501, 1963.

Lowry, Philip. *Green Cathedrals: The Ultimate Celebration of All 273 Major League and Negro League Ballparks.* Reading, MA: Addison-Wesley, 1992.

McConnell, Bob, and David Vincent (eds.). *SABR Presents The Home Run Encyclopedia.* New York: Macmillan, 1996.

McNeil, William F. *The King of Swat: An Analysis of Baseball's Home Run Hitters from the Major, Minor, Negro and Japanese Leagues.* Jefferson, NC: McFarland, 1997.

Neyer, Rob, and Eddie Epstein. *Baseball Dynasties: The Greatest Teams of All Time.* New York: W. W. Norton, 2000.

O'Rourke, Frank. *The Heavenly World Series.* New York: Carroll & Graf, 2002.

Pietrusza, David, Matthew Silverman, and Michael Gershman (eds.). *Baseball: The Biographical Encyclopedia.* Kingston, NY: Total Sports, 2000.

Roberts, Russell. *Stolen! A History of Base Stealing.* Jefferson, NC: McFarland, 1999.

Schell, Michael J. *Baseball's All-Time Best Hitters: How Statistics Can Level the Playing Field.* Princeton, NJ: Princeton University Press, 1999.

Siwoff, Seymour, Steve Hirdt, and Pete Hirdt. *The 1985 Elias Baseball Analyst.* New York: Macmillan, 1985. [See also *Elias Baseball Analyst* for the years 1986–93. The 1989–93 editions have a fourth coauthor, Tom Hirdt; in 1991, Fireside became the publisher.]

STATS Inc., and Bill James. *Bill James Presents . . . STATS Major League Handbook.* Morton Grove, IL: STATS, Inc., 1999.

STATS Player Profiles 1998. Skokie, IL: STATS, Inc., 1997.

Thomas, G. Scott. *Leveling the Field: An Encyclopedia of Baseball's All-Time Great Performances as Revealed through Adjusted Statistics.* New York: Black Dog & Leventhal, 2002.

Thorn, John, and Pete Palmer. *The Hidden Game of Baseball: A Revolutionary Approach to Baseball and Its Statistics.* Garden City, NY: Doubleday, 1985.

——— (eds.). *Total Baseball,* Fourth Edition. New York: Viking Penguin, 1995.

Thorn, John, Pete Palmer, and Michael Gershman (eds.). *Total Baseball,* Seventh Edition. Kingston, NY: Total Sports, 2001.

Thorn, John, Pete Palmer, Michael Gershman, and David Pietrusza (eds.). *Total Baseball,* Fifth Edition. New York: Viking, 1997.

Verducci, Tom. "The Best Hitter since Ted Williams." *Sports Illustrated,* July 28, 1997.

Westcott, Rich. *Philadelphia's Old Ballparks.* Philadelphia: Temple University Press, 1996.

Wright, Russell O. *The Evolution of Baseball: A History of the Major Leagues in Graphs, 1903–1989.* Jefferson, NC: McFarland, 1992.

PLAYER INDEX

The index includes players who are in one or more of the most significant lists in the book: multiple single-seasons among the top 100, top 10 single-seasons, or productive careers for the basic or derived offensive events presented in Chapters 7–14; career batter rating; position-adjusted career batter rating; top players by career position; and players active in 2004 who are candidates for top 100 CBR or CBR+ rankings. Career batter rating and, after the semicolon, career position and ranking obtained from Tables 15.1–15.9 are listed in parentheses after the player's name.